16807

McCOOK COMMUNITY COLLEGE
Learning Resource Center

D1202045

CULTURE AND
DEMOCRACY

CULTURE AND DEMOCRACY

The Struggle for Form in Society and Architecture
in Chicago and the Middle West during the Life and
Times of Louis H. Sullivan

HUGH DALZIEL DUNCAN

THE BEDMINSTER PRESS

1 9 6 5

16807

McCOOK COMMUNITY COLLEGE
Learning Resource Center

Copyright © 1965 by The Bedminster Press, Incorporated
Library of Congress Catalogue Card Number: 65–24660
Manufactured in the United States of America
by H. Wolff, New York

Readers of this book are invited to send their names and addresses to
The Bedminster Press, Vreeland Avenue, Totowa, New Jersey, U.S.A.
to receive announcements and literature about other books
in the social sciences published by The Bedminster Press.

McCOOK COMMUNITY COLLEGE
Learning Resource Center

*To all Chicagoans who struggle to keep alive
the soul of a city guarded by the spirit of
Louis Henri Sullivan*

Acknowledgments

Many debts to persons and institutions have piled up over the years in writing this book. If it does something to bring attention to the struggle in Chicago to create a democratic culture, some of these debts will be repaid. Financial aid in the form of a Fellowship from the Graham Foundation for Advanced Studies in the Fine Arts has helped greatly in writing this book. Richard Nickel's photographs speak for themselves, but these are only a small part of a devotion to the memory of Louis Henri Sullivan and Dankmar Adler, and the architecture of Chicago, which helps Chicagoans to treasure their heritage of greatness.

H . D . D .

May 4, 1965
Southern Illinois University
Carbondale, Illinois

Contents

PART FIVE

The Struggle to Create an American Architecture in Chicago

PART SIX

Sullivan's Creation of an American Philosophy of Architecture: A Resolution of Culture and Democracy

Illustrations

Introduction: Culture and Architecture in Chicago

ONE OF THE great ironies of our time is the sense of inferiority Chicagoans have about the culture of their city. The image of Chicago as a city of violence, crime, and political graft is familiar enough. But the image of Chicago as a white city, whose gleaming towers would stand beside an inland sea to create a new Athens in America—the image that captured the imagination and disciplined the spirit of Root, Sullivan, Wright, and Burnham and still touches the spirit of our best Chicago architects—is not so well known. Chicago has inspired men and women—for evil as well as good—but it has not yet inspired great, or even significant, cultural analysis. And this is very strange, for of few modern American cities can it be said, as of Chicago, that in its architecture lies the history of the struggle for the form of a new civilization, the civilization of America which emerged after the Civil War.

Critical opinion on the significance of Chicago architecture has changed greatly since Fiske Kimball's *American Architecture* appeared in 1928. What was then thought to be a style—and not a very important style, at that—is now accepted as a world order of architecture. We no longer send our architects to Paris or Rome; now Europeans come to America, and specifically to Chicago. In his *Architecture USA* the British architect and critic Ian McCallum says: "For the young European architect an American Grand Tour is becoming as important as the Italian was to the eighteenth-century English gentleman." [1] In 1940 Sigfried Giedion, whose *Space, Time and Architecture: The Growth of a New Tradition* is now a standard work on modern design, said: "From 1880 to the time of the Columbian Exposition of 1893 the 'Loop' area in Chicago (its business quarter) was the center of architectural development not merely for the United States but for the whole world." [2]

Our first complete history of modern architecture, *Architecture: Nineteenth and Twentieth Centuries*, by Henry-Russell Hitchcock,[3] sums up the Chicago achievement by saying: "The whole picture of architecture in the twentieth century, so different from the picture of architecture before 1850, was modified by the developments that culminated in the Chicago skyscrapers." And while Hitchcock strives to establish historical continuity for the modern movements as a whole, he emphasizes the greatness of the Chicago architectural achievement as such. He says: "Enlightened commercial patrons demanded and often received the best architecture of their day. Undoubtedly the functional and technical challenges of commercial building brought out the capacities . . . of architects as no other commissions did so consistently." If we compare, Hitchcock goes on to point out, civic and religious architecture with commercial, "the strictly *architectural,* as well as the technical and social, significance of the major commercial monuments of the nineteenth century will be evident." [4] Even in the new city of Chicago, religious, civic, and scholastic tradition weighed too heavily on architecture. It was the businessman of Chicago, not her priests, politicians, or educators, who made possible the great architecture of the Chicago School.[5]

In his 1939 London lectures, Frank Lloyd Wright said: "Now, America begins west of Buffalo. The greatest and most nearly beautiful city of our young nation is probably Chicago. Eventually, I think that Chicago will be the most beautiful great city left in the modern world." [6] Wright thought this would happen because businessmen would accept modern American architects as cultural guides. "To say that 'business' will some day know good architecture suited to its purpose, before art, science, education and religion are able to recognize it, may be astonishing but I believe, nevertheless, true. . . . The manufacturer, world over, in this has been a leader. Perhaps this is because 'culture,' in quotation marks, had no place for it but in the final decisions of business—the mind of the superior businessman was more free than the pseudo-cultural academic to accept the change that is progress." [7] His vision of Chicago as the most beautiful city in the world staggered Wright's London audiences.[8] In answer to the question: "Why do you consider that Chicago is going to be the most beautiful city in the world?"—Wright replied:

First of all because it has a generous park system, the greatest on earth. You may drive nearly the whole day without going away from the boulevard and park system of Chicago. And the parks are as well looked after as your own London parks, which is very well indeed. Another reason is that, thanks to an architect, Dan Burnham, Chicago seems to be the only great city in our States to have discovered its own waterfront. Moreover, to a greater extent than any other city it has a life of its own. Chicago takes pride in building things in a big, substantial, broad way. Even when the city goes in for gangsters it does so on a big scale, although I think you'll find more gangsters in New York City than in Chicago and a more dangerous gangster mind there too. I deplore its narrow provinciality but I like to go occasionally to New York. But, well, I like Chicago.

The British philosopher Alfred North Whitehead was deeply moved by Chicago. In his talks with Lucien Price he said: "I fancy the place I have been in that was most like Greece was a gathering of university scholars at Chicago! The city was disorderly but very much alive. The Greeks weren't studying the best models to be had abroad. They were making their own. That, I fancy, is the most Greek thing a man can do." [9] In a later conversation he returns to this again. "I think the one place where I have been that is most like ancient Athens is the University of Chicago. You see, I am looking for your American equivalent of the Aegean, and I believe it is the Midwest." [10] Chicago's greatness was in its sense of adventure, its determination to create indigenous American forms of life, art, and thought. "The Midwesterners have the great advantage of being naïve. In New York, for example, your type tends to be blasé; they have heard everything, and consider that the simple subjects are hackneyed. So they are. But great art is a dealing with simple subjects freshly. . . . Europe has collapsed; civilization is in your hands, . . ." [11] "America, as I see it, is the only hope. There is adventure here, and a welcome for novelty." [12]

Henry L. Mencken, who delighted in baiting the British and affected profound distaste for Harvard, stands far from Whitehead, the British philosopher who taught at Harvard. Yet in 1917 he told the readers of the Chicago *Sunday Tribune:* "The most civilized city in America? Chicago, of course! And per corollary the most thoroughly American . . . in Chicago there is the mysterious something . . . in Chicago a spirit broods upon the face of the waters . . . all American literary movements that have youth in them, and a fresh point of view, and the authentic bounce and verve of the country and the true character and philosophy of its people—all these came out of Chicago." [13] Robert Morss Lovett in his article "The Future of the Middle West," [14] written some twenty years later, said:

In the Middle West today progress and reaction seem fairly in balance, with a tendency toward the latter. But progress is the natural and characteristic mood of this region, to which it is conditioned by origins and history. . . . One need not go back to Lincoln and Douglas. It is only necessary to recall in politics the group of statesmen of whom Senator Norris is today the only survivor; in business the men who built railroads, sleeping cars, great stores, packing plants, agricultural machinery and automobiles; in culture the founders of universities, orchestras, art galleries, whose monument was the Columbian Exposition of 1893. These men were mostly rugged individualists; they were among the destructive as well as the constructive elements which shaped the Middle West; but in their later generation they shared leadership with such men and women of social vision as Tom Johnson, Jane Addams, W. R. Harper, Julius Rosenwald, John Peter Altgeld, Clarence Darrow and Eugene Debs. All these, selfishly or generously, contributed to the stimulus and release of energy in the community and in energy it had its distinctive character.[15]

New orders of architecture are not born every day. Few cities can say they produced not only great buildings, but urban and regional plans destined to become a point of departure for every planning discussion in our time. Whatever we say about Chicago, however we explain that Chicago is not a great culture center after all, the fact still remains that more significant modern commercial and domestic architecture exists in and around Chicago (as of 1964) than anywhere in the world. Chicago has built and torn down more significant modern buildings than other large cities such as New York possess. Chicago became the stage, first for the genius of Sullivan and Wright, and finally, in our time, for the talent of Mies van der Rohe, whose forms now dominate world architecture. To characterize Chicago, as Giedion did, as a "spontaneously growing center of force [which] embodies, as few other places do, that brutal and inventive vitality of the nineteenth century" [16] is to repeat what has been said before, and no doubt will be said again: that Chicago's culture is to be accounted for, not by intelligence, imagination, and will, but by some mysterious eruption of social energy. Ascriptions of causes for "social energy" change. God, Fate, Destiny, the folk-soul, the spirit of the times, the class struggle, or historical necessity have been invoked; now it is some kind of deification of social force, as in the "natural tendency for social units to equilibrate."

Chicago did not grow "spontaneously." It grew because men of courage, will, intelligence, and imagination wanted to make it a great city. Whatever their motives—money, holiness, power, love, or beauty—Chicagoans from 1875 to 1915 created a unique vision of a great city: a new kind of city, where men and women of all stations of life could walk the streets in dignity, in freedom, and in beauty. Chicago architects and engineers who designed the industrial town of Pullman, the stockyards, and the large commercial buildings in the Loop created not only forms of architecture but of community itself. Americans everywhere copied such forms as the skyscraper because these buildings alone could house the new urban communities which were replacing the villages, towns, and neighborhoods of a rural America. Cincinnati and St. Louis were great river and railway centers long before Chicago, but Chicago soon surpassed them because it had architects, engineers, and businessmen who created stages on which the new urban drama of our time could unfold. By 1890 St. Louis possessed some of Sullivan's great works, notably the Wainwright Building, and in 1893 his design for another great building, the Trust and Savings Bank Building, was ready for construction in St. Louis. It was never built. The Wainwright Building stands as solitary tribute to Sullivan in the business section of St. Louis. Chicago and its suburbs, on the other hand, contain hundreds of buildings created by Sullivan and his followers in the Chicago School of the eighties.

If we argue that social conditions "caused" the rapid development of Chicago, we must explain why the same conditions did not produce equally great architecture in other cities. Boston had a great fire, and it also had a great architect in Richardson, but the forms of life so characteristic of modern America did not come out of Boston, but Chicago. And even Richardson himself had to come to Chicago to do the great work of his last years. New York far surpassed Chicago in size and in commercial activity, yet none of its architects developed the large business buildings of Chicago which are now so common throughout the cities of the world. Indeed, until about 1910, New Yorkers imported Chicagoans to design and build their skyscrapers. Great building requires a high degree of social organization and the closest collaboration of architect, builder, and client. Many minds, hands, and resources must be brought together to make even a single building possible. As long as cultural historians were content to think of Jenney, Root, Sullivan, Holabird and Roche, and Wright as creators of a style among styles, there was little need for concern over Chicago. But as evidence accumulates, and as convictions deepen, that Sullivan and Wright are great authentic American voices like those of Lincoln and Mark Twain, we must either deny Chicago's greatness or develop a new cultural history.

There is little in traditional humanistic training which prepares us to deal with great art arising out of commerce and engineering. Many Chicago architects and engineers themselves could not quite believe, even in the years of their greatest achievement, that what they were doing was great art. Jenney, Burnham, Cobb, Root, Adler, as well as Sullivan himself, were in little doubt about the significance of Chicago achievements in engineering, but they were not so sure of their achievement in art. Charles Moore, Burnham's biographer, in speaking of the final decision to make the Chicago Fair of 1893 classical, argued that "commercial architecture" was not art, and that classical form was really the traditional American form, hence its adoption in 1891 was "but a return to our better selves." [17] The art of Chicago and the Middle West cannot be treated at all unless we are willing to discard theories of cultural expression based on "fine" art. This is hardly a matter of choice. For if we are to say anything about the cultural expression of the Middle West from 1875 to 1905, when the great buildings of the Chicago School appeared, we must learn to think about a civilization which was highly expressive but not "artistic"—as those who follow the canons of fine art define "artistic." The arts of the Middle West were applied arts. Lincoln may have spoken for the ages, but this was not why he was asked to speak, and it was not what he thought he was doing when he spoke. He was never a highly self-conscious oratorical stylist. For him oratory was a craft, a tool, useful in getting votes, raising troops, commemorating the dead, and persuading others to follow his leadership.

Jenney, Adler, Burnham, Root, Sullivan, and other Chicago engineers and architects, erected the steel cage we now see reaching its final expression in the work of Mies van der Rohe. Jenney's architecture was not conceived of as fine art, but as a solution for the space needs of businessmen in the Loop of Chicago. Sullivan even denied that Jenney *was* an architect, as when he tells us in his autobiography that Jenney "was not an architect except by courtesy of terms. His true profession was that of engineer." The architecture which was to "belong to the ages" was turned over to McKim and Mead, classicists of the Chicago Fair of 1893, whose devotion to the ages doomed the Chicago School and all but destroyed indigenous American architecture. Few would be foolhardy enough to say now that, from the time of Lincoln's address to the "People of Sangamon County" in 1831 to Sullivan's Schlesinger and Mayer department store of 1899, the Middle West was an aesthetic void. The oratory of Lincoln, the novels of Mark Twain, the steel frame of Jenney, the Tacoma Building of Holabird and Roche, the Reliance Building of Atwood and Burnham, and the Schlesinger and Mayer store (now Carson, Pirie, Scott) of Sullivan are not found in cultural wastelands.

If the resources of the student of culture who believes culture to be determined by art as much as by economics, politics, religion, or the family are not adequate to deal with such art, he must develop new theories and methods of cultural analysis. The cultural achievements of the Middle West do not need to be "discovered." The Carson Pirie Scott store stands on the "busiest corner in the world," Madison and State streets in Chicago. And it stands in Chicago—not Boston, New York, London, or Paris. Western artists have been hearing for the past century that they must measure themselves against the great enduring classics of the past, for these create the eternal standards against which new art must be judged. In November of 1863 Lincoln's great political oratory was considered crude beside the "classical" style of Edward Everett. In 1891 Chicago architects, who had created their wonderful towers of glass and steel, were told to subordinate themselves to the classicists McKim, Mead, and White; for these cultural emissaries from the East were to bring universal standards to refine Western taste. In 1900 Browne, editor of the old Chicago *Dial,* warned Chicago writers of their need for classical standards in literature. In 1941 Chicago citizens heard again that only the "Great Books of the Western World" could save us from the evils of parochialism.

Chicago artists have not been, nor are they now, ignorant men and women who design as they do because they are "urban primitives." Chicago artists such as Sullivan and Wright were not unlettered, nor were they unfamiliar with the great cultural traditions of Europe. Sullivan left Chicago to study in Paris, so that his art would not suffer from parochialism. Wright studied and traveled widely, both in Japan and Europe. But to these great artists, as to other artists of the Middle West, the problem of using "universal" standards was one of relevance to the American life shaping in her new cities. No one struggled more deeply than Sullivan to create a universal form, a form "so broad as to admit of no exceptions," as he tells us in his *Autobiography of an Idea*. Sullivan and Wright both rejected Hamlin Garland's and Lorado Taft's attempts to deny the past of Europe by substituting a romantic pioneer past of America. Pasts, Sullivan and Wright argued, of America as of Europe, must be tested by some principle of form which could bring order into the content of the new *American* life in the cities and plains of the great valley.

In Chicago from 1875 to 1915 many traditions were examined, just as many ideal cities of the future were proposed. In architecture, Jenney, Root, Burnham, Sullivan, and Wright had very different conceptions of the role of architecture in democratic society. Turner, Veblen, Harper, Dewey, and Park also differed widely on the relationship between culture and democracy. In literature, the voices of Garland, Browne, Fuller, Masters, Dreiser, Sandburg, and Anderson seldom agreed on how to create a great democratic art. Pullman, Gage, and Charles R. Crane differed on how capitalism could flourish in democracy. Struggles between anarchists, socialists, communists, the American Federation of Labor and the Congress for Industrial Organization were long and bitter. There was sharp disagreement between New England bluestockings and Southern belles on the role of the new woman in Chicago society, just as there was sharp disagreement on whether British models of the gentlemen could serve as models for the new gentleman of the Middle West.

Discussion, argument, debate, struggle of all kinds—sometimes violent, always intense and prolonged—characterized Chicago from 1875 to 1916. It was the resolution of contending voices, not the overwhelming power of any one voice, which produced the greatness of Chicago. Wright cannot be understood if we do not understand his struggle against the classicists and the academicians. Sullivan cannot be understood unless we understand his attempt to resolve the struggle among engineers, architects, businessmen, clergymen, intellectuals, and artists for spiritual and material domination of Chicago. Veblen's attack on cosmopolitan forms of taste makes little sense if we know nothing about Mrs. Potter Palmer's "Rhine Castle" on Michigan Boulevard, the Chicago Committee of the American Academy in Rome, or the Gothic architecture of the University of Chicago, where Veblen taught and began his career.

Dewey's convictions on the democratic role of the school in society were formed in the great Middle Western argument among religious, commercial, and educational interests over the context and form of democratic education. The University of Chicago, under Harper's leadership, was born in debate over the function of learning and the role of the university in democratic society. The development of the social studies at the University of Chicago under Dewey, Veblen, Mead, Freund, Pound, Thomas, Park, and Ogburn, like the social and economic analysis of Ely, Ross, Commons, and Van Hise at Wisconsin, grew out of the demand in business and politics that learning become a guide for action in democracy. La Follette wanted scholarship at Wisconsin to serve the politician so that he could legislate wisely. Harper at Chicago wanted teachers trained, and scholars developed, who could bring knowledge into the active life of the democratic community. The University of Chicago created great stores of knowledge and inspired searching study of the city. No other group of urban social scientists studied their own localities so intensively and tried to serve their communities in so many different ways. No city in the modern world has been so well studied as an economic, political, and social entity as Chicago.[18]

In his review of Theodore Roosevelt's *The Winning of the West,* published in August of 1889, Frederick Jackson Turner said: "America's historians have for the most part, like the wise men of old, come from the East; and as a result our history has been written from the point of view of the Atlantic coast. . . . But the American occupation of the Mississippi basin has not found its historian. General United States history should be built upon the fact that the centre of gravity of the nation has passed across the mountains into this region."[19] Insofar as cultural history and certainly the history of architecture is concerned, this quotation still stands true. The region which produced Lincoln, Mark Twain, U. S. Grant, W. T. Sherman, Turner, Veblen, Sullivan, Wright, Dreiser, and harbored Mies van der Rohe—men whose forms of expression in politics, history, sociology, literature, war, and architecture did so much to create the American civilization of our time—has not yet found scholars capable of interpreting its greatness.

The specific intellectual contributions of the Middle West are beginning to be recognized. In *The American Mind: An Interpretation of American Thought and Character since the 1880's,* by Henry Steel Commager, Chapter XIX "Architecture and Society" is one of our newest discussions of Chicago architecture as a form of cultural expression. David Riesman, in his work *Thorstein Veblen: A Critical Interpretation,* discusses Veblen and Mark Twain, as well as Veblen and Henry Ford. But in neither of these is there mention of the importance of the great debate in Chicago among classicists, cosmopolitans, humanists, engineers, academicians, architects, and artists over how to create democratic forms of life, thought, and art. The importance of Chicago as a stage of struggle to achieve a new democratic society is recognized, but Chicago's contributions to the *forms* of American expression are not. It is a common mistake to think of the Middle West only in economic and political terms. Turner's argument that American history must be studied in terms of westward expansion, searching as it is, neglects art. Yet even as early as 1893 Chicago was significant enough to produce a great World's Fair and to evoke a separate chapter in *The Education of Henry Adams.* And it was at this World's Fair that Turner himself read to the American Historical Association his essay, "The Significance of the Frontier in American History," which was to revolutionize the study of American history.

We look back now from a world where Sullivan's principles of architecture are international. We have seen the ideals of the Chicago school of 1880 to 1910 infuse Art Nouveau in 1898, arouse secessionisms under Wagner and Hoffman in Germany and the North countries in 1910, and inspire the work of Le Corbusier, Gropius, and the other European "Young Pioneers" of 1914. In the twenties and the thirties Richard Neutra, Mies van der Rohe, Moholy-Nagy, Walter Gropius, and Alvar Aalto came to America. Chicago's great tradition in architecture found new expression with the arrival of Laszlo Moholy-Nagy and his Bauhaus group, who founded the Chicago Institute of Design, and in the work of Ludwig Mies van der Rohe, who became director of the architectural department of the Illinois Institute of Technology in 1938. Chicago continues to be the home of great architecture, both as a living workshop and as the bearer of a great tradition. Since 1880 Chicago has been a world center of engineering, planning, and architecture. In many ways it has been *the* world center. And finally, in 1964, a building is under construction in the Chicago Loop, designed by a great Chicago architect, Mies van der Rohe, on commission from the Federal government. The young radicals of the eighties whose Chicago Design was the first great integration of art and science, now begin their reincarnation as official architects. The spirit of Sullivan, who died in poverty and despair but a few blocks from the new buildings of the Loop and the Illinois Institute of Technology, now triumphs. His spirit still guards the city he loved.

Notes

[1] Ian McCallum, *Architecture USA* (London: Architectural Press, 1959), p. 9.

[2] Sigfried Giedion, *Space, Time and Architecture,* 3d ed., enlarged (Cambridge: Harvard University Press, 1954). As Giedion tells us in the foreword to the first edition of 1940, this book was the outgrowth of lectures and seminars given at Harvard during his tenure as Charles Eliot Norton Professor for 1938–39. Part V, "American Development," is almost wholly devoted to Chicago. Despite our great debt to Giedion, he created a damaging stereotype about the "anonymous architecture" of the Chicago School. As we hope to show, there was nothing "anonymous" about Chicago's cultural achievements.

[3] Henry-Russell Hitchcock, *Architecture: Nineteenth and Twentieth Centuries* (Baltimore: Penguin Books, 1959). Since this was selected for publication in *The Pelican History of Art,* edited by Nikolaus Pevsner, the distinguished British critic and historian of modern architecture, we may assume that it will stand as a definite historical statement on the achievements of the Chicago school. In view of this, it is all the more regrettable that this work is marred by such careless mistakes as a reference to Dankmar Adler as a Dane.

[4] See p. 252 of Hitchcock's *Architecture* for discussion of this point.

[5] As they made possible the University of Chicago, which still has a far larger percentage of businessmen on its board than Harvard, Yale, or Columbia. The incongruity between the Gothic architecture, a business board, and the progressivism of the University is one of the many paradoxes in the Chicago spirit.

[6] Frank Lloyd Wright, *The Future of Architecture* (New York: The Horizon Press, 1953), p. 260.

[7] Frank Lloyd Wright, *The Living City* (New York: The Horizon Press, 1958), p. 164.

[8] It always left New York audiences in a state of amused bewilderment.

[9] Lucien Price, *Dialogues of Alfred North Whitehead as Recorded by Julien Price* (Boston: Little, Brown and Company, 1954), p. 56. These took place from 1932 to 1947. R. M. Hutchins was then introducing his "Chicago Plan" for higher education.

[10] *Ibid.,* p. 180.

[11] *Ibid.,* p. 181.

[12] *Ibid.,* p. 255.

[13] This appeared in the book section on October 28, 1917.

[14] In *The New Republic,* November 8, 1939.

[15] *Ibid.,* p. 56.

[16] See Sigfried Giedion, *Mechanization Takes Command: A Contribution to Anonymous History* (New York: Oxford University Press, 1948). See pp. 218ff. for discussion of this view of history.

[17] Charles Moore, *Daniel H. Burnham, Architect, Planner of Cities,* 2 vols. (Boston and New York: Houghton, Mifflin Co., 1921), Vol. I, p. 91.

[18] Chicago's population, social composition, etc., has been studied continuously and well for many years at the University of Chicago. Such studies have been—and will be —of great value to planners now creating a new city based on Chicago's great planning heritage of the Burnham Plan of 1906.

[19] Quoted from *The Early Writings of Frederick Jackson Turner* by Everett E. Edwards (Madison, Wis.: University of Wisconsin Press, 1938), p. 22.

PART ONE

The Search for Community in the Middle West

1

Forms of Settlement in the Chicago Region

THE PEOPLING of the prairies and forests of the Mississippi Valley is one of the great sagas of our civilization. Within three short generations a new kind of human community developed on the Middle Border of America. This was a community of families dwelling on their own farms and freeholds, people of widely different types ranging from "outliers," the lone wolves who lived beyond the rim of settlement, to highly educated youths seeking fortune and adventure. The outlier loved the wilderness. As enshrined in American legend, Daniel Boone and Kit Carson opened the wilderness to civilization. But these scouts were sometimes little more than savages, even if we grant them legendary stature as noble savages. Contemporary depictions of artists like Mark Twain, the reminiscences of itinerant preachers like Peter Cartwright or of political leaders like Lincoln say little about nobility. These lone wolves were frequently at odds with permanent settlers, although everyone admired their awesome journeys into the forests and plains of America. Many settlers would never have reached their homesteads without the lessons supplied by these scouts.

After these outliers came the squatter, who lived by hunting and from the corn grown in acreage cleared by himself and his family. "Clearin' folk" seldom stayed more than a few months or years; usually they sold their improved land and cabin to more permanent settlers and moved on. Squatters were often shiftless and lazy, but often, too, they were simply without a "stake," or capital, which would have allowed them to settle and prosper. The farmer followed the squatter. He came with stock or capital and did not settle on any land save what he owned or expected to buy. His first living arrangements differed little from the outlier or the squatter. Often he began with a half-faced camp of logs piled up to give shelter on three sides, with an open fire on the fourth. This was succeeded as soon as possible by a single or double log cabin with puncheoned floors and chinked walls. But the farmer intended to make a permanent home. Unlike the outlier, he wanted to create a settlement which could become a permanent community. Farmers of this type were the backbone of the new communities of Illinois.

But alongside these hardy pioneers was another pioneer type soon to become equally typical of America. He appears very early in the Middle West. The small trader, as storekeeper, peddler, or innkeeper, was familiar enough in older parts of America, but the new Middle Western businessman was a promoter, a dealer in "futures." He first appears as a land speculator. These "Boomers," later called "Boosters," stalk through pioneer accounts and depictions of frontier life long before they are fixed in American letters as indigenous types by Mark Twain, George Ade, and Sinclair Lewis; in American letters and life as Colonel Sellers, the Chicago "drummer," and George F. Babbitt, the Zenith real-estate promoter. As early as 1839 we meet "Mr. Mazard, the Land-Shark" in Caroline M. Kirkland's *A New Home, or Life in the Clearings,* an account of frontier life in Michigan. Farmers and townsmen alike shared a common interest in real-estate speculation. Even in 1835 it was common practice for farmers to "take up" more land than could be cultivated. "The possession of a large number of acres is esteemed a great good," Kirkland tells us. When Tocqueville and Beaumont visited Michigan in the early thirties, the same years as Mrs. Kirkland, they discovered that every farmer was a realtor. Few were so devoted to the land they had cleared and worked that they were unwilling to "pull up stakes," make a "deal," and move on to repeat the process if possible. American "futures" in land, glowing visions of cities rising in swamps and forest, reminded some European travelers of the mad visions of Don Quixote. Others found American visions of the future nothing but lies used to deceive the gullible. Were these new Americans, with their dreams of great cities springing out of mud, madmen, fools, liars, or prophets?

The panic of 1837 and the repudiation of its bonds by Illinois in 1841 inclined men of the East to think of Western boomers as windbags and cheats —fools, perhaps, but sometimes dangerous. Many in the West laughed at their real-estate prophets; but Western laughter was raised in love, not scorn. The glory of the Middle West was in the future, and it was this future, not the past, which bound together the people of the West. When visions of golden futures vanished, tedium, despair, and gloom settled. Cut off from their own past, mingling with strange and alien people, the settlers of Illinois and Chicago found a present unlighted by a golden future unbearable. When visions died, the new Athens glowing in the visions of the future changed swiftly into the decay and filth of the Arkansas town Mark Twain describes in *Huckleberry Finn.*

All the streets and lanes was just mud; they warn't nothing else *but* mud—mud as black as tar and nigh about a foot deep in some places, and two or three inches deep in *all* the places. The hogs loafed and grunted around everywheres. You'd see a muddy sow and a litter of pigs come lazying along the street and whollop herself right down in the way, where folks had to walk around her, and she'd stretch out and shut her eyes and wave her ears whilst the pigs was milking her, and look as happy as if she was on salary. And pretty soon you'd hear a loafer sing out, "Hi! *so* boy! sick him, Tige!" and away the sow would go, squealing most horrible, with a dog or two swinging to each ear, and three or four dozen more a-coming; and then you would see all the loafers get up and watch the thing out of sight, and laugh at the fun and look grateful for the noise. Then they'd settle back again till there was a dog-fight. There couldn't anything wake them up all over, and make them happy all over, like a dog-fight—unless it might be putting turpentine on a stray dog and setting fire to him, or tying a tin pan to his tail and see him run himself to death.

The present was grim enough. As the first generation of rural pioneers in southern and central Illinois cleared virgin forests and broke prairie sod never touched by man, vast masses of decaying vegetable matter were exposed to the sun. Dense underbrush, decaying logs, stagnant pools, and stinking swamps soon became breeding grounds for all kinds of wasting diseases. Fever, ague, the "milk sickness" so deeply feared each spring, wrecked the health of strong men and women. The weak died young; the unlucky who injured themselves in the dangerous and solitary labor of clearing and plowing, or, like Lincoln's father, were attacked by Indians, died without help. As Tocqueville's host at Pontiac in his Michigan trip of 1831 said, "All clearing is a dangerous enterprise . . . it is almost without example that the pioneer and his family escape the woods fever during the first year." Faced with this, pioneers resigned themselves and awaited a better future. When Tocqueville asked about doctors, his host replied: "The nearest doctor often lives sixty miles from their [the pioneers'] house. They do like the Indians: they die or get well, as it pleases God."

In the years between 1849 and 1856 the population of Illinois changed rapidly. Until 1800 Illinois was a part of the Northwest Territory; from 1800 to 1809 it was part of Indiana Territory. It was only with the creation of Illinois Territory in 1809 and with subsequent statehood in 1818 that the people of Illinois had much control over their own destiny. The officials sent out by Congress to govern these new territories ruled as aristocrats over French and Americans who still conceded gentlemen the right to political as well as social leadership. By 1800 there were about 2,500 new Americans in Illinois. The French and Americans who lived a rude life in stockaded stations were almost evenly divided.

The shift from the old village settlement of New England and Europe to the farmstead of the Middle West had profound effects on the forms of community life. As religious control over the settlements declined and the power of the General Court became less strict, land grants were secured on a strictly commercial basis, often by persons who had no intention of settling personally on land so obtained. Thus, in less than a hundred years, the traffic in lands changed from a governmental monopoly rigidly controlled in the interest of close group settlement on the village plan, to wild speculation. The abundance of land in the Middle West made squatting easy. In such extralegal settlements, a man could be sure of his land only by "sitting down" or "squatting" upon it. This inevitably meant scattered farmsteads in the new areas of the West.

The vision which bound these settlers together was the vision of each man on his freehold of land. The early settlers of the Chicago region and of Illinois created a new form of land settlement, the homestead: a freehold in which each farm was located among the fields worked by the family. New England village settlements were determined by close and intimate relations, but in these scattered and isolated farmsteads the homes of the farmers were widely separated. The more that tracts of land were held in squares, the more impossible it became for farmers to construct their homes in proximity to each other. This checkerboard pattern of land settlement, so characteristic of early Illinois, separated landholdings and isolated farm homes to a degree unknown to any previous American settlement. The freehold created a new ideal of life. A family, *every* family, had a right to its own land. The home with a yard around it, and the fields stretching beyond, became the ideal American homestead, for farmer and townsman alike. And, as we see in the development of Frank Lloyd Wright's "prairie houses," it became the ideal of Chicago architects responsible for house design. Even the Prairie avenue homes (as well as later suburban homes) of the new urban plutocrats of Chicago were homes with a yard. All sides of the house were open to the yard and the street. Great porches ran across whole house fronts, sometimes even around two or three sides of the house. Few of the early Prairie avenue houses are enclosed by great walls or even by high fences; they open freely to the yard and to the street beyond. They share this form with very simple dwellings, such as the white Greek Revival cottages of the Middle West towns. Perhaps suburbia itself, the flight from the city apartment we now hear so much about, is but a symbolic return to a homestead form of life.[1] The urban people of the Middle West are, it seems, not urban in any European sense at all. They follow still a tradition which was established by the first settlers of their land and continue to create a new type of settlement, the region, which is neither urban nor rural but something of each.

By 1850 the restless frontier people of pioneer Illinois were flowing out to the newer West. Images of gold, the opening of Kansas and Nebraska, "Pike's Peak or Bust," seized the American imagination. But people poured in far more rapidly than they poured out; southern and eastern Illinois were settled by 1850. These new people came from New England. They also came from Germany, where political idealists, seeking a land of liberty after the disaster of 1848, knew the price of freedom and free thought. Other parts of Europe also sent their quotas: there were colonies of Frenchmen as at Nauvoo, of French-Canadians in the Kankakee country, of Swedes at Bishop Hill. Norwegians soon arrived. By 1860 Chicago had more foreign- than native-born among its people. Yet these "foreigners" with their babel of tongues and accents, so alien to the older Americans of New England, nominated Lincoln and, once the Civil War began, supported the Union as much, and perhaps even more, than any state and city of the North. By July of 1861 Illinois had enrolled four times as many troops as could be accepted in service. By October, forty-three regiments were in service—more than New York State could supply. Thousands of youngsters from Illinois and Chicago, impatient at delay, joined Wisconsin, Missouri, or Indiana regiments in order to get to the front. By this time Illinois had seventy-three thousand men under arms. All classes, all creeds, marched together. The Irish Brigade stirred Chicagoans' hearts with its exploits at Lexington, Missouri. The Jews of Chicago raised and armed a company in 1862. In four years of a new and terrible war, Illinois sent 231,488 men into the Northern army. On the basis of population this was far above that of any other state. All these men were volunteers. Chicago alone sent fifteen thousand out of a population that numbered one hundred thousand in 1861 and one hundred and seventy thousand in 1865. Only fifty-eight of these men were conscripts.

It was not only the foreign-born who had to be assimilated. From the Old South, as from Kentucky and Tennessee, came many of the first settlers in the southern counties of Illinois. The foreign-born settled in towns, the people from the South stayed on the land. Thus began a sectional split in Illinois which still dominates state politics. Once their first reaction of sympathy with the South passed, the devotion of these farmers—so-called Egypt— was unsurpassed. On October 1, 1863, the ten southern counties were credited with enlistments of 50 per cent over their quota. In eighteen months Union County furnished nineteen companies out of a voting population of 2,030, including but 157 Republicans.

When Illinois land speculators bought up the claims of veterans of the War of 1812 to tracts of 160 acres in the Military Tract between the Illinois and the Mississippi rivers, they chose uplands timbered with hard woods. The broad, fertile prairie, the "American Bottom" which was soon to feed America and support the largest armies ever put into the field, originally were considered fit only for grazing. The first settlers of Illinois were axmen. As William Cobbett wrote in 1817:

An *axe* is their tool, and with that tool, at *cutting down* trees or *cutting them up,* they will do *ten times* as much in a day as any other men that I ever saw. Set one of these men upon a wood of timber trees, and his slaughter will astonish you. A neighbor of mine tells me a story of an Irishman, who promised he could *do anything,* and whom, therefore, the employer sent into the wood to cut down a load of wood to burn. He stayed a long while away with the team, and the farmer went to him, fearing some accident had happened. The man was hacking away at a hickory tree, but had not got it half down; and that was all he had done. An American, black or white, would have had a dozen trees cut down, cut up into lengths, put upon the carriage, and brought home in the time.[2]

Easterners, accustomed to valleys separated by hills and mountains, found they must learn to live and work in new ways. As land holdings increased in size and people became more separate in space there was greater need for new forms of transportation and communication to cover large areas peopled by new Americans, alien to New England and Southern traditions alike. The routing of roads and railways meant riches or poverty to the prairie farmer. As a "cash cropper" he raised for markets which must be reached quickly and cheaply. The pioneer farmer of Lincoln's youth could place his family on a flatboat, strike out into the wilderness, cut out his clearing, and, with little or no capital, go on to independence. The small craftsman could set up his shop, buy his materials and tools from neighbors, and sell to nearby customers. To the town dweller of New England or the backwoodsman of the Carolinas, place evoked a deep sense of communal identification. The soil on which ancestors had fallen in battle, the house of birth, marriage, and death, the home as the sacred meeting place of the clan did not exist in the Middle West. Place, like time, was a future, a hope, a vision, not a tradition. Space belonged to the future, and the design of land and buildings, and, indeed, the whole community, was envisioned in terms of this future.

The prairie farmer and townsman built his silos and adopted geometrical patterns for planting, not because he was more skillful or intelligent than his forebears in Europe or New England, but because he was able to take new attitudes toward land use. Paxton's Crystal Palace and Eiffel's Tower were great engineering constructions, but they were not designed for use in everyday life, as were the grain elevators, farm silo, bridges, railway sheds, department stores, or office buildings of the Chicago region. An old landmark, a graveyard, all places infused with traditional values, cannot be treated in the same manner as land infused with visions of a future. Ever-increasing acreage yield of corn, like the ever-increasing urban standard of living, are visions whose power moves us by their promise of things to come. When building forms become sacred, as in Gothic form, it is very difficult to change them or to adopt new forms. Even when new materials such as steel are used

A home in the "clearings" depended on a supply of timber as well as food and water. *An engraving after a painting by George Harvey. Courtesy Chicago Historical Society*

they are shaped into traditional forms. It is customary to think of the sacred in terms of the past, but the sacred is not the only profound determinant of taste and style. Manners, customs, and traditions weigh heavily upon taste. They form a social past which has power over us because their use brought order into social relationships. A style, and particularly architectural style, is an identification. It relates us to each other as actors upon a stage of life. The Colonial house evokes an American past, a past of founding fathers. We ritualize the use of such past forms to gain a sense of identity with others who do the same. But in the newer regions of America the future as well as the past is used to create and sustain a sense of belonging. New, as well as traditional styles, become highly evocative. A Colonial house must be the "newest model" of Colonial. Thus, the future, like the past, becomes a "tradition." Evoking the future in quick acceptance of new styles becomes as powerful a social motive as the recapture of hallowed pasts in traditional observance.

The ideal community role of the pioneer gentleman in the expanding Middle West, and certainly the ideal of Chicago's founders, was a combination of community service and self-interest. As one pioneer wrote to friends in the East: "It is a universal rule here to help one another, each one keeping an eye single to his own interest." In early times community service meant survival. Frontier towns of the Middle West were too isolated from military garrisons to allow much military protection from permanent army posts. The army opened pathways through the Middle West, but it could not guard them. Pioneers expected to do their own fighting. In struggles with Indians and lawless elements in their own communities, every pioneer was a soldier as well as a hunter and farmer. When the need for concerted action against the Indian arose, every man was expected to volunteer. Assembled volunteers elected officers from their own ranks who would drill them and lead them into battle. The pioneer needed much help to survive in the struggle with his physical environment. It was easy enough to take up land, but to clear land, sow and reap a crop of corn, build a cabin, raise and slaughter hogs and cattle, survive disease, and obtain tools necessary to "cash-crop" a pioneer farm, was not easy. Log-rolling, house-raising, corn-husking, apple-paring, quilting bees, in which neighbors gathered to help one another, taught the newly arrived pioneers the need for joining together to satisfy individual needs through common action. Squatters' associations, organized for protection against land speculators, camp meeting, vigilantes, and the use of "gentlemen's agreements," grew out of voluntary pioneer associations. In the Middle Border, a new kind of community was emerging, a community of individuals who could band together in their own free will as individuals.

A new community, based on rules representing the will of equals who reached agreement through argument and discussion, was struggling to birth.

As settlers increased and travelers became more common, frontier groups became more heterogeneous. This was especially true of Illinois, and later of Chicago. Every gathering of people included people of widely different backgrounds, traditions, and class. Scotch-Irish and Palatine Germans, or "Pennsylvania Dutch," made up the dominant element in the stock of the colonial frontier. As Governor Spotswood of Virginia wrote in 1717, "The inhabitants of our frontiers are composed generally of such as have been transported hither as servants, and, being out of their time, settle themselves where land is to be taken up and that will produce the necessarys of life with little labor." Between the "lower orders" and those of a higher station in the older parts of America there was little communication. In the South, as in New England, each class kept to itself. In some communities in Pennsylvania, English was not used. Christina Tillson's observations on Pennsylvania indicate the basis for Edmund Burke's fear that Pennsylvania might become "wholly foreign." "We stopped every night [on her journey to Illinois], and between Philadelphia and Lancaster found ourselves in houses where they could not speak a word of English, and our pantomime performances were very amusing." [3]

But on the new frontier, being a neighbor involved frequent and sometimes heavy responsibilities in sharing labor, tools, skills, and time. The custom of borrowing and the habit of "dropping in" unannounced struck many observers of frontier life. As Francis Grierson said:

And what a gulf there was between the customs of the old country and the customs usual in the new West! Visitors appeared unannounced and at almost any hour. Today a neighbor would come two miles to borrow some sugar; tomorrow another would come still farther to borrow tea or coffee. All were received as if they were old and tried friends. My mother attended to the wants of those who came to borrow things for the table, while my father did his best to satisfy the men who came to borrow ploughs, spades, saws, wagons, and even horses. [4]

Hospitality was a necessity as well as a pleasure. Settlers who were as widely separated in space as in social background and tradition could not wait for town life to develop slowly into community life. They had to make their own community.

Middle Western settlers lived not in towns but on their own land. The town was for public life, the home on the land for private family life and for making a living. The older, village type of settlement, common to New England and adopted by communistic or cooperative colonies such as the Shakers, New Harmony, the Amana colony, the "little Landers," Bishop Hill, and New Llano, was abandoned in the Middle West. Responsibility shifted from governmental to proprietorial organizations in the new settlements. Intensive settlement was encouraged—one township or group of townships was granted at a time, and these grants were made to actual settlers. When Daniel Boone and his contemporaries pushed through the passes of the Appalachian Mountains and established their homes, each person selected the land that best suited him, seated himself on it, and set forth the limits of his claim with convenient trees, stones, creeks, and other natural objects. Few times in history has there been such freedom of location. This system, or lack of system, was changed in 1785, when lands were allocated as parts of regularly surveyed blocks or sections containing 640 acres each.

Government ownership and survey of the land did little to change land habits in the Middle West. The land belonged to those who worked it, not those who owned it. To Easterners squatting was simply thievery, but to the people of the Middle West whoever improved land earned a right to possess it. By 1850 the squatter ideal of individual freedom to compete unrestrictedly for the resources of the continent became political doctrine. Delegate Sibley of Minnesota, later to be the State's first governor, a regent of its university, president of its historical society, and a doctor of laws of Princeton, spoke out in favor of squatters. In a speech given in Congress in 1852, he declared that laws punishing "hardy lumbermen" for trespassing on the public domain should be "expunged as a disgrace to the country and the nineteenth century." The forests belonged to those who "penetrated to the remotest wilds of the Northwest [now the Middle West] to drag from their recesses the materials for building up towns and cities in the great valley of the Mississippi. . . ."

The domestic and social life of the Middle West brought together widely divergent social types. Women found themselves forced to associate with others of very different religions, family lineage, education, and manners. On her arrival in Illinois, Mrs. Tillson found that older Southern women would refer openly to a Southerner as a "white man" to distinguish him from a Yankee, a Northerner, or an Indian. An old Tennessee woman is quoted as saying: "I am getting skeery about them'ere Yankees; there is such a power of them coming in that they and the Injuns will squatch out all the white folks." [5] Children passed on to each other such rhymes as:

> The Irish and the Dutch [Germans],
> They don't amount to much.

Women of superior education and station discovered that few frontier women were willing to be permanent servants. Mrs. Kirkland tells us: "I

have . . . seen the interior of many a wretched dwelling, with almost literally nothing in it but a bed, a chest, and a table; children ragged to the last
degree, and potatoes the only fare; but never yet saw I one where the daughter was willing to own herself obliged to live out at service. She would 'hire
out' long enough to buy some articles of dress perhaps, or 'because our folks
have been sick, and want a little money to pay the doctor,' or for some such
special reason; but never as a regular calling, or with an acknowledgment
of inferior station." [6] Living with someone for wages was considered by common consent a favor. For women reared to think of social class as a necessary
frame to good society the frontier was a rude shock. As Mrs. Kirkland told
her Eastern readers, certain habits of behavior usual in Eastern society would
be considered ridiculous in the wilderness. "What can be more absurd than
a feeling of proud distinction, where a stray spark of fire, a sudden illness,
or a day's contre-temps, may throw you entirely upon the kindness of your
humblest neighbor? If I treat Mrs. Timson with neglect today can I with any
face borrow her broom to-morrow? And what would become of me, if in
revenge for my declining her invitation to tea this afternoon, she should
decline coming to my washing on Monday?"

Notes

[1] Row housing has never been popular in Chicago and is not developing in the
newer suburbs.

[2] Quoted from *America Through British Eyes*, compiled and edited by Allan Nevins
(New York: Oxford University Press, 1948), p. 66.

[3] Christiana Holmes Tillson, *A Woman's Story of Pioneer Illinois*, ed. by Milo Milton
Quaife (Chicago: R. R. Donnelly & Sons, 1919), p. 36.

[4] Francis Grierson, *The Valley of Shadows* (Boston: Houghton Mifflin, 1948), p. 30.

[5] Tillson, *op. cit.*, p. 25.

[6] Caroline M. Kirkland, *A New Home, or Life in the Clearings*, ed. and with an
intro. by John Nerber (New York: Putnam, 1953), pp. 66–67. The passing of the hired
girl who ate with the family, to the servant who lived back-stairs, is often noted in
discussion and stories on the change from country to city life in Chicago from 1885 to
1905.

2

The Search for Community in Religious Expression

In his sermons, as in the staging of revivals, the frontier preacher fought a devil who walked the wilderness beside him and his flock. The frontier sermon was the true sacrament of the church. The drama of conversion was a drama of struggle and violence, not in some far-off Armageddon but in daily life itself. Brother Axley, who rode the backwoods with Cartwright, often said that in superfluous dress, whisky, and slavery he had "a trinity of devils to fight." As British travelers noted, the new Americans of the West took their religion very literally. Preachers did not enter into disputation over the existence of Heaven and Hell or the nature of Death and Judgment; they dramatized them in terrible but glorious dramas of salvation. Peter Cartwright of Illinois delighted in depicting the struggle between God and the Devil for the soul of men. His God and his Devil were gods of struggle. And these struggles took place in daily life within all individuals, rich and poor alike. There was no vicarious atonement by an established priesthood. Individuals must struggle for salvation and atone for their sins. They must search out the devil in themselves, grapple with him, and, with God's help, cast him down.

In the days following the meeting of the Great Revival almost every expression of life was infused with religious value. The choice of clothes, food, and drink became a moral choice. Even at corn-husking time, a time of merrymaking, love-making, gaiety, dancing, and drinking, nothing stronger than coffee was drunk in the cabins of the devout during periods of intense religious zeal. Among "Abolition Methodists" there was no separation of politics and morals. "Sin in politics is ekil to sin in religion—there ain't no dividin' line," said the man of God in Francis Grierson's *The Valley of Shadows*. For such people, justice was achieved in revelation, not in debate. Under the power of such truth, religion became a guide to the smallest and the daily details of life. Preachers like Peter Cartwright spoke out against whisky, gambling, jewelry, and fine clothes; they defined clearly, frequently, and with great authority how one should *act* (not "think") as a religious person. Higher education was denounced because it substituted thought for action and produced preachers who moved people to think about religion but not how to act as members of a religious community. To Cartwright, Uncle Jimmy Painter, or Samuel Thornton Scott the Word alone was important. Rank, wealth, lineage, beauty, or elegance meant little to these proud men of God. At dinner with the governor of Illinois, Cartwright stopped the service by saying, "Hold on, Governor, ask the blessing." When the governor admitted that he did not know how to do so, Cartwright pronounced the blessing and afterward rebuked the governor for not being a practicing Christian. Even though a Jackson democrat, Cartwright would not humble himself to his leader in the house of the Lord. In story and legend the authority of the preacher speaks out. "Peter Cartwright was a-preachin' when Old Hickory walked in. The presidin' elder sez to the preacher: 'Thet's Andrew Jackson,' but Pete Cartwright didn't noways keer. 'Who's Andrew Jackson?' he sez. 'If he's a sinner God'll damn him the same ez He would a Guinea nigger.' En he went right on preachin'."

Seizures of religious ecstasy in which sinners announced their freedom from the bondage of sin were frequent and intense. Bishop Asbury and the simple preacher Cartwright agree in their descriptions of the extraordinary vehemence of religious expression in rolling, running, dancing, and even barking. Most common was the falling exercise which, as Cartwright tells us, affected "saints and sinners of every age and of every grade." "With a piercing scream," those taken would "fall like a log on the floor or ground seemingly dead, sometimes lying thus for hours at a time." Worshipers were seized by jerks. These convulsive movements of the body might affect only the legs, arms, or the head. Frequently the whole body would be convulsed. Cartwright tells us the only cure was not to strive against these jerks but to "pray in good earnest." He tells us of seeing more than five hundred persons jerking at one time. "The first jerk or so, you would see their fine bonnets, caps and combs fly; and so sudden would be the jerking of the head that their long loose hair would crack almost as loud as a wagoner's whip."[1] Injuries, sometimes even death, occurred. We hear of "a large drinking man" who tried to fight his seizure with whisky. As he "cursed and swore very profanely," his jerks increased. Finally he "fetched a very violent jerk, snapped his neck, fell, and soon expired."

Ecstasy of joy in the Lord was expressed in chants, songs, gleeful screams, and frenzied dances. The Sweezyites or Holy Rollers rolled back and forth on the floor. Even laughter found religious expression among the "Holy Laughers," who moved their audience by shouting and laughing. Laughing to God became a form of prayer which lasted for hours. Primitive Baptist preachers developed the "holy tone," or "holy whine," a sing-song method of speaking, in which the sound "ah" occurs at the end of each breath pause and the taking of a fresh breath is intentionally made audible. The Shakers reached ecstatic union with God through dancing and handclapping. Inner symbolic struggles with the Devil were often matched in real battle with his fleshly minions, the rowdies and rogues who came to break up religious gatherings. Cartwright tells us, "They came drunk, and armed with dirks, clubs, knives, and horse-whips, and swore they would break up the meeting. After interrupting us very much on Saturday night, they collected early on Sunday morning, determined on a general riot." In the middle of his sermon two young men "marched into the congregation with loaded whips, and hats on, and rose up and stood in the midst of the ladies, and began to laugh and talk." Appeals to camp magistrates to stop them were of no avail. Cartwright decided he must vanquish his own devils.

I advanced toward them. They ordered me to stand off, but I advanced. One of them made a pass at my head with his whip, but I closed with him, and jerked him off the seat. A regular scuffle ensued. The congregation by this time were all in commotion. I heard the magistrates give general orders, commanding all friends of order to aid in suppressing the riot. In the scuffle I threw my prisoner down, and held him fast; he tried his best to get loose; I told him to be quiet, or I would pound his chest well. The mob rose, and rushed to the rescue of the two prisoners. . . . An old and drunken magistrate came up to me, and ordered me to let my prisoner go. I told him I should not. He swore if I did not, he would knock me down. I told him to crack away. Then one of my friends, at my request, took hold of my prisoner, and the drunken justice made a pass at me; but I parried the stroke, and seized him by the collar and the hair of the head, and fetching him a sudden jerk forward, brought him to the ground, and jumped on him. I told him to be quiet, or I would pound him well. The mob then rushed to the scene; they knocked down seven magistrates, and several preachers and others. I gave up my drunken prisoners to another, and threw myself in front of the friends of order. Just at this moment the ringleader of the mob and I met; he made three passes at me, intending to knock me down. The last time he struck at me, by the force of his own effort he threw the side of his face toward me. It seemed at that moment I had not power to resist temptation, and I struck a sudden blow in the burr of the ear and dropped him to the earth. Just at that moment the friends of order rushed by the hundreds on the mob, knocking them down in every direction. In a few minutes, the place became too strait for the mob, and they wheeled and fled in every direction, but we secured about thirty prisoners, marched them off to a vacant tent, and put them under guard till Monday morning, when they were tried, and every man was fined to the utmost limits of the law.[2]

The violent ecstasies of the sects signaled a search for new forms of religious expression. From the days of the Great Revivals in religion to the rise of urban revivalists like Billy Sunday, an extraordinary sense of style marks religious revivals in the Middle West. It was not the style of the East, certainly not that of Europe. Godly settlers inveighed against "art" because for them art was style, fashion, fine art—the worldly art of effeminate dudes of

aesthetic rapture in drama, was created in carefully formed expression in which participants achieved a profound sense of communion. The Cane Ridge meeting of 1801 in Bourbon County, Kentucky, was attended by crowds (variously estimated at from 10,000 to 25,000) who stayed in worship for several days. Similar camp meetings soon followed throughout the Middle West. Bishop Asbury states in his *Journal* for 1811 that there were four hundred camp meetings held in that year alone. Eye witnesses of these meetings agree on their overwhelming dramatic power.

Great numbers were on the ground from Friday until the Thursday following, night and day without intermission, engaged in some religious act of worship. They are commonly collected in small circles of 10 or 12, close adjoining another circle and all engaged in singing . . . hymns; and then a minister steps upon a stump or log, and begins an exhortation or sermon, when as many as can hear collect around him. On Sabbath I saw above 100 candles burning at once and I saw 100 persons at once on the ground crying for mercy, of all ages from 8 to 60 years. . . . When a person is struck down he is carried by others out of the congregation, when some minister converses with and prays for him; afterwards a few gather around and sing a hymn suitable to the case. The whole number brought to the ground, under convictions, were about 1,000, not less. The sensible, the weak, etc., learned and unlearned, the rich and poor are subjects of it.[5]

Night camp meetings created deeply impressive moments in the community drama of frontier life.

The glare of the blazing camp-fires falling on a dense assemblage . . . and reflected back from long ranges of tents upon every side; hundreds of candles and lamps suspended among the trees, together with numerous torches flashing to and fro, throwing an uncertain light upon the tremulous foliage, and giving an appearance of dim and indefinite extent to the depth of the forest; the solemn chanting of hymns swelling and falling on the night wind; the impassioned exhortations; the earnest prayers; the sobs, shrieks, or shouts, bursting from persons under intense agitation of mind; the sudden spasms which seize upon scores, that unexpectedly dashed them to the ground; all conspired to work up feelings to the highest pitch of excitement.[6]

Camp meetings were a new kind of religious art and a new form of community drama. For the devout as for the sinner they were a supreme moment of identification. The devout lived through these meetings, not as commemorative gatherings of civic life, but as living dramas of atonement and redemption, of the birth and rebirth of the self and the community in Christ. People looked forward to meeting times for weeks on end. They hungered and yearned for the moment when they could again become brothers in Christ. Immediately before the meeting expectancy mounted to a high pitch. During the meeting itself people prayed for the great moment of salvation and redemption, the moment when the soul found God and men found each other in an ecstasy of brotherhood. The enactment of the great religious drama of salvation, redemption, and communion moved thousands of worshipers to joy in brotherhood. As they clasped hands and marched together they were no longer alone and separate. In the Christian love feast they become brothers and sisters in Christ, in and of the earth as of heaven. Worshipers turned homeward in deep serenity. So long as the radiance of love lasted there was no fear or loneliness in the pioneer homes scattered over the plains and forests of the Middle Border.

The trip to the meeting was a pilgrimage. For some it was a journey of many days, for others but a few hours. Thousands of people poured into the meeting grounds. They came in wagons, buggies, and on horseback. Many of the horses "carried double." Whole families, with provisions for a long journey, rode in big covered wagons. Blinding dust filled the air and covered the clothes of travelers, who closed in and greeted each other as they drew closer to the camp site. Francis Grierson, out of a boyhood spent in frontier Illinois, tells of the arrival:

As we got within two miles of the grounds the whole populace, for a radius of many miles, seemed to be on the move, converging towards one point. From a slight eminence which we had just attained, commanding a view on all sides, a scraggly line of white-topped wagons could be seen descending a slope to the right, while to the left, a little below us, another line of twisting vehicles ascended in a slow, weary train, enveloped in clouds of dust, now partly hidden behind clumps of trees, now emerging like the remnant of some scattered army crawling towards the precincts of a friendly country. Once in a while we were passed by young men on horseback who galloped their horses; others, in light buggies, shot past the heavy wagons and were soon out of sight; hundreds were on foot, looking neither to the right nor to the left, and these, as Uriah Busby observed, were the ones in dead earnest, bound to get there no matter how. . . . We drove into the camp grounds about one o'clock, and found two or three thousand persons there already, with others pouring in by the hundred.[7]

Frontier sadness and melancholy, noted by Crèvecoeur and Tocqueville, and so deeply etched in Lincoln's face, was born of a tragic vision of life. Long before the Civil War brought tragedy into the daily lives of all Americans, the frontier people of the Middle West faced sickness and death. In the fall of 1818 and the winter of 1829 epidemics of "the milk sick" ravaged the Indiana frontier. Within hours and days, the healthy, strong bodies of men and cattle wasted away. Whole districts were depopulated. There was no cure for this or for other dread diseases. Those who survived fled to other sections, like the Lincolns, Hankses, and Sparrows, who were driven from Pigeon Creek in Indiana to Sangamon county in Illinois. The stricken waited on "God's will." Those who were spared often watched their loved ones wither and die. As Sandburg tells us: "Abe and his sister Sarah waited on their mother. . . . There was no physician nearer than thirty-five miles. The

Camp meeting sermons were a moment of high drama in the frontier community.
Courtesy Chicago Historical Society

mother knew she was going to die, and called the children to her bedside. She was very weak, and the children leaned over while she gave her last message. Placing her feeble hand on little Abe's head she told him to be kind and good to his father and sister; to both she said, 'Be good to one another,' expressing a hope that they might live, as they had been taught by her, to love their kindred and worship God." Months later, near the end of winter, Lincoln, then nine years old, helped to get David Elkin, an itinerant preacher, to consecrate his mother's grave.

These frontiersmen of the Middle West knew the extremes of good and evil, as they knew suffering and death. In the midst of the violence of frontier life sects like the Separatists of Zoar lived lives free of lust, greed, or violence. Joseph Baumeler, who led his congregation into the Ohio wilderness in 1817, taught that "a Christian cannot murder his enemy, much less his friend." Other utopian American societies were scattered through the Middle West. If there were men of fire and the sword, there were men, too, of peace, light, and art. Zoarites had no preacher or minister, but the church at Zoar had an organ. Many of the households, poor as they were, had pianos; the boys were taught to read music and to play in the band.

As they plunged deeper and deeper into the wilderness of the Ohio River Valley, pioneers often found it necessary to brutalize themselves. Any group of whites, women and children alike, were subject to attack by hostile Indians. A solitary farmer clearing land or tilling his plot of corn beyond the outposts of the nearest fort or station might be found lying dead beside his plow. Lincoln's father and his uncles saw their father shot down. Men whose boyhood memories were haunted by such visions hated Indians with deadly hate. Indian-killing for them was a duty—sometimes, indeed, a kind of sport. News of Indians loose anywhere within a half-day's riding aroused Mordecai Lincoln, brother of Abraham Lincoln, the grandfather of the President, to gather his best rifles, pistols, and knives and join the manhunt. Preachers such as Cartwright spoke almost casually of Indian-killing. Sherman's terse remark in 1869 that "the only good Indians I ever saw were dead," would have excited little discussion in the Bloody Ground of Kentucky. But exterminating Indians was cruel work. Life became increasingly savage on the frontier. Crimes lay heavy on the conscience of men, and especially of women, whose religious and social heritage taught them not to kill. Cursing, blaspheming, drunkenness, savage fighting, killing Indians, and mob rule—as in the murder of Elijah P. Lovejoy, the abolitionist, at Alton, Illinois—might be condoned, but they could not be forgotten. Terrible childhood memories of violence, suffering, and death haunted many settlers. Mothers and fathers saw their children waste and die of disease; children saw their parents die.

Lincoln watched his mother die and later in life buried his own second child.

These new Puritans on the frontier and their descendants in the cities had little regard for art that did not serve religion or could be used to meet the trials of life. And while every man could be his own priest, he could do so only through the Bible, which he must hear spoken out or be able to read for himself. The Bible and its sayings soon became part of the community imagery of the West. The Methodist Church, as did all frontier churches, translated its liturgy into the vernacular of the West. The American Tract Society, formed in 1825, sent agents into every section of the country supplying the poor and the neglected, and, as the cities developed, the immigrant, with tracts and books. The translation of the Bible into American vernacular was done in speech, as well as in writing. As Tocqueville observed: "In the United States [circa 1835] the influence of religion is not confined to the manners, but extends to the intelligence of the people."

The Methodists in England, like the Shakers in America, laid great stress upon the song as part of worship. The Methodist movement in eighteenth-century England was to a great extent a singing movement, and the hymns of the Wesleys were more effective in bringing Methodist theology to the people than even the preaching. Many of the Wesleyan hymns were set to popular tunes, as were many of the early Lutheran hymns. Between 1805 and 1843 at least seventeen religious songbooks appeared. These songs were based on the daily experience of the people, and whether of death, the day of judgment, future punishment, heaven, hell—the great popular drama of salvation—they were created for religious communication among people who often could not read or write. And among those who could, life in America was often so strange and new that traditional forms of expression were almost meaningless. Even the English texts of Watts and Wesley, created for the common people of England, required a certain exercise of learning and knowledge of cadences and rhythms of speech not indigenous to the frontier.

Rural American religious versemakers, such as Granade and Leland, turned to old British and British-American folk tunes, which everybody could sing in words that spoke from the heart in the language of the common man. Thus the traditional ballad "In Seaport Town" the recurring phrase:

> Till at last they came to that lonesome valley

becomes the beautiful spiritual "Lonesome Valley"

> You got to go to that lonesome valley,
> You got to go there by yourself.

whose tune is very close to that of the secular song. The revival spiritual songs are another step toward simplification and expression in the new speech of America. At the camp meetings it was not a question of inducing everyone to sing, but of letting everyone sing, of letting all sing songs which were so simple that they offered an irresistible temptation to join in.[8] The religious search for community in the camp meeting was always a search for communion through some kind of symbolic expression. There was no standard liturgy, and even commonly used hymns were altered to suit the demand of local preachers and their congregations. Camp meetings were community affairs drawn from the whole community not from any particular class.

Methodists, Baptists, and Disciples agreed that no amount of theological education could make up for a preacher's lack of ability to preach the "simple gospel" or lead songs of the faith. The struggle for communication in some kind of vernacular reached a climax in camp meetings, where it was discovered that only songs of very simple texts could be shared by all alike. Even the older folk hymns of New England and Britain, simple as they were, were inadequate. They were progressively simplified until an organically constructed tune was achieved. The verse of the song was mastered by comparatively few singers, even though it was "lined out" by the song leader. But the whole assemblage had its chance to join lustily in singing the chorus. (Such songs were sometimes called "choruses.") One short phrase might be sung three times, and then followed by a one-phrase refrain.

> Where are the Hebrew children?
> Where are the Hebrew children?
> Where are the Hebrew children?
> *Safe in the promised land.*

Final brevity and simplicity was reached when one short phrase or sentence, sung over and over, filled out the whole frame as a stanza.

In these songs, as later in the vernacular of the Chicago school of architecture in the seventies and eighties, people sought to create forms in which experience could be shared in common. The violent, cruel, ugly life of the frontier, as later of the new, raw city of Chicago, needed beauty as much as it needed religion. For if religion was called upon in suffering and death, art was invoked to create joy and gladness in life. And if we can say that religion made early forms of American art possible, we must also say that art made many forms of American religion possible. For there could be no religion until ceremonies and rituals existed for communicating belief. Religious expression is always a search for deep communion with a living God. On the frontier of the Middle West separation of people on their homesteads, the lack of established community life, the guilt and terror of living in violence and danger made the search for God necessary to social as well as religious life. The call to meeting and the journey through the woods began the pilgrimage of people yearning for community with a God who would also bring them into community with each other. In such meetings they sought what they called a "glory moment." This moment of ecstasy in song, shout, and dance carried people out of the woods and the prairies to some world beyond, but it also created and re-created social bonds. Frontier people wanted a sense of being together, of being one in common purpose with their fellow beings, for without this the burden of freedom and the responsibilities of individuality could scarcely be born. These "rugged individualists," living on their own freeholds, discovered that in the new America the individual could exist only if he found some kind of social bond which would not make loneliness and isolation the price of individuality. No one, not even the hardy pioneer on his freehold, the freest man thus far known in civilization, could enjoy his new freedom if he could not enjoy it in community with other free men.

The camp meeting was religious ritual drama, a drama in which the religious community of the frontier was born and reborn. But it was also a social drama.[9] Meeting sessions often began with the "handshake ceremony," in which, with all the congregation standing, each turned to his right and then to his left and shook hands with whoever stood next to him. At such moments the burdens of inequality, as well as the specific religious burden of sin, was transformed into deeply felt equality and neighborliness. In the eyes of God all men were equal, as the popular camp meeting ditty reminded them:

> Come hungry, come thirsty, come ragged, come bare,
> Come filthy, come lousy, come just as you are.

The spirit of this call was carried out to the letter. No one was allowed to go without food, shelter, or clothes. All travelers, hostile and sympathetic alike, agree that the Western camp meeting was the very heart and soul of hospitality and kindness. The parting ceremonies of a Portsmouth, Ohio, camp meeting of 1818 tell what it meant for the pioneer families to meet together in brotherhood of Christ: "The thoughts of parting to meet no more, or of meeting to part no more, produced the medley of those groans and shouts which far exceed all description. When we for the last time marched in order around the camp and sang our parting hymn, the scene was truly solemn and impressive. The tents struck; the wagons in readiness; weeping circles of young converts folded in each other's arms; ministers surrounded with weeping hundreds, crying out as they presented the parting hand, "pray for me and mine!" [10]

Notes

[1] Peter Cartwright, *Autobiography of Peter Cartwright, The Backwoods Preacher,* ed. by W. P. Strickland (New York: Nelson & Phillips, 1856), p. 49.

[2] *Ibid.,* pp. 91–92. Like Shaw's Christian, Ferrovius, in *Androcles and the Lion,* Cartwright's laying on of hands was sometimes a violent and painful memory to the converted. He often succumbed to the temptation of battle.

[3] As we shall see, men were not conscripted as soldiers in the armies of the North and South, but exhorted to join and to remain in the ranks, through song and oratory.

[4] Quoted from Charles Nordhoff, *The Communistic Societies of the United States* (New York: Hillary House, 1961), pp. 170ff.

[5] Quoted from W. W. Sweet, *The Story of Religion in America* (New York: Scribners, 1950), p. 229. For other accounts, see C. C. Cleveland, *The Great Revival in the West, 1797–1805* (Chicago: University of Chicago Press, 1916), Appendix V., pp. 183–89.

[6] Quoted from Sweet, *op. cit.,* p. 229.

[7] Francis Grierson, *The Valley of Shadows* (Boston: Houghton, Mifflin, 1948), p. 135.

[8] For discussion of this, see the introduction to *Spiritual Folksongs of Early America* (New York: Locust Valley, 1853), by G. P. Jackson.

[9] Jackson tells us in his studies of the spiritual folk songs of early America that "the camp meetings at Rock Springs, Lincoln County, North Carolina . . . had been the 'mating grounds' for that state for fifty years" (i.e. from 1830 to 1880).

[10] Quoted from Charles A. Johnson, *Frontier Camp Meeting: Religion's Harvest Time* (Dallas, Texas: Southern Methodist University Press, 1955), p. 228.

3

Western Styles of Expression

THE GREAT utterances of Lincoln, and the incarnation of the American egalitarian spirit in *Huckleberry Finn,* could not have developed in a common, low, and vulgar language. *Huckleberry Finn* and Lincoln's Gettysburg Address, Farewell Address, Second Inaugural Address, and his earlier "Concluding Speech" of the campaign of 1858 are peaks of American expression. Lincoln's political genius often blinds us to the fact that he was an artist—and a very great artist—in a new kind of American speech, the speech of the Middle West. Like Mark Twain and so many readers of the Middle West, he *heard* words. Lincoln punctuated for pause and emphasis as one accustomed to speak rather than to write for print. He spoke instead of writing, because it was the only way to be a literary artist on the frontier. His love of words and his lifelong desire to entertain and to fashion tales and comic parables found expression in the spoken drama of politics. But with all his genius, Lincoln—no more than Mark Twain, Louis H. Sullivan, or Frank Lloyd Wright—could not have created his great forms unless the language and all expressive form in the Middle West possessed resources which could be made into art. Lincoln was not a simple, plain, homespun speaker. His appeals were not made to audiences of illiterates or ignoramuses. His speech was not artless with little debt to rhetoric. On the contrary, his speech was rich in figures, his anecdotes told with high drama. His sentences flow easily. His diction, while simple enough, contains rich patterns of assonance, alliteration, and other rhetorical devices. Phrases and clauses are often separated by caesuras and grouped in balanced staves of two or more phrase units. His style is marked by repetition. He seems to be searching for some way to resolve contending voices within and without himself. But there is a calm, sure deliberation in his search, and it is expressed in words simple enough to be understood by everyone.

Western religious and political leaders faced many problems in communication. Local leadership was gained through skill in common speech and manners. But the manners and speech which carried men to local leadership in the political styles of campaigning in the West often served as a handicap in the national stage. Opponents in the Middle West did not discuss issues in well-ordered debate, or in "book" English. An opponent was a villain in a drama whose outcome determined the fate of the community. Vilification, blessing, cursing, mockery, ridicule, and all the resources of rhetoric were used. Months before election day campaigns became so feverish, and tempers so frayed, that deep personal friendships were endangered. Politics, like religion among the devout, intruded into all aspects of life. Every candidate boasted of his log-cabin and hard-cider origins. In dress, manner, speech, conviviality, and worship, candidates struggled to achieve a "plain-folks" appeal. The surest shaft against an opponent was to prove that he held himself superior to common men. Thus "Long John Wentworth" of Illinois, who campaigned in and around Chicago in the forties, accused the Whig incumbent, Benjamin Raymond, of being a "wealthy merchant" whereas Wentworth's candidate was "a builder and a contractor who worked among the people." "While Mr. Raymond will be found perfumed in a lady's parlor," said Wentworth, "our candidate can be seen with his coat off shingling back houses." [1]

"Plain folk" appeal was necessary to success in the West. Men like Wentworth, a Dartmouth graduate, learned soon enough that to communicate successfully with constituents in Chicago and Illinois they must dress, speak, and act as Westerners. This means such things as laying aside new clothes for a shabbier outfit suitable to horse-and-wagon travel, even though other Americans found this shabbiness uncouth and vulgar. A correspondent for a Boston paper in 1857 reported on Wentworth's appearance on the streets of Chicago during his term as mayor. He was, the reporter said, a "shabby, elephantine individual," with a good-natured countenance, who wore an old straw hat turned down all around, a poorly fitted linen coat, unblacked shoes that seemed three sizes too large, and loose trousers which looked "as if he had jumped too far into them and hadn't time to go back." [2] Western politicians dressed this way because it identified them with the people, not because they were ignorant of niceties in dress. This identification went far beyond tricks of political staging. Educated men like Wentworth often began their careers in the West with a self-conscious identification with the people, but many ended their lives believing in the virtue of such identification. To be a leader of free men, to lead them in prayer, in search for justice under law, and finally into battle, was glory enough. In the arts, too, Mark Twain, Sullivan, Wright, Dreiser, the poets Vachel Lindsay and Carl Sandburg all found glory in designing and speaking for the people. They were well aware that as they pleased the people, they alienated the standard-bearers of culture. Western artists, such as Sullivan, were not people's artists because of ignorance but from choice. They were in no sense "primitives"—any more than Lincoln was a "primitive" in politics.

Revolt against Eastern elegance was both religious and social. Cartwright said, in speaking of his early years as a backwoods preacher: "When I joined the Church, her ministers and members were a plain people; plain in dress and address. You could know a Methodist preacher by his plain dress as far as you could see him. The members were also plain, very plain in dress. They wore no jewelry, nor were they permitted to wear jewelry, or superfluous ornament, or extravagant dress of any kind." Such dress, Cartwright goes on to explain, was not the result of poverty but of a religious conviction that "ornaments engender pride, and lead to many hurtful lusts." And although "we knew then as well as we do now, that the religion of the Lord Jesus Christ did not consist in dress, or the cut of the garment," yet simple dress was "the rule by which we walked, whether poor or rich, young or old."[3] And if dress was a self-conscious identification in religious life so, too, was speech. Cartwright preached as he did because it was the only way to reach people. But he never thought of himself as preaching down to the people. Nor did he concern himself with the traditional arts of pulpit rhetoric. He was aware that preaching in the vernacular, with direct, homely, and dramatic appeals to his audience, was considered vulgar and ignorant in the East. ". . . [A]lmost all [the Yankees] I had seen in the West had assumed such high ground, professed such mighty educational attainments, that we poor illiterate Western backwoods preachers could hardly hold an intelligible conversation with them; . . . we were afraid to start any proposition whatever; and when we met them, we could only stand and look at them, and make ready to answer questions."

When the Methodists held their first General Conference in the East, at Boston in 1852, several Western preachers attended. Cartwright tried twice and failed each time to move his audiences as he had moved them so often in Illinois. When Brother Taylor asked him to preach at his church, Cartwright told him: "Brother Taylor, you need not think that any of us Western men are anxious about preaching to you in Boston; your way of worship here is so different from ours in the West, that we are confused. There's your old wooden god, the organ, bellowing up in the gallery, and a few dandified singers lead in singing, and really do it all. The congregation won't sing, and when you pray, they sit down instead of kneeling. We don't worship God in the West by proxy, or substitution." Cartwright said he would preach only if he could "preach in the Western manner." Brother Taylor replied: "Brother, you must preach to us at Bethel; and roll up your sleeves, and un-

16807

McCOOK COMMUNITY COLLEGE
Learning Resource Center

As this French engraving of 1854, "The Country Election," shows, the great game of politics dominated the frontier community. *Courtesy Chicago Historical Society*

button your collar, and give us a real Western cut." Cartwright agreed. "I took my text from Matthew xi, 12; [4] and after a few commonplace remarks, I commenced giving them some Western anecdotes, which had a thrilling effect on the congregation, and excited them immoderately, I cannot say religiously; but I thought if ever I saw animal excitement, it was then and there. This broke the charm. During my stay after this, I could pass anywhere for Peter Cartwright, the old pioneer of the West." He found the Boston people generous, hospitable, and social. Their "sociability and friendly greetings reminded me more of our Western manners than anything I ever found among total strangers, and many of them are sincere, devout Christians. . . ." [5]

During the Civil War, Western troops in the armies of the North dressed, marched, talked, and carried themselves differently from those of the East. Eastern soldiers disparaged their Western comrades as crude, undisciplined, and slovenly, while Yanks from the Middle West denounced those of Massachusetts, New York, or Pennsylvania as effete, liquor-soaked, money-mad dandies—"bandbox" troops, fit only for parade and garrison. In his comments on preparations for the great victory parade in Washington at the war's end, Theodore Upson, the young Hoosier who fought under Grant at Vicksburg and Chattanooga and followed Sherman through Georgia and the Carolinas, tells how careful Sherman's "Bummers" were not to ape the "polished shoes and brass trimmings"—the "rifles burnished till they shone, the new uniforms and nearly all white gloves"—of the armies of the East. "Our Army is to march as they had been marching—just as we came from the front without any extra fuss or feathers. . . . So I put on my soiled uniform again, took up my rifle and blankets ready to go to my company. . . . When we started down the Avenue our boys fell into the long swinging step, every man in perfect time, . . . and it seemed to me that the men never had marched so well." As they passed the reviewing stand, General Grant and the "great men of the nation, and many from other nations . . . all rose to their feet and with bared heads cheered and cheered. I glanced down the line of our Platoon—every man had his eyes front, every step was perfect; *on the face of the men was what one might call a glory look*." [6]

Grant was very careful not to fan the flames of sectional jealousy, but his account in the *Memoirs* of the Grand Review marks proudly the Western characteristics of Sherman's armies. They had fought continuously, for they "had been engaged in all the battles of the West and had marched from the Mississippi through the Southern States to the sea. . . . [They] had passed over many of the battlefields of the Army of the Potomac, thus having seen, to a greater extent than any other body of troops, the entire theatre of the four years' war for the preservation of the Union. . . . I doubt whether an equal body of men of any nation, take them man for man, officer for officer, was ever gotten together that would have proved their equal in battle." He notes the differences between his Western and Eastern armies:

Sherman's army made a different appearance from that of the Army of the Potomac. . . . Sherman's army was not so well-dressed as the Army of the Potomac, but their marching could not be excelled; they gave the appearance of men who had been thoroughly drilled to endure hardships, either by long and continuous marches or through exposure to any climate, without the ordinary shelter of a camp. They exhibited also some of the order of march through Georgia. . . . In the rear of a company there would be a captured horse or mule loaded with small cooking utensils, captured chickens and other food picked up for the use of the men. Negro families who had followed the army would sometimes come along in the rear of a company, with three or four children packed upon a single mule, and the mother leading it.[7]

Western attitude toward dress is told by Hamlin Garland in the chapter, "London and Evening Dress," of his *A Daughter of the Middle Border:*

Up to my thirty-ninth year in 1899 I had never worn a swallow-tail evening coat, and the question of conforming to the growing sartorial custom was becoming, each day, of more acute concern to my friends as well as to myself. . . . The claw-hammer suit was to me, as to my fellow artists, "the livery of privilege" worn only by monopolistic brigands and the poor parasites who fawned upon and served them, whereas the double-breasted black coat [the Prince Albert frock coat] . . . was associated in my mind with judges, professors, senators and doctors of divinity [for the frock coat] remained the uniform of professional men throughout the Middle Border.

But the World's Fair in 1893 brought to Chicago "many of the discriminating social customs of the East, [and] guests from the old world to whom dress was a formal, almost sacred routine." In his sixties, Garland can joke about his concern over the "livery of privilege," but he stresses that such changes of dress were really changes of identity for the artists of the Middle Border. In London he was invited to an authors' dinner at which, Zangwill told him, he must wear evening dress, "the accursed suit in which I was about to lose my identity."

British authors were highly amused at such concern, but Garland tells us that it was not just a matter of giving up a style of dress.

In stating my case I am stating the perplexities of thousands of my fellow citizens of the Middle Border. It has its humorous phases—this reversal of social habit in me, but it also has wide significance. My surrender was coincidental with similar changes of thought in millions of other young men throughout the West. It was but another indication that the customs of the Border were fading to a memory, and that Western society, which had long been dominated by the stately figures of the minister and the judge, was on its way to adopt the manners and customs of the openly derided but secretly admired "four hundred." To abandon western dress was to part company with Walt Whitman, Joaquin Miller, John Burroughs, and other illustrious non-conformists to whom long beards, easy collars, and short coats were natural and becoming. To take the other was to follow Lowell and Stedman and Howells. To shorten my beard—or remove it altogether—to wear a standing collar, and attached cuffs—to abandon my western wide-rimmed hat—these and many other "reforms" were involved in my decision.

Garland jokes about the consternation of his fellow Chicago artists when they saw him, after his return from London, in evening dress at the Annual Reception of the Chicago Art Institute. "I met two of my fellow republicans in Prince Albert frock suits. At sight of me they started with surprise—surprise and sorrow—exclaiming, 'Look at Hamlin Garland!'" Eugene Field, the first of the Chicago newspaper humorists, also expressed his sorrow over the surrender of "the sturdy opponent of the swallow-tail suit." But the joking wears thin, and Garland ends his discussion of his surrender by agreeing with Burroughs. "Howells . . . heartily approved of my action, but Burroughs regarded it as a weak surrender. 'A silk hat and steel-pen coat on a Whitman Democrat,' he said, 'seems like a make-believe,' which in a sense it was." [8]

Garland's forebodings about his change of identity were correct. His realistic portrayals of rural life, which opened the way in Chicago writing for the revolt against the genteel tradition of the East and the South, all done when he identified himself as a Westerner, changed in 1902 to *The Captain of the Gray-Horse Troop,* where sentiment and the romance of the West supplant the depiction of farm life as in *A Little Norsk* (1892) and *Rose of Dutcher's Coolly* (1895). The "veritism" of *Crumbling Idols* (1894) where Garland joined in spirit with Sullivan, Wright, Altgeld, Veblen, Edelman, Harper, and Ade in their search for urban democratic forms of expression in life, art, and thought, dies in Garland's New York years. Garland's loss of identity in Chicago, where he could not relate to the new people of the urban West, was a loss of creative force. He shook off the sickness and despair of his last days in Chicago only when he recaptured in memory the West he had lost in reality and became the literary spokesman for the passing agrarian frontier.

Like the classicists who fought the Chicago school of architecture, the self-styled "cosmopolites"—later to call themselves internationalists—who took over the studio life of the Fine Arts Building in Chicago nearly destroyed the indigenous art of the city. The "cosmopolites," who bought their art in Europe and discovered their aesthetic standards in the schools, drove the young writers of the next generation into the city rooms of Chicago newspapers. By 1905 the Press Club, the White Chapel, and Loop saloons were the gathering places for Chicago writers.

Notes

[1] Quoted from D. E. Fehrenbacher, *Chicago Giant: A Biography of Long John Wentworth* (Madison, Wis.: University of Wisconsin Press, 1957), p. 31.

[2] *Ibid.,* p. 147.

[3] Chapter xxxiii, "Methodist Usages," of Cartwright's *Autobiography,* contains these and other comments on religious customs in early Illinois.

[4] "And from the days of John the Baptist until now the kingdom of heaven suffereth violence, and the violent take it by force."

[5] Peter Cartwright, *Autobiography of Peter Cartwright, The Backwoods Preacher* (New York: Nelson and Phillips, 1856), pp. 477–78.

[6] Theodore F. Upson, *With Sherman to the Sea,* ed. by O. O. Winther (Bloomington, Ind.: University of Indiana Press, 1958), pp. 175–77. Upson's italics.

[7] *Personal Memoirs of U. S. Grant,* ed. with notes and introduction by E. B. Long (Cleveland & New York: World Publishing Co., 1952), p. 579. It was in this army that Jenney and Adler, the great Chicago builders, served—Jenney as an engineer corps officer, Adler as a topographical draftsman.

[8] Hamlin Garland, *A Daughter of the Middle Border* (New York: Macmillan, 1921), p. 96. All quotations above are taken from Chapter 7, "London and Evening Dress."

4

Oral Art and American Vernacular in the Middle West

Lincoln's Gettysburg Address and Mark Twain's *Huckleberry Finn* made clear that the new speech of the West had taken American speech into new realms of art. The syntax, idioms, and above all the vocabulary of the Middle West became an instrument for the genius of Lincoln and Mark Twain, who made a literary medium of the new American language. Since the appearance of *Huckleberry Finn,* our writers have been able to write in confidence, and sometimes in glory, as *American* writers. Mark Twain was the first great American writer who was also a popular writer. For the first time in literature of the highest rank, the Middle Western American becomes heroic and his speech beautiful.

Political oratory in the Middle West also rose to high art. In her autobiography, *A Poet's Life,* Harriet Monroe tells how this great oratory moved the soul of a young poet. "The afternoon session [of the Democratic convention of 1896, held in Chicago] had scarcely begun when the chairman recognized a dark-haired young man of powerful build with a voice like the Bull of Bashan. Here was a speaker, who, unlike the morning's whisperers, could be heard to the last row of the highest gallery—indeed, I thought he might be heard in Indiana. Who was he—this William J. Bryan of Nebraska? Nobody around me had ever heard of him, but we all listened with ears and eyes wide open while the 'Cross of Gold' oration rolled out toward the resounding roof." When he finished, the delegates "went mad with such excitement as I have never seen matched anywhere—we looked down breathless at the wildly joyous antics of hundreds of men below us. . . . It was not merely that they cheered . . . not merely that they gathered to gather the standards of the states—always seemingly a drunken orgy—and marched the young orator around to the sound of bands and raucous singing . . . but that they put into it such a passion of hope and faith as no other convention of my experience has ever been inspired by." [1]

Bryce, in his great study, *The American Commonwealth,* admired, like Tocqueville, the passion and conviction of American political oratory. He found lectures "usually well arranged, well composed to meet the taste of the audience, and above all, well delivered." What he called the oratory of occasion, when the Orator of the Day held forth, often ended in pompous and affected style. He explains that European lecturers are often upset by the apparent coldness of the audience. "This grave reserve in American listeners surprises Europeans, especially those who have observed the excitability shown on presidential campaigns." But the real greatness of American oratory, Bryce concludes, is the "lighter ornamental style, such as the after-dinner speech." "The fondness of the people for anecdotes, and their skill in telling them, the general diffusion of humour, the readiness in catching the spirit of an occasion, all contribute to make their efforts in this direction more easy and happy than those of the English, while furnishing less temptation for the characteristic fault of a straining after effect. I have already observed that they shine in stump speaking, properly so called—that is, in speaking which rouses any audience but ought not to be reported."

Yet even in the days of Mark Twain, and with the memory of Abraham Lincoln still fresh, Bryce cannot rise above his British models. He finds the greatest American orators in New England. In the West, fashion in oratory and speech could not be set by the capacities "of the cultivated few." In Europe, "the leading speakers and writers have nearly all belonged to the cultivated classes and, feeling themselves raised above their audiences, have been in the habit of obeying their own taste and that of their class rather than the appetite of those whom they addressed." In England the standard of speaking was set by parliamentary debate, where many of the leading British politicians won their reputation. "They carried their parliamentary style with them into popular meetings, and aspirants of all classes imitated this style. It sometimes erred in being too formal and too prolix; but its taste was good, and its very plainness obliged the speaker to have solid matter." In America, on the other hand, stump oratory was older than, or at least quite as old as, congressional oratory. The latter never gained "that hold on the ideas and habits of the people which parliamentary debate held in England. As a result, American speaking moved on a somewhat lower level. . . ." True, there were brilliant popular orators in the first days of the Republic, such as Patrick Henry, and majestic parliamentary orators, such as Daniel Webster, but "the volume of stump speaking was so much greater than in England that the fashion could not be set by a few of the greatest men, but was determined by the capacities of the average man. The taste of the average man was not raised by the cultivated few to their own standard, but tended to lower the practice, and to some extent even the taste, of the cultivated few." To seem wiser or more refined than the multitude, to incur the suspicion of talking down to the multitude and treating them as inferiors, "would have offended the sentiment of the country, and injured the prospects of a statesman." [2] Because of this, plain speech has flourished in the West, while the most polished speakers generally belonged to New England, where the level of average taste and knowledge was exceptionally high.

The American people were far better equipped to criticize the art of the speaker than of the writer, musician, painter, sculptor, or architect. From 1700 to 1900, Americans had given and listened to more speeches than any other people of their age. Audiences were very large and met often. Perhaps this was to be expected in a new republic dedicated to the belief that every man was qualified to judge and discuss, or take the stump, on all problems of state, finance, or even international relations. Middle Westerners were connoisseurs of political oratory in all its styles. Their training in oratory, after the days of a settlement, was not left to chance. McGuffey's Readers, the common reader of schools of the Middle West, were written to train the voice in debate and declamation. The Fifth Reader contained instructions, not on the lessons to be learned from the printed selections from masterpieces, nor on the meaning of the authors, but on how to read aloud. To the parents of the children learning from McGuffey, oratory was far more than training in proper speech. It was character training, and training in leadership, as Garland stresses in his memoirs. It was the custom at the close of every week's work to bring a section of the pupils on the platform as essayists or orators, and these "exercises" formed "the most interesting and the most passionately dreaded feature of the entire school. No pupil who took part in it ever forgot his first appearance. It was at once a pillory and a burning. It called for self-possession, memory, grace of gesture and a voice." [3]

In this speech, the hopes and fears of American democracy found its first great modern voice. Until the rise of Sullivan and Wright in architecture, the voices of Lincoln and Mark Twain were the great and characteristic expressions of the Great Valley, and in our time, of America. But the voices of the "Westerners" were not easily heard. Mark Twain's rejection by cosmopolites was shared by Sullivan and Wright. As late as 1946, we read in Bernard de Voto's introduction to the Viking Portable edition of Mark Twain. "Shortly before this Introduction was written, the most pontifical American critic guessed that Mark must have turned to the vernacular of *Huckleberry Finn* because he lacked education, was unacquainted with literary traditions, and therefore wrote thin or awkward prose." [4] As we shall see, it was the same attitude toward the "ugliness" and "utility" of Chicago architecture in the eighties which killed Sullivan and all but destroyed American architecture. The "official" critics of the schools and the cosmopolites of high society were concerned with what they called standards. The standard of "correct" American taste was debatable; it might be classical, Gothic, English, French, or Italian, but it could not be American. It was inconceivable that the language used in the stories in the corner store, the smoking room of trains, or in the homely parables of Lincoln were the stuff of art. Literary art was written, and it was in books. The men and women in the towns, villages, and cities of the new West did not read books; they read newspapers when they read at all. They spoke in a vernacular, which, so the guardians of taste held, must be refined before it could become good usage, let alone art. Art already existed in "universal forms of beauty," and these forms must be brought to the West to lift its popular art in the realm of "pure art."

People of Chicago and the Middle West said things in a new way because they were doing new things. The spoken word was related to action. Speaker and hearer searched faces, weighed tones, and watched gestures in their face-to-face meetings with each other. From the woods-clearing family, listening intently to the visitor's account of the news, to the halls of Congress, where John Quincy Adams listened to Stephen A. Douglas, the "Little Giant" of Illinois, "roaring" over the outrages of the government of Mexico against the United States, speech stirred the hearts and minds of men to action. The heroes of the New West were forensic heroes who created in speech great community dramas of struggle between good and evil. Men faced each other in political meetings, in the courtroom, and in debate, because they believed speech a way to action. In church, courtroom, political rallies, schools, even in business, great speakers were the heroes of the day. A man (and a woman) was supposed to speak up and be heard. The people of Chicago and of the new towns of the Middle West accepted people at "face value." As a man talked, so he was. He must, in the vernacular, "put up or shut up." These new Americans believed that discussion could determine human destiny. What people said, they did—indeed *must* do. A man's words must match his acts. If he did not talk true he debased all communication in a society where face-to-face communication created and sustained social bonds among men.

To Europeans and older Americans of the East this new speech was a great shock. Chicago talk stunned Rudyard Kipling. He refused to call the speech of Chicagoans a language. It was at best "dialect, slang, provincialism, accent . . ." Even sacred speech, as in Chicago church services, was hopelessly vulgar. It was a circus:

As we see in this Currier and Ives lithograph of 1855, "Arguing the Point," frontiersmen delighted in argument and talk. Their "jawing," as British observers
described it, was a new kind of speech which became the speech of modern America.
Courtesy Chicago Historical Society

. . . a congregation of savages [led by a] wonderful man completely in the confidence of their God, who he treated colloquially and exploited very much as a newspaper reporter would exploit a foreign potentate. With a voice of silver and with imagery borrowed from the auction-room, he built up for his hearers a heaven on the lines of the Palmer House [but with all the gilding real gold and all the plate-glass diamond] and set in the centre of it a loud-voiced, argumentative, and very shrewd creation that he called God. . . . Apropos of some question of the Judgment Day [the minister said]: No! I tell you God don't do business that way. . . . He interlarded his performance with the slang of the streets, the counter, and the Exchange, and he said that religion ought to enter into daily life.[5]

Yet the popular speech of Douglas, Lincoln, Altgeld, Bryan, Ingersoll, or Moody—like that of Mark Twain—was carefully formed, if not in ways considered so by Bostonians. The formal, cultural, and intellectual life of the Middle West was heavily marked by oratory and speech. Large and small groups underwrote lecture-discussion courses which were given in the local church, opera house, or Masonic Hall. Until the rise of the press, oratory and lecturing were the chief means of mass communication. The two main lecture circuits, those of James Redpath and Major J. B. Pond and on which Mark Twain spoke, were developed out of the use of lecturers for antislavery agitation and propaganda work during the Civil War. The two most respected professions in the towns of the Middle West depended on oratorical skill. Law was considered a training ground for politics, and legal debate was considered to be a debate over justice, not technicalities of the law. Until the rise of the "office lawyer" after 1900, a legal career was often a prelude to a public career. Political debate was both public business and entertainment. A speaker was expected to reason closely and debate with vigor. A political speaker was judged as an actor in a community drama.

Political campaigns were frequent and intensive in the Middle West. People dramatized their community life as a great forensic struggle between heroes and villains whose dialogue was an exhortation to act, not a disquisition on how to think about action or how to judge it like some distant god. Altgeld, one of the great political leaders of the Middle West, stresses the importance of oratory in the opening sentence of his treatise on oratory: "Oratory is the greatest art known to man and embraces a number of great arts." For him it is a dramatic art, for "when all has been said, *delivery— action*—is the vital essence of oratory." The great orator who holds audiences of many thousands spellbound for hours must think of oratory as music. The orator must give his words a rhythmic arrangement which must be delivered with all the care of the singer. "Delivery requires as much attention to voice as given by a singer. But oratory is greater than music. It is the 'masculine of music,' but however vigorous a declamator the orator may be, he must not forget that oratory is governed by the same laws of 'rhythm, cadence, measure, harmony, and at times even melody.'" The orator must think of his audience as he would a neighbor. This will not reduce his art to "utilitarian talk," for the "universal intelligence among the people, and the presence of cultivated women, have tended to give high character to public meetings. Neither Demosthenes nor Cicero ever saw such inspiring audiences as greet the modern orator." The American people "average higher than any others as all around talkers and stump speakers." This is owing to "the nature of our institutions and the fact that all the people participated in the discussions of every public question." For, "Oratory is the child of democracy." It is "the product of Free Institutions; it grows in a republic, it withers in a despotism." [6]

Westerners argued and discussed because they believed disputation to be a way to truth. Speakers such as Douglas and Lincoln went out among the people to hear them as well as to talk to them. Civil War soldiers were persuaded to stay in service by spoken appeals. Grant credited Logan's oratory for the enlistment of his first regiment. "Logan followed McClernand [the first speaker appealing to the troops to re-enlist] in a speech . . . [which] breathed a loyalty and devotion to the Union which inspired my men to such a point that they would have volunteered to remain in the army as long as an enemy of the country continued to bear arms against it." Logan's appeal was colloquial and intimate, as well as oratorical and formal. After painting the glories of defending the flag, he said:

You can't fall out now. If you go home now to Mary, she will say, "Why, Tom, are you home from the war so soon?"
"Yes."
"How far did you get?"
"Mattoon." (Mattoon was but a short distance from their homes.)

As the laughter and cheers of the men increased, Grant knew that he had a command. [7]

Oratory was no less important in recruitment of men in the cities and towns behind the front. The Chicago Loop echoed throughout the day, and sometimes through the night, with the roll of recruiting drums. Court House Square was filled with recruiting tents. Chicagoans followed the fortunes of the armies of the West in deep excitement. On February 15, 1862, news of the capture of Ft. Donelson was celebrated as a city holiday. Business was suspended; the Board of Trade resolved itself into a war meeting. Men shook each other by the hand and rushed around the next corner to shake hands again. Great crowds surged into Bryant Hall, facing the recruiting tents in the Square. Orators mounted platforms and harangued the crowd. Far into the night the voices of orators and people rose in "The Battle Hymn of the Republic," "John Brown's Body," "Hail, Columbia," and other songs.[8]

In the search to create symbols which would make possible a democratic art and thus a democratic community, law and religion acted in common. Even frontier church discipline, which was enacted in courtroom style, played a large part in the social life of the church and community. When a frontier church was organized its members agreed among themselves through discussion and debate on rules of conduct. In the monthly meetings of the Baptist churches, all members were required to be present. Charges brought against members for fighting, lying, harmful gossip, stealing, adultery, horse racing, dishonest business dealings (such as selling an unsound horse), quarrels over boundaries, and drunkenness (most common of all) were discussed. Some of the charges on which Methodists were tried were dishonest business dealings, breach of promise, gross immorality, fraud, lying, stealing a pig, selling unsound millstones, and dishonest land transactions. These trials were conducted in a formal and orderly manner, and a full record of the proceedings was kept. As "moral courts" these trials set the standards of the community. Individual church members submitted to these extralegal decisions; the voice of the church was the voice of God. Loss of church membership meant loss of honor among the "decent" folk of the community. Thus each member knew he was being tried by social, as well as sacred, powers. When he broke a church law he was breaking rules agreed to by himself and created in free and open discussion. He was being tried before judges who spoke, not as bearers of revealed truths, but as judges of courts, under rules made by those who were being judged by the rules.

Political and social experience of equality, the legal right to trial by a jury, and the moral experience of judgment by peers in church courts intensified the egalitarian quality of community life in the Middle Border. Subordination to the will of the church congregation was submission to the will of equals. The individual was bound through his own will; he was free to leave the congregation at any time, and as a member of the congregation he could challenge the decisions of his leaders.

Church courts were limited to their own membership, but secular courts served the whole community. Law stood beside religion in the drama of justice, and the lawyer stood beside the minister as a public hero in the enactment of justice. County seat lawyers visited smaller towns as orators on all public occasions, such as the Fourth of July. In political campaigns, as well as on holidays, they spoke to the people. In court, they carried the forensic drama of argument and debate to great heights before audiences of their neighbors. In the years before and after the Civil War, these juries of neighbors were supreme in legal decision. The right to trial by jury was revered as the gospel of the Law. Few cases were taken from the jury, although an expedient existed by which the judge could decide that the verdict was against the weight of the evidence, and on that ground then seek to have the verdict set aside. This practice was jealously circumscribed by rules and precedents. The great objective of a trial and the central moment in forensic drama was the winning of the jury.

Edgar Lee Masters, Illinois poet, lawyer, and son of an early Illinois lawyer who practiced in Lincoln's county, describes the enactment of law in these times. "The farmer and village audience gathers; and sits in benches outside the railing which bars the privileged space for lawyers, the jury and the judge. The jury has rattan chairs, or benches for its use; the judge is throned somewhat above the jury. A long trial table is at the right or left of the judge's seat where the lawyers sit with their clients back of them, and the witness chair is at one side or the other of the judge, sometimes a little above the level of the trial table, sometimes not; but in any case the witness is facing the lawyers, and the judge can look down upon him, frowning or doubting, or admonishing him to speak louder, or commanding him to repeat what he has said or to do so." [9] Here in such rooms the lawyer acted in his community role as champion of justice. Here justice was made dramatic and meaningful to all people, and from such stages men might, as Lincoln did, go on to local, national, and finally world leadership. Juries were addressed in colloquial and familiar manner. Lawyers such as Lincoln spoke as actors seeking to move an audience to love and hate as well as to "weigh the facts." In such courts law was a drama. The jury, like the chorus of the Greek drama, was appealed to as the conscience of the community. The judge upheld rules of law which he arbitrated but did not create or could not change. The audience to the trial represented the general public as well as the conscience of the community. It was their right to express approval or disapproval of the conduct of the trial. Contesting lawyers attacked each other as heroes and villains of a great drama of justice. Justice was related to life within the community, not to a body of abstract legal principles or the authority of judges.

Lawyers played for an audience, but this was not a mass audience. There were really several audiences of different capacities, talents, and values. The courtroom audience of friend, enemies, and relatives of the accused was gathered not to applaud the decisions of authority but to weigh them. The jury was asked by the judge to judge according to due process of law as he interpreted it. But the Western judge, like the umpire in games, also adjudicated performances through rules. The opposing lawyers, like actors in a dialogue, determined the course of each other's argument. Democratic principles of domination by rules which represented the will of equals were the guiding spirit of the American trial. Men and women rose to eminence in their communities through ability to communicate these great democratic principles to people of widely different traditions. No single tradition was strong enough to fix meaning in speech. Only in the great moving visions of a new commonwealth of free men could the past become prologue to the future. The men and women of the town, cities, and plains of the Great Valley of the Ohio and the Mississippi lived in wonder over the promise of a new community of free men.

In the rapidly shifting and changing society of the Middle West, talk was often an adventure in itself. The mingling of the dialects in search for common meaning produced color and vigor in speech among people who spoke to each other frequently and freely because they spoke as equals. Early travelers delight in studding their accounts with local turns of speech. Frontier Americans soon established reputations as great talkers; their virtuosity at "jawing" was marked by many observers. In 1884, in his explanatory note at the beginning of *Huckleberry Finn,* Mark Twain tells us: "In this book a number of dialects are used. . . . I make this explanation for the reason that without it many readers would suppose that all these characters were trying to talk alike and not succeeding." Humor was of equal importance to serious and tragic discourse in religion, law, and politics. The profound incongruities of frontier life were met in laughter as well as tears. Differences in language, rank, station, religion, politics, region, race, and national origin, differences which had never before been overcome—and which not even America would overcome without a terrible war—were often resolved in laughter. The new people of Illinois and Chicago were very much aware of the incongruities in their lives. There were many perplexities in being a Westerner. Westerners knew they were not like older Americans; they learned early through hardship and suffering that their community could not solve its problems as problems had been solved in the East. Yet it was easier for Westerners to say what they were not than to say what they were. What did it really mean to be a Middle Westerner? How did it differ from being a Yankee or a Southerner? Even on the level of daily talk, what *was* proper usage? On formal social occasions, what constituted genteel standards of speech?

Common speech required the development of the vernacular. If a man wanted to be widely understood, certainly if he wanted to be a leader, he must become highly skilled in vernacular usage. People in a town like Springfield, as later in Chicago, might be impressed by those who upheld polished usage or speech modeled after written classics, but they elected few such men to office, listened to few of their sermons, and seldom voted to follow them in war. Herndon tells us that Lincoln was not a master of British English nor in any sense a bookish man. But he is careful to add that while Lincoln may not have read deeply, he talked deeply. He turned to the vernacular of the frontier in his jokes, stories, and sayings because it "contained [resources for expressing] the exact coloring power, and shape of his ideas." [10] Even among its scholars and writers, the culture of the Middle West was not bookish. Herndon tells us that Lincoln "never in his life sat down and read a book through, and yet he could readily quote any number of passages from the few volumes whose pages he had hastily scanned." Lincoln, like Mark Twain and later the architects Sullivan and Wright, thought of art in relation to action. Lincoln's mode of self-expression was in oratory; the audience he wanted to reach was the people. He was interested not in commemorating the grandeur of the past but in solving the problems of the present. Like Mark Twain, he thought the comic view of life equal, perhaps indeed superior, to the tragic. For him, comedy faced the incongruities of life. It was a *method* for understanding because it was a method of communicating, not simply an escape or merely "fun." Comedy exposed traditions and utopias to the test of action in the present. It resolved problems through reason because it opened them to discussion. So long as there was trust and confidence there was laughter, and in laughter, as frontier people soon discovered, trust and confidence were born. Only equals can laugh *with* each other; superiors and inferiors laugh *at* each other.

This new oral tradition was shaping the symbolic experience of America.[11] It was creating a new language, the American lauguage, for use by the writers of the new generation. Until this was accomplished, until the West possessed such a language, it could not become a community. It needed a new lauguage because it was creating a new life. For many situations there were simply no words. Railroading, for example, required a whole new vocabulary. It was not intended to be literary. "Literature" was what appeared in New England publications. This usage was the best speech of New Englanders of Emerson's day. It was not, however, the best speech of the Middle Western gentry, certainly not of men whose interests (and hence, their speech) were based in the religion of the Bible, politics as a drama of community life, and business as a development of community resources. Women shared the perplexity of their men over what constituted proper speech. Traditional feminine roles were changing rapidly in the shift from familial to public life. Proper speech in both familial and public roles was one of the required "female" accomplishments. Such speech was taught as manners, not art or oratory. And since this speech was taught by teachers trained in New England and British traditions, female schooling of upper-class girls was conducted in a language alien to the common speech of the Middle West, and especially to the speech of men in politics, war, business, and the informal masculine social life of the tavern and corner store.

From 1890 to 1920 women of the Middle West moved rapidly into public life of all kinds.[12] Their entry into teaching, libraries, newspapers, magazine and book publishing, and the creation of women's clubs (where lectures soon became standard parts of each program) spread the power of women as guardians of propriety and culture far beyond the family.[13] The split between this genteel feminine speech, based on New England British usage, and the speech of the Chicago region was widened even more by the great influx of non-Anglo-Saxon immigrant stock. The German, Irish, Italian, Pole, Bohemian—each in turn was required to write English based on New England literary models. But the Americans of the Middle Border did not speak as they wrote. It was impossible to fix the idioms and forms of their speech—even if they wanted to do so. Perhaps this is why no other tongue of modern time admits foreign words and phrases more readily. We are more careless of precedents and show greater fecundity and originality of fancy in speech because for us speech is a highly practical art, an art in which we strive to be understood by many publics with whom we must learn to communicate if we are to have any community at all.

Notes

[1] Harriet Monroe, *A Poet's Life: Seventy Years in a Changing World* (New York: Macmillan, 1938), pp. 43–44.

[2] See Chapter CXIV, "American Oratory," in Vol. II of the third edition of *The American Commonwealth* (New York and London: Macmillan, 1895) for these quotations.

[3] Hamlin Garland, *A Son of the Middle Border* (New York: Macmillan, 1923), p. 197.

[4] See *The Portable Mark Twain*, ed. by Bernard de Voto (New York: Viking Press, 1946), p. 27.

[5] These quotes are taken from *As Others See Chicago: Impressions of Visitors, 1673–1933*, compiled and edited by Bessie Louise Pierce (University of Chicago Press: Chicago, Illinois, 1933), pp. 253–54.

[6] John P. Altgeld, *Oratory, Its Requirements and Its Rewards* (Chicago: Charles H. Kerr and Co., 1901). These quotations are taken from the Lakeside Press edition, published by R. R. Donnelly & Sons, Chicago (n.d.). Altgeld thought that newspapers, "instead of destroying oratory, simply prepare the ground for a higher order of elo-

quence. They educate the public as to the facts, and thus partially relieve the speaker of dry detail, so that he can devote himself more largely to a discussion of principles than he otherwise could do. At the same time they multiply his audience by the thousand. [Newspapers often printed speeches in full.] Once the speaker reached only the people before him, now he reached millions. . . ." (p. 49)

7 Military oratory is still highly valued by some general officers. In his doctrine of command, General Montgomery says: "The troops must be brought to a state of wild enthusiasm. . . ." before battle. "In achieving this . . . it is the spoken word which counts; from the commander to his troops, plain speech is far more effective than any written word."

8 Chicago was one of the great centers of war song, as it was of military oratory.

9 Edgar Lee Masters, *Lincoln the Man* (New York: Dodd, Mead, 1931), pp. 118–19.

10 See Chapter XX of Herndon's *Life of Lincoln* (Cleveland and New York: The World Publishing Co., 1949) for his discussion of this.

11 Our younger writers are returning again to oral traditions in poetry and jazz. Our popular arts, radio, television, and the movies, are now spoken as well as visual arts.

12 As we shall see in later discussion, businessmen feminized American life when they made the American woman the Great American Customer. Our matriarchy is a new type, a public as well as a familial matriarchy, whose power is based on spending money. This has little to do with the matriarchies discussed by anthropologists or older European scholars.

13 Huckleberry Finn's flight from civilization is a flight from women as well as men. Discipline for Huck and Tom is feminine. Huck's father is little better than a drunken brute. Huck's social problem is one of masculine *identity;* his father's masculinity, like that of many town males, is savage and brutal.

5

Chicago Journalism and
the New Urban Speech of Chicago

Artists of the towns and villages of the Middle Border followed the New England tradition, which set patterns for all American literary "art." Champions of this tradition fought against the debasement of literature by "journalists." Journalists, and particularly Western journalists, accused the New England guardians of culture of being highbrow, academic "stuffed shirts" and literary "dudes." Differences between the "journalists" and the "professors" soon passed into open hostility. Creative writers in Chicago of 1920, like the architects of the eighties and nineties, had little faith in schools of art.[1] The American Academy of Arts and Letters (notably in the February 22, 1917, meeting) concerned itself with "the conservation of the English language in its beauty and purity." Hamlin Garland and many of the older writers were active in this. In opposition to the American Academy, Chicago editors opened their pages to Mr. Dooley, Pink Marsh, and other heroes of new American speech. The results, like Mark Twain's earlier assaults on standard English, were dramatic. As "Mr. Dooley" (Dunne) told his Chicago readers: "When we Americans are through with the English language, it will look as if it had been run over by a musical comedy." George Ade said: "The American must go to England in order to learn for a dead certainty that he does not speak the English language. This pitiful fact comes home to every American when he arrives in London—that there are two languages, the English and American. One is correct; the other is incorrect. One is a pure and limpid stream; the other is a stagnant pool swarming with bacilli."[2] The problem faced by Chicago writers was not only how to present characters and draw up plots, but what *language* to use in doing so. Their readers knew little, and seemed to care less, about the "proper" usage of the small group in the upper class who cultivated Briticisms in their speech.

The higher the expectancy of literacy on the part of the public being addressed, the more "refined" the language. Church news and the editorial page were written in "literary language." The sports page was written in a new language. Chicago newspaper writers did not invent characters because they were ignorant of proper usage. As George Ade said: "People in my stories had talked slang, but only when they had to do so in order to be plausible and probable. If I used a word or a phrase which was reasonably under suspicion, I would hang up the quotation marks so that the reader might know that I was not approving the language, but merely utilizing it for more picturesque effect." [3] Chicago publics accepted, but they did not create (out of some kind of "folk-soul"), the new vernacular. It was created instead by a long line of Chicago writers, who, like all artists, struggled to give form to the speech of their time. Ade, Opie Read, Eugene Field, Finley Peter Dunne, Dreiser, Sandburg, Lewis, and Lardner—like the older writers Fuller, Hamlin Garland, Robert Herrick, Francis Fisher Browne (of the *Dial*), and Will Payne—tried to give form to the speech they heard in the streets and homes of Chicago and to depict characters and incidents which would characterize the new life of the West. In one sense they urbanized an already existing frontier newspaper *genre*,[4] the colorful, boisterous, fantastic "tall tales" of people who wanted drama and life in their speech. This school of writing, both amateur and professional, was already established by 1850—but it was established as a rural and village tradition. The task of shaping this tradition into urban forms was undertaken by the "newspaper gang," as Garland called Chicago journalists.

Both Frances Trollope and her son Anthony, writing a generation apart about their American experiences, stress the importance of the newspaper in the West. Mrs. Trollope's account of her conversation with a milkman tells us much about early attitudes toward the newspaper. The milkman asks her: "Your papers ben't like ourn, I reckon? Now we says and prints what we likes." Mrs. Trollope replies: "You spend a good deal of time reading the newspapers." Her milkman asks: "And I'd like you to tell me how we can spend it better. How should freemen spend their time, but looking after their government, and watching that them fellers as we gives offices to, doos their duty, and give themselves no airs?" To Mrs. Trollope's somewhat acid reply that time could be taken away from newspaper reading to mend roads, the milkman replies: "The Lord! to see how little you knows of a free country! Why, what's the smoothness of a road, put against the freedom of a free-born American? And what does a broken zigzag signify, comparable to knowing that the men what we have been pleased to send up to Congress, speaks handsome and straight, as we chooses they should." [5]

Her son Anthony, the novelist, was even more impressed with the American habit of newspaper reading. "Newspapers in the United States . . . may be said to be the one chief necessary of life." This was not because the American newspapers printed the truth or taught their readers how to think dispassionately about local or national issues. On the contrary, the American press was biased and partisan, its language informal and loose, its view of the present always determined by what was to happen in a golden future. There was very little straight reporting in these early papers. Cover of town events was done through commentary and dramatization, not documentary reporting of facts. What "happened," the simple bare facts of an event, could easily and quickly be told. But the meaning of what happened, the human interest of an event could be given only by writers interested in creating a drama of community life. Newspaper writers like those in Chicago created a whole series of new American urban types. The local colorists of the last part of the century experimented with dialects from various parts of the country, yet this movement, which offered so much to the writer, attracted few professional writers. Even the genius of Mark Twain in *Huckleberry Finn,* or the great talents of James Russell Lowell in *The Biglow Papers,* failed to create the American language necessary to our modern national literature. The vigorous and widely popular humor of J. C. Neal, Artemus Ward, and Josh Billings did not take root in the cities. The language used by these writers needed to be urbanized, and, above all, it needed to be enriched by the usages of non-Anglo-Saxon immigrants before it could become the common language of the writers of the new cities of the West, and later of all America.

America received these additions soon enough, and it received them first and to the highest degree of excellence in Chicago newspaper writing. As Mencken points out: "The enormous dialect literature of twenty years ago left [the American language] untouched. Localisms were explored diligently, but the general dialect went virtually unobserved. It is not in 'Chimmie Fadden'; it is not in 'David Harum'; it is not even in the prefable stories of George Ade, perhaps the most acute observer of average, undistinguished American types, urban and rustic, that American literature has yet produced." [6] It was the task of expressing the American language in print that had to wait for Ring W. Lardner, a Chicago newspaper reporter. "In his grotesque tales of base-ball players, so immediately and so deservedly successful, Lardner reports the common speech not only with humor, but also with the utmost accuracy. . . . In a single story by Lardner, in truth, it is usually possible to discover examples of almost every logical and grammatical peculiarity of the emerging language, and he always resists very stoutly the temptation to overdo the thing." [7]

The "literary" artists in Chicago from 1890 to 1910 were as acutely aware of the need for a new language as Mark Twain had been in his struggles to give symbolic form to the life of the new American townspeople of the West. But *how* was one to write of Chicago characters and Chicago life in a language which was created in a tradition and for audiences so different from those of older America? The same problem faced businessmen. How was one to advertise products to urban people who knew little about "correct" or "proper," to say nothing of "literary," usage? How did one write about the new horseless carriage? What could one say about a motor oil? No one knew how to meet these new needs in expression, but it was generally agreed that, if anyone knew, it must be newspaper writers. The "poetry" of industrialism was launched in the press. The thousands of images of specific social types used in newspaper ads, the stereotyping of social classes and types in advertising depictions, the invention of hundreds of new words, as well as new linguistic forms, soon became an important part of the struggle to achieve a new urban language.

In the Chicago papers of the nineties, sports writing was not a small department, it was front page news. The best reporter on the staff was sent to cover the great sporting events. The highest paid Chicago journalist without executive responsibilities, Eugene Field, was a rabid baseball fan. His usual copy did not differ greatly from regular editorial matter, but his column contained poetry, baseball, political editorials—indeed, anything that struck his fancy. This freedom was given Field, Ade, Dooley and their followers because their writing increased circulation. The *Evening News* printed baseball news (written by Finley Peter Dunne) in place of simply printing the results of the game for the first time in 1887. Sports reporting became highly inventive, and its language rich in slang and new turns of phrase. By 1920 a very large part of current American slang was propagated by the newspapers, and much of it was invented by newspaper writers, as we know from the development of baseball slang. Such phrases as "to clout the sphere," "the initial sock," "to slam the pill," and "the dexter meadow" were obviously not created in the bleachers by the urban "folk." As Mencken said: "There is not enough imagination in that depressing army to devise such things; more often than not, there is not even enough intelligence to comprehend them." The true place of their origin was the desk of newspaper reporters, whose competence and compensation were largely estimated on papers of wide circulation by their capacity for inventing novelties. The inventiveness of sports writers was so great that connoisseurship soon developed; a skilled slangmaker soon became a local hero of the press and the reading public somewhat after the fashion of the village swearer whose profanity moved the ungodly to admiration.

In the linguistic expression of Chicagoans, relations between words and acts were close. A great number of phrases used by Ade, Dunne, Dreiser, and Sandburg are closely related to action, and especially of action in the new urban world that was developing so rapidly after the Civil War. The language of sports, business, and politics dramatized the peculiarly urban social qualities of such experience. Writers of the school and the studio knew that newspaper writers were creating an indigenous American urban language. Howells, Garland, and Fuller realized that Ade's galaxy of lower middle-class urban types was authentic characterization. Howells and Fuller begged Ade to do an American novel, just as the "intellectuals" whom Lardner so disliked begged him to realize himself more fully in "art." Fuller wrote to Ade: "When you feel the disposition to write the 'Chicago novel' that people are beginning to expect of you, I don't know of anybody who wouldn't be glad to pull off to one side and give you all the room you need. . . . The urban pinhead [Cousin Walter Miller in the story of the same name] who passes for a 'wise city mug'—is one of the most obvious and perennial of the types, but you are about the first to capture him. I don't know why the thing that lies right in the way should be the thing that everybody passes by." [8]

Hobart Chatfield-Taylor, Fuller, Garland, and Herrick, like Henry James of the East, did not attempt to create authentic American types. They knew it should be done, but they did not know how to do it. Nothing in their urban or rural lives or in their education and training as artists prepared them for the characters we meet in Ade's sketches. Henry Blake Fuller, like Louis Sullivan, prowled endlessly through the city, immersing himself in the changing life of the streets of Chicago. His changes of residence, his "disappearances" from elite studio life, his avowals that the best thing the Chicago writer could do was to write about Chicago, led to fine studies of Chicago life, but they failed (and no one was more conscious of the failure than Fuller) because the streets of Chicago did not engage him as they did Ade, Dreiser, Lardner, and Sandburg. Fuller's flights to Italy, in art as in life, were like Burnham's flight from the vulgarity of the commercial architecture of Chicago to the serene classical architecture of Greece and Rome. These flights to "eternal beauty" offered escape from the tensions of life in the new American city, Chicago.

Fuller's paradise was in Italy, an Italy of art and of men and women whose lives were shaped by the quest for beauty. The Italian notebooks of his youth and his Italian novels of later years are a cry of the heart against the ugliness of Chicago's business civilization. His Chicago novels are an admission, not so much of the failure of art in life but of the irrelevance of traditional art to the kind of art Chicago required. His Italian Chevalier, the aesthetic hero wandering in Italy, finds no peace beyond a kind of sad irony over the inability of men like himself to break through their dilettantism to some kind of creative identity as artists. Fuller's Chicago heroes and heroines, the generous builders of a new city, may be narrow and parochial, but they are real. When the decent, hard-working businessman, the mother, daughter, or even the career woman begin to express themselves through money, they find that it was the vision of what it could buy, not the possession of it, that made money exciting. It is the struggle, not the victory, the memories of youth, a time of building and a time of hope, which sustains Chicagoans of Fuller's and Sullivan's time. Chicago was a future whose present and past were endurable only in the radiance of the vision of a great democratic city.

The young city in 1890 soon became a giant among cities. As it lunged into a new world of technology and money, it smashed many cherished aesthetic traditions. Fuller's wonder over Chicago ends in irony over both Italy, the home of art, and Chicago, the home of money and business. Yet, as Fuller describes his longing for beauty, and his despair and horror over the corruption and depravity of life without art, it was not the failure of Chicago but of himself as an "aesthetic pioneer" which darkened his life. He simply could not confront the city. He understood well that aesthetic pioneers were needed to match the business, political, and educational pioneers who were bringing Chicago to fame in so short a time, but, unlike the architects Root, Sullivan, and Wright, Fuller never found a form that would express the great Chicago vision of a democratic community. He died, as Sullivan died, in loneliness, but he never lived, as did Sullivan, in deep belief and love of Chicago's fulfillment as a leading city of America's art. Fuller never shared Sullivan's conviction that men—*all* men—could lift their eyes to visions of a democratic life lived in cities, as well as in the forests and the prairies of the Middle West.

The "studio" writers of 1890–1905 had none of the experience with language, and few of the social values, possessed by newspaper men. Newspaper depiction of Chicago life was vivid and fanciful, full of life and vigor. There was nothing "intellectual," "witty," or "refined" about this style. Chicago newspaper controversies were not "refined," any more than discussion of the opposing baseball teams was "refined." A "discussion" of an opposing point of view invoked invective abuse, slander, ridicule, humor, sarcasm, and all the arts of verbal mayhem. The Chicago journalists knew (and if they forgot, they were reminded forcefully) that they were not writing for a "literary" reader. They were writing for people who did not want wit, subtlety, compactness, or logic, but action, feeling, emotion, and color expressed with vigor, humor, and exaggeration. The journalist was expected to "take sides," to speak up plainly about his likes and dislikes. He could be comic or tragic. He could even be ironic, but it must be a heavily underscored irony. Above all, he must dramatize the news, not from the view of a dispassionate witness but from that of a participant who spits on his hands, rolls up his sleeves, and jumps into the fight.

This does not mean that writers on *The Tribune,* the *Evening Post,* or the

Daily News did not espouse the cause of literature. But the guardians of culture in the press, such as Burton Roscoe, knew they had to make news, even on a "highbrow" page, if they were to continue writing about books. To do so Roscoe (as he tells us) "engineered dogfights and got up controversies." The important thing in these controversies was not that art was judged by some universal standard, but that it was kept close to the intellectual and moral interests of the city. The battles over books in Chicago newspapers from the days of the controversy between Hamlin Garland and Mrs. Elia W. Peattie, to Margaret Anderson's and Ben Hecht's vigorous defense of art against "morals" read like reports from the front. Actors in these symbolic struggles jumped into the struggle like soldiers hurling themselves into battle. A style became a weapon. As early as 1919 Mencken pointed out, "what the public wants eternally—at least the American public—is rough work. It delights in vituperation. It revels in scandal . . . violent and effective denunciation . . . ceaseless querulous and bellicose [argument]." [9]

The relationship between the cub reporter and the newspaper employing him was very close to the apprentice–master relationship in craft work. The cub was given little theoretical training. He was expected to accept someone among the older reporters as his mentor and to learn from him. This was not formalized in any way; there was complete freedom on the part of either to end the relationship. The cub could go along on practically any local mission. He was watched closely for any signs of a "bent" or "talent," and, once this was discovered, it was developed by master newspapermen. This made recruitment and training a relatively simple affair. In the studio each writer, young or old, was treated as an artist in his own right. It was assumed that his apprenticeship was over and he was now ready to enter the world of art as a professional. He depended on public critics, as well as masters, to judge his work. Older artists within the studio may have taken an "interest" in younger writers, but this interest was not expressed in the daily contact which existed in the newspaper world.

Chicago studio life from 1865 to 1905 was related as much to "society" as to art. The newspaper world demanded a complete commitment to the craft of journalism. In the early days of Chicago newspaper life, marriage was considered a threat to the career of a journalist. As late as 1925 we still find Chicago newspapermen assuming that a good newspaperman will spend very little time away from his paper. It was also assumed that journalists would be free to go anywhere. Such factors mitigated heavily toward any "outside" influences affecting the development of the young newspaperman. It was also assumed that the club would get whatever education he needed. "Education" on the Chicago newspapers was construed very broadly. It was assumed that every good newspaperman possessed a general culture, and a knowledge of what we now call the social sciences, sufficient to allow him to write well on a very wide range of topics. But knowledge of the city had to be particular and detailed. It is still necessary for a journalist to know his city, but today "leg men" get the news and "turn in" the story, verbally reported or hastily written up, and the rewrite men turn out the story as printed.

In the period from 1885 to 1915, a Chicago reporter was expected to get his own story and to write it up. Further, he was expected to write it up with a great deal of "color." As Dreiser describes it, Chicago journalism in the nineties was "still in that discursive stage which loved long-winded yarns upon almost any topic. . . ." But, as he soon found out, the color must be local urban color, not simply "purple patches" about life. It was always necessary for the reporter to know the neighborhoods, and reader interest could be created and sustained only when qualities peculiar to these neighborhoods were evoked. Chicagoans wanted local news as well as "downtown" news. Editors like Lawson of the *Daily News* were anxious to get their papers into homes. This required a shift from masculine to feminine human interest stories. Until about 1900 Chicago newspapers were edited largely for male readers. The development of a newspaper to be read by both men and women, what was to be called a family newspaper, intensified interest in intimate and personal problems in family life in local neighborhoods. The school of life for the young reporter, as for the young architect, was the streets of Chicago. George Ade told Kelly: "If we had been blindfolded and led along on familiar city trails, we could have called the corners and the landmarks because of the aromatic variations." [10]

The discovery that reading markets could be greatly enlarged through techniques common to commodity distribution soon changed the distribution of literary material. When Munsey, McClure, Hearst and other newspaper editors began distribution of stories to millions of readers and undertook to offer their readers new material at gradually shortening intervals, demand for literary wares increased. Writing became a commodity. One immediate effect was an increasing differentiation within the profession of writing. Browne's type of general editor in Chicago letters gave way to the "experts" and the "specialists" of our own time. Now the editor of the book section need not be a critic, but an editor with "connections" among "experts" who "know a field." Newspaper writers soon became famous for a certain kind of story, a certain type of writing, even for a certain character, like the actor who is famous for one or two roles. The same differentiation took place in all the arts. The art administrator, who "organizes talents" and who now dominates so much of our art, was born, and American writers began their new existence as "corporation writers."

The new publics forming in Chicago were composed of native and foreign immigrants who did not settle and take root but remained highly mobile. Very few writers—or their readers—stayed where they were born. Moving about from one town to another, from the farm to town, or from town to city was a characteristic experience for Chicago writers and their readers. Chicago readers, whether native or foreign, could not enjoy the "sense of place," nor feel the deep roots of a tradition developing over many generations. As the diffusion of urban literature increased with the development of transportation and the consequent distribution of urban literary products, depictions of urban life penetrated rapidly and widely into rural areas. The drama of urbanization as depicted in the press (as later in the movies, radio, and now on television) reached those who stayed at home, as well as those who came to the city. The symbolic drama of America became an urban drama.

The youthfulness of characters in Chicago literary depictions, the emphasis on finding a way of life, of getting a job, struggling to success, meeting a girl, falling in—or out—of love, getting married, learning about "life" in the city —such experiences were shared by readers who themselves were young. There are few depictions of old age, and few old people in Chicago literature —just as there are few Chicago writers who produced the bulk or the best part of their work after middle age. It is a literature written by young men and women in a city of youth. The native rural tradition of America was broken in the Chicago region from 1865 to 1910. Young immigrants who had no sense of the American rural and village past arrived in the same years. Native American women who came to the city "to get a job" needed to know how to act in situations new to their elders, as to themselves. Traditional roles as sweethearts, wives, and mothers were refashioned. Editors and writers discovered that these "new" women, like their men, needed "new" writing. Feminism in Chicago soon broadened into a social as well as an economic and political quest. Mrs. Potter Palmer, Jane Addams, and Frances Willard wanted to be "ladies" as well as "feminists." Jane Addams called her settlement a "house"—Hull House—and taught her workers to think of the people around them as neighbors and to meet them in warmth and friendliness. The "new women" of Chicago, like their men, were convinced that women, as well as men, could contribute to the making of a great new city in America.

Notes

1 Sullivan's attack on the schools began in the nineties.

2 George Ade, *In Pastures New* (New York: McClure, Phillips, 1906), p. 6.

3 Fred C. Kelly, *George Ade: Warmhearted Satirist* (Indianapolis: Bobbs-Merrill, 1947), p. 136.

4 Bernard De Voto and Franklin Mein describe this tradition in their work. See Bernard De Voto, *Mark Twain's America* (Cambridge: Houghton-Mifflin, 1932).

5 Frances Trollope, *Domestic Manners of the Americans* (New York: Dodd, Mead & Co., 1927), p. 85. Her observations were made in the years 1827–30; Anthony Trollope's in 1861 and 1862.

6 H. L. Mencken, *The American Language: An Inquiry into the Development of English in the United States,* 3d ed. (New York: Alfred A. Knopf, 1930), p. 275.

7 *Ibid.,* pp. 276–77.

8 Quoted by Fred C. Kelly in his study of George Ade (*op. cit.*), p. 122.

9 H. L. Mencken, *Prejudices: First Series* (New York: Knopf, 1919), pp. 179–80.

10 Kelly, *op. cit.,* p. 108.

6

Equality and Leadership in the Middle West

THE MINGLING of people of diverse nations, religions, creeds, and races in the Mississippi Valley had many historic parallels. Greece, Rome, Islam, and Britain created empires through harmonizing widely different peoples. But never before in the history of civilization had this been done within three generations. The sons of men who fought in the American Revolutionary War watched their sons march off to the Civil War. Men left farms and towns of rural America to fight a war where men suffered and died in terrifying numbers, and these same men returned to a life rapidly coming under the domination of cities strange and alien to rural Americans. American cities were being transformed, as the war had been transformed, by a technology based on money.

Between the Civil War and World War I, a span of some fifty years, almost every value known to the American people was to undergo a profound transformation, a symbolic transformation which created new forms of life because it created new forms of communication. The civilization of the Middle West, and the development of its great city, Chicago, waited upon the development of communication. No people in America had separated themselves physically so much by their form of settlement; never before had people been able to establish freeholds on such a completely individual basis. Forms of communication and transportation familiar to New England, the Middle Atlantic States, and the South meant little to people who were settling land in new ways and relating to each other in ways new to traditional forms of communication. "Manifest destiny," like the "melting pot" of later years, were ideals based on utopian futures, not traditions of a hallowed past. Traditional economic, political, and ecclesiastical forms of expression were of little value because religion, politics, and culture were now being democratized through communicative forms which were new, strange, and, indeed, incomprehensible to those bound by the traditions of Europe, New England, or the South.

The new people of Illinois wanted freedom to live their own lives on freeholds of their own choosing.[1] But they soon discovered that homesteads so widely separated in space, and lives rooted in such different traditions, could not exist without communal life. In older areas, community was taken for granted. The church and the state assumed responsibility for the individual. The individual was born into a community which had been created long before his birth and which, he was taught, would continue long after his death. But in the Middle West there was no community; it had to be created. Men were isolated geographically; they hungered for companionship, yet there was little use in coming together if they could not communicate. And they could not communicate if they did not share certain beliefs in common. It mattered little whether these beliefs were based on traditions, utopias, manners, customs, or religion; consensus had to be established. Even trade demanded this, for unless buyers and sellers had some common set of expectations how could they trade? The search for community in the Middle West, as in Chicago, was a search for forms which people of widely different backgrounds and language could use to act together in politics, business, religion, and society.

The opening of the Middle West, and the Far West, is often told as a dramatic moment of struggle between man and his physical environment. It is strange how this image holds the American imagination. Yet what, after all, is a "physical" environment and how do we experience it? We experience our environment through symbols which must be created if we are to create and sustain social order.[2] To invoke environment under the guise of "the exploitation of resources" does not absolve us from the difficult task of explaining why such exploitation takes one form and not another, and why such forms (as in architecture) arise in one place and not another. In the search for new ways to transport, travel, and communicate, France, Germany, Britain, and America alike possessed brilliant engineers. The Frenchman Eiffel built a great steel tower; the Americans Roebling and Eads built great steel bridges; Jenney, Adler, Root, and Sullivan of Chicago built great steel office buildings, now known as skyscrapers; and Wright built "prairie homes" which were the beginning of all modern homes.

It is also said frequently that desire for economic betterment brought people into the plains and forests of the Middle West. But the decisive question is why this desire was expressed in certain forms—and, for our purposes here, in forms specific to the Middle West of America. Cartwright's preaching, Lincoln's statesmanship, Grant's style of war, McCormick's way of making and selling reapers, Mark Twain's comedies of Western life, Sullivan's business buildings, Wright's prairie and forest houses are *forms,* not "forces," and they were forms indigenous to the Middle West. Bostonians, Philadelphians, and New Yorkers were as eager as Chicagoans to do business, but none of their architects created the great office buildings which the architects of the Chicago school sent soaring into the skies of Chicago. The American family was not created in Chicago, but the great houses of Frank Lloyd Wright, which did so much to change American family life, were designed for the suburbs of Chicago and the towns and cities of the Middle West. Form in itself is a social force; it does not simply "reflect" but creates social relationships. Buildings in Chicago intended for manufacturing, distribution, or selling are significant because they *created* stages for new kinds of human relationships, not because they were a "reflection" of economic forces.

Those involved in creating and sustaining Middle Western social institutions realized the necessity of developing a new theory and practice of community life. Many old institutions could be adapted to new uses. The people of the Middle West did not have to create anew the institutions of the family, the farm, the school, or the church. But they were not able to transplant any of these without great modifications. There seemed little in the character or situation of the frontier to give hope for the emergence of a democratic civilization of the Middle West. There was even a long record of failure by the great powers, France, England, and Spain, to create bonds which could evolve into democratic community. The new American states of the East, themselves born in rebellion, could not contain the rebellion of their new states in the West. The first wave of frontiersmen and squatters who preceded the farmer in the settlement of the Illinois territory lived rude, savage, and often short lives. The town life of settled farmers was marked by violence and drunkenness. Feuds were settled by savage violence. In Mark Twain's *Huckleberry Finn,* cold ferocity rings in the voices of the Shepherdsons as they run along the river bank shooting at the wounded Granderford boys, who try to escape by swimming downcurrent in the river.

In the lives of the Shepherdsons, and all the clansmen of the day, a gentleman was determined as much by capacity for sustained hatred of enemies as by love of friends. As Sandburg tells us of Lincoln's time in New Salem: "Between some families there was bitter hate year on year; . . . Once two men met on the New Salem side of the river, spat hate at each other across the river before a crowd of men, and then decided to go alone and fight it out. They crossed over, stripped their clothes, and fought as wolves fight, with claw, tooth, and fang, till men came from over the river, parted them, and made them shake hands. One of the fighters was sick for a year and then died of his wounds and gouges." The mingling of peoples of diverse and hostile religious, racial, national, and social views was not "predestined" to democracy. Law and order, the foundations of community life, were not given, but created. Often they were created out of violence and hate. Feuds, killings, and lynchings were common. Peter Cartwright, the "backwoods preacher" of the Middle West, tells of the efforts of honest citizens to make laws respected.

Murderers, horse thieves, highway robbers, and counterfeiters . . . carried on such violence and outrage that the honest part of the citizens seemed to be driven to the necessity of uniting and combining together, and taking the law into their own hands, under the name of Regulators. . . . Soon a quarrel commenced, and a general battle ensued between the rogues and Regulators, and they fought with guns, pistols, dirks, knives, and clubs. Some were actually killed, many wounded, the rogues proved victors, kept the ground, and drove the Regulators out of town. The Regulators rallied again, hunted, killed, and lynched many of the rogues, until several of them fled, and left for parts unknown. Many lives were lost on both sides, to the great scandal of civilized people.[3]

The men of the Middle West loved contests of every kind. Racing, gambling, "wraslin," "fist-fighting," argument—all kinds of sharp competition were popular. Mythical frontier heroes of the Middle Border and the Ohio watercourse such as Mike Fink, "half horse and half alligator," were heroes of battles. "I can outrun, outhop, outjump, throw down, drag out, and lick any man in the country; I'm a Salt River roarer; I love the [women] and I'm chockfull of fight," . . . so Mike Fink tells us in story and legend. Among river bad men, rough-and-tumble fighting included eye-gouging, thumb-chewing, knee-lifting, head-butting, biting off noses and ears, and tearing loose of underlips with the teeth. But among honest men who pitted themselves against each other in wrestling, horse racing, foot racing, or rough-and-tumble fights, wounding and killing an opponent was a crime, not the brave act of a gentleman. In the Middle West there was no "Code of Honor," as in the South, which concerned itself with the stylistic niceties involved in "proper" killing and wounding according to the codes and conventions of the duel.

In his first campaign for office in 1832, Lincoln grappled with local wrestlers who were eager to test his strength and skill. Lincoln's wrestling matches with Needham, Armstrong, and Thompson tell us much about the development of the hero in the Middle West. Unlike the private Southern duel with sword or pistol, a Middle Western match was widely publicized, conducted openly, and discussed freely. Betting of all kinds was encouraged. The highly stylized etiquette of the dueling code proscribed such publicity and limited dueling to the gentry. The dueler's honor rested with his seconds, whose judgments were final. Elders of the dueling field were deferred to as guardians of the code. They knew how to insult deftly, how to take an affront in polite style, how to shoot with courtesy, and how to die in a fashion sure to bring honor to one's family. But the wrestler's honor in Illinois was determined by rules which were guarded jealously by those who watched the match. As the contestants panted and heaved in the dust, shouts and cries arose from the audience. Each man was expected to fight hard, but he must abide by rules and he must not forget the element of play in the contest. It was not honorable to injure or kill an opponent. No frontier gentleman carried a fight with his equal beyond his opponent's admission that he was beaten. It was good to win, but one must win fairly and playfully and then shake hands, laugh, and share drinks together.

Middle Westerners believed the individual should defer to the community, or delegates of the community, because the social bonds of community life were created in the will of equals. Laws made by the people themselves should rule, just as laws hated by people should be changed. In 1836 Lincoln told the Young Men's Lyceum at Springfield: "Whenever the vicious portion of population shall be permitted to gather in bands of hundreds and thousands, and burn churches, ravage and rob provision stores, throw printing-presses into rivers, shoot editors, and hang and burn obnoxious persons at pleasure and with impunity, depend upon it, this government cannot last." The law, and the courts where law was adjudicated, were sacred. High- and low-born alike must take their disputes before the delegates of the community in the courts. Laws, like rules, could not please everyone, but so long as they were binding on all and every man was treated alike in their application, justice was done. Bad laws should be changed in open, free, and informed discussion. No one must take the law into his own hands, for once he did so the power of the community as an expression of the will of equals vanished.

The frontier individualism of the Middle West was far different from that of the South. The Southern ideal of social responsibility remained narrow and purely personal. The Southern gentleman was kind and gentle to "his own." He assumed personal responsibility for his slaves and for the poor whites he considered his neighbors. He had nothing but contempt for those who beat, starved, or overworked their slaves. But while he was willing enough to ameliorate the lot of an individual, or deal with a specific instance of injustice, he believed that every man was completely and wholly responsible for himself. Appeals for justice to courts of law, the creation of a wide range of voluntary associations, the submission of family to neighborhood demands, so characteristic of the Middle West, were almost unknown in the South. As we read in *Pudd'nhead Wilson* and *Huckleberry Finn,* recourse to courts of law for adjustment of grievances was considered the art of a coward. Judge Driscoll in *Pudd'nhead Wilson* is horrified to discover that his son Tom has gone to court. He berates Tom: "You cur! You scum! You vermin! Do you mean to tell me that blood of my race has suffered a blow and crawled to a court of law about it? Answer!"

Learning to live by rules was not easy or "natural" to the settlers of the Middle Border. "Bowie knife Southerners," "cow-milking Yankee Puritans," "beer-drinking Germans," "wild Irishmen," were all part of the Illinois scene. Germans, English, Irish, and Scandinavians, strange (sometimes deeply hostile) to each other in the Old World, transcended their ancient differences within one short generation in the new America of the Middle West. Many settlers from the Middle Western frontier were of good birth, and those who were not brought with them social prejudices and habits of speech and dress which set them apart from those of more common origins. They soon discovered that the education, taste, and manners which had given them superior status in the East or the South meant little in the Middle West. Indeed, far from helping them to rise or keep their place, such manners were a hindrance. The new people of the Middle West were deeply suspicious of Eastern or Southern manners, but social and regional differences had not yet hardened into class differences. In the memoirs, novels, diaries, and letters of life in the Middle Border before the Civil War, regional differences are clearly indicated, while class differences are but lightly marked, or if marked, drawn in irony and slapstick, not awe and reverence.

Leadership developed swiftly in frontier settlements, but it was a leadership based on possession of qualities serviceable to a young society. Many of these Western leaders, such as Clay, Jackson, Harrison, and Lincoln, became national, and in the case of Lincoln of Illinois, world heroes. The lady and gentleman of the South and of New England, the Cavalier and the Yankee, were familiar types in Illinois society. Each was highly conscious of his heritage and sought to impress it on others. Westerners respected both, but found it impossible to become either. The Westerner, unlike the New Englander, had no village tradition in manners, morals, or law. He lived on his freehold, and his sons did the same when they became strong enough to work their own land. Plantation life based on slavery was repugnant to a society where a man was expected to work the land he owned. Working for others as a servant put one in an inferior social position. "Hiring out" to "help" a neighbor, or to become a "hired hand" who ate in common with those who paid his wages, did not.

Lurking behind all claims for equality were many new kinds of inequality in political, community, military, educational, religious, and social life. Those of higher station who settled on the frontier soon learned this. If they were to lead they must learn to do so in terms which made sense to a new people.

The first thing they must learn was how to communicate in a language which, seemingly English, was really American. Educated settlers discovered they must discard much of the speech held proper in the East. The new Americans of the Middle West were not impressed by the speech of the East and the South. Boston and Charleston ladies were amazed at the new turns of speech considered proper on the frontier. And this new speech, like so much in Middle Western society, was being created at the bottom and the middle, as well as the top, of society. The ideal of service opened ways to different kinds of leadership. A man was not given leadership because of birth or wealth alone. Skill in things necessary to community survival counted for more. As skills proved their worth, the men possessing them rose to power. In times of stress and danger, such as the Black Hawk War, military leadership was determined by community vote (as were officers in the Civil War). People listened to their leaders, as their leaders listened to them, to decide how to act together. When the leader had done his job he returned to the ranks until another chance to lead occurred. But a leader's expression of power was always that of being first among equals, the most delicate of all forms of leadership. "In this country one man is as good as another; and for the matter of that very often a great deal better." Or "New Salem neighborhood has no principal citizen; every man there is a principal citizen." Lincoln's proverbial sayings on leadership were treasured in the Middle West.

Where all are considered equal, rules determine leadership. Where the leader is voted in and out of power by his equals he must learn to communicate his designs and listen to the suggestions of his followers. He must not only "accept" but inspire discussion. He must be prepared to step back into the ranks and follow other leaders in actions where other skills are required. Under differential status of this kind, equality demands skill in being led, as well as in leading. In Lincoln's days in the frontier town of New Salem, differential status based on the man, as well as his office, was very marked. Kirkpatrick, a sawmill owner who had hired Lincoln to move logs, and Lincoln were both elected to lead a company of volunteers in the Black Hawk War. Lincoln won out over his employer. Yet when Lincoln first ran for state office he lost, placing seventh among twelve candidates. In frontier society, leaders among equals found it necessary to become highly skilled in persuasive communication in open and free discussion. Equals appointed leaders and followed orders; they did not "obey" their leaders so much as "agree" with them.

Unlike people separated widely in space and through historical time, leaders and followers of rural and village America met face to face. In such meetings, communication involved the whole person. What a man said, how he said it, his gestures, his voice, and his eyes determined the force of his meaning. He prepared to persuade as well as command. Rhetoric became a tool, not an ornament, of discourse. Leadership of this type, so characteristic of the Middle West, was often misunderstood. Spokesmen for the East thought the men who followed Lincoln were lawless. Tocqueville feared that equality would lead to a conformity so oppressive that leadership could not flourish.

When the conditions of men are almost equal, they do not easily allow themselves to be persuaded by one another. As they all live in close intercourse, as they have learned the same things together, and as they lead the same life, they are not naturally disposed to take one of themselves for a guide and to follow him implicitly. Men seldom take the opinion of their equal or of a man like themselves upon trust.[4]

Herndon's account of Lincoln's command in the Black Hawk War illustrates these conditions of frontier leadership. On being elected captain, Lincoln replied in a brief response of modest and thankful acceptance. But as Lincoln himself tells us, his authority had to be won before it could be exercised. The first order he gave as captain got the response: "Go to hell." In spite of many such unsoldierlike civilities between Lincoln and his men, he gradually gained their respect. But it was a respect hard won and sustained with little help from the glamor of office. As commanding officer he was asked to champion his own men in a wrestling match with a soldier from the ranks of another company. This soldier threw Lincoln twice in succession. Lincoln's men shouted that Lincoln had been fouled, but Lincoln told his men: "Boys, give up your bets. If this man hasn't thrown me fairly, he could." The man, as well as the office, determined respect among such men.

We read in the Lincoln legends of an old Indian who strayed, hungry and helpless, into camp, where he was set upon by Lincoln's men. They wanted to kill him as a spy, but Lincoln refused. One of the men called Lincoln a coward who was taking advantage of his rank. Lincoln stood by the frightened, trembling old Indian and quietly told the angry mob of soldiers: "If any man thinks I am a coward, let him test it." There was a cry: "Lincoln, you're bigger and heavier than we are." Lincoln replied swiftly: "You can guard against that—choose your weapons!" Hot tempers cooled. The men understood they had a captain who would not hide behind his office. One of the men who served with him characterized his leadership as "freedom without familiarity." His "courtesy without condescension" won the respect of his rude but appreciative men. Such was Lincoln's first experience of leadership over Middle Westerners.[5]

Struggle for position and rank, like the struggle for existence in the wilderness itself, was often violent. A new schoolmaster expected to do battle with the class bully. If they fought, and they often did, whoever won dominated the school. A teacher who was not prepared to fight might teach a summer school "when nothin' but children come." But as the young Hoosier schoolmaster of Edward Eggleston's novel is told, ". . . it takes a right smart *man* to be schoolmaster in Flat Crick in the winter. They'd pitch you out of doors, sonny, neck and heels, afore Christmas." A teacher was measured by his ability to keep order. That he did so with violence did not seem strange to people who lived in violence. Lincoln described the frontier school in his autobiographical letter to Fell:

> There were some schools, so called, but no qualification was ever required of a teacher beyond readin', writin', and cipherin' to the rule of three.
> If a straggler, supposed to understand Latin, happened to sojourn in the neighborhood, he was looked upon as a wizard. There was absolutely nothing to excite ambition for education. Of course, when I came of age I did not know much, still somehow I could read, write, and cipher to the rule of three: but that was all.[6]

Clearly, there were many differences among the new people of the Middle Border. These differences were often so great that few observers believed they could be harmonized into any kind of community life. Foreign observers could not discover any "organic root" of community in this new world. As late as 1904, in his visit to Chicago on the way to St. Louis, the great German sociologist Max Weber used the image of the killing ground of America, the Chicago stockyards, where the entrails of animals were "laid bare" for all to see, as his image of the city. But Weber learned from young members of German clubs in America that the American boss, unlike the German-American boss, did not condescend toward his office help. He was able to meet his workers as equals, just as the worker, in turn, was able to look his boss in the eye and talk to him as a man.

Even the greatest social analysts of our time, such as Tocqueville and Weber, could not believe that the new democracy of the Middle Border could endure without forging traditional bonds of community. Equality at best was but a transitional stage to authority, and authority, as everyone in Europe knew, was grounded in religion, tradition, and custom and was enforced by a central power which could bring force against those who disobeyed or rebelled. But there was no such central power in the Middle Border, and its inhabitants, far from yearning for such power, were deeply hostile to it. Yet this powerless vacuum was no "primitive" community. As hundreds, then thousands, and soon millions, poured into the Great Valley of the Middle West, it became obvious that a new kind of social power and authority was being born in America.

This was the power of rules as a binding force among equals. Equals could agree because they could submit themselves to what Jefferson called "umpirage." The umpire, like the contestants, was bound by rules which were made, or accepted, by all those making use of them. The umpire was not a "sacred" figure who ruled by divine fiat, nor was he an individual whose judgments were correct because they were the judgments of a superior. And certainly his judgments were not based on his charisma as a person. The umpire's office, if not his person, bound men to it because it was an office which represented the will of equals who found in rules the fairest ways to reach decisions binding on all. Under rules, honor changed from adherence to custom and tradition which were guarded jealously by the "best" people, to the acceptance of rules which were reached in common discussion and upheld before publics who could challenge them at any time. If the challenge made sense in open and free discussion, it was accepted and the rule changed.

Rules existed only among equals. Inferiors could not be bound by rules, indeed, it was a mark of their inferiority that they could not accept rules. Anyone who needed "centralized power" backed by force to govern his relations with people could not be equal. A man who broke rules or who made rules to his own advantage was not to be trusted. A rule made by a superior without the consent of the inferior need not be kept. Only those who could make their own rules and submit themselves to rules of their own making were fit to be equals. For, as Jefferson had argued and the people of the Middle Border believed, rules were good and bad to the degree that they made consensus possible. The first rule, and indeed the basis for all rules in this new society, was the rule of discussion. As Jefferson said in the first section of his *Manual of Parliamentary Practice:* "It is much more material that there should be a rule to go by than what that rule is; that there may be a uniformity of proceeding in business not subject to the caprice of the speaker or captiousness of the members." Order in society depended on order in discussion, and thus the forms or rules of discussion became the forms of social order on informal as well as formal levels of action.

Notes

[1] As we shall see, this always remained Frank Lloyd Wright's ideal of family life.

[2] We cannot assume "community" as a type of social relationship, and then describe "forces" which have brought the community into being. Social, economic, or political

"conditions" affect men only as they become meanings under whose sign we act to-gether in love and hate. Such meanings are created by men and women struggling to achieve forms of sociation in which they can satisfy love and hate. Until such forms are created, there can be no communication, and hence no community. For, when all is said and done, it is how they *express* themselves in their search for relationships which determines how they relate.

[3] Peter Cartwright, *Autobiography of Peter Cartwright, The Backwoods Preacher* (New York: Nelson and Phillips, 1856), p. 25.

[4] Alexis de Tocqueville, *Democracy in America,* ed. by Phillips Bradley, 2 vols. (New York: Vintage Books, 1956), Vol II, p. 273. Tocqueville was sensitive to the relationship between the Middle Western form of settlement and equality. "When social conditions are equal, every man is apt to live apart, centered in himself and forgetful of the public. If the rulers of democratic nations were either to neglect to correct this fatal tendency or to encourage it from a notion that it weans men from political passions and this wards off revolutions, they might eventually produce the evil they seek to avoid, and a time might come when the inordinate passions of a few men, aided by the unintelli-gent selfishness of the pusillanimity of the greater number, would ultimately compel society to pass through strange vicissitudes." *Ibid.,* Vol. II, p. 270. He sensed the dangers of tyranny inherent in the lack of community, but we see now that his cure, religion, can be perverted into worship of a state (as by Hitler and Stalin). Whenever the truths of worship are placed beyond reason, equality cannot exist.

[5] *Herndon's Life of Lincoln,* with notes and introduction by Paul M. Angle (Cleve-land and New York: The World Publishing Co., 1949), pp. 77–83, is the source for these quotations.

[6] *Ibid.,* p. 34.

7

Comedy and Society in the Middle West

THE TRAGIC religious drama of salvation was but one of the great community dramas of the frontier. In their search for community men turned to tragic and comic art as well as religion. Tragic art in song, dance, and sermon lived beside the altar, as it has from time immemorial. But comic art dwelt apart. The laughing gods of the frontier lived among their people, and were kept alive by their artists. There were no laughing gods in frontier religion. "Make us cry—make us cry: don't make us laugh," an "old gray-headed man, with straight-breasted coat" begged Peter Cartwright, who opened his Roaring River Meeting with "anecdotes . . . well calculated to excite . . . risibilities." Chroniclers of the meeting like preacher Stone tell us of laughing seizures. He called it the "laughing exercise." Other chroniclers call it the "holy laugh." Stone explains that this loud hearty laughter came from only a few of the worshipers, and, unlike the rolling, dancing, running, and singing "exercises" of the "fallers," was not infectious.

Tragic euphoria was balanced by a deep and profound comic joy. For if men must weep to atone for their sins they must laugh to open their minds to reason in society. There was great laughter on the frontier, and as early as the fifties this frontier laughter was shaking America. From the mid-thirties on through the forties, the printing, as well as the telling, of uproarious yarns dealing with frontier characters and happenings was widespread. By 1852 enough of these tall tales, as this characteristic Western humor was called, existed to be brought into an anthology by Haliburton in his *Traits of American Humor* (1852) and *The Americans at Home* (1854). The *Nasby Papers* of Petroleum V. Nasby appeared in 1864, "Artemus Ward's Sayings" began to appear in the Cleveland *Plain Dealer* in 1857, and the first volume of Orpheus C. Kerr's *Papers* was published in 1862. Mark Twain wrote his first sketches for the Virginia City *Enterprise* in 1862. By mid-1863 several large editions of Lincoln joke books, such as *Old Abe's Jokes—Fresh from Abraham's Bosom* and *Old Abe's Joker, or Wit at the White House,* had been printed and sold. By 1884 Western comedy reached full expression in *Huckleberry Finn,* the American literary masterpiece of our time. A few years later the comic genius of the Middle West shifted to Chicago. Comic writers such as George Ade, Eugene Field, Finley Peter Dunne, and Ring Lardner urbanized the speech of the West and carried on the search for an American vernacular in writing, as well as speech.

Within twenty years, from 1864 to 1884, the humor of the West carried the American vernacular to the White House. Like the great Chicago architecture of the eighties and nineties, this humor was a popular, not an elite, art. It was created by people who lived on the frontier and in the new cities, its main emphasis was on the people themselves, and it was art to the people long before it was even recognized by the guardians of American culture. Burlesque and exaggeration characterize much of this humor, but it was the realistic portrayal of characters facing the many incongruities of society which distinguished it. New social types were given forms which made possible an *American* drama of community life. These humorists did much to create the language and social types which came to be characteristic of America from 1860 to 1920, the birth time of the urban America we know. The idealization of the American democrat in Lincoln, and the emergence of an indigenous American artist on the world's stage in Mark Twain, did not occur in any traditional literary world. It was not the product of fine art, academic sponsorship, or the patronage of an elite. Like the art of Sullivan and Wright, or the later art of Chaplin, it came from artists who were content with a popular audience. It was an art whose themes came from the bottom, not the top, of its society. And, indeed, as we shall see, it was not even recognized as "art," any more than the commercial and domestic architecture of Sullivan and Wright was recognized as "art" by the guardians of architectural tradition in America.

The East smiled and enjoyed popular humorists such as Artemus Ward, Josh Billings, and Mark Twain. The fool might be funny, occasionally he might be wise, but he was seldom considered an artist. A Westerner like Bret Harte or Hamlin Garland could be measured against a well-understood literary tradition. Harte spoke a language Bostonians could understand. His humor, his pathos, his point of view were all recognizable. It was an art already standardized by many masters. But Mark Twain and the Chicagoans Ade, Dunne, and Lardner spoke a new and startling tongue, and they depicted low characters and relations between high and low characters from the viewpoint of the "little fellow," the man of the people. The clash between established traditions and the new problems of frontier life created incongruities which could not be resolved easily, if at all. Much of Mark Twain's humor is simply a statement of deep perplexity. As in much of Lincoln's humor, the statement of monstrous incongruity is comic enough. Contrast in life between how one must act in the Middle West and how one had been taught to act in the older tradition of the East was highly incongruous. To meet such frequent and profound incongruities in frontier life required great flexibility. There were few rituals—in sacred as well as secular aspects of community life—which could be invoked. Even the simplest social functions and the most traditional manners could not be carried on as they had been in the East. The stages on which Eastern traditions and manners were mounted no longer existed in the Middle Border. In the face of the incongruities between the ideals of the East or the South and the reality of his own life, the Middle Westerner found laughter a necessity to community life. Caroline Kirkland, writing of Michigan frontier life in 1839, points out that pride without laughter soon made community life impossible. "[H]owever we may justify certain exclusive habits in populous places, they are strikingly and confessedly ridiculous in the wilderness." [1]

Huck's struggles with the conventions and manners of genteel folk was experienced by every frontiersman who tried to settle and become a good citizen of the new American community in the Great Valley. His search is a search for brotherhood, for a life among men who could live as equals without surrendering dignity and freedom. In this search he found good and evil among the people of the river. No one has depicted the cruelty, violence, and cowardice of the frontier better than Mark Twain. Yet no one loved more the great promise of a new day of love and freedom in equality. As we listen to Huck and Jim we hear the search for democracy, just as later in the buildings of Sullivan and Wright we see the search for a peoples' architecture. But we hear it through laughter, for how else could the great distance between traditions and the new life of America be explored safely? Tragedy had been invoked in a terrible war. The empty chairs around family tables and the thousands of maimed veterans hobbling down the streets of America were eloquent witnesses to the failure of the tragic spirit.

Americans, and particularly Americans in the Middle West, turned to comedy because comedy alone could refresh the springs of community life after the Civil War. As Americans laughed and played together they reaffirmed their equality. We laugh *at* inferiors or superiors (when they cannot hear us), but we laugh *with* equals. We also laugh to endure what we cannot, or will not, change. Men of the East did not always find the Westerner comic. Often they thought him grotesque. Sometimes the clown's role was the only one possible to the Westerner. Lincoln, like Mark Twain, Ade, Dunne, Lardner, and Sinclair Lewis, often played the fool, and in doing so was often accused of bad taste by official guardians of manners. Lincoln and Mark Twain (in spite of all attempts to clean up their historical image as American

In city and country alike the drama of politics often ended in laughter and fun in which the whole community took part. Elections were great contests in which many bets were made. Here in the "Lost Bet," printed in Chicago in 1893 from the painting by Joseph Klir, the artist used as models his friends and neighbors, many of whom were from Czechoslovakia. *Courtesy Chicago Historical Society*

In this etching the anti-Lincoln cartoonist, Adalbert J. Volck (1828–1912), indicates how difficult it was for "serious" Americans to relate the gift of comedy to political leadership. *Courtesy Chicago Historical Society*

GREAT AMERICAN TRAGEDIANS, COMEDIANS
CLOWNS AND ROPE-DANZERS IN
THEIR FAVORITE CHARACTERS.

Your honours players are come to play a pleasant comedy.... Is it a
Comedy....a Christmas Gambol or a tumbling trick.....No my Lord to
is more pleasing stuff....it is a kind of history.

demigods) were often obscene. But they seldom turned their humor or their obscene ridicule on the weak and the oppressed. They saved their shafts for those who separate men and women. For a golden moment in the Middle West it was believed that laughter could save us from hate. We could laugh at our differences because in democracy difference could be harmonized.

The traditions of New England and the South were put under heavy strain in the Great Valley. Often, indeed, they were completely irrelevant. In a land where there were few servants and when dress must be kept simple, how did one play the role of lady? Among men of small learning who must be addressed as equals, how did one speak? In travel where there was no separation of classes, how did one guard his privacy and respect the privacy of others? In teaching children of communities where vernacular speech was common, what was the relevance of British or even New England classics? In commanding men at war, how did one discipline troops who were volunteers, who elected their own officers, and who had to be persuaded, not ordered, to stay on when their enlistment time was up? In courting women, how could one use the conventions of romantic love with women one worked beside or saw working at all kinds of tasks every day? How did one trade with people who thought of trade as a kind of social event, and made stores into an informal club? How did one campaign for political office among people who wanted to see and hear their candidates, entertain them in their homes, and make politics a community drama of parade, picnics, and stump speaking? Even religion offered its own brand of incongruity. Methodists, Baptists, Presbyterians, Campbellites—almost every sect known, and indeed some unknown anywhere else—preached the "true" gospel. And where the "call" alone was sufficient warrant to assume the right to preach to others, interpretations of Holy Writ were highly individual. The camp meetings where devotion rose to such ecstasy were a strange mixture of the sacred and the profane. To those not seized with the holy spirit, the confusion and excitement of the camp meeting conversions easily became ridiculous. Sometimes, indeed, it was too much even for the devout. Preacher Cartwright admits bursting out in laughter: "To see those proud young gentlemen and young ladies, dressed in their silks, jewelry, and prunella, from top to toe, take the *Jerks,* would often excite my risibilities." [2]

We read of mock sacraments being held in the woods near the sacred altar itself. Whisky served as the lubricating agent, and tipsy "mourners" acting their parts at make-believe altars.[3] Satire on the camp meetings appeared very early in the newspapers. Hooper's Captain Suggs stories appeared in the forties; they tell how Captain Suggs swindled camp meeting worshipers (a similar episode is in *Huckleberry Finn*). In these stories, ridicule and satire of religious services at the meetings is sharp and deep. Captain Suggs even suggests that preachers were moved by lust as well as Christian love in their ministration to women: "Wonder what's the reason these here preachers never hugs up the old, ugly women? Never seed one do it in my life—the sperrit never moves 'em that way! It's nater tho'; and the women! They never flocks around one o' the old dried-up breethring. . . . Well! who blames 'em? Nater will be nater, all the world over; and judge of I was a preacher, I should save the purtiest souls fust, myself!" [4] *The Harp of A Thousand Strings: A Hard-Shell Baptist Sermon,* first published in the 1850s, is really a mock sermon. The story of a recruit who could not name his father telling his officers: "Captain, sir, I guess I'm just a camp-meetin' baby," was told by Lincoln himself.[5]

Middle Western comedy was a popular art. Mark Twain wrote to Andrew Lang in 1890: "It is not that little minority who are already saved [for culture] that are best worth trying to uplift, I should think, but the mighty mass of the uncultivated who are underneath." In reference to his own career, Mark Twain says: "I have never tried in even one single instance, to help cultivate the cultivated classes. I was not equipped for it, either by native gifts or training. And I never had any ambition in that direction, but always hunted for bigger game—the masses. I have seldom deliberately tried to instruct them, but have done my best to entertain them . . . for amusement is a good preparation for study and a good healer of fatigue after it. My audience is dumb, it has no voice in print, and so I cannot know whether I have won its approbation or only got its censure." [6]

Yet while Mark Twain was content to be a popular writer he did not pander to the people. He was very much aware of the problems of his time, so aware that people read Henry Wheeler Shaw ("Josh Billings"), Robert H. Newell ("Orpheus C. Kerr"), Dunne, and Mark Twain as we now read political cartoons. We turn to our comic political art for help in thinking about affairs of the day, and for expressing clearly passions which we have experienced but cannot communicate easily. Mark Twain's identification with the Western view of American life, like his identification with the genteel tradition of the East in his domestic and social life, was a self-conscious one. The Middle Western view of life, and especially the comic view, in Lincoln and Mark Twain was born in attempts to resolve the incongruity between demands of a new life in the West and the older ideals of the East. What struck Westerners as comic was smug arrogance born of ignorance among Easterners who knew little of life in the Middle West. In consternation, anger, and sometimes rage, the Westerner saw Easterners dismiss the West as vulgar, crude, and ignorant. Their humorists admitted these charges.

But they reminded the world that if the new man of the West was often a braggart, he was so because he lived in hope and confidence in the future of America. His braggarts, like his prophets, all lived in a future "over the hills and far away." Westerners who walked town streets which were often little better than hog wallows were aware of the mud, filth, and stink. But as they walked in mud, they could lift their eyes to the stars, where they saw ideal commonwealths. In the West, visionaries were not grotesque, or madmen, or fools, but prophets of a new day.

In the mud and filth of the towns of the Middle Border, they saw Athens—but an Athens without slaves. These new Americans were determined to create a commonwealth of free individuals, where differences could become a source of strength and where, in open debate and discussion, new resources of thought and spirit could be tapped. When their hopes waned and died, men turned from their Utopias of freedom, the future died, and laughter and tolerance died with it. The dark god of tragedy took the stage to punish in hate and violence those whose differences were once a source of joy and laughter. The spirit of the Middle West was sustained in great laughter, for it was through laughter that America's new citizens could confront the many incongruities in their lives. The spectacle of ignorant, crude, and often violent and undisciplined men aspiring to leadership over other men was always perilously close to comedy. Mark Twain agreed with Brooks and Henry Adams that democracy was an unrealized Utopia, perhaps even a mad dream. His personal despair, like that of Sullivan, was deep and agonizing. His faith in democracy was born and sustained in love of the common man of the West. This love, like all great love, was conceived in joy but sustained in sorrow. The laughter of the Middle West, like all great laughter, was sustained in tears. But in our laughter at Huck, Jim, and Tom there is hope. Without such hope, Americans who had seen their sons march off to suffer and die in a terrible war could not have returned to their great task of creating a democratic commonwealth.

Notes

[1] Caroline M. Kirkland, *A New Home or Life in the Clearings,* ed. and with an intro. by John Nerber (New York: Putnam, 1953), p. 102.

[2] Peter Cartwright, *Autobiography* (New York: Nelson and Phillips, 1856), pp. 48–49.

[3] Charles A. Johnson, *The Frontier Camp Meeting: Religion Harvest Time* (Dallas: Southern Methodist University Press, 1955), p. 224.

[4] Quoted from V. L. O. Chittick, ed., *Ring-Tailed Roarers: Tall Tales of the American Frontier 1830–1860* (Caldwell, Idaho: The Caxton Printers, 1943), p. 238.

⁵ Sandburg tells us John Hay heard Lincoln tell it. See *Abraham Lincoln: The War Years,* 4 vols. (New York: Harcourt, 1939), Vol. III, p. 330.

⁶ This letter is reprinted in *The Portable Mark Twain,* ed. by Bernard De Voto (New York: The Viking Press, 1946), pp. 770–73.

PART TWO

Money as a Symbol of Life
in the Middle West

8

The Emergence of Chicago in the American Mind

IN THE YEARS between the Chicago Fire of 1871 and the Chicago Fair of 1893, Chicago architects created forms which were to become characteristic of all forms of modern technology.[1] Much of what is now loved, hated, and feared in the "Americanization" of Europe and Asia found expression in Chicago during these years. The Chicago Fair of 1893 shifted the drama of the American spirit from New England and New York to Chicago. Thoughtful Americans and Europeans began to realize that Chicago forms of life, thought, and architecture, so alien and strange to New England and Europe, were the dawn of a new day in American culture. Henry Adams understood that Chicago's presentation of itself to the world in the Fair marked the beginning of a new era in American civilization. He said: "The exposition itself defied philosophy. . . . As a scenic display, Paris had never approached it, but the inconceivable scenic display consisted in its being there at all— more surprising than anything else on the continent, Niagara Falls, the Yellowstone Geysers, and the whole railway system thrown in. . . ." When Adams sat down to brood as he had never brooded "on the benches of Harvard College, either as student or professor," he was "ashamed of the childlike ignorance and babbling futility" of an education which had not prepared him for the shock of Chicago.

"Chicago," Adams continues, "was the first expression of American thought as a unity." If anyone wished to understand the future of America, and thus of the world, he "must start there." For over a century the American people had "hesitated, vacillated, swayed forward and back, between two forces. . . . In 1893 . . . the majority at last declared itself, once for all, in favor of the capitalistic system with all its necessary machinery." This new unity was, for Adams, a force. He was not quite sure what this force was, but, whatever it was, it was not art. "On one side, at the Louvre and at Chartres . . . was the highest energy ever known to man . . . and yet this energy was unknown to the American mind. An American Virgin would never dare command; an American Venus would never dare exist." Americans "felt a railway train as power; yet they, and all other artists, constantly complained that the power embodied in a railway train could never be embodied in art."

The only art Adams saw in Chicago was the Beaux-Arts classicism of the Fair. Adams did not ask whether Sullivan's Transportation Building should be preferred to Charles B. Atwood's Fine Arts Building. He does not even mention the Transportation Building. "If the people of the Northwest actually knew what was good when they saw it, they would some day talk about Hunt and Richardson, La Farge and St. Gaudens, Burnham and McKim, and Stanford White when their politicians and millionaires were otherwise forgotten." Burnham is the only Chicago architect mentioned, and it is Burnham the classicist, not the architect of the Reliance Building. "[A]rt, to the Western people, was a stage decoration; a diamond shirt-stud; a paper collar . . ." as the Eastern artists told Adams. The Tacoma or the Reliance buildings, like the Cunard steamers, were not art but "forces" to be summed up in the image of the dynamo. The twentieth century would be a struggle between art (the Virgin) and science as technology (the Dynamo). The disenchantment of the world would soon be complete for the engineer had routed the artist and the humanist. Thus Adams, like so many thinkers of his generation, saw in Chicago a clear and ominous portent of a new age of machines and technology where the humane spirit of democracy would survive—if it did survive—in ways unlike anything envisioned by the founders of the American commonwealth.

Henry Adams was not alone in his backward walk into the twentieth century. Henry James failed to understand the new art of technology as well as the businessmen of the West, who were establishing themselves as guardians of a new art based on technology. Harriet Monroe, who wrote so understandingly in 1896 of John Wellborn Root's life and work and who was to make Chicago an international headquarters for the new poetry of her time, faltered in her championship of an equally new architecture. In 1915, it was the "White City in Jackson Park," not the Transportation Building with its Golden Door, which stirred her memories of the Fair. "No other festal city has been so spacious by land and water, with buildings so nobly grouped beside large lagoons. . . . [There] was a passion of great beauty evoked out of dust and fire; for a moment all unreal things were real, and dreams had the hardihood of marble." [2] Chicago artists outside the field of architecture show little recognition of the greatness of Chicago design. [3] The letters and memoirs of the artists who were to make Chicago the literary capital of America in the years before World War I make little reference to the architectural achievements of their own city. Art for Fuller, Dreiser, Garland, Stone and Kimball of the *Chap-Book,* Chatfield-Taylor, as well as Masters,

The expression of American thought "as a unity" (as described by Henry Adams in his chapter on Chicago in *The Education of Henry Adams*) in the development of architectural form as an expression of social function, was nowhere seen better than at State and Madison streets in the Chicago Loop.
Courtesy Chicago Historical Society

Sandburg, Sherwood Anderson, and Floyd Dell, had little to do with the buildings going up about them. Even Garland, whose *Crumbling Idols* of 1894 attacked literary imitation of the "last epics of feudalism" and repetitions of "the dying echoes of Romance," was deeply moved by the "wonder and beauty" of the classical Fair.

Yet on the near-by streets of the new city stood over a hundred buildings designed in what was to be known as "contemporary" style. By 1893, almost every characteristic of the Chicago School and what we now think of as modern style, was in evidence. Even the "curtain wall" was already clearly stated in the Tacoma Building (1889) of Holabird and Roche, and the Reliance Building (1890) of Burnham and Root. Jenney's first Leiter Building was built in 1879; Burnham and Root's Montauk Building, Chicago's first ten-story building, was built in 1882; Adler and Sullivan's Kennedy Bakery in 1883; Jenney's Home Insurance, the first "skeleton" skyscraper, in 1884; Burnham and Root's Rookery Building in 1886, and their Phoenix Insurance Company Building (now Austin Building), in 1886. Richardson's Marshall Field Wholesale Warehouse, a block-square, seven-story building, which expressed its masonry structure clearly and eloquently, was built in 1887. Adler and Sullivan's Auditorium Theatre, Hotel, and Office Building of 1886–90, a huge structure, housed a complex of facilities. Jenney's Manhattan Building, Chicago's tallest building, was erected in 1890. Burnham and Root's Monadnock Building, this country's highest wall-bearing building, went up in 1891. Sullivan's tower in the Schiller Building of 1892 seemed to soar upwards into the sky. Burnham and Root's Masonic Temple of 1892, the tallest building in America until 1900, was one of Chicago's famous "sights." Even at the Fair itself, Adler and Sullivan's Transportation Building with its golden door, the first fully developed statement of Sullivan's architectural ornament, was to be awarded medals by the *Union Centrale des Arts Décoratifs*—the only building so honored by any foreign institution.

But these great buildings, soaring into the sky to house a new breed of "cliff dwellers," were not all. H. H. Richardson, America's greatest architect of the years after the Civil War and the designer of Henry Adams's own home in Washington, completed the Glessner house in 1886. This was his finest house, just as the Marshall Field Warehouse was his most significant expression of masonry. Frank Lloyd Wright's residence (1889) in Oak Park and the Charnley residence on Astor Street (1892) already indicated the spatial articulation and structural expression of his later work. Even sacred architecture had been touched by the new spirit. The Kehilath Anshe Ma'ariv Synagogue of Adler and Sullivan, like the Auditorium Theatre, enhanced the beauty of sound and created new possibilities for religious architecture.

But even those who saw beauty in cathedrals where people worshiped, but not in buildings where they worked, should have understood the Getty Tomb of 1890, in Graceland Cemetery. Here the hierarchy of content, which decreed that architecture must be used only for dignified and majestic occasions, was preserved. One of the oldest architectural forms, the tomb, found new beauty in the creation of a young Chicago "functionalist." Its beauty is purely architectural, a harmony in mass, plane and line, which subordinates ornament to architectural composition. As his pupil, Frank Lloyd Wright, who carried the glory of Sullivan's spirit to the world, said in 1949, "The Getty Tomb in Graceland Cemetery was entirely his own; fine sculpture. A Statue. A great poem addressed to human sensibilities as such. Outside the realm of music what finer requiem?"

The new society of Chicago which produced this new art was based on money. Money, as everyone said, was a new symbol of life. Certainly it was a perplexing one. Simmel, the German sociologist who became the master of Robert Ezra Park, who, in turn, brought sociology in Chicago to national and international fame, described money as the most abstract of all symbols of power. As he pointed out, money has no intrinsic value in itself. Unlike land, which evokes a spirit of continuity as it becomes the hallowed scene of family and community life, money as such evokes nothing. It must be transformed into other symbols, whose radiance moves us by their majestic identifications with a sacred past or with a prophetic belief in the glory of things to come. At the same time, these sacred symbols must be made comprehensible to all. The dilemma of money as a symbol of power is that we must use it to be exclusive, yet not so exclusive that audiences cannot comprehend our exclusiveness. We cannot place ourselves so far beyond the comprehension of the audiences that they think us strange and peculiar, not majestic and sublime. In Europe it has been common to translate money into land, titles, and office. Under such conditions, money is powerful, not because it binds its possessor to the common people as an audience to his wealth, but because it is a way of raising oneself above the common people to a sublime aristocracy whose traditional symbols of prestige are not "vulgar" expressions of money. Among such aristocrats rank, lineage, and skill reduce money to a means, not an end, in status enactment.

The social mystique of aristocracy exists in the values of family lineage as expressed in the dramatization of dynastic traditions as community traditions. The power of money, like the power of any symbol, is determined by the nature of the symbol as well as by the political, economic, and social environment in which the symbol is used. A symbol which begins as a weapon in a struggle for power, in victory often becomes an end in itself. Those who safeguard the sanctity of such symbols want fixed, sacred meanings for their symbols, and they want to communicate them through ritual. For in such ritual, the symbol becomes an end in itself. It is invested with "spirit" and its power lies beyond reason. Belief may be explained through appeal to reason, but this is not the social basis for its acceptance. Social beliefs arise out of conviction that proper use of a symbol is necessary to the continuance of the community. Symbols based in such convictions attain a radiance and glory, a transcendence, whose power comes from their enhancement of the sense of community among men.

Chicago businessmen understood that success depended on skill in glamorizing their symbol of success, money. To make earning, and particularly spending, a value beyond doubt and question demanded that the materialism of money be spiritualized through some new kind of identification with American values. Earning money had been related to divine purpose in the traditions of the Puritan conception of the stewardship of wealth. But Chicagoans added a new dimension to their Puritan tradition by spiritualizing spending through relating it to brotherhood in community life. As Wesley taught, and Carnegie practiced, great earning could be justified only through *giving* money to the community. But Chicago businessmen wanted individuals to spend as well as to earn, and they wanted Chicagoans to spend on themselves as well as the community. For until individuals could become customers, as well as stewards of wealth or heroes of philanthropy, business could not develop. Only a *resolution* of individual and community spending could bring money full power because it was only through some such identification that money could be spiritualized as an expression of community. To compete for markets in a purely economic sense with already established cities such as Cincinnati, St. Louis, or New York could not bring supremacy to Chicago traders. William Bross recognized this as early as 1856, when he urged Chicagoans to listen faithfully to their "divine" call to trade. The future of Chicago, Bross told his Canadian listeners at the Great Railway Celebration held in Montreal in 1856, was in divine hands: "The Creator when he formed the Great Lakes and the St. Lawrence, intended that the commerce of the mighty and teeming West should be borne on their broad bosom to the ocean, and I think, Sir, it requires no great amount of geographical and philosophical sagacity to discover that while Chicago is to be the great central commercial city of the North American continent, Montreal is to be one of the great commercial emporiums of the seaboard." [4]

Chicago "boomers" like "Deacon" Bross and John Stephen Wright should not be confused with Colonel Sellers of *The Gilded Age,* or George F. Babbitt of *Babbitt.* Bross and Wright, Chicago boomers all their lives, thought of themselves as founders of a new way of life as well as traders booming a new city. They hoped to found their own fortunes as well as the fortunes of others. Wright admitted openly in his letters to newspapers, and in the series of circulars on railroads and Western real estate opportunities which he turned out in such great numbers, that he expected to make money through Chicago's growth. But he hoped to make his money in a city where money would be used to humanize the existence of the common man. His *Chicago, Past, Present, Future,* published three years before the great fire of 1871, and his writings of the last years of a life which began in the frontier settlement of Chicago in 1832, is really a hymn to the spirit of plutocracy. Wright thought of businessmen as honest and earnest stewards who would employ their wealth to advance the "cause of God and humanity." For Wright there was no conflict between business and morality so long as businessmen assumed their responsibilities to the city. When monopolies formed and held back land for sale at reasonable prices (as was done by the Illinois Central) Wright fought them. Although an advocate of land grants to the railroads, Wright did not believe in corporate control of land. Business was justified only so long as it benefited the people—*all* the people. Like Henry Ford, he believed money must justify itself by its ability to create and sustain an ever-increasing standard of life for the common people. Chicagoans of 1870 who agreed with this view had little reason to question the social value of capitalism. If businessmen could supply great armies in the field, raise the farmer above a brute struggle with nature, supply funds for public education from childhood to youth, develop railways linking the South with the North and thus heal the wounds of a terrible war, then money-making was justified.

John Stephen Wright understood well the perversions of the Puritan ethic in making money. He warned his fellow businessmen that they must teach the Americans and themselves how to consume as well as produce wealth in a Christian fashion. More than any other great Chicagoan of the years before the Fire, he taught the gospel of public spending. Such spending was good for business—as it was for the people—because it developed community resources. These in turn created greater opportunities for business. In this spirit, businessmen were urged to spend for public education, transportation, parks, and community facilities of all kinds. Schools, churches, and civic buildings were good for the people, but they were also good for business since they enhanced neighborhood real-estate values. This was the Lord's work for Jew, Catholic, and Protestant alike. A sound community produced good Christians and good Americans because it produced good customers. The revolt against business which characterized the younger generation of 1840 in Boston and the sharp distinction made between the gentleman and the trader in the South were not evident in Chicago. Townsmen and farmer alike shared dreams of wealth. The farmer must become an efficient businessman, not simply a workman who exerted himself to make his farm support him. It was common practice to "take up" more land than could be cultivated. Holding these idle and semi-idle acres intact was costly, since farm credit was notoriously usurious. Mrs. Kirkland, writing in 1839, says:

Comforts do not seem to abound in proportion to land increase, but often on the contrary, are really diminished for the sake of it: and the habit of selling out so frequently makes that *home*-feeling, which is so large an ingredient in happiness elsewhere, almost a nonentity in Michigan. The man who holds himself ready to accept the first advantageous offer, will not be very solicitous to provide those minor accommodations, which, although essential to domestic comfort, will not add to the moneyed value of his farm, which he considers merely an article of trade, and which he knows his successor will look upon in the same light.

It was not until the eighties and nineties that Chicagoans thought of money as a divisive factor in community life. Wright and Bross taught that money brought men together in "Christian service." Fortunes made in lumber, grain, beef, pork, reapers, and railroads were reinvested in the city—indeed, they had to be, if the city was to provide the means to greater prosperity. To the second generation of Chicagoans, money meant well-fed, clothed, and armed Union troops. In 1871 it meant the rebuilding of a city all but destroyed by fire. In 1891 money created the great Chicago Fair and founded one of America's great universities, the University of Chicago. Thus from the very beginning of the city, the role of the businessman in Chicago was a civic role. He thought of himself as a community leader, a man of affairs. The glory of money was in its community identification. Money must be "put to work" because through its workings individual and the community alike benefited. The frontier transvaluation of land into real estate makes this clear.[5] "Passion for acquisition," as well as "workmanship," characterized the farmer of the Middle West, as Veblen stressed. Veblen held that in a business society, real estate was the one community interest which bound townsmen and farmer together. "Habitually and with singular uniformity the American farmers have aimed to acquire real estate at the same time they have worked at their trade as husbandmen." Caroline Kirkland's Montacute, Mark Twain's and Charles Dudley Warner's city of Napoleon, as fictive towns differ only in degree from the real practice of "town plating" in the Middle West. Colonel Sellers and Mr. Mazard, like their real counterparts in Chicago, Stephen Wright and "Deacon" Bross, envisioned towns and cities where duller eyes saw only swamps and bogs.

Rural, village, and urban pioneers alike were seeking to develop a society based on money before European and native Americans found the promise of dignity and freedom in this new symbol. Native Americans hoped that money would produce a commonwealth of free men who could live without fear of starvation or want. As the older symbols of office, rank, and family were transformed it was hoped that money could do for the new urban community what land as a freehold had done in rural communities to create an independent rural citizenry capable of governing themselves. The new glory of money was not the power of gold which gleams and glows in the wonder tales of older societies. Nor was it the achievement of a quality of rank or station as in the status drama of the British gentlemen. The Chicago drama was one of movement up and down the social ladder. It was the movement, the fame, the rivalry, the "money-game," not the arrival, which fascinated Chicagoans. The strange and mysterious quality of this drama is the continual movement "with the procession," as Fuller called it in his novel by this name which appeared in 1895. The drama of money to Veblen, Fuller, Dreiser, Burnham, and Fitzgerald was not in the increase in standards of living, but the *ever*-increasing standard of living. Beyond what one had, which once had seemed so radiant and mysterious, was another golden future. The present was but a step to a future which in turn would become a step to another future.

Chicagoans of the seventies and eighties were not interested in creating a past. The future destroyed the past in Chicago. Richardson's Romanesque died in his great Chicago building, the Marshall Field Warehouse. For, although this was a Romanesque expression, it was the expression of a new kind of structure—a great sales bazaar. The genteel tradition in American literature also died in Chicago. Indeed, to many it seemed as if all traditional values were dying. As Fuller said, Chicago "was the only great city in the world to which all of its great citizens have come for the avowed purpose of making money. There you have its genesis, its growth, its object; and there are but few of us who are not attending to that object very strictly." [6] When Marshall Field was asked to supply information for a genealogical chart carrying Field ancestors back to 1630, he replied, "I have nothing to give you," and then in turn asked the question that seemed natural to Chicagoans: "Why do we need a genealogy?" Wealth earned in certain ways needed no dignification beyond itself. The only past Chicagoans of 1885 honored deeply was their own past. And for them this was a trader's past—but a new kind of trader. Business was accepted as far more than a training ground for making money. Older aristocratic virtues were supplanted by a new kind of plutocratic honor and gentility. The "old settlers" honored in Chicago society were the old settlers who had made money. For such Chicago novelists as Juliette

Kinzie, trade was a new kind of gentility. In *Mark Logan, the Bourgeoise,* written in 1870, she says of the expedition managers of the American Fur Company: "One characteristic of these young men has been much remarked by strangers, particularly by foreign travellers—the fact, namely, that so far from becoming rough and coarse under the exposure and associations incidental to their service, they were, as a class, noticeable for the graceful ease and courtly refinement of their manners. Even at this day we hear it said, —'What a well-bred man is H, or K, or M!' And then comes the answer, 'Certainly; he was brought up in the American Fur Company.'"

In her *Wau-Bun* of 1856, the first "Chicago novel," Mrs. Kinzie created the accepted business legend of Chicago's founding. John Kinzie in reality was scarcely the enlightened and genteel trader of the legend. But the genteel trader was the myth Chicagoans wanted. "So thoroughly has her narrative of the Kinzie family . . . permeated the local mind, that all the efforts of all the historians, probably, will never succeed in replacing it with a more correct and judicial concept." [7] Others in the city pointed out that chevaliers and Jesuits of France, Indians, and even American soldiers had as much to do with the founding of Chicago as the trader John Kinzie. There were many legends Chicagoans could shape into a conventional myth of origin. But Chicagoans selected the past they preferred, just as today they still write their history in political and economic terms and solve their future in economic planning as they staff their boards and civic committees with businessmen. [8]

Few Chicagoans of the seventies or eighties wanted to make money so that they could do something else besides making money. There were—and are— few men of leisure in Chicago. As Kipling, writing in the nineties, said: "They told me to go to the Palmer House . . . and there I found a huge ball of tesellated marble, crammed with people talking about money and spitting about everywhere. Other barbarians charged in and out of this inferno with letters and telegrams in their hands, and yet others shouted at each other." [9] Chicagoans might have objected to the spitting, but talk about money, far from being vulgar, was highly acceptable. What else was there to talk about? Even women were at work behind counters and in offices. Some, such as Mrs. Newbury, who ran the Boston Store for 42 years, were a match for men in their devotion to money. [10] But this devotion to money has little to do with avarice, or the older Puritan ethic of holy earning as a steward of the Lord. Chicago businessmen were famous for the money they risked and spent, not for what they hoarded and saved. Miserliness was despised. The farmer or immigrant who would not put his money in the bank was a butt of popular humor. The "tight wad" was a stock comic character. [11] Much of the action of such novels as *With the Procession* and of Ade's *Fables* (as indeed of *Silas*

Lapham, Howell's business novel) centers around getting "Pa" to spend money on a house, on a trip to Europe, or to marry off a daughter. "City slickers" fleecing a "rube"—or anyone else—was a much enjoyed burlesque act in local theatres. Chicagoans laughed heartily at stories of swindlers and confidence men who victimized small town bankers, notorious for their thrift. Cheating a man who wanted great returns at no risk was against the law, but not against the popular notion that the only risk brought honor.

The pursuit of money, the "money-game," as Will Payne called it in his Chicago novels, was the drama of wealth for the man, just as spending money —"putting on the dog," "keeping up with the Joneses," or "conspicuous consumption," as spending was called in various circles in Chicago—was a drama for women. When Philip D. Armour was asked about retirement he said quite simply and openly: "I have no other interest in life but my business. I do not want more money. . . . I have more than I want. I do not love money, what I do love is the getting of it, the making it. . . . I do not read, I do not take any part in politics, what can I do? But in my counting house I am in my element: there I live and the struggle is the very breath of life to me." [12] The Chicagoans Pullman, Armour, and Field were feudal enough in their attitude toward power, but they did not consider themselves speculators or "robber barons." Like every great American city from 1875 to 1900, Chicago had its plungers. The wheat pit of the Chicago Board of Trade was the economic pivot of America from the depression of 1873 to 1900. The Chicago market set the price of the world's bread. Frank Norris, the novelist, turned to Chicago for the second volume of his projected trilogy, *The Epic of the Wheat.* This novel, *The Pit,* is subtitled *A Story of Chicago.* Jadwin, the hero of the "Battle of the Street," had his counterpart in Benjamin P. Hutchinson ("Old Hutch"), the Chicago grain plunger who controlled the world's wheat during his great September *coup* in 1888. Local newspaper reports of 1888 are scarcely less dramatic than the novel of 1902. In such stories we read that whenever "Old Hutch" even engaged in conversation in the pit, all conversation died and business stopped. Theodore Dreiser selected another Chicago speculator, Charles T. Yerkes, as the model for Cowperwood, the hero of *The Financier* and *The Titan.*

But in the eyes of Chicago, businessmen like Armour, Leiter and Yerkes were really not proper Chicago businessmen at all. A businessman created something more than money. He helped harvest the world's wheat, like McCormick, transported a nation, like Pullman, clothed a city, like Field, or fed the world, like Armour. In 1900, Professor Oscar Lovell Triggs of the English department of the University of Chicago said: "Given a suffering world, just starting, there was no doubt that men like Field, who lessen the cost of living, would be of more value than men like Shakespeare, because people suffering from cold and hunger could not possibly get any good from the poets, and could only be ready for Shakespeare after Field and Company had warmed and fed them." [13] Even Godkin of the *Nation* scored the development of a leisure class in America as nothing more than "idleness and immorality." Chicago publicized but did not honor its speculators. "Old Hutch" was feared and respected for his daring, but was not honored as were Field, Pullman, and Armour. Samuel Insull, too, was feared and respected, but he was never accepted by Chicago society, and the city turned against him when he failed. By 1880 the Chicago businessman who made his life in what Armour called the "counting house," and what soon came to be called the "office," was already affecting the social drama of American life. He lived for his business, but he thought Chicago was his business too. The city of Chicago was his creation. What was good for business was good for Chicago, and if Field's prospered, so did the city. If capital accumulated it was not squandered but poured back into the business. If the city needed schools, hospitals, parks, and churches to make it a great city, money was raised. It was believed that such improvements (like Burnham's Chicago Plan) were good for business.[14] They enhanced real-estate values, and thus enriched businessmen, who, in turn, supplied jobs to the people of the city. Chicagoans believed that their business leaders, not their politicians, certainly not their labor leaders, created and safeguarded the jobs of the people who worked for them.

Notes

[1] New York's small role in the development of contemporary architecture is one of the great puzzles in American cultural history. The city with the greatest concentration of money and talent in America, and the largest number of skyscrapers in America, continues to put up one mediocre building after another.

[2] Harriet Monroe, *A Poet's Life: Seventy Years in a Changing World* (New York: Macmillan, 1938), p. 138.

[3] Lack of comprehension on the relationship of engineering and art is not limited to general art publics in America. Until very recently our architects and our artists (especially our literary artists) have been strangers to each other. Architectural criticism is just beginning to appear beside criticism of other arts in our journals. It has not been accepted by newspaper publishers and editors as part of their art pages.

[4] William Bross, *History of Chicago* (Chicago: Jansen, McClurg & Co., 1876), p. 75.

[5] Lewis selected a real-estate broker, Babbitt, to characterize the Middle Western businessman and his society, just as Colonel Sellers of *The Gilded Age* represented the earlier real-estate visionary, the "boomer," of the frontier. It is the saver—the banker, not the spender, the promoter, or real-estate operator—who is the villain in depictions

of business life in writing from 1875 to 1915. The spender was often a clown but seldom a villain in the new West.

[6] Quoted from *Fabulous Chicago* by Emmett Dedmon (New York: Random House, 1953), p. 186. Sullivan said much the same in his autobiography. Like Veblen, he understood that it was the ability to create wants, not simply to satisfy wants already created, which characterized American business. "The passion to sell is the impelling power in American life. Manufacturing is subsidiary and adventitious."

[7] See the Lakeside Classics edition of *Wau-Bun: The "Early Day" in the North-West,* with a historical introduction by Milo Milton Quaife (Lakeside Press: Chicago, 1932), p. liii.

[8] This is done in the belief that businessmen will have a broader "community view" than the "expert" and thus should dominate the "expert." A library board of business-men will openly admit to small knowledge of books, but will argue that, as businessmen, they represent the community and know how to hire experts who will carry out the community view. Much of Veblen's irony over "the hire learning" stems from the incongruity of unlearned men shaping the policy of learned institutions.

[9] *As Others See Chicago: Impressions of Visitors, 1673–1933,* ed. by Bessie Louise Pierce (University of Chicago Press: Chicago, 1933), p. 251.

[10] She is quoted in *Time,* July 29, 1946, as saying that she and her husband "talked business just as other people talked love."

[11] He still is. Jack Benny, one of our highest paid comedians, is the all-American miser. Even his Negro houseman is permitted to joke openly at the miserliness of his white master.

[12] Quoted from Dedmon, *op. cit.,* p. 186.

[13] Quoted in Edward Chase Kirkland, *Dream and Thought in the Business Community: 1860–1900* (Cornell University Press: Ithaca, 1956), p. 166. As radical writers were quick to point out, Field was clothing only those who could afford to pay prices which brought Field's its handsome profits. But Chicagoans believed, at least until the Pullman strike of 1894, that such profits were a proper return for enterprise and hard work. The church taught that the poor were poor not because of Field's low wages, but because of their own depravity and shiftlessness.

[14] In suburban real-estate developments churches were often offered support by pro-moters who believed that a church building helped sales. In 1959 builders are beginning to subsidize schools for the same reason. Billboards exhort Chicagoans to give to their community fund because "mercy pays."

9

The Emergence of New Roles for Women in Chicago

F or the Chicago businessmen's wives who became the feminine society leaders of Chicago the house was a great stage for mounting frequent, large, and costly entertainments. Since social reputations were made and sustained in the newspaper, these entertainments had to be made communicable to the public. Reliance on the press required social leaders to stage social affairs which could be made interesting to their guests and, at the same time, exciting to newspaper readers. The mystique of the Chicago plutocracy was its wealth, but the "society" expression of this wealth, the drama of spending which moved Chicagoans, and the kind of newspaper communication over wealth which increased circulation was controlled in private and domestic spheres almost exclusively by women. Mrs. Potter Palmer and Mrs. Rockefeller McCormick were social queens in every sense of the word. In the social sphere they reigned without men, or reduced their consorts to very subordinate roles. We even hear of Potter Palmer eating alone while his wife served and entertained her guests in the lavish splendor of their "Rhine Castle."

Mrs. Palmer was one of the first American society leaders to understand the new role of the press in creating and sustaining social prestige. Unlike the wives of New York plutocrats of the eighties and nineties, Mrs. Palmer cultivated newspaper men. They in turn taught her much about the art of public relations and reported her social triumphs so well that her public reputation outside her own set was far greater than her reputation in society proper.[1] Her enactment of her role as a social leader was peculiarly adapted to Chicago. Meeker tells us that "she was never able to make an impression in the more sophisticated fields she tardily attempted to cultivate. She bored Newport and London."[2] But she did not bore Chicagoans, or at least those who read the papers. She understood that plutocrats and their wives must interest the people who give them power. Her "castle on the drive" was designed by Henry Ives Cobb and Charles Sumner Frost. As Tallmadge tells us in *Architecture in Old Chicago,* it was "the most famous, probably the largest, and by all odds the most imposing house in our city . . . a mansion to end all mansions. . . . Built in 1882 it came very early in the Romanesque Queen Anne regimen . . . it [was] Gothic—English of the later square headed variety." The interior was done in a luxurious eclectic style. Contemporary newspaper descriptions of the Rhine castle interior abound in superlatives: "Upon being admitted to the Palmer mansion, the visitor stepped into an octagonal hall three stories high, its floor a mosaic of marble and its walls heavily obscured by large Gobelin tapestries. From the hall he might be taken to a French drawing room, a Spanish music room, an English dining room . . . or through a Moorish corridor into a Turkish parlor or perhaps a Greek or Japanese parlor. . . . Mrs. Palmer slept in a Louis XVI bed ten feet high."

Mrs. Palmer styled her appearance as carefully as her house. As the new American dowager she soon stood beside the "Gibson Girl" of the East in the pantheon of American women. Her grey marcelled coiffure, tiara of diamonds, and "dog-collar" of pearls or diamonds became fixed in the popular image of such dowagers as Maggie in the cartoon strip "Maggie and Jiggs," Marie Dressler, the hostess of "swell" parties in Chaplin's early comedies, Margaret Dumont, the rich lady pursued so sedulously by Groucho Marx, and finally Mae West with her ropes of pearls. In McCutcheon's illustrations to Ade's Chicago stories of breaking into society, she becomes the dowager who, "in the mad race for culture, is always first over the fence." In her own time in Chicago she becomes the prototype of the most famous of all depictions of American women—the "Gibson Girl," created by the illustrator of high society life, William Dana Gibson.

In playing her role as a leader of Chicago society, Mrs. Palmer faced the dilemma common to leaders of every institution in Chicago. Social leadership was based on effective communication. It was not enough to spend in ways judged tasteful by members of a sophisticated class whose standards were set by cosmopolites who knew the traditional art of Europe or by connoisseurs such as the Glessner family who commissioned Richardson to design their house. Mrs. Palmer's house, which was built early in the Romanesque Queen Anne vogue in Chicago domestic architecture, was really neither Romanesque Queen Anne, nor even pure Gothic, but "an American architect's best thought of what a baronial castle should be," Tallmadge tells us. Her entertainments, no less than her house, conformed to what Veblen (a fellow Chicagoan during these years) aptly called "pecuniary canons of taste." Press reports of social events in the Palmer home translated the poetry of society, its traditional glory of taste and beauty, into a plutocratic litany. Cost, not beauty, created the glamor of the occasion. In contemporary accounts of Palmer entertainments and receptions little distinction is made between beauty and costliness. Yet it would be a great mistake to think that women like Mrs. Palmer were simply traders' wives devoted to upholding pecuniary canons of taste. If this were so there would be no Frank Lloyd Wright houses in the Chicago area, just as there are none in New York. The nucleus of the fine collection of French Impressionists now displayed in the Art Institute of Chicago once graced the walls of Mrs. Palmer's home. When Strauss's *Salome* became a moral as well as an aesthetic issue in Europe, Mrs. Palmer had it performed in her Mayfair house in London. Here, too, Pavlova danced. At a reception for her son Honoré and his wife in her Paris home she offered a performance of the Russian ballet.

But if Mrs. Palmer, unlike the next generation of society leaders in Chicago such as Edith Rockefeller McCormick, Mrs. Arthur Ryerson, Mrs. John Alden Carpenter, Margaret Ayer Barnes, and Janet Ayer Fairbank, did not relate feminine social prestige in Chicago to the patronage of fine arts, it does not follow that her reign was marked by "empty frivolity" (as Wecter in his *Sage of American Society* would have us believe). Mrs. Palmer was intelligent and more than held her own among a generation of Chicago women whose public, as well as domestic, accomplishments broke new paths for American women. Chicagoans who knew the Palmers, and those whose education and taste add significance to their estimate of her creation of the role of society leader in Chicago, tell us that, if anything, Mrs. Palmer was too serious about the "new woman" of Chicago. Fuller suggests in his novels that the new social leaders of Chicago, as portrayed by Susan Bates in *With the Procession,* were always somewhat detached about their role as social leaders. For them society was at best a game, as business was a game to their husbands.

Mrs. Palmer was an early champion of working women. She encouraged her son Honoré to run for alderman of the Twenty-first Ward, and she acted successfully as his political manager. She linked her New Year's Day reception (which determined social position in the city for the following year) to an annual Charity Ball, which soon became a civic institution. In doing this, Mrs. Palmer pioneered the relationship between charity and society which became so characteristic of high society in Chicago. She accepted the presidency of the Board of Lady Managers of the World's Columbian Exposition in 1890 and inspired and administered the design and building of the Woman's Building which was to "present a complete picture of the condition of women in every country of the world . . . and more particularly of those women who are bread winners." Long before New York society leaders found it expedient to do so, Mrs. Palmer became an ardent feminist. Like Jane Addams, she advocated a feminism that would bring freedom to women as women. She wanted women to be independent because she thought the skill of women necessary to public as well as private life. Her address to the Fortnightly Club of April 10, 1891, sets forth her aims, and indeed the aims of a generation of Chicago women leaders who opened new paths for women in America. The range of feminine accomplishments in Chicago from 1880 to 1930 was the greatest of any American city.[3]

The establishment of new roles for women in the home and the community was of great importance to domestic architecture. Wright's prairie houses, which were first published in the *Ladies' Home Journal* in 1901 and publicized widely by Edward Bok (who instigated their design), were intended as architectural stages for a new kind of domestic life. How indigenous this was to Chicago we learn from Manson, who points out in his study of Wright's early work: "These two original and revolutionary Prairie Houses, accorded the widest publicity then possible among American homeowners, had no immediate effect in the nation at large. . . . For the period [Wright's work up to 1910] the circumference of Wright's work was virtually limited to Chicagoland and Buffalo."[4] Mrs. Palmer, Wright, and Veblen—socialite, architect and sociologist—all agreed on the new role of women in Chicago. In her address delivered on Oct. 12, 1892, at the dedicatory ceremonies of the World's Columbian Exposition, Mrs. Palmer explained the purposes of the Woman's Building and its exhibits. "Of all the changes that have resulted from the great ingenuity and inventiveness of the race, there is none that equals in importance to woman the application of machinery to the performance of the never-ending tasks that have previously been hers. . . . Women have been liberated. They now have time to think, to be educated, to plan and pursue careers of their own choosing. . . . As a result of the freedom and training now granted them, we may confidently await, not a renaissance, but the first blooming of the perfect flower of woman hood." But while this freedom and education is to prepare women for a new life it must not be a life apart from men. "Our utmost hope is, that woman may become a more congenial companion and fit partner for her illustrious mate."[5]

The "useless" woman who evoked a "poetry of society" in Amiel and Proust was not at home in Chicago. She was scorned equally by society leaders, social philosophers, novelists, and Chicago's great and highly vocal contingent of radicals. Perhaps the most representative view of Chicagoans of the nineties over the new role of society leader is found in Henry Blake Fuller's novels, *With the Procession* (1895) and *The Cliff-Dwellers* (1893). No honor is given to the "social butterfly." High society must exist for some purpose beyond display of wealth or the development of plutocratic taste. As Susan Bates of *With the Procession* tells us, society entertainments are not enough for a woman of spirit. Like her man, she did not want to be a social butterfly or a mistress of the art of entertainment, but a creative force in the building of a new city. The salon spirit in which the woman inspires and guides the expression of culture found no home in the houses of Chicago plutocrats. The excitement of talk in Chicago was over what was "doing" in the city. Chicago businessmen fused social and business life so completely that it was impossible to say where one ended and the other began.

The effect of this new mingling of social and business life was disastrous to the forms of talk common to polite gatherings in older American and European cities. Observers from these cities often commented on how men and women in Chicago came together at parties only to separate so that men could talk about business and politics and the women of their families and friends. But these observers failed to notice that new kinds of relationships between men and women were forming in Chicago. In meetings over civic or institutional affairs, men and women mingled freely as individuals. Much of the social life of Chicagoans was determined by gatherings devoted to various civic causes. Men and women may not have shared each other's company in purely social affairs but they met frequently at many gatherings where the work of voluntary associations was accomplished. Without the voluntary help of its countless committees, the community life of Chicago and its suburbs could not have developed. From decisions reached in such meetings, a city was created, rebuilt after a terrible fire, staged as a classical forum in the great Chicago Fair of 1893, and finally planned as a model for all modern cities in the Chicago Plan of 1906. None of these accomplishments would have been possible without official action, but such action was the result of action taken in voluntary groups.

Secularization of public life in the cities did not lessen the seriousness or scope of community affairs, although it did involve changes in its expression. Much of the planning and preparation for the Columbian Exposition was done at informal gatherings at luncheons and dinners. Women as well as men chaired such meetings and led discussion groups. In such meetings, new social forms of public and private life were created. Chicagoans reaching for success learned the arts of extemporaneous speaking, committee leadership, and public relations necessary to the success of civic and institutional enterprise of all kinds. Community decisions were reached in talk, debate, and discussion. Politics and business, the great community dramas of Chicago, were created and sustained in talk and oratory. The great public stages in Chicago, such as Adler's Exposition Opera Hall in Grant Park, his Central

Music Hall, and Adler and Sullivan's Auditorium, all designed before 1889, were stages for the human voice.[6]

Women soon discovered the excitement and pleasure of a public life based on talk, discussion, and oratory. Chicago men worked hard, but they enjoyed their work. They fused social and business life so firmly that Easterners often failed to discover any social life in Chicago. The Chicago habit of "doing business" over meals, or of inviting business acquaintances of only a few days' standing to their homes, where men and women talked as equals, baffled Easterners and Europeans who were accustomed to separating business and social life and to separate and very distinct roles for men and women. Chicago women, they observed, talked as much about their city as did their men, whose eternal boasting about the city was considered one of the trials to be endured in visiting Chicago. It was strange for many Eastern men, and certainly for Europeans, to find themselves talking to women whose intelligence was directed toward civic affairs. Even the traditional concern of women over cultural life was not the same in Chicago. Few Chicagoans, certainly few men, seemed to enjoy art for its own sake, but all were agreed that if art could be useful it could be "good." Chicago women asked to be regarded as public as well as private individuals. The frank, open, and friendly talk of "these daughters of the West," the way they joked and teased men, intrigued writers of the nineties. Oscar Wilde reminded Londoners that these new American girls were one of the wonders of the new world. Henry James saw in them a new social type whose "innocence" of European vice and corruption offered hope for a better life in America. Henry Adams found the wives of American senators and men of affairs to be superior to their husbands.

Writers like Julian Ralph of *Harper's Magazine,* and Montgomery Schuyler of the New York *Times,* pointed out that the Chicago Loop buildings really housed whole communities of men and women. In these new buildings, unlike the warehouses and loft buildings along Canal and Franklin Streets, new roles for women were developing. A customer in these new offices was treated as a visiting guest in a home. A girl who worked in the building was not asked to seclude herself behind partitions, but to talk with clients or customers and to make their visit as pleasant as possible. At eating places in the building she met other men and women as an equal. She was an individual, a person to whom one related as a person. It was the creation of the office building as a new kind of social stage, as well as a work place, which made these new buildings so significant. The business novels of Dreiser and Fuller describe the luxury and elegance of these new Chicago offices. Selfridge of Field's talked of making the store a "downtown home" for Chicago women. In *The Cliff-Dwellers* the office of the Massachusetts Brass Company on the tenth floor of the Clifton is described as "cause enough for envy in that small square of velvety Axminister, in the harmonious tinting of the walls, in the polished brightness of the cherry desk-tops, in the fresh blotting-pads and the immaculate ink-stand. To sit in this pleasant little apartment for half an hour is to receive quite a new impression of the possible luxury of business, the ultimate elegance of trade."

In such offices, as in stores like Field's, girls of all classes learned to play independent roles. Sister Carrie gazed in wonder at the "swell" clothes in Field's windows. Cornelia McNabb used the Clifton as a training ground in manners to help her catch a businessman. She explains to Ogden, the genteel Easterner,[7] that these new Loop buildings were the best place for a girl on her own to find a husband. In traditional courtship her family determined her chances of marriage; in these Loop buildings she could meet men and women "on her own." The new world of business was supplanting the home and the neighborhood. In the Chicago novels of Herrick, Fuller, and Floyd Dell, we meet an independent woman who is determined to relate to her men as a friend and colleague as well as an erotic or romantic partner. The Chicago story, told by Dreiser in *Sister Carrie* and *Jeannie Gerhardt* and later developed in *An American Tragedy,* is the story of women who wanted a new kind of relationship with men. Attempts to escape from traditional roles becomes central to the literature as it does to the architecture of Chicago and the Middle West.

Chicago stories begin where Eastern writers like Edith Wharton end their novels. Sister Carrie, unlike Lily Bart, enters into sexual relations as a natural part of her relationship to men. Her moral concern is not so much over sex as over the character and destiny of her lover and her role as a woman in a business society. In Chicago writing the woman is really far stronger than the man, for she is more concerned over the human meaning of new relationships and new symbols. Chicago admired and respected the new types of women emerging in Chicago. Veblen's mordant irony lightens when it touches on feminine roles. He sympathized with women who must relate to predatory males who reduce them to "trophies of the raid" or use them as "delegate consumers," and who must affect uselessness and wastefulness in their dress and the decoration of their houses to uphold the feudal majesty of their men. By 1895 Veblen decided that the women he was meeting in the 57th Street studios,[8] in Hull House, the Fine Arts Building, and on the campus of the University of Chicago (where women were teachers as well as students) would soon lead women out of the "class of unfree subjects" to the male.

Chicago's new women accepted Veblen's attack on conspicuous consumption and pecuniary canons of taste as a vindication of their own struggle. In his *Theory of the Leisure Class* of 1899 Veblen makes clear that his attack on plutocratic canons of taste is directed mainly against women of the leisure class. Such women, he holds, do not stand in any direct organic relationship to the workaday industrial world. They carry over into the realm of the supernatural the logic and the logical processes of an everyday life of status and vicarious leisure and are at home and content in a range of ideas which are "alien and imbecile" to adult men and women. The wealthier class of the North, as Veblen observed them in the nineties, was rapidly taking on "devotional habits" of feudal society. Weddings, funerals, and like honorific events were solemnized with some special degree of "religious circumstance." Naïve, sensational methods of appeal were used more in the sacred architecture of the upper leisure class than in that of the lower and middle classes. Veblen's ironic vision confronts the incongruities of feudal forms of expression developing in a city where money and what he called "the industrial process" marked so much of life. Unlike other Chicago writers who wrote for the people, Veblen masks his irony in erudite and esoteric phrases suitable to learned journals. Few American writers have hurled such invective at businessmen. Yet business apologists found Veblen difficult to attack because he hid himself behind a mask of scientific detachment. He was merely "recording" a social process which, like gravity, was a force independent of the will of individuals. His images of the incongruities arising out of attempts to graft conspicuous forms of spending money to feudal rituals of rank and status soon became part of all social thought and art in Chicago. Intellectuals and artists knew the hero of Chicago, the businessman, was being savagely ridiculed—if the businessman himself did not.

Sullivan, Wright, all the young radicals of the Chicago school, benefited greatly from Veblen's analysis of the clash between feudal and democratic forms of expression. Sullivan makes use of the same imagery. In his architecture he struggled to give form to a democratic architecture. This architecture, unlike the Gothic, "with its thought far above with Christ in the heavens, seeing but little here below . . . must be supplanted by an architecture which will return men to nature and to each other here on this earth." For Sullivan, as for Veblen, the power of Gothic forms was rooted in fear and superstition. Newspaper writers like Field, Ade and Dunne, the "Chicago humorists" who wrote for the people, not for the cultivated few like Veblen, were equally sensitive to the incongruities between traditional roles and the new life of the city. Ade and Field poke fun at the use of imported cultural forms by social climbers. In Ade's *Breaking into So-ciety, People You Know,* and his collections of "fables in slang," upper-class and would-be upper-class women are shown toiling unsuccessfully to make "swells" out of husbands who cannot understand why "they should ape the manners of people who make less money than they do." Thus in his fable, "The Attempt to Spruce Up the Family and Give It Standing," Ma meets the "Lady Managers of Society," [9] who inspire her to lead her family into the "High Life." Father is not easily moved by the glory of "High Life." "He said he didn't purpose to strain himself being Polite to a lot of Four-Flushers who owed him Money. That was the Trouble with Father. He was President of the Company, and seemed to think that his Official Position gave him a Right to break Crackers into his Soup. He refused to wear a White Tie with his Evening Clothes just because some cheap Department Manager had set the Style."

Chicago comedies of manners were born of anger over betrayal of demo-cratic virtues and rooted in suspicion of an elite which was not based on money earned through hard work. Money, in turn, was acceptable as a symbol of community life because it was believed that it could be used to benefit everyone. While all joined in laughter at the vulgarity of self-made merchants, there was respect and love as well as ridicule in such laughter. Western manners were crude, no doubt, but they were still to be preferred to Eastern snobbery. Chicagoans of the Fair generation laughed at their parvenus, not because their imitations of Eastern upper-class manners were so bad, but because they were imitations of a standard deemed highly ir-relevant to their own lives. Chicagoans believed deeply in the democracy of town and rural life, even though they were not sure how to sustain democracy in their new urban world. Their first city, the "Garden City" with its white houses, green lawns, and shade trees, merely expanded the village image. But as the city changed into the "Phoenix City" which would arise from its ashes, the will to create a democratic city shifted from re-capturing a village past to creating a new urban life. In this city, a white new city shining beside a blue inland sea, men would walk the streets in dignity and freedom because the new power of urban technology could be used to free people from want and fear.

Every Chicago institution was measured against such democratic visions. In her address delivered at the opening of the Woman's Building at the Fair on May 1, 1893, Mrs. Potter Palmer spoke out as sharply as any radical against the exploitation of women. She accused "conservative people" who argued that woman belongs in the home, of making it possible for manu-facturers and producers "to disparage her work and obtain her services for a nominal price, thus profiting largely by the necessities and helplessness of their victim." Such conservative thinking, she said, was feudal thinking. "Men of the finest and most chivalric type, who have poetic theories about the sanctity of the home and the refining, elevating influence of woman in it—theories inherited from the days of romance and chivalry . . . these men have asked many times whether the Board of Lady Managers thinks it well to promote a sentiment which may tend to destroy the home by encouraging occupations for women which take them out of it." Such men, Mrs. Palmer stresses, are really very ignorant of the world. "Would that the eyes of these idealists could be thoroughly opened that they might see, not the fortunate few of a favored class, with whom they are in daily contact, but the general status of the labor market. . . ." They would discover that every woman is not dwelling in a home where she is queen with a "manly and loving arm to shield her from rough contact with life." Widows with dependent children, wives of drunkards and criminals, and other women work because they must live, not because they wish to give up their homes. "The necessity for their work under present conditions is too evident and too urgent to be questioned. They must work or they must starve."

In her other speeches Mrs. Palmer discussed clearly the effects of monopoly on the small business concerns which employed so many women. Large companies, she points out, can afford to advertise and thus create tastes for mass-produced products. But the small firm cannot, since its owners lack capital and labor. Thus, she warns, the Woman's Building dairy exhibits are biased in favor of big business. These speeches of Chicago's "great lady" were not abstract economic discussions, nor were they homilies from a "lady bountiful." They were concerned with how the individual woman makes her living. Thus, while there was none of the cultural sophistication of the New England bluestocking, the glamorous luxury of New York society or the romance of the Southern Belle about Mrs. Palmer, there was sophistication of another kind. In her role as a society leader she styled herself as a civic leader, deeply concerned about the impact of industry on the lives of women in Chicago and the Middle West. No other society leaders in America of these years showed such concern over the meaning of democracy to women.

Ade hated whatever kept men and women from cherishing one another as individuals. In his popular story "Effie Whittlesy," Ed Wallace comes home to dinner to discover that his wife has hired Effie, an old family friend of his youth, as a servant. As she recognizes him but waits to see how he will greet her, Ed Wallace speaks to her as an equal, for he "had been reared in the democracy of a small community, and the democratic spirit came uppermost." Mrs. Wallace wants her husband to treat Effie as a servant but he refuses to do so. He explains that he was born and raised in a small town and that such a town was a "very poor schooling for a fellow who wants to be a snob." But Ed sees that his wife, a "Twombley of Baltimore . . . with relatives in Virginia," insists on treating Effie as a servant. He will not have Effie treated so and offers her money to return to Brainer, her home town. He tells her why. "Effie, you see—you're an old friend of mine and I don't like the idea of your being here in my house as a—well, as a hired girl." Effie offers to stay. "I guess I'm a servant now. I used to be a hired girl when I worked for your ma, but now I am a servant. I don't see as it makes any difference what you call me, as long as the work's the same."

But Ed Wallace makes clear that he will not have Effie in the house as a servant, and that he will not tolerate his wife reducing her to a servant.

"You understand what I mean, don't you? Any time you come here to my house I want you to come as an old acquaintance—a visitor, not a servant."

"Ed Wallace, don't be foolish. I'd as soon work for you as anyone, and a good deal sooner."

"I know, but I wouldn't like to see my wife giving orders to an old friend, as you are. You understand, don't you?"

After they say goodbye, Mrs. Wallace indicates her relief at seeing the last of Effie. But Ed turns to his wife and says quietly, "I've invited her to call when she comes back." And then begins the dialogue between a Twombley of Baltimore and a townsman of Illinois and now a Chicagoan.

"To call—here?"

"Most assuredly. I told her you'd be delighted to see her at any time."

"The idea! Did you invite her, really?"

"Of course I did! And I'm reasonably certain that she'll come."

"What shall I do?"

"I think you can manage it, even if you never did live in Brainer!"

Even a Twombley of Baltimore bows before such feeling for the importance of the individual: "Then the revulsion came and Mrs. Wallace, with a full return of pride in her husband, said she would try." [10]

Few Chicagoans and, indeed, few Americans, read "Effie Whittlesy" without a cry of the heart over the democracy of their lost youth in the towns and the farms of the Middle West. Love, trust, and laughter echoed in the memories of a younger time when they knew no fear and lived in simple, intimate, egalitarian relations with each other. These memories increased in poignancy as immigrants who had never walked the earth as free men and who had known only the slums of European cities poured into Chicago. For some, these new people shattered forever the faith in democracy born and nourished in the town and village life of their childhood and youth. But for others, and for the young architects Root, Sullivan, and Wright, the quest for democracy in their new city soon became the great quest of the time. As the memory of the Garden City died in the smoke and murk of the metropolis, architects envisioned a new kind of city—a city where every individual could not only live, but live beautifully, and in so doing live as a neighbor. Others like Jane Addams searched for ways to adapt traditional village roles to urban life. The neighborhood settlement, even when it became a complex of buildings, was called a "house." In these settlements a type of woman emerged whose traditional feminine warmth and charm was never reduced to the harsh, black-suited, unfeminine doctor and social worker of cartoon and legend. Jane Addams taught her female assistants in Hull House that there was no conflict between femininity and civic responsibility. To her, people were neighbors who had all the rights of the traditional frontier neighborhood where houses opened to the street and children ran in and out of whatever house they happened to be near, and where "dropping in" unannounced was as much a part of visiting as formally arranging calls.

Jane Addams urbanized the village tradition of neighborliness. Workers at Hull House were trained to live among the new Americans of the neighborhood. They were asked to regard them as equals, and to understand them as they would friends. Jane Addams and her colleagues created the role of the social worker, not as a trained technician or civil servant, but as a neighbor who would help people to help themselves. In the eyes of her slum neighbors she was a great mother living in a house whose doors were always open to her large family. No one was given food, clothing, shelter, or money without being given at the same time a feeling of his importance as an individual. Jane Addams saw nothing wrong with money,[11] so long as money was used as a means to better the life of the whole community. But she insisted that the heart must go with the purse, and with terrible simplicity she taught that democracy was brotherly love. This love developed in the strong tradition of welfare work among Chicago women. Two great catastrophes, the Civil War and the Great Fire of 1871, gave Chicago women ample opportunity to develop welfare skills. In the early months of the war a "Soldiers' Rest," where hundreds of thousands of meals were served to soldiers, was established. No regiment was allowed to pass through the city without being entertained. Two great Sanitary Fairs were organized in 1863 and 1865. Camp hospitals were equipped and supplied with nurses and medical supplies; fresh and home-canned foods were supplied to troops. The Sanitary Fair of 1863, which was organized to aid the Sanitary Com-

(*Above*) Ladies' Garment Workers parade during the strike of 1912. (*Below*) Jane Addams (shown holding flag) and her colleagues in a suffragette parade of 1912. These women had seen much of the misery of urban life. *Courtesy Chicago Historical Society*

mission, served as a model for similar fairs held throughout the country. Lincoln thought so highly of the accomplishments of the Mrs. Livermore, Hoge, and Hosmer of Chicago that he gave them the original copy of the Emancipation Proclamation to be auctioned off for money to run the Fair. These Chicago women often worked with and through men, but their capacity for large-scale organization soon made them a match for men in this new kind of public work.

Jane Addams's predicament, like that of Sullivan and Wright, was not whether one ought to accept money as a symbol of life, but *how* to humanize money in the new urban civilization of Chicago. Hull House, and the program of social betterment which reached intellectual expression in the work of Graham Taylor, Albion Small, and Robert Park in the social studies at the University of Chicago, was never based on a denial of American ideals of an ever-increasing standard of living. Jane Addams thought Chicago businessmen who worked for the betterment of their workers and the city ought to be trusted as civic leaders. For if Chicago had its Pullman it also had its Lyman Gage. In Jane Addams's teachings businessmen were not to be condemned categorically any more than "systems" such as socialism were to be followed because of their theoretical consistency. Jane Addams wanted to purify the businessman, not to abolish him. The heart of democracy in the Middle West she had grown up in was neighborliness, and, as she insisted, neighborliness to all, whether rich or poor, black or grown, illiterate or educated. As professed socialists and Marxists were always discovering to their chagrin, it was the human quality of the individual and the warmth of relationships among people she prized. Dogmas, creeds, reforms of all kinds were measured by their effect on the relationships of individuals as equals. For her the only kind of leadership was leadership among equals. She was fully aware of the difficulties of being first among equals, and no one ever accused her of refusing to take power when such power was necessary to getting a job done. But she led by example, when she could, and insisted always that love must be tempered by intelligence and knowledge.

There really were few tribal villains in her world, and the resident-worker within the house soon learned the fallacies of all social stereotypes—even those against the rich. Jane Addams taught her residents to think of people as individuals and to measure what individuals taught by how they acted, not by what they said. Brotherhood for her was an act, not a preachment. And it was an act of the mind as well as the heart. Hull House became a forum for the mind, as well as a haven for the spirit. Everyone had a right to speak in Hull House, but he also had an obligation to listen, and he must be prepared to open his views to free and searching discussion. For if the heart must be open to suffering, so, too, the mind. Understanding social injustice was an intellectual as well as a spiritual or emotional process. Out of this belief, shared so deeply by all thoughtful Chicagoans, the study of sociology was born at the University of Chicago—the first university in America to create a department of sociology.

There were no revealed truths in Hull House. Truth was subject to reason because it was tested in open and free discussion. The first generation of sociologists and social philosophers in Chicago believed in rigorous thinking about society, but they wanted it to be about action, not reflection, in society. They wanted to know how to act, as well as how to think about how to act. Mead, Dewey, Sullivan, Jane Addams—all of the various Chicago schools—prized reflection. As William James pointed out, few groups thought harder about philosophy than Chicagoans, but unlike others they thought about reason as an act in society, not as an ordering of knowledge or discovery of laws of nature. The dominant question for these Chicagoans was not how do we know, but how do we act?

Men who fell under the influence of Hull House and the University learned not only how the poor and humble lived, but also how to associate with women of mind and spirit who were determined to be individuals in their own right and who thought of marriage and indeed all relationships as a partnership of equals. Relating to the "new" women of Hull House and the University of Chicago was a chastening experience for young masculine intellectuals. Living in Hull House offered young female intellectuals opportunities to develop as women in relation to other women, as well as in relation to men. All who lived in Hull House experienced in Jane Addams a new kind of feminine community leadership. She became the model for a new American heroine whose call to public service challenged the traditional community leadership of men.[12] The fact that a woman became the conscience of Chicago made possible a whole new conception of public leadership for women. Women moved into public roles, and it was not long until they were championed not only as equals but even as superiors to men in some kinds of civic leadership in Chicago. The problem for the Chicago woman was not whether she would have a public role, but what happened to her relationships with men and to her conception of herself as a woman when she did. Eastern novelists often subordinate their men to the women of their novels but these women play very traditional roles. Chicago novelists, even as early as Fuller, depicted heroines of a "rare and even new kind," as Howells said. These heroines possess a very high degree of social consciousness, and they open to doubt and question social issues which Eastern novelists do not even touch. The church also offered Chicago women new roles.

Temperance and prohibition societies reached national importance by 1900. The Salvation Army, the Young Women's Christian Association, and many other social and philanthropic organizations dominated by the churches were staffed largely by women. Chicago welfare circles owed much to the churches for giving to women positions of leadership that gave them training for roles which were to lead into the profession of social work. The Christian Science Church, which was founded by a woman and which continued to fill its holy office with women, grew rapidly in the Middle West. By 1890 the Woman's Christian Temperance Union reached the height of its power through the leadership of Frances Willard of Evanston and Chicago. She became one of the nation's most famous personages through her administrative skill in leading an organization which influenced national and state legislation.

Chicago women rose to fame in many fields. Harriet Monroe founded *Poetry* magazine and introduced modern poetry to America. The reputations of Jane Addams, Frances Willard, and Mrs. Potter Palmer soon passed beyond Chicago to all America. Most remarkable of all was the range of ability of Chicago women. Saintly women like Jane Addams were almost equaled in fame by Minna and Ada Everleigh, whose Everleigh Club at 2131–33 South Dearborn Street was the most notorious bordello in America. From 1890 to 1912 Chicago was famous for its Levee district. Here madams such as Frankie Wright, Vina Fields, and Vic Shaw created a new kind of erotic expression—a drama in which money was used to inspire lust.

Minna and Ada Everleigh changed the role of the prostitute. Their "girls" became plutocratic courtesans who staged a drama of lust and money. Their services were so expensive that a visit to the Club was an indication of financial, if not of sexual, power. Minna Everleigh tells us that among her patrons money often dominated lust. In her later years she said: "Admitting that women are a risk, I still say that men prefer dice, cards, or a wheel of fortune to a frolic with a charmer. I have watched men, embraced in the arms of the most bewitching sirens in our club, dump their feminine flesh from their laps for a roll of the dice." [13] In recalling her Chicago years Minna stated: "Gambling diverts men faster than lechery." The Everleigh girls were taught to imitate the dress and mannerisms of the plutocratic lady. The Club was decorated as an elegant mansion; a well-stocked library graced the lower floor. Sumptuous formal dinners with music supplied by a string ensemble were given in rooms adjacent to the library. Patrons were entertained in richly furnished parlors styled as Moorish, Japanese, Egyptian, and Chinese. The greatest room of all, the Gold Room with its glittering gold piano, was polished every day and refinished each year in gold leaf. Even the spittoons were of gold. In these rooms the ladies of the Club wore evening dress and greeted clients as if they were gentlemen callers. No vulgarities were permitted. Minna and Ada played the role of sophisticated women of the plutocratic world who desired to charm through wit as well as money and sex. They were careful to keep informed on politics and business as well as the arts. And, like all Chicagoans seeking renown, the Everleighs cultivated the press. Important journalists were given the free run of the house.

Chicago architecture owed much to Chicago women. They became the great clients of domestic architecture necessary to develop the genius of Frank Lloyd Wright. But their influence was not limited to domestic architecture. One of Chicago's most famous Loop buildings was commissioned by a woman's organization. In the typical Chicago fashion of supporting good causes out of profits earned by good works, the Temperance Union commissioned Burnham and Root to design a building that would be at once a monument to women and a source of profit. A site at the southwest corner of Monroe and La Salle streets was secured from Marshall Field. Plans were begun in 1891. The building was thirteen stories high and built around an H plan, a radical innovation for such a building. Harriet Monroe tells us that Root and Burnham gave much time and thought to the building in order to avoid simply repeating the square, tall office building plan. Nor was Root content to follow Richardson's masculine Romanesque style in a building for women.

The Chicago school of architects was helped by Harriet Monroe, who continued to write and talk about architecture,[14] as well as about poetry. She was one of the first Chicago artists to notice the young radicals around Sullivan and to mention the work of his great pupil, Wright. Her understanding of modern poetry was far greater than her understanding of modern architecture, but she did much to keep the cause of architecture alive [15] and helped guide the taste of women who commissioned houses from the radical young Chicago architects at a time when such patronage was far from fashionable. Jane Addams sponsored discussion groups and lectures on architecture. Frank Lloyd Wright's lecture, "The Art and Craft of the Machine," was given first at Hull House in 1901. Without these new women of Chicago, the prairie house of Wright and the development of his great architecture would have been very different. For if businessmen in the Loop made Sullivan's career possible, women of Chicago and its suburbs made Wright's first "golden age" of design possible. His houses could have been done in and around other cities; Bok's publication of the prairie house in the *Ladies' Home Journal* gave Wright wide publicity. But it was the women of Chicagoland and the Middle West who continued to commission houses from the young radicals of the Chicago school. Like their businessmen husbands they were not ashamed to patronize their own artists. They knew the kind of life they wanted to lead as women of a new city. And, like their husbands in their Loop offices, they had courage enough in their own convictions to seek out artists who would help give these convictions architectural form. Out of such conviction came the wonderful houses of Wright, which made possible a new kind of family life in America.

Notes

[1] Arthur Meeker, Chicago socialite and son of a socially prominent family of the Palmer generation, discusses this in his *Chicago, With Love* (New York: Knopf, 1955) in the chapter, "Queens for a Day."

[2] *Ibid.,* p. 45.

[3] The "independent woman" was already a stock figure in Chicago fiction by 1893. She appears in Henry Blake Fuller's *Cliff-Dwellers* (New York: Harper's, 1893) and in Dreiser's *Sister Carrie* (New York: Dodge, 1900). New York writers, like Edith Wharton in her *House of Mirth* (New York: Scribner's, 1905), use the failure of the New York woman to achieve any kind of independence as a tragic theme. Chicago novelists take it for granted that independence and careers are possible for women. They do not ask whether women *should* be independent but what happens to them when they are. In novels such as *Sister Carrie* and Fuller's *With the Procession* (New York: Harper's, 1895), the women, not the men, motivate the action.

[4] Grant Carpenter Manson, *Frank Lloyd Wright to 1910: The First Golden Age* (New York: Reinhold, 1958), p. 106.

[5] See *Addresses and Reports of Mrs. Potter Palmer* (Chicago: Rand, McNally, 1894), pp. 116–19.

[6] Adler's success was based on his reputation as an acoustical engineer. He was consultant for Carnegie Hall in New York, and the basis for the fame of Adler and Sullivan was their skill in solving acoustical problems in theatres.

[7] This type is often used in the Chicago novel as the "outsider" to whom the peculiarities of Chicago life can be explained.

[8] By 1910, these "studios" (really temporary structures built for the Fair in 1893 as a row of small shops fronting Jackson Park on either side of 57th Street between Stony Island and the Illinois Central Railroad) were the art center of Chicago. Sherwood Anderson, Floyd Dell, Carl Sandburg, Margaret Anderson, teachers and students from the nearby University of Chicago gathered at parties given by Margery Currey and other resident artists.

[9] Mrs. Potter Palmer's official title as organizer of the women's exposition at the Fair had been "President of the Board of Lady Managers, World's Columbian Commission."

[10] This is reprinted in *The Permanent Ade: The Living Writings of George Ade,* ed. by Fred C. Kelly (Indianapolis and Chicago: Bobbs-Merrill, 1947), pp. 129–36.

[11] Her rejection of Tolstoy's program of "bread labor" in the fields as a solution to poverty was that "exigent and unremitting labor grants the poor no leisure even in the supreme moments of human suffering. . . ."

[12] "Adams owed more to the American woman than to all the American men he ever heard of. . . . woman was the superior. . . ." Henry Adams, *The Education of Henry Adams* (Boston and New York: Houghton, Mifflin Co., 1930), p. 442.

[13] The career of the Everleighs is told by Charles Washburn in his *Come into My Parlor: A Biography of the Aristocratic Everleigh Sisters of Chicago* (New York: Knickerbocker, 1934).

[14] For instance, she wrote *John Wellborn Root: A Study of His Life and Work* (Boston and New York: Houghton, Mifflin, 1896).

[15] Sullivan's "Wherefore the Poet," a selection from "Democracy: A Man-Search," was published in *Poetry*, Vol. 7 (March, 1916), pp. 305–7.

10

The Glamorization of Spending in Chicago

DURING the eighties woman became the chief object of social expenditure in Chicago, and her stage, the plutocratic household, a center of great luxury and extravagance. The new feminine social leaders of Chicago played their roles in great luxury, which they were careful to stage in the full glare of publicity. Detailed and glamorous reporting of society events soon rivaled sports, politics, and business in reader interest. The typical society story in the press was a drama of opulent spending. Thus we read in the Chicago press that during one of her transatlantic voyages Mrs. Palmer's appearance in a tiara of diamonds the size of Tokay grapes—accompanied by a diamond sunburst of nearly ten inches, a stomacher of more diamonds, a collar of pearls, and a corsage pinned to a base of diamonds—stopped Alois Burgstaller of the Metropolitan Opera in the middle of an aria. One of Mrs. Palmer's collars, reporters were fond of recording, contained 2,268 pearls and seven large diamonds. In his *The Chatelaine of La Trinité* of 1892, as in his article of 1897 on the upward movement in Chicago, Fuller agrees with Veblen that Chicago opulence was both "conspicuous" and "feudal." But, unlike Veblen, he believes that women, not men, are the masters of plutocracy. It is not the predatory male but the predatory female who determines American life.[1] "America," he says, "was now suffering under the rule of an aristocracy, novel indeed, all pervasive, and ultra-tyrannical—the aristocracy of sex." What was American society, he asks, "but a magnificent galley in which husbands and fathers toiled at the oars, while wives and daughters sat above in perfumed idleness?" He characterizes the American male as "the helots whose labors make possible the mental expansion of the feminine aristocracy." It was an aristocracy, as the Chicago novelists and architects were quick to point out, whose power was based on spending.

At the time of his death in 1906, Field's thirty-six acres of floor space and seven thousand employees had become the great shopping center for women of Chicago and the West. Its lunchrooms, which created new forms of genteel eating for women shoppers, seated two thousand. Women came not only to shop, but to lunch, write letters, rest, and meet friends. State Street window displays in Field's and other stores mounted elaborate and changing dramas of elegance. Arthur Frazer of Field's changed window displays from a simple presentation of merchandise against authentic backgrounds, to vivid tableaux of elegance in sumptuous rooms peopled by slender and graceful mannequins. "Window shopping," as Chicagoans called it, soon became a city habit. Immigrant women, girls from farms and small towns of the Middle West, clerks hurrying to work stood in awe before these dumb shows of plutocratic elegance. The majesty and power of a ruling class was no longer secret and mysterious or hidden away to be seen only in great ceremonials or feast days, but was communicated openly and daily. The drama in these windows was no fantasy nor a tableau of strange doings of a fabled aristocracy played before a select court. The plutocratic drama was a new kind of ceremonial community drama which went far beyond the older status dramas based on the mystery and enchantment of the strange and distant. Mass communication gave commercial artists a new kind of power— the power to bombard their audiences monthly, weekly, daily, and now, in our time, hourly with glamorous images of what money will buy. Commercial art soon passed beyond the simple messages of the artisan to a new kind of urban magic. American plutocrats were able to cast their spell over a whole civilization by making style, as well as family, social position, ownership, and skill, the determinant of social status.

In this plutocratic realm there were no formal or informal sumptuary laws determining who could wear what kind of adornment. For the first time in history, all, regardless of rank, sex, race, religion, age, or birth, were urged to buy. These tableaux of slender, immaculate gods and goddesses of plutocracy, with their "heiress look," standing before rich draperies parted like clouds opening to paradise, communicated the mystery and wonder of wealth to the thousands of young Chicagoans who poured daily and hourly into the Loop. The life within the mansions gleaming through the trees along Sheridan Road, behind the shuttered windows of the houses of the McCormick family on the near north side, or in the stately homes of the first families on Prairie Avenue was no longer a secret and remote fantasy but a public display mounted in great luxury and ever-changing drama. Yet how close to fantasy and dream these fabulous tableaux remained! Like the images of the dream, the images of plutocracy, mounted behind a "façade" architecture (as in its commerce), were highly visual. In town and village life people met to speak, and how one spoke had as much to do with social position as dress, house, or carriage. But the city was not designed for talk, and, until the return of speech in talking movies, phonograph records, and now television, communication to large audiences was visual. Business art soon

Marshall Field and his executives were masters of plutocratic showmanship. They made Field's into a great stage of consumption. The "carriage trade" soon became public heroes to Chicago shoppers, as we see in this early photograph of the State Street entrance. *Courtesy Chicago Historical Society*

In the department store he designed for Schlesinger and Mayer, later known as the Carson Pirie Scott Store, Sullivan brought the feminized drama of retail shopping to new heights of elegance. *Photograph by J. Blair, for the Sullivan Project of the Institute of Design, Illinois Institute of Technology*

became a visual art. Photography, the movies, a whole new world of print where the image was controlled and fed to passive audiences, soon dominated all forms of communication.

The Loop became a vast promenade of huge glass windows in which mannequins stood as mistresses of taste to teach people how to embody their secret longings for status in things of great price. Newspapers, magazines, store windows, silent movies, billboards—visual art of all kinds turned into poster art. The human eye was extended and its power magnified. The visual images of the dream, the fantasy of the fairy tale, and the forgotten art of the mime became forms in a new art, the magical visual commercial art of business. To the thousands of Sister Carries fresh from the towns of the Middle West, as for the new immigrants from eastern and southern Europe, these glass-enclosed State Street tableaux were an enchanted land. For all, these things, these radiant things of price, promised a refined and elegant life among the immaculately dressed and poised plutocrats who moved serenely through rooms aglow with mahogany, silver, and silks. All the treasurable things of the earth, once only dreams, wishes, or mysteries conjured up by demonic powers, waited for the inspection of all who could buy and fired the longings of those who could not. The demon of money promised equality, but it also satisfied unspoken yearnings for superiority. It destroyed the injustice of traditional status based on rank and family to carry on the ancient drama of status based on a new symbol of status, money.

The problem of making people customers could not be solved simply by wide appeals to mass audiences. For mass appeal, if tasteless and repeated too often, could easily vulgarize symbols whose power depended on mystery and glamor. If money was vulgarized too much those who had aspirations to a higher class might be alienated, just as the people of feudal society had been alienated by leaders who profaned and vulgarized their sacred symbols of power. Plutocratic as well as aristocratic majesty and glamor is born and sustained in communication, but communication of a mystery witnessed in fear and trembling. Even the distant, remote, and mysterious caliphs of *The Arabian Nights* needed to keep their mystery alive and powerful through communication with people greatly inferior in rank but necessary as audiences to their superiority. The American urbanite had to become an audience for plutocratic majesty. Plutocrats, like kings holding court, had to allow themselves to become an audience to inferiors passing in review before them. The glamor of money could not insure power to businessmen if they let themselves become too remote from their people. Power passed to those willing to *communicate* their glory, which in the case of Chicago was the glory of money. The plutocrats of Chicago avoided the mistakes of New

Yorkers, who set themselves apart from the people and soon found themselves condemned as robber barons or wastrels who cared little for anything but luxury and pleasure. Chicago businessmen and their wives styled themselves carefully as civic leaders. Business was dramatized as a civic enterprise. Good relations with the local press were cultivated. The press, in turn, glorified the businessman. For several decades any great business event—a store opening, a big sale, business forecasts by business executives—was front-page news. As early as 1875, Field's was regarded as a civic institution, along with the school and church. Business stories were human interest stories, not simply financial news. Dignitaries, and indeed even royalty, were expected to visit Field's. Here they signed a guest book and were escorted through the store, which now became the court of a new aristocracy, the "merchant princes" of Chicago.

Field, John G. Shedd, and all Field executives, considered the plutocratic drama of consumption to be a status drama of taste and studied how to translate taste into money. For the new people of Chicago, taste must become taste in spending. Immigrant women, women from small towns of the Middle West, and all those seeking to rise in society must be persuaded to come to Field's to learn how to spend properly. Styles must be transformed into new kinds of status identification. The woman fingering a costly lace tablecloth spread out before her by the admiring clerk, was coached to identify with a class higher than her own. She was not only "permitted" to be dissatisfied, but goaded into dissatisfaction with her own lot. To do this, Chicago merchants had to change traditional status symbols of blood, rank, and skill into symbols of money. The Europeans pouring into Chicago from 1880 to 1920 were a far different stock than the older Anglo-Saxon stock of earlier years. Success in the older class system of Europe had been determined by family lineage within a class position, ownership or attachment to land, and skills necessary to a community based on craft skills. Under such conditions, freedom to spend was very limited. Sumptuary laws, as well as traditional religious and status inhibitions ("knowing one's place") inhibited the development of attitudes necessary to the creation of a standard of life based on spending. If we can believe Max Weber, there was a "calling" to earn as a steward of the Lord. But spending was an aristocratic virtue, and thus highly suspect by the Puritan.

The immigrant woman in America was no longer taught to "know her place" and keep it. To aspire for better things was no longer a matter for guilt. Her discontent, like the Puritan discontent of old, was divine because it was a mark of aspiration for higher things. Frequently changed styles challenged worship of the old with an equally devout worship of the new. Even economists began to talk of "psychological obsolescence," as Veblen talked of "social obsolescence." The tradition of the old, the heirloom, was replaced by the tradition of the new, which was a pure expression of money. The price of the new plutocratic stages and stage properties—homes, cars, clothes, travel, all the status trappings of the plutocracy—could be communicated openly so long as its cost could be communicated easily. What a thing cost became a measure of its social value. The Chicago woman went to Field's to learn how to play her own social role correctly. To the newly arrived immigrants, anxious to assimilate with Americans, stores like Field's offered a stage for vicarious identification with an envied class of plutocrats. The speech, dress, and deportment of Field's clerks were considered models of plutocratic gentility. The store itself, with its classical motifs in decorative and architectural details, the careful dress of the clerks, the majestic floor-walkers with their muted voices and refined bearing, offered a continual pantomime of plutocratic status enactment in which the humblest woman could play a part through her role as customer or shopper.

The beauty and charm of "salesladies," the glamorous elevator girls, the draped mannequin—all these evoked desire and at the same time taught that such desire could be satisfied through money. The technique of staging the luxury of spending on things as developed in Field's windows by Arthur Fraser, soon passed into formally staged revues which rivaled the "gorgeous" tableaux of the Ziegfeld Follies. Florenz Ziegfeld, who began his career in Chicago, presented tall, stately girls, "radiant with youth," draped in "priceless costumes of furs, gems, laces, ribbons and flowers," who paraded "with patrician grace" before the footlights.[2] He changed the musical comedy into a pageant of sex and money. Great humorists such as W. C. Fields were used only to entertain the audience while the "girls" changed clothes and sets which enhanced the splendor and luxury of money were being shifted.[3]

Ziegfeld girls were trained in the arts of plutocratic spending. He demanded that they be well groomed in the streets, hotels, restaurants, or "wherever they were seen by the public." He insisted upon gloves, hats, high heels, and stockings at all times. "Too much rouge, mascara or lipstick off stage was as forbidden as wearing a costume with the slightest variation from his dictates."[4] The first of Ziegfeld's "glorified" beauties, Lillian Lorraine, was never without a gold vanity case initialed in diamonds. Her floor-length ermine evening wrap dazzled Broadway. From 1907 until 1931, when the private spending of money lost some of its magical power over American life, the glory of the Ziegfeld girl was her expense. Unlike the Folies Bergère of Paris, Ziegfeld used the nude sparingly. "Bare legs were never as enticing as legs sheathed in the finest silks." Ziegfeld girls received "an average salary of $75 a week but they wore ermines, sables, mink, and diamonds. And if anyone gave a party for them [and many plutocrats did] they took for granted emeralds or at least thousand-dollar bills tucked into their vanity cases as their just due." [5] In the stores and streets of the Chicago Loop of his youth Ziegfeld saw the greatest public stage of plutocratic "elegance" in America. Until the Follies lost their public in the thirties he created in his own life, as he did on the stage, a drama of ostentatious spending. Gold telephones stood on his office desk. His luxurious house, the Burkely Crest estate, cost $10,000 a month to operate. He entertained lavishly on week ends, "not caring much who [his guests were] so long as they were personages." He lived in the manner of "a grandee." Such luxury was a communication to others, and thus to himself, that so long as he was spending he was important. We are told by those who knew him that Ziegfeld "measured things by outward symbols, of which the most important were wealth and its ostentatious habiliments. He had very little inner life." [6]

The Middle West had inherited a Puritan tradition which sanctioned earning but not spending—or at least not spending on oneself. This tradition had both sacred and secular roots. Luxury was sinful in the eyes of God, and it was the mark of a hated aristocracy among men. Among Puritans of America, as of England, simple dress was an ascetic virtue, a positive act of grace, but it was also a radical and public denial of aristocratic elegance. Simple dress expressed hatred of the aristocrat at the same time that it indicated membership in the "community of saints." Frontier usage in America dramatized this social and religious linkage. A dude was scorned by the preachers, because his foppish dress was sinful, and by the laity because dressing as a "gentleman" was a sign of snobbery, the cardinal sin of the frontier.

But the aristocratic luxury of the dude, which the people of the American frontier were taught to scorn by their preachers, at least allowed the individual to glorify himself on his own terms. The right to wear a powdered wig, to carry a sword, and to adorn shoes with silver buckles was a status right. It indicated membership in the aristocratic community, and because of the power of sumptuary laws and tradition which upheld such laws, luxurious equipage communicated authority over common people who could dream of luxury but not realize it. The somber Puritan in black and white indicated his membership in a community too. This "community of saints" may not have been an aristocracy of the world; but, in the world beyond, the Puritan elect were to rule supreme over the hated aristocrats of this world. And, as we know from the history of New England, the "saints" in America soon created an aristocracy as autocratic as any known in Europe.

As long as the iron discipline of the Puritan church held, individuals could express themselves only through the hierarchy of the church. And even when the symbols of money and trade challenged religious symbols, they were related to the sacred symbols of Puritanism through the creation of what Max Weber has taught us to call the Puritan Ethic. Money could be earned by the elect, but it must be regarded as corporate, not individual earning. A rich man was a "steward of the Lord," and his earnings, while held individually, were really held for the Lord. As John Wesley said, what you earn is not your own. It belongs to God, and must be used to further his purposes here on earth. In this teaching Wesley and his followers on the frontier, like the preacher Peter Cartwright, hoped to remove the taint of sin from money.

This ideal of corporate wealth in which the individual earned and spent for the community was equally strong in business life. Private gain must lead to public good. Public spending was justified because it developed community resources and thus benefited everyone. Taxes for roads, canals, railways, and whatever the community "needed" to develop as a commercial center were just taxes. True, corporations as well as individuals enriched themselves, but they did so in developing the community. To spend on individual luxuries, such as great houses, elegant clothes, beautiful gardens, or personal service, was wrong because this benefited the individual, not the community. The "plain necessaries" in dress, houses, food, and travel were enough for the individual.

But for people who had known the bondage of sumptuary laws, or the inhibitions of "keeping one's place" through "proper" spending, a corporate role was not enough. If it was the privilege of the gentleman and the lady to stage themselves as they liked, and in doing so to communicate their individual glory to others, why was it not possible for all? For, as Goethe made clear in *Wilhelm Meister,* the aristocrat not only enjoyed his individuality, but he enjoyed it in public. He possessed the right to a public life which was denied the burgher. Even as late as 1914 in the British army most officers were gentlemen by birth. The great stages of public life where the high and the mighty ruled and the destinies of nations and men were decided were all but closed to commoners.

When the individual was free to spend as he liked he could communicate his success to whatever publics he could reach. It was the attraction of new public roles which created the glamor of spending money in America. What a man earned by sweat or skill, he could spend as he saw fit. For the first time in history, men were free to spend and, through the magic of symbolic transformation, freedom itself soon became freedom to spend, as well as to worship gods of one's choice, or to vote without fear. And so the American customer emerged. In Chicago, under the leadership of the State Street merchants, not only the familiar wholesale customer, but a new customer, the individual retail customer, emerged. This freed spending from its corporate forms; and the individual customer, who is flattered, cajoled, and courted in all the arts of commercial magic, was born.

The linkage of spending with sex and courtship, as well as with religion and public life, was another powerful element in the glamorization of spending. The Puritans, as we have been told so often, hope to contain Eros within the family. But Puritans never solved the problems of what to do about sex outside of the family. It was easy enough in settled rural communities to arrange marriages, formally or informally, and to marry off the young at an early age. But when family life was broken up in the movement westward, and in the ever-increasing social and spatial mobility of democratic life, familial control of sex broke down. If the young had to find their own mates with little or no parental help, it was only natural that they should develop their own forms of courtship. If they were to meet in public as well as private roles they must learn to stage themselves so as to attract other individuals.

Staging of the self as an individual involved status skills in *both* sex and status appeal. And since status was no longer expressed in traditional familial roles, and highly mobile individuals must attract each other quickly, money and all the arts of the expression of real and imputed wealth soon supplanted traditional symbols of courtship. Money could be used quickly and easily; a fine dress could be bought for the asking, so long as it was proper to ask and one could pay. Family lineage, rank, skill, long residence, and all the traditional symbols of status soon changed among people who, as the Americans said of themselves, were "here today and gone tomorrow."

The connection between sex and glamor which was to introduce the "sexual sell" so familiar to us, had already been forged by the Puritan fathers. On both class and religious levels, the arts of glamorizing the self had been condemned. Aristocratic elegance was condemned in the eyes of God and hated in the eyes of men who had struggled so long to gain their freedom from the tyranny of these elegant aristocrats. In countless sermons, pamphlets, and books, the "sin of the eye" was condemned. But in making spending a sin, the Puritans also invested it with dark mysteries. The linkage of spending with aristocratic decadence, sexual license, pride, seductiveness, and worldliness, as a grand negation of all the Puritan virtues, only served to make spending on the self more exciting. Shopping became more than a necessity; it became a risk. Money now offered more than security, it offered danger; and it lifted trading from "bargaining" to an adventure.

Notes

[1] Thus the attack as well as the glorification of the female plutocrat begins at the same time in Chicago. Irony and laughter over the new female plutocrat was also common in Chicago. Perhaps, indeed, irony was more common than acceptance or rejection. In the writings of Veblen, Fuller, Herrick, Ade, as in the domestic architecture of Root and Wright, the "new woman" is treated with compassion and dignity. Even Veblen, whose irony was often cruel and savage, is gentle with the wives of the plutocrats he ridiculed. There is little glorification of the traditional American woman in Chicago art. Evidently the "new woman" was a highly significant audience and client to the Chicago artist. They turned to Veblen, Fuller, Dreiser, Masters, and Herrick for depictions of the social role of the modern woman. They followed other Chicagoans such as Dewey, Mead, and Parker in education, and they supported Jane Addams in Hull House, because they were in revolt against traditional feminine roles. But they were in revolt, too, against the new role of "heroic spending" which Veblen, Fuller, Ade, and other Chicagoans satirized.

[2] Marjorie Farnsworth, *The Ziegfeld Follies: A History in Text and Pictures* (New York: Putnam, 1956), p. 28. W. C. Fields objected to his subordination as a clown to these plutocratic mimes. He nicknamed Ziegfeld beauties "camels" because of their long slender legs and strutting walk.

[3] Just as they are now used on television to hold audiences until the commercial, when "glamor girls" excite us to drink beer or refined ladies urge us to purchase certain brands of toilet paper.

[4] Farnsworth, *Ziegfeld,* p. 84.

[5] *Ibid.,*

[6] *Ibid.,* p. 152.

11

Setting the Stage for a New Urban Drama, the Drama of Shopping

THE PRIDE of the Chicagoan in his role as Chicagoan soon became legendary. The traditional role of the male plutocrat with his great house and lavish entertainment engrossed the Chicago businessman far less than his role in the city.[1] For this role he needed a new stage, just as his wife needed a new house. In their search, Chicago businessmen turned to their architects for buildings which would dignify their roles by creating stages proper to their heroic conception of their role in the business drama of Chicago.

But the newest drama, and the one which was to determine the character of all business life in the Chicago Loop, was shopping. Making it possible for women to spend money in the Loop required many changes in the public role of women. Unaccompanied women or women not accompanied by men were greatly restricted in their public movements. Hotels, department stores, public and private institutions alike had to create respectable ways for women to use their services. The unescorted lady was not served in public restaurants, or, if she was, only where a discreet sign (still to be seen on old Chicago neighborhood restaurant windows) saying "ladies invited" made plain her welcome. There were no tearooms or clubrooms for women. Beauty shops for women did not exist; hotel barbers cut men's but not women's hair. There were few female clerks, even in Potter Palmer's stores. Until the eighties the Chicago Loop was restricted to men; customers were usually wholesale, not retail, buyers.

By 1880 Chicagoans observed a new kind of shopper on State Street. Even as early as the fifties masculine irony over the shopping mania of the new female shopper was almost a convention in newspaper reports. By the fifties "bargain sales" in Chicago retail stores were enough of an event to attract the attention of national magazine editors. A *Harper's* writer reports: "I had to storm *cheveaux de frise* of hoops to reach the counter. . . . Observe your wife at dry goods if you would know her. She may be sweet in the parlor, but she is like a ghoul at the counter, as if she might steal a dress or tear out the eyes of a clerk who refused to abate the price. . . . The shopping mania is a disease peculiar to women. It is a species of insanity." The November fire of 1877 in the Field and Leiter Store was reported in the Chicago *Tribune* with heavy masculine irony over the foibles of women shoppers. "The destruction of St. Peter's at Rome could hardly have aroused an apparently deeper interest than the destruction of this palatial dry goods establishment. It is questionable whether the death of the Pope or the burning up of the Vatican could have excited such a keen local interest. . . . This was the place of worship of thousands of our female fellow-citizens. It was the only shrine at which they paid their devotions." [2]

The Chicago retail merchant, unlike the industrialist, was not yet thought of as a heroic developer of "community resources." Salesmanship and all the arts of persuasion used to create customers were far lower in public esteem in 1890 than banking, manufacturing, or railroading. The salesman sold service, not a thing, or, as we now say, a "package." Selling, and particularly retail selling, was too closely linked in frontier memory with servility. Retail service, "waiting on people," was menial. It was also an "art" rather than a "science." Motivating people to buy could not be reduced to hard and fast rules. Manufacturing and distribution could become a science; quantification techniques based on motion studies of efficient production could be applied. Even in Veblen the relationship between technology and consumption is never made clear. The consumer is taken for granted; his "needs" are to be satisfied. Who is to determine his "need"? Evidently the same technocrats who supply them. In Veblen's view, salesmanship to increase individual or "pecuniary" wants was wasteful (as, in older views, luxury had been sinful). The view of Bruce Barton in 1925, that "Jesus was really a business man at heart," [3] and the development of spending at Christmastime as a kind of secular prayer were very remote from the attitudes toward spending commonly held in the years before and after the Civil War.

Chicago merchants made their stores great stages for the enactment of their roles as "servants of the public." Far from being too proud to clerk in their stores, they gloried in the art of presenting themselves to customers as friendly yet elegant hosts and appearing before their clerks as grand masters in all the arts of management. Chicagoans thought of their stores as social centers. Prairie Avenue ladies did their own shopping and often used the store as a place to meet friends. By the nineties neighborhood shopping was a well enough developed social event to require proper dress. Going to the store was often a family affair. Children of steady customers were welcomed with gifts of candy. Retail merchants were friendly, and so were their customers. For who could tell? The shopkeeper of today was often the plutocrat of tomorrow. Palmer, Leiter, and Field started behind a counter. Many retail shopkeepers listed in city directories of the fifties are prominent in Chicago society of the nineties.

The shift in the drama of shopping from wholesale to retail and the consequent feminization of shopping took place in one generation. In 1887, nearly thirty years after the opening of Potter Palmer's store on Lake Street, Marshall Field backed fully the change from wholesale to retail trade. Wholesale trade had a long tradition as a man's game. Potter Palmer's "marble palace," built for Field and Leiter at Washington and State streets in 1868 and "Chicago's pride" in these years, was devoted primarily to wholesale. Only the first floor was used for retail selling. Here the drama of retail merchandising was played to a feminine audience, a new audience of women who visited the stores to see and to be seen. But for years to come, profits were derived from wholesale not retail trade. Field's retail profits from 1871 to 1877 were but some $300,000, while wholesale profits were $5,286,000. Because of this, Leiter argued that the future of Leiter and Field was in wholesale and urged the firm to concentrate on their wholesale store.

In trying to create a great public drama of shopping, Chicago merchants faced class as well as sexual taboos. If only lower-class women could shop in the Loop, how was it to be made acceptable to upper-class women? And if upper-class women did come to State Street stores, how could the exclusiveness of the stores be retained, without at the same time alienating lower-class women? The "shawl trade" and the "carriage trade" were necessary audiences to each other in the new drama of shopping. The presence of "society ladies" added to the status excitement of shopping for the "shawl trade," while the open admiration of clerks, managers, and customers enhanced the pleasure of shopping for customers who found the status drama of purchase much easier to sustain than the traditional status drama of entertainment at home. Being a lady at home required training in manners and skills necessary to staging genteel entertainments; shopping required money which could be spent on a stage set by others, and before audiences who were not guests but customers.

Potter Palmer began the feminization of Chicago shopping during the fifties. He welcomed unescorted women to his store, where they were treated with deference and encouraged to shop at leisure. Clerks were required to dress as gentlemen and to greet women shoppers of all classes politely and courteously.[4] Ladies entering his store were greeted with a smile and a bow by Potter Palmer himself, dressed in a frock coat.[5] Women were urged to take goods home on approval. Prices were plainly marked. Items were selected as sales leaders and priced very low, but at the same time quality and style in women's apparel were emphasized. Goods were imported directly from Paris. This attracted wealthy women, whose patronage soon made public shopping fashionable. Since there was no haggling over prices, time was not spent on bargaining but in helping the customer select pleasing items.

Thus shopping became a status drama, a moment of individual choice in which the clerk acted as a friendly guide or instructor in matters of taste, style, and propriety. Potter Palmer and his imitators acted out their roles as merchant princes on stages thronged with women. These new audiences changed daily and hourly; thousands of customers, clerks, and office workers offered great audiences before whom merchants could play frequent and varied roles. To the clerks behind the counters, Field's daily appearance was the triumphal entry and processional of a hero. To the customers and clerks alike, he was a courtly merchant prince. Ernest Poole, the Chicago novelist, tells in his memoirs that Marshall Field was the "courtly merchant whom I used to see long ago, when I went with my mother downtown to shop. . . . A man still in his fifties then, with a low soft voice and charming manners, gray mustache and hair, as he moved about the store with bright observing smiling eyes, he had such a patrician air, I used to stare at him—Marshall Field, the richest man in Chicago and ace merchant of the West." [6]

Palmer and Field did more than run stores; they transformed shopping into a drama of spending in a new kind of court, the plutocratic bazaar—the department store. The first stage these merchants asked their architects to design was the store building itself. But Palmer soon realized that the inside of a store was not sufficient in itself to mount a highly profitable drama of shopping. The street and the sidewalks must serve as a promenade for customers. And if women, and especially upper-class women, were to be attracted to the downtown area, streets must be designed far differently from Lake Street, "The Street of Merchants." Here on hot summer days the filth and smell required women to hold scented lace handkerchiefs to their noses as they picked their way along rickety walks among cordage shops, tailor shops, cheap hotels, spice stores, coffee stores, groceries, saloons, and butcher shops, before an audience of stevedores, peddlers, waterfront loungers, fishmongers, drunks, and gamblers. Potter Palmer was not alone in his search for greater gentility in shopping.

Chicago architects and engineers realized that customers could not reach the Loop until not only the streets, but the whole city was planned for shopping. The high-rise building could carry people from floor to floor and keep them in easy communication, but transportation to and from these buildings must be provided. In 1890, as in 1964, talk about the strangulation of the

Chicago Loop was common. As the buildings went higher and brought more people to work and shop, congestion increased. When the automobile appeared, Frank Lloyd Wright warned Chicagoans that the future of the Loop and, indeed, the whole city would be determined by a race between the elevator and the automobile. By 1900 Chicago architects were betting on the automobile. The Chicago Plan, the first great American urban plan of modern times, was created by Burnham out of his experience in the World's Fair in coordinating the movement and servicing of millions of Fair visitors and creating a whole new "White City" in Jackson Park. The Chicago Plan, like so many to follow, was a plan for getting customers and those who supplied and waited on them in and out of the Loop.

In the first few years of his career Potter Palmer tried to attract the carriage trade, believing, unlike his competitors, that his fashionable customers would serve as a lure to attract women of lower station. He treated all classes of women with great courtesy.[7] Signs in the stores read: "If, when you get your goods home, you do not find them entirely satisfactory, please return them and your money will be refunded." The main floor of the "marble palace" of 1868 was outfitted in a luxurious style new to store design. Walnut counters, frescoed walls, brilliant lights, window and floor displays of silks and furs created a stage rich enough for the wealthiest families. Displays of twelve-hundred-dollar shawls and thousand-dollar lace tablecloths made clear to Chicago plutocrats that they could become heroic spenders in Chicago, as well as New York, London, or Paris. The feminization of spending (as Potter Palmer realized in his many plutocratic roles as merchant, hotel operator, real estate dealer, and husband of Chicago's great lady) depended on the transformation of traditional woman's role as mother, mistress, wife, and lady. As mothers, Chicago women must be taught to spend properly for their families; as mistresses, they must translate erotic appeal into money; as wives, they must learn the nuances of the "pecuniary canons of taste" required in public and private appearance. All must learn how to translate traditional forms of gentility into pecuniary forms of gentility. It was not simply a matter of giving the lady what she wanted, but of seeing to it that she wanted things and services that money alone could buy.

But, as Potter Palmer discovered in 1852, making shopping genteel was not easy. Lake Street was the shopping center of what was to become the Chicago Loop, and the most concentrated shopping center in the world. This street lay along the river on low ground. Like most Loop streets of the time it was little better than a mud slough. Sidewalks were made of wooden planks through which mud spurted, making it impossible to keep clean while walking. The level of the town was only two feet above the river.

Engineers reported that the town must be raised at least twelve feet and that this would require twelve hundred acres of fill. Until street grades could be established by law, builders were free to construct foundations at different levels. In some Loop streets it was necessary to walk up and down stairs to pass by only a block of stores. It was said jokingly that when a genuine Chicagoan visited New York he could not abide walking too long on a level surface and was obliged to turn into an adjacent building every block or so and run up and down a stairway to keep himself in trim.

But the mud and filth of the streets and the stink of the sewage-clogged river were not the only problems in creating a shopping area refined enough for ladies. From its founding in the thirties until its great Fair of 1893 Chicago was a man's town. It was also for many years a city of single men, who far outnumbered women in the social life of middle- and upper-class families. By the seventies Chicago was the rail hub of America. It became the greatest labor mart in America for railroad jobs and finally for all kinds of itinerant labor. During these years Chicago was also one of the leading ports of the nation. Lake traffic in timber, ore, and grain was handled by sailors, who made Chicago their headquarters. Seventeen grain elevators holding 6,500,000 bushels linked the wheat of the northwest with the railroads of America. All along the river stood coal yards, great warehouses, wholesale storage buildings, distilleries, flour mills. In 1964 many of these buildings still stand. The river front, which contains some of the most dramatic sites in Chicago, is just beginning to be developed.

The Loop and its environs was a city of homeless men and women. From the flophouses on Lake Street to the Palmer House on State Street, Chicago was filled with men whose roots were not in the city yet whose continued presence determined the form and spirit of urban life. These new mobile urbanites were to shape Chicago's commercial architecture, just as neighborhood and suburban family life created the conditions which inspired the great domestic architecture of Root, Wright, and the Chicago school. In the seventies, differences between traditional and Middle Western urban styles of family and civic life began to appear. Chicagoans lived in neighborhoods. Everyone used the Loop, but few families lived in it. Even so fine a building as Beman's Pullman Building with its famous Tip Top Inn and suites of residential apartments did not keep its apartments for long. The Loop was a place in which to "do business"; the neighborhood, and later the suburb, the place to live and raise a family. The Loop was a place to buy something, not a place to walk or to sit and talk. Hotels and restaurants catered to transients or to businessmen who did not live in the Loop. After the Fair of 1893 the Loop changed into a great commercial and shopping center, probably the most concentrated in the world. This, if anything, only intensified the transiency of its daily population.

As the mobility of American business increased and Chicago became a great rail hub, the city became one of the great "convention towns" of America. "Conventioneers," like the cattlemen, sailors, and laborers of Chicago after the Civil War, related to others as mobile individuals, not as members of families. Their presence created the dilemma now so familiar to all urban planning: How do we create a city for families and yet, at the same time, for transitory individuals who care little for the stability or future of the city as a community of homes? Beyond the crowded streets of the Loop in 1871 stretched the "Garden City." In the year of the Chicago Fire there were no tenement houses. Workmen owned or rented houses located among shops and factories in the streets west of LaSalle Street. During these years, and until World War I, Chicago plutocrats lived in the city. Within a few years after the Fire, Field, Pullman, and Armour built their homes on Prairie Avenue. In contrast to the homes of New York plutocrats such as Frick, these homes had spacious yards, large windows opening to all sides of the house, bay windows permitting a view up and down the street, wide porches, and stairs to the front door (as well as a carriage entry on one side). The grounds, or the yard, as it was called, were surrounded by low fences which bounded but did not enclose the property. In Prairie Avenue, as on the West Side, the informal spirit of the Garden City prevailed. On mild evenings the front steps and the stoop were transformed into an outdoor living room. Families made themselves comfortable with rugs and cushions, as children played in the yard. Mandolin and guitar parties filled the evening with laughter and song.

Neighborhoods and suburbs developed outside of the Loop. Here people lived in homes as families [8] bound together by religion, nationality, race, occupation, and income. Old residents of Chicago tell us that early neighborhoods corresponded to parochial lines. North of the river, McCormickville (as the region around Rush Street was called, because so many of the McCormick families lived there) was divided between communicants of the North Presbyterian and St. James Episcopal churches. Meeker, who was raised on Prairie Avenue as a child, tells us that Prairie and Calumet avenues were the first neighborhoods in Chicago that were bounded by secular rather than ecclesiastical ties. In his novel *Prairie Avenue* and his memoir, *Chicago, With Love,* Meeker depicts life in Chicago neighborhoods as centered about church and family. The decline of ecclesiastical power over social life in Chicago began with the increase of travel and the secularization of popular communication through the rise of a metropolitan press. By 1893 "cosmopolitanism" was in high fashion. European travel, trips through America, mass travel of all kinds soon joined standardized mass communication in breaking the control of small intimate groups gathered around religious institutions.

The shift to "pecuniary canons of taste" soon went far beyond that of taste in dress. The church, the school, and the state itself were soon dominated by pecuniary values. As Veblen's subtitle to *The Higher Learning in America* —"A Memorandum on the Conduct of Universities by Business Men"—indicated, the power of money was taking new forms. The American university,[9] Veblen argues, existed to indoctrinate the young with pecuniary ideals of earning and spending. "[By] engendering spendthrift and sportsmanlike habits . . . businesslike management diverts the undergraduate students from going in for the disinterested pursuit of knowledge, and so from entering on what is properly university work. . . ."[10] Business attempts to transform universities into training grounds for customers and workers were also noted by the sociologist, Lester Ward, whose influence on Middle Western and University of Chicago students of society was very great. Like Veblen, he argued against business domination. Education, he argued, cannot be conducted on "business principles." There is no "demand" for education in the economic sense. The child knows nothing of its value and the parent rarely desires it. "Society is the only interest that can be said to demand it, and society must supply its own demand. Those who found educational institutions or promote educational enterprises put themselves in the place of society and assume to speak and act for society, and not for any economic interest."[11] Thus Ward, like Veblen, Fuller, Sullivan, and Wright, warned Americans to keep an eye on the swift domination of Chicago by the "money powers."

Notes

[1] Chicago is still the despair of high society. In his study on metropolitan elites, Baltzell points out that Chicago in 1940 had twice as many individuals listed in *Who's Who,* and less than half as many families listed in the *Social Register,* as Philadelphia. (See E. Digby Baltzell, *Philadelphia Gentlemen: The Making of a National Upper Class* [Glencoe, Illinois: The Free Press, 1958] pp. 29–30.) Dixon Wecter in *The Saga of American Society: A Record of Social Aspiration 1607–1937* (New York: Scribner's, 1937), states ". . . the paradise of parvenus is Chicago. In this Midwestern metropolis one's social passport is given a mere perfunctory glance, particularly if it bears the visa of wealth" (p. 143). Even Arthur Meeker, scion of one of the old Chicago packing families, says: "Who with all the world to choose from in the year 1955, would pick Chicago? . . . Detroit or St. Louis or Minneapolis or Cleveland . . . have a perfect

right to be hick towns if they like. Chicago hasn't that right any more. . . ." (See *Chicago, With Love: A Polite and Personal History* [New York: Knopf, 1955], p. 283.)

2 Quoted from L. Wendt and H. Kogan, *Give the Lady What She Wants* (Chicago: Rand McNally, 1952), p. 147.

3 See Bruce Barton, *The Man Nobody Knows: A Discovery of the Real Jesus* (Indianapolis: Bobbs-Merrill, 1925). This was the most widely read nonfiction book of the year 1925. His mystique of money is matched by Fitzgerald's "golden girls" and great spenders in his novels of the same period. Depictions of luxurious spending were stock scenes in all popular art, but they were frequent, too, in serious literature and art of the time.

4 The rudeness of store clerks (from 1850 to 1880) to women of the lower classes was so common that it evoked editorial comment in the Chicago press.

5 Formal dress during the day was not limited to rich merchants. All those who aspired to "dignified" gentility—in professional life as well as business—wore frock coats, silk hats or homburgs, etc.

6 Ernest Poole, *Giants Gone: Men Who Made Chicago* (New York and London: McGraw-Hill, 1943), p. 115.

7 Rudeness of clerks to the "shawl" as well as the "carriage" trade was cause for instant dismissal.

8 Chicago has always been noted for its high percentage of homeowners. It has been a suburban, home-owned community, as well as an urban, transient center, since 1875. "Escaping" to the suburbs is as old a tradition in Chicago as promoting it as the "Convention City of America." Row housing has never been acceptable to Chicagoans.

9 His observations are based on his life in Chicago and as a professor at the University of Chicago.

10 Thorstein Veblen, *The Higher Learning in America: A Memorandum on the Conduct of Universities by Business Men* (Stanford: Stanford University Press, 1954), p. 225.

11 Veblen refers to him throughout his work. So, too, do Cooley and Albion Small, the founder of sociology at the University of Chicago. Ward argues that man creates telic factors, or values, whose symbolic expression makes society possible. He does not disavow genesis in the evolutionary sense, but insists that genesis cannot be understood without telesis. Ward's writings range from *Dynamic Sociology* (1883) to *Glimpses of the Cosmos* (6 vols., 1913–18). Ward trusted the common people, and like most Chicago artists and thinkers argued that the strength of the artist and thinker came from his relationship to his people. He thought that individual freedom could be guaranteed only by the state, not by what he called "the money powers."

12

The Urban Drama of Status

THE SUCCESS of Chicago businessmen in changing traditional feminine roles fascinated Chicago artists and thinkers of the eighties and nineties. Veblen's article, "The Economic Theory of Woman's Dress," appeared in 1894.[1] He argued that woman's dress sets forth the wealth of the household to which she belongs. The first principle of dress is "conspicuous expensiveness." The second fundamental principle is the "evidence of expenditure afforded by a constant suppression of one wasteful garment or trinket by a new one." The flux, change, and novelty of fashion are "demanded by the central principle of all dress—conspicuous waste." Underlying these principles is the use of dress to indicate "conspicuous abstention from useful effort." The plutocratic woman must show evidence that she leads a "useless life," because this indicates that her husband is successful enough to support a woman who cannot earn and is even "wasteful." The ideal of such dress "is to demonstrate to all observers, and to compel observation of the fact, that the wearer is manifestly incapable of doing anything that is of use. The modern civilized woman's dress attempts this demonstration of habitual idleness and succeeds measurably."

In sum, expensiveness, novelty, and ineptitude (that is, evidence of incapacitating the wearer for any gainful occupation), are the three cardinal principles of the plutocratic woman's dress. Besides these three principles there is a "principle of adornment, in the aesthetic sense." This has a certain degree of economic importance and applies "with a good deal of generality." Actually the function of the principle of adornment in dress is that of handmaid to the principle of novelty, rather than that of an independent or coordinate factor. For so long as the chance of rivalry between persons in respect of wealth remains nothing can set aside the use of clothes to express the great central requisite of conspicuous waste. Such conspicuous waste is largely feminine, but men and children make similar use of clothes. "The child in the hands of the civilized woman is an accessory organ of conspicuous consumption, much as any tool in the hands of a laborer is an accessory organ of productive efficiency." And while it is true that there is a class of men who express themselves in clothes as do women, such men are really "persons who in the crude biological sense [only] are men. . . ."

Veblen saw downtown Chicago become a series of canyons intersecting great glass-windowed blocks devoted to satisfying such pecuniary canons of taste. The Loop, with its magnificent waterfront, soon became one of the world's most highly concentrated stages for customers. But State Street merchants in Chicago were determined to make shopping "beautiful" as well as efficient. All roads led to the department store, for these were the reason for being of the Chicago Loop. The Chicago Loop was not (and is not) a place to stroll and chat as one glances in the windows. Nor is it a leisurely place to eat with friends. The river front, which might easily contain very beautiful urban stages of life, is just beginning (in 1964) to escape its shabby past. The ground floors, or indeed any floor, of the great Loop buildings offers few places to sit. The streets have few benches. Public comfort stations are neither clean nor comfortable. The screech and roar of trains running on tracks elevated over the streets, combined with the noise of trucks, buses, and automobiles, make any kind of talk impossible. Despite the presence everywhere of great numbers of people there is no sound of human voices; the urban crowd is both lonely and mute. As one enters a bar or restaurant the roar of the streets dies away to be replaced by other sharp mechanical noises. In many bars and restaurants television blares away; even small bars have singers, pianists, or organists who perform on perchlike platforms surrounded by gleaming displays of whisky bottles. Restaurants provide entertainment with their meals. Silence or muted talk is "dead," noise and movement, "live."

As Chicagoans of 1900 stepped within the doors of Sullivan's great Schlesinger and Mayer department store, the status drama of the streets shifted from the eye alone to the ear. The noise and ugliness of the street were transformed into quiet serenity and elegance. Clerks were not servile, hurried, or surly. They had no control of price, so there was no bargaining. Goods were not hidden away to be brought out at the discretion of the clerk but displayed openly in and upon gleaming glass cases. The clerk's job was to find out what his customer wanted, not simply to tell him what was in stock. He was taught to "personalize shopping" by acting as a counselor and guide in making a selection. He did not harangue or coax; indeed, he could even criticize goods which he and the customer examined together. Sometimes he disagreed with his customer's choice and suggested that something else be tried. In playing his role he identified with the customer as well as with the buyers and managers of the store. Unlike the bureaucratic clerk, the clerk of State Street tried to give his customers a sense of individuality;

but in turn he asked that he, too, be regarded as an individual. The clerk and the customer became partners in a search for individual expression, an expression which must stage the self in forms understood by all yet varied enough to be an expression of individuality. One must be acceptable to others yet distinguished from them. The weight and dignity of traditional dress were transformed through style and fashion into a personal expression. Chicago merchants knew that traditional forms were used to identify with a sacred and hallowed past. Such identifications could be expressed in "antiques" and "old masters" by the rich, but for those who could not afford genuine antiques, imitations (even of worm holes in wood) were created. The tradition of imitation, but a *new* imitation of the old, soon took root in plutocratic expression of status. Veblen's account of the incongruity in Chicago of "pecuniary canons of taste" based on the "archaic traits" of a "predatory feudal" businessman was easy enough for Chicagoans to understand. By 1900 popular writers were describing the local plutocrats as "money barons." But another tradition was emerging. This was the tradition of the new. At worst, this was what we now call "built-in obsolescence," but at best it created a spirit in Chicago which made possible the great work of Sullivan, Wright, and Burnham, as well as the miraculous growth of the University of Chicago.

Successful sales clerks on State Street were trained to subordinate themselves to the customer, but such subordination was not confused with personal servility. It was subordination to a principle of merchandising which bound together Field, the "merchant prince," the lowest shipping clerk, and the great and poor among his customers. Store executives dignified the act of retail selling. Clerks were not allowed to rush toward customers as they entered their department. As H. Gordon Selfridge said, "undue urging of merchandise upon customers is not desired." Field and Selfridge taught that dignified personal service and courtesy was the touchstone of good salesmanship. Subordination to the customer, as to the store, was not servility, but subordination to a great institution, Marshall Field's of Chicago, whose customers were being taught "to share in the good things in life" in their "downtown home."

Selfridge never criticized employees before customers or other clerks. He asked his workers to treat each other courteously. They were to address each other with "dignity, respect and care" for a "careless word or an act of familiarity may, in the mind of some passing customer, cause a reflection to the discredit of those who are responsible for same, or allow customers to wrongfully interpret words or gestures, and this we wish to avoid." Clerks, doormen, and floorwalkers were instructed not to call each other by their first names or nicknames. They addressed each other as "Mr. Smith" or "Miss Jones." Customers were not addressed familiarly as "Dearie" or "my dear." "Yes, madam," was proper address. "Gents' Furnishings" became "Gentlemen's Furnishings." [2] Clerks were warned against eating while on duty and advised not to lean on the counter for a gossip with visiting friends. Only those who could speak without accent (or who could learn quickly how to do so) and knew the refined conventions of speech, dress, and deportment were fit to wait upon customers at Field's.

But in this new urban plutocratic drama of shopping, the Field manager himself was the hero. Field, Selfridge, and Shedd, like Potter Palmer, walked the broad aisles of the store like gods descending from on high. Selfridge spent much of his time going through the store. In his daily processionals he wore expensive frock coats, wing collars, and gleaming patent leather shoes. He often changed clothes two or three times a day. C. P. L. Lyman, whom Field and Leiter brought from the East to open their new store in 1873, "flitted from counter to counter, brushing imaginary dust from his Prince Albert coat with a large silk handkerchief." At the opening in 1907 of the present building, Shedd wore a dark, braid-trimmed suit, mauve vest, high wing collar, and billowing cravat ornamented with a pearl stickpin. Thus, if these merchants did not find stages in high society, they did so in their stores and on the streets of Chicago.[3] The high moment in the drama of purchase could be seen in the public greeting by Field or Selfridge of a society leader such as Mrs. Palmer. Upon her arrival at the Washington Street entrance Mrs. Palmer was helped out of her carriage by Charlie Pritzlaff, the doorman, who memorized names in the society Blue Book in order to personalize his greeting to the great ladies as he helped them into the store.[4] Here she was greeted by Field himself, dressed in black with white gloves. In dress, bearing, speech, and deportment he studied and perfected the role of the "patrician plutocrat." Field changed the boisterous, back-slapping, fast-talking, affable wholesale executive into a reserved yet courteous retail salesman in cutaway. His patrician air convinced Chicagoans that Field could pass in Europe for a nobleman or a diplomat. Patrician grace and elegance reached new dimensions in the glamor and mystery of the "business gentleman," the new social type of the Middle West. The "patrician plutocrat" soon became a model for the perfect salesman. Soon we hear of "gentlemen salesmen in cutaway" such as Duveen, the art dealer, who added coyness to elegance and "allowed" his Morgans and Mellons to make him part (at great price) with pictures he loved.

This drama of genteel selling was repeated on every floor and in every department. As business increased, the original heroes, department store

Mrs. Potter (Bertha Honore) Palmer, as photographed about the time of the World's Columbian Exposition in Chicago, where she did so much to present the problems of the American woman to Fair visitors. Mrs. Palmer created a link between high society and welfare work that greatly affected the role of society women in Chicago and all America. *Courtesy Chicago Historical Society*

(*Right top*) The Potter Palmer residence, Chicago's "Rhine Castle" on Lake Shore Drive, was a civic monument to plutocratic power. As Veblen taught his students at the University of Chicago, it was a glaring example of "conspicuous consumption." *Courtesy Chicago Historical Society*

(*Right bottom*) Chicago plutocrats favored a "cosmopolitan art" in their own homes, if not in their business buildings, as this interior view of the Potter Palmer residence shows. *Courtesy Chicago Historical Society*

executives, could no longer meet their increased and varied publics. Symbolic counterparts were created in the floorwalker. Like gentlemen of ancient courts, these floorwalkers simulated the radiance of their masters in dress and manner. These tall, elderly, or dignified actors, elegant in dress and speech, were highly skilled in surrounding the act of purchase with an air of plutocratic majesty. Their purely formal existence indicated that selling was no longer an "efficient" service but an art. The act of purchase was now a drama requiring a stage, scenery, actors, lines, chorus, and audience. As they strolled up and down the aisle of the store, women of every station could anticipate a courteous greeting. Inquiries and questions were answered with dignified politeness. Sales slips were signed with an authoritative air, greetings returned in dignified low tones, customers directed graciously to other departments, where they were greeted in turn by other floorwalkers. To the clerks, as to the public, floorwalkers were a constant reminder of the dignity and majesty of the store. They served as living reminders of plutocratic and managerial dignity to the clerks, who in turn served as audience[5] to the elegance and decorum of the floorwalker. Thus by 1900 the role of the patrician plutocrats of the store had become so fixed that it could be played like a stock part in popular drama. The daily dramas of purchase kept the act of spending and the art of retail salesmanship living enactments of plutocratic grace.

State Street merchants soon discovered they must plan a whole city, not just a store, to produce their ideal stages for the drama of spending. Their buildings were designed to serve the needs of individuals who were now thought of as dwellers in a "downtown home," as Selfridge called it. In his novel *The Cliff Dwellers* (1893), Fuller describes the Tacoma, the Monadnock, "and a great host of other modern monsters" as a new kind of human community. These towers in which "hundreds of windows glitter with multitudinous letterings in gold and silver" and through which "clambering hordes" swarm, aimed to be complete colonies within themselves. "The tribe inhabiting the Clifton is large and rather heterogeneous. All told, it numbers about four thousand souls. It includes bankers, capitalists, lawyers, 'promoters'; brokers in bonds, stocks, pork, oil, mortgages; real-estate people and railroad people and insurance people . . . a host of principals, agents, middlemen, clerks, cashiers, stenographers, and errand-boys; and the necessary force of engineers, janitors, scrub-women, and elevator-hands."[6]

In these "downtown homes," Chicagoans soon learned to express almost every event of their lives in money. They turned to their stores to learn how to stage the arrival of a baby, to present a child in public, to give proper pecuniary expression to marriage rites, to buy proper clothes for the opening of school, to dress a corpse properly, and finally to celebrate the holy days of Christmas, Easter, and Thanksgiving. Merchants even created new days of family and community celebrations, such as Mother's and Father's Day, where social bonds were expressed solely through purchased gifts. On all such days gift exchange became an exchange not of time but of money or something money could buy. The forms of erotic life, from the lowest forms of prostitution to the most subtle forms of courtship (commercial art glamorized the "heiress look") were soon communicated through the symbol of money. The hierarchal gods in family and community were worshiped through spending. Chicagoans were taught to *spend* their way to beauty, wisdom, and love—and even to God, for Michigan Avenue billboards reminded Chicagoans that "mercy pays."

Money's power to transform even sacred rites into shopping rites soon taught Chicagoans that money had reached a new level of power. The new power of money had little to do with utilitarian promise of comfort or efficiency. Palmer, Field, Armour, Pullman, and certainly the plungers of the Chicago Pit as dramatized by Norris, never even pretended that money excited them because it promised security. It was the risk, the excitement, the drama of the "money game," which moved them, just as it was the drama of pecuniary emulation which moved their wives. It was these new attitudes toward money and technology which brought the Western businessman to power. There were no markets waiting for Chicago businessmen to exploit. When Chicago became the rail hub of the country it made possible distribution of goods throughout the Middle West. But roads run two ways, and if it became easier for Chicago business to ship to Western markets it also became easier for Eastern businessmen to invade the same markets. What McClurg, Sears and Roebuck, Montgomery Ward, and McCormick distributed could be distributed by firms of far greater capital and organization. Chicago businessmen knew that markets would not "open themselves up"; they must be created and then sustained as new markets. The secularization of life, which Veblen, Wright, and Ford so well understood, was not a "force," a "condition," or an environment which was its own cause and effect. It was created, as all symbols are created. As Veblen said: "Invention is the mother of necessity." Money rose to power because it was spiritualized. By 1890 money was regarded as a supernatural force in Chicago.

In societies where stability is sought through tradition and ritual we are punished if we undeservedly wear the uniform of an officer, the garb of a priest, or the insignia of a public official. But in a plutocracy when we wear clothes beyond our means we find admiring audiences to our masquerade. We are not impostors who do not know our place, but rather ambitious Americans acting out pecuniary discontent, the divine discontent of a plutocracy. Desire to go beyond our station and discontent with what we can afford are highly proper. For only so long as we yearn for what we do not have and allow ourselves to be goaded into not wanting what we do have, do we uphold the magic of money. Rapid changes in styles are used to communicate our ambition to become something different from what we were. Our ability to change is an indication of our ability to spend and of our desire to do what other spenders significant to us are doing. Such spending has little to do with actual need: it is a symbol of identification, an indication to others that we want to be one of them, and to ourselves that we are members of a group whose values we share.

Public, frequent, and open display of the self to large anonymous audiences blurs individual expression and creates anxiety, for when we communicate with audiences from whom we have little or limited response we are never sure we have communicated or that our communication is approved. So long as we wish to communicate with large or poorly defined publics so must we dress and conduct ourselves in ways comprehensible to great numbers of people. We must show that we follow styles considered proper by our group, for such style is a form of identification with the group. But we must in turn give form to our individuality, a self which in being acceptable to the group is yet different from others in the group. And, since plutocratic style must be expensive and new, it must evoke the future, not the past. It plunges us into a new kind of time, a time which flows from a present into a future, and from a future back into a present. In the drama of purchase determined by style we do not evoke a changeless, sacred tradition, but such invocation of the future is no less "sacred" than evocation of the past.

Notes

[1] In *Popular Science Monthly,* Vol. XLVI (November, 1894).

[2] Quoted from L. Wendt and H. Kogan, *Give the Lady What She Wants* (Chicago: Rand McNally, 1952), p. 222.

[3] The modest business suit of our time was not worn by Field. Even on his way to lunch he wore formal morning dress. We read accounts of his stately greeting to fellow plutocrats on State Street by "doffing his silk hat."

[4] We read of doormen who cultivated a "Boston accent."

[5] The clerks were a somewhat ironic audience, at times, since they and other workers in the store knew that the floorwalker had little real power. Perhaps it would be better

to say they functioned like the chorus in a Gilbert and Sullivan opera. Such a chorus is inferior to the hero, but far superior to the general audience. In all modern public staging some such group of spending actors is used to symbolize through dress and bearing the elegance and dignity of money.

[6] Henry Blake Fuller, *The Cliff-Dwellers* (New York: Harper's, 1893), pp. 4-5.

13

The Glamorization of Money in Art

Dreiser's plutocratic heroes of Chicago are mythical figures who motivate action because, like all such figures, they are the ultimate value which determines dramatic action. His plutocrats are different in kind, not degree, from the middle and lower class. His great plutocrats—like Mann's Mynheer Peeperkorn in *The Magic Mountain,* who embodies passion and feeling—represent a principle whose mystery moves the artists (and the artists' public) because it is the principle of social order around which their community is organized. The scenes in *The Great Gatsby* where Nick, Daisy, and Gatsby walk through the huge, luxurious mansion show how great spending becomes an organizing mystery in Fitzgerald's work. Overwhelmed by the magnificence of a great pile of handmade English shirts, Daisy bows her head and weeps "stormily." Sex, love, every phase of the erotic turns on the symbol of money. Gatsby has lost his girl because he has no money. Daisy has married Tom, a wealthy, well-born Easterner. The habits of wealth enhance Daisy's charm. " 'She's got an indiscreet voice,' [Nick] remarked. 'It's full of ——' [he] hesitated. 'Her voice is full of money,' [Gatsby] said suddenly. That was it. I'd never understood before. It was full of money—that was the inexhaustible charm that rose and fell in it, the jingle of it, the cymbals' song of it. . . . High in a white palace the king's daughter, the golden girl. . . ." [1]

For Thomas Mann's young Germans of the nineties money destroys love, even life itself, as in *Buddenbrooks,* where the businessman is shown as vulgar, greedy, corrupt, and weak. For Fitzgerald's young Americans, money creates the "golden girl." Fitzgerald's characters are sexually and spiritually aroused by money; Mann's are made impotent. In D. H. Lawrence, money is pitted against sex, which for him is a sacramental act of communion. Money destroys men and women because it robs them of their ability to commit themselves to each other. Money makes them cold, hard, and calculating. The heart dies in the ascendancy of an intellect which must learn how to calculate because it must be used to deal with money. Dreiser's characters (women as well as men) are deeply involved with money. The Chicago story of Cowperwood's rise to power is highly dramatic so long as he is earning and Ailene, his wife, is spending. Unlike the heroes and villains of James and Wharton, who are staged in scenes filled with traditional art images, the Chicago characters of Norris, Dreiser, Fuller, and Herrick move in scenes of great opulence and luxury. Cowperwood's aura does not depend on his ability to spend in good taste, but to earn in struggle and competition with powerful rivals. In these struggles men and women rise and fall in the social hierarchy of Chicago. Status ascent "from rags to riches" becomes a common theme in elite and popular art of the Middle West. The radiance of things in these stories is not their evocation of tradition, like the heirlooms in *The Spoils of Poynton* of James, but of money which promises ascent into what Fitzgerald called an "orgiastic future."

The dignification of wealth through spending on heirlooms, old homes, and titles to match the sanctification of wealth through earning as a "steward of the Lord" was not so central a concern to Chicago plutocrats as to those of the East. The marriage of Consuelo Vanderbilt to the Duke of Marlborough, of Anna Gould to Count Boni de Castellane, of Mary Leiter[2] to the Marquis Curzon of Kedleston, and of Pauline Whitney to Sir Almeric Paget in 1895 were climaxed in 1899 by the marriage of Prince Michael Cantacuzene of Russia to Julia Grant, the daughter of the President. But aside from occasional marriage into European aristocracy, Chicagoans spent money on their own businesses and on their own city. To be a great civic figure known and honored throughout Chicago was renown enough for most plutocrats. Chicagoans succumbed, like everyone else, to the lure of Europe. By 1893 over 90,000 Americans visited Europe each year; those who could not buy a title bought objects of art, pictures, and things which identified them with past aristocracies. From Fifth Avenue to Prairie Avenue and Nob Hill the turrets of French châteaux, the spires and crenelations of Rhenish castles, and the gables of English manor houses offered new American identification with an alien past. Those who could not afford a grand marital alliance, the Grand Tour, or the grand house enjoyed a pinchbeck splendor in joining the Colonial Order of the Crown for descendants of Charlemagne or the Order of the Crown of America composed of those ostensibly related to other royalty. But such identifications with Europe, strong as they were among Chicago parvenus, did not obliterate the vigorous Americanism of Chicagoans.

Dreiser's wonder of rich spending in Chicago has a far different content from that of James, although the power of money as an expression of hierarchy is equally great in both. The things money buys, in Dreiser, are not of the hallowed world of European culture. They are from the windows and counters of Chicago department stores, whose opulence excited the Sister Carries pouring into Chicago from the towns and farms of the Middle West. Her story, the story of a simple girl making her way in the big city, became a legend for rural and village youth throughout America. The wonder and enchantment of Chicago for them was the wonder of money. Clothes, houses, department stores, and furnishings, like the jewels, silks, and perfumes of *The Arabian Nights,* were infused with hierarchical magic and mystery. Hurstwood's superiority over Drouet, Carrie's first lover, is foreshadowed through the imagery of clothes, whose hierarchical radiance arises from a new kind of elegance, the elegance of price. Hurstwood's clothes

were particularly new and rich in appearance. The coat lapels stood out with that medium stiffness which excellent cloth possesses. The vest was of a rich Scotch plaid, set with a double row of round mother-of-pearl buttons. His cravat was a shiny combination of silken threads, not loud, ·not inconspicuous. What he wore did not strike the eye so forcibly as that which Drouet had on, but Carrie could see the elegance of the material. [His shoes] were of soft, black calf, polished only to a dull shine. Drouet wore patent leather, but Carrie could not help feeling that there was a distinction in favour of the soft leather, where all else was so rich. She noticed these things almost unconsciously.[3]

As Sister Carrie moves up the social ladder, the mystery and power of money deepens until it becomes a "force" like nature. As Dreiser says, "Finally one is led to conclude that by and large, the financial type is the coldest, the most selfish, and the most useful of all living phenomena. Plainly it is a highly specialized machine for the accomplishment of some end which Nature has in view. Often humorless, sharklike, avid, yet among the greatest constructive forces imaginable; absolutely opposed to democracy in practise, yet as useful an implement for its accomplishment as for autocracy." Yerkes, like his fictive Chicago financier Cowperwood, becomes demonic: "A rebellious Lucifer this, glorious in his somber conception of the value of power. A night-black pool his world will seem to some, played over by fulgurous gleams of his own individualistic and truly titanic mind . . . a clear suggestion of the inscrutable forces of life. . . ."[4] Edith Wharton makes villains out of Dreiser's heroes. They are the "new people" whom "New York was beginning to dread and yet be drawn to. . . ." For New York, "as far back as the mind of man could travel, had been divided into two great fundamental groups," those who cared about eating, sex, clothes, and money, and those who were devoted to travel, the creation of beautiful homes and gardens, and culture. In her early novels, such as the *House of Mirth,* making money is not only common and vulgar, but even vulgarizing and degrading to genteel people. Only Jews really lived by money. "[Mr.

Rosedale] had his race's accuracy in the appraisal of values, and to be seen walking down the platform at the crowded afternoon hour in the company of Miss Lily Bart would have been money in his pocket, as he himself might have phrased it." Tasteful spending and well-ordered luxury creates a spiritual aura about Wharton's characters. But in her final analysis of New York society, irony replaces condemnation of her businessmen and her idealization of families based on tradition and culture. Social power in New York was in the last analysis "simply the power of money . . . social credit was based on an impregnable bank account." [5]

Radical Westerners in architecture as in literature did not deny the transcendence of money. The architects Root, Sullivan, and Wright sought to dignify capitalistic earning and spending. The office building, the factory, even the "grocer's warehouse" should be beautiful. This was not the beauty of austerity, but of wealth. The "simple" Monadnock building of Root, the great Auditorium of Adler and Sullivan, like the simple homes of Wright, were very costly. In place of crenelated towers they offer us clean, soaring planes in space filled with interlocking cubes of glass and steel. But these "simple" cubes, where, as Mies van der Rohe tells us, "less becomes more," are very expensive. And thus even art proper, like religion, becomes subordinate to money as a symbol of life. We spend our way to beauty as we do to God. As we see in the work of Veblen, Root, Sullivan, Wright, and the Chicago humorists, Ade, Field, and Dooley, the dilemma of spending to beauty and goodness was a common problem. Veblen argued that the meaning of what he called "the true, the good, and the beautiful," is determined by who controls the symbols in which they are communicated. Where older social philosophers argued that *all* display is communication of pride, Veblen argued that conspicuous consumption of money alone is pride. The canons of "pecuniary decency" are reducible to waste, futility, and ferocity. And where Mandeville or La Rochefoucauld justify their exposure of pride through the understanding to be gained in the confrontation of pride by critical intelligence, Veblen holds that awareness of the "invidious" nature of money will make us recognize and honor the "instinct of workmanship." Behind the ignoble capitalist consumer stands the noble technological worker and engineer. These were Veblen's heroes, and, as we shall see, the heroes of the Chicago school of architecture.

As a device for exposing the incongruities of money and technology, Veblen's innocent technocrat, who works only for the "community" and who looks over in amazed wonder at the spending antics of those under the spell of pecuniary motives, is highly effective. By making the Puritan "stewards of the Lord" predatory beasts and low clowns, he desanctifies the symbol of money. By treating the use of money as a kind of false rhetoric when it is used for private spending, Veblen uncovers many incongruities in capitalism. In *The Higher Learning in America: A Memorandum on the Conduct of Universities by Business Men* he shows universities ostensibly devoted to learning actually destroying learning through emphasis on the dignification of wealth. Academicians teach not the art of thought, but of "genteel expenditure." For, he argues, in a world where spending determines reputability, skill in such spending must be taught by those who want plutocratic support. Even learning itself must be translated into forms whose expense can be communicated to the people. We spend, not to satisfy needs, but to glorify money. What we cannot spend on we cannot value. What is not on the market cannot be priced. What cannot be priced cannot be cherished. Teachers cannot be well paid because they do not make profit, and therefore must be written off as a loss under "deficit financing." Only when poor schools threaten urban and suburban real-estate values, turn out students with low spending morale, or subject the symbol of money itself to savage attack does the school really evoke much concern. Just as we seek to purify the symbol of money from individual greed by spending on gifts to individuals and communities, so do we attempt further purification through spending on learning. As we pay our teachers more we increase respect for them, not because people know much more about the glory of teaching or even what is being taught, but because the glory of money has shed its radiance over our schools.

Chicago artists, scholars, and philosophers followed Veblen in pointing out that the specific contribution of America to our symbolic resources was the development of money as a symbol of hierarchy. This was done by freeing spending as well as earning from religious and social inhibitions. Symbols of exchange, as Sullivan and Veblen stressed, were treated as basic motives of all human relations. We deduce freedom itself from a free market because we believe that such a market supplies the conditions for freedom. American discussion of "freedom" was becoming a discussion of freedom to earn and to spend. God's laws as well as nature's laws, formerly considered the grounds for freedom, were being replaced by market laws (law of supply and demand, the iron law of profit, etc.). Money was no longer thought of as a means, a medium of exchange, but as the purpose or end of economic action. We do not use money to produce, distribute, and consume more goods and services, but to make more money.[6]

The promise of American life, Chicago businessmen taught, was not an increased but an *ever-increasing* standard of living. What we have now is more than we had in the past, and is but a promise of what is to come.

Businessmen killed the past through style (annual and seasonal). The present was infused with a future, both orgiastic and spiritual. No material want need be denied ourselves or others, because in making ourselves prosperous we increase the prosperity of the community. We have a "right" to spend as we see fit—so long as we spend on the market. It is "unjust" to prevent anyone from spending. Adolescents (and even children) have a "right" to spend their own money, and indeed are coached in how to do so in many kinds of commercial art. Prosperity is a sign that God loves us; making and spending money are really acts of service. Spending, like earning, is a duty, a community benefaction. At Christmastime spending becomes a new kind of prayer, a secular prayer. The market place has replaced the cathedral.

The commercial magicians and priests of consumption in Chicago did not urge people to buy things because they would last. On the contrary, they taught that it was precisely because of their promise of not lasting, of being merely a step toward another thing, a token of an infinitely expanding future of bigger and better things, that we must buy. Hierarchical usefulness, not simple utility, determined purchase. Even the car "made to last" must be traded in for a new model. As Chicago businessmen understood, the power of style in America is derived from its power to *communicate* to others, strange and even remote to us, our power to spend freely and frequently. Bankers in Chicago urged people to spend *before,* not *after,* they earned. This was in sharp contrast to the Puritan Ethic which taught us to abhor debt. We work to pay off debts for houses, cars, or clothes, which we have already used. We go in debt for more things and services (but much more for things) we do not have, to satisfy the demands of a pecuniary propriety which does not allow us to be satisfied with what we have. As money infuses technology, obsolescence becomes our standard of value. This is because we have shifted spending from the abhorred luxury of the aristocracy so deeply hated by the Puritans, to a common "right." We are worth what we spend, and our discontent with what we have is but a mark of ambition to spend more, or as we say "to get ahead." As we spend we enhance our community, just as the industrialist who spends on new machinery, or the state that builds new roads, develops community resources as well as the resources of his own corporation.

The spiritualization of money in Chicago is best illustrated in the development of Christmas celebrations in the Loop. The first commercial exploitation of our holy days in Chicago began about 1890, when merchants "recognized the commercial potentialities" of holy days. By 1920 the business exploitation of Christmas in Chicago became a community celebration. By 1950 December sales ranged from 11 to nearly 23 per cent of the year's sales.[7]

Merchants open the "Christmas shopping season" on the Monday after Thanksgiving (also celebrated by great spending on food and liquor). Carols, both sacred and secular, blare through business streets. Everything from garbage cans to automobiles is advertised under headings describing the "joy of Christmas" as the "spirit of giving." A great parade welcoming Santa Claus is held in the Loop. Nativity scenes appear in advertisements for any kind of commodity under captions of "peace on earth, good will to men." As the newspapers themselves tell us, the "annual shopping spree" is under way. The traditional English "Father Christmas" and the German "St. Nicholas" and "Knecht Rupprecht," who symbolized the gaiety and feasting of Christmas Eve, have been transformed into gift bringers. Gifts, which formerly had been made by hand and selected with great care, are now supplanted by purchased gifts, lavishly wrapped and sent by mail.[8] The master of revels, Santa Claus, has become a patron of children and the family. Older folk customs of convivial drinking and song have changed. Christmas is now a family celebration centering around a gift-laden tree. Women now buy and prepare most of the gifts. Even in stores where men wrap and prepare merchandise for mailing and delivery throughout the year, women are hired as gift wrappers for the Christmas season.

Santa, once a Falstaffian knight or a kindly father, now has a soft androgynous body. He is fat, jolly, old—no longer masculine, but maternal. The Christmas woman herself is transformed. During December, erotic, romantic, and occupational roles must be replaced in advertising (as in life) by maternal and familial images. This strengthens other festive images of the American Madonna, who gives, not her breast, but gifts bought for money. Santa no longer comes down the chimney; he comes to State Street,[9] where he is enthroned in the toy departments of the stores to hear children's wishes for gifts. The master of revels is now a confessor of hidden desires for gifts that only money will buy. The older folk Christmas revels, so repugnant to the Puritans and banished from the home by the ascendancy of mother and child, have been revived in business life. Work slackens, time for shopping is allowed, vacations and holidays are given, a Christmas bonus distributed, and office parties are held. The older American custom among male workers of drinking and joking together on the job throughout the day before Christmas has now been changed into a party where inhibitions of rank and sex are forgotten in drinking, song, jokes, pranks, and sex play.

The infusion of money with supernatural values, and the use, in turn, of money as communication of such value, can also be seen in our funeral practices. Few funerals in the Middle West are conducted now in homes. Yet, as late as 1910 it was difficult, and sometimes impossible, to get permission to remove a body from the home. Families insisted on bringing their dead from hospitals, or wherever death occurred, to the house as soon as possible. Funeral parlors were used by those who had no home of their own, or had no friends or relatives willing to offer their homes. In the home the body was laid out by the bereaved, or by friends in the neighborhood experienced in handling the dead. Washed, dressed in the best or favorite suit or dress, the body was moved to the parlor, where it was put on view even before the casket arrived. Friends visited the bereaved home as soon as news of the death reached them; members of the family seated themselves in the living room to receive condolences. Each caller tiptoed into the parlor to see the corpse. The kitchen was soon piled high with cakes, pies, and meats brought by friends and neighbors. Services at the home were long, solemn, and sad. The mystery of death was a promise of eternal life. Life was tragic and sinful, death was a welcome release from suffering and guilt.

By 1900 funeral homes in Chicago were already advertising their "homelike rooms" and elegant parlors. By 1950 the funeral chapel had become a standard part of nearly all urban and many town and village funeral homes. Funeral "artists," working from a photograph of the deceased, restore the corpse to an appearance of health and life. Powder, rouge, lipstick, mascara, and other beauty aids are used to fit the body for the elegance of the casket and its floral backdrop. The custom of sitting with the dead and holding nightlong wakes is no longer thought proper to the "routine of modern funeral home operations." Now the funeral ceremony is held in the funeral home as well as in the church. Funeral homes of the 1950s, unlike those of 1880, do not emphasize the "parlor" and do not stress "hominess." They are built around the chapel, "modern in every particular, air-conditioned throughout with the latest development in livery equipment (limousines), luxuriously appointed rooms, beautifully landscaped grounds where everything moves smoothly with a reserved elegance." And as the undertakers' advertisement goes on to say: "All this costs no more than an ordinary funeral." The architecture of funeral homes varies widely from Early Colonial to "modern." But, whatever the style, the building must be imposing, accessible to transportation, highly public, and kept in good order. Funeral homes are community showpieces, a fitting background for the funeral director who thinks of himself as a person who carries out his vocation in neat, sanitary, dignified, and even "beautiful" surroundings.

The "elegant reserve" and "dignity" of the funeral home is not created through ageless and traditional forms. The archaic forms of "conspicuous waste" which Veblen found so characteristic of devout observances in Chicago in 1890, and which characterized the old family mansion taken over as a funeral home, are now replaced by funeral homes which are "the most modern in all America" or "new modern funeral homes." The crude coffin of colonial times and the pine box of pioneer days have been replaced by ornate caskets. Casket styles are changing more rapidly each year. A funeral director who bought caskets by the hundreds in 1910 would now consider ten caskets a precarious inventory. The undertaker—now a mortician, mortuary consultant, funeral counselor, or more generally, a funeral director —no longer takes the corpse wrapped in a shroud to a graveyard in a hearse. He takes the "patient" in a funeral car or casket coach, dressed in a slumber robe, from the reposing room to a memorial park. Here there is no ground burial but mausoleum entombment in pretentious and costly tombs of every conceivable style from Gothic to Modern.

Death, like the celebration of the Nativity, has been made salable, and hence subject to the mystery of money. We now bury our dead "in style" —that is, pecuniary style. Obsolescence in products and services necessary to decent burial of the dead is a matter of style, not decay. Long before funeral cars wear out they become obsolete, and long before funeral homes actually begin to look shabby many funeral directors feel the urge to redecorate. We submit to the rising costs of funerals because we believe there is a direct connection between the money spent on the funeral and the respect given to the dead. In this moment of symbolic transformation, quantity becomes *quality* and the hierarchical mystery of money fastens its spell upon us.

It is a mistake to think of the pecuniary expression of Christmas and of death as "secularization." Death has lost none of its mystery or power. The clerk who spends several hundred dollars, which he must borrow and pay back in small installments, for his father's funeral is not "secularizing" funeral rites. Funerals have shifted from churches and homes to commercial funeral homes because spending money in itself has become a way of showing respect, and now, in our time, of showing reverence. The indigent family which sinks further into debt to provide an expensive funeral is practicing a kind of mortification. Such spending is a penance, a self-punishment. For in going into debt the debtor pledges many future hours of work to his creditor. He thus pledges himself to present and future sacrifice. And he does it in a highly public fashion before guests at the funeral and those who accompany the body to the grave. These serve as witnesses to his heroic spending which will be paid for in many months of toil.

As theologians tell us, Christ's law of mortification implies something more than mere self-restraint; it implies the use of what Jeremy Taylor calls "rudeness" against oneself. Christian temperance implies the control of appetite at those points where its demands are most importunate and difficult to resist. The aim of the temperate Christian is positive, not negative. He aims not merely at the subjugation of greed, but at the cultivation of moral and spiritual power. He makes circumstances subservient to his spiritual progress and "passes through them upwards and onwards to God." Possession of money, to the modern "steward of the Lord," means that he has struggled against temptation to sloth. Going into debt to bury our dead is a pious risk, and in the supernatural as well as the social realm risk-taking brings us glory. Willingness to take risks is our grasp of faith. In a system of hierarchy based on money risk is always honored so long as it is risk of money.

Chicago businessmen, the new "feudal barons" of America, as Chicagoans themselves called them, understood that money must become radiant and mysterious to become a powerful symbol of community. If the businessman did not spend lavishly, and his artists did not publicize it, no one would know the glory of wealth. If Chicagoans refused to believe that money brought success in courtship, dignity in citizenship, and majesty in social relations, its power would vanish. But such belief rested not simply on the possession of money, but on its communication and glamorization as a symbol of community in heaven as here below. The mysterious power of celestial symbols, as Chicagoans were quick to understand, does not lie in their remoteness or exclusiveness, but in their promise of a higher life. Money must be accessible to everyone, but beside the promise of equality stands the promise of inequality. At the moment I spend I am as good as the next man, yet at the same time I am better than those who do not, or will not, spend. In every stage of spending there is immanence of a higher life, what we call our ever-increasing standard of living. This "upward way" of money does not end in a state of financial bliss where everybody will have "enough" and be content. For in the American capitalistic paradise, discontent is truly divine. Waste itself becomes a virtue. Saving betrays lack of faith in the orgiastic future of an ever-spending capitalism.

But the mystery of money, which was so well exploited by Chicago businessmen, was also completely debunked in Chicago. For if Chicago was the business center of the West it was also the center of radical and searching thought over the value of business to democracy. The struggles between businessmen and their adversaries in Chicago soon reached an intensity unknown to any city in America. Money's greatest evil, to the opponents of the businessman, was that it destroyed equality. Without equality life was feudal, and democracy nothing but a haunting memory of an agrarian and village past. Was the "money baron," Chicagoans asked, any better than the feudal baron? Was the surrender of freedom in Pullman towns the price we must pay under capitalism for a life without want and starvation?

Notes

[1] F. Scott Fitzgerald, *The Great Gatsby* (New York: Bantam Books, 1945), p. 128.

[2] Mrs. Leiter's "social ambitions," as the Chicago press put it, were considered one of the reasons for Leiter's break with Field. Social prestige for Field and his fellow businessmen, if not always for their wives, was local prestige.

[3] *Sister Carrie* (New York: Dodge, 1907), pp. 197–98. See also the scene in *A Book about Myself* (New York: Boni and Liveright, 1922) at the end of Chapter VIII, where Dreiser describes his own enchantment over the "new, sunny prosperity" of the Chicago of the nineties. Elias, Dreiser's biographer, tells us of Dreiser's belief that a satin-lined overcoat with gloves and cane would make him irresistible to women.

[4] Quoted in Robert H. Elias, *Theodore Dreiser: Apostle of Nature* (New York: Alfred A. Knopf, 1949), pp. 175–76.

[5] Edith Wharton, *The House of Mirth* (New York: Scribner's, 1905), pp. 22–25.

[6] It was *not* only radicals like Henry Demarest Lloyd, academicians like Veblen, or novelists like Fuller who pointed this out. Henry Ford argued that money is a means to the "creative" businessman. "Wall Street Bankers" (evil men, all) teach us that money is an end in itself. Ford insisted he wanted to "get Fords to the people," not to amass wealth. The new value added here is expense. The function of advertising magic is to change all values into money and then to help us to become dissatisfied with how we spend our money. This was well understood in Chicago by 1895. The problem as discussed in Chicago (notably by Veblen) was whether it was good for human relationships to have so much time and energy put into being able to "afford to pay the difference."

[7] In his study, *The American Christmas* (New York: Macmillan, 1954), James H. Barnett gives the following figures as percentages of yearly sales made up by December sales: Building materials 7.0; Department stores 14.8; Drug stores 11.0; Eating and drinking places 8.9; Family and other apparel 15.0; General merchandising 14.5; Jewelry 22.7; Liquor 15.0; Men's clothing and furnishings 16.0; Women's apparel and accessories 13.1. If sales were constant, each month would account for approximately 8.3 of the annual total.

[8] A "boughten" gift was thought vulgar or common unless given by a bachelor or someone who could not make his own.

[9] In 1959 Santa arrived in a snorkel, an elevated, bucketlike platform which the fire department uses to reach into the upper stories of buildings. Indignant letters to the press castigated this as bad taste. Santa now arrives in his traditional sled drawn by reindeers—even on State Street.

PART THREE

The Struggle for Power in Chicago

14

Feudal Forms of Control: George H. Pullman and His Model Industrial Town

From 1871 to 1891, the years between the great Fire and the Fair, Chicago was the staging ground of a new world architecture. During these years engineers and architects struggled to create a grammar of form at the same time as they struggled to define its meaning for democratic community life. Sullivan believed the architect to be as important to democracy as the businessman, politician, priest, and educator. Even those who, like Burnham, disagreed with Sullivan's style agreed with the importance of the struggle to make architecture an art and science of community life. With all its timid classicism, Burnham's Chicago Plan is a great assertion of the social importance of architecture. His Chicago Plan of 1906 is a plan for an urban people, just as Beman's Pullman Town Plan was a plan for an ideal community of workers.

John Root, too, was very explicit about the democratic virtues of life in Chicago and responsibilities of the architect in creating and preserving them.[1] Henry Ives Cobb turned away from the principles of the Chicago school to produce a Gothic campus at the University of Chicago, but he believed that a university campus must be thought of as a community. The university was unique among American universities for its plan (if not for its architecture) and its provisions for future expansion. The stage set for shopping in the Chicago Loop was in itself a great engineering and architectural achievement, whatever the intentions of those who paid for it. Chicago architects disagreed about design, but all agreed on the significance of architecture to the quality of human relationships in the city. This conviction was shared by Chicago writers, artists, and scholars, such as Herrick, Fuller, Veblen, Dewey, and Mead. Democratic society must be created and sustained through art, as well as economics, politics, and religion.

Discussion of design in Root, Burnham, Sullivan, and Wright is moral and social as well as aesthetic. Sullivan stresses continuously that a building is an act, a *social* act. In his writing, "function" is a social as well as a formal term; there is no discussion in Sullivan of "machines to live in." The function of a building is good in so far as it enhances humane qualities in democratic relationships. Such discussion involved Sullivan and others, in much new and complex thought on the function of art in society. For if architecture were to determine human relations in the city, and if urban democratic human relations, in turn, were to determine architecture, each must be defined in its own terms as well as in terms of the other. Sullivan struggled to clarify his understanding of the relation between art and society. His defeat by the classicists deepened his concern with the effect of architecture on human relationships. He shared this with other Chicagoans like Dewey, Veblen, and Mead. Sullivan understood clearly that *how* we express ourselves determines *what* we express. Democracy, he argued, must be related to forms of art as well as the contents or "forces" of economics, politics, and religion.

Sullivan and Wright accept Jeffersonian and Whitmanesque ideals of American democracy. There is little significant discussion over political, ethical, or moral problems as such in their writings. And what there is, as in Sullivan's *Democracy: A Man Search* is important mainly for what it tells us about Sullivan's architecture. Wright, too, who wrote and talked all his long life about democracy, said nothing very new about the political principles of democracy. But what Sullivan, the master, and Wright, his pupil, did say that was new, and is still new, is that the fate of democracy would be determined by architecture. Their discussion, like all great discussion about art in society, is about the *morality* of form.

A bad building horrified Sullivan. His horror was moral as well as aesthetic; a bad architect was not simply a bad artist, but a traitor to his people. Like Jefferson (and Wright), Sullivan held himself responsible for his acts, and believed that until we master ourselves we cannot master others. But he believed that democratic leaders must be responsive to their people and rule through persuasion created in open and free communication. Leaders of architecture in democracy (like Jefferson) who ruled by reason, and particularly the reasoned imagination of the artist, not those who ruled by magic and fear, would be the glory and salvation of architecture and thus of democracy. Architects must make clear to themselves what architectural form meant to democracy, for only then could they provide a democratic community with forms necessary to its existence as a community of free men. Sullivan spoke out against bad buildings on every occasion, and he spoke with the vehemence and force of the prophet and seer.

Frank Lloyd Wright's son, John, who knew great discourse about architecture, describes Sullivan's prophetic talk. He visited Sullivan when he was still occupying his offices on the top floor of the Auditorium Tower. "The fifty-board drafting room adjoining was without a single draftsman—no secretary, no office force, just Louis H. Sullivan—alone." Since he had no work as an architect, he was expressing himself the only way he could—in writing about architecture. As John finished telling Sullivan about himself, Sullivan sat in silence, eyeing him quizzically. He then picked up a manuscript and in his low musical voice read to the young architect. In the visits that followed, the young architect listened to the greatest utterance he ever heard on the mission of the architect in democratic society.[2]

Sullivan spoke to Wright's son, as he spoke to all who would listen, as a prophet of democracy. But he was a new kind of prophet, the art prophet. The people of Sullivan's generation in the Middle West knew great political utterance on democracy. They had listened to Lincoln, Douglas, Bryan, and Altgeld. They read and loved *Huckleberry Finn.* Now they were hearing an architect who told his people that until Chicago was a city of good buildings, it could not be a city of good people. The salvation of Chicago, and of America, lay in the imagination of the architect. In the fire and exaltation of great architecture American cities would find their spirit, just as agrarian America found its soul in Thoreau's *Walden,* Whitman's *Leaves of Grass,* and Lincoln's speeches.

Root, Burnham, Sullivan, Wright, and other members of the Chicago school wrote and spoke much about architecture. They spoke to all kinds of groups and published essays in magazines ranging from architectural and engineers' journals to contractors' magazines. They founded the *Inland Architect* and *Western Architect* to give Western architects a professional voice. The publics they wanted to reach were not those of the established art groups, nor the cosmopolites of high society. Their ideal clients in Chicago were men and women who had enough courage in themselves, and enough love for the creation of living art, to trust design problems to their own architects. They wrote for their own profession, and above all for young architects.[3] While they inspired as prophets, they reasoned as critics. Sullivan's prophetic and lyric outbursts in poetry and prose are not a flight from reason. His mysticism, like Wright's, is the mysticism of action governed by reason in society. It is in every sense worldly, because its values are social and of a present, not a Utopian or Edenic, society. Imagination, emotion, and the heart transcend the intellect, because the end or consummation of action in democratic society is conceived through the imagination. Because man can imagine the ends of his acts he is able to create his own environment. As Sullivan said, "Deep down within [man] lies that power we call Imagination, the power instantly or slowly to picture forth, the power to act in advance of action; the power that knows no limitations, no boundaries, that renders vivid both giving and receiving; the inscrutable dynamic power that energizes all other powers. Think of man as Imagination."[4]

Sullivan taught that democracy without a poetic architecture degenerates into feudal barbarism. But at the same time he argued that poetry removed from democratic action becomes sterile. He did not think Chicago businessmen who commissioned bad buildings were practical, for in setting false stages for business they ridiculed themselves and degraded the symbolic power of money. A bank that looked like a Roman temple inspired awe and fear, but this, Sullivan argued, would eventually alienate people from business and banking. A democratic people wanted their bankers to treat them as equals, not inferiors. Nor did he respect academicians who judged the past so glibly but could not, or would not, judge the present. The essence of architecture was the creation of a poetry of action which would enhance the quality of life within space. Architectural space was space to be acted within, not to be looked at, and certainly never to be made so inhuman that movement within it must be reduced merely to efficient movement. A building, a city—all architecture was a great stage whose structure *determined* action as a relationship between people, not simply movement in space and time.

Sullivan did not reach such conclusions alone. Chicago raged with debates on the political meaning of urban democracy, the role of architecture in democracy, as well as the problem of form in architecture. The passion and depth of these discussions swept young architects to heights of creative tension unique to Chicago. Sullivan did not think of himself as a lonesome genius among primitive giants or as determined by the "anonymous force" of technology. Nor did he think of the businessmen of Chicago as simpletons who could be tricked into patronizing good design. The Chicago braggarts whose favorite phrase was "biggest in the world" amused him at first, but he soon came to believe, like Dreiser, that Chicago's great businessmen embodied a new kind of social power. As he said: "These men had vision. What they saw was real; they saw it as destiny." [5] Sullivan accepted these visionary Chicagoans as his peers in strength and will, if not in art. He found some of their visions evil, but never trivial.

In the end these feudal barons of Chicago, as Sullivan and Veblen called them, killed Sullivan. But Sullivan's spirit, like that of Lincoln, Mark Twain, Grant, Veblen, and later Wright, reached greatness because it was challenged by great adversaries. Both Sullivan and his adversaries were fighting for a principle, the principle of democracy, whose value was never in doubt. Sullivan knew despair at his death, as he knew rage and hate in life, over his neglect by his own people. But he never knew the horror of the modern artist, who has seen men torture and kill each other in the greatest numbers and in the most terrible ways known to history. The modern artist doubts himself because he doubts the truth of art. He fights despair, not against the Philistines, but against the absurdity of having struggled at all.

George Pullman, who typified for Chicagoans and the Middle West, the feudal baron at his best—and worst—was a powerful adversary. He was a stern and pious plutocrat, and, like Field, a man with little humor. Pullman believed in the power of architecture. Making available well-designed homes, parks, good schools, shopping centers, churches, and recreation halls would reduce discontent among workers. He had seen Chicago become the capital of a militant labor movement and had heard himself and other Chicago businessmen called tyrants and bloodsuckers by the Chicago radicals. He joined Chicago businessmen in their struggle with labor, a struggle which had broken into open war on the streets of the city. Pullman was as determined as Leiter, Field, and Armour to dominate labor. But as a feudal baron he was determined that feudal rights should be balanced by feudal duties. He refused to follow other members of the Pullman board, who argued for the construction of cheap frame houses which workers could rent for a nominal sum, and to permit haphazard construction of houses and tenements by landlords, workers, and speculators. He set himself resolutely to the task of building a beautiful town that would be exemplary in a time when living conditions for labor were notoriously bad.

There was nothing philanthropic about Pullman's plans. If Pullman workers could pay rent to landlords, why should they not do this for Pullman? Pullman did not think of his workers as customers—this enlightened plutocratic view of the worker did not come until the days of Ford. Pullman was committed to the paternal ideal of business stewardship. The workers were his "wards" who needed to be protected from "baneful influences." For providing his workers with a community free from such influences Pullman asked for a return of six per cent on the actual investment of capital. Any profits made from increased values on surrounding land were to go to the company as a reward for its initial risk of capital. In return for a secure life in a beautiful community, workers were expected to be "faithful" to the company, and the company in turn expected to profit by increased production from such loyal workers and from increasing values in land and rent. "The object in building Pullman," Pullman stated clearly, "was the establishment of a great manufacturing business on the most substantial basis possible, recognizing as we did, and do now, that the working people are the most important element which enters into a successful operation of any manufacturing enterprise."

To accomplish this the company purchased more than four thousand acres of prairie land, the bulk of it comprising a compact unit on the western shore of Lake Calumet, some twelve miles south of the business district of Chicago.[6] Chicago was believed to be sufficiently far removed to allow the experiment to be conducted free of any "debasing" influences. "We decided to build in close proximity to the shops homes for workingmen of such character and surroundings as would prove so attractive as to cause the best class of mechanics to seek that place for employment in preference to others. We also desired to establish the place on such a basis as would exclude all baneful influences, believing that such a policy would result in the greatest measure of success, both from a commercial point of view and also—what was equally important, or perhaps of greater importance—in a tendency toward continued elevation and improvement of the condition not only of the working people themselves, but of their children growing up around them." [7]

Pullman prepared carefully. Prior to the founding of Pullman there were in Europe three active company towns: Saltaire in England; Guise in France; and Essen in Germany. These received wide publicity during the seventies and eighties. Saltaire has been suggested [8] as Pullman's model. We know that Pullman visited England in 1873, and it seems probable that he visited Saltaire while there. But large-scale planning was not new to Chicago. By 1884 Chicago had created the greatest urban American system of parks and boulevards.[9] In 1890 these parks, comprising almost two thousand acres, stretched for many miles along the lake front. As early as 1865 "Packing-town," as the stockyards area was called, covered 120 acres. By 1896 the yards comprised 340 acres, and with its contiguous area made up a neighborhood of forty thousand men, women, and children. Fifty thousand cattle, two hundred thousand hogs, thirty thousand sheep, and five hundred horses could be moved, watered, fed and processed at one time. Over sixty thousand animals could be slaughtered in one day.

Pullman brought the young architect, Solon Spencer Beman, to Chicago in 1879. He commissioned him to design the model town and to serve as general supervisor of all construction work. Pond, who served as a draftsman for Beman in the building of Pullman, tells us that Beman was interested in architectural planning. This involved designing building groups related according to some assumption of common needs. Such needs were poorly understood, if they were understood at all, by the school architects of the time. But Chicago had never depended much on formally trained architects. John B. Sherman, who laid out the stockyards and served for twenty-five years as a South Park Commissioner, had no formal schooling. Yet he planned and supervised a community in which many features of assembly line production were developed long before they were used elsewhere. Cyrus

Residences built in 1880–84 by George M. Pullman for Pullman employees.
Courtesy Chicago Historical Society

Hall McCormick was not an architect, yet his plant layouts became models. In early press accounts of the McCormick Chicago River Works of the fifties we read of

> . . . little wheels of steel attached to horizontal, upright and oblique shafts. . . . Rude pieces of wood without form or comeliness are hourly approaching them upon little railways, as if drawn thither by some mysterious attraction. They touch them and *presto,* grooved, scalloped, rounded, on they go, with a little help from an attendant, who seems to have an easy time of it, and transferred to another railway when down comes a guillotine-like contrivance—they are morticed, bored, and whirled away, where the tireless planes without hands, like a boatswain, whistle the rough plank into polish, and it is turned out smoothed, shaped, and fitted for its place in the Reaper or the Harvester.[10]

Beman, like Sullivan, was stirred by the problem central to Chicago design: how to resolve the conflict between engineering and architecture. Engineers like Jenney, Baumann, and Adler did not think in styles, but in terms of problems. Their relationships with clients were not over the "art" but the "use" of structure. Sherman wanted to use gravity flow for handling animal carcasses in the stockyards. How to meet this problem, not the "style" of the yards, determined how they were built. The problem of continuous production was a problem of how to keep slaughtered animals moving to the worker. McCormick wanted the same kind of movement, but his problem was one of continuous assembly, not the disassembly involved in cutting up a whole carcass. After the Fire, businessmen needed great amounts of space for production, storage, distribution, and sales. Chicago businessmen like Pullman and promoters like Peck, who made the Auditorium possible, knew how to create large organizations. They gave architects the kind of leadership required for working in the groups which made possible large building and planning enterprises. By 1880, when Pullman began the construction of his village, there were already in Chicago several great private and public achievements which were the result of successful collaboration between engineers, architects, businessmen, labor, and public officials. "Chicago construction," in these years meant different things to architects, engineers, artists, critics, and philosophers. But to the bankers, as to the people, it meant the ability to create large buildings, such as the Auditorium; whole communities, such as Pullman; the Chicago parks; the World's Fair; and finally Burnham's Chicago Plan of 1906.[11]

In the years following the Fire several buildings covering whole blocks, known by such names as the Portland Block and the Borden Block, were built. These enormous structures, like Richardson's Marshall Field Warehouse, brought the large masonry-wall building as far as it could go in terms of land prices in a booming city. By 1880 Chicago architects faced an impasse.

They knew how to build large buildings along the ground, but they did not know how to build them in the air. The syndicates of businessmen who organized money and labor for these large buildings could no longer make profit out of buildings that required hundreds of feet of frontage on streets where land costs were high and going higher every day. But, whatever the costs, businessmen needed enormous amounts of space, and the business district must be highly concentrated to be convenient to customers and the staffs of workers required to service them. The problem was clear enough, if the solution was not.

In magnitude and in the types of obstacles which had to be overcome, the building of Pullman village, which began in 1880 with Beman in charge, was the equal of the largest and best engineering and architectural enterprises of the time. An example of this was the handling of sewage. Surface water could be disposed of easily enough by laying pipes that would insure a rapid gravity discharge into Lake Calumet. Sewage could have been pumped into Lake Michigan, but this required over six miles of pipe. A sewage farm was established three miles south of the town. All sewage was carried by force of gravity into a large reservoir under the water tower, and from there it was immediately pumped to the model farm for distribution. All land was carefully underdrained with three- and four-inch farm tile; hydrants were located conveniently for the distribution of sewage by means of hose. Solid waste was absorbed by the soil and growing vegetation, and the water was carried off through drains to Lake Calumet. By 1882 the farm was self-supporting. In 1883 it yielded 8 per cent on the investment. Almost any crop could be produced on the irrigated, well-fertilized soil.

The building of Pullman was one of the great architectural and engineering dramas of Chicago. During the spring of 1880 thousands of laborers were employed. Some traveled daily from Chicago in special trains over the Illinois Central Railroad. A roughly constructed frame building called "Hotel de Grab" furnished meals. Pullman did not contract for the building of the town. The Pullman Company hired its own workmen, established its own carpentry shops and brickyards. Sashes, doors, paneling, sills, and moldings were prefabricated in the shops. Clay was dredged from the bottom of Lake Calumet to make the millions of cream-colored bricks which the homes of the village required. Construction costs were watched carefully, and only in a few buildings, such as the theater and the library, was there any approach to luxury. Despite a very severe winter, work progressed rapidly. In January of 1881 the first permanent resident moved in. By April the Pullman car shops were in operation; by May three hundred and fifty people were living in Pullman. A fully developed town was in operation by 1884.

Pullman homes differed widely. The brickyard dwellings (which Pullman denied were a part of the town) were small shanties without sewer or other conveniences. The tenement neighborhood on Fulton Street consisted of ten large buildings. These three-story buildings contained two- and four-room flats; each building accommodated from twelve to forty-eight families. Tenement families had only one water faucet for each group of five families and the same toilet for two or more families. In sharp contrast to these were the spacious nine-room homes for Pullman executives in the vicinity of the Florence Hotel. These were steam heated and equipped with a large fireplace, a bathroom, many closets, a laundry, and large bay windows. In 1885 there were fourteen hundred tenements; by 1894 there were about eighteen hundred. All the dwellings were of brick with stone trimmings and roofed with slate. The typical dwelling was a two-story row house. Houses were built in blocks of two or more, except for a dozen of the very best dwellings. A two-story row house consisted of five rooms furnished with a sink, water tap, toilet facilities, and ample closet and pantry space. All had roomy, well-ventilated basements; they were furnished with gas, water, and excellent sewage facilities. They were designed to have an abundance of fresh air and sunlight, and to be clean and livable. They were priced at seventeen hundred dollars, including a charge of three hundred dollars for the lot. The company sodded the lawns, inclosed the back yard with a high fence, and, toward the rear near the macadamized alley, built a coal-and-wood shed.

When completed at a cost of eight million dollars, Pullman became one of the sights of Chicago. Visitors heaped praise on the harmony between architecture, landscaping, and engineering. One visitor said: "I stepped from the cars. Beauty, grace and art met me on every hand. I had seen landscape gardening elsewhere. Here was also architectural gardening." The Chicago *Inter Ocean* reflected the judgment of many newspapers and magazines when it reported in 1885: "It is famous already as one of the wonders of the West. Splendid provision has been made for the present comfort of its eight thousand residents, its four thousand workmen. . . . More completely and on a larger scale than was probably ever before attempted, there is seen here a sympathetic blending of the useful and beautiful." [12] In 1896 the town of Pullman was honored by the jury of the second International Hygienic and Pharmaceutical Exposition held at Prague, Bohemia. After weighing the merits of various outstanding towns, the committee judged Pullman to be the most perfect in the world, and awarded George Pullman two magnificent medals and a handsome diploma. In the matter of homes, sanitation, water system, shops, public halls, churches, and parks, the town of Pullman was without an equal.

Although Pullman was highly industrialized, the average death rate from 1881 to 1895 ranged from 7 to 15 per thousand, in contrast with average rates of 22.5 per thousand for other American cities. A report to the state of Illinois in 1895 disclosed that there had been no cases of cholera, no yellow fever or typhoid, only two cases of smallpox, and a few of diphtheria and scarlatina. Saloons and brothels were strictly prohibited. Everything possible was done to discourage drinking. There was little drunkenness in the town, and all agreed that moral conditions in Pullman were very satisfactory. Education on all levels was encouraged. Every child was assured of an eighth-grade education. A free kindergarten was opened to all children between the ages of four and six. The school board planned in 1884 to provide high school studies whenever demand arose. This was finally done in an evening school. Adult education was fostered by the Pullman Library, which was dedicated with great ceremony in the spring of 1883. The Library was given five thousand volumes by George Pullman. Great care was taken to create a good collection of books. By 1895 the well-balanced collection had reached eighty-five hundred volumes. Study groups, extension courses, and lectures were organized and given in the library.

Recreation of all kinds was encouraged. The Arcade Theatre was opened by an audience of three hundred notables in full dress. Only high-quality plays were given, and some of the best theatrical talent in the world performed in it. The Pullman Military Band soon became famous. In 1893 there were at least forty lodges, clubs, and other social organizations in the village. The Pullman Athletic Association with ten thousand dollars in its treasury, promoted regattas, cycling contests, track meets, cricket matches, baseball games, and other sports. Spring Games were held on Memorial Day. These were fashioned after the Olympic Games. The climax of the games was the bicycle race, in which over four hundred cyclists competed for three thousand dollars in prize money.

The diversity of Pullman's population demanded great tact and skill in every sort of community enterprise. In 1884 fifty-one per cent of the population was foreign born. This increased to 72 per cent in 1892. In this year Scandinavians made up 23 per cent, British and German 12 per cent, Dutch 10 per cent, and the Irish 5 per cent of the population. Large numbers of the village population were unnaturalized. In 1887 there were eight hundred British subjects who made no attempt to become American citizens. George Pullman decided on the creation of a union church as the only way to meet the diverse religious needs of such a population. He built the Green Stone Church, the "most beautiful structure in Pullman," as contemporary accounts tell us. This was made large enough to satisfy the needs of every religious denomination. George Pullman stubbornly refused to allow the construction of any other church building in the town.

Pullman identified himself very closely with his town. It represented for him a triumph of engineering, architecture, and what Flinn's Chicago guidebook of 1891 called "strict business principles." It also proved to Pullman, and to many of his contemporaries, that through the reward of profit, business could produce a good society. Pullman and his apologists argued that benevolence, far from being costly, actually was profitable. The Pullman worker was more productive because he was given a richer community life and protected from "baneful influences." As Pullman said, "During the eleven years the town has been in existence, the Pullman workingman has developed into a distinctive type—distinct in appearance, in tidiness of dress, in fact in all the external indications of self-respect. . . . It is within the mark to say that a representative gathering of Pullman workmen would be quite forty per cent better in evidence of thrift and refinement and in all the outward indications of a wholesome habit of life, than would be a representative gathering of any corresponding group of workingmen which could be assembled elsewhere in the country." [13]

Pullman thus proved, as was pointed out in many public lectures and newspaper stories, that it paid in hard, practical dollars and cents to raise the living standard of labor. Dr. David Swing, the renowned liberal pastor of Central Church in Chicago, contrasted the benevolence of Pullman and his civic devotion with that of a New York millionaire. "There is nothing inexplicable or mysterious in the gold applied by the founder of this library," Swing told his audience of prominent citizens on the opening of the Pullman Library. "But should this gentleman give a Vanderbilt Ball [as was done in New York] we might well be amazed, for there a hundred thousand dollars, less or more, were lavished on the last point between something and nothing. . . . Such pageants should come but rarely into our world, and indeed they are fading away. They were frequent in Rome in times of war and plunder, but as reason advances, such applications of money and labor decline. We hope the rich men of the West will always prefer libraries, and parks, and music temples, and even good theatres to the perishable display of the ballroom." [14]

Pullman soon became a national shrine of paternalistic businessmen. Thousands of distinguished men and women visited the town. George Pullman was particularly anxious that businessmen see it. In 1891 he played host to a distinguished group of American businessmen, including Cornelius Vanderbilt and Chauncey M. Depew. In 1893 the model town was overrun by Chicago Fair visitors, at least ten thousand of whom were foreigners. University professors and their students journeyed to Pullman to see the new industrial Utopia. George Pullman often invited groups to use his parlor car to take them to Pullman. Here they were greeted by officials who pictured the Pullman experiment as a model for all American business. Many visitors left deeply convinced that a new era in industrialism was beginning in Chicago, where so much that was new and hopeful for the future of America was coming into being.

Notes

[1] Root talks about the gentility of design, but this should not be confused with the genteel tradition of the East. He thought a businessman could be a gentleman and that money could find a home in American art and life as well as in politics and business. A house, he said, should not "shout." Design, not ornament, and composition, not costly façades, should determine Chicago buildings, domestic and commercial alike. Root, unlike Sullivan, welcomed commissions to do houses, and in his homes of the eighties he is far more radical than Sullivan.

[2] John Lloyd Wright, *My Father Who Is on Earth* (New York: Putnam, 1946), p. 104. Sullivan's spoken comments, as passed on by those who knew him, were often unprintable. His rage against those he thought were betraying architecture is still very much alive in Chicago tales and legends about Sullivan. Sullivan was a man of great rages and deep hate, but he laughed and loved deeply too. To young architects trying to be good architects, he was the soul of kindness. *Kindergarten Chats,* like Dewey's *The School and Society* and *The Child and the Curriculum,* is written from a teacher's point of view. But Sullivan as a teacher is very different from Dewey. He teases and jokes; he allows his students to talk back and even tease him. He turns irony on his own rage, as he does on all Chicago society. He is always genial and sometimes merry. The student is a comrade in art. *Democracy: A Man Search* (1906) has none of this humor and geniality. Here Sullivan speaks as an angry prophet without honor in his own land.

[3] Sullivan disdained architects who were not completely and devoutly committed to the glory of architecture. He despised draftsmen. When anyone close to him seemed to deny the nobility of the architect and the importance of architecture to democracy he turned on them with cold fury. He never forgave Adler for giving up his practice to sell elevators. He refused to hear Wright out when his great and proud pupil stood before him to confess shame over designing the Harlan house outside office hours, thus breaking his contract with Adler and Sullivan. Their estrangement of twenty years was overcome at last, but Wright was haunted all his days by his master's rejection, for Wright knew that Sullivan was the soul of architecture and that in failing his master, he failed himself.

[4] Louis H. Sullivan, *The Autobiography of an Idea* (New York: Press of the American Institute of Architects, 1926), p. 269. Chapter XIV, "Face to Face," summarizes Sullivan's ideas on man.

[5] It was easy enough to be amused by Chicago braggarts of the eighties. But amusement often passed to wonder, and sometimes deep affection. For their boasts sometimes became prophecies. As William James said, "The rest of the world has made merry over the legendary Chicago man's saying that 'Chicago hasn't had time to get round

to culture yet, but when she does strike her, she'll make her hum.'" But only a few years later the prophecy was fulfilled in a dazzling manner by the creation of a "Chicago School of Philosophy," as James called the work of John Dewey, George Herbert Mead, James H. Tuft, and Addison Moore, who founded the Chicago School of Philosophy during the decade from 1894 to 1904.

[6] Pullman expected Lake Calumet to become a great inland port area. His "rosy predictions" were considered "fantastic" until the opening in 1959 of the St. Lawrence Seaway, which now makes Lake Calumet a world port.

[7] Taken from Pullman's testimony before the United States Strike Commission in 1894. Quoted from *Chicago: Its History and Its Builders,* by J. Seymour Currey, 3 vols. (Chicago: S. J. Clarke, 1918), Vol. III, p. 205.

[8] Grant argues that Pullman used Saltaire as a model. See Thomas B. Grant, "Pullman and Its Lessons," *American Journal of Politics,* V (1894), 190–204.

[9] As we shall see in later discussion, both the parks and the stockyards were planned in terms of *movement* of animals and men.

[10] Quoted from *The Century of the Reaper* by Cyrus McCormick (Boston and New York: Appleton, 1931), p. 37. By 1856 the McCormick works could produce forty reapers a day.

[11] As we shall see, it was Chicago's ability to plan and build such large-scale projects that had much to do with winning the struggle in 1891 to be the site of the World's Columbian Exposition.

[12] Quoted from Almond Lindsey, *The Pullman Strike: The Story of a Unique Experiment and of a Great Labor Upheaval* (Chicago: University of Chicago Press,' 1942), p. 48.

[13] *The Story of Pullman,* pp. 23–24. (A pamphlet distributed by the Pullman Company at its exhibit at the World's Columbian Exposition, Chicago, 1893.)

[14] The Vanderbilt Ball of March 26, 1883, which took place a few weeks before the opening of the Pullman Library, was the most ornate and expensive party in the history of American high society until 1897, the year of the Bradley Martin Ball. Every New York paper gave it precedence over all other news. It soon became nationally famous and was made into a symbol of the "feudal arrogance and waste" of the idle rich. In 1892 Mrs. Vanderbilt spent nine million dollars on furnishing and building Marble House, greatest of Newport villas. This was more than George Pullman spent on the whole town of Pullman. The contrast between the spending of Chicago and New York plutocrats was noted by many observers.

15

Chicago Labor Fights Back: From the Haymarket Riots to the Pullman Strike

Bᴜᴛ Chicagoans were soon to see this planned industrial paradise turn into a hell of misery and hate. Violent conflict broke out between management and labor. Federal troops were called in; soon after their departure George Pullman sickened and died. Like a great feudal lord, he died in despair over the "black ingratitude" of his workers. The failure of Pullman destroyed faith in the benevolence of business leaders. The old battle lines of class war in Europe, which Americans had struggled so valiantly to overcome, were drawn once again in the new city of Chicago. Architectural planning of industrial communities died, and "company town" became an epithet instead of a symbol of planned benevolence and security. Chicago engineers and architects learned that their new architecture could degrade as well as ennoble the common lot of man. Utilitarian structures like railway bridges and roads could be discussed as purely functional problems, but a village was not a bridge where "form followed function." The village Pullman and Beman created became the most hated village in America. From 1880 to 1907, the years of Pullman as a company town, Chicago architects and engineers discovered that architectural planning involved social as well as architectural and engineering functions. Architectural space was not a neutral space to be conceived of in terms of motion, or what Veblen called the "machine process." It was inhabited space, a lived-in space, which determined the quality of life within its bounds.

In Pullman human relations were completely feudal. Architectural planning served to sustain autocratic capitalistic power, whose measure of success was profit. The model town of Pullman and the Pullman shops were controlled by different agencies all responsible to the Pullman corporation. Direct management of the town was lodged in a town agent whose appointment and tenure of office rested with George Pullman. All town officials were appointed by the Pullman Corporation. Members of the school board were elected, but they were Pullman employees and hence subject to the influence of George Pullman. The *Pullman Journal* supported all policies of George Pullman and published nothing that would reflect on the merits of paternalism. Free speech was denied. Labor agitators and radical speakers were barred from the town by denying them the right to rent or use public halls. Labor unions were anathema to George Pullman, and he fought them with all the resources of money and power at his command. Pullman villagers were afraid to discuss public issues openly, and few were willing to have their name used in any criticism of village policy. It was widely believed that George Pullman used "spotters"—paid eavesdroppers—to mingle with the villagers and report any sign or word expressing disapproval or criticism of the authorities. In the judgment of the Reverend William Carwardine, pastor of the First Methodist Episcopal Church of Pullman, weekly reports on what inhabitants were doing and what they were discussing were submitted to headquarters.

No property was for sale in Pullman village. Individual home ownership was not permitted. Pullman rents averaged 20 to 25 per cent higher than rents in Chicago or surrounding communities. Rentals from sixty frame houses in the brickyard returned 40 per cent on the investment. Rentals for public buildings, stores, and offices were very high. The market building rents earned 19 per cent on invested capital. The company reserved the right at any time to enter the premise for inspection. Any lease could be voided within ten days by either party. George Pullman explained to Graham Taylor that this "ten day clause" enabled him to get rid of undesirable renters without giving them due recourse to law. In signing the lease the renter agreed to observe all rules which the company might choose to make. The grounds surrounding the dwelling could not be dug or planted without permission; nor were mechanical work, calcimining, or painting allowed on any premise without official consent. Company rules on the use of dwellings were very detailed. In one clause alone we read: "Tenants should always enter or leave the building quietly; always avoid entering the halls with muddy feet; never permit hammering, pounding or splitting of wood upon the floors or in the cellars, or anything which disturbs and annoys those occupying neighboring rooms; avoid the use of musical instruments after bed time; avoid all loud noises or boisterous conduct that might annoy others or disturb the sick and weary; avoid loitering in the stairways; avoid smoking in the cellars; always fill and trim lamps in the forenoon; . . . always leave some ashes in the bottom of the stove. . . ."[1]

In his study of Pullman village Richard L. Ely of the University of Wisconsin said in 1885, five years after the founding of the town and at the time of its greatest renown: "In looking over all the facts of the case, the conclusion is unavoidable that the ideal of Pullman is un-American. It is a nearer approach than anything the writer has seen to what appears to be the ideal

of the Great German Chancellor. It is not the American ideal. It is benevolent well-wishing feudalism, which desires the happiness of the people, but
in such a way as to please the authorities." [2] No one questioned that workers
in Pullman village enjoyed a higher levelt of comfort than other workers. But
the price they paid for this comfort was the complete surrender of their rights
as individuals and the denial of the basic democratic role of citizen. Chicago
architects, engineers, sociologists—all those who would now be called "planners"—learned from the experience of Pullman that they could no longer
divorce form and content in architecture. For if all their skills in design
could not produce a democratic society, what was the good of their new
architecture?

Even before Pullman made clear how autocratic control would affect
democratic life, radical labor leaders in Chicago were telling their audiences
that plutocratic benevolence was paid for in the sweat and blood of the
worker. Thus from 1875 to 1895 the powerful plutocrats of Chicago were
challenged by equally powerful labor leaders. From 1870 to 1891 Chicago
was the national capital of various workingmen's associations, and also the
national center of radicalism. The Socialist Labor party of Chicago was the
leader of the socialist movement in America. Chicago radicals such as Albert
Parsons and George Schilling were bold and shrewd strike tacticians, highly
skilled in all the arts of radical rhetoric. Chicago socialists taught the doctrine of class war. One element in the party advocated open violence and
organized "Revolutionary Clubs" to do battle with their enemies, the plutocrats of Chicago. A national convention of the Revolutionary Clubs was held
in Chicago, and the Revolutionary Socialist party soon began to compete
with the Socialist Labor party. The extremists talked of violence, dynamite,
and political assassination, but it was not until the arrival of Johann Most
that talk turned into action. He advocated openly the extermination of all
politicians and exploiters of the people. "Let us rely upon the unquenchable
spirit of destruction and annihilation which is the perpetual spring of new
life. The joy of destruction is a creative joy!" He was a frequent visitor to
Chicago, and under his influence *Die Arbeiter Zeitung,* a Socialist paper,
turned anarchist. Albert Parsons also accepted Most's ideas and leadership in
his editing of his paper, *Alarm,* where open violence was advocated. "Dynamite," the *Alarm* cried on February 21, 1895, ". . . is a genuine boon for the
disinherited. . . . A pound of this good stuff beats a bushel of dollars all
hollow."

These calls to violence found ready ears. The memory of the riots at the
McCormick Reaper Works still rankled. Albert R. Parsons had been told to
quit addressing the strikers and was warned by Mayor Monroe Heath to go

back to Texas, for "Those Board of Trade Men would as leave hang you to a lamppost as not." Parsons refused and had tried to explain that his was a peaceful strike for a living wage, not an armed revolution. He was thrown out by the Mayor. The conservative press branded him as the "leader of the Commune." Police broke up an assemblage of three thousand workers waiting to hear him speak. In haste Parsons and his comrades in the Workingmen's party tried to direct the strike and hold down violence. Rioting began. The police fought with a mob on the Randolph Street Bridge. A pitched battle was fought at the viaduct between Halsted and Archer avenues. Soon twenty thousand men, police and citizens were under arms. Squads of householders shouldered rifles and patrolled residence districts. Saloons were closed. Farwell, Field, and Leiter offered their delivery wagons for use as police transport. Terror-stricken businessmen met in the Moody and Sankey Tabernacle and demanded five thousand additional militiamen to put down "the ragged commune wretches." Many upper-class families left the city. Two companies of United States regulars, fresh from the Indian campaigns in the Northwest, arrived and marched down the streets of Chicago. At their head was Lieutenant Colonel Frederick Dent Grant, son of the great war leader and President.

After the riots of 1877 faith weakened in peaceful political means of social change. Socialists made rapid gains in Chicago, but anarchists soon rose to power within the party. Although probably never exceeding three thousand members, the skill and devotion of the anarchist leaders soon raised them to great power in radical ranks. The eloquence and daring of Schwab (of the German paper *Die Arbeiter Zeitung*) Samuel Fielden, a Methodist lay preacher and teamster, Neebe, organizer of beer wagon drivers, Fischer, a typesetter, Engle, a toymaker, and Lingg, a colorful organizer for the Brotherhood of Carpenters, soon made Chicago the anarchist capital of America. The ringing speeches of Johann Most haunted the minds of radicals and liberals alike. His sneers at American liberty bit deep. "Of what value is it? Has anyone ever been able to clothe himself with it, to house himself in it, or to satisfy with it the cravings of his stomach?" Chicago businessmen countered the rising anarchist strength by developing their own police. By 1860 Allan Pinkerton had developed a corps of night watchmen to guard business houses. In 1885 the Pinkerton agency was able to offer plants a fully armed police force, trained and armed for violence.

On the "Black Road" leading to the McCormick plant, where some of the worst riots of 1877 had taken place, the "Pinkertons" and strikers met. Fights broke out, shots were fired, and rioting began. A mob gathered at the foot of La Salle Street to jeer and howl at Chicago's leading financiers, who were meeting in the new Board of Trade building for its inaugural banquet. Parsons and other radical leaders, now calling themselves the International Working People's party, addressed workers carrying red and black flags—red for the common blood of humanity, black for starvation. Parsons declared that they should march on what he called the "Board of Thieves" singing the Marseillaise. Through the summer of 1885 small strikes continued. Streetcar employees walked out. The public supported their demands, and Carter Harrison, now entering his fourth consecutive term as mayor, declared that he would never allow troops to be brought into Chicago to shoot down striking workingmen. He upheld the right of free speech. The streetcar employees eventually forced the streetcar company to surrender. There was some rioting, but juries quickly freed prisoners brought in by the police. Again serious trouble was averted. But in February of 1886 the McCormick works declared for "open shop." Scabs were hired. Union men from all over the city threw their strength behind the picketing of the plant. Scabs were waylaid and beaten. Pinkerton detectives and police hurried to the defense of the plant as rioting spread throughout the city.

Parsons and his fellow anarchists agreed to cooperate with union labor leaders. Five hundred Bohemian, Polish, and Hungarian "tailor-girls" marched under red flags. The police fired on crowds gathered outside the McCormick works. Six men were killed. August Spies's speech to a gathering of some five thousand Slavs on the Black Road to the plant was interrupted by the volley. He hurried to the *Arbeiter Zeitung* office and wrote a proclamation, "Revenge," which he sent over the city in both German and English. It read: "Your masters sent out their bloodhounds—the police. They killed six of your brothers at McCormick's this afternoon. They killed the poor wretches because they, like you, had the courage to disobey the supreme will of your bosses. . . . If you are men, destroy the hideous monster that seeks to destroy you. To arms! We call you to arms!" A great mass meeting was called for 7:30 the next evening, May 4th, in the Haymarket, Randolph Street, between Desplaines and Halsted. During the speech Mayor Harrison mingled with the crowds listening to Spies and Parsons. He wanted, he said, "to let the people know their mayor is here."

The gathering seemed peaceable enough. Mayor Harrison and the chief of police went home, leaving Inspector Bonfield in charge. During Fielden's speech, which was to end the meeting, a scout ran from the meeting and told Bonfield that violence was being advocated. Bonfield ordered out 176 policemen and marched them toward the crowd, calling for the meeting to break up. Fielden replied that it was peaceable and that the police had no right to interfere. Suddenly an explosion ripped through the ranks of the police.

Bonfield ordered his men to fire. Their poorly aimed fire flew in all directions, wounding and killing police as well as bystanders. People broke in panic, trampling each other in frenzied escape from the wild fire of the maddened police. Police clubs fell on women and men alike. Wounded dragged themselves into doorways. When the smoke cleared sixty-seven officers lay wounded. Seven of these officers died. No one ever knew how many of the crowd were killed or wounded. The police insisted that the anarchists spirited away their dead and wounded.

Chicago and America were stunned. The narrow middle ground of tolerance, where differences could be resolved in discussion and debate, vanished. The police raided wildly. Workingmen's homes were searched for bombs. The press whipped the police to greater efforts, the police in turn announced new discoveries of dynamite in "dynamiter's lairs," as they called workingmen's homes. The conservative Protestant religious press described the workers as "wild beasts" and "reckless desperadoes" who must be clubbed into submission or mowed down with cannon and Gatling guns.[3] After wholesale arrests a grand jury indicted Fielden, Parsons, Spies, Schwab, Fischer, Engel, Lingg, Neebe, Seliger, and Schnaubelt. Parsons and Schnaubelt escaped, the former to a Wisconsin farm, the latter to Europe, from which he never returned. The case against Seliger was dropped. The accused were rushed to trial.

At the opening of the trial, Parsons walked in, shook hands quietly with his comrades, and sat down to await his sentence to death. As the trial progressed it became clear that punishment, not justice, was its purpose. The public, goaded by an incendiary press, demanded death. No creditable evidence linked any of the accused with the throwing of the bomb; no bomb thrower was ever discovered. The charge was that the dynamiter, whoever he was, had been incited by the radical speeches and publications of the prisoners. The jury voted "guilty." Judge Gary passed a death sentence on Parsons, Spies, Lingg, Fielden, Schwab, Fischer, and Engel, and sentenced Oscar Neebe to fifteen years' imprisonment. The verdict was sustained by the Supreme Court, making it clear that the organized passions of Chicago were widely shared. Governor Oglesby commuted the sentences of Schwab and Fielden to life imprisonment. Lingg killed himself in his cell by exploding a dynamite cartridge between his teeth. Six years later Governor Altgeld pardoned Neebe, Schwab, and Fielden.

There was no question that anarchists had advocated violent overthrow of the government. Altgeld's conclusion that the "eight defendants had been convicted not because they had been proved guilty of murder, but because they were anarchists," did not represent liberal opinion of the eighties. Even

Graham Taylor, who did as much as any man in Chicago to further liberal causes, tells us: "I . . . shared the country-wide indorsement of their conviction and penalty. . . ." [4] Chicagoans were told that they must make a choice between anarchy and law. It was not a matter of the guilt or innocence of the anarchists, but of destroying those who sought to destroy the foundations of social order. Anarchists, in short, must be treated as enemies of the people. Businessmen, like Field, Pullman, Armour, and McCormick were guardians of society. Attacking their interests or challenging their will was really attacking the weak as well as the strong. For was it not these strong, powerful, hard-working business leaders who created the jobs which kept workers from poverty and hunger? Who were these anarchists after all? Foreigners and immigrants (Parsons was a Texan and a former Confederate soldier). Instead of being grateful and working hard to rise in industry like Pullman, Armour, or Field, what had they done but cause trouble and incite others to trouble? Such attitudes were common to all levels of society in these years. Very little information on the immigrant and his problems existed in the eighties. Nor, indeed, was general knowledge of the worker, native or immigrant, much more prevalent. Even liberal and humane Chicago writers, such as Fuller, Dreiser, and Herrick, used anti-Semitic stereotypes of the Jew in their novels. Grant's famous general order Number 11 of December 17, 1862, forbade Jews entry to his military department, on the grounds that "as a class" they were "violating every regulation of trade. . . ." [5]

Business interests and their political allies controlled the Chicago press. German socialists and their sympathizers controlled the radical foreign-language press in Chicago.[6] Thoughtful citizens of American backgrounds could not read the radical press; they formed their opinions on what they read in a heavily biased press and what they heard from an equally biased pulpit. The older forms of community life, where the lot of neighbors was a common lot and where discussion in face-to-face meeting prevailed, no longer existed. In place of open and free discussion and meetings at which anyone could challenge the speaker was the urban newspaper which represented the interests of management and a Protestant urban church with little interest in the non-Protestant workingman. The speaker–audience relationship of debate and discussion and the many voices of a village press were silent. The public forum which produced the great debates of Lincoln and Douglas had been replaced by the mass oratory of editors, preachers, and public speakers who exhorted but did not discuss. Opponents became enemies, not disputants, as force replaced persuasion.

But the thoughtful Chicagoans, who had been shocked by the violence of strikers, were soon to be deeply disturbed by the ruthlessness of management. On May 11, 1894, the workers of Pullman village, the American worker's Utopia, went on strike. The employees expected a speedy settlement. Their grievance was against their "straw bosses." They believed that when George Pullman understood their grievances the strike would be settled in the spirit of benevolence which, the world had been told by the press and pulpit, ruled George Pullman and his model town. But when the strikers asked the company to arbitrate they were told: "We have nothing to arbitrate." The Pullman Corporation made it clear that it intended to break the strike—by starving its workers, if need be. When the strike was broken, only nonunion labor would be employed and production would be resumed on company terms. The model town of Pullman, so peaceful and serene during its fourteen years of renown, was now the stage for a showdown between the new forces of labor and capital. Pullman workers turned to the American Railway Union for help. A boycott of all Pullman cars was declared. Railroad companies formed a General Managers' Association to fight the strikers. The Civic Federation of Chicago created a conciliation board of which Jane Addams was a member. Pullman again refused to arbitrate. Every request for arbitration, even those from big manufacturers such as Erskine M. Phelps, was refused. Pullman declared that a great principle was involved—whether or not a factory owner should operate his plant in his own way, completely free of labor or "outside interests." The questions at issue, he asserted, were matters of fact and hence not suitable for arbitration. For if the law of supply and demand determined wages, how could a law be arbitrated?

Although there was no rioting and the Illinois militia was available to keep order, federal troops were sent to the city. Riots soon followed. There was no purpose or leadership in the rioting mobs, and later investigations proved that if any direct connection between mob violence and the strike existed, it was on the side of management, not labor. On July 6 mobs descended upon railway yards. Incendiaries ignited cars with torches and waste taken from axle boxes. While furnishing protection to a wrecking train, a company of militia was assaulted by an angry mob. After a bayonet charge, which wounded several people, failed to disperse the mob, soldiers fired at will. Four rioters were killed and some twenty wounded, among whom were a few women. The conservative Chicago press, headed by the Chicago *Herald, Inter Ocean, Tribune, Journal,* and *Evening Post,* instructed their reporters [7] to magnify every disturbance into a scene of "riot, terror, and pillage." Scare headlines were used to sell extras and increase circulation. On June 30 the Chicago *Tribune* captioned its major news story with

"MOB IS IN CONTROL." On July 5 readers were told: "GUNS AWE THEM NOT—DRUNKEN STOCKYARDS RIOTERS DEFY UNCLE SAM'S TROOPS—MOBS INVITE DEATH." The *Inter Ocean* for July 7 declared: "FLAMES MAKE HAVOC—UNPARALLELED SCENES OF RIOT, TERROR AND PILLAGE—ANARCHY IS RAMPANT—MOBS AT PULLMAN AND BURNSIDE APPLY THE TORCH—CITY AN ARMED CAMP—U.S. TROOPS AND MILITIA AT THE DANGER POINTS PREPARED TO FIGHT." Papers outside of Chicago took up the cry. The Washington *Post* for July 7 headlined its story: "CHICAGO AT THE MERCY OF THE INCENDIARY'S TORCH." Readers were told further that "anarchists and socialists [are] said to be planning the destruction and looting of the treasury." The New York *Times* on July 9 questioned Debs's sanity. It was reported that Debs was a drunkard and of a "disordered condition of mind and body. . . ." The front cover of *Harper's Weekly* for July 21 carried an impressive cartoon entitled "The Vanguard of Anarchy." Even the *Nation* declared that Debs's leadership "puts this country before the world as the sport of lunatics and madmen."

Not all Chicago newspapers favored Pullman and the railroad management. The Chicago *Daily News* carried on its distinguished record of impartial reporting established during the strikes of 1877, when, at the request of Leiter and Chicago business leaders, it refused to suspend publication of fresh editions reporting the progress of the strikes. The Chicago *Record* reported impartially, while the *Dispatch, Mail,* and the *Times* backed the strikers. The *Herald* denounced both George Pullman and the strikers. The *Tribune* had no sympathy for the American Railway Union, but neither did it approve of Pullman's refusal to arbitrate. The *Times* hated Pullman and attacked him at every turn. In the highly personal and vigorously expressed traditions of Chicago journalism, the *Times* for July 4, 1894, described Pullman as a "cold-hearted, cold-blooded autocrat. . . . A pair of small, piggish eyes gleam out from above the puffed cheeks, and the glitter of avarice is plainly apparent in their depths. Mr. Pullman's usual expression is one of supercilious contempt for the world at large, mingled with traces of self-satisfaction at his own comfortable state." In an effort to mediate the strike and alleviate the sufferings of Pullman strikers Governor Altgeld visited Pullman village. He found poverty and hunger. The relief committee had exhausted its resources in giving to each family two pounds of oatmeal and the same amount of cornmeal. Pullman refused to help his workers. Altgeld then appealed to the people of Illinois in behalf of the Pullman inhabitants. Various Chicago newspapers responded magnificently by portraying vividly conditions in the model town. Contributions poured in from all quarters. Sympathy for the strikers was marked on the streets of Chicago by wearing bits of white ribbon.

The Pullman Strike destroyed forever the easy faith of Chicagoans in the enlightenment of paternalistic business leaders as benevolent guardians of society. For if the Haymarket anarchists had been willing to use violence, George Pullman was willing to use violence and to starve his workers into submission. Chicagoans now experienced at first hand the meaning of class war. As Jane Addams said, "The Pullman strike afforded much illumination to many Chicago people. Before it there had been nothing in my experience to reveal that distinct cleavage of society, which a general strike at least momentarily affords. Certainly, during all those dark days of the Pullman strike, the growth of class bitterness was most obvious. The fact that the Settlement maintained avenues of intercourse with both sides seemed to give it opportunity for nothing but a realization of the bitterness and division along class lines." [8] For Sullivan the struggle between men like Pullman and Altgeld was but another form of the same struggle in architecture. As he said of Burnham: "Daniel Burnham was obsessed by the feudal idea of power. . . . Burnham's megalomania concerning the largest, the tallest, the most costly and sensational, moved on its sure orbit, as he painfully learned to use the jargon of big business. . . . So matters stood in the early eighties and onward." In 1882, Sullivan tells us, he "was too young to grasp the truth that the fair-appearing civilization within which he lived was but a huge invisible man-trap, man-made. . . ." [9] The defeat in 1891 of the young radicals of the Chicago school at the hands of Burnham's classicists at the World's Fair and the victory of the Pullman Company in 1894 taught Sullivan that the new architecture he envisioned could exist only in a new society. He saw the new men of Chicago turn away from their own architects to the feudal monuments of the past, just as in business they had turned away from democracy to feudal forms of control. The task of the architect in 1900 was no longer purely architectural, it was now social. It was also moral, for, if architecture was not to produce a society where democracy could exist, what was the use of being an architect?

Notes

[1] Quoted in Almond Lindsey, *The Pullman Strike: The Story of a Unique Experiment and of a Great Labor Upheaval* (Chicago: University of Chicago Press, 1942), p. 70.

[2] *Ibid.,* p. 86.

[3] See Richard Hofstadter, *The Age of Reform* (New York: Knopf, 1955), pp. 149–52 for discussion of this.

[4] See Graham Taylor, *Pioneering on Social Frontiers* (Chicago: University of Chicago Press, 1930), p. 136.

[5] Bruce Catton, in his *Grant Moves South* (Boston: Little, Brown, 1960), gives the history of this incident. See pages 353–56.

[6] Chicago had three radical papers before New York had even one. The *Verboten* was founded in 1872, the *Arbeiter Zeitung* in 1876, and the *Fackel* in 1879. It was not until 1886 that the *Hlas Lidu,* a Bohemian paper, was founded in New York. See Robert E. Park, *The Immigrant Press and Its Control* (New York and London: Harper's, 1922).

[7] Editorial bias was so flagrantly misused that one reporter for the Chicago *Tribune* refused to declare authentic a distorted version of an interview he had with Eugene Debs. The statement was so garbled that the reporter was not able to recognize it. He refused to perjure himself to keep his job.

[8] Jane Addams, *Twenty Years at Hull House* (New York: Macmillan, 1914), p. 214.

[9] Louis H. Sullivan, *The Autobiography of an Idea* (New York: Press of the American Institute of Architects, 1926), p. 289.

16

The Search for a Middle Ground: I

THE ANARCHISM of the Haymarket rioters and the feudalism of George Pullman formed a vicious circle which Chicagoans knew they must break if democracy was to survive. The democratic traditions of New England and the frontier no longer applied to the city. It was plain now that every American tradition must be reexamined in the light of its relevance to urban life. The first problem was one of communication. Democratic action assumed that contending voices could become a source of strength as long as they could be resolved. But these contending voices must be heard, and they must be understood. Public opinion had to be formed and communicated in new ways among people who could no longer be brought together in face-to-face groups, who no longer spoke a common tongue or shared a common heritage.

By 1890 fully 68 per cent of Chicago's 1,208,676 people were foreign born, while of the 32 per cent native born many were children of old residents among the German and Irish groups. Many immigrants, such as Scandinavians, knew nothing of any other region of America. They came directly to the Middle West and Chicago. To them the older American traditions of New England were as strange and remote as were those of Europe to native Americans. And even those who were steeped in the traditions of American democracy, and whose faith had been reborn in the terrible battles of the Civil War, discovered that they simply did not know how to combat the anarchists. They were equally powerless to deal with captains of industry who were turning back to feudal forms of control. It was obvious that new forms of community must be established. Native Americans, Chicagoans who had settled the city, and the new immigrants knew little about each other. The gaps between classes, religions, races, and generations were so wide that communication seemed impossible. Yet unless there was communication, there could be no community. And if communication was controlled by any group to the exclusion of others, there could be no democracy.

Most perplexing of all was the problem of equality. In rural American society economic equality was based on rights to land. Anyone in the West who was willing to work hard enough could take up land. The law, and especially law in the West, was framed to create and uphold the rights of those who worked land, as well as those who owned it. "Giving people a start" meant settling them on land; American Utopias were based on land settlement. Even among highly urbanized people such as the European Jewry, attempts at land settlement were made in the Chicago region. A Jewish philanthropist, Renau, sent an agent from New York to Chicago in the forties to investigate the possibility of founding a Jewish settlement. A colonization project was started in Schaumburg, Cook County. But the new immigrants of 1870 to 1900 who settled in cities brought little experience of equality in their social and cultural life. Many, indeed, did not even know what it was to be a public person. The Latvian Jews who came to Chicago in the seventies came from a village world, where the affairs of their synagogue were the only public life they knew.[1] Poor immigrants, such as the Russian Jews who came to Chicago in great numbers from 1880 to 1890, took it more or less for granted that they did not possess equal rights before the law. Local political leaders among the immigrants did nothing to dispel such notions, for so long as they existed they could rule the new immigrant in ways common to those he knew in Europe. Such neighborhoods as the Maxwell Street market, the great outdoor market of the ghetto, were organized in terms of the "fix" and the "pay-off." Politicians built up a system of private patronage and "protection." In 1926 it was estimated that $250,000 was extorted annually from street vendors as payment for their right to make a living of even the humblest kind.

Another new experience was the American way of working and using money. Deeply rooted in the American consciousness was the idea that work should be joyful and creative, as well as profitable. The new immigrants to Chicago discovered that American businessmen and workers mingled social and business life so thoroughly that it was impossible to distinguish one from another. But strangest of all was the American public life of voluntary associations conducted by rule. American labor unions conducted meetings controlled by rules established by constitutions, as well as by leaders who based their rule on personal authority. The whole concept of rules was very strange. Commandments of sacred and secular authorities were familiar enough, but the expression of the will of equals in rules whose power resided only in the consent of all those bound by them was new. Ideas such as "playing the game," being "fair," and arbitrating differences before public bodies were not part of many immigrant traditions. Equality in religion, where all men were equal in the eyes of God, was understood, but this was an equality "not of this world." Equality under law was accepted as a polite fiction by Europeans who were accustomed to bribe authorities with money and deference.

"Feudal barons" like Pullman, who talked of labor as a commodity, won power in Chicago but they did not win the conscience of the city. They failed to establish tyranny over the spirit of Chicago because liberals within the church, school, newspaper, government, and art fought to keep communication open. They upheld the democratic ideal of reaching decisions through public discussion and of keeping laws and rules open to constant revision in continuing discussion. The liberal view was based on the assumption that democratic truth was subject to reason, but a reason which originated and was tested in debate and discussion. Rational demonstration of "immutable social laws" which must be followed, not discussed, were no better than feudal commands where the voice of the lord was the voice of God. As Jane Addams said, liberals did not want to be bullied into belief by millionaires who would not arbitrate, any more than by socialists who were deaf to the revealed truths of religion, but not to those of "historical necessity."

Chicago liberals were not alone in their alarm over Pullman's refusal to arbitrate. The conservative Chicago *Tribune* argued that while certain labor leaders were to blame for workers' taking the law into their own hands, this did not relieve Pullman from the responsibility of not seeking a peaceful solution through arbitration. Liberal churchmen of the city discovered to their horror that men like Pullman considered themselves to be "stewards of the Lord" and that many churchmen agreed with the Reverend Oggel of the Green Stone Church in Pullman, who delivered a Christian panegyric just three weeks before the strike on "George M. Pullman, his services to his age, his country, and humanity," using as his text: "Thou hast made him a little lower than the angels and hast crowned him with glory and honor." Reverend William Carwardine, pastor of the Pullman Methodist Church, and other liberal clergymen of the city, disagreed with the conservative clergy. They found no evidence of Christian stewardship in Pullman.

In orthodox eyes, a striker was at worst a sinner whose sin was disobedience; at best, a malcontent rebelling against benevolent masters. The famous letter of George F. Baer, President of the Philadelphia and Reading Railway and spokesman for the operators in the coal strike of 1902, made this clear. In response to a letter appealing for an end to the strike from a citizen of Wilkes-Barre, Baer replied:

I do not know who you are. I see that you are a religious man; but you are evidently biased in favor of the right of the working man to control a business in which he has no other interest than to secure fair wages for the work he does.

I beg of you not to be discouraged. The rights and interests of the laboring man will be protected and cared for—not by the labor agitators, but by the Christian men to whom God in His infinite wisdom has given the control of the property interests of the country, and upon the successful Management of which so much depends. Do not be discouraged. Pray earnestly that right may triumph, always remembering that the Lord God Omnipotent still reigns, and that His reign is one of law and order, and not of violence and crime.[2]

Clergymen in Chicago, Protestant, Catholic, and Jewish alike, began to realize the danger to the Church in business use of sacred symbols. The Catholic church in Chicago had always been the church of the poor immigrant. The new immigrants from southern and eastern Europe who poured into Chicago from 1870 to 1900, like the Irish who came earlier, were absorbed into an urban church. Where many Chicago Protestant churches were abandoned in the old and crowded neighborhoods of the south and west sides of the city, the Catholic church stayed close to the heart of the city. It was the church of the poor and the workingman. Catholic priests did not have to move to Hull House, the Chicago Commons, or the University of Chicago Settlement House to learn what it was like to be poor. They lived, worked, and prayed in the "lower depths" of the city, and they assumed the burden of providing social and spiritual security. Until the rise of the Protestant "Social Gospel" in Graham Taylor's course in sociology at the Chicago Seminary in 1892, the Catholic church of Chicago was the church of the people. Cardinal Gibbons warned the Holy See in 1887 that it would be a fatal mistake to condemn the Knights of Labor, who were, he said, only seeking redress of just grievances from capitalists who abused their power and wealth.

By 1902 Protestant churchmen admitted what they could not admit in the Haymarket Riots of 1886, or the Pullman strike of 1894. Their church had become identified with plutocracy. Hearst's New York *American and Journal* described the "sacred" plutocrat as a pious pirate in modern form and went on to warn the church that the relations between a just God and the thieving trusts must receive adequate treatment in the pulpit if Protestantism was to survive. *Watchman,* a Baptist religious paper, warned its readers against the new feudalism: "The doctrine of the divine right of kings was bad enough, but not so intolerable as the doctrine of the divine right of plutocrats to administer things in general with the presumption that what it pleases them to do is the will of God." But the Protestant conscience within the church proper was slow to condemn economic and political injustice as evil. As liberal churchmen of the nineties pointed out to their congregations, the Protestant sense of sin did not relate enough to the realities of urban life. In summing up the Baptist role in Chicago, Stackhouse says of the church which did so much for the city by founding the University of Chicago: ". . . the Baptist conscience was more sensitive concerning the evils of Sabbath desecration, the liquor traffic, gambling, and prostitution than it was on the exploitation of the hewers of wood and drawers of water by millionaire corporations." Even as late as 1933 he goes on to say: "Bad housing, child labor, juvenile delinquency, starvation wages, and excessive hours of labor for women and working men have not become subjects of resolutions at Baptist associations." [3]

The Jews of Chicago, like the Catholics, learned their public civic roles under the tutelage of an urban church. The synagogue was the center of life for the newly arrived Jew. But even before the Civil War Chicago Jews were seeking a broader identification with American community life. The question of reform in the sacred and secular life of the synagogue and the ghetto soon became a vital issue. In their new freedom as citizens of a free community the Jews of Chicago were determined to identify themselves with their city as well as with their faith. The reform section, which founded one of the outstanding bodies in American Jewry, Sinai congregation, broke away from the Kehilath Anshe Maarab congregation. One of the issues was assimilation. The Sinai congregation desired to expunge from the liturgy the hope that all Jews would someday return to Jerusalem. They wanted Jews to retain their religion, but to give up their separate existence as Jews. This new spirit had already found expression in the organization of a company of Jews during the Civil War. Although the Jewish population of Chicago did not exceed a thousand, one hundred men enlisted, and over $11,000 was raised to support them.

But the greatest contribution of Chicago Jews was not their generous support of community enterprises or their devoted support of Jewish immigrants. Of far more importance to the future of Chicago, and of profound importance to the development of art in Chicago, was the place they gave to learning and culture in their own community.[4] Family status in the Jewish community had always depended to a considerable degree upon the learning of their children. In the Old World this was mainly religious learning, but in America, and especially among such reform congregations as Sinai, secular learning often substituted for orthodox religious learning. Among orthodox and reformed groups alike the intellectual was a clearly defined and respected social type. In the ghetto a poor but learned talmudic student was a desirable candidate for a son-in-law of a prosperous merchant, while among reformed Jews, doctors, lawyers, professors, writers, painters, architects, and engineers occupied an equally high place.

The high place given to intellectual achievement among Chicago Jews affected the city in many ways. In 1890 the Standard Club, the great Jewish club of the city, voted unanimously to raise $25,000 for the new University of Chicago. Although the University was founded by Baptists, Chicago Jews gave and continued to give notable support to the University. Emil G. Hirsch, rabbi of the Sinai congregation, was appointed Professor of Rabbinical Literature and Philosophy. President Harper was himself a notable Hebrew scholar and by his teaching and writing on the Bible did much to illumine the relationship between Judaism and Christianity. The University received generous support from the Epstein, Mandel, Rosenberger, and Rosenwald families. The German Jews made education and culture necessary to success within their group, and, since they were the oldest and most powerful group in Chicago Jewry, they served as models for all Chicago Jews. The effect on this among students at the University was very marked. As Hyde Park and the South Side became centers of Jewish life, more Jewish students were drawn from the neighborhood of the University. As Robert Morss Lovett tells us in his autobiography, "In early years the female students came, on the whole, from a higher social level than the male." [5] Robert Herrick, in his novel *Chimes,* a story of the University as seen through the eyes of one of its great teachers, says much the same. Most of the women "were as able, even abler, than the men, and were generally of a superior social class, with a more cultivated background, especially the young women from rich Jewish families." [6]

The opening of the University of Chicago to students of every race, color, and creed and to men and women alike created an intellectual environment which produced one of the cultural miracles of modern times—the rise of the University of Chicago within a single generation to a great institution of learning. This miracle was accomplished through making the University a true forum of the mind. It was a community of scholars in the traditional sense—Harper had seen to that by his raids on the faculties of American and European universities—but more than this, the University was, from 1893 to 1916, the greatest center in America of the search for the meaning of democracy in urban society. The University of Chicago did not become great because of the erudition of its scholars, nor simply because of Rockefeller money. The older universities had far superior scholars, greater libraries, and much more money. But they were not able to use these resources to launch inquiries relevant to the great questions of their time, or to fire scholars with the passion and conviction of men who believed they were creating, as well as serving, a democratic commonwealth. In the social studies few equaled Sumner in knowledge. Yet with all his learning and the vast resources of Yale at his command, his work, and that of his students take a minor place beside that of the new scholars of the Middle West such as Cooley, Ward, Veblen, Dewey, Mead, and Park. As William James said of these thinkers, "what strikes me most in [their thought] is the great sense of concrete reality with which it is filled." This concrete reality was seen in Chicago, and not in Cambridge or New Haven, because the University opened its doors to the new people of America who challenged upholders of native tradition to submit their beliefs to inquiry.

If the University did nothing else it created a forum where doubt and question were considered the beginning of wisdom, not of heresy. It extended the range of skepticism from purely intellectual to social and economic realms. For, as teachers from the East such as Robert Herrick and Robert Morss Lovett (members of what was called President Harper's "Harvard Gang") discovered, their students did not want information alone, nor did they believe deeply enough in any conception of the gentleman or the lady to allow this to create a fixed set of attitudes toward learning. Chicagoans did not know what a Middle Western lady or gentleman was, and even when they learned to recognize Boston and Cambridge models, considered them to be of dubious relevance to life in Chicago. University classes were very mixed. Candidates for higher degrees, schoolteachers, casual listeners from the city, "irregulars" of all kinds, immigrants and native born, Jew and gentile, rich and poor, orthodox believers and atheists, all walked the campus together. They shared in a great search, the search for the meaning of democratic community. They sought, as Herrick tells us, "for something with which to enlarge their consciousness of life." The glory of teaching such students was in their quick and eager response to whatever gave them this sense of enlargement. These students, and their best teachers, wanted to learn not only how to think about democracy but how to act in it.

No other institution in the United States exhibited such tolerance of unorthodox opinion and behavior and forced so many different types of people to stand up in discourse with one another. Traditional attitudes were challenged at every turn. Even on social levels it was impossible to fall back on tradition. While Howells and Wharton were turning out endless variations on romantic love themes, Herrick and Lovett found themselves in company with women who were openly contemptuous of such romance. They wanted to work beside their men, to share lives of common effort. Easterners also found themselves confronted with immigrants who, like Veblen, found the sacred genteel traditions of the East highly comic when they were not vicious and corrupt. But they found, too, new types of American businessmen, such as Martin A. Ryerson and Charles L. Hutchinson, who carried the ambitious cultural projects of the city, including the University and the

World's Fair, through the financial panic of 1893. Such businessmen wanted to do more than buy culture; they wanted to create it.

For one generation the University of Chicago was a haven for those in passage from old to new faiths. As Veblen said in his essay on the Jews, "It appears to be only when the gifted Jew escapes from the cultural environment created and fed by the particular genius of his own people, only when he falls into the alien lines of gentile inquiry and becomes a naturalized, though hyphenate, citizen in the gentile republic of learning, that he comes into his own as a creative leader in the world's intellectual enterprise. It is by loss of allegiance, or at the best by force of a divided allegiance to the people of his origins that he finds himself in the vanguard of modern inquiry." [7] As many have pointed out, what Veblen said of the Jew could be said of Veblen himself and of every intellectual in the Middle West who found traditional American and European values irrelevant to the new experience of life in the new cities of America. The skepticism of University intellectuals was not simply a negation. It was, as thoughtful Easterners pointed out, an affirmation of a new faith. It made skepticism an instrument of discourse, a way to truth. Men like Veblen, Dewey, and Mead were able to submit traditions and absolutes to doubt because they believed in a democratic world where the search for truth could become a guide for all, not for the privileged few. These new thinkers were not outsiders suffering alienation from an established world. They were creating a world of their own, and a world which they deeply believed would be a better world for all. The home of their thought was in the future, not the past, but it was a future as securely held as the past of older American tradition.

Notes

[1] Louis Wirth's *The Ghetto* (Chicago: University of Chicago Press, 1928) describes the urban drama of assimilation in Chicago.

[2] Quoted in Mark Sullivan, *Our Times: America Finding Herself* (New York and London: Charles Scribner's Sons, 1927), p. 426.

[3] Perry J. Stackhouse, *Chicago and the Baptists: A Century of Progress* (Chicago: University of Chicago Press, 1933), p. 142.

[4] Dankmar Adler, Sullivan's partner, was a Jew and had a large following among Chicago Jews, who were responsible for many of Sullivan's designs. The Schlesinger and Mayer Building, now known as the Carson Pirie Scott Building, is the most notable example.

[5] Robert Morss Lovett, *All Our Years: The Autobiography of Robert Morss Lovett* (New York: Viking, 1948).

[6] Robert Herrick, *Chimes* (New York: Macmillan, 1926), pp. 59–60.

[7] This is reprinted in Thorstein Veblen, *Essays in Our Changing Order*, ed. by Leon Ardzrooni (New York: Viking, 1934). Quotation given here is from p. 226.

17

The Search for a Middle Ground: II. Hull House and the Settlement House Movement in Chicago

CHICAGO LIBERALS believed that public opinion in democratic society could be formed in discourse between opponents who were willing to discuss and debate before informed publics. Older American forms of public discussion, such as the town meeting of New England and the stump speaking of the Middle West, were rural and village forms of discussions. In Chicago search began for forms of discussion which could create consensus of a new kind based on urban relationships. Liberals realized that new forms of urban communication must supplant the old. It was easy enough to say that communication was the basis of community, but the relationship between communication and one certain kind of community, the urban democratic commonwealth, was not easy to grasp. Indeed, in the writings of Europeans such as Burckhardt, Nietzsche, and the great analyst of American life, Tocqueville, modern urban dwellers were described as a kind of inert formless mass waiting to be awakened by demagogues. Even the great American prophets of individualism, Emerson and Thoreau, were openly fearful of the new urban "masses," as the people of the cities were called by European social philosophers. As Emerson said in his *Conduct of Life:* "Masses are rude, . . . pernicious in their demands and influence, and need not to be flattered but to be schooled. I wish not to concede anything to them, but to tame, drill, divide, and break them up, and draw individuals out of them."

One of the earliest Chicago associations devoted to open, free, and informed discussion was the Sunset Club. A group of business and professional men headed by Lyman J. Gage, president of the First National Bank of Chicago and later Secretary of the Treasury in the cabinets of Presidents McKinley and Theodore Roosevelt, sponsored such meetings. Gage's prestige was enough to attract other powerful men and women of the city. The Chicago press gave every meeting full coverage. Chicago liberalism became a force in its own right, as well as a means for communicating views which it did not itself create but simply reported for thoughtful consideration. Gaps between classes narrowed, until by 1900 Chicago became a great liberal, as well as radical and conservative, center of discussion. By 1905 faith in progressive liberalism ran deep. A new vision of American democracy as an urban democracy was formed in Chicago.

The Chicago school of architects discovered that they shared basic concerns over the function of art in democratic society with the Chicago school of writers and Chicago school of philosophers (as William James called them) at the University of Chicago. By 1900 the creative literary center of America had shifted from Boston to Chicago, where writers were creating a new language, the American language of Dreiser, Lewis, and Hemingway. Chicago newspapers, the patrons of these new writers, soon became famous. Young reporters flocked to Chicago, the "greatest newspaper town of them all." In October of 1912 Harriet Monroe started her *Poetry: A Magazine of Verse*. By 1914, the "glorious year of 1914," as Masters, the Chicago poet, calls it in his autobiography, "a re-arisen liberty was blossoming . . . in Chicago, where vitality and youth, almost abandoned in its assertion of freedom and delight, streamed along Michigan Avenue carrying . . . new books under their arms, or congregated at Bohemian restaurants to talk poetry and the drama. All this came to my eyes as though I had been confined to darkness and had suddenly come into the sunlight. . . . [This] revived all my slumbering humanism and gave me eyes for a thousand new phases of life and for appreciation of the new life in Chicago, which was growing more beautiful as it had become more interesting." [1]

The years from 1885 to the beginning of World War I were times of great debate in Chicago. Belief in the public forum as a way to truth became a settled conviction. The great talk and discussion in Chicago of this time were not intended to "manipulate the masses," or to communicate decisions already reached by leaders or committees. Mead taught that no self exists or knows itself save through the response of another. It was believed, by one generation at least, that words (and indeed all art) *created,* not simply discovered, truth. The high level of discourse and talk, the faith and skill in rhetoric as a means to truth, and the emphasis on the spoken word struck many observers. Among artists Chicago became a great American city because for them it exemplified the hope of urban democracy. Hutchins Hapgood, Dreiser, Upton Sinclair, and many other artists selected Chicago and Middle Western types as the characteristic American types for their depictions of the new America. Hapgood said in 1907:

. . . when I became interested in the laborer . . . it seemed to me that I should be more likely to find such a man in Chicago than anywhere else. In the democratic Middle West . . . the common man is probably more expressive than anywhere else in the world. Labor, there, is more self-conscious and socially, if not politically, more

powerful than elsewhere. The proletariat of America, and more especially of the progressive and intensely vital Middle West, is no real proletariat, in the dumb and crushed
European sense, but in its hopefulness and early activity, in the breadth of its interests;
in its mental joyousness and vitality, seems to have the quality of a Renaissance.[2]

Hull House became one of the great forums of America. Here anyone
could say anything, provided he was willing to let others have their say.
Faiths could be defended at Hull House, but they had to be defended in
discussion and sustained in debate before audiences treated as equals. Truth,
so the residents of Hull House believed, was born in action and could be
perfected in reasoned discourse among free and informed people only if
their deliberations led to action. As many lecturers discovered, sometimes to
their dismay, Hull House audiences were intelligent, well informed, and
widely experienced in the actual life of their time. University professors,
students, businessmen, anarchists, socialists, poets, artists, architects, politicians, labor leaders, feminists, society leaders, immigrants who scarcely spoke
English, descendants of great American families—all met together, often
for the first time, in Hull House. Outside of the University community and
the liberal press such as the *Daily News* Hull House was the greatest liberal
influence in Chicago. Certainly it was the center of liberal action. The
Deweys were regular visitors and made friends among the residents, especially with Jane Addams. "They found contact with many types of persons
there the most interesting and stimulating part of their non-professional life."
Dewey became a trustee of Hull House. He learned much from his settlement experience, and, as he tells us, persons and situations influenced his
intellectual development more than books. His daughters tell us: "Dewey's
faith in democracy as a guiding force in education took on both a sharper
and a deeper meaning because of Hull House and Jane Addams. For, as
Jane Addams taught, democracy was a way of life or it was nothing." [3]

Most important of all, discussants at Hull House met as equals. All,
speaker, discussants, and moderators alike, subordinated themselves to rules
of discussion which guaranteed a hearing to all who would abide by them.
In the rough and tumble of these discussions the power of rank and status
was soon forgotten. What a man said, not who he was, counted. For immigrants who had never spoken out in public as individuals, students bound
by the conventions of the lecture hall, and those considered enemies of
society, such as the anarchists, these meetings were a discovery. For those
securely established in American society and for those in power in the city,
Hull House meetings were also a discovery. For those who held cherished
beliefs which they had never put to the test of public discussion, Hull House
meetings were often a revelation.

Jane Addams taught that people must learn *how* to be equal. Submitting decisions to open and free discussion was a new experience. But such discussion had to be learned and its value understood by both workers and management, poor and rich, uneducated and educated, as well as self-educated intellectuals and academicians. The Haymarket Riot and its dismal aftermath in the courts haunted the minds of just men. For when all the fine points of law had been argued and all the evidence presented, the fact remained that free speech and free assembly had been denied. Whether the anarchists were guilty or not, democratic procedure had not been used to convict them. Pullman, too, by his refusal to arbitrate, denied fundamental democratic rights—the right to be judged by peers and to reach agreement with them for common action. Thoughtful citizens like Gage, Jane Addams, and Graham Taylor of the Chicago Commons, realized that the gaps between groups in the city must be bridged before they were closed fast.

Lack of democratic communication, not failure of democratic ideals, was the cause of the hate and discontent which were threatening the stability of Chicago in the nineties, Jane Addams argued. Democratic communication, she argued further, was endangered by all who believed in one truth— whether it was revealed by God or Karl Marx. Democratic consciousness was born and sustained in argument and debate where truth was resolved under self-imposed rules of discourse. In this spirit she created at Hull House the Working People's Social Economic Club, whose purpose was: "To give opportunity for representatives of various economic theories to modify each other, and at least to learn tolerance and the futility of endeavoring to convince all the world of the truth of one position." For, she said, "Fanaticism is engendered only when men, finding no contradiction to their theories, at last believe that the very universe lends itself as an exemplification of one point of view." [4] Jane Addams, Graham Taylor, and other settlement leaders argued that what Veblen and Sullivan described as the "feudal mentality" was born in secrecy and nourished in fear. They argued that forcing workers to discuss their grievances in secret gatherings only strengthened the power of those who urged violence as the only means to change in society.

They asked those who upheld the revealed truths of religion why such truths could not bear the light of discussion. They asked the conservative press of the city not to give up criticism of liberal and radical policies, but to give both sides of the case so that some kind of common ground for communication on social issues could be established. Settlement leaders wanted to solve concrete social problems. Knowledge of society, they argued, must be knowledge of relationships among people. And such knowledge could originate only in understanding, not simply witnessing or judging

(*Top*) It was the sight of poor children such as these in the "back of the yards" neighborhood of Chicago that moved the great heart and mind of Jane Addams. She thought welfare work should be carried out in a house—a neighborhood house, not an office. Hull House soon became a national and international center of welfare, or what we now call social work. It has been preserved as a shrine to her memory. *Courtesy Chicago Historical Society*

(*Bottom*) Chicagoans in all walks of life recognized their responsibility in the Americanization of the immigrant worker. "Americanization classes" were held in schools, plants, and settlement houses. *Courtesy Chicago Historical Society*

action in society. Social facts were facts of emotion and will, as well as of the mind. As facts of emotion and will they could be understood only in the living drama of experience. Settlement leaders asked their residents and leaders of Chicago life to understand the human meaning of being poor and unemployed, of being in jail charged with crime, and of suffering the weight of oppression and misery. The simple but basic question they posed was: How does power in democratic society really work? This question had been asked before, but it had never been asked about democratic power in cities teeming with immigrants strange to American traditions, as well as native Americans from farms and towns where communication over democratic problems had taken place in discussion in small, intimate, face-to-face groups.

Settlement leaders and the intellectuals who gathered about them found themselves under heavy attack from many quarters. The orthodox clergy argued that settlement house workers confused ignorance and sin. The virulence of this attack from orthodox quarters mounted until it was openly said that settlement house workers were really inspiring evil by studying crime instead of punishing it. The lead editorial of the Chicago *Chronicle* of November 30, 1903, entitled "Socialism, Sociology and Crime," thundered: ". . . those who commit robbery with incidental murder are your practical sociologists." For, your "sociologist being a very scientific man, and of course dispassionate, is not horror-stricken in the presence of monstrous crime. He has no feeling about the protection of society against moral monsters who commit such crimes. He is not disturbed by any feeling of indignation." The sinfulness, not the ignorance, of man was responsible for crime. "These men of science are careful to exonerate those who commit the atrocious deeds, to throw the burden of the blame upon ancestry, or upon society, or upon any and every person and thing except the criminal himself." [5]

The *Chronicle* was soon joined by the Chicago *Inter Ocean* in attacks on the introduction of "Sociological teaching" to the curriculum of the Chicago Theological Seminary. In an editorial leader for December 26, 1903, called "Sociology and Theology," Graham Taylor, "a prominent socialist, best known for his connection with the Chicago Commons," was accused of undermining the church and the pulpit. "This is exactly what might have been expected from a substitute of socialism for Christianity, and politics for preaching. Socialism aims directly at the destruction of the family and the church. Christianity is not a system of sociology. It is a method of getting sin pardoned through vicarious atonement so as to escape hell and reach heaven. The trouble with a large section of the Christian ministry is that they are trying to substitute sociology for theology and the result is that many of them are losing their jobs and the seminaries are closing their doors." [6] The advocacy of class war in the radical press and vituperation over the treason and violence of the anarchists in the conservative press also plagued thoughtful Chicagoans. The use of police power to suppress anarchism and the plutocratic use of illegal means to uphold the majesty of the law could not be reconciled. For how could democratic ends be achieved by nondemocratic means? And if businessmen were so wise and so powerful, why were they in such fear of radicals, who were, after all, few in number, without money, and with small means for communicating widely their tales of injustice?

Notes

[1] Edgar Lee Masters, *Across Spoon River: An Autobiography* (New York: Farrar & Rinehart, 1936), p. 339.

[2] Hutchins Hapgood, *The Spirit of Labor* (New York: Harper's, 1907), p. 11.

[3] See Jane Dewey in *The Philosophy of John Dewey,* ed. by Paul Arthur Schilpp (New York: Tudor, 1951), p. 29.

[4] Quoted in Graham Taylor, *Chicago Commons through Forty Years* (Chicago: University of Chicago Press, 1936), pp. 124–25.

[5] *Ibid.,* p. 145.

[6] *Ibid.,* p. 146.

18

Chicago Searches Its Conscience

Discussions on art at Hull House focused on the function of art in democracy, just as those at the University of Chicago between Mead and Dewey focused on the relation of art to knowledge in social action as well as perception. Basic to all thought about art and, as Sullivan argued in his talks and writings, to the creation of a new architecture in America was a specific definition of art as experience. It was easy enough to say that art was autonomous, an "experience in its own right," but what kind of experience was it? And how did it differ from other "autonomous experiences" in religion, science, and philosophy? Little was added to the answer by saying that art was social. For, as Mead, Dewey, Veblen, Sullivan, and Wright argued, the problem was not only the general one of the relation of art to society, but of art to democratic society.

It was easy enough to say also that art was a form of knowledge, but what kind of knowledge could be ascribed to art forms? What, for example, was the meaning of a building? For whatever was said about art must be said in terms of its forms. This was the strongest point in the aesthetic approach. But, like the social approach, this, too, soon developed characteristic incongruities. What, really, did "pure form" mean? The eternally fixed archetypes of beauty to which forms must correspond seemed capable of everything but demonstration, and even when understood could account for everything but change in art. In actual use these absolutes often seemed nothing more than pious evocation. Their power arose in evocation and repetition, not in demonstration. Clearly, there was not much in traditional aesthetics, or for that matter in philosophy itself, which could be of great help in thinking about the function of art in a democratic society based on money and technology.

Art, then, must somehow be brought back into experience, but not at the expense of losing its quality as art. Experience, on the other hand, must be thought of as art but as the forms of art peculiar to a democratic society based on money and technology. Thought itself must be re-examined, for if thinking must be related to democratic action, how would this affect judgments and truths commonly held in authoritarian society? And finally, what was meant by "democratic" relationships among people? In what sense were they really different from autocratic relationships? How could we clarify the meaning of equality? Did relationships among equals have any special psychological qualities of their own? If so, how did this affect the development of community in democratic life, and finally what was the difference between the communication of authority in democratic as compared with autocratic communities?

The Chicago pragmatism of Mead, Dewey, Veblen, and Sullivan was a profound shift in beliefs on authority as well as on thought. As we now see, it was really a shift in education from the authority of persons and transcendental absolutes (as well as supernatural authority) to an authority of method. Today technique often dominates method,[1] and we suffer from a worship of technology which often places it in the realm of ritual beyond rational judgment. Because of this it is easy to forget how Americans of 1890 suffered from the tyranny of absolutes and laws, both natural and supernatural, which could be "discovered" and "demonstrated," but not changed. In 1890 the struggle to supplant absolutism with experimentalism was a revolutionary struggle. Science, the Chicagoans argued, was more than a method; it was a way of life with values of its own. Laboratory research was group or team research in which the individual was subordinated to the group. Facts, not points of view; manipulation, not discourse; proof (usually quantitative), not the logic of discourse determined thought. In business and industry mass production, machine process, and rationalization of management control through increased quantification was changing the whole concept of work. The machine was no longer being related to the workers and managers, instead, they were being related to the machine. The image of society used by sociologists was taken from a model of "process" and, as Veblen said, of "machine process." Thus even the social act, the relatedness of people, was reduced to a study of motion.

Doctrines of efficiency, and the reduction of process to motion, were not new to Chicagoans. For nearly thirty years they had been accustomed to the sight, sound, and above all, the smell of the stockyards. Here, as popular accounts of the time tell us, steer carcasses rolled so rapidly along overhead tracks that "men have not even time to crack a joke, resembling automatic machines in the rapidity and regularity of their movements." In Cincinnati, and finally in Chicago about 1865, modern straight line production was perfected enough to serve as a model for all subsequent assembly lines. When Armour opened his first hog house, the carcass was hoisted by man power to dressing rails. Hanging the carcasses on a moving chain and passing it before cutters who removed a part or parts of the carcass made meatcutting an assembly line process. This was the process Henry Ford saw on his visits to the stockyards and the one he adapted for the development of the automobile assembly line. The principle of "gravity-flow," whereby hogs were driven up inclines to the top floor of the killing rooms and then moved down chutes to the ground floor, was used by Sullivan in his Kennedy Bakery of 1883-84, where all the ingredients were hoisted to the upper story and moved downward by their own weight as various stages of their processing were completed.

A visit to the 340 acres of yards devoted to the efficient mechanization of death was an experience which few forgot. By 1895 the yards were one of the great industrial achievements of the modern world. "Packingtown," as it was called, with its five thousand pens, stables, railroad stations, unloading platforms, horse pavilion, hotels, inns, and saloons, and the dwellings of its workers made up a community of over forty thousand. Immediately outside the yard palings stretched rows of dwellings, hotels, liveries, blacksmitheries, furniture stores, groceries, meat markets and over two hundred saloons which served free lunches to workers who bought drinks. As the guidebooks tell us: "The din of activity from city and yards rising from early dawn till far into the night" united in sounds "of enterprise which are the business man's anthem."

But there were other sounds whose echoes made terribly clear that the "machine process" must be thought of as more than technique. "As the wheel turned, a hog was suddenly jerked off his feet and borne aloft." Soon "the ear was assailed by a most terrifying shriek." This was followed by another, "louder and yet more agonizing—for once started upon that journey, the hog never came back; at the top of the wheel he was shunted off upon a trolley, and went sailing down the room. And meantime another was swung up, and then another, until there was a double line of them, each dangling by a foot and kicking in frenzy—and squealing." As the din mounted the squealing became appalling, "perilous to the eardrums," until one feared that the room itself would burst.[2] Sullivan never forgot the stockyards. Writing in the last months of his life, he observed: "There was huge slaughter at the Stock Yards, as droves of steers, hogs and sheep moved bellowing, squealing, bleating or silently anxious as they crowded the runways to their reward. The agonized look in the eyes of a steer as his nose was pulled silently down tight to the floor ring, in useless protest, the blow on the crown of the skull . . . a pandemonium of terror. . . . Then comes the next one and the next one and the next, as they have been coming ever since, and will come!"

Planning and constructing the stockyards was one of Chicago's great achievements. As Sullivan tells us in his autobiography,

> . . . all distinguished strangers, upon arrival in the city, at once were taken to the Stock Yards . . . to view with salutary wonder the prodigious goings on, and to be crammed with statistics and oratory concerning how Chicago feeds the world; and inasmuch as the reporter's first query would be: How do you like Chicago? Next, invariably: Have you seen the Stock Yards? and the third, possible: Have you viewed our beautiful system of parks and boulevards? It may be assumed that in the cultural system prevailing in those days of long ago, the butcher stood at the peak of social eminence, while slightly below him were ranged the overlords of grain, lumber, and merchandising. Of manufacturing, ordinarily so-called, there was little, and the units were scattering and small.

But in his last poignant soliloquy on Chicago, the final chapter, "Retrospect," of his autobiography, whose completed copy reached Sullivan just a few days before his death, he voices the fear of all those seeking to humanize technology. The capacity of men for slaughtering their fellow beings has now become so great that, "upon reflection, what about [babies]at the breast today? Are they to grow up within a culture which shall demand of them their immolation? or shall they not?" [3]

Men had always killed to live, but never before had killing been done without some attempt to conciliate the gods of the family, the community, or the church. Killing had always been regarded as a sacred act. Taking life was proper only to those who gave it—the gods. Engineers and businessmen had reduced space and time to motion in their canals and railroads; now they were reducing life itself to the same process. As Sullivan said wryly, the animals in the yards were not even murdered, they were slaughtered. Before such suffering and death, impersonal as it was, men and women stood in silence. Laughter died quickly, men looked at each other; "women [stood] with hands clenched, and the blood rushing to their faces, and the tears starting in their eyes." [4] Even the guidebooks warned of the ordeal. It was a common Chicago joke that everyone was a vegetarian after his visit to the yards. Chicagoans boasted to the world of their stockyards, and urged everyone to see them. Animals had to die if millions were to be fed, just as they had died to feed Union soldiers and give them the hides they needed for shoes, boots, cartridge boxes, saddles, and harness.

It was the impersonalization of death, in this terrible linkage of technology and death, which was so disturbing. As the stench of death filled the air, Chicagoans had daily reminders that technology could become a curse as well as a blessing. World War I taught that killing machines could be turned against men as well as animals. In his last months of life, horrible images of men going to their death like animals to the slaughter pens in

The stockyards of Chicago were an early example of the great talent of Chicagoans for large-scale planning in industry as well as in public projects. Chicago businessmen were among the first in America to grasp the implications of technology for business. *Courtesy Chicago Historical Society*

the yards haunted Sullivan. In the last chapter of his autobiography there are images of "hog's background of culture" and his journey to death in answer to "his country's call . . . to fill little holes in the ground where poppies grow and bloom." In final, terrible irony, Sullivan asks his Chicagoans, who have developed such marvelous killing machines, why they are so sure that someday men may not turn their terrible machines against each other as well as against animals? As he wrote *Democracy: A Man Search* Sullivan's conviction deepened that the battle of the twentieth century would be between feudal powers of death and democratic powers of life.[5]

Feudal power, he argued, seeks to enslave and kill. Merchants of death sell poisoned food and drink in our cities, manufacturers sicken and kill their workers in workshops so foul that animals could not exist in them. And the church, formed in the image of Christ's love and charity, has been betrayed in the unholy alliance between the church and the moneychangers. The "man in the street" walks within the "confines of a world-trap, a human rat-trap of fictions which he calls business, real life, education, and other like names. The man who buys men takes them for granted—He will kill them if he can. For when he says 'money talks' it is the same as saying, 'I will kill them if I can.'—for what they say life is, such is death." And then Sullivan's agony over the betrayal of a democratic architecture by the feudal merchants of death bursts into the frenzy of his poem, "The Dance of Death." This chapter is the most savage outburst in all of Sullivan's writing. For a terrible moment the predatory feudal barons have won, and hell now opens up to earth, as the mad dance of death begins. The venal predatory businessman of Veblen now becomes a devil who walks the earth only to visit suffering and death among men. Sullivan's ironic mask drops, the plutocrat is no longer a clown, but a villain of dark tragedy.

As the depression of 1893 wore on, the contrast increased between the white city shining beside the blue waters of Lake Michigan and the filthy stinking slums just a few blocks from the Lake. The University of Chicago was adjacent to the Fair grounds in a neighborhood of hotels, rooming houses, restaurants, and shops which had been built to profit from the Fair. As the Fair closed, whole blocks became vacant, hotels were boarded up, and the University found itself almost overnight in the midst of a desolated area. As Herrick described it out of his experience as an instructor at the University in 1893, Cottage Grove Avenue stretched block "after block, mile after mile. . . . No other city on the globe could present quite this combination of tawdriness, slackness, dirt, vulgarity. . . . India, the Spanish-American countries, might show something fouler as far as mere filth, but nothing so incomparably mean and long." [6]

But worst of all, Lovett tells us in his autobiography, "was the spectacle of poverty—men, women, and children marching to the garbage dumps and, in spite of unoccupied buildings galore, sleeping in jails or the City Hall. From our windows in Graduates Hall [at the University of Chicago] we saw Coxey's army of unemployed straggle north to seek shelter and food in the city." The scholars gathering in the ugly, desolate University neighborhood found no ivory towers waiting for them. And, unlike Chicagoans who still basked in the assurance that their Fair was the most splendid civic presentation ever created in America, they did not share glowing visions of a future which alone made the present supportable. "The campus was a rough sand-lot with a swamp marked by a few scrub oak trees, where frogs croaked us to sleep at night . . . all bleak and grim," [7] Lovett tells us.

But even the hardy breed of Chicago boosters did not bask long in their glory. They were rudely shaken by an arraignment which, so Chicagoans were told, had not been surpassed since the Hebrew prophets denounced Babylon. This was the publication of *If Christ Came to Chicago: A Plea for the Union of All Who Love in the Service of All Who Suffer* by William T. Stead, the widely known London journalist who came to report the Fair and stayed to study the city. Night and day for several weeks he tramped the streets, exploring cheap lodginghouses and saloons, visiting with citizens in the corridors of the City Hall, talking with the madams of the Levee bordellos, frequenting the haunts of the unemployed and people broken by the cruelty of life in the city. He found much of Chicago a "disgrace to a civilized country," and went on in speech and writing to say why he thought so. Stead listed owners of houses of prostitution, exposed startling discrepancies in tax assessments, and described the horrors of life among the poor and unemployed. Exposure of Chicago vice, crime, and corruption was not new—indeed, it had become a genre of Chicago writing. As the Chicago *Herald* editorialized, "The book contains nothing that is novel. Much of it is a mere paraphrase of old newspaper reports relating to past events." To Stead's statement that the only place where a poor man can exist free in Chicago was a saloon, or to his harrowing descriptions of the homeless and hungry unemployed searching through garbage for food, replies were easy enough. Chicagoans had heard this "anarchist propaganda" before. But when Stead attacked the church by saying that if "Christ came to Chicago and sought to discover His Church He would not be likely to mistake any of the existing ecclesiastical sectarian institutions for the society which He founded for the purpose of carrying on the work of the redemption of the world," he shifted the burden of sin from the "depraved" poor to the shoulders of the saints themselves.

Chicago businessmen, pillars of the church, whose wealth was given them to serve as "stewards of the Lord," were no better than their priests in Stead's indictment. Stead told the churches that the City Hall, with all its iniquities, would be "Christ's cathedral" if he came to Chicago. The churches had withdrawn from civic life and refused to preach about the social and civic duties of the Christian. They had violated the fundamental principle of the Christian brotherhood. Brotherhood, now dead in the Christian church, was being kept alive in politics and in settlement houses where true Christianity now existed. "In the citizen-ship of Chicago, as in the old Christian Church, there is neither Greek nor Jew, bond nor free, Barbarian nor Scythian—all are one before the ballot-box."

Chicago girls who worked in State Street stores were driven to prostitution because they could not live on weekly salaries of two dollars and fifty cents. He even went so far as to say in print that the head of the dressmaking department in "one of the largest dry-goods stores in Chicago" was the manager of a house of ill-fame down in the Levee. She found this "combination very convenient, as she recruited in one establishment by day for assistants in the other at night." Stead's "Black List" of property, some of which was used for houses of prostitution and gambling, gave the names of the "prominent citizens" who owned it. Many old Puritan families, it turned out, were pocketing rents from the vice traffic. He published a map of the Levee district, showing "streets of sin," where whole blocks were given up to brothels. Chicago's feudal barons, Stead argued, were not even very feudal in their concern with their city. While Chicago had accomplished much and was still capable of becoming a great city of ten million souls, it could no longer rely on men like the Fields, the Pullmans, and the Armours to lead it. Chicago businessmen and the leaders of the established church had betrayed the city. All that could save Chicago now was a new kind of religion, a new social concept of sin, and a willingness to face the facts of urban life.

These attacks were made openly and received wide publicity. Encouraged by the response, and especially by that of trade unions, Stead issued a call for a mass meeting to be held November 12, 1893, under trade-union auspices at Central Music Hall. As Graham Taylor, who spoke at the meeting, said, "Such a gathering Chicago had never seen before, and is not likely to see again." The floors and galleries of the city's greatest forum (designed by Dankmar Adler) were filled by men and women of all ranks, races, sects, and conditions. On the stage sitting side by side were leading businessmen and labor leaders, politicians, members of exclusive clubs, preachers, saloon-keepers, gamblers, professors of theology, society matrons, madams from Levee houses, judges of the courts, and even one of the men convicted in the

Haymarket Riot trial who had recently been pardoned by Governor Altgeld. Stead opened with a prayer for mutual understanding and then described conditions in the city. Thomas Morgan, the veteran leader of the socialists, came to respond for labor. He pointed out that what Christ would condemn most was "the crime of silence—a silence which had been broken here almost for the first time in the history of our city." However harsh his indictment, Stead voiced no doubt over the ability of Chicago leaders to create a great city. Like Sullivan, he found the secret of Chicago in the broad and powerful visions of its new leaders. He gives a prophetic vision of what Chicago will be like when it is a city of between three and four millions. He tells us that he is a new kind of prophet, a sociological prophet who fashions Utopias to give direction to life here on earth, and in the present, not an ideal future. "Unlike most writers who enter the field of imaginary prediction, I have endeavoured scrupulously to confine myself to the practical. In describing Chicago as it might be in the twentieth century, I have refrained from colouring the picture by introducing any element that is not well within the grasp of her citizens, if only they would give their minds to the task of obtaining it."

By 1960, Stead prophesied, Chicago would be the "greatest seaport of the world." Atlantic steamers will plough their way direct from Europe to Lake Michigan. The Federal Government will be transferred from Washington to Chicago, the "continental centre," and housed in marble buildings which recapture the "architectural glories of the World's Fair." [8] And, although Chicago of 1960 will become more than ever a "city of magnificent distances," the population will be more compact "due to the more general utilization of lofty buildings for purposes of cooperative housekeeping." Gas will be the common fuel of the city, and anyone whose chimney smokes for more than five minutes will be liable to imprisonment in the Bridewell. A central furnace in each block will enable the municipality to provide heat at a fixed charge for every room on the block. Garbage will be used, along with gas, as fuel. All streets will be paved and washed every day. The city will be serviced, and its people transported, in a series of underground tunnels.

The "skyscrapers," built for the purpose of co-operative housekeeping, will contain restaurants (run by first-class French chefs), libraries, reading rooms, concert rooms, and other cultural facilities. Branch establishments of these co-operative homes will be established in the country for use in the summer time. "Roads [will be] so good that there is nothing to prevent the [workers] from cycling backwards and forwards to their place of business and their summer retreat. . . ." [9] Owing to the general introduction of taller buildings in the residential quarters, great spaces [are] cleared and devoted to parks and recreation grounds. Each nationality [will have] its own playing ground, in which it pursued its national sports." In 1960, he prophesied, the streets will be planted with shade trees, fountains play in all the public places, and in winter time the squares will be converted into heated winter gardens, where music and society are enjoyed in the winter as they are in parks during the summer.

All this has been done by a new kind of urban community guardian. "The great civic revival . . . brought into existence what in an ecclesiastical age would have been called a religious order, but which in this age was simply the appearance of a body of men and women who were known as 'helpers.'" These citizens will have dedicated themselves to the service of the city, as the followers of Loyola dedicated themselves to the service of the church. "It was the first instance of an order or a society of consecrated souls dedicated to the redemption of the municipal and social system." The model of civic revival has been the ideal of the family, hence women must not only be permitted but even compelled to take a full and fair share with men in all civic work. "The result of this infusion of the more refined and cultured and graceful element into municipal work was everywhere apparent." In the skyscrapers devoted to cooperative housekeeping, domestic service has become a profession. Cooks and housemaids will have at least the position of a stenographer or a retail clerk. They work in relays, and after they finish they are as free to go and come as any clerk in an office or store.

The theater has now become the "greatest reinforcement of all the moral forces of the city." The churches, far from censoring the theater,[10] encourage the drama as a special means of cultivating the mind and "reaching the heart of the population, and especially of the scholars." Every school and every Sunday school will have its own dramatic society, and it is a proud day for the pious parent when her daughter is permitted to make her debut on the boards of the municipal theater. There should be a circus in every park and a theater in every ward. A city ward without its municipal theater will be "regarded as being in a state of spiritual destitution which called for the prayers of the churches, and their immediate assistance to supply the want." There will be a "Church of Chicago" which includes all religions. Archbishop Ireland has become the head of this municipal church, with Reverend Jenkins Lloyd Jones, the Unitarian, as the first vice-president. With centralized control, spiritual or moral evil in one district is the concern of all.

Every morning ministers will sit with their assistants to listen to the distressed, to give counsel, and to compose the difficulties of their parishioners. The churches have become the center of their communities. They are open all night and have been transformed into picture galleries and museums of sculpture, as well as places of worship.[11] Every church will also contain a reading room, and all classrooms will be open to students who cannot find privacy in their boardinghouses or homes. In working-class districts every church is also a concert room at the dinner hour. "Nothing could be more remarkable than to see the church edifices crowded with grimy, brawny workmen eating out of their dinner pails and listening to organ recitals and vocal and instrumental music."

The churches themselves will be held responsible for the sins of their congregation. When a church member sins, as in the birth of an illegitimate child, the church will be draped in black to point up its failings. For such a scandal could not occur if the church had done its duty. "As the church had not been able to prove that it had done all that it might have done to have remedied the evil from which this seduction sprang, it was doomed to wear penitential garb on this day of public rejoicing."

Medical services will be provided free for all the citizens. "Mr. George M. Pullman on his retirement from business had handed over three-quarters of his immense wealth to be employed in conveying convalescents and consumptives by Pullman cars to regions where their recovery would be expedited. Floating hospitals were anchored in the Lake during the summer."

Civic hospitality will have reached new heights. The hospitality of the mayors of Chicago has become world famous. Under the mayoralty of Mrs. Potter Palmer, who will make the year 1900 memorable in the history of America, Chicago will have entertained, as a matter of course, every distinguished visitor who arrived on the American continent. All citizens will regard it as an honor to keep open house for any stranger. Millionaires no longer keep their art treasures to themselves and a select circle of friends. On visiting days the poorest citizen in Chicago may drink in his fill of beauty in the picture galleries of the richest millionaire on Prairie Avenue. A citizen who possesses valuable pictures and excludes citizens from seeing them will be regarded "virtually as a thief, and when due representation has been made, and made in vain, was boycotted by his neighbors and excommunicated by the church."

Such changes are to be made possible by a complete change in the plutocratic status system of Chicago. The post of Superintendent of Schools will be the most important in the city after those of the Mayor, the Chairman of the Civic Federation, the President of Hull House, and the Chairman of the Church of Chicago. Every ward of the city will have an outpost of Hull House, which has gradually extended its borders until it has become the greatest social center of the city with affiliates in every one of the two thousand precincts. Settlement workers will live among the people, share their lives, and constantly interchange their experience to bring the help of all to the aid of each. After the Superintendent of Schools the most important official in town is the Chief of Police. The scions of Chicago's first families compete for positions in the police and fire departments. The police force is composed largely of women, who have raised the moral tone of the force. Great Chicago merchants have now become provisioners to the people. All services have been municipalized.

The necessities of life will be sold directly to the consumer without the interference of the middleman. Mr. Marshall Field and Mr. Leiter will have decided that they have made enough money and gave their stores, fully stocked and with adequate capital to carry on the business, to the people of Chicago. Other millionaires followed this example, and soon the city was making enough from such stores to pay for its civic programs. The City Council, which will run these enterprises, will be staffed by the best citizens of Chicago, who consider it a sacred trust to run such enterprises for the people. Mr. Kohlsaat has given his bakery for the city to be used as an experimental station for supplying well-cooked food at a minimum cost. Pageants and celebrations will be numerous and splendid. On all such days, Chicago will honor its great citizens and present itself to the world as the ideal city of the world.

Stead's attack, the publicity given his condemnation of the church, and, above all, his concrete visions of what Chicago could become initiated a reform movement. Orthodox clergymen held that the cause of poverty was depravity. Liberals argued that poverty was not the result but the cause of depravity. For the moment orthodox opinion was victorious. The poor, the unemployed, the delinquent were all shiftless, lazy, and corrupt. Even good workmen were too ignorant, and subject to too few restraints, to be trusted to take care of themselves. They must be kept in custody by businessmen who would see to it that they had steady work. But as the debate raged a new tone crept into the arguments of the orthodox. For the first time they admitted the existence of a great amount of suffering and were shaken in their belief that depravity caused poverty. The debate was no longer over the fact of poverty and want, but its cause.

The events of the summer of 1894, which followed Stead's exposures by only a few months, soon made clear to Chicagoans that a serious breakdown had occurred in American society. The Pullman strike spread to all railroads having connections in Chicago. On the pretext that strikers were interfering with the mails (a charge hotly denied by Governor Altgeld) federal troops were ordered into the city. President Cleveland sent investigators, among them John Graham Brooks, to find out what was happening and to report back directly to him. During visits and discussions with members of the University of Chicago community, he stated that burning cars were fired by the railroad companies for propaganda purposes. Campus conservatives such as Professor James Laurence Laughlin upheld the rights of management. The intensity of the debate mounted as students and faculty became involved in the fate of the strikers. Rioting and violence crept closer to the campus. Lovett tells us, "Night after night we [the faculty and students] saw the western sky red with the light of burning cars. Grant Park was white with the tents of soldiers."

Notes

[1] Making technique an absolute beyond reason has produced incongruities no less dangerous than the older and better-understood incongruity of basing reason in supernatural faith.

[2] Upton Sinclair, *The Jungle* (New York: Viking, 1946). This Viking Press edition has an introduction by Sinclair in which he tells of his days in Chicago in 1904, when he gathered material for his novel. His account of the effects of the trip through the killing rooms is matched by several other accounts. See, for example, Paul Bourget's *Outre-Mer: Impressions of America* (New York: Scribner's, 1895). Even popular accounts stress the shock and terror of facing the mechanization of death.

[3] Sullivan is speaking here in 1922 or 1923, when he wrote *The Autobiography of an Idea*. The "days of long ago" before large-scale manufacturing were the decades from 1870 to 1890. These quotations are from pages 307 and 308.

[4] Sinclair, *op. cit.,* p. 35.

[5] This accurate vision of the rise of authoritarian states was shared by Veblen, whose *Imperial Germany and the Industrial Revolution* (New York: Viking, 1917) is an uncanny forecast of the rise to power of the "feudal mind" in our time. He argued that the only kind of social control understood by Germans was authoritarian control and that, since the state, not the business community, would control technology, we would see technology perverted to feudal uses far worse than those of the predatory capitalists, who, at least, competed with each other and thus slackened the process of centralization of power.

[6] Robert Herrick, *The Web of Life* (New York: Macmillan, 1900). The novels of Fuller, Herrick, and Dreiser are all, to one degree or another, novels of Chicago.

[7] *All Our Years: The Autobiography of Robert Morss Lovett* (New York: The Viking Press, 1948), p. 54.

[8] Stead agitated for the preservation of the classical Fair buildings. The preservation of Atwood's Fine Arts Building in Jackson Park was greatly aided by his efforts. The architecture in most American Utopias of those years was classical—as it was in the new Christian Science Church and in most civic buildings.

[9] Chicago businessmen were quick to grasp the significance of mechanized movement in the railroad and bicycle, but they failed to understand the automobile and did nothing to attract the automobile industry. This failure really marks the beginning of Chicago's decline as "the wonder city."

[10] Actors, and especially actresses, were not considered fit guests in many pious

families of the nineties. Chicago "blue-stockings," unlike their Boston counterparts, did not find cultural interests necessary to prestige. "Good works," not "good taste," determined social prestige among women. Businessmen could organize and finance art, but they could not, even as amateurs, practice it. Edgar Lee Masters, the Chicago poet and law partner of Clarence Darrow, tells how suspicious Chicago businessmen were of a male poet. To succeed as a lawyer it was necessary to mask and hide his poetry. *Spoon River Anthology* was published under an assumed name to protect his law practice.

[11] The wedding of art and religion was vigorously advocated by liberal clergymen such as Swing and Gunsaulus. Because of this, Sullivan and Wright were able to show how their new "utilitarian" architecture could be used for sacred purposes. The religious work of the Chicago school has received far too little stress.

19

The Chicago School of Thought: I. Veblen Clears the Ground for a Reconsideration of Art in a Democratic Society

U NLIKE most American universities in 1894, the University of Chicago was an intimate part of a city. This was a moral as well as a physical relationship. President Harper made clear that he wanted no split between "town and gown"; University of Chicago teachers and scholars were to take part in the social and civic life of the city. Rockefeller's gifts, generous though they were, were conditioned on local support. President Harper understood, if his faculty sometimes did not, that the University must root itself in the community. This required communicating the purposes of the University in forms comprehensible to interest groups who agreed on the need for a great University but for very different reasons based on widely different definitions of greatness. Businessmen of the city wanted their sons to learn how to make money, while their daughters must be inspired to uphold what Veblen called "pecuniary canons of taste." Secondary school superintendents wanted their students admitted to the University by certificate, not by exam. Business alumni identified athletic success of the University with the greatness of Chicago. Local churchmen wanted the University to uphold "Christian ethics." Liberal journalists, clergymen and artists, as well as settlement house workers wanted the University to champion liberal thought and social action. Nor was communication within the University much easier. To appeal to faculty audiences ranging from radicals such as Veblen to conservatives such as Laughlin or the distinguished German scholar Professor Herman E. von Holst required great skill.

President Harper was prepared for free inquiry in theology, but the radical and liberal press of the nation, Harper soon discovered, thought of academic freedom in terms of economic and political as well as theological doctrine. The country was highly skeptical about a "Rockefeller university" harboring anything but plutocratic doctrines. But, to the glory of Chicago and the amazement of the country, the University struck out boldly on many new paths of thought and action which were sustained by Chicago plutocrats as well as by Rockefeller himself. President Harper was determined that a liberal position be maintained, but he argued that liberalism must be made relevant to life off the campus as well as on. His arguments with those who upheld the universality of the classics, such as Herrick and Lovett of the "Harvard Gang," was over the communication of the classics, and, indeed, the communication of learning in democracy. He argued that the University must not only create but communicate knowledge.

President Harper succeeded in gathering about him an extraordinary faculty—perhaps the most stimulating group of scholars in the country, certainly the one with the most varied traditions and backgrounds. All, radical and conservative alike, have left eloquent testimony to the greatness of President Harper. Robert Morss Lovett, a target of conservatives during the witchhunts after World War I and in Senator McCarthy's time, said: "No one can testify with better right than I to the fact that no other institution in the United States ever exhibited such tolerance of unorthodox opinion and behavior as the University of Chicago." [1]

President Harper's public was the people of Chicago, not just the plutocracy. He wanted to train an educational elite for the Middle West, but he also wanted this elite to be recruited from the people, or if this was not possible, to train an elite which would remain highly responsive to the people. From the first the University was in every sense an institution of public service, as well as a community of "detached" scholars. To international scholars and those from the established seats of learning in the East there was no problem about founding a community of scholars. But the problem of the responsibility of scholars to their community was far more complex. Harper believed that the University could rise no higher than its source of strength, the city of Chicago. Yet few of the scholars just beginning their careers, and even fewer of the famous scholars attracted to the University, knew much about the people of Chicago. Even those who had been raised in New England and the Middle West and who were instinctively democratic knew little about urban life and less about the strange and alien immigrants pouring into Chicago from all corners of the earth. Any good reporter on the Chicago press knew more of the city and how it worked than most of the faculty of the new University.

The sight of Coxey's Army (the most publicized of many bands of unemployed men who marched to Washington, D.C., in 1894) of ragged and hungry unemployed workers straggling through the Midway in search of food and shelter in the city, the contrast between the radiance of the Fair and the squalor and filth of the city lit up by the flames of burning railroad cars in the sky to the west of the campus, shocked even the detached scholars. Many understood for the first time in their careers that if scholarship was to survive there must be a community to sustain it. Men could not think, any more than they could live, in fear and distrust. If the price of democracy was hunger and degradation, who could blame men for taking to the streets to gain the democratic rights by force that they could not obtain by law? New Englanders on the faculty knew that their ancestors had done so. Middle Westerners still remembered the silence and tears of their mothers and sisters over the bodies of soldiers who fought, suffered, and died to preserve the Union. If men were free, but free only to starve, what good was democracy?

The great argument among the first generation of scholars, teachers, and students at the University was not limited to the relationship between capitalism and democracy or the specific role of the scholar in shaping American society. The relevance of literature, art, science, and the whole life of the mind to poverty, hunger, and degradation in the lives of thousands of Chicago unemployed workers was examined. For younger scholars such as Dewey, Mead, and Veblen, the lack of relevance between classical universals and the particular problems of Chicago soon became acute. What, for example, was the use of teaching the sons and daughters of businessmen Plato's *Republic*—a Utopia in which merchants were not considered fit to be free citizens let alone community guardians. How should Athenian "democracy" based on slavery be taught to the children of soldiers who had fought and died in the cause of a union of free men? What was the use of spinning out more romantic tales of love for men and women who wanted to find a new kind of love in shared experience? How, Herrick asked, could one go on making Chicago heroines in the image of the women of Howells, Wharton, or James? Chicago women at the University, Hull House, and even in high society were not interested in being romantic heroines. Harriett Monroe, Mrs. Palmer, Jane Addams, Frances Willard, and the younger women led by Margaret Anderson refused to mount romantic pedestals. They wanted to work and create in the same manner as men. Even Mrs. Palmer, "Mrs. Chicago" to the world of fashion, warned women that masculine chivalry was based on the subjugation of women.

And what was one to do with the son of an immigrant who was the first of the family to reach for a higher education, yet whose eagerness and capacity to learn stood in such poignant relief against his ignorance? It became harder and harder for the gifted young aesthetes and scholars of the campus to turn back in the evenings to manuscripts that upheld a tradition that had taken so little account of such a world as Chicago. Making a university in the new city of Chicago, it turned out, really required making a new community, both in the city and on the campus. It was an exhausting task. Many broke under the strain, others fled the campus never to return.

Even the best often knew weariness and despair. As Moody, the poet, said, "Every time I give a good lecture a poem dies." But in moments of black despair, a vision gleamed of freedom and dignity. The battle of democracy was being fought in the classroom. Whoever won the minds of the students of 1900 won America. But even those fired by the challenge of Chicago and the Middle West often yearned for escape. Memories of Harvard and Yale and the mellow culture of the East haunted the raw Chicago campus. The Harvard of 1888–93 was, says Lovett, "a golden age in the history of Harvard. The setting sun of the classics cast a mellow glow from the horizon, like Christianity in an age of science." But, Lovett came to believe, it was the glow of a dying sun. The new people of the Middle West lived in a present lighted by a future. Their present was determined by gleaming futures, not the golden pasts of Boston or Europe. As Dewey, Mead, and Veblen said, the future, not the past, must be searched diligently to create goals which could determine action in the present. The hallowed past of New England was, for Dewey, Mead, Veblen, and Sullivan, a "bookish" past. In New England the nerve between action and thought had been cut.

If the classics were accepted as absolutes, how were these absolutes to be applied to the life of the city, and how were they to be related to the sciences and technology which were determining the new life of America? Arrivals to the campus soon found that what they had taken for granted in the East must now be defended. There were even men on the faculty who argued that the classics should be abolished! [2] As the debate raged it soon became obvious that absolutes of all kinds must be tested for their relevance to the new life of an urban democratic community. The city itself, its meaning for the future of America, thus became the new stage of the American spirit. The drama of Chicago from 1895 to 1915 soon engrossed University scholars as it already had engrossed architects and engineers such as Adler, Sullivan, Root, Edelmann, and Burnham from 1870 to 1895. But the task of clearing ground for new thinking about democracy was formidable. Understanding American life, and especially the new life of the Middle West where the democracy of our time was born, was not easy for scholars trained in other traditions. It was difficult, too, for Americans to say that democracy must work, when no one knew exactly what "working" meant and what kinds of tests could be applied to it. If traditional theological, philosophical, and cultural norms no longer applied, what did? If democracy depended so greatly on capitalism, why had capitalism failed to vanquish poverty and want? If technology was to determine the way men worked, what was to become of the joy of craftsmanship? If technology was to be controlled by businessmen, what reason was there to hope that giving them new and greater power would abolish the poverty and want capitalism had already created in the great cities of the world?

Dewey, Veblen, and Mead shifted the whole basis of argument over the relationships of humanism and science. They argued that it was not up to the new scientists and artists to justify their ways to the humanists, but it was the humanists, with their transcendental absolutes, who must explain the relevance of the humanities to science and the new art struggling for birth in technology. Dewey argued that there was nothing real, whether as being, or relations between things, that was not a direct matter of the senses. He placed the locus of thought at specifically the point where idealists found it missing, namely, in the ambiguities arising out of conflict between the old and new. Mead argued that it was the social process itself which was responsible for the appearance of the self, since there could be no self apart from social experience. Veblen argued that the observable data of business enterprise, the forms of consumption in which a business society expressed itself (its rhetoric, so to speak), confirmed none of the benefits to the community claimed by businessmen. On the contrary, business rule was nothing but a feudal rule which condemned the modern democratic urban community to a reign of waste, futility, and violence. In his eyes, businessmen were not only useless but vicious.

No one, not even Sullivan, hated Chicago's "captains of industry" more than Veblen. He believed that business enterprise was simply feudal enterprise in new dress. It was, he argued, a regime devoted to waste and futility at the hands of predatory leaders whose power was based on ferocity, cunning, and magic. Only one thing might save democracy: the stupidity of these feudal monsters and the discipline of technology which was habituating men to ways of thought and work necessary to survival in the new age. In this he agreed with Chicago socialists and reformers such as Henry Demarest Lloyd. But where they preached, Veblen analyzed. To Veblen the businessman was not only a villain but a clown filled with low cunning. He realized that before the businessman could be attacked successfully he must be desanctified. So long as he was a sacred figure criticism was blasphemous and heretical.

Veblen's highly esoteric irony, when translated into the simpler language of political progressivism, soon stripped the businessman of his sacred halo. Where the anarchists and socialists made the businessman a devil, Veblen made him a fool. Veblen even goes beyond comedy into the grotesque. Like Sullivan, he drops his ironic mask and bursts out in savage invective against a plutocracy he found corrupt and evil. This belief runs like a great chord through all his writing. His range of imagery, like his comic variations on the theme of the predatory feudal businessman, is very wide. There are few comic devices which Veblen does not use at one time or another in his attacks. But there is an element beyond comedy, a moment when hate breaks through irony. It is like a scream of rage or horror, in the midst of laughter. At other times the horror is not even lightened by ironic smiles; it becomes a terrible grotesque, like the monsters of a nightmare.[3]

In his early essays of 1894, "The Economic Theory of Woman's Dress," Veblen argues that if we are to understand society, and specifically the workings of a money society such as ours, we must examine how wealth is communicated. His three "cardinal principles" of dress are "expense, novelty, and ineptitude." Capitalistic dress is "evidence of incapacitating the wearer for any gainful occupation; . . . [which] should also make it apparent that she is permanently unfit for any useful effort, even after the restraint of the apparel is removed." Besides these three, Veblen admits a fourth: the "principle of adornment," which plays some part in the aesthetic sense in dress. But this is by no means imperatively present. And indeed, "The office of the principle of adornment in dress is that of handmaid to the principle of novelty," or style. Thus, despite variations and some slight aesthetic tinge, the arts of dress in a plutocratic world "are derivatives of the great central requisite of conspicuous waste."

Veblen's *The Higher Learning in America: A Memorandum on the Conduct of Universities by Business Men,* was written about the same time as the *Kindergarten Chats* of Sullivan, and, like it, was based on life in Chicago. Sullivan and Veblen agreed that higher education was anti-democratic—a commonplace charge in Chicago. Businessmen echoed the attacks on traditional schooling led by Sullivan in architecture, Dewey in educational philosophy, Veblen in sociology, and Francis Wayland Parker in the education of children. Veblen's pun on higher learning as "hire learning" was often quoted in campus circles. In Veblen's eyes campus ceremonials, and indeed all of campus life, were a kind of primitive magic used by feudal barons to keep the minds of scholars and their students away from the important problems of the city or any examination of the incongruities of life among a "community of scholars." In his discussion of architecture Veblen argued that American universities were dominated by a spirit of business enterprise which expressed itself in "decorative real-estate, spectacular pageantry, bureaucratic magnificence, elusive statistics, vocational training, genteel solemnities, and sweatshop instruction."[4] University architecture, and particularly the Univeristy of Chicago campus designed by Henry Ives Cobb, was "designed to impress not the academic personnel, or the scholarly element at large, but the laity." Thus, "under the compulsion of the business principles of publicity, it will be found . . . that the exterior and the decorative appointments are the chief object of the designer's attention." [5] The building and grounds of the university must be interpreted in terms of "advertising art," not architecture.

In the pages which follow these introductory remarks in the chapter "The Material Equipment," the importance of architecture to all social observers in Chicago from 1880 to 1900 is made clear. Like Sullivan and Dewey, Veblen is concerned with the relation of architecture to technology and democracy. He shares Sullivan's convictions on the moral and social effects of architecture. An "eclectic and modified Gothic" is "consistently and unavoidably meretricious." Housing the quest for truth in buildings gaudily and deceitfully ornamented to serve as a stage for indoctrinating students of a democratic society with the attitudes and skills of a predatory business class was for Veblen highly immoral. "These architectural vagaries serve no useful end in academic life. As an object lesson they conduce, in their measure, to inculcate in the students a spirit of disingenuousness." [6]

Veblen's architectural criticism is very precise. He is concerned not only with why campus architecture is traditional, but why it is of one tradition, the Gothic, and finally what the effect will be of such architecture in a democratic society. Moore, Burnham's official biographer, argued that the adoption of classical forms by the Chicago Fair was a return to a colonial American past and thus to "a better self." This was necessary because the architecture of the Chicago school was materialistic and thus without "spirit." Classical architecture was the architecture of the American gentlemen, as Jefferson's example indicated. Veblen argues that the source of the "conventional preconception that . . . scholastic edifices should show something of the revered traits of ecclesiastical and monastic real-estate" [7] derives from the need of businessmen to communicate widely their ability to spend money. In the "more sprightly and exuberant effects of decoration and magnificence to which the modern concert-hall, the more expensive cafes and clubrooms, and the Pullman coaches have given a degree of authentication" we see architecture used to communicate the power of money.

In the chapter "Devout Observances" of *The Theory of the Leisure Class* Veblen tells why he thinks Gothic was selected by the businessmen who commissioned Henry Ives Cobb to design the University of Chicago campus. Businessmen, he argues, think of society as "a structure based on status. The pervading norm in the predatory community's scheme of life is the relation of superior and inferior, noble and base, dominant and subservient, persons and classes, master and slave." The devout edifices of such a class, like the buildings of gentlemen of leisure, must be expensive and set apart for the

The early planning of Chicago's park commissioners made possible the excellent site and plan of the University of Chicago. The "Monastic real estate" of the University evoked Veblen's scorn in *The Higher Learning in America,* but critics such as Montgomery Schuyler, who did much to spread the fame of the Chicago school of architecture, were careful to point out that Cobb's plan for the future development of the University was of great significance in University campus planning.

Courtesy Chicago Historical Society

benefit of the person served. They must not be common in kind or grade but "always show a large element of conspicuous waste." And they are invariably "of an archaic cast in their structure and fittings." Archaism in architecture is a kind of ceremonial cleanliness, intended to remove devout observance from any suggestion of industrial occupation "or any habitual addiction to such employments as are of material use." [8]

The process of selective adaptation of designs to the end of conspicuous waste, and the substitution of "pecuniary beauty for aesthetic beauty, has been especially effective in the development of architecture," Veblen argues in his chapter "Pecuniary Canons of Taste" in *The Theory of the Leisure Class*. From his life in the Middle West, which began as a student under John Bates Clark at Carleton College [9] in the late seventies, through his seven-year residence on farms near Northfield, Minnesota, and Stacyville, Iowa, and finally as an instructor at the University of Chicago, Veblen decided that plutocratic architecture turned to traditional forms to uphold a principle of "honorific waste." "The endless variety of fronts presented by the better class of tenements and apartment houses in our cities is an endless variety of architectural distress and of suggestions of expensive discomfort."

This process has gone so far, Veblen stresses, that such structures cannot even be thought beautiful.

The diversion of expenditure to honorific waste . . . is not uncommon enough to cause surprise or even to raise a smile. An appreciable share of the funds is spent in the construction of an edifice faced with some aesthetically objectionable but expensive stone, covered with grotesque and incongruous details, and designed, in its battlemented walls and turrets and its massive portals and strategic approaches, to suggest certain barbaric methods of warfare. The interior of the structure shows the same pervasive guidance of the canons of conspicuous waste and predatory exploit. The windows, for instance, to go no further into detail, are placed with a view to impress their pecuniary excellence upon the chance beholder from the outside, rather than with a view to effectiveness for their ostensible end in the convenience or comfort of the beneficiaries within; and the detail of interior arrangement is required to conform itself as best it may to this alien but imperious requirement of pecuniary beauty.[10]

Good architecture, Veblen argued, is simple and straightforward. "Considered as objects of beauty, the dead walls of the sides and backs of [plutocratic structures], left untouched by the hands of the artist, are commonly the best feature of the building." The architecture of the future will fall in line with the exigencies of machine technology, which is indispensable to modern culture. The industrial art method of continuing the ideals of the handicraft era, and the architecture which uses the machine simply to copy and imitate hand-made forms, is not democratic—for a democratic architecture will require low cost and a large, thoroughly standardized output of buildings. Not even Sullivan or Wright, in all their essays and utterances on architecture, surpassed Veblen in his understanding of architecture as a communication of plutocratic power in modern society. His attack on business use of art went far beyond Edelmann's because he analyzed carefully, and communicated so well, the relationship between money and art as a new kind of social rhetoric.

Notes

[1] Robert Morss Lovett, *All Our Years* (New York: Viking, 1948), p. 60.

[2] Veblen said: "The canons of reputable living act to throw such intellectual interest as seeks expression among the class on the side of classical and formal erudition, rather than on the side of the sciences that bear some relation to the community's industrial life." For Veblen the sciences were the field of learning within which "cognition or intellectual interest" is dominant. Sullivan hated the classical curriculum of the architectural schools and argued that liberal studies must turn away from the past. He thought social studies, and particularly sociology, should be central to democratic education in the arts.

[3] See, for example, the footnote to p. 243 of Thorstein Veblen, *The Higher Learning in America: A Memorandum on the Conduct of Universities by Business Men* (New York: Huebsch, 1918), where he describes "incumbents and aspirants for academic office . . . visibly affected with those characteristic pathological hypertrophy of the abdomen, varicose veins, particularly of the facial tissues, a blear eye and a colouration suggestive of bile and apoplexy."

[4] *Ibid.*, pp. 175–76.

[5] *Ibid.*, p. 143.

[6] *Ibid.*, pp. 146–47. Veblen used words with great precision. The dictionary definitions of meretricious are 1. "characteristic of, or being, a prostitute; . . ." 2. "alluring by false show; gaudily and deceitfully ornamented; tawdry; . . ." He makes clear in his introduction to *The Higher Learning* that his observations are based on his Chicago experience and he makes clear throughout that art used for communications of wealth alone is a prostituted art.

[7] *Ibid.*, p. 145.

[8] Thorstein Veblen, *The Theory of the Leisure Class: An Economic Study of Institutions* (New York: The Modern Library, 1934), p. 309.

[9] Where he is not yet (as of 1964) honored by a plaque or statue.

[10] This quotation is taken from the end of Chap. IV, "Academic Prestige and the Material Equipment," of *The Higher Learning*.

20

The Chicago School of Thought: II. Democratic Reconstruction in Philosophy in the Work of Dewey and Mead

J OHN D EWEY, who was at the University of Minnesota from 1888–89, Michigan from 1889–94, and Chicago, where he was director of the School of Education from 1894–1904, agreed with Chicagoans on the "feudal" dangers of elite education. "What the best and wisest parent wants for his own child, that must the community want for all its children." [1] He pointed out in 1900 that hardly one per cent of the entire school population "ever attain to what we call higher education; only five per cent to the grade of our high school, while much more than half leave on or before the completion of the fifth year of the elementary grade." [2] Dewey does not raise the question of whether we should educate the people: for him, as for Sullivan, Veblen, and Harper, democracy could not exist without educational opportunities for all. And, as both Harper and Sullivan advocated, this must be a continuing education, not just a few years during youth.

Sullivan thought community agencies such as the newspaper would further adult education. Harper thought adult education should be a function of the university itself, as did Dewey and Mead. But all agreed on providing the widest possible base for popular education. Sullivan's faith in the free press was born and nourished by living in a community with vigorous, well-written newspapers. Even the conservative press, such as the Chicago *Tribune,* allowed reporters to depart from editorial policy. Both conservative and liberal newspapers agreed that their central task was the interpretation of life in Chicago. Dewey and Veblen agreed that education must come to terms with science and technology. Dewey argued, as did the architects of the Chicago school, that modern education must be created for those who want "to make, to do, to create, to produce, whether in the form of utility or art." He describes the education of his time in the same feudal imagery used by Sullivan and Veblen. Such education appeals "to the intellectual aspect of our natures, our desire to learn, to accumulate information, and to get control of the symbols of learning." This "medieval conception of learning" was causing a dangerous split in American society. Students interested in shop courses, the arts, and the sciences were looked down on as "technical students." The result is, says Dewey, that we see about us everywhere the division into "cultured" people and "workers," the "separation of theory and practice." [3]

In his essay, "Poetry and Philosophy," written in 1891 [4] Dewey says: "I do not understand how that can be true for the imagination, for the emotions, which is not also true for intelligence." [5] In his work in education at the University, as in his later writings, Dewey made intelligence a quality of human conduct which is completely realized when experience becomes an intelligently cultivated art. As Ratner tells us in Schilpp's collection of essays on Dewey, "It is not unnatural therefore that one finds Dewey's best and profoundest exposition of his integral conception of philosophy, or the nature of intelligence, in his *Art as Experience*." [6] In his own "Rejoinder" to the various essays on his own work, Dewey points out that making his theory of instrumentalism synonymous with knowledge reached through techniques based on quantification is foreign to his whole philosophy.[7]

Both Dewey and Mead argued that there could be no intelligence without imagination, and no experience without art. "Art has been the means of keeping alive the sense of purposes that outrun evidence and of meanings that transcend indurated habit." [8] Mead pointed out that purpose always lies in a future and that images of the future, while imagined, are constructed forms and thus subject to control in consciousness. No one can "prove" a future, yet without images of the future, or end of the act, we cannot act. For the image of the future, like the image of the past, "organizes the present in which we must act." The unit of reality which art teaches us to understand is the act. The specific aesthetic moment in the act is the moment of consummation. The common element in all the arts is organization of energy as a means to produce a result. "Literature conveys the meaning of the past that is significant in present experience and is prophetic of the larger movements of the future. . . . The first stirrings of dissatisfaction and the first intimations of a better future are always found in works of art. . . . Factual science may collect statistics and make charts. But its predictions are . . . but past history reversed. Change in the climate of the imagination is the precursor of the changes that affect more than the details of life." [9]

Dewey, along with Mead and Cooley, argued that the degradation of art to mere ornament or as a communicator of wealth or majesty was possible only because men failed to understand the social function of art. Imagination, as developed in art, is the great instrument of moral good, for the way we treat others depends on our ability to put ourselves in their place in the imagination as we act together. Thus the ideal factors in every moral outlook are imaginative. In the historic alliance between art and religion, Dewey continued, art has often been more moral than religious moralities. The latter tend to become consecrations of the *status quo,* reflections of custom, and thus reinforce the established order. The moral prophets of humanity have always been poets. The "bureaucratization of the imagination" which follows every revolution in society is not the fault of art, but the bad use of art by priests, politicians, educators, and administrators who use it to communicate ideologies and dogmas necessary to their power.

History teaches us, Dewey held, that economic and political power is insignificant in comparison with the influence of architecture, the novel, or the drama, for the "political and economic arts that may furnish security and competency are no warrants of a rich and abundant human life save as they are attended by the flourishing of the arts that determine culture." [10] George Herbert Mead's theory of the genesis of self and the nature of the social bond depends on a theory of language as the communication of significant symbols. He thinks of social acts in terms of democratic experience in play, games, and conversation. He uses the term play in a very broad sense, ranging from simple mimicry and make-believe to the drama of great art. Through the use of such forms, he argues, we anticipate the response of others, as they in turn anticipate ours. Thus we organize our own response by our capacity for dramatic rehearsal in the imagination. It is just because the individual finds himself taking the attitudes of others with whom he acts, that he is able to become an object to himself. For it is only by taking the role of others that we can come back to ourselves. Even in the deepest moments of self-awareness, as when we talk to ourselves in soliloquy, we take the attitudes of others toward ourselves. Like Hamlet, we argue with other selves, whom we create within us to make clear to ourselves what we really are.

We organize the attitudes of others, and our response to them, into systems of symbols. Property becomes a system, not of exchange of goods and services, but of economic symbols. The individual stimulates himself to buy by a prospective offer to sell. Buying and selling are thus involved in each other through dramatic rehearsal in the imagination of the role of the buyer and the seller in their response to each other. "Something that can be exchanged can exist in the experience of the individual only in so far as he has in his own make-up the tendency to sell when he has also the tendency to buy." [11] In the transaction we assume that we have certain rights because we assume the assent of all members of the community in what we do. "We take the role of what may be called the "generalized other." In doing so we become a social self. Buying and selling, the most "utilitarian" of all acts, is symbolic, and thus is as dependent on created forms of expression as any other act.

There are two stages in the attainment of self-consciousness. The first is that of play, the second that of the game, where these two are really distin-

guished from each other. In play the child enacts roles. He is continually acting as a parent, a teacher, a preacher, a grocery man, a policeman, a pirate, a
cowboy, or an Indian. In doing so, the child is acquiring the roles of those
who belong to his society. Role taking is possible because the child excites in
himself the responses to his own social acts. He learns to do so because in his
great dependence on others in infancy, he is peculiarly sensitive to the responses of others to his pleas for their response. In playing with a doll, the
child responds to the imagined appeals of the doll as his parents have responded to his cries and gurgles. This has been called imitation, but it really
is not, for we can imitate only in so far as the so-called imitated act can be
called out in the individual by his appropriate stimulation of himself. That is,
one tends to call out in himself the same response that he calls out in the other.

Play comes before games in the experience of the child. The game is distinguished from play by the existence of regulated procedures and rules. "The
child must not only take the role of the other, as he does in play, but he must
assume the various roles of all the participants in the game, and govern his
action accordingly. If he plays first base, it is as the one to whom the ball will
be thrown from the field or from the catcher. He has imbedded their organized reactions to him in his own playing of the different positions, and this
organized reaction becomes . . . the "generalized other" that accompanies
and controls his conduct." And it is this generalized other in his experience
which provides him with a social self, for in such moments we act in terms of
the assumed acts of others.

How does the individual stimulate others to respond to him in the same
way as he arouses in himself tendencies to the same reactions? This begins
with the gestures of the child. In making movements, vocal sounds, or in
grasping he acts. He learns to organize his world through manipulating it,
not only through looking at it. The hand, more than the eye, is the clue to
the genesis of human understanding. For the child, unlike the amoeba, does
not experience the objects in his environment directly, but indirectly through
his hands, which he uses to bring things to his body. Unlike the eye, which
sees others but does not see itself, the hand and the voice can be experienced
by the self as they can be experienced by others. The sounds we make assail
our ears in the same physiological fashion as they affect the ears of others. We
see or feel movements of our hands as others see and feel them.

Society arises in and continues through the communication of symbols.
Social organization is symbolic, for how we create and order symbols determines how we create and order our social relations. We do not have an experience and then communicate about it, but we have an experience because
in communication we discover ourselves through others, as we discover

others through ourselves. Our thinking, Mead taught, is really an inner conversation in which we take the roles of others toward ourselves. Three basic kinds of role may be distinguished. There is a generalized community role (the "generalized other"). This generalized other is the group's representative in the individual. Even in the absence of others, or in moments of no direct communication with others who are present and necessary to the group activity (as players in a game or a drama), the individual can yet organize his behavior with regard to his conception of their related attitudes. There is a localization within the self of the generalized other. Not Christian duty in general, but *my* Christian duty, is what we respond to within our selves. And finally, there is a unique and individual response, the "I," which is not like the generalized other (the "they") or the localized generalized other (the "me"), although it is only through conversation with its "I" that "me" reaches expression.

The "they" and the "me" are there in our environment as relatively fixed meanings, as in social tradition and family custom. But when action is blocked traditions no longer work. Yet neither do the most carefully rehearsed goals or futures of the act work out as we have intended. We start out to do something in terms of a plan, an imagined future, which we use to organize the present in which we must act. Something often interferes; we soon discover that results are, at best, a little different from what we had anticipated. Thus all action is problematic, and all imagined ends and recalled traditions are hypothetical at best. Movement into the future always brings novelty into action. As we press toward our goals we must deal with aspects of the situation which are simply unpredictable. Confusion, ambiguity, and incongruities of all kinds arise.

The critical importance of language (and all art) in the development of society lies in the fact that the stimulus of such symbols affects the speaking individual as it reacts upon the other who listens. The individual can hear what he says, and in hearing what he says he is tending to respond as the other person responds. Such responses are made up of a series of steps which take place in time as well as in space. These steps follow each other like the rhythms in art, or the acts in a play. That is, they do not simply follow each other, they determine each other, as when we say the child is not the precursor but the father of the man. All expressions, and certainly all conscious expression, are part of a larger social act. Conscious communication arises when symbols become significant socially, when the response within one's self is one which is a stimulus to the individual as well as a response to others. Where the response of the other person is called out and becomes a stimulus to control his own action, we have meaningful control.

Aesthetic experience, Mead argues, is unique in its power to "catch the enjoyment that belongs to the consummation, the outcome, of an undertaking and to give to the implements, the objects that are instrumental in the undertaking, and to the acts that compose it, something of the joy and satisfaction that suffuse its successful accomplishment." To so construct an object "that it shall catch this joy of consummation is the achievement of the artist." Aesthetic experience is part of the attempt to interpret complex social life "in terms of the goals toward which our efforts run." Other experience, religious, political, educational, hygienic, and technical undertakings, also look into the future to select and fashion ends in terms of which we can organize conduct in the present. But none of these endeavors carries with it the satisfaction that belongs to finalities as we experience them in the delight of art. For the practical acts of community life are, says Dewey, "infected by the interest which belongs to the fashioning of means into ends, to the shaping and testing of hypotheses, to invention and discovery, to the exercise of artisanship, and to the excitement of adventure in every field." This, however, is the province of action, not that of appreciation. "Our affective experience, that of emotion, of interest, of pleasure and pain, of satisfaction and dissatisfaction, may be roughly divided between that of doing and enjoying and their opposites, and it is that which attaches to finalities that characterizes aesthetic experience." In the fashioning of means into ends, in the use of tools, we attend to only whatever will further the enterprise. We see and hear only enough to recognize and use, and we pass from the recognition to the operation. But in appreciation "we contemplate, and abide, and rest in our presentations. The artisan who stops to sense the nice perfection of a tool or a machine has interrupted its use to appreciate it and is in an aesthetic mood."

At the moment of consummation all the adjectives of value obtain immediately. There objects are possessed, are good, bad, indifferent, beautiful or ugly, and lovable or noxious. Physical things alone can never do this, for they are means, and means for ends and values which often must be discovered. They have an existence which is indifferent to ends and constitutes the field of mechanism. Their hypothetical character is to be distinguished from the attainment of the end. When the individual stops in his common labor and effort to feel the surety of his colleagues, the loyalty of his supporters, the response of the public, to enjoy the community of life in the family, or profession, or party, or church, or country—to taste in Whitmanesque manner the commonality of experience—his attitude is aesthetic. Social moments in action are infused with aesthetic delight in festivals and solemn concourses when the community presents itself in terms of values, ends, and purposes. We import the finalities of past victories and defeats into the finalities of the uncertain future. Without such moments, without the consummatory moment of art, society could not exist because it could never know what social values mean as acts. Thus, in Dewey and Mead, as in Sullivan, social experience depends on art, for only in art do we have the symbols we need for communication and the symbolic experience of the end of an act which makes possible organization of our action in the present. Acts are not "processes," nor do they take place in "fields." "For life," says Dewey, "is no uniform uninterrupted march or flow. It is a thing of histories, each with its own plot, its own inception and movement toward a close." The aesthetic quality that rounds out an experience to completeness is emotional as well as intellectual. All emotions are qualifications of a drama, and they change as the drama develops. That is why we must look to drama, and all art, for real accounts of experience, for art deals with experience as a unified act, and until we know the ends of acts we do not know their social meaning.

The significance of such thinking did not escape William James. In a letter to Mrs. Henry Whitman, dated from Cambridge, October 29, 1903, he wrote: "I have the duty on Monday of reporting at a 'Philosophical Conference' on the Chicago School of Thought. Chicago University has during the past six months given birth to the fruit of its ten years of gestation under John Dewey. The result is wonderful—*a real school,* and *real Thought.* Important thought, too! Did you ever hear of such a city or such a University? Here we have thought, but no school. At Yale a school, but no thought. Chicago has both. . . ." [12] In his review of Dewey's *Studies in Logical Theory,* which included essays by Mead, Moore, and Angell, James warns his colleagues that the legendary Chicagoan who said that "Chicago hasn't had time to get round to culture yet, but when she does strike her, she'll make her hum" was right after all. "Already the prophecy is fulfilling itself in a dazzling manner. Chicago has a School of Thought! . . . It probably has a great future, and is certainly something of which Americans may be proud." [13] He was right. Other schools soon discovered that the creative center of American philosophy had shifted to Chicago, where the twenty-year-old struggle to resolve the relationships of democracy, technology, and art was beginning to show results in philosophy as well as in architecture, education, and literature.

The development of their struggle in Chicago indicates how clearly Chicagoans understood the nature of the struggle for power in the new urban society of America. They were the first trenchant American critics of a business civilization. They understood that power in American society was shifting, not to those who controlled money as such, but to those who controlled the forms in which it was communicated. Henry Adams wrote about money, and in his *Education* he speaks of it as a power in American society. But his image of the "dynamo" is highly abstract. Money, science, and technology are social "forces" whose laws can be discovered like any of nature's laws. Chicagoans thought of the dynamo as an *act,* not a "process." Sullivan, Dewey, Mead, and Veblen believed that man determined life, as well as was determined by it. Man created symbols whose forms made possible communication which, in turn, determined social relations because it was only in and through the communication of symbols that society could exist.

The Chicago image of society was a dramatic image, a struggle between heroes and villains for the soul of democracy. Sullivan, Veblen, Fuller, Dreiser, Sandburg, and Wright speak as actors to other actors, and they speak in dialogue addressed to audiences who can be warned of evil and persuaded to good. Like all actors on great stages, they speak through tragic, comic, and ironic masks to audiences they respect and cherish. They believed that man was responsible for his own acts, and while they spoke much of the people, they never spoke of the people as masses. Sullivan, Veblen, and Dewey were radical enough, yet they were never Marxists. In their image of society, man was essentially an artist, what Dewey called a "maker and a doer," and the most human moment in social action was the moment of consummation, when experience was meaningful because it was infused with a finality that is characteristic of all experience infused with art. Man was often a victim, but a victim of his own folly, not of forces beyond his control in a nature he could know but never affect.[14]

There is very little dispassionate treatment of the businessman in the writings of Chicagoans. He is hated or he is loved. Nowhere else in American art, not even in the proletarian literature of our time, is the businessman so vilified.[15] Even the anarchists, socialists, communists, and populists of Chicago, who yielded to none in the vigor of their attack on conservatives like Pullman, do not surpass, or even equal, the violence of Sullivan's and Veblen's imagery. There is no talk in Sullivan of the "capitalistic system," the "class war," or "the proletariat," or of abstract forces which affect each other like chemicals or atoms. Man does not exist in a field of force, but in a great social drama where he chooses his roles and enacts them in terms of how others enact theirs. "This one word, choice, stands for the sole and single power; it is the name of the mystery that lies behind the veil of all human appearances."[16]

Where Sullivan makes his evil money men monsters, Veblen makes them fools, degenerates, or pious frauds. Predatory and bestial imagery of the businessman is common in both Sullivan and Veblen. Veblen's ironic mask seldom slips, but when it does we recoil at the hatred seething beneath it. Unlike

Sullivan, Veblen created the fiction of a dispassionate observer who reports, as from a field trip among strange and faraway people, incongruities between the ideals and the practices of a business society. He argued that a business city like Chicago was a regime of status, led by a ruling class, devoted to "waste, futility, and ferocity." The machine in modern industry involves standardization of processes, goods, and services and requires a new set of rulers who can think of the community good in impersonal, standardized terms. Such thought can come only from those who, like the engineer and the engineer-artist, learn to think of industrial efficiency in relation to the "machine process" and the human community.

The emergence of the engineer and architect as hero in Veblen was the end, not the beginning, of a Chicago tradition. Chicago, like Venice, depended on engineers and architects for its very existence. By the fifties it was well understood that the bogs and swamps at the mouth of the Chicago River could not become the site of a big town, let alone a city, until they could be reclaimed through the skill of engineers. The destruction of the city in the Chicago Fire of 1871, the difficult soil conditions, violent extremes in temperature, and the difficulties created by the course of the Chicago River forced engineers and architects to develop new methods of building. By 1880 Chicago was the undisputed architectural engineering capital of America. By 1890 hopes for the greatest exposition America had yet seen, and a Fair which would be expressed in American forms by architects who could plan and build as well as draw, ran high. In the struggle between the "feudal barons" and the architects of the new city, it seemed for a golden moment as if the architects could bend the businessmen of their city to their will. For Chicago businessmen were patronizing their own architects, and their architects in turn were accepting their needs as valid for the creation of high art.

Notes

[1] See "The School and Social Progress" in *The Child and the Curriculum* (Chicago: University of Chicago Press, Phoenix Books, n.d.).

[2] *Ibid.*

[3] *Ibid.*

[4] This was published in *The Andover Review,* August, 1891, and republished in *Characters and Events* (New York: Henry Holt, 1929).

[5] Sullivan agreed that what is true for imagination *must* be true for intellect, for imagination transcends intellect.

[6] Ratner discusses this point in his article on Dewey in *The Philosophy of John Dewey,* ed. by P. A. Schilpp (New York: Tudor, 1939).

[7] See pp. 520–21 of Schilpp (*op. cit.*).

[8] John Dewey, *Art as Experience* (New York: Minton, Balch, 1934), p. 348.

[9] *Ibid.,* pp. 345–46.

[10] For Dewey's discussion of this, see Chapter XIV, "Art and Civilization," of *Art as Experience.*

[11] George Herbert Mead, *The Philosophy of the Present,* ed. by Arthur E. Murphy, with prefatory remarks by John Dewey (Chicago: Open Court Publishing Co., 1932), p. 185. "The Genesis of the Self and Social Control," *International Journal of Ethics,* XXXV (1924–25), pp. 251–77; and "The Nature of Aesthetic Experience," *International Journal of Ethics,* XXXVI (1926), pp. 382–92, were written and thought out carefully by Mead himself. His books—with the exception of a good share of *The Philosophy of the Present*—are compiled from students' notes or from manuscripts he had not yet published at his death.

[12] See *The Letters of William James,* ed. by his son, Henry James (London: Longmans, Green, 1926), pp. 201–2.

[13] *Psychological Bulletin,* Vol. I, No. 1 (January 15, 1904), pp. 1–5.

[14] See Veblen's careful discussion of instinct in his introductory remarks to *The Instinct of Workmanship and the State of Industrial Arts.*

[15] Upton Sinclair's *The Jungle* (1906) is a socialistic novel, but its exposé of Chicago business tactics was not a new theme in Chicago writing. Herrick (among others) depicted the unholy alliance between business and politics in *The Common Lot* (1904), in which a young Chicago architect succumbs to the temptation of get-rich-quick methods and builds a flimsy tenement that burns and destroys its tenants. *The Memoirs of an American Citizen* (1905) by Robert Herrick is the story of Van Harrington, an unscrupulous industrialist. Criticism of business corruption was well established in 1895. Wright, as we shall see, assumes, as early as 1900, that the American city has failed as a stage for humane relationships. Like Sullivan, he argues that architecture, not religion, politics, and certainly not the higher education of his day, will cure the ills of democracy.

[16] Louis H. Sullivan, *The Autobiography of an Idea* (New York: Press of American Institute of Architects, 1926), p. 267.

The Chicago Debate on the Function of Art in Society

PART FOUR

The Chicago Debate on the Function of Art in Society

21

Sullivan on the Meaning of Architecture in Democratic Society

I N 1894, the year of Dewey's arrival at the University of Chicago and the beginning of the decade in which the "Chicago school of thought" (as James called it) developed, Sullivan was thirty-eight years old. He had designed over a hundred structures—factories, stores, houses, libraries, schools, churches, theaters, suburban railway stations, clubhouses, burial tombs, and hotels. His Auditorium Building was, as Frank Lloyd Wright said, "the greatest building achievement of the period: and to this day probably is the best room for opera, all things considered, yet built in the world." [1] It was an outstanding engineering achievement, as well as an architectural masterpiece—the heaviest structure yet carried on floating foundations. This great landmark in American architecture was the work of young men. Sullivan was thirty, Adler forty-two when the Auditorium was begun.

Thus some forty years before Dewey was able to create a new American philosophy of art, Sullivan made clear that the art existed if the philosophy did not. And in his speeches, essays, poetry, and articles of the years from 1885 to 1900, when he composed *Kindergarten Chats*, the most profound book yet written on American architecture, the range and power of Sullivan's thought on architecture often reaches philosophic depth. It was not until 1934, the year of Dewey's *Art as Experience*, which now ranks as the best American pragmatic statement of aesthetic theory, that any American work approached *Kindergarten Chats*. Dewey's treatment of art in *The Child and the Curriculum* and *The School and Society*, in 1899 and 1900, is very thin and pale beside the richness of Sullivan's thoughts on art in education. Yet by 1950 *The Child and the Curriculum* had gone through a quarter of a hundred printings, while *Kindergarten Chats* (which was serialized in *Interstate Architect and Builder* from February 16, 1901, to February 8, 1902, and was revised by Sullivan in 1918) appeared for the first time in book form in 1934. Even this was a limited edition, and it was not until 1947 that a readily available edition even existed. [2] Analysis of Sullivan's writings on architecture, therefore, becomes more than a recapitulation of what others have said, or an attempt to bring some kind of order into his thinking. [3]

The earliest statement of Sullivan's we possess is his address, "Character-istics and Tendencies of American Architecture," delivered to the Western Association of Architects in 1885. This is the first Chicago statement of the "realistic" theory of art which was to become characteristic of all Chicago criticism. It antedates by nine years Garland's *Crumbling Idols,* which warned Chicago artists against copying the "last epics of feudalism" and repeating "the dying echoes of Romance." Thus some ten years before the literary revolt, twenty years before the first significant publications of the Chicago school of philosophy, and nearly forty years before the rise of Chi-cago jazz, Sullivan and other Chicago architects, Adler, Root, Edelmann and Wright, raised issues which determined the course of art criticism for their time and ours as well. Sullivan thought of himself as an architect, but he did not think that solutions to the problems of American architecture could be found within the profession as it was practiced in his time. He argued that the problems of architecture in America were common to every art and to the whole culture of America. The absence of a distinctively American style in architecture, he argued, cannot be overcome in architec-ture (or in any art) by contemplating the matured beauty of Old World art, and then grafting or transplanting such form to American forms of expres-sion. These views ignore the complex fact that a national style must be a growth in which "slow and gradual assimilation of nutriment and a struggle against obstacles are necessary adjuncts to the purblind process of growth." [4] We must therefore, Sullivan says, "disregard these dreams of a Minerva-like architectural splendor springing full-formed into being."

The American architect must seek in himself signs of a spontaneous archi-tectural feeling "arising in sympathy with the emotions latent or conspicuous in our people." A study of the people will show that the individual seeks ex-pedients to shape his immediate surroundings into a realization of his de-sires. These expedients should be taken very seriously, for the people's at-tempts at architectural form "has already in many cases produced significant and valuable results." To test such a hypothesis we have but to look into the daily life of our architecture as it now exists, in search for the existence of spontaneous and characteristic popular emotional feeling "as an element of warmth tingeing scholastic formalism; sometimes as a seemingly paradoxical inspiration in the works of the uncultivated." [5] The architect must learn from other arts, for what happens to them will happen to architecture. American literature is the only national art which has been given serious recognition at home or abroad.[6] What are the characteristics of this art? "Excessive regard for minute detail, painful self-consciousness of finish, timidity and embarrass-ment in the delineation of all but the well-behaved and docile emotions, and a tacit fiction as to the passions: all beautifully executed with much patient, earnest labor, and diplomatically tempered to the understanding." American literature is exquisite, but not virile, "too much a matter of heart and fingers, and too little an offspring of brain and soul." American romanticism, in architecture as in all art, is far too dependent on verbal explanation and comment. The architect must learn to beware of words, for words are often used to justify architectural absurdities.[7] Yet even in the curious *mélange* of "super-sentimentalisms" there is "ingenuity in device, or superb flow of spirits —all more or less leavened with stubborn common sense." As we investigate such art we need not despair, for behind "a somewhat uncertain vision resides a marvelous instinct."

American artists lack conviction,[8] and until conviction is developed creative power cannot develop. Architects are unable to develop elementary ideas "organically." In this the architect is far inferior to the businessman and financier, whose capacity to expand "a simple congenial idea, once fixed, into subtle, manifold and consistent ramifications" is admirable and a shining example which we have often ignored. For what businessmen understand, and architects do not, is the element of power. "Until this element is widely introduced into our work, giving it the impress of brilliancy, intuition and great depth of feeling, that work, exhaustively considered, will remain but little more than a temporary expedient." The presence of power as a mental characteristic in one class of our people (businessmen) augurs well for the belief that it may pervade the ranks of architects. True, the power of the new businessmen of Chicago is often crude. But the beginnings of all power in society are usually so "crude and harsh as to be revolting to refined taste." Yet such power, if "subtilized, flushed with emotion and guided by clear insight," can produce great architecture. For if the American businessman creates and understands power, the people, too, have within them a germ of artistic greatness. No "people on earth [possess] more of innate poetic feeling, more of ideality, greater capacity to adore the beautiful, than our own people."

American architects, Sullivan continues, have found it more expedient to maintain tradition than "to promulgate vitalizing thought." We are weak, and "should sentiment gain a pronounced ascendency, we may remain weak." While some of the responsibility for the weakness of our architecture rests with the public, a far greater share of blame must be taken by architects themselves. "We have at times individually sought to lead the public, when we more wisely should have followed it; and have, as a body, often followed, when, with beneficent results we could have led." But, in any case, no architectural style can become "a finality, that runs counter to popular feeling." Such feeling must be deeply respected, for it is the heart of creative energy.

"The desire at once to follow and to lead the public should be the initial attitude of our profession toward the formation of a national style. For while we conduct the technical operations, the shaping and controlling process is mainly in the hands of the public." Public demands are to be respected, for they are the reality which keeps the architect "within bounds." The public can only partially and imperfectly state its wants. The architect without a national architectural tradition must experiment with forms which bring the hopes and aspirations of the people into reality.

If the public accepts its architects as leaders and learns to go directly to them and responds readily to the intuition of those who anticipate its desires, it will gain provisionally, year by year, all the satisfaction possible to a new society. Thus, while one recognized style after another will pass through "the hands of the architect, to be tried and finally rejected in the search for permanent satisfaction," if there is a good relationship between the architect and his public "a modified residuum from each will doubtless be added to a fund representing our growth in emotional and spiritual wealth." This process will be slow, involving the lives of many generations. In the practical world, of course, we must work at short range and for immediate results. But if there is general agreement among architects on "our status, our tendencies and our policy," an abiding *esprit de corps* will be infused into the profession of architecture in America, and it will surely achieve greatness.

The problem of the architect is how to keep standards of excellence alive within himself, when he is constantly harassed by cares and responsibilities of daily life in a new city where too much is done too quickly. Chicago architects of the eighties have within them, Sullivan says, "an insuppressible yearning toward ideals." [9] These ideals must be protected "until the thrilling radiance of power shall awaken them to action." For only when "ideal thought and effective action" are one in architecture do we have a vital substance which makes it live. If the American architect will be true to himself and his art he will achieve the "mellowed spontaneity of a national style."

In his first published statement on form in architecture, "What Is the Just Subordination, in Architectural Design, of Details to Mass?" [10] Sullivan continues his argument that form in American architecture must be "in the direction of indigenous and sincere results." Only when "we become justly sympathetic, ward off extraneous and irrelevant influences, and make an honest effort to reach zeal and intense results," will the American architect find an answer on how to produce a great American architecture. The answer, the ultimate form which will become the great American form, cannot be predicted. "As for me, I do not yet know what the answer is to be, though I believe I share with others a premonition of its nature." But while we cannot predict the characteristic forms of American architecture, we can say how great indigenous forms will be achieved. "The contemplation of nature and humanity is the only source of inspiration." A building is not an inanimate thing, it lives with "intense, if quiescent life." This is because it springs from the life of its architect, and this is why present theories of art are useless. The only substantial facts which remain after "all the rubbish, dust and scientific-analytic-aesthetic cobwebs are brushed away are these facts, which each man may take to himself, namely: That I am, that I am immersed in nature here with my fellow men; that we are all striving for something which we do not now possess; that there is an inscrutable power of permeating all, and the cause of it all." Desire is the "deepest of human emotions, and . . . prudence is its correlative; [desire] is the precursor, the creator, the arbiter of all others." In great art "great desire and great prudence must precede great results."

Desire and prudence in art are linked through imagination, which is the home of reason in art. Art is never escape or simply make-believe. In art, as in religion, we must face the great reality of life—death. The power of art is, in the last analysis, the power of life over death. All "we see and feel and know, without and within us, is one mighty poem of striving." This poem is a "vast and subtle tragedy." To remain "unperturbed and serene within this turbulent and drifting flow of hope and sorrow, light and darkness, is the uttermost position and fact attainable to the soul, the only permanent link between the finite and the infinite." This is why only the spiritual results of architecture are really important. All inspiration in art contains an element of pathos, for it has "too much of the calm of nature's mysterious decadence, to permit the forgetfulness, for more than a passing moment, of this deep-down conviction, that an idea lives according solely as by its power and prudence it compromises with death." [11] In his last essay, "Ornament in Architecture," [12] before the hard lessons of the rejection of the Chicago school for the classical forms of the Fair, Sullivan restates his belief that the architect must be responsive to the people, and that the people are ready to accept an indigenous American architecture. "I can proceed," he says, "only on the supposition that our culture has progressed to the stage wherein an imitative or reminiscential art does not wholly satisfy, and that there exists an actual desire for spontaneous expression. I assume too, that we are to begin, not by shutting our eyes and ears to the unspeakable past, but rather by opening our hearts, in enlightened sympathy and filial regard, to the voice of our times. . . . America is the only land in the whole earth wherein a dream like this may be realized; for here alone tradition is without shackles, and the soul of man is free to grow, to mature, to seek its own."

In the last months of his life, when he was composing *The Autobiography of an Idea,* Sullivan characterized these early essays as products of his age of innocence. He "was too young to grasp the truth that the fair-appearing civilization [of Chicago and America] was but a huge invisible man-trap, man made." He was, he tells us, grossly ignorant. "Of politics he knew nothing and suspected nothing, all seemed fair on the surface. Of man's betrayal by man on a colossal scale he knew nothing and suspected nothing. He had heard of the State, but had not a glimmering of the meaning of the State. He had dutifully read some books on political economy because he thought he had to, and had accepted their statements as fact. He had also heard vaguely something about finance and what a mystery it was. In other words, Louis was absurdly, grotesquely credulous. How could it be otherwise with him? He believed that most people were honest and intelligent. How could he suspect the eminent?" [13] But as the dying artist looks back after thirty years in Chicago, he realizes that these years of blind faith in democracy and in the architect's capacity to shape a new civilization were a blessing in disguise. It was well he lived in illusion, for had the hideous truth come to him suddenly it might have destroyed him. As it was, he "kept on with his innocent studies, becoming more and more enamored of the sciences, particularly those dealing with forms of life and the aspects of life's urging, called functions." He "noted that invariably the form expressed the function. . . . [He then] discovered that in truth it was not simply a matter of form expressing function, but the vital idea was this: That the function *created* or organized its form." Hence "Louis began to regard all functions in nature as powers, manifestations of the all-power of Life, and thus man's power came into direct relationship with all other powers."

Until the bitter lessons of the Fair, Sullivan thought as an artist. And while he talked about architecture as the self-expression of free men, he exhorted and preached as much as he criticized. His outbursts in prose and poetry, are at once mystical and lyric.[14] He turns to nature, not to society, for his early images of man. He evokes nature through a kind of aesthetic incantation. Thus at the very end of his first oration on architecture, "Characteristics and Tendencies of American Architecture," he turns suddenly from argument to invocation. "The soft beams of the full-orbed moon failed with pathetic caress upon the slumbering life of the world; paling with the dawn, her tender vigil ended, she melts in the infinite depths when the ruddy herald of day proudly summons the workers. So does the soul watch over its greater ideals until the thrilling radiance of power shall awaken them to action." These outbursts affected his contemporaries in different ways. Some, like

Frank Lloyd Wright, often found his aesthetic mysticism sentimental. In the chapter, "The Master," of his *Autobiography,* Wright says:

He was absorbed in what seemed extravagant worship of Wagner at the time. I could not share this but I could understand. He would often try to sing the leitmotifs for me and described the scenes to which they belonged, as he sat by my drawing board. He adored Whitman, as I did. And, explain it however you can, was deep in Herbert Spencer. He gave Spencer's "Synthetic Philosophy" to me to take home and read. He himself had just written "Inspiration." He gave it to me. I thought it a kind of baying at the moon. Again too sentimental. I never liked his writing in those early days. Here again was this insidious sentimentality showing even in him. What had been suspicion now began to ripen into rebellion against sentimentality in general.[15]

Despite his deep belief that art and democracy could not survive without each other, Sullivan never possessed or cultivated the common touch. Steele, one of Sullivan's draftsmen during the Auditorium days, says: "We did not love him, but we had a great respect for him, and a great admiration for his vigorous personality. . . . He was a natural leader of men, but was either too independent, or too indifferent, to lend himself to any of the arts of the politician." He was profoundly interested in his theory of democracy, "especially in its relation to art as the self-expression of free men. On the other hand, in his way of life, his mode of dress, his manner of speech, he was an aristocrat of whom any old Bourbon might have been proud. Wilful, passionate, ambitious, domineering; a hard taskmaster as well as a fine raconteur and bon vivant, he held his handsome head high." [16]

In his *Autobiography* Wright tells us: "The Master's very walk at this time bore dangerous resemblance to a strut." But, as all admitted, the young Sullivan had a right to his pride. Adler and Sullivan had been entrusted with Chicago's greatest civic enterprise—the Chicago Auditorium, which was to seat five thousand people.[17] For several years there had been talk about Chicago's need for a grand opera house, but, as Sullivan tells us, "the several schemes advanced were too aristocratic and exclusive to meet the general approval. In 1885 there appeared the man of the hour, Ferdinand W. Peck . . . who wished to give birth to a great hall within which the multitude might gather for all sorts of purposes including grand opera." There were to be boxes, but only a few, for high society. Peck, Adler, and Sullivan—promoter, engineer, and architect—agreed the Chicago Auditorium should be for the people of the city and that, even though it was for the people, it was to be the finest large hall in the world.

Every city has some building that represents it to the world. The Auditorium is Chicago's most characteristic cultural statement. It was conceived, financed, designed, and built by Chicagoans. It stands as a great monument to a generation of businessmen who had enough confidence in themselves to go directly to their own engineers, architects, and artists.[18] For one great moment in Chicago, money, technology, and art reached harmonious expression. Chicago had built factories and stockyards that were world famous. Her parks and boulevards set new standards in civic planning. Now Chicago was to express her cultural ambitions in a building of equal scope and power. And, as American businessmen noted carefully, this revolutionary stage for the arts, glittering society balls, and political conventions was underwritten by private capital; not as a civic charity but as a sound business venture. Commodore Peck wanted culture in Chicago, but he wanted it to pay its own way. He was determined to show that culture in Chicago would "hum" because it could be made to "hum" at a profit.

Notes

[1] Frank Lloyd Wright, *An Autobiography* (New York: Duell, Sloan, and Pearce, 1943), pp. 105–6. In his Autobiography Sullivan tells us that he and Adler worked on "this enormous, unprecedented work" for "four long years." See p. 294.

[2] And even this, excellent as it is, has no index and is bound in paper.

[3] There are many reasons for this strange neglect of Sullivan as a thinker and teacher. Most important of all is the failure of the architects themselves to carry on the tradition of independent criticism of architecture developed in Chicago with the founding of such journals as *The Inland Architect* and *Western Architect* and the discussions on art which went on in Hull House and in educational circles in Chicago from 1895 to 1915. There is so little independent criticism of architecture in America today that it is hard to defend architects against the frequently raised criticism (by Frank Lloyd Wright, among others) that architecture is no longer a profession, but a trade. In most universities, architecture, unlike literature, music, drama, dance, and indeed almost every art, is not taught as a cultural study, but as a craft in engineering schools. In some circles it is even argued that architecture cannot be criticized because a building is "property," not art, and that since adverse criticism might affect "money value" it should not be permitted. Yet even much berated television programs are criticized openly and frequently by the same press which shows such timidity about architecture. The history of how architecture became "property," and no longer art, would help us to understand the relationship between art and money in our society. With the recent television scandals and dissatisfaction with business control of mass communications this is now a national problem.

[4] "Characteristics and Tendencies of American Architecture," as reprinted in *Kindergarten Chats on Architecture, Education, and Democracy,* ed. by Isabella Athey (New York: George Wittenborn, 1947), p. 177.

[5] Ralph Adams Cram, the leading Gothic exponent of these years, argued that democracy degraded art and society. Sullivan's "feudal" opponents were not straw men —in art, or in society.

[6] Sullivan was speaking here of the situation in 1885.

[7] Sullivan tells us in his autobiography and in *Kindergarten Chats* how the architect must learn to think without words.

[8] Henry Adams, after reading Henry James's biography of the sculptor, W. W. Story, in 1903, wrote to James: "The painful truth is that all of my New England generation, counting the half century, 1820–1870, were in actual fact only one mind and nature. . . . One cannot exaggerate the profundity of ignorance of Story in becoming a sculptor. . . . God knows that we knew our want of knowledge! The self-consciousness—irritable dislike of America, and antipathy to Boston. . . . Improvised Europeans, we were, and —Lord God!—now this!" *Letters of Henry Adams, 1892–1918,* ed. Worthington Chauncey Ford (Boston: Houghton, Mifflin Co., 1918), p. 414.

[9] Sullivan spoke in the eighties not as an outsider or rebel but as a leader of Chicago architects. After the Fair and his break with Adler, Sullivan's power within the profession declined as Burnham's rose.

[10] This was the title of a discussion at the regular meeting of the Illinois Association of Architects, held April 2, 1887, in the form of a symposium. It is reprinted in the 1947 edition of *Kindergarten Chats,* pp. 182–86.

[11] These lines were uttered by Sullivan in 1887 when he was thirty-one years old. Although hostile to the established church, Sullivan believed that if art was to become a great power it must help men to master death. His three great tombs, the Ryerson of 1889, the Getty Tomb of 1890, and the Wainwright Tomb of 1892, are serene witnesses to his confrontation of death. Frank Lloyd Wright considered the Getty Tomb one of Sullivan's greatest works. His tombs are in every sense "unperturbed and serene" and represent a side of Sullivan's art that stands in forgotten contrast to the power of his commercial buildings.

[12] Published in *The Engineering Magazine,* August, 1892. This is reprinted in the 1947 edition of *Kindergarten Chats,* pp. 187–90.

[13] Louis H. Sullivan, *The Autobiography of an Idea* (New York: Press of The American Institute of Architects, 1926), p. 289.

[14] Wright tells us that Sullivan often talked as one possessed.

[15] As we shall see in the discussion on form, this soon ripened into a very basic aesthetic difference between Wright and Sullivan. Wright felt that Sullivan's early ornament was "efflorescence pure and simple," while from "the very beginning my T-squares were easy media of expression for my geometrical sense of things." In the last years of his life, however, Wright turned back to Sullivan's "plastic" doctrines. Even the steel cage, as indeed all structure, must become more plastic. The "skin" wall, the hemicycle, and other "free-form" houses of Wright's and others, continue the search for a plastic containment of space—or, as we now say, a molded space.

[16] Quoted from Hugh Morrison, *Louis Sullivan: Prophet of Modern Architecture* (New York: Norton, 1935), p. 179.

[17] The Auditorium Building was not put out for bids, but was given directly to Adler and Sullivan.

[18] That is, they did not turn their buildings over to "experts" who "surveyed the field" and then reported "as a committee." In this generation Chicago businessmen made their own decisions and worked through individuals.

22

The Education of the Architect: I

THE FINISH of the Auditorium was a turning point in Sullivan's life. He tells us in his *Autobiography*: "Louis's heart went into this structure. It is old-time now, but its tower holds its head in the air, as a tower should." It was the culmination of Louis's "masonry period." [1] It was more than a culmination of a period; it was a death and rebirth of the spirit. "For four long years Dankmar Adler and his partner labored on this enormous, unprecedented work. . . . The unremitting strain . . . doubtless shortened Adler's life. He did not collapse at the end as Louis did; rather the effect was deadly and constitutional. Louis's case was one of utter weariness." In flight from Chicago to a land where there would be no "enterprise," no "progress," no "booming," "no factories, no anxious faces, no glare of the dollar hunter, no land agents, no hustlers, no drummers, no white-staked lonely subdivisions," he found peace near Ocean Springs, Mississippi, in a tract of stately forest "of immense short-leaved pines, sheer eighty feet to their stiff gnarled crowns; graceful swamp pines, very tall, delicately plumed; slender vertical Loblolly pines in dense masses; patriarchal sweet gums and black gums with their younger broods; maples, hickories, myrtles; in the undergrowth, dogwoods, azaleas, sloe plums, buckeyes and azaleas, all in a riot of bloom; a giant magnolia gradiflora near the front—all grouped and arranged as though by the hand of an unseen poet." [2]

It was here that "Louis underwent that morphosis which is all there is of him, that spiritual illumination which knows no why and no wherefore, no hither and no hence, that peace which is life's sublimation, timeless and spaceless. . . . here Louis did his finest purest thinking. . . . here he saw the flow of life, that all life became a flowing for him, and so the thoughts and works of man. . . . here he saw the witchery of nature's fleeting moods—those dramas gauged in seconds. . . . here he gazed into the depths of that flowing, as the mystery of countless living functions moved silently into the mystery of palpable or imponderable form." Looking back on this moment after many years of suffering and seeming defeat, Sullivan describes this illumination as moral and social as well as aesthetic. "Yet he never lost

Here at Ocean Springs, Mississippi, where he built a summer home, Sullivan refreshed his spirit and his body by immersing himself in nature. *Chicago Architectural Photographing Company*

Sullivan at Ocean Springs during his great years in architecture. *From the files of Richard Nickel* his footing on the earth; never came the sense of immortality: One life surely is enough if lived and fulfilled: That we have yet to learn the true significance of man; to realize the destruction we have wrought; to come to a consciousness of our moral instability: For man is god-like enough did he but know it—did he but choose, did he but remove his wrappings and his blinders, and say good-bye to his superstitions and his fear." [3]

The God Sullivan found within him was the artist. He returned to Chicago in March of 1890, no longer simply a talented architect, but a genius possessed by visions of a new world of form. His Auditorium design was a powerful statement, but of a tradition which Richardson, not Sullivan, had established. But there was greatness in the theater. Here, as Sullivan's young draftsman, Frank Lloyd Wright, saw it:

A great genius had appeared in the world of architecture. . . . Intricate gilded reliefs swept over the succession of elliptical arches forming the vast ceiling. Exquisitely modeled ornament was everywhere delicately glistening and dancing overhead and to be found in unexpected places almost anywhere alongside. The catenary curve of the main floor on which the audience rested wore all this as a golden aura. . . . Acoustics had now come to architecture. Owing to this repeated recession of elliptical arches forming the great overhead and extending from the proscenium [widest in the world] into the body of the house like a magnified trumpet, the big chief [Adler] had struck a principle that created a miracle in the projection and extension of sound. . . . Not alone had a miracle of appropriate beauty arrived but also a great triumph in acoustics. [4]

Sullivan's return to Chicago in 1890 marked the beginning of a great outburst of creative energy. In the next ten years Sullivan inaugurated a new era in American, and, as we now know, world architecture. If he had done nothing more than the Getty Tomb (1890–91), the Dooly Block (1890–91), the Wainwright Building (1891), the Transportation Building at the World's Fair (1893–94), the Guaranty Building (1895), and finally the Schlesinger and Mayer department store (1899–1904), Sullivan's contribution to modern architecture would be very great. But these structures, important as they are, do not express the full power of Sullivan's genius. As Wright says: "The buildings he has left with us for a brief time are the least of him." It was his struggle to create a principle of architecture as an aesthetic and moral force in democracy that constituted his genius and that, in turn, stirred the genius of Frank Lloyd Wright.

Four years after his birth as an artist, Sullivan addressed the American Institute of Architects in New York. He had felt the touch of death again. But this time it was not within himself, but in the city, and among architects he hoped to lead in the struggle to create a new American culture. Burnham betrayed Western architecture by offering all the work of the Fair to Eastern architects, as Sullivan reports, [5] "on account of their surpassing culture."

Only the intervention of Edward T. Jefferey, a self-educated machinist who had become a Chicago railroad executive and served as Chairman of the Committee on Buildings and Grounds, saved some of the work for Chicago architects. In one afternoon Sullivan saw his hopes and visions for a new power in American life—the power of an indigenous American architecture and the rise of the American architect to equality in the councils of business-men, priests, politicians, and professors—destroyed. Chicago architects and engineers who so proudly heralded the opening in 1899 of the great Audi-torium now, only two short years later, shifted allegiance to Burnham, who rejected as crude and vulgar whatever was truly indigenous in the work of the Chicago school.

What had gone wrong? The answer to this occupied Sullivan until the day of his death. His New York address, given a few months after the closing of the Fair, is his first attempt to answer. The struggle, he then thought, was between two traditions in architecture, as the title of his essay makes clear: "Emotional Architecture as Compared with Intellectual: A Study in Subjective and Objective." [6] He begins by saying that the cultural failure of Americans is the result of education that fails to build on the nat-ural, unspirited, sensitivity of Americans. "So familiarly has he [the Amer-ican] fared with sunshine and air and the living things, that they seem, as indeed they are, every-day and common to him. . . . Breathing the same air as they, maturing in the same glowing sunshine . . . he and they expand side by side, defining themselves intimately to each other; and the boy, growing always, after a while feels himself to be not only with them but of them." The American grows into a "brotherhood with the trees; . . . he softens to the flowers; he has a comely friendship for them all . . . he lives as only a boy can live—his lively sensibilities always in physical touch with his surroundings, in the full and irrepressible enjoyment of his five senses."

American education rejects art and thus robs the mind of imagination and sensitivity. The five senses which interpret nature to the growing boy, the "ready language" which keeps him in such natural sympathy, are so thoroughly destroyed "that he does not for a moment realize that he is then and there doing that which education, so called, once having made inop-erative in him, he will in after years, poet though he be, reacquire only with the utmost difficulty the power to do." What the simple youth does in his relationship with nature and the "physical and psychic state that it implies, we call *Touch*." For touch is to be related to action, not simply tactile stimuli. Touch means "not the touch of the painter, not the touch of the sculptor, not the mechanical and technical touch of the fingers only, not quite their negligent contact with things, but the exquisite touch of the sensibilities, the warm physical touch of the body, the touch of a sound head and a responsive heart, the touch of the native one, the poet, out of doors, in spontaneous communion with Nature." Without this even the mind cannot develop powers of abstract thought. For such direct apprehension is the first essential prerequisite in the early analytical strivings of the mind, and it is this perfect concrete analysis by the senses and the sympathies which serves as a basis for the abstract analyses of the intellect.

Sullivan thus grounds education of the young, and certainly of the architect, in the senses. And while his main concern in education is with the education of the young architect, he argues that such education could become a model for all education because in relating men to nature, and to each other as individuals, we teach them how to act, not only as architects but as members of a free society. In the essays before *Kindergarten Chats,* Sullivan seeks to ground art in experience common to all men. He argues that the greatest community experience of art lies in architecture, and that the architect in turn develops only when he relies on his natural human capacities, which he finds most purely expressed in the wonder of childhood. The child has in his breast "the true architectural afflatus, and will some day come forth the Messiah of our art. For he has that early and sure understanding by the eyes that will survive the future uncertainties of the brain."

Art is not something added to experience like ornament on a building, it *is* experience. For until the artist creates forms we cannot communicate and we cannot act together, and thus cannot achieve community. Imagination, unlike make-believe or thought based on quantification or logic, is born of a desire to act. The fully developed act involves *imagination, thought,* and *expression.* Imagination is the beginning of action because it is "a sympathy that lives in both our sense and our intellect—the flash between the past and the future, the middle link in that living chain or sequence leading from nature unto art, and that lies deep down in the emotions and will." Thought cannot exist without imagination because "in that supreme moment when ideas are born," only imagination "reveals the end with the beginning." [7]

Thus Sullivan joins Dewey and Mead in his stress on what they called the "consummatory moment" in art. That is, art deals in the finalities or ends of action, not motion, as do the physical sciences (and all theories of perception based on them), and art is thus more characteristic of *human* action than any other kind of experience. Through our use of art we learn what ends in action mean in human relationships. As Mead tells us in his *Philosophy of the Present,* we recapture pasts and envision futures in art in order to organize action in a present. Thought alone, unlike imagination, Sullivan continues, "doubts and inquires . . . recognizes time and space and the material limitations, . . . [and] eventually arrives at a science of logical statement that shall shape and define the scheme and structure that is to underlie, penetrate and support the form of an art work. [Thought] is hard, the bony structure, it is the tough, tendinous fibre; it may be at times perhaps as limber as the lips that move, yet is never the need of smiling—never the smile." The "smile," the joy of life we find in shared experience, is born and sustained in art.

Expression, third and last in the trinity of elements which must exist in harmony within the individual for action to reach its highest power, is "open-armed and free, supple, active, dramatic, changeable, beautifully pensive, persuasive and wonderful." Through expression we clothe the structure of art with a form of beauty; "for she is the perfection of the physical, she is the physical itself, and the uttermost attainment of emotionality. Hers is an infinite tenderness, an adorable and sweet fascination. In her companionship, imaginative Thought, long searching, has found its own, and lives anew, immortal, filled with sensibility, graciousness and the warm blood of a fully rounded maturity." And thus art "comes into Life! Thus Life comes into Art!" Imagination, thought, and expression in art arise in the longing of men to be at peace with "Nature and the Inscrutable Spirit of Man." The struggle within man which the artist struggles to resolve is between his objective and subjective powers. Some men believe only in what they can see, others in what they cannot see. Often the man who can see with the outer eye cannot see with the inner eye, "because the other man rhapsodizing with the clear insight of faith, had no thought for the things of this world. Neither has believed in the virtue of the other. Neither has inferred, from the presence of the other, the necessary existence of a balancing but hidden power." When an individual possesses both subjective and objective capacities within himself, and goes to the unfailing bounty of nature, he then "by virtue of his passionate adoration," transcends the objective to enter the "extraordinary communion that the sacred writers called to walk with God."

Religious longing for identification with God is not the only way to complete unity of being. There is also art which is born of desire to be at peace with "Nature and Spirit." Great art "typifies a realization of this ardent, patient longing." All efforts of the body, all undertakings of the mind, "tend, consciously or unconsciously, toward this consummation, tend toward this final peace: the peace of perfect equilibrium, the repose of absolute unity, the serenity of a complete identification." Such identification is known to all in childhood experiences with nature, whose forms, like the forms of art, are the means by which we reach a deep sense of harmony with ourselves.

In childhood experiences of nature we have our first and most profound intimations of what we will later experience in art. This is joy, the joy of creating and appreciating forms which make possible community among men because men find themselves in each other by sharing joy and love as they act together in the forms given by life to art.

Education's great crime is that it "has removed us from Nature." Now, in place of a happy people, "open-eyed children of Nature teeming with beautiful impulses," we are lost in darkness, groping under a sooty and lurid sky. As a result of a "brutish and mean system of guidance," we face life in fear and hate. The architect in each of us, and certainly the architect seeking to learn his craft in school, is killed because only the objective aspects and forms of architecture are taught. The student has been told that "grammar was a book, algebra was a book, geometry another book," geography, chemistry, physics still other books. Educators never tell the young architect that "these things are actually intense symbols, complex ratios, representing man's relation to Nature and his fellow man; they never told him that his mathematics came into being in response to a *desire* in the human breast to come nearer to nature—that the full moon looked round to the human eye ages before the circle was dreamed of."

The technical training of the architect is intellectual training, but this creates no understanding of architecture. The conscientious student knows a thousand and one specific facts concerning the shapes and measurements and ratios of the whole and the parts of said buildings, and can neatly and deftly draw and color them to scale. He has read that architecture gives one an excellent idea of civilization. The student takes all this literally. He is told that architecture "is fixed, a real, a specific, a definite thing, that it's all done, that it's all known, arranged, tabulated, and put away neatly in handy packages called books." He is encouraged to believe that when his turn comes, if he wishes to create an architecture for Americans or for his generation at large, "he can dip it out of his books with the same facility that dubs a grocer dipping beans out of a bin." He learns from the logic of events that "architecture in practice is a commercial article, like a patent medicine, unknown in its mixture and sold exclusively to the public exclusively on the brand."

But architecture is not what we so stupidly call a reality, but a "most complex, a glowing and gloriously wrought metaphor, embodying as no other form under the sun can do, the pure, clean and deep inspiration of the race flowing as a stream of living water from its well-spring to the sea." The architect, to be a true exponent of his time, must possess "first, last and always the sympathy, the intuition of the poet," for this is the "one real, vital principle that survives all places and all time." The search for "a natural expression of our lives, of our thoughts, our meditations, our feelings, is the architectural art as I understand it: and it is because I so understand it, that, ignoring the viciousness of the past, I gladly make appeal to the good that is in human nature—that goodness of heart and soundness of head, that ready and natural response of the soul in which I have always trusted and shall always trust. It is to this sane and wholesome quality that I plead for the abiding sincerity and nobility of our art. It is to this *manliness* that I call to come before the judgment seat and make an answer for us."

For centuries it has been taught that intellect and emotions are two separate and antagonistic things. But this is wrong, for no nature in which either is wanting can become a fully rounded nature. Greek classical architecture was one-sided and incomplete because it was almost exculsively intellectual. Emotional architecture, especially the Gothic, was also one-sided and incomplete, "however great and beautiful its development of feeling, because of the almost total absence of mentality." No complete architecture has yet appeared, because men, in architecture alone, have "obstinately sought to express themselves solely in terms either of the head or of the heart." Architectural art has failed to reach its highest development as a form of imagination, thought, and expression because "it has not yet found a way to become truly plastic; it does not yet respond to the poet's touch." It is "the only art for which the multitudinous rhythms of outward nature, the manifold fluctuations of man's inner being have no significance, no place." Greek architecture, though "perfect in its eyesight, definite in its desires, clear in its purpose," was not "resourceful in forms: . . . it lacked the flexibility and the humanity to respond to the varied and constantly shifting desires of the heart. . . . It was a pure, it was a noble art, wherefore we call it classic." But it was "an apologetic art," possessing serenity yet lacking "the divinely human element of mobility." The Greeks never caught the secret of "the changing of the seasons, the orderly and complete sequences of their rhythm within the calmly moving year." Nor did the Greeks know "what we now know of Nature's bounty, for music in those days had not been born: this lovely friend, approaching man to man, had not yet begun to bloom as a rose, to exhale its wondrous perfume."

Gothic architecture, on the other hand, was too far removed from men. With "sombre ecstatic eye" and with thought far above "with Christ in the heavens, seeing but little here below, feverish and overwrought, taking comfort in gardening and plant life, sympathizing deeply with Nature's visible forms, [it] evolved a copious and rich variety of incidental expressions but lacked the unitary comprehension, the absolute consciousness and mastery of pure form that can come alone of unclouded and serene contemplation, of perfect repose and peace of mind." The Greek "knew the static, the Goth the dynamics," of architecture. But neither suspected "the mobile equilibrium [8] of it: neither of them divined the movement and stability of nature." Both will pass when the true, the "Poetic Architecture" will arise—the architecture which will speak clearly, eloquently, and warmly of the "fullness, the completeness of man's intercourse with Nature and with his fellow men." Even the greatest architecture of the past lacked resources now readily available. Human beings have become "too rich in possessions, too well equipped, too magnificently endowed," for any past architecture to have even "hinted at its resources, much less to have exhausted them by anticipation."

We have a rich heritage from the past, but this becomes meaningful only if we use it as a basis for the creation of a new civilization. The Hindu, "soaring in contemplation"; the Hebrew giving us the "One Great Spirit"; the sombre Egyptians who struggled so courageously with fate; the lonely man of Nazareth breathing "a spirit of gentleness" new to the world; the Greeks, "lovers of the physical, accurate thinkers, worshipers of beauty"; the Goths, who created emotion as we now experience it; modern science, which teaches us not to fear; and modern music, "arising in glory as the heart took wings—*a new thing under the sun*" [9]—all these have taught us much. But we must think deeply for ourselves over the meaning of democracy as the "utterance of freedom, the beginning of the Individual Man." For now at last in machinery and steam power man possesses the capacity to annihilate distance in his new means of communication. Thus, if we but have the wisdom and the will, Americans can achieve the greatest community of all—a humane society. "Think, as we stand here, not in a new land, a Promised Land that is ours, think how passionately latent, how marvelous to contemplate is America our country. *Think that here destiny has decreed there shall be enacted the final part in the drama of man's emancipation—the redemption of his soul!*" [10] Our age, "the darkest of the dark ages," stirs with change. An era of spiritual splendor is about to dawn in America. If American architects rise to this challenge they will lead the world to a new golden age.

Notes

[1] Louis H. Sullivan, *The Autobiography of an Idea* (New York: Press of the American Institute of Architects, 1926), p. 303.

[2] *Ibid.*, p. 297.

[3] *Ibid.*, pp. 297–98.

[4] Frank Lloyd Wright, *Genius and the Mobocracy* (New York: Duell, Sloan and Pearce, 1949), pp. 50–51. It should be noted how much credit Wright gives to Adler. Adler has been greatly neglected. Actually, it was because of Adler that the firm obtained the Auditorium; as Sullivan discovered after their break in 1895, the clients of Adler and Sullivan were Adler's clients.

[5] Sullivan was secretary of the architectural committee.

[6] The word "Classical" appeared in the title as a misprint for "Intellectual," says Isabella Athey, the editor of the 1947 Wittenborn edition of *Kindergarten Chats*. This essay is reprinted in this edition. All quotations from here to the end of the chapter are taken from pp. 191–201. The relationship between "subjective" and "objective" has been, of course, of lasting interest to all thought. Sullivan enters the discussion in much the same way as William James—namely, to attack the copy or correspondence theory of knowledge, which taught that what went on in the mind went on in nature. Sullivan seems to take the idealist position in favor of mind, but Sullivan's mind is the mind of the artist, not that of the metaphysician, scientist, or priest.

[7] Mead distinguished four stages in the act—impulse, perception, manipulation, and consummation—in his *Philosophy of the Act* (Chicago: University of Chicago Press, 1938).

[8] If there is any key to Sullivan's theory of form, it is in the phrase "mobile equilibrium."

[9] Sullivan's italics. Sullivan's love of Wagner, and his love for Handel, many of whose scores were in his library, is well known. John Root was also very musical. Frank Lloyd Wright's father was an excellent musician. The influence of music in the development of Chicago architects was very great, and in their writings on the aesthetics of architecture we find many musical images. Sullivan taught that music was the sister art of architecture.

[10] Sullivan's italics.

23

The Education of the Architect: II.
Kindergarten Chats

Kindergarten Chats *is the American architectural testament of faith in democratic art. It is a strange and moving book. Like *Huckleberry Finn* it is colloquial, episodic, bombastic, filled with laughter and teasing and golden flashes of faith and love. The hero of *Kindergarten Chats* is also a youngster and, like Huck, a voyager. Here the voyage is not a mystic return to brotherhood by Jim, the Negro, and Huck, the son of an evil white father, but a journey through the streets of Chicago, led by Sullivan himself, of a young man fresh from architectural school, into the grandeur and misery of urban architecture. It is an architectural voyage, reported in the "free form of dialogue." The physical journey is simple enough. It is easy for a Chicagoan to distinguish the buildings Sullivan and his young architect pause before as they point up arguments in their talk. But there is also a spiritual journey, a journey into ecstasy or what Sullivan called "illumination." In all of Sullivan's major writings the expression of this journey, the allegory of the spiritual voyage, is a description of awakening to the spirit to art. In these moments of illumination the individual finds a democratic spirit of art within himself which makes him yearn for a moment of supreme identification with man in nature and society. In *Kindergarten Chats* this moment occurs during a summer storm.[1] In his *Autobiography* the moment of "morphosis," as he calls it, occurs at Ocean Springs in the "stately forest" untouched by the hand of man. Such conversions occur in nature because there is a direct psychic and physical relationship between man and nature. Nature's rhythms, the progression of the seasons from spring through winter, are the great rhythms "discernible alike in nature and human affairs."

Sullivan's allegory of man in nature appears in his early writings, continues in the writing of his middle years, and again in the work of the last months of his life. In 1886, the year he began the design of the Auditorium, he read his poetical essay, "Inspiration," to a convention of the Western Association of Architects. This allegory falls into three parts: GROWTHS: A Spring Song; DECADENCE: An Autumn Reverie; THE INFINITE: A Song of the Sea. As Sullivan tells us, democratic art must face and master death, which transcends life in the feudal spirit. This feudal spirit mastered death, but only by making it supreme over life, and by condemning men to live forever in fear and hate because they denied life. In 1889 Sullivan placed two invocations on opposite walls of the Auditorium Theatre. "O, soft, melodious Springtime! First-born of life and love!" and, "A great life has passed into the tomb, and there, awaits the requiem of Winter's snows." [2] By 1900, when Sullivan began writing *Kindergarten Chats,* the allegory of nature as the allegory of the human spirit reaches the form we find in all Sullivan's subsequent work. [3]

In Sullivan the action of the allegory is a struggle between conventional American architecture and expression, which is "literal, objective . . . cynical, and brutal, and philistine," and an art conceived of as a "specialized social activity inextricably interwoven with the thoughts, and the aspirations of the people." [4] The structure of the allegory is the passage of the seasons. Summer represents the awakening of the spirit of the artist. In the fullness of nature's bloom he discovers that "form follows the function," an aesthetic principle which will guide him in architecture. Autumn is a time of serene, searching thought and an understanding of nature's rhythms, the "exquisitely balanced modulation from moving into quiescent life." Winter brings us "face to face with the wall against which men have broken their hearts." To be an artist we must learn to face loneliness, suffering, and death. In winter the artist discovers his solitude and his power. He can face winter, or death, because deep in the artist's heart there is belief in spring. Spring, "the melody of procreation," teaches us that great art is born in love, the "power of powers" which makes art immortal.

Toward the end of their journey together, the master turns to his pupil, the young architect, and explains to him that he has taken him to nature and will continue to do so, because she is the "unfailing source" of creative energy and because form and content taken by the drama of nature is also that of man's spiritual drama. Our moods "parallel [nature's] moods. . . . her problems parallel our problems. . . . you find there, now and forevermore, the key to solutions." We must learn to read "in Nature's book so that her processes may be our processes." The greatest of these is the progression in nature "from function into form" which determines poetic finalities of art. Man must seek and find within his own spirit a sure anchorage "within the visible and invisible universe, upon the earth, his home, and in the world and the hearts of his fellow men." For in man's adjustment with "Nature and his kind lies his happiness, in discord lies his misery." [5]

In his letters to Lyndon P. Smith, a friend of Sullivan's who collaborated on the Bayard Building in New York City, and to Claude Bragdon, architect and critic whose essays on Sullivan did so much to keep his name alive,[6] Sullivan tells what he is trying to do in *Kindergarten Chats*. On December 13, 1900, he writes Smith: "I have arranged to write 52 articles on American architecture for the *Interstate Architect and Builder* of Cleveland—In reality the 52 articles will constitute *one* argument and will all be interrelated." Some weeks later he writes to Smith: "The 'Kindergarten Chats' will strike deeper than you are inclined to imagine. As a psychological study they will be far and away beyond anything I have hitherto attempted. The key to them, you will find, as the development proceeds, slowly but elaborately,— in the development of the character and artistic nature of the young man, *from within*."[7] In a letter to Bragdon, which is quoted in the Introduction to the Scarab edition[8] of the *Kindergarten Chats,* the purpose of the *Chats* is outlined. "I subject [the young man] to certain experiences and allow the impression they make on him to infiltrate, and, as I note the effect, I gradually use a guiding hand. . . . It remains then to determine carefully the kind of experiences to which I shall subject the lad, and in what order, or logical (and especially psychological) sequence." Sullivan continues: "I begin, then, with aspects that are literal, objective, more or less cynical, and brutal, and philistine. A little at a time I introduce the subjective, the refined, the altruistic; and by and to-and-fro, increasingly intense rhythm of these two opposing themes, worked so to speak in counterpoint, I reach a preliminary climax; of brutality tempered by a longing for nobler, purer things." Then comes his revulsion and flight from the city to the country. In his first experience of nature, and during the summer storm, the young architect finds his soul as he discovers that creative architecture "is in essence a dramatic art, and an art of eloquence: of subtle rhythmic beauty, power and tenderness."

He cautions Smith that he would like to have the *Chats* "circulated as extensively as possible among the *laity*." For the "architects will not understand much of what is in them, but the laity, more open-minded, will. . . . It is among the *people* that we want to work."[9] The *Chats* will, Sullivan again writes Smith in the same month, "be the first serious attempt ever made to test architecture by human nature and democracy.—Don't let a certain flippancy of treatment mislead you. Try to spread them as far as you can among the laity, for they will be free from technicalities. I am writing for the people, not for architects." In the revision of *Kindergarten Chats,* which Sullivan worked on during the summer months of 1918, the stress on appeal to the laity is increased. "[*Kindergarten Chats*] was originally written for young architects. In its present form it has been sufficiently recast to broaden and extend its appeal to all those who may be interested in the nature of Architecture as a creative art. The work is free of technicalities, is couched in easy dialogue form and its doctrine should be intelligible to all: for it is based on the realities of every-day life and is essentially democratic in its belief in the aesthetic soundness of our common natural powers."

The central purpose of the work, Sullivan tells us in the foreword to the revised edition of 1918, "is to liberate the mind from serfdom to tradition, and to exhibit man's natural powers in their creative capabilities when expanding in the open-air-of-the-spirit-of-responsible-freedom; in other words, in the true spirit of democracy." The battle of our time is between the "feudal" and "democratic mind." The operation of the historic feudal mind and the advancing democratic mind are placed in sharp contrast. The appeal therefore is to broaden the intelligence of the public mind "seeking not only a knowledge and understanding of architecture as a plastic art, but, as well, a clear view of its social basis as an art of expression." To think well about democracy we must learn to distinguish between "the basic nature of democracy as contrasted with its merely political aspect." This demands a statement about art as power in society and its specific relation to democracy.[10]

The walk taken through the streets of Chicago by master and apprentice, the comments made on various buildings, the problems stated and resolved, are depicted in the city whose fate, Sullivan argues, will be the fate of America. Thus in content and purpose *Kindergarten Chats* is as much a Chicago book as Sandburg's *Chicago Poems* of 1916; John Dewey's *The School and Society* of 1899; Veblen's *Theory of the Leisure Class* of 1899, *The Theory of Business Enterprise* of 1904, and *The Higher Learning in America* (published in 1918 but written in 1904); Fuller's *Cliff-Dwellers* of 1893 and *With the Procession* of 1895; Dreiser's *Sister Carrie* of 1900 and *The Financier* of 1912; and the articles and lectures of George Herbert Mead beginning in 1900 at the University of Chicago on the social emergence of the self.[11]

Until the moment of conversion in *Chat* XXIV, "Summer: The Storm," the young architect fails to understand much of what is told him and often doubts what he does understand. The master is comic, ironic, witty, lyric, and prophetic in turn. He treats his pupil as an equal and allows himself to be teased and chaffed. Sullivan's genial comedy stands in sharp contrast to his lyric and prophetic utterance.[12] The basis of his humor is the incongruity of using traditional art, born of a feudal society, to express the needs of a democratic city. This was also the basis for much of the comedy of Veblen, Ade, Fuller, Dunne, and Field. Veblen's famous irony over the "monastic real-estate" of the University of Chicago was based in his belief that all historic styles of architecture were simply pious frauds used by "Captains of Erudition," as he called college presidents, to create belief that solemn and majestic thought was finding a home in their city, and thus to convince businessmen and those under the spell of money that education was reputable because it was archaic and expensive. Sullivan, too, was amused at the use of architecture as a form of conspicuous consumption, but he found other aspects of the deception equally comic. Chicago imitations of Roman forms, as in her Loop banks, weren't even good imitations. Thus while Burnham and his followers intoned piously the need for bringing copies of "the imperishable masterpieces of the past" to develop the architectural taste of Chicagoans, they were palming off buildings that were not really Roman at all. And, Sullivan asks, why was architecture alone copied from the past? Bankers so enamored of Roman styles ought to wear togas, sandals, and conduct their business in "the venerated Latin tongue—oral and written."

At the beginning of their walk the master singles out the Montgomery Ward (now Tower) Building at 6 North Michigan Avenue, with its 22½-foot sculpture ("Progress Lighting the Way for Commerce") atop seventeen stories and a three-story tower. It is, the master tells his apprentice as they pass down Michigan Boulevard, "an ill-compounded salad, with a rather rancid New Yorky flavor." The master warns his pupil that such buildings are really pathological. And, like a medical lecturer warning students that cadavers can be dissected only by those with strong stomachs, Sullivan warns his pupil that if he is to look deeply into American architecture he must steel himself to face the horrors of a world of forms created by madmen and lunatics.[13] To his pupil's reply that he cannot see what political and social discussion has to do with architecture, the master says: The "critical study of architecture becomes not merely the direct study of an art—for that is but a minor phase of a great phenomenon—but, *in extenso,* a study of the social conditions producing it; the study of a newly shaping type of civilization. By this light the study of architecture becomes naturally and logically a branch of social science." The pupil is bewildered: "But I can never learn how to do this. I feel that it requires the eye of a poet." The master replies: "We are all poets. . . . You will understand. So, when I tell you that this wretchedly tormented structure, this alleged railway station, is in the public-be-damned style, is degenerate and corrupt, I repeat to you only what the building says to me." [14]

As they walk together the master warns his young architect that his architectural school training has been too abstract and too intellectual. He must learn to return to the faculties which nature gave him at birth but which now are shriveled. These must be revivified "to send out new roots, to grow, to expand, and to bring forth as nature intended." The teacher must be like a gardener who plants seeds in pupils, "under the broad sky of humanity," and cares for these seeds with "the water of life, drawn from nature's well-spring." But the garden which must be cultivated is the garden of the heart and the imagination. The teacher must have beauty in his own heart before he can cultivate in others the will of the "Creative Dreamer," who alone possesses the "power of vision needed to harness Imagination, to harness the intellect, to make science do his will, to make the emotions serve him." For without emotion the intellect cannot come to life.[15]

As they pause before a State Street department store (probably Field's at Randolph and State) Sullivan tells his pupil that this building is not designed as a department store, but as a hotel, a bad copy of the New York Imperial Hotel. "Surely, if it were a department store, all masonry would be reduced to a minimum, and there would be an expanse of glass for light and display. . . . The structure is a hotel . . . , the lower two stories of which have, probably, been rented to some merchant." If it were designed well as an office building it would suggest that function. "There would be that regular and equable spacing of windows, that general suggestion of business and business housing, which would be unmistakable." In Chicago, the master goes on to say, "There are a number of well arranged office structures. . . . This particular building [Field's] is . . . not characteristic of the West. It lacks, utterly, western frankness, directness—crudity, if you will. It is merely a weak-rooted cutting from the eastern hothouse. . . . It merely serves to . . . make its owner ridiculous and pitiful. . . . To say . . . that this building is canting and hypocritical is to couch our definition in mildest terms." [16]

They stop before Richardson's Marshall Field Wholesale Warehouse. Here at last is architecture in all its greatness.

Four-square and brown, it stands, in physical fact, a monument to trade, to the organized commercial spirit, to the power and progress of the age, to the strength and resources of individuality and force of character; spiritually, it stands as the index of a mind, large enough, courageous enough to cope with these things, master them, absorb them and give them forth again, impressed with the stamp of large and forceful personality; artistically, it stands as the oration of one who knows well how to choose his words, who has something to say and says it—and says it as the outpouring of a copious, direct, large and simple mind. . . . in a world of barren pettiness, [it is] a male; for it sings the song of procreant power, as the others have squealed of miscegenation.

Richardson's great building moves the master to warn his pupil that he has come into architecture at a most critical period, a period in which "the forces that make for growth or decay are in strenuous but delicate balance." Architecture will be of crucial importance in tipping this balance. "Whichever way our country goes, so will go our architecture: it is the same proposition stated in different ways. . . . That the bulk of our architecture is rotten to the core, is a statement which does not admit of one solitary doubt. That there is in our national life, in the genius of our people, a fruitful germ, and that there are a handful who perceive this, is likewise beyond question." The task of the architect is to create a living art, "an art of and for democracy, an art of and for the American people." [17]

Notes

[1] *Kindergarten Chats and Other Writings,* ed. by Isabella Athey (New York: George Wittenborn, 1947). See *Chat* XXIV, "Summer: The Storm."

[2] These legends, speaking from the golden beauty of the theater, have nourished the spirit of Chicagoans who find art as well as science and religion a way to truth. These invocations in the Auditorium to life as the lord of death, his poetry, and the creation of his great tombs, all took place as Sullivan was passing into his thirties.

[3] As we shall see in the discussion of architectural form, his ornament is fashioned after models taken from nature.

[4] See *Chat* XLIX, "The Art of Expression."

[5] *Chat* XLVIII, "On Poetry."

[6] See Claude Bragdon, *Architecture and Democracy* (New York: Knopf, 1918), for his essay, "Louis Sullivan, Prophet of Democracy," and his *Merely Players* (New York: Knopf, 1929), where "The First American Modernist" appears.

[7] Sullivan's italics. These letters are reprinted in *Kindergarten Chats, op. cit.*

[8] The *Chats* appeared in 52 issues from February 16, 1901, to February 8, 1902. They appeared in book form for the first time in an edition edited by Claude F. Bragdon and published by the Scarab Fraternity Press, Lawrence, Kansas. Appendix E of Athey's edition contains a discussion of manuscripts, revisions, publication, etc. of the *Kindergarten Chats.*

[9] Letter of February 18, 1901, to Lyndon P. Smith, as quoted in Athey's edition, p. 243. Sullivan's italics. In this letter, he also says: "The composition of the articles is going along merrily. I have 27 written. In the 24th I get the "young man" out of doors on a hot summer's day, and the *awakening* begins."

[10] Sullivan, *op. cit.,* p. 15. The Athey edition contains photographs which "illustrate buildings to which Sullivan was referring in fact if not by name, or to which he might have been referring." The buildings so named are used here. References will be given to the name of the essay from which quotations are taken so that any edition may be used.

[11] See George Herbert Mead, *Mind, Self, and Society,* ed. by C. W. Morris (Chicago: University of Chicago Press, 1934). Mead's work on the social basis for consciousness was a very great contribution to American social thought. It offers a philosophical base for a democratic theory of personality, for it teaches that in the response of the other we discover our self, as in turn the other discovers himself in our response to him. Thus the self not only "needs" or "depends" on others, but *exists* in communication with them. Mead holds that the self is born in conversation—which reaches its highest development only between equals—whatever maximizes opportunities to share expression is good. Mead and Dewey believed that democracy created more chances than autocracy for the self and others to share.

[12] Those who knew Sullivan agree that his profound sense of comedy ranged widely from very subtle irony to broad Rabelaisian humor. Wright comments frequently, as do others, on the deep twinkle of humor in Sullivan's eyes. Some of his quoted remarks about architects and his descriptions of Chicago buildings are unprintable. Veblen delighted in poking fun at the solemnities of the Gothic architecture of the University of Chicago.

[13] Like Goya, Sullivan often passed beyond irony and comedy into the grotesque that is born of horror, not laughter. No Chicago artist possessed a deeper sense of comedy than Sullivan, but his sense of outrage (which in his private life sometimes passed into more than verbal violence) over the betrayal of architecture in Chicago often went beyond laughter and tears.

[14] Sullivan, *op. cit.,* "A Terminal Station," p. 24. From his question, "Why does not the lake engulf it?"—it seems reasonable to conclude that reference is made to Chicago's only terminal on the lake, namely the Illinois Central Station at Twelfth Street and Michigan. For information on this and other Chicago buildings, see Frank A. Randall's *History of the Development of Building Construction in Chicago* (Urbana: University of Illinois Press, 1949). This chronological account of Chicago buildings gives locations, dates of construction, and the names of architects and engineers responsible for Chicago buildings from 1830 to 1948. It is one of the indispensable books on Chicago building. Our debt to the Randall family is further increased by John D. Randall, who carries on his father's tradition in his publications, *A Guide to Significant Chicago Architecture of 1872 to 1922* (Box 345, Glencoe, Illinois: privately printed, 1958).

[15] Louis H. Sullivan, *The Autobiography of an Idea* (New York: Press of the American Institute of Architects, 1926).

[16] Sullivan, *op. cit., Chat* V, "An Hotel."

[17] *Ibid.,* "*The Key.*"

24

The Education of the Architect: III.
Kindergarten Chats

In *Chat* XXIV, "Summer: The Storm," the young architect awakens to the spirit of art, but as the euphoria passes he is seized by doubt and despair. "I have had my little emotional, and intellectual, and moral and spiritual, and democratic, and feudal jag." He turns against his master. "I . . . have been philosophized to the death, burdened, darkened, nauseated and made rebellious by your psychology, or perhaps I had better say, your pseudomysticism." Even if the master is right about art, how can any sane man believe such mystical nonsense about democracy and democratic art? "Democracy is a humbug and a wild, disordered dream, a fanatical dream which disturbs, distorts, and distracts all realities." How, the master is asked, can a real man exist in a democracy? Democracy is the refuge of the common, the average, the vulgar.

Look at [the people of democracy]: all cheap, the richer the cheaper. Look at the faces: see them shudder—all sordid, all pigeyed, all self-centered in their democratic savagery; all cave-dwellers, troglodytes, men of a modern stone age, with dirt under their brainclaws, crafty and cruel, selfish, noxious—a poisonous snob! You talk of men! I am looking for men!! But I shall never find men under the cloud and murk of democracy. I want men who are men—men of distinction, men of quality, men of tone, men of elevation of mind and spirit, men of humanity and *savoir faire*—and you can't show them to me here [in Chicago]. . . . I *see* realities. I am of the new generation, . . . and I tell you that there is only one thing that any pair of eyes can see with absolute certainty nowadays, and that is the DOLLAR! To deny its reality, to refuse to worship, means ruin.[1]

In his final outburst of hate and despair over democracy, the student makes his master's enemy, the feudal baron, his hero. "Democracy is a herd of cattle, a herd without a driver, without a whip. They huddle, and press, and trample in their own dung." The people of democracy are a "dull-eyed, patient crew; helpless and inert without a leader. . . . Democracy means, merely, the liberation of numbers, the wandering and huddling of helpless units." Democracy means "disorder, filth, brutal unity, coarse appetites—a stifling crowd! . . . Give me an autocrat! Give me a MAN, a real man!

A man big enough and strong enough and willful enough to guide and to govern. The herd wish to be governed; they need a powerful, a dominating hand. . . . It takes brains to govern and guide and foresee! The very disease of which . . . you have been talking is *democracy itself;* for democracy is, in itself, a disease." Men are *not* born equal. Some are born to rule, some to serve. Only the herd fears death. "Sentiment is a strength of the heart, the weak know no real sentiment; and tenderness, truly, is a power of the heart. . . . You should not have left me alone in the country, for it has defeated your object. . . . I have seen how Nature works—how she despises the weak and exalts the strong." [2]

In the next *Chat,* "Democracy," the student repents, but he still cannot shake off doubt and despair. He asks his master to help him "dispel the heavy gloom" of despair and his sickness of heart over the failure of democracy to produce good architecture. But even in his cry for help he mocks his master's bombast. "Like a fire I go out in ashes. You are the 'Promethean heat that shall that light relume.' Oh, let not the spark expire! I make genuflections, obeisances, salaams, oblations; I kiss the hem of your garment." After some banter, the master admits that he has not been very clear about democratic art, and that it is his responsibility to clarify for himself, as for others, just what is meant by a democratic art. He begins by rejecting the identification of democracy with the mob, with political action alone. *"Democracy is primarily of the individual!"* It is not "a mere political fabric, a form of government; that is but one phase of it—an incidental phase. Democracy is a *moral* principle, a *spiritual* law, a perennial subjective reality in the realm of man's spirit." Democracy "is not, as you might infer from superficial observation, merely a modern notion of a government by and for the people; it is a force, latent, and old as earth; a force for whose fulfillment the ages have been preparing the way." It is the "serene forces of nature that are most powerful; and that force which we call Democracy, lying inexpressibly deep in the spirit of man is now as ever seeking expression." [3]

Christianity is really democracy. "When the spirit of man first discerned One Infinite Spirit, after ages of groping, the way was opened which leads toward the discovery of man by man as a spirit." Christ was really the first democrat. He came into a world "crushed under the hell of absolutism, spoke eloquently to the lowly; he taught that the individual possessed his own soul. He outlined the need for self-government, the value of kindness; he preached man's unity with the divine, the immanence of the spirit. For these and other sayings in opposition to the established order, he was crucified. But his gentle, luminous doctrine has survived, because it is an utterance of nature's urge, which found, through this compassionate dream, a long-sought outlet through the soul." [4]

Religion, morals, and government, as well as art, reach their highest expression only in democracy, and since democracy has reached its highest expression in America, the ultimate form of democracy as a commonwealth of free men will be reached here. Primitive democracy was a unitary conception which has now been subdivided into "three separate conceptions—of government, religion, and morals." This separation soon led to conflicting interests (political, sacerdotal, and ethical) in which democratic expression was restrained. But in America there are varied currents that are dissolving these broken thoughts and are bringing them to a synthesis. This synthesis will reach full expression in a conception of conduct where the great forces of religion, morals, and government will be harmonized. In this light, the master continues, America is the land of destiny, for here nature has prepared through the ages a slumbering continent, a virgin wilderness, "to be the home of free men—free in their bodies, free in their souls"; so that the "working calm and the power of the wilderness, the potency of the soil, of the waters and air might permeate them physically, mentally, morally, and spiritually, and lift them up to be a great people animated by a great purpose, a great force, a great beauty—the beauty and the power and the glory of democracy—the divine altitude of man's humanity." [5]

The young architect is deeply moved by the words of his master. He now understands that greatness in architecture in America depends on how to give form to democratic society. But, he asks his master, how can we create a theory of democratic art? The master begins by restating his theory of functions. The spirit of democracy is a "function seeking expression in organized social form." It is true that the concept of function seems very abstract, and that talk about the relationship between function and spirit seems obscure. But function simply means a need, "whatever it may be, which is seeking or finding fulfillment. If you put an acorn in the ground, that acorn, containing the function oak, will seek the form oak, and, in process of time, will become an oak-tree." So, "if I say that a certain function, aspirant democracy, is seeking a certain form of expression, democratic architecture, . . . I am making a statement that does not differ in essence from what I said concerning the acorn." [6]

The idea of function is simple enough, the master continues, but we do not know how to think about function seeking expression in organized form because teachers of architecture are not preparing students to think about the relationship between democracy and art. Teachers in architectural schools fail to exhibit to the student "the simple basis of architectural phenomena and [to make] that basic principle clear and manageable." Instead they impose upon students "formulas of learning and attitudes of mind toward learning which have descended to us from times when education was for the gentleman—for the few, for a class: that education which separates one from his people by the violence of alienation and uselessness." The teachers in the schools do not have a clear idea of the function of architecture in our time. Like people of refinement, cultivation, and good manners—to say nothing of the newly rich, the vulgar rich, and the hard-headed, practical businessman—such teachers hold, often unconsciously, that the life of our time is vulgar and unrefined. To them the clamor and unrest is not a sign of strength but chaos. They want something manageable, something culturally domesticated, something that will stand still. They seek a sleek peace, not achievement; tranquillity, not strife. They are really ashamed of America. They weaken our culture, not so much by taking refuge in the past as by their refusal to help the young architect understand the relationship of architecture to his own time. Sound scholarship must bear "a relation of unmistakable value to the day and generation of the scholar—otherwise it has no function."

American scholarship must question the past, not worship it. It must teach us to solve the pressing problems of democracy which confront us, just as the great architects of the past helped their own age to confront its problems. The touchstone of architectural scholarship is its ability to make us think of architecture as solutions to problems. Yet when we turn to our architectural scholars we find them talking soulfully about styles, not about solutions to "any one of a hundred directly and distinctly modern American problems hitherto unsolved." They continue to design Greek, Gothic, and Roman libraries for American universities, twenty-story office buildings to look like Greek temples, or Doric columns as memorials to the Great Lakes, the land of the primeval forest and the hardy voyagers. Such architects betray scholarship, for they turn our minds and hearts away from trying to understand the glory of the creative impulse in men. "Of true scholarship you can never have too much. It never burdens and wearies, nor does it dull the mind and dry the heart; rather does it give wings to the spirit, serenity to the mind, and to the heart eternal youth!" [7]

The great spiritual flaw in architectural teaching is its neglect of "the social value of democracy and of creative art." Schools of architecture are "inculcating the meretricious in their pseudo-explanations of the architectural art." [8] Methods of architectural instruction are archaic at a time when other departments of education have made positive strides in advance. The study of the child and of the young has been pursued with intelligence and devotion; and the kindergarten has brought bloom to the mind of many a child. "But there is, alas! no *architectural kindergarten*—a garden of the heart." The architectural schools have failed to keep pace with the general progress of educational philosophy and the teaching art; indeed, they have flouted such progress. "Unfamiliar with the immense educational value of metaphysics and psychology as the groundwork of the teaching art, they lack the ground-plan of a naturalistic philosophy of architecture in its historical and creative aspects: hence they fail utterly to illuminate the architectural art past, present, and prospective." [9]

Democratic education should be concerned with man's powers to act. By nature man is a wanderer, a toiler, a worker, an artisan, and finally an artist: "for these things mean the power to do—to create." Man has the "urging power" of curiosity, but his intellectual nature is not his greatest power. Man as the worker, the inquirer, the thinker, "may be purely material, strictly utilitarian, altogether objective in the ordinary sense." His powers in action may become purely intellectual and physical. But man has the power of emotion, and great powers of his inner life, "hence man is The Poet." And man also has the power to "vision forth: hence is he dreamer of dreams, spectator of visions: *The Prophet!* His emotions and dreams, like his visions and forecasts, vitalize his thinking, his speculations, and his work." [10] But man is also spirit and needs union with spirit, for man is not determined but has the power of choice. In this ability to choose lies the central power of the Ego. We must study man's nature and activities; "his actions . . . as exhibited in what he does—the record he himself makes of himself." We must ask, not what powers man has, but what man really does with his powers. This "most urgent of all present human inquiries" exists in what is called sociology. This is the "art, the science" of man. It is a unitary science, but also a poem and drama which makes sociology the precursor of democracy—"its explorer, its evangel." If man's moral power is his supreme constructive power, we must study how the choices man makes affect social values. It is the "business of democratic sociology to simplify and clarify all things, to exhibit and elucidate these powers of man which energize his power of choice and the dramatic consequences of such choice." [11]

In the study of American society we must turn to Chicago, not New York, as the greatest American city. "New York is not the country. It is in this land physically to be sure, but spiritually it is on the outskirts. It is *sui generis* a border town." For in New York "money is God, and God is money." This has produced in New York an architecture completely devoid of art. "For Art is not in the hearts of [New York] men. Gold is in the hearts of men here and fills arteries, capillaries, veins, with its maddening stream." The culture of New York is a fraud. The spectacle of a New York businessman stepping out of his French château, a Château de Blois on a street corner, could make anyone laugh—or weep. A New Yorker may live in such a house physically, but he cannot live in it morally, mentally, or spiritually. He and his home are simply a paradox. Even worse are New York office buildings, "with one barbarism heaped upon another until the incongruous mass reaches the limit of its idiocy in height, and culminates, perchance, in a Greek temple?—a solecism more extravagant, if possible, than the château." So stands New York as a "negation of democracy," its gigantic energy gone wrong. All we can hope for is that its "contagion" will not spread.[12]

This attack on New York is too much for the young architect, who has been suffering from the ugliness of Chicago. "And what, doctor mine, shall we say of this flat smear, this endless drawl of streets and shanties. . . . Is *this* a true exponent of democracy? . . . Are filth in the air, and slime under foot, or dust in the nostrils, indices of enlightenment?" New York "may be revolting to you, but this Chicago thing is infinitely repulsive to me. *There* at least was a physical . . . cleanliness." But "this foul spot on the smiling prairie, this blotch on the fair face of Nature! Why have you brought me here again? . . . I thought it well understood that no one stays here who can get away; that it is no place for a civilized human being to live. What are we here for?" [13] The master admits that Chicago leaves much to be desired, but insists that it is "pole-opposite" to New York. "Seventy years ago it was a mudhole—today it is a human swamp. It is the *City of Indifference*. Its nominal shibboleth, 'I will'—its actuality, 'I won't'; with the subscription: 'Not how good but how cheap'! It is the *'City of Contrasts.'* " Look out over the "sumptuous beauty, the color, the spread, the open far horizon of Lake Michigan, and then turn to this ugliness and horror on its shore . . . a city sunk in solitary gloom." Chicagoans and their leaders will not accept democracy because they refuse to face the "immediate responsibility of the individual" and respond not to coercion, "but to [the] inner prompting, [the] rectitude and pride, which makes for self-respect and self-control."

Chicago is a failure of the individual, the so-called man in the street, who lives in apathy and fear. True, there are libraries, universities, and art galleries, but what are books "but folly, and what is art but a curse—when they touch not the heart and impel it not to action." But the leaders of the city are no better. They are doing just what the mob are doing—nothing. There is no "tangible, forceful great ideal, physically, broadly, to be seen." And yet the "Great Lake and the Prairie, emblems of pride, fertility and power and graciousness, encircle and enfold the city as a wistful mother holds a sub-normal child. This City of vacant, sullen materialism, brooding and morose within the splendor, presents a spectacle unparalleled in history: the spec-tacle of Man's abject spiritual beggary." Yet at least there is hope in Chicago. "There is a leaven here, I WILL!" But there are ferments in the life of Chicago which may leaven the mass. "The materialistic humus may have already made a fertile soil: who knows? The rose springs from decayed things, and betimes it blooms in a passionate outburst of beauty." American architecture, as, indeed, all American civilization, is closely linked to the fate of Chicago. The "case [of] 'Chicago' is not more hopeless, seemingly, to him who can weigh values, than is that of the architectural art at large; it is not a whit more impoverished, spiritually, nor inept physically; not at all more apathetic; and if we may hope for the latter as we do, why not for the former as we may?"

Chicago has youth and hope. The sins of its youth have been fierce and debilitating, and almost fatal, "but there are a few sparks remaining in the ashes of its short life." The democratic fire which made Chicago great may flame again. "It is a chance—a chance only—but youth is here; a tremen-dous under-strength is here. The critical turn is at hand—we shall see what we shall see—and we shall see it soon." Chicago is not New York, and is not to be judged by it. There is "no common standard of comparison—New York is old—its sins are fixed, the damage is done. Chicago is young, clumsy, foolish; its architectural sins are unstable, captious and fleeting; it can pull itself down and rebuild itself in a generation, if it will: it has done and can do great things when the mood is on. There can be no new New York, but there may be a new Chicago. . . . All greatness is born of dreams. Chicago is a city of dream and ecstasy. Perhaps these dreams are foolish. One must be incurably optimistic even momentarily to dream such a dream." Yet how easy it is to dream of architectural beauty in Chicago with its incomparable lake and "strong, silent, lovely prairies." Dreams of beauty in Chicago are never sheer fantasy. For "the Lake is there, awaiting, in all its glory; and the sky is there above, awaiting, in its eternal beauty; and the Prairie, the ever-fertile prairie is awaiting. And they, all three, as a trinity, in one, are dreaming—some prophetic dream: I am aware: even as the Big City dreams its sordid introspective dream. And he who looks upon them, all in one, in pulchritude of his heart, in rejuvenescence of his spirit, may perchance in turn dream something of their dream—who knows? There may be unknown dreamers here!" [14]

Perhaps, when all is said and done, we take Chicago and New York too seriously. The cities are "great battle-grounds, they are not great breeding-grounds." Great men may go to the cities but they are not generally speaking born and bred in the cities. Great minds are born and nourished in solitude. "In the quiet, in the silence, alone with itself and Nature, and alone with the subtly interchanging influences and aspirations of Nature and of Self [are born] the thoughts which mold and make a civilization." The big cities are "breeders of distraction, of noise, of racket, hurly-burly, turmoil and worry, jostle, wear and tear, by-products of a most intense pitch of mental and material activity." The great open country breeds mind, spirit and heart as it brings forth its wheat, its trees, its rains, its rivers and its lakes, its mountains and plains and forests, its glories of the seasons, its poems of the night and the day, its expanse of the heavens, and its repose of the earth." [15]

The young architect is fired by the master's talk. "I don't know [the country] very well. . . . And yet I feel, . . . vaguely, and wistfully, what you mean. . . . the country, the out-of-doors, is the prime source of power; and the city, the arena in which the power is dissipated for good or ill; or, to broaden the view, that Nature is the true source of all power of the heart and the spirit, and likewise the source of the power of the great cities." Perhaps this is why Americans have "something of that feeling for out-of-doors; else why this love of golf and country clubs, this annual flowing of people to the parks, to the lakes and woods, to the seashore and the mountains?" The master replies: "That is instinctive and shows that we are not indefinitely to remain a nation of city-dyspeptics and weary melancholics. It is part of our semi-conscious need of racial self-preservation." The restful, expansive beauty of America is prophetic of a new race of men, "such as the world has not known." Here on American soil will arise "the greatest race of creative artists in history; creative minds in every walk of life; and I predicate it on the soil, the waters, and the air, and on the spirit of Democracy which has mated and shall fully mate with them." Democracy, "and the open air of a serene continent, shall bring forth this superb race; and the eminent, the thinkers, poets, artists of that race, in turn shall bring forth in their works that which the urge of Democracy and a luxuriantly vital continent have imparted to them and to their people."

And then the master turns to his pupil and speaks of his love for America. The mask of the ironic teacher drops, as his heart opens and he utters his testament of faith.

I have in my heart a profound reverence for the great self-centered body of the American people, for the inexhaustible activity and imaginative flexibility of the American mind, for the wealth of sentiment resident in the American heart, and for the inexhaustible energy of the American continent, which, after the subtle manner of Nature's processes, is slowly infiltrating the American heart, mind and spirit. To take a less broad, less vital view of our land and people, would mean inevitably that the art philosophy which I am expounding to you would rest on a basis less broad and less vital than the land and the people. I am unfolding to you a philosophy of art simpler and deeper than the world has hitherto known, because, through my love of my land, of my people, of Democracy, and of the Infinite Creator, has come the insight and the power so to do.

The master then tells his pupil about the sources of his art.

My conclusions have been reached not in the racket of cities, nor in the study of garrulous philosophies, nor in libraries, nor in schools, but in the bounteous open air, within the infinite peace of Nature, alone in the solitudes, where the soul in contemplation became peaceful as the dawn, and mirrored the infinite in its own calm. I have communed more with trees than with books, and have exchanged greetings with the broad sky and the broad sea, with snow-capped mountains and the far-flung plain and prairie, with river and lake and tiny pool, with the sun in his rising, his high course and his majestic setting, with the moon in all her infinitely sweet, sad moods, and I have as a devoted lover followed the seasons through their beauteous rhythm, and have known the modulated solitudes of the starry night, and the brilliant ever-varying glories of the day.

The people of America, like the land itself, helped the master to discover his mission. "And I have been with that hitherto enigmatic creature we call man, in all his complex attitudes of heart, of mind, of soul. And from the contemplation of these has slowly emerged into the light of our day and our land, the conception of a creative art, for and by the people, which I am now engaged in imparting to you." The master has found among the people, not the cultivated few, the great clients architects will need. The basis of the new democratic art of architecture is "too simple, too natural, too unaffected and too straight-forward for a schoolman or a man of 'culture' to understand, to grasp, or to sympathize with." But there are minds and natures like that of the young architect, that have not yet become "wholly sophisticated, artificial and inert." Such minds exist "in abundance among the American people; particularly in the rising generation." And just so soon as the "immense feudal scare-crow of scholarship and culture and eminence is destroyed for them, the ground cleared, and the idea of a personal spiritual freedom conjoined with a personal responsibility and accountability"—then will the new generation in America reach greatness.

The new generation rising to power must believe in the dignity of man, but this dignity rests on "self-responsibility and self-government." New York and Chicago have failed to develop democratic communities. "True, there are righteous forces within these cities, but they are not characteristic of them, and the balance of forces at present is heavily against them." American cities are losing their character. "The originally vigorous Puritanism of Boston, the Catholicism of Baltimore, the Quakerism of Philadelphia, the slave-holding oligarchism of New Orleans and other southern cities, the 'river' epoch of Cincinnati, and other 'river' towns, the mining craze of San Francisco—were forces now long ago on the wane, and no definite rehabilitation of aspiring energies has led, in any of these instances, to a new and marked definition of character. The transition stage has been singularly protracted." And since we must study contemporaneous, not historical, American architecture and civilization, "they can offer us but little of suggestion, except in a negative or neutral sense." The two cities of "oppressively modern individuality, however harsh and discordant, are unquestionably Chicago and New York." There is so little differentiation now among American cities that we must turn to the country and the people for "the characteristic force against which these two cities must be balanced."

Notes

[1] Louis H. Sullivan, *Kindergarten Chats and Other Writings,* ed. by Isabella Athey (New York: George Wittenborn, 1947), *Chat* XXVIII, "Revulsion."

[2] *Ibid.*

[3] *Ibid., Chat* XXIX, "Democracy."

[4] *Ibid.* As we shall see in the discussion of *Democracy: A Man Search,* Sullivan thought the artist a better guide than the priest to the spirit of life. He rejected any trend of appeal to a supernatural beyond reason, but his reason was in the imagination of the artist, who described how men could act in the world, not merely think about it or witness it like a god.

[5] Sullivan, *op. cit., Chat* XXIX, "Democracy."

[6] *Ibid., Chat* XXX, "Education."

[7] *Ibid., Chat* XL, "On Scholarship."

[8] This is almost the exact phrase Veblen used about the "monastic real-estate" of the University of Chicago, in *The Higher Learning in America,* which was written some ten years later than *Kindergarten Chats.*

[9] Sullivan, *op. cit., Chat* XXX, "Education."

[10] *Ibid., Chat* XXXI, "Man's Powers."

[11] *Ibid., Chat* XXXI, "Man's Powers." This dramatistic conception of sociology was shared by Charles Horton Cooley, Lester Ward, John Dewey, George Herbert Mead, and in our time, Kenneth Burke. Basic to this view is the assumption that society arises in, and exists through, the communication of expressive symbols which men use in acting—that is, playing their roles—in society.

[12] *Ibid., Chat* XXXIII, "Our City."

[13] *Ibid., Chat* XXXIV, "Another City."

[14] *Ibid.*

[15] *Ibid., Chat* XXXV, "A Survey." This belief in man's place in nature was developed in the work of Wright and Jens Jensen.

25

Sullivan's Search for a Philosophy of Architecture

ARCHITECTURAL THINKING (Sullivan continues in *Kindergarten Chats,* as he turns to the problem of form), as distinguished from other types of thought, is thinking about the human function of structure in space. Function for the architect is not mechanical function. The architect must learn how to "engineer" his structures, but this is only an elementary part of his task. The great task of the architect is to create structures whose forms determine action within space. The art of architecture is a dramatic art; the humanity of a structure is determined by the joy and pleasure it creates in the lives of those who enact their roles within it. A building is not only spaced to be "used," but to be "lived in," and the quality of life within it will be determined by the architect. In democratic society the architect must think of the life of all the citizens and respect all their needs.[1] Architectural thinking must not rely too much on words. "[Y]ou must think in terms of *images,* of pictures, of states of feeling, of rhythm. The well-trained, well-organized, well-disciplined mind works with remarkable rapidity and with luminous intensity; it will body forth combinations, in mass, so complex, so far-reaching that you could not write them down in years. Writing is but the slow, snail like creeping of words, climbing, laboriously, over a little structure that *resembles* the thought: meanwhile the mind has gone on and on, here and yonder and back and out and back again." The test of all thought "will always be—results; for thinking brings real results." Real thinking is not a discovery of existing laws in nature, nor is it logic. It is creative. "You cannot create unless you think, and you cannot truly think without creating in thought."[2]

In his final statement on architectural thought, *Chat* XLIV, "On Knowledge and Understanding," which was completely rewritten in the 1918 version, Sullivan says: "My ostensible thesis has been Architecture as a social function, as an art of expression. My real thesis underlying that one and all others of all other men is that within man, a spiritual being, resides a spiritual power capable of infinite unfolding. . . . That power in its becoming I call Democracy, and hail as man's becoming."[3] Thus, democracy, as Sullivan uses the term, is not only a political system but an art of life. This art must never be set apart from reason or put in opposition to science. Art and thought are as closely related as science and thought. Science teaches us how to measure, or how to deal in abstractions of motion, but architecture teaches us how to understand human acts because it creates the stages within which human relationships unfold. Sullivan distinguishes between knowledge and understanding. Knowledge is of the head, understanding of the heart. Knowledge is of the intellect, understanding of emotion. It is often argued that understanding will increase with knowledge, but history warrants no such confidence in knowledge. "It is strange, a strange role in the strange drama, that intellect, proclaimed by man his highest power, tends ever to forsake man." Man's intellect has examined and systematized. It has produced vastly erudite accounts of man's career, but it has made one fatal mistake. "It has erected its own conception of man in its own intellectual image: THEREFORE, it has utterly failed to understand man. It neither sought nor found him. What it sought and found was an abstract intellectual concept—a complete inversion of the reality." [4]

The men who have understood men have not been scientists, logicians, philosophers, not theologians, but "compassionate dreamers overflowing with love." The wise could not understand them. Only the common people "could glimpse an understanding; for the multitude also are compassionate—they are near to the earth." If ever there has been an example of "that pride which goeth before destruction, and that haughty spirit which goeth before a fall, it is this unique colossal failure of the intellect to discern and welcome man; to reveal him to his own perturbed and anxious self." Intellect, having forsaken emotion, cannot understand man. This must be done through the heart, for it is the heart alone that understands. The unique characteristic of intellect is that alone, "uncontrolled and unsupported, it is peculiarly unstable; it tends ever toward insanity, toward self-destruction. . . . Those diseases, selfishness, greed, domination, suppression, usually attributed to the heart, are distinctly attitudes [not attributes] of the intellect in its unbalance. To speak of a man as hard of heart is foolish: to speak of him as hard in intellect is the truth. For ages man has been the victim of his intellect, and such victim he is today." [5]

The biblical story of the Fall tells a great truth. As man evolved, intellect became more active and dominant, while instinct declined. "Ego chose intellect for its counselor and guide, through fear. And here began selfishness, here Feudalism began its long career." Here began man's sin of pride in his intellect, so vividly portrayed in Genesis in the spiritual allegory of the garden. "Here began sin: the sin of intellect. Verily he tasted of the fruit of the tree of Knowledge. What a price he has since paid! For when man parted with Instinct the conserver, the preserver, the sure sustainer, he parted company with himself, and became a wanderer." In his loneliness man sought with his intellect to create a companion. "He put forth an image of his loneliness which took shape in dual philosophies," but man in becoming dual lost his integrity. Yet deep within man a vision of oneness remained. The heart yearned for understanding. The intellect could find no stabilizing thought: "Knowledge and Understanding were far apart." [6] How shall knowledge and understanding be reconciled? "There is but one agency, SYMPATHY." For sympathy is the power, long dormant in man, which may harmonize his thoughts. "For Sympathy is of the Spirit. It is at once the Searcher, the Visionary, the INTERPRETER. Its ethereal power underlies and enfolds both knowledge and understanding. . . . It is man's greatest unused power. . . . To possess knowledge without understanding is not only a misfortune, it is socially dangerous." Only sympathy saves man from destruction because it interprets, stabilizes and guides. [7]

Thought exists in time, not outside of it. And the reality of thought is in the present. "You cannot think *in* the past, you can think only *of* the past. You cannot think *in* the future, you can think only *of* the future. By great power of imagination you may think of the past and of the future *almost* in terms of the present: the one is the function of the historian, the other that of the prophet. But *reality* is of, in, by and for the present, and the present only. . . . The present is the *organic moment,* the *living moment.* The past and the future do not exist: the one is dead, the other unborn." [8] Time is dramatic, not historical. Actors invoke a past or envision a future to solve problems in the present. We use the past and the future to organize action so we can press forward toward desired goals.

Like Sullivan, Chicago artists and thinkers were deeply involved with the problem of time. It was easy enough to deny the past; indeed, if any new work was to be done, it was necessary. The domination of the Fair by Burnham and his classicists taught Chicago artists that tradition could be invoked to uphold bad as well as good art. Sullivan taught that when a tradition is no longer of relevance to the artist's search for form it must be abandoned —no matter how fixed or sacred it has become. He argued, too, that time in architecture was like dramatic time. A building was a stage, a form in which human activity achieved qualities of experience which could not have been achieved without it. The actor within the space created by the architect is not there to recall a past, or invoke a glorious future. He exists in a present which calls for characteristic actions of its own. Thus the act of buying and selling in Chicago cannot take place in a Roman temple, because trading is

The Kennedy Bakery, 1883–84. Detail of the façade. *Photo by Richard Nickel*

The Dooly Block of 1890–91 in Salt Lake City was an early attempt by Sullivan to create buildings whose form enhanced the function within (here commerce). *Photo by Richard Nickel*

not an act of worship, and it certainly is not Roman. The architect must give form to the act of buying and selling as it occurs on State Street, not invoke through stylistic identifications with the past, another, and very different, kind of trading.

As Sullivan, Dewey, Veblen, and Mead observed, appeals to tradition often went far beyond mere revivals of style. In 1890 history was invoked to explain social causation and, at the same time, to justify a moral standard. The classicists, as well as the medievalists, taught that return to the past (i.e., their past) was really a discovery of "a better self." The past was a "standard" against which the present and the future could be measured. In evolutionary thought as well as the new psychology of Freud, the past determined the present. Sumner of Yale taught that "millionaires are a product of natural selection, acting on the whole body of men to pick out those who can meet the requirement of certain work to be done. . . . [Thus they] may fairly be regarded as the naturally selected agents of society for certain work." [9] As Westerners such as Lester F. Ward, Dewey, and Veblen pointed out, the past discovered at Yale and Harvard was often what Sullivan called a feudal past. In his sociology, which influenced greatly the work of Veblen, Dewey, Mead, and Sullivan, Ward argued against confusing human with natural laws. Man is determined by natural selection, but he also determines himself through "telesis," in which he applies his intellect to his own improvement. In his *Dynamic Sociology* of 1883 he argued that all action consists in efforts to attain desired ends, and that the "end is present to the mind before the action is attempted." [10] Ends are created in deliberately constructed futures which are used to organize action in a present.

Sullivan's democratic man, who was to become the "great audience" of a new architecture, could oust the aristocrat only if he was really capable of becoming conscious of his own acts, and could test the relevance of his choices to the community good. The problem of self-consciousness seemed capable of solution through discussion, for in a land of equality discussion would be a sure way to truth because it thrives among equals. Democratic public opinion could be trusted to reach truth because it was the result of open, free, and informed discussion.[11] But the problem of testing acts, and especially architecture, for relevance to the good life of a modern democratic community was a much more complex problem. There was no theory of democratic architecture; it had to be created. It was easy enough to say that man lived in society, not in nature, and that society, unlike nature, had a future which was formed by man. But what kind of man was to form the future, and what kind of thinking was required to form it? And how was one to avoid domination by fanatics who appointed themselves guardians of the future, as the academic critics of the East had appointed themselves guardians of a hallowed classical past in architecture. How could the democratic artist *transcend* the future, as he had the past? And if social truths existed in art, not outside of art, in religion, politics, or economics, what was the nature of the truths of art?

The artist imagines the ideal, gives it form, and thus "by holding up the picture fires men to pursue [the ideal]." [12] He deals with human action; he is interested in character and fate as determined by social relationships. He tries to depict the ends of acts in terms of the human satisfaction experienced in such ends. The artist struggles to give ends forms, so we can know what such ends are. Unlike the priest, the artist tries to depict the satisfaction ends will bring here and now, in our relationship with each other, in a present whose values can be tested by reason, not some power beyond reason. Unlike the historian the artist does not reconstruct a past to discover "what really happened," but to tell us what *can* happen. Sullivan set himself resolutely against any approach to art which would take it beyond reason, or out of society into a realm of "pure essence." He argued to the very last that art, like science, must stand the test of reason in society. And even though Cooley, Dewey, and Mead, unlike Sullivan, were not trying to think as artists, yet they turned to art for models of actions in society. For, as Dewey said in *Experience and Nature,* "A thing is more significantly what it makes possible than what it immediately is. . . . Knowledge or science, as a work of art, like any other work of art, confers upon things traits and potentialities which did not *previously* belong to them." [13] Or, as Mead taught, only in art can we experience emergence and novelty, which must be explained, if we are to explain human action, not as motion, but as emotion.

In his essay, "The Roots of Social Knowledge," Charles Horton Cooley argued that there are two kinds of knowledge, "spatial or material knowledge" and "personal or social knowledge." The second is developed from contact with the minds of other men through communication. "It might also be described as sympathetic, or, in its more active forms, as dramatic, since it is apt to consist of a visualization of behavior accompanied by imagination of corresponding mental processes." And in almost the same terminology used by Sullivan some thirty years prior to this essay, Cooley says: "In relation to social phenomena the merely spatial conception of knowledge indicates an abstract way of thinking that does not envisage the facts. It is not, in this field, in accord with common sense. . . . If the distinctive trait of spatial knowledge is that it is mensurative, that of social knowledge is, perhaps, that it is dramatic. . . . although our knowledge of people is likewise behavioristic, it has no penetration, no distinctly human insight, unless it is sympathetic also." [14] But to say that art was the most characteristic human experience was only a beginning. For there to be any rigorous thinking about art, about art in society, or about society in the image of art, clear definitions were needed. What *kind* of art should supply the model for the image of society? Even when dramatic images were invoked, what *kind* of drama should be used? And even when images of communication, conversation, dialogue, role, play, or the game were invoked, exactly what structure of what function was involved? For until something was said about the nature of aesthetic experience as experience to be tested in observation of social relationships, there was nothing to be gained by saying that art experience was the characteristic social experience.

Notes

[1] Oscar Niemeyer, the designer of Brasília, restates Sullivan's credo. "The specific function of architecture is to serve the human being without social discrimination." Like Sullivan, he is quick to add that this does not mean without social *differentiation,* however. "Mass" architecture may be feudal, as well as democratic.

[2] Louis H. Sullivan, *Kindergarten Chats and Other Writings,* ed. by Isabella Athey (New York: George Wittenborn, 1947), *Chat* XV, "Thought."

[3] *Ibid., Chat* XLIV, "On Knowledge and Understanding."

[4] *Ibid.*

[5] *Ibid.*

[6] *Ibid.*

[7] *Chat* XLIV, "On Knowledge and Understanding." Cooley, like Mead and Dewey, argued that sympathetic introspection and sympathetic projection into the lives of others were the basis of social knowledge.

[8] *Ibid., Chat* XV, "Thought," Sullivan's italics. In his *Philosophy of the Present,* Mead, too, argues that the locus of reality is in the present.

[9] William Graham Sumner, *The Challenge of Facts and Other Essays* (New Haven: Yale University Press, 1914), p. 90

[10] See Lester F. Ward, *Dynamic Sociology,* 2 vols. (New York and London: Appleton, 1883), Vol. II, Chap. XI, "Action." Ward's telesis found its way into Dewey's psychology and Mead's social psychology. We select the kind of stimuli we need to activate us to responses which lead to desired ends. Sullivan insisted that only if we allowed man choices of ends could art have any meaning in society.

[11] Sullivan thought of the press as a competitive institution. In his view, newspapers would always present different points of view, and would be subject to criticism. Universities and schools were feudal because they did not open themselves to criticism, confused history with truth, and reduced reason to intellectual abstractions.

[12] The theories of action held by Cooley, Mead, Dewey, Veblen, and, indeed, by almost every progressive thinker in the Middle West, such as Lloyd, depended on accepting "culture," the "social," or art as the most *characteristic* human experience. This was the basis of pragmatic social theory, as we see in Dewey's *Experience and Nature.*

13 John Dewey, *Experience and Nature* (New York: Norton, 1929). Chap. IX, "Experience, Nature and Art."

14 Charles Horton Cooley, "The Roots of Social Knowledge." This paper was read as the Presidential Address before the Michigan Academy of Science, Arts, and Letters, March 31, 1926, and was published in *The American Journal of Sociology*, XXXII, No. 1 (July, 1926), pp. 59–79. It is reprinted in *Sociological Theory and Social Research: Being Selected Papers of Charles Horton Cooley* (New York: Henry Holt, 1930).

26

Art Considered as a Form of Sociation in Chicago Thought: I. Mead

SULLIVAN'S ARGUMENT that democracy depended on art was shared by Cooley, Veblen, Dewey, and Mead. John Ruskin and William Morris had said many things about art in society, but Sullivan and the sociologists, psychologists, and philosophers of the Chicago school were concerned not only with the general function of art in society but with its specific democratic function in an industrial society based on technology. There was very little concern in Chicago writing with purely aesthetic questions; the philosophy of art for Chicago artists was a social philosophy. There was nothing particularly new in relating art to society. But what was new was their assertion that art created forms (indeed *was* the form) which determined society. The assertion that only as we understand art do we understand society was new to American social thought of their time.[1] Sullivan's concern with the function of art in society, and his search for a theory of how art determines society, antedates that of Dewey and Mead by many years. His early essays were published some ten years before Veblen's *Theory of the Leisure Class,* an American classic in the sociology of art.[2] Sullivan's debt to Dewey is obvious, but we must not forget that it was Sullivan and the Chicago architects and engineers of the eighties who initiated the type of thinking that stimulated Veblen, Dewey, Cooley, and Mead. The Chicago School of Philosophy and the equally important Chicago School of Sociology and Education (under Dewey) was born in the Chicago School of Architecture of the eighties.

Cooley, the sociologist, believed that art, and particularly dramatic art, was the characteristic form of human sociation because communication was the basic social act. In social activity, relations between the self and others are regulated and modified by their struggle to achieve a common goal. Language, and all communication, thus becomes a development within social interaction. Individual and social roles are born in communication and are but different aspects of the same reality. Personality develops only in a social context, and society, in turn, exists only in and through persons who are in communication with each other.

Veblen, as economist and sociologist writing for an academic audience of social scientists, argued that "fine art" had become the phony rhetoric of plutocrats who used art to legitimize their power in forms expressing conspicuous consumption of time and money. In an industrial society, Veblen taught, art must become technological art. His term for such art is "the instinct of workmanship." [3] The artist of the handicraft era who worked at a craft must be replaced by an engineer-artist who expresses himself through machines. "He will be proficient in his craft in much the same degree in which he is master of the matter-of-fact logic involved in mechanical processes of pressure, velocity, displacement and the like." [4] In his review of Professor Trigg's *Chapters in the History of the Arts and Crafts Movement,* Veblen argues that industrial art which does not work through and in the spirit of the machine technology is, at best, an exotic with no chance of life "beyond the hothouse shelter of decadent aestheticism." The enduring characteristic of art and industry is not an aristocratic ideal of fine art, but an "insistence on sensuous beauty of line and color and on visible serviceability in all the objects which it touches." And these results can be better attained in full measure through "the technological expedients of which the machine process disposes than by any means within the reach of the industry of a past age."

Mead thought about art in terms of the emergence of the self in society. He argued that the self cannot be conceived outside of social experience. Man becomes man in dramatic dialogue with other men. The individual takes the attitudes of the others who are involved in his conduct, and thus becomes an object to himself. "It is only by taking the roles of others that we [are] able to come back to ourselves." We become "self-conscious" in so far as we take the attitude toward ourselves that others take toward us. In play we assume the roles of others so we can respond to them, or to our own imitation of their roles, like the child playing "grownup" before a mirror. In games we create procedures and rules. We not only take the role of the other, as in play, but assume the different roles of all the participants in the game, and govern our action accordingly. If we play first base on a baesball team, we play as the one to whom the ball will be thrown from the field or from the catcher. We create within ourselves the organized responses of others to the role we play. Thus in the game, as in play, the actor who stimulates others to response is at the same time arousing in himself tendencies to the same reactions. [5]

The third, and most characteristic form of sociation, is conversation. This is what distinguishes men from animals. Animals play, and they organize play into games, but they do not converse. This is because they do not have "significant symbols," as Mead calls the symbols created by the artist and used for expression in role-taking. The speaker is able to produce in himself the same intellectual and emotional effect he produces in his audience. He can import the attitudes of the audiences into himself. In the act of reflection we become audiences to ourselves through holding conversations with ourselves. We correct our own inner conversations through imaginary audiences. The "I" beholds its "Me," both of which, in turn, are corrected from the standpoint of a "they"—the "generalized other," which is, according to Mead, the attitude of the whole community, where man lives in a world of meaning. Even physical things constitute both "the hard physical realities of science, and the other, the material out of which to build the world of our heart's desire, the stuff that dreams are made of." [6] Such breaks between physical things that constitute the means and the ends, and values of community life have made economics a "dismal science, . . . mechanized and anatomized psychology . . . made ethics utilitarian, and aesthetics an affair of esoteric formulae." This bifurcation of our world cannot be "healed by a new philosophic formula." We must turn to experience of art to understand how the technical and the final intersect in experience.

"What is peculiar to aesthetic experience," Mead continues, "is its power to catch the enjoyment that belongs to the consummation, the outcome, of an undertaking, and to give the implements, the objects that are instrumental in the undertaking, and to the acts that compose it something of the joy and satisfaction that suffuse its successful accomplishment. . . . The beatitude that permeates the common striving of men after an infinite God of their salvation, belongs to the cathedral. . . . To so construct the object that it shall catch this joy of consummation is the achievement of the artist." Aesthetic experience as a social experience is therefore an attempt to give form to the ends which we are trying to achieve. But these ends exist *within* art, not in some reality beyond art which art can express but never create. Religious, political, educational, hygienic, and technical undertakings look into a future too. Indeed, every act must assume a future, or a goal, if only to organize immediate conduct in the act. But such endeavors do not carry with them "the satisfactions that belong to finalities." They belong in the province of action, "not that of appreciation." Our affective experience, "that of emotion, of interest, of pleasure and pain, of satisfaction and dissatisfaction, may be roughly divided between that of doing, and enjoying, and their opposites, and it is that which attaches to finalities that characterizes aesthetic experience." [7]

Mead, like Sullivan, made careful distinctions between intellectual and emotional experience. The intellect seeks to pass from recognition to operation; "we give attention only to that which forwards [an] undertaking; we see and hear only enough to recognize and use." But in appreciation "we contemplate, and abide, and rest in our presentations." When one stops to feel the surety of his colleagues, the loyalty of his supporters, the response of his public, or to enjoy the community of life in the family, profession, party, church, or country, "to taste in Whitmanesque manner the commonality of existence, his attitude is aesthetic." In social life art becomes a kind of poetry of action, as in community festivals and ceremonies where we dramatize goals and ends so that we can appreciate them. Thus the community, like the individual, stages ends and values to discover what they are. While the aesthetic attitude accompanies, inspires, and dedicates common action, which finds its moment of ideal significance in future achievement, the material in which its significance and beauty are fashioned is historic as well as Utopian. The creative imagination draws from the storehouses and quarries of the past. But aesthetic use of the past is really an interpretation to be used in a present. History is also an interpretation of the present, for art and history give us not only "the direction and trend of events, the reliable uniformities and laws of affairs, but [also] the irrevocableness of the pattern of what has occurred, in which to embody the still uncertain and unsubstantial objects we would achieve. The solidity and definitiveness and clarity of our undertakings are the donation of the past." [8]

Society could not exist without aesthetic experience, for without it we would not know what the ends of acts mean to man as an actor in social life. The perfection of aesthetic form may be reached in fine art, but art also involves the creative imagination and aesthetic appreciation of the least artistically endowed. Creative joy can be common to experience only when it belongs to the co-ordinated efforts of many in the community, when the "role of the other in the production is aroused in each worker at the common task; when the sense of team play, esprit de corps, inspires interrelated activities. In these situations something of the delight of consummation can crown all intermediate processes." [9] In our competitive industrial society work often lacks aesthetic delight. But it is folly to say that men do not have such delight because they do not want it. Men still hunger for enjoyment in work and seek to use the imagination to achieve healthy and normal satisfaction in the kind of consummation we experience in art. Daydreaming is substituted for art when the goal of an act is too far removed in time and too difficult of approach. Then the imagination leaps to ultimate satisfactions which cannot be related to the uninteresting details of preparation. The nerve of action is cut, the relation between means and ends is perverted. Ends are not expressed in action; they are not earned in shared experience.

Men turn to bad art to escape, not to share, common experience, which has become tedious, degrading, and painful.

Arts used for escape are like dreams. The visual imagery of popular movies is like the images of dreams, where there is no real shared experience. The movie, like the dream, has no active, responsive audience; its audience is not a community but a collection of strange and anonymous individuals. The unseen audience does not inspire the moving speech of the great actor or fire the imagination of the great orator. As a member of the audience under the power of an orator, one "is in the perspective of the whole community." Even the morning paper is shared with others, but the members of the movie audience, isolated from each other as persons, yet so compact physically, do not communicate. No one is bound to the other because no one assumes any responsibility to the audience as a whole. Since all are free to come and go, there is no group form which controls the individual.[10]

Art must enter into the active and practical lives of men in society. It is silly and inept to deify fine art, to "undertake by the spread of so-called culture to replace consummatory objects in men's reveries by the imagery of artists, or to replace machine production by medieval artisanship." [11] Those who inveigh against "machine industry" [12] as crushing out the artistic impulse "are indulging in reverie." While we must admit that "the factory organization of drudgery" makes reverie inevitable, if only to lift the pain of hard and ugly work, we must realize that this is a pathological condition. As Freud teaches, such reverie, like the infantile wish, is an escape from reality." [13] In a fully developed democratic society a man's work would be interesting, because every worker would have a sense of the whole that he is completing in his work. With advances in production and technology there ought to be a deeper sense of shared experience, and this, as Dewey [14] reminds us, is the greatest of human goods and the greatest value of a democratic society. Just so far as we can endow men with a gift of artisanship and creative impulse of any kind, and provide them with an opportunity to express it, we give them opportunity for aesthetic delight in labor. With society organized as it now is, this is impossible. But to the degree to which it is possible to add creative interest to work, we add aesthetic delight and thus humanize labor. Until we do so the worker in democratic society must find in daydreams what he cannot find in reality. Unless this is checked, the worker falls prey to inferiority complexes which render him unfit for responsible participation in democratic community life.

The democratization of industry offers an escape from the degradation of ugly and menial work. But, Mead continues, returning to craft organizations, as advocated by the Guild Socialists, is not the way to socialize industry.

New inventions bring men closer together, so that they realize their interdependence and increase their shared experience. This makes it more possible for them to put themselves in each other's places. Every form of communication which enables men to participate in each other's minds increases the socialization of the industrial community. The isolated individual is one of the great problems in modern society. Man's hunger for community, his yearning to escape isolation and loneliness, will determine the social forms of technology. Pressure for new inventions in communication and for greater sharing of aesthetic experience will not cease until the isolation of man within society has passed away.

The function of art in democratic society is exemplified in the newspaper.[15] A newspaper reporter is sent out to get a story, not the "facts." Readers demand that news take forms which conform (as far as this is possible) to the results desired by the various groups of readers. Thus it is the realm of reverie, of imagined enjoyable results, that dictates the policy of the daily press. This form of enjoyed result has an aesthetic function only when such stories, after being put into forms acceptable to newspaper publics, serve to interpret to the reader his experience as the shared experience of the community of which he feels himself to be a part. The enjoyable imagery may hardly rise above "unsatisfied animal impulses of gain, sex, or hate, but in so far as it has what is called the human appeal, or that of nation, town, or class, it serves to give the man the gratification of his experience as shared by the community to which he belongs." For such forms, the forms created in art, are "the determining forms which interpret . . . social experience."[16]

The movies, unlike the press, are more private and particular in the reverie that dominates the movie audience. Reverie provides us with an imagery of common values through the experience of common moments of consummation, but it also provides us with compensations for our defeats, our inferiorities, and our unconfessed failures. We learn from the average movie that the hidden unsatisfied longings of the average man and woman are very immediate, simple, and primitive. But this is not without its consolations. The confessed defeats of men, as expressed in popular art, are not defeats of altruistic and generous impulses. It is the primitive impulses which are repulsed in our society. If this is true, it may be assumed that men's defeats to reach greater social good have at least been alleviated by their shared experiences. Compensatory and escape values are not the only values that find expression in popular art such as the movies, even though they dominate and fix much of public taste, as we now know it.

Audiences who laugh heartily at Charlie Chaplin are presumably finding compensation for repressed primitive tendencies to inflict suffering and pain upon their enemies. But is this unreproved enjoyment of the terrors and enjoyment of another really only a release of primitive impulses which renders us callous to the sufferings of others? Can we really say that art teaches men to enjoy torture and violence? No, for aesthetic experience is a catharsis, not a reversion to a primitive state. The physically timid man does not become more courageous from watching the hero wipe out a nest of bandits. "But there should be a certain release, and relief from restraint, which comes from the fulfilment of the escape reaction with a richness of imagery which the inner imagination can never offer. If these escape reactions play any legitimate part in the economy of keeping house with one's self, and I think they do, elaboration of them at just the point where the imagination fails should emphasize that function."[17] Under such conditions, the enjoyed imagery is genuinely aesthetic.

Popular art, Mead believed, is not all escape art. Some movies appeal simply to interest in a story vividly told, to a sympathetic love of adventure, to a response to beauty in nature, and to delight in picturesque and distant scenes. We capture something of the same values that we experience in real travel and adventure. In such moments, a genuine aesthetic effect is produced. We are apt to consider the aesthetic experience of Joyce's *Ulysses* as a purely private affair. Such experience seems to be "infected with privacy and therefore subject to disintegration." But it passes into the universal meanings of "common discourse and cooperative effort," and out of it arise the forms of "universal beauty, the intuitions of the inventor, the hypotheses of the scientist, and the creation of the artist." It is "that part of the life of the inner life of man which cannot be given its implicated meaning of the incompleteness of social organization. It marks man's isolation within society."[18]

Notes

[1] It is one of the many paradoxes of American culture that art should have been made into a social category in Chicago, "hog butcher for the world." Artists, C. Wright Mills tells us in *The Sociological Imagination* (New York: Oxford, 1959), in the absence "of an adequate social science . . . have been the major, and often the only, formulators of private troubles and even of public issues . . . but still not with the intellectual clarity required for their understanding or relief today. Art does not and cannot formulate these feelings as problems containing the troubles and issues men must now confront if they are to overcome [them]" (p. 18). This is said by one of the "angry men" of sociology, not one of the accepted authorities such as Parsons. That is, even a so-called "radical" sociologist gives art no constituent place in his theory of society. And this is said a generation after the appearance of Dewey's *Art as Experience,* and two generations after Sullivan's *Kindergarten Chats.*

[2] The sociology of art is still so little understood that Veblen, like Machiavelli, is now being discussed as a "comic artist." This, upon close examination, turns out to mean that Veblen does not write in the sociological jargon so popular among our academicians. In 1964 a sociologist "reports research," and such reports are "scientific" to the degree they are expressed in a language taken very largely from the physical sciences. Few physical scientists agree that sociology is scientific at all. Even sociologists themselves admit that communication in American sociology is very poor. The American sociologist is not concerned with how well, but how "scientifically," he says something. That is, he has voted for one style as the proper style and thus is limited by that style. He must reduce motives to motion, and thus strip them of emotion, because his techniques were developed to study motion. The dogmatic minds that Sullivan inveighed against in the schools are as strong as ever, and unfortunately, far more numerous than in Sullivan's day. The kind of thinking about art in society which Sullivan thought necessary to the preservation of democracy is now being done in literary criticism, not in the social sciences, where social reality lies outside of art in economics, politics, the family, or "society." Common sense alone indicates that whatever the "nature" of the social bond, it arises in and is sustained through communication, which takes place in the expressive forms created in the kind of activity we call art.

[3] *The Instinct of Workmanship and the State of the Industrial Arts* (New York: Macmillan, 1914), as the title indicates, is a book about art in society. Dorfman tells us that after "he had ceased writing Veblen declared that *The Instinct of Workmanship* was his only important book." See Joseph Dorfman, *Thorstein Veblen and His America* (New York: Viking, 1934), p. 324. Veblen's discussion, along with those of Adler, Root, Sullivan, Wright and Dewey, antedates that of Le Corbusier by almost thirty years. When Le Corbusier said, "I am an American" he meant "I am a Chicagoan," for it was the engineers and architects of Chicago he was thinking about when he identified himself with America.

[4] See Chapter VII, "The Machine Industry," of *The Instinct of Workmanship.*

[5] This account of Mead's theory of the social self is taken from his article, "The Genesis of the Self and Social Control," which appeared in *The International Journal of Ethics,* Vol. 35, No. 3 (April, 1925). This is also reprinted in *The Philosophy of the Present* (Chicago: Open Court, 1932). Mead understood that it was not enough to say we take roles without at the same time discussing how roles are staged. That is, granting interaction as basic to all social intercourse, what specific *forms* of social interaction can we distinguish? It is the same with communication. We do not just communicate, but communicate with each other in certain social groups which are staged in various ways to enact roles necessary to certain acts. Mead discusses such forms of staging as play, games, conversation, and drama, but conversation is his basic image of social interaction.

[6] Mead, like Dewey and Sullivan, was careful *not* to limit meaning to verbal experience alone. "What [man] sees and hears means what he will or might handle," Mead tells us in "The Nature of Aesthetic Experience." Sullivan's warning to architects not to think in words and to develop a sense of what he called "tough," is a further example of this. Meaning is expression, and expression involves all the senses. Any theory of meaning based on art as action must be essentially a dramatistic theory.

[7] See "The Nature of Aesthetic Experience."

[8] "The Nature of Aesthetic Experience." That is, the past as tradition or custom affects us as much as the future or the ideal. The past may even become a future, or goal, as when classicists preached that American architecture in the future must *return* to its better self, i.e., its classical past. The past, however, must be re-enacted in a present if it is to be kept as a living tradition. "Unused" pasts or traditions soon die— just as do "unused" futures, ideals, or visions.

[9] "The Nature of Aesthetic Experience," *International Journal of Ethics,* XXXVI (1926), pp. 382–92.

[10] The same is true of modern ballroom dancing. Unlike dances in the minuet, the modern couple dance together and enter and leave as they choose. Individuals can even change partners while the dance goes on. The modern dance is often done in dim light. In such intimate dancing one exists for one other but not for the group.

[11] Mead, like Veblen and Sullivan, had little use for "monastic real-estate" or "the feudal mind."

[12] This was Veblen's phrase.

[13] Mead's use of Freud in this context is one of the few stresses in Mead on the pathological aspects of conduct. Mead, like Dewey, overlooked the fact that we share evil as we do good. That is, sharing in itself is not good—as our generation learned to its horror as we watched Germans torture and murder millions of Jews in their death camps.

[14] In a footnote to the title of his article, "The Nature of Aesthetic Experience," Mead says: "I have not made specific acknowledgements in the article to Professor Dewey, but the reader who is familiar with *Experience and Nature* will realize that it was written under the influence of that treatise." All those who knew Dewey well stress that, while Mead was indebted to Dewey, Dewey, in turn, was deeply indebted to Mead. The relationship between Dewey, Mead, and Cooley is touched upon in *Dialogue on John Dewey* by Farrell, Johnson, Kallen, and others, edited by Corliss Lamont (New York: Horizon Press, 1959).

[15] Mead, like Sullivan, considered a free press to be a foundation stone of democratic society. Unlike most who stress "information" and "facts" as the truth of the newspaper, Mead stressed its dramatic function or what we now call its "human interest."

[16] "The Nature of Aesthetic Experience," *op. cit.*

[17] *Ibid.*

[18] *Ibid.*

27

Art Considered as a Form of Sociation in Chicago Thought: II

M EAD was interested in art because of his interest in the genesis of the self through communication in society. Dewey, and certainly the Dewey of the Chicago years, was interested in art in education and its relation to knowledge and mind. His early "instrumentalism" is an attempt to bring intellect into some kind of relationship with emotion. Both Mead and Dewey thought of the act as the basic unit of human experience. They argued that knowledge should not be thought of merely in terms of vision—which was the traditional model for what we call perception—but first as manipulation, and finally as action. As Dewey told Frederick Woodbridge (his colleague in philosophy at Columbia), who held that the visible world and vision were the clue to any theory of understanding, "I think this whole problem of understanding should be approached not from the point of view of the eyes, but from the point of view of the hands." [1] Mead said much the same: "Man lives in a world of Meaning. What he sees and hears means what he will or might handle. . . . The world of perceptual reality, the world of physical things is the world of our contacts and our manipulations, and the distance experience of the eye and the ear means first of all these physical things." [2]

Perception for Mead was part of an act. "All perception involves an immediate sensuous stimulation and an attitude toward this stimulation, which is that of the reaction of the individual to the stimulation." A perception has in it, therefore, "all the elements of an act—the stimulation, the response represented by the attitude, and the ultimate experience which follows upon the reaction, represented by the imagery arising out of past reactions." He realized that the central task in basing a philosophy on democratic social action was not simply to bring action back into society, but to show *how* the act took *form*. It was easy enough to say that an act was "social," for if it was not social what was it? But it was not very logical to explain acts by "society," and then some paragraphs later to explain society by acts. [3] The real question was over the forms in which the act took place, *how* the self was presented, the *ways* in which groups staged themselves.

Even when art was invoked as a model for thinking about sociation, some *kind* of art, not just "art," must be specified. This was also true in discussion over communication. Sullivan argued that inner dialogue was carried on best *without* words and exhorted his young architect to learn to think without words. At times, indeed, he relates verbal art to feudalism, and certainly he was suspicious of all literary treatment of architecture. Meaning in society, Sullivan insisted, was architectural as well as verbal. Architectural structure determined the spatial qualities of action, as stage designers fashioned spatial tones and atmospheres in the dramatic environment of the stage scene and set conditions in which action takes place.

By 1885 in America, meaning had already been brought into close relation to action by James's theory of the emotions. To say that we are afraid because we run away from a bear, are gay because we laugh, or angry because we fight (as in James's familiar illustrations) implied that emotion was born in action between a self and an other, and was therefore of social origin. Cooley, Mead, Dewey, Veblen, and Sullivan did not have to bring meaning back to action, nor action back into society. But what they had to do, and what is significant about their social thought, is the manner in which they struggled to find forms of social action which would reduce the general theoretical category "social" to *specific forms* of socialization which could be used to observe action in society.[4] Mead argued that the physical aspects of things are means. "They have an existence which is indifferent . . . to ends, and constitute the field of mechanism." They become ends when we invest them with intention. We see objects as we will handle them. We are conscious of "that in the perceptual world which suggests confirmation, direct or indirect, in fulfilled manipulation. . . . The dagger before Macbeth is not there until he grasps it. . . . the dagger's reality, which his hand sought to grasp, lay in the future. He was conscious of what implicated that futurity."[5] Thus while the end or future of an act is an ideal, its reality is not in the mind alone (as a kind of Platonic essence), but in the relationship between the assumed end and action in a present. In tactile experience it is not the image of the resistance of that which will be grasped, but the readiness (the "body-set") to grasp it, which make the reality of the precept.

This distinction, which is basic in the thought of Mead and Dewey, is also basic to Sullivan's famous formula: "Form follows function." If we assume that architectural forms are copies of some kind of ideal form, we shift reality into a transcendent Platonic essence, for that which is copied must be antecedent to its copy.[6] If we assume, on the other hand, that ideal functions already exist (as physical scientists do with such fictions as "frictionless functioning") and that all the scientist or artist needs to do is to discover them, then function is but a crude expression of pure form. But if we assume, as did the Chicago school, that forms arise in attempts to solve problems in social action, form and function are real, not because of their relationship to an essence outside of or beyond action, but *within* action in society.[7] Such forms are subject to reason because they must be tested continually in terms of their usefulness in solving problems in human relationships.

The problems we are trying to solve always involve physical objects whose reality lies in how we manipulate them or imagine how to manipulate them, and in a time whose reality exists in our ability to organize recalled pasts and imagined futures for action in a present. In his discussion of form and function Sullivan says: "For Man there is nothing but the physical; what he calls his spirituality is but the most exalted reach of his animalism. Little by little, Man, through his senses, divines the Infinite. His highest thoughts, like his most delicate yearnings, arise, through an imperceptible birth, and growth, from the material sense of touch." The language of function and form is rhythm, which is "the very wedding-march and ceremonial that quickens into song the unison of form and function." This unison is determined in solutions to problems in a present, not by forms designed to solve problems in the past.

At the beginning of *Chat* XIII, "Function and Form (2)," Sullivan's student breaks in, teasing his master for his high-flown language.

It seems to me that I could have gotten a clearer idea of your recent harangue on function and form, if you had used half as many words. Still, I think I catch your meaning after a fashion. The gist of it is, I take it, that behind every form we see there is a vital something or other which we do not see, yet which makes itself visible to us in that very form. In other words, in a state of nature the form exists *because* of the function, and this something behind the form is neither more nor less than a manifestation of what you call the infinitive creative spirit, and what I call God. . . . what you want me to understand and hold to is, that, just as every form contains its function, and exists by virtue of it, so every function finds or is engaged in finding its form. And furthermore, while this is true of the every-day things we see about us in nature and in the reflection of nature we call human life, it is just as true, because it is a universal law, of everything that the mind can take hold of.

The student then asks of the master what all this has to do with the specific problem of designing a building. The master asks the student why thinking about building should differ from thinking about any other form or function. The student is led to discover for himself the relationship between a theory of functionalism and a functional theory of architecture. He tells his master: "I suppose if I call a building a form, then there should be a function, a purpose, a reason for each building, a definite explainable relation between the form, the development of each building, and the causes that bring it into that particular shape; and that the building, to be good architecture, must, first of all, clearly correspond with its function, must be its image, as you would say." But the student is still puzzled. He can see the logic of functional theory, but what has it to do with art?

To think about art, the master replies, we must learn to think "organically." In seeking a "reasonably solid grasp on the value of the word organic, we should at the beginning fix in mind the values of the correlated words, organism, structure, function, growth, development, form." Organic qualities of form are not to be understood through words: "architecture, for the past several centuries, has suffered from a growing accretion of words: it is now in fact so overgrown and stifled with words that the reality has been lost to view. Words and phrases have usurped the place of function and form. Finally phrase-making has come to be an accepted substitute for architecture-making." [8] This is why so much of the architecture of our time is bad: "Its features have a pallid leer. . . . Its eye is lustreless, its ear is dulled, its vitals atrophied. So moves it wearily on its crutch of scholarship—groping through spectacles of words." [9] Organic architecture, the new architecture of our time, will be created by

a generative man, who is the creative man—A man having five senses all awake; eyes that fully see, ears that are attuned to every sound; a man living in his present, knowing and feeling the vibrancy of that ever-moving moment, with heart to draw it in and mind to put it out: that incessant, that portentous birth, that fertile moment we call TODAY! As a man who knows his day, who loves his day, who knows and loves the exercise of life, who rightly values strength and kindliness, whose feet are on the earth, whose brain is keyed to the ceaseless song of his kind: who sees the past with kindly eye, who sees the future in a kindling vision: a man who wills to create: So shall our art be. For to live, wholly to live, is the manifest consummation of existence.[10]

Expression in organic architecture must change from feudal to democratic forms. It must include every human activity. A democratic art of expression is founded on man's "high moral power of choice." It will guide him in the exercise of various powers as "Worker, Inquirer, Thinker, and Dreamer." Man has thus far lived by fear, but democracy will abolish fear because democratic men qualify, each in his own way, in the "all-inclusive art of expression." The art of developing democracy into a complete working civilization is the "one great art of expression confronting man today." That is why, Sullivan continues, "my object all along has been, first, to isolate the architectural art as a specialized social activity and then to show how inextricably, in its genuine state, it is interwoven with the needs, the thoughts, the aspirations of the people, [so] that it cannot have a real life without them." [11]

But this is only the first step in architecture. Democratic architecture must respond to the people's needs, but it must raise these needs into "higher realms of interpretation." It must "take its vigorous origin in the direct, practical, utilitarian needs," and make use of every modern resource. It must "first fully satisfy the needs, fully utilize the resources." For then, and then only, "is it justified in entering the realms of sentiment and poetic imagination; and then only for the purpose of giving to the utilitarian its needed aspect of beauty, thus contributing its share to the happiness of mankind —to the poem of Democracy." [12] Nature furnishes the

materials and you have but to use them with intelligence, and feeling. All geometric forms are at your disposal, they are universal; it is for you to utilize them, to manipulate them, to transmute them, with feeling and intelligence. Engineering science has substantially solved all problems of construction. The industrial arts, the so-called fine arts, mechanical skill, craftsmanship are at your disposal. The organized building arts, transportation, communication are at your disposal; language is at your disposal. Nature's manifold expressions of function and form are at your disposal. . . . To make these things, these instrumentalities, plastic to your ends is your business.

Finally, the architect must understand that every problem contains and suggests its own solution. It is a waste of time to look elsewhere.[13]

Toward the end of his long life, Dewey pointed out that he had not wanted only to establish knowledge in a better and more solid form, "but to establish the sphere of values, of human desires and aims, on the same basis and in an analogous form as the system of knowledge." [14] In his early essays on education he is concerned with the training of the emotions. Thus in "The Aesthetic Element in Education," [15] Dewey, like Sullivan talking to his pupil, tells us that by the aesthetic he means "a certain phase of all education, rather than a particular group of studies." Modern theory and practice in education, he goes on, "have laid relatively too much stress upon the volitional training in practical control and intellectual training in the acquisition of information, and too little upon the training of responsiveness. . . . We need to return more to the Greek conception, which defined education as the attaching of pleasure and pain to the right objects and ideals in the right way. This ideal overemphasized the emotional element, but we have now gone to the opposite extreme."

Dewey was attracted to art in education because art teaches us to express ourselves. "Responsiveness," he told teachers, "an emotional reaction to ideas and arts, is a necessary factor in moral character." It is also necessary and highly practical, since it supplies "a delicacy and quickness in the face of practical situations." Responsiveness must be directed in certain ways. The emotions, like the intellect, must be trained. As Dewey indicates in his review in 1893 of Bosanquet's *History of Aesthetic,* the gap between feeling and reason must be closed. When "it is shown that beauty or morality are products of a purely 'natural' development, their reality is in nowise impugned; the reality is neither in the first state merely as such, nor in the latter in its isolation, but in the law or movement which holds all in one unity. . . . the specific problem common to both metaphysic and aesthetic [is] how to reconcile feeling and reason; how sense material may be pregnant with meaning." The good society must have right emotions, as well as right thoughts, if it is to have good acts.

Dewey's writings during his Chicago years [16] assign no such high place to art in experience as we find in Sullivan's essays of the same period. For Sullivan art is the supreme experience of man. Art is "understanding," philosophy and science are "knowledge." Art teaches us how to act, intelligence how to think about acting. Art is of the heart and teaches us joy and love, intellect is of the mind and kills whatever it abstracts. Science deals with motion, art with emotion. And, finally, art is of nature, and thus in harmony with all creation.

Up to the first version of *Experience and Nature,* in 1925, Dewey relates intelligence and art in such a way that neither transcends the other, but they find their unity in "experience"—without really defining what "experience" is. Later in his writing, art becomes the kind of shared experience which makes community possible. "Human experience in the large, in its coarse and conspicuous features, has for one of its most striking features pre-occupation with direct enjoyment, feasting and festivities; ornamentation, dance, song, dramatic pantomime, telling yarns and enacting stories." But we find that in art (or at least the aesthetic moment in art) "objects are possessed and appreciated, but they are not *known*." And when we confuse the creation of art with aesthetic contemplation of it, and then insist that all final objects must be thought about in ways similar to the contemplation of beauty, science cannot develop.

Or at least it could not develop into the kind of knowledge we need to live well in society. Classical thought regarded possession, contemplations, as the essence of science, and thought of science as a complete possession of reality which incorporated it with mind. Knowledge thus became an immediate possession of Being. Even when the actual conditions of knowing changed radically, this conception of science as a grasp of reality in its final self-sufficing form, in contrast to the imperfect, confused, and perverted modes of experience in art, continued. The question we must ask, according to Dewey, is —"If the proper object of science is a mathematic-mechanical world (as the achievements of science have proved to be the case) and if the object of science defines the true and perfect reality (as the perpetuation of the classic tradition asserted), then how can the objects of love, appreciation—whether sensory or ideal—and devotion be included within true reality?" [17]

Notes

[1] This is reported by Schneider in *Dialogue on John Dewey* (New York: Horizon Press, 1959), p. 95. We sometimes forget that in the classical theory of art there is a hierarchy of the senses. As Francis Bacon says: "The arts which relate to the eye and the ear, are above the rest, accounted liberal; these two senses being the more pure, and the sciences thereof more learned, as having mathematics to attend them. . . . The pleasure of the other senses, and the arts employed about them are in less repute, as approaching nearer to sensuality than magnificence." *The Advancement of Learning,* Fourth Book, Chapter II, next to last paragraph.

[2] This is taken from the first paragraph of Mead's "The Nature of Aesthetic Experience," *International Journal of Ethics,* XXXVI (1926), pp. 382–92. Many passages in Sullivan on the primacy of "touch" in architectural understanding and creation, could be quoted in agreement with Dewey and Mead. Relating senses other than sight to meaning as an intellectual experience, brings all the arts into the realm of thought. Chicago thinkers, such as Sullivan in his quest for a philosophy of architecture, argued that perception was an act involving far more than the eye alone. Sullivan's imagery of vision, of how we see a building, is not the imagery of an object perceived in space, but of a dramatic action on a stage. Buildings literally "spoke" to Sullivan.

[3] This kind of circularity is not so rare as the high title of "Social philosophy" might indicate. All theories of social process are peculiarly liable to it. For if we invoke process, without at the same time taking into account the agent affected by process we soon end with a model of society which has everything but acting human beings within it.

[4] That is, just as Freud created a model of family life, the Oedipus complex, to help him understand love and hate, so did Chicago artists and philosophers try to create a model of democratic action which would help them to understand community life. In their thought "the social" as a category became a category of community action, and this in turn was described as a form of democratic action.

[5] See discussion, "Perspective Theory of Perception," in George Herbert Mead, *The Philosophy of the Act* (Chicago: University of Chicago Press, 1936).

[6] This was, of course, the view of the traditionalists in architecture. Interpreted literally, it soon became the basis of the view that, since there were many beautiful buildings in the world, all the Chicago architect had to do was to copy them. The only problem then was *which* "beauty" to copy.

[7] Mead, far more than Dewey, was interested in how such a view affected our understanding of time, as well as space. In *The Philosophy of the Present,* Mead argues that time exists within a present because we use pasts and futures to organize action in a present. In this philosophy we do not "return" to pasts, nor are we "empelled" or "driven" by a past—any more than we are "attracted" to a future. We are trying to solve problems in action. The architectural theories of the Chicago school are very closely related to these views of the Chicago philosophers and sociologists.

[8] See Louis H. Sullivan, *Kindergarten Chats and Other Writings,* ed. by Isabella Athey (New York: George Wittenborn, 1947), *Chat* XIV, "Growth and Decay."

[9] For a man who warns architects against words, Sullivan pays great homage to the

power of words. His personifications of buildings, the images in which he depicts the psychological and human effect of structure, are among his best passages. His theory of architecture as a dramatic art is reflected in the images of buildings as actors and as stages which determine action. This imagery of building is usually a *dramatic* image.

10 Sullivan, *op. cit., Chat* XIV, "Growth and Decay." In this, and other similar passages, Sullivan makes the artist, and particularly the architect, a hero in the struggle for democracy in Chicago. It is significant that no other artists made heroes out of themselves. Often, as in Dreiser or Fuller, they depict artists (but *not* architects) as weaklings, clowns, or even villains. The architect, as depicted in the novel, relates to the world of men, as well as women. Other artists move within a wholly feminized world where art is a pastime or a decoration.

11 Sullivan, *op. cit., Chat* XLIX, "The Art of Expression."

12 This was John Root's point too. There is no hierarchy of content, or of social class, in the Chicago school. Until (as Wright taught) the meanest citizen is housed beautifully the architect in democracy has failed.

13 Sullivan, *op. cit., Chat* XLIX, "The Art of Expression."

14 See "The Philosopher Replies" in *The Philosophy of John Dewey . . . A Critical Analysis and Evaluation* by Russell, Santayana, *et al.,* including a new, authoritative bibliography and John Dewey's Reply to His Critics, ed. by Paul Arthur Schilpp (New York and London: Tudor, 1939).

15 In National Education Association, *Addresses and Proceedings,* 1897.

16 In 1900 Chicago was a radical center of education as it was of architecture and philosophy—and was to become of literature and jazz.

17 This is discussed in chapter four, "Nature, Means and Knowledge," of Dewey's *Experience and Nature* (New York: Norton, 1929).

28

Art and Science in Chicago Thought and Art

D EWEY'S QUESTION haunted Chicago thought. Sullivan faced it before he began to design the Auditorium. Sullivan's first great moment of illumination in his mature life (which preceded his second by some fifteen years) was born of science, not art. Monsieur Clopet, his tutor in mathematics, who was preparing him for the Beaux-Arts entrance examinations, launched him on his spiritual journey in quest of an "engineer's aesthetic." "Now observe," Monsieur Clopet said about a book on geometry which Sullivan was showing him,

> Here is a problem with five exceptions or special cases; here is a theorem, three special cases; another nine, and so on and on, a procession of exceptions and special cases. I suggest you place the book in the waste basket; we shall not need it here, *for here our demonstrations shall be so broad as to admit of* NO EXCEPTION!"
> At these amazing words Louis stood as one whose body had turned to hot stone, while his brain was raging. Instantly the words had flashed, there arose a vision and a fixed resolve; an instantaneous inquiry and an instant answer. The inquiry: If this can be done in Mathematics, why not in Architecture? The instant answer: It can, and it shall be! *No one has—I will!* [1]

And thus began Sullivan's search for a principle of form in architecture which would match the generality and beauty of mathematical demonstration. In the "immense seconds of this eidolon," [2] he dedicated his life to this pursuit. "It may be years from now, before I find what I seek, but I shall find what I seek." And he will find it in society, among men. "The world of men, of thoughts, of things, shall be mine. . . . the world is filled with evidence. I shall explore that world to seek, to find." [3]

If true of mathematics, why not of art? This question, in one form or another, soon became as central to American thought as the debate over science and religion. Religious "truths" had been banished to a supernatural beyond reason. But if one rejected the revealed truths of religion, or the quantitative truths of science, what then was the truth of art? If the truths of art did not rest simply on belief, and yet were far different from those of science, then what were they? All agreed with the accepted view that aesthetic experience existed in its own right. But as James, Dewey, and Mead observed, far more was known about art as aesthetic than as communication. Common sense taught that art was a great part of life, and that community life would be infinitely poorer without it, but no one seemed able to say just why this was so.

In Chicago discussion on the social function of art focused on architecture, as Sullivan discovered upon his return from Europe. His reading of Taine stimulated him to think about art in society. "From these works he derived three strong impressions, novel shocks: First, that there *existed* such a thing as a Philosophy of Art; second, that according to M. Taine's philosophy the art of a people is a reflex or direct expression of the life of that people; third, that one must become well acquainted with that life in order to see into the art." All this, Sullivan tells us of his return to Chicago, "was new and shining." He knew it was true of "Boston and Chicago." But what he was not prepared for in Chicago was the challenge to philosophies of fine art which had been so widely accepted in Europe.[4]

In his search for a principle of art which would rival the universality of Monsieur Clopet's demonstrations in mathematics, Sullivan turned first to the engineers. There was a positive quality in their thought; they transformed mathematical formula into structure. "Louis found himself drifting towards the engineering point of view, or state of mind, as he began to discern that the engineers were the only men who could face a problem squarely; who knew a problem when they saw it. Their minds were trained to deal with real things, as far as they knew them, as far as they could ascertain them, while the architectural mind lacked this directness, this simplicity, this singleness of purpose—it had no standard of reference, no bench-mark one might say."[5] Differences between architects and engineers in Chicago ranged from mild teasing to violent disputes. "The architect," Sullivan tells us, "could not or would not understand the real working of the engineering mind because it was hidden in deadly literal attitudes and results, because of the horrors it had brought forth as misbegotten stigmata; while the engineer regarded the architect as a frivolous person of small-rule-of-thumb consequence." But it was the engineers, not the architects, who first dramatized structure in the Middle West. Two great engineering works, Eades's triple arch bridge to cross the Mississippi at Saint Louis and C. Shaler Smith's great cantilever bridge to cross the chasm of the Kentucky River for the use of the Cincinnati Southern Railroad, excited Sullivan. "As the drama of these two bridges unfolded in the pages of the *Railway Gazette,* Sullivan identified more and more with the engineers. . . . Louis followed every detail of design, every measurement, every operation as the two works progressed from the sinking of the caissons in the bed of the Mississippi, and the start in the wild of the initial cantilevers from the face of the cliff. . . . Every difficulty encountered he felt to be his own; every expedient, every device, he shared in." [6]

The drama of the two bridges so captured his imagination that he dreamed briefly of becoming a great bridge engineer. The idea of spanning a void appealed to him as masterful in thought and deed. His interest in these bridges soon passed from engineering to science in general. What attracted him in the scientific mind was "its honest search for stability in truth." Hitherto he had regarded his mathematics as an art; he had not followed far enough to see it as a science. "Indeed he had hitherto regarded every constructive human effort as an art, and to this view he had been held through the consistent unfolding of the Idea." [7] But what at once impressed Louis as new and vital was what was known as "The Scientific Method." He now felt he had in his hands the instrument he needed in his search for a universal principle in architecture. But if science and engineering were enough, what then *was* the function of art in architecture and in society? If science could tell us so much about power in nature, and intellect so much about power in thought, what was the power of art? What distinguished art from science and philosophy? What did one mean by the "art" of a building, and how could one explain art to tough-minded engineers like Baumann, Jenney, Adler, Smith, or Strobel, who openly sneered that architects were not designers but decorators? How could the artist hold his own in conversation with Frederick Baumann, "who found all human beings ridiculous," and especially architects in Chicago? What could one say to Edelmann, who could draw like an angel, think like an engineer, and talk like a philosopher? And finally what could the artist do in argument against Veblen, who insisted that the fine art of architecture was really nothing but a pious fraud or a kind of plutocratic magic used to communicate the majesty of pecuniary canons of life?

Sullivan soon distinguished between science as a technique and science as a way of thinking.[8] Science, he saw, "could not go either fast or far were it not for Imagination's glowing light and warmth. By nature it is rigid and prosaic—and Louis early noted that the free spirits within its field were men of vision—masters of imagination, men of courage, great adventurers —men of one big, dominant idea." [9] And the engineers, for all their tough. talk and ability to face and solve problems in structure, showed little concern over the social meanings of their structures. He discerned, as he tells us, "that in truth the science of engineering is a science of *reaction,* while the science of architectural design—were such a science to be presupposed—must

be a science of action." [10] But in what form, in what idea, could art be cast
as a model of action? If society was a work of art, what *kind* of art work was
it? And if architecture was to determine democratic society, what form
must such architecture take? Science dealt with man in space. William
James stressed that time and space relations, unlike those of art, are impressed
from without. Science, so the current belief ran, had discovered realities
which exist in nature, not the mind alone. When (as James said) "you give
things mathematical and mechanical names and call them just so many
solids in just such positions, describing just such paths with just such veloci-
ties, all is changed. Your sagacity finds its rewards in the verification by
nature of all the deductions which you may next proceed to make. Your
'things' realize all the consequences of the name by which you classed them."
But call "the things of nature as much as you like by sentimental, moral,
and aesthetic names, no natural consequences follow from the naming." [11]

For, when we pass from scientific to aesthetic and ethical systems,

> every one readily admits that, although the elements are matters of experience, the
> peculiar forms of relation into which they are woven are incongruent with the order
> of passively received experience (as in our knowledge of nature). The world of aes-
> thetics and ethics is an ideal world, a Utopia, a world which the outer relations persist
> in contradicting, but which we as stubbornly persist in striving to make actual. Why
> do we thus invincibly crave to alter the given order of nature? Simply because other
> relations among things are far more interesting to us and more charming than the
> mere rates of frequency of their time- and space-conjunctions. These other relations are
> all secondary and brain-born, "spontaneous variations" most of them, of our sensibility,
> whereby certain elements of experience, and certain arrangements in time and space,
> have acquired an agreeableness which otherwise would not have been felt.[12]

And, when all is said about art and ethics, James concluded, there really
is no way we can relate them to our "outer" experience of nature. *"There
are then ideal and inward relations amongst the objects of our thought
which can in no intelligible sense whatever be interpreted as reproductions
of the order of outer experience."* Indeed, the aesthetic realm of "ideal and
inward relations," *conflicts* with the "order of outer experience." Aesthetic
kingdoms, the city beautiful in the vision of the architect, is not of this earth,
and for it to become so the city we now know must be destroyed. But, says
James, the

> peculiarity of those relations among objects of our thought which are dubbed "scientific"
> is this, that although they no more are inward *reproductions* of the outer order than
> the ethical and aesthetic relations are, yet they do not conflict with that order, but,
> once having sprung up by the play of inward forces, are found—some of them at least,
> namely the only ones which have survived long enough to be matters of record—to
> be *congruent* with the time- and space-relations which our impressions affect. . . . In

other words, though nature's materials lent themselves slowly and discouragingly to our translation of them into ethical forms, but more readily into aesthetic forms; to translation into scientific forms they lend themselves with relative ease and completeness.[13]

In his discussion of aesthetic and moral principles in the chapter on "Necessary Truths," James tells us that "aesthetic principles are at bottom such axioms as that a note sounds good with its third and fifth, or that potatoes need salt!" The mathematical world-formula of science butchers "at a blow" the "sentimental facts and relations" of art and ethics. But the "rationality yielded is so superbly complete in *form* that to many minds this atones for the loss, and reconciles the thinker to the notion of a purposeless universe, in which all the things and qualities men love . . . are but illusions of our fancy attached to accidental clouds of dust which will be dissipated by the eternal cosmic weather as carelessly as they were formed." [14]

James brings his *Psychology* to a close by denying that "the couplings of terms within the mind are simple copies of corresponding couplings impressed upon it by the environment." And even if we agree that such simple copies exist, "so far as logical and mathematical, ethical, aesthetical, and metaphysical propositions go, such an assertion is not only untrue but altogether unintelligible." The causes "of our mental structure are doubtless natural. . . ." and we must assume that they are connected in some way with our "nervous structure." But the best an honest thinker can say in the present state of knowledge, is that we cannot account for our mental structure. "Our interests, our tendencies of attention, our motor impulses, the aesthetic, moral, and theoretic combinations we delight in, the extent of our power of apprehending schemes of relation, just like the elementary relations themselves, time, space, difference and similarity, and the elementary kinds of feeling, have all grown up in ways of which at present we can give no account." [15]

Thus, while James admits that it has proved easier to identify nature's objects with mental terms of the mechanical than with forms of sentient order, and that philosophy can at best offer "postulates, not propositions," with regard to the real world outside, he is careful to point out that much of human experience cannot be described by any mechanical model. Some twelve years later, in 1902, the same year as the publication of Sullivan's *Kindergarten Chats,* James makes clear his refusal to accept science as an adequate description of experience. "The whole drift of my education goes to persuade me that the world of our present consciousness is only one out of many worlds of consciousness that exist, and that these other worlds must contain experiences which have a meaning for our life also. . . . I *can,* of course, put myself into the sectarian scientist's attitude, and imagine vividly that the world of sensations and of scientific laws and objects may be all. But whenever I do this, I hear that inward monitor . . . whispering the word "bosh!" Humbug is humbug, even though it bear the scientific name, and the total expression of human experience, as I view it objectively, invincibly urges me beyond the narrow 'scientific' bounds." [16]

Unfortunately for art, but not for religion, James broke through the narrow "scientism" of Herbert Spencer and John Stuart Mill, by his great study of the psychology of religious life. Thus we have *The Varieties of Religious Experience* but no corresponding work on aesthetic experience.[17] Our only clue to what James might have done with some form of "The Varieties of Aesthetic Experience," comes from Lecture XIX, "Other Characteristics," of *The Varieties of Religious Experience*. Here he points out that much of the power of religion comes from "the way in which [ecclesiastical systems] satisfy aesthetic needs." He understands that the hold of such systems is based in their dramatization of authority. He then goes on to discuss aesthetic depiction of religious experience.

Although some persons aim most at intellectual purity and simplification, for others *richness* is the supreme imaginative requirement. . . . The inner need is . . . of something institutional and complex, majestic in the hierarchic inter-relatedness of its parts, with authority descending from stage to stage, and at every stage objects for adjectives of mystery and splendour, derived in the last resort from the Godhead who is the fountain and culmination of the system. . . . one gets the honorific vibration coming from every quarter. Compared with such a noble complexity, in which ascending and descending seem in no way to jar upon stability, in which no single item, however humble, is insignificant, because so many august institutions hold it in place.[18]

What he seems to mean by "richness" is the ways in which institutions and individuals *present* themselves, as his use of the following passage from Newman's *Apologia* indicates:

I loved to act in the sight of my bishop, as if I was, as it were, in the sight of God. . . . It was not a mere formal obedience to rule that I put before me, but I desired to please him personally, as I considered him set over me by the Divine Hand. I was strict in observing my clerical engagements, not only because they *were* engagements, but because I considered myself simply as the servant and instrument of my bishop. I did not care much for the bench of bishops . . . all these matters seemed to me to be *jure ecclesiastico*, but what to me was *jure divino* was the voice of my bishop in his own person. My own bishop was my pope; I knew of no other; the successor of the apostles, the vicar of Christ. This was but a practical exhibition of the Anglican theory of church government, as I had already drawn it out myself.[19]

And even in his care to honor the uniqueness of religious experience, and its great power in society, James is always sensitive to the fact that religious experience must be communicated, and that those who control and create the symbols upon which such communication depends, will determine much of the form and content of religious life. For, if religion determines art, art, too, determines religion.[20] In his discussion of the dramatization of religious expression in Protestantism and Catholicism, James says:

How flat does evangelical Protestantism appear, how bare the atmosphere of those isolated religious lives whose boast it is that "man in the bush with God may meet." What a pulverization and leveling of what a gloriously piled-up structure! To an imagi- nation used to the perspectives of dignity and glory, the naked gospel scheme seems to offer an almhouse for a palace. . . . It is much like the patriotic sentiment of those brought up in ancient empires. How many emotions must be frustrated of their object, when one gives up the titles of dignity, the crimson lights and blare of brass, the gold embroidery, the plumed troops, the fear and trembling, and puts up with a president in a black coat who shakes hands with you, and comes, it may be, from a "home" upon a veldt or prairie with one sitting room and a Bible on its centre-table. It pauperizes the monarchial imagination![21]

James admonishes us (in comic tones) that aesthetic elements, the need for dramatization in expression, can easily subvert religion.[22] "Compare the informality of Protestantism, where the 'meek lover of the good,' alone with his God, visits the sick, etc., for their own sakes, with the elaborate 'business' that goes on in Catholic devotion, and carries with it the social excitement of all more complex businesses. An essentially worldly-minded Catholic woman can become a visitor of the sick on purely coquettish principles, with her confessor and director, her 'merit' storing up, her patron saints, her privi- leged relation to the Almighty, drawing his attention as a professional *dévote,* her definite 'exercises,' and her definitely recognized social *pose* in the organization."[23]

Notes

[1] Louis H. Sullivan, *The Autobiography of an Idea* (New York: Press of the Ameri- can Institute of Architects, New York, 1926) pp. 220–21. Sullivan's italics and capitaliza- tion.

[2] This is Whitman's usage of this term.

[3] This illumination, his first great conversion to art as a way of life, is described in the chapter on Paris in *The Autobiography of an Idea*. Sullivan loved Paris because it reminded him of Chicago. "Paris, though filled with historic monuments did not seem old; it gave rather an impress of ever-renewing youth and its people seemed light hearted." This was because the "two people [of Paris and Chicago] appeared to possess the same light-hearted spirit of adventure."

[4] Some thirty years had to pass before Le Corbusier could bring discussion of archi- tecture in France to the same point it had reached in Chicago by 1890.

[5] Sullivan, *op. cit.,* p. 246.

[6] *Ibid.,* pp. 246–47.

[7] His reading at this time included "Spencer, Darwin, Huxley, Tyndall, and the Germans."

[8] Similarly, Veblen, in *The Instinct of Workmanship,* describes how "the facts of technological use and wont are fundamental and definitive, in the sense that they underlie and condition the scope and method of civilization in other than the technological respect, but not in such a sense as to preclude or overlook the degree in which these other conventions of any given civilization in their turn react on the state of the industrial arts" (p. vii).

[9] Sullivan, *op. cit.,* p. 250.

[10] *Ibid.,* p. 246.

[11] These points are discussed in chapter XXVIII, "Necessary Truths and the Effects of Experience," of *The Principles of Psychology* (New York: Henry Holt, 1890). James and Sullivan matured in the same decade, 1880–90.

[12] *Ibid.,* p. 639.

[13] These quotations are taken from the section, "The Genesis of the Elementary Mental Categories," in chapter XXVIII of James's *Psychology.* James's italics.

[14] There is a kind of sad poetry over ideals and beliefs held far away and long ago in James's disenchantment. Even as he commemorates the victory of science over art, the victor's strength does not attract him. He is not very enthusiastic about the brave new world of science and technology. This is not true of Veblen, Sullivan, Dewey, or Mead. They welcome the future. In their eyes the sun is rising, not setting. It should be noted, too, that the satisfaction which makes the death of the gods bearable is the enjoyment of *form* which *creates* life.

[15] These quotations are taken from the last paragraph of the *Psychology.*

[16] See the last paragraph of "Conclusions," Lecture XX, of *Varieties of Religious Experience.*

[17] Nor do we have one now, although material abounds for such study.

[18] William James, *The Varieties of Religious Experience* (New York: Modern Library, n.d.), p. 450.

[19] John Henry Cardinal Newman, *Apologia Pro Vita Sua* (London and New York: Everyman's Library, 1949), pp. 68–69. Newman (to whom James refers in his discussion of art) realized that too much stress on the dramatic enactment of religious duty might place religion under the sway of art, which, he warned the faithful, has "ends of its own." His criticism of elaborate Gothic staging for worship is a curious corroboration of Veblen's animus against "monastic real-estate." ". . . I think that that style which, whatever be its origin, is called Gothic is endowed with a profound and a commanding beauty such as no other style possesses with which we are acquainted, and which probably the Church will not surpass until it attain to the Celestial City. . . . But this feeling should not blind us, rather it should awaken us, to the danger lest what is really a divine gift be incautiously used as an end rather than a means. . . . We are not living in an age of wealth and loyalty, of pomp and stateliness, of time-honored establishments, of pilgrimage and penance, or heritages and convents in the wild, and of fervent populations supplying the want of education by love, and apprehending in form and symbol what they cannot read in books. Our rules and our rubrics have been altered now to meet the times, and hence an obsolete discipline may be a present heresy."

[20] No one is more conscious of this than the fathers of the various churches. All, Jew, Catholic, and Protestant alike, warn against the power of art in its "graven images."

[21] *The Varieties of Religious Experience,* p. 450.

[22] To be more precise, it may subvert Catholicism as a religion. His sense of comedy

over Protestantism is not so well developed. The Protestant drama is verbal and musical, as in Milton and Bach. Its great dramatic text is the Bible. This "inner" drama seems more profound and individual to the Protestant than to the Catholic. The "idols" Protestants and Jews inveigh against are visual, not auditory idols. The Catholic might well argue that the Protestant, too, has his idols.

23 *The Varieties of Religious Experience,* p. 451. James's italics.

29

Sullivan's Search for Principles of Form in Architecture

SULLIVAN was an architect, not a social philosopher like James, Dewey, Mead, and Veblen. His problem was the problem of the artist—how to form, not how to perceive a world. He spoke and wrote a great deal because he was anxious to communicate through words what he had not been able to communicate through architecture. He thought of the architect as a form-giver who created the spirit of civilization by shaping the human environment into stages of action. Sullivan taught that the architect must make clear what his creations meant to society as well as to himself. And finally, since the democratic architect was responsible to the people, he must learn to communicate his purposes to them. Sullivan writes in many roles as critic, poet, architect, autobiographer, teacher, and social philosopher. But in even the most inward moments of prophecy he addresses his audience as equals. He never writes down, and even his moments of prophecy are lyric as well as hortatory. He wants the reader to share his revelation, not to obey it as a commandment.

In *Kindergarten Chats* he teases his apprentice and he lets himself be teased in turn. He is eager to submit his revelations to reason so long as it is the reason of discourse. He hated obscurity in words as in architecture. And if he did not always think the voice of the people was the voice of God, he did believe that the people were capable of reaching reasonable conclusions. To discover that Sullivan used a stock of ideas common to Ward, Cooley, James, Dewey, Mead, and Veblen does not in any way diminish the importance of his search. That they often said things about art in society and about the function of art in the genesis of the self, does not change the fact that Sullivan said much about the function of art in society many years before either Dewey, Mead, or Veblen. Ten years before Veblen, and some thirty years before Dewey or Mead, he argued that until we recognize the reciprocal relations between art and society we can have no theory of art, and, what was more to the point for the development of social philosophy, no theory of democratic society.[1] And while Sullivan's hopes for a sociology based on the experience of art have not been realized,[2] this does not mean that Sullivan was wrong. Dewey admits, at the end of a long philosophical career, that art is not only experience, but the most *characteristic* human experience.

If Sullivan had never designed a building his writings on architecture as art and social experience would still be important. It is easy enough to see in them the influence of the Chicago school of thought, the psychology of William James, and the philosophy of Dewey. From Sullivan's own copy of Dewey's *Reconstruction in Philosophy* we have some clues as to what interested him in Dewey's work. But while Sullivan said many of the things about art in society that Dewey said, he said them some thirty years earlier and he said them to help create a great new school of architecture. As those close to Dewey tell us, and as Dewey himself often said, his years in the Middle West and Chicago were seminal years in his life. He tells us that he learned more from men than from books, and the men and women he learned from in his formative years were in the Middle West and Chicago.[3] Sullivan thought of himself as an architect, but he thought architects must assume responsibility for developing and communicating the standard and values of their craft. Few artists have been as careful as Sullivan to warn their apprentices against the pitfalls of a literary approach to art, but Sullivan understood that in democratic society it was the architect's *responsibility* to communicate the values of his art to the people.

Sullivan began to speak and write about form in architecture at the same time he began the design of the Auditorium. We have a record of one of his early discussions, "What Is the Just Subordination, in Architectural Design, of Details to Mass?"[4] This is an early but characteristic statement of the architectural views of the Chicago school. Mass meant structure, detail meant ornament. As architecture was commonly practiced in Chicago during the eighties, structure was "engineering," ornamentation was "art."[5] Architects in Europe were familiar with this distinction through reading Viollet-le-Duc's *Entretiens sur l'architecture* (the first volume appeared in 1863, the second in 1872).[6] American architects also found a discussion in Viollet-le-Duc on the relationship between what he called the "programme" and the "constructive" process, or, as we now say, function and form. They knew, too, his statement: "Architecture is the sister of Science; the former undergoes modifications and advances hand in hand with the latter, and reaches its point of greatest splendour when Science itself has just passed a glorious stage in its career. . . . Architecture, whose principles are based more directly than any other art on Science, may disregard this support to such a degree as to be entirely unconscious of its value, and so decline. And it can only recover itself by immersion in the vivifying fount of science." Greek and

Roman architecture, the revival of architecture in the West toward the middle of the twelfth century, and the close relations established between architecture and the physical and mathematical sciences in the twelfth and sixteenth centuries made this clear, Viollet-le-Duc argues.

And the end of Viollet-le-Duc's discussion on the relation of science and architecture, and, indeed, at the very end of his work, he says in 1872 what Sullivan said many times in later years: Few ages can compare with our own in the glory of its scientific achievement. But do our architects, like their predecessors, "eagerly avail themselves of this source of aesthetic renovation?" They do not, but "prefer to ignore the close connection of science with art." Thus we suffer from buildings, and especially public buildings, "of a hybrid style," influenced by the "debased architecture of the last two centuries." Viollet-le-Duc then closes his book with a warning that it was not the engineer who needed the architect, but the architect who needed the engineer. If "they [architects] thus persist in rejecting that light, and in refusing that aid which science would gladly give them, the function of the architect is obsolete; while that of the engineer is commencing—that of men really devoted to construction, and who will make purely scientific knowledge their starting-point to constitute an art deduced from that knowledge and from the requirements of the time." [7]

Thus there was no need for Sullivan to repeat generalities over the relation between science and architecture. Viollet-le-Duc's statement that engineers, not architects, might create the great building of the future was widely accepted in Chicago. As we have seen, Sullivan thought for a time of becoming an engineer and, even after he decided on architecture, searched continuously for a principle of design similar in scope and application to the principles of mathematics he had learned in Paris. He admits openly in the 1887 symposium that he does not yet know the solution to the problem of how to relate "details to mass." For him the question must be answered in specific and logical terms. He wanted "indigenous and sincere" results which could be tested "today and here in Chicago." Sullivan argued that it was not a question of subordinating detail to mass, but of *differentiating* detail from mass. "I do believe in the differentiation of detail from mass (the idea of subordination occurring incidentally and as of no controlling import), because this word symbolizes to my mind an idea which is very congenial to it, namely, that of an expansive and rhythmic growth, in a building, of a single, germinal impulse or idea, which shall permeate the mass and its every detail with the same spirit, to such an extent indeed, that it would be as difficult to determine (not, surely, as a matter of arithmetical ratio, but rather as a factor in the total complex impression on the beholder) which is the more important, which in fact subordinates detail or mass. . . ." And the proper image for the architect to have before him as he thinks of ornament and structure is a tree. For when we think of the form of a tree the question, "Which is more to us, the leaves or the tree?" becomes meaningless.

The image of the tree looms large in Sullivan's description of architectural form.[8] In *The Autobiography of an Idea* he describes how he "became infiltrated, suffused, inspired with the fateful sense of beauty" of a lovely elm which stood "solitary in the meadow where he wandered as a child." [9] From his use of the image of the tree we learn what he really meant by saying that the form follows function. "Which is more to us, the leaves or the tree?"— such a question, Sullivan argues, is almost meaningless. "Should the leaves be large, and hide the branches, as in the horse chestnut, or should they be frivolous and dainty things, coquettishly exposing the branches? Should the trunk prevail, as in the proud and mournful southern pine, or should the trunk be short and sturdy, as the oak, with powerful gnarled and spreading branches, bared and grim before the tempest? . . . For my part I find their thousand ways all charming, and fruitful in suggestion." [10]

Sullivan understands that his use of animate terms to describe inanimate objects, such as buildings, is confusing. "It may be said that I am at fault in comparing animate with inanimate things; but this is the very heart of a mysterious subject; for I insist strenuously, that a building should live with intense, if quiescent life, because it is sprung from the life of its architect. On no other basis are results of permanent value to be attained." To Mr. Pierce's remarks that a building must be considered in terms of mechanical and abstract terms as implied by the words radiation, repetition, or unity in variety, Sullivan replies: "I value spiritual results only. I say spiritual results precede all other results, and indicate them. I can see no efficient way of handling this subject on any other than a spiritual or psychic basis." And then Sullivan states, as he does so many times, his credo as an architect. "The only substantial facts which remain after all this rubbish, dust and scientific-analytic-aesthetic cobwebs are brushed away are these facts, which each man may take to himself, namely: That I am; that I am immersed here in nature here with my fellow men; that we are all striving after something which we do not now possess; that there is an inscrutable power permeating all, and the cause of it all." A tragic sense of life, in which the artist must find some kind of meaning, is the price of art. "And I say that all we see and feel and know, without and within us, is one mighty poem of striving, one vast and subtle tragedy. That to remain unperturbed and serene within this turbulent and drifting flow of hope and sorrow, light and darkness, is the uttermost position and fact attainable to the soul, the only permanent link between the finite and infinite."

The whole inquiry as to the just subordination of details to mass, in so far as it contains the implication of a fixed rule, is "simply a pedagogic scarecrow." Contemplation of nature and humanity "is the only source" of inspiration. If "cultivated mediocrity is what is wanted, the question can be answered readily and specifically for each historic style. If the culture of action is demanded, then indeed we have a task before us to find an answer." Every problem for the Chicago architect is "as yet, unsolved." We are like "pioneers in a primeval forest." And while the work done by Chicago architects can only be small, "so long as it is the fruit of great desires, it may speak of greatness." But if this is to happen, Chicago architects must learn that mechanists who pride themselves on their realism are not realistic at all; spiritual and psychic facts are the only real facts of art.[11] Sullivan returns again to these themes in his article, "Ornament in Architecture." [12] "I take it as self-evident that a building, quite devoid of ornament, may convey a noble and dignified sentiment by virtue of mass and proportion. It is not evident to me that ornament can intrinsically heighten these elemental qualities. Why, then, should we use ornament? Is not a noble and simple dignity sufficient: Why should we ask for more?" There is no question that in 1892 ornament was the bane of architecture. It "would be greatly for our aesthetic good if we should refrain entirely from the use of ornament for a period of years, in order that our thought might concentrate acutely upon the production of buildings well formed and comely in the nude. We should thus perforce eschew many undesirable things, and learn by contrast how effective it is to think in a natural vigorous and wholesome way."

But "mass-composition," while "more profound" than ornamentation, is not enough. A building which is a work of art is "an emotional expression." It must have "a life." There is much misunderstanding of ornament because it has been the fashion to speak of ornament as a thing to be put on or omitted. But this is false, for the presence or absence of ornament should be determined "at the very beginning of design." For creative architecture "is an art so fine that its power is manifest in rhythms of great subtlety, as much so indeed as those of musical art, its nearest relative." Ornament in design "will be more beautiful if it seems a part of the surface or substance that receives it than if it looks 'stuck on.' " Ornament should appear as if it had come forth from the very substance of the material and "was there by the same right that a flower appears amid the leaves of its parent plant."

It follows then by the logic of growth that "a certain kind of ornament should appear on a certain kind of structure, just as a certain kind of leaf must appear on a certain kind of tree." Nor should the ornamental systems of buildings of any various sorts be interchangeable as between these buildings. For buildings should possess an individuality as marked as that which exists among men, making them distinctly separable from each other, however strong the racial or family resemblance may be. "The possibilities of ornament conceived as organic expression with structure are marvelous. Reflect now the light of this conception full and free upon joint considerations of mass-considerations of mass-composition, and how serious, how eloquent, how inspiring is the imagery, how noble the dramatic force that shall make sublime our future architecture." But for this we must turn back to nature "to learn how to see the rhythmic cadences and endless variations of her forms." But we must turn to our own people, too, for America is the "only land in the whole earth wherein a dream like this may be realized; for here tradition is without shackles, and the soul of man free to grow, to mature, to seek its own." [13]

In 1894, three years after the rejection of the Chicago school at the Fair, and with much of his best work behind him, Sullivan began work on his address for the annual convention of the American Institute of Architects. He had taken the lessons of his defeat to heart. The main reason for the degradation of architecture was not that businessmen used it for profit, but that architects themselves, and particularly those who taught in the schools, did not believe American art to be a constituent force in our society. They had "obstinately sought to express themselves solely in terms either of the head or of the heart." Architectural art had failed to reach its highest form of expression in Chicago because it had not yet found a way to become "truly plastic." Both Greek and Gothic fail because they do not resolve tension between the intellect and the emotions, between statics and dynamics in art, or between men's relations to each other and their relationship to nature. To understand this principle of resolution we turn to the simplest vertical element in architecture, namely, the pier. Whatever its shape or material the pier rests upon ground; "it thus has support but it already aspires, for it rises vertically from its ground-support into the air. It is stable, for it has both weight and strength. It is serene because within itself are balanced the two great forces, the simplest elemental rhythms of Nature, to wit, the rhythm of growth, of aspiration, of that which would rise into the air: which impulse we shall call the Rhythm of Life: and the counter-rhythm of decadence, of destruction, of that which would crush to the earth, of that which makes for a return to the elements of earth, the Rhythm of Death." [14]

Notes

[1] The notion that pragmatism's instrumentalism exalts science and banishes art is not based on any close reading of Mead or Dewey. Both make the consummatory moment in the experience of art a cornerstone of the pragmatic theory of knowledge as it arises within the act in society.

[2] Of 999 research projects listed in their bulletin, *Current Sociological Research, 1960,* the American Sociological Association lists only *three* in the sociology of art and mentions that even these were added as "a 25th category, [namely, the] Sociology of Science and Arts. . . ." The hopes of Sullivan—to say nothing of Ward, Cooley, Veblen, Mead, James, and Dewey—for a sociology of art which would clarify social (as well as art) theory have not been fulfilled. Actually there is *less* interest now in 1964 in art as social experience than there was in the years from 1885 to 1925.

[3] In his *Social Ideas of American Educators* (Paterson, N. J.: Littlefield, 1962), Merle Curti, on the basis of an interview with Dewey on December 21, 1932, says Dewey told him that residence in Michigan and Chicago during his formative period gave him a first-hand acquaintance with a type of life still colored by the pioneer heritage of social democracy (p. 500). Kallen argued that "It was the old Vermont town-meeting idea and that conception of democracy that seemed to come out on top in his [Dewey's] mind." But Schneider, Dewey's colleague in philosophy at Columbia, denies this [as do Gutmann and Farrell]. "[Dewey] told me he left that Godforsaken country [Vermont] as soon as he could." Randall said Dewey told him: "I don't see why you fellows want to get back to summer places in Vermont. I got out as soon as I could." Dewey's statement, "Democracy begins in conversation," was commonplace in the work of Cooley, Mead, and Sullivan. Dewey's debt to the Middle West and Chicago is discussed in *Dialogue on John Dewey,* ed. by Corliss Lamont (New York: Horizon Press, New York: 1959).

[4] This took place at the regular meeting of the Illinois Association of Architects, held April 2, 1887, in a symposium with talks by Louis H. Sullivan, L. D. Cleveland, and O. J. Pierce, and a summary by Louis H. Sullivan. It is reprinted in *Kindergarten Chats,* ed. by Isabella Athey (New York: George Wittenborn, 1947).

[5] Nor should we forget that in the communication of the building for sales purposes, "artistic renderings," not engineer's prints, were used.

[6] Translations were soon available in *Discourses on Architecture,* 2 vols., Boston, 1875, 1881, and *Lectures on Architecture,* 2 vols., London, 1877, 1881.

[7] These quotations are taken from the last paragraph of *Discourses on Architecture,* tr. by Benjamin Bucknall, in the Grove Press Edition published in 1959 (a reprint of the edition published in 1889 by Ticknor of Boston).

[8] As it does in Wright's descriptions of the cantilever principle and the relationship of a house to its site.

[9] This is from Chapter IV, "A Vacation." Sullivan agreed with Wordsworth that the child is father of the man—and especially of man as artist. His memories of childhood were written in the last months of his life. His love and reverence for the awakening of the artist in the child inspire some of the most affecting passages Sullivan ever wrote. His memories of youth and maturity are filled with tender irony over the lives of his friends and peers. The savage irony and black hatred of *Democracy: A Man Search* is gone. Wonderment and reverence at the birth of the young artist in nature suffuses his memories of a golden childhood in nature.

[10] "What Is the Just Subordination, in Architectural Design, of Details to Mass?" as printed in "Additional Papers" in the Athey edition of *Kindergarten Chats.*

[11] These statements make clear that Sullivan's "functionalism" has nothing to do with the "function of a machine to live in."

[12] This essay, published in *The Engineering Magazine,* August, 1892, is reprinted in the Athey edition of *Kindergarten Chats.*

[13] "Ornament in Architecture," in the Athey edition of *Kindergarten Chats,* pp. 187–90.

[14] *Op. cit., Chat* XXXVII, "The Elements of Architecture: Objective and Subjective: (1) Pier and Lintel."

30

Sullivan's Principle of Mobile Equilibrium

SULLIVAN BELIEVED that the creative spirit of the artist was created and re-created in moments of "illumination." These great moments of deep understanding are moments of possession which end in salvation and birth. They are what Sullivan called "subjective" moments, deeply inward yet outward, too, because they illumine the meaning of the objective world [1] and thus break down the customary barriers between the subjective self and the objective world. Without such illuminations the artist dies. Illuminations, the master tells his pupil, "will remain with you forever. You are born again. For illumination is but that cataclysm of birth of which you have heard me speak." The artist is immortal because art is immortal; without the forms created by the artist there could be no society. The spirit of art, of joy and gladness in creation, never dies. Art is necessary to community life, for without art men have no joy and gladness in each other, and without the forms of art they could never communicate and hence could not relate to each other.

There are several descriptions of these illuminations in Sullivan's writings. It is customary to dismiss these as expressions of his alleged weakness, what Frank Lloyd Wright calls his "sentimental exuberance." [2] Wright did not like his master's writings, and he even tells us that he made it a point not to read them.

The Sullivanian philosophy, so far as it was personal to him, is written in that chosen language of his most clearly and if you are going to read him at all, it is there to be read at level best. Not in the remarkable buildings built by the firm nor in his own writings (so I felt then and now think) were the perfect expressions of Louis H. Sullivan to be found. As I could see even then, the buildings were often far from it. His writing at that time (let's mention "Inspiration—A Spring Song," which he read to me) seemed to me a kind of "baying at the moon," as I once risked telling him with no good results where I was concerned. Or where he was concerned either. So I seldom read what he wrote. There was no need. He would sometimes read passages to me or, better still, talk about himself in his own way. Probably "trying it out on the 'pup' "? But always I preferred his drawings. Naturally enough, because I shared in them. He may have been ridiculous when he wrote: I don't know. He was miraculous when he drew. I always wanted him to "draw"! But soon he began to draw less and less. . . .

Early in my life he gave me Spencer and Whitman to read. . . . Most of all I *preferred* that he "draw." I never had occasion to be ashamed of myself with him then.[3]

But Sullivan's "mystical" moments are his most characteristic moments. Wright admits that Sullivan liked to write, and those who knew Sullivan tell us of the strange fascination of his talk. The "Great Spirit" which Sullivan invoked was very real to him if not to others. This Spirit for Sullivan was the spirit of art. Like the religious mystic seeking to describe union with God, Sullivan struggles to re-create his experience or art so we can share it with him. For him intellect was on a lower order of experience than imagination brought into consciousness through art. He did not deny the power of intellect, but in his ascent to truth the intellect was of value only as it was *related* to emotion. By emotion he does not mean feeling, or any kind of somatic discharge, but a dramatic moment which he describes by metaphors of the heart, of tenderness, and of love. Nor does he mean orgiastic states of possession. Emotion *contains* reason; in life emotion depends on form which is real because it is in and through such forms that we experience the world of men and things.

If we disregard Sullivan's transcendent moments we fail to understand him. Even in discussion on form in architecture he moves swiftly beyond what he himself called "mechanical" considerations. Thus in one of his most famous essays on architectural form, "The Tall Office Building Artistically Considered," he begins by stating the "conditions" of the building "in the plainest manner." But a statement of the mechanics of the building, or the social conditions (congestion, etc.) is not a statement of the problem of form for Sullivan, as we see at once in his statement on the problems of designing a tall building. "Problem: How shall we impart to this sterile pile, this crude, harsh, brutal agglomeration, this stark, staring exclamation of eternal strife, the graciousness of those high forms of sensibility and culture that rest on the lower and fiercer passions? How shall we proclaim from the dizzy height of this strange, weird, modern house top the peaceful evangel of sentiment, of beauty, the cult of a higher life?"

What did Sullivan mean by "higher life?" He certainly did not mean anything like what was implied by current clichés on what Veblen called mockingly "the true, the good, and the beautiful." In his essay, "The Young Man in Architecture,"[4] he warns his young architect to beware of the "purring of the select company of Ruskinites. The gasping of the Emersonites. The rasping of the Spencerites. The moaning of the Tennysonites. The whimper of the aesthetes. We are commanded to know that there is much of mystery, much of the esoteric, in the so-called 'pure art' which the hand of the Modern may not profane. So be it. Let us be the Cat. And let the pure art be the King. We will look at him. And we will look at the good king's children, the great styles. And at his retinue of bastards, the so-called 'other styles.'" The "higher life" for Sullivan was life where men lived in harmony with nature, and with each other, in a democratic community. We will have great American architecture when "we know and feel that Nature is our friend, not our implacable enemy [5]—that an afternoon in the country, an hour by the sea, a full open view of one single day, through dawn, high noon, and twilight, will suggest to us so much that is rhythmical, deep and eternal in the vast art of architecture. . . ." Such an architecture will live because it will be "of the people, for the people, and by the people." [6]

In his writing on form in architecture, Sullivan defines form by how it *affects* human beings, as he makes clear in his essays on the basic elements of architectural form. The pier form is the simplest of architectural elements. "It is equilibrium—at seeming rest." It is a resolution through architectural form of a tension between two opposing principles. While it seems aspiring, it seems also solidly based: "It impresses us as immovable, as static: as timeless." Simple as it seems and is to our sense of sight, "it is nevertheless compound; for it is the field of operation of the two synchronous forces—downward and upward." A pier may stand alone as a monument, memorial, a boundary, a guide; even as a boulder; "yet with it the architectural art literally begins." But with the lintel a new element, "a most subtle, strange and abstruse element," appears. The moment the lintel is laid upon two piers and connects their activities—"Presto! by the subtlest of conceivable magic, instantly the Science of Architecture comes into being. . . . This phenomenon in Nature, the exact opposite of catastrophe or sudden death —it is sudden, instant BIRTH!" [7] The pier and lintel lying flat on the earth cannot be distinguished one from the other: their potentiality is the same. "It is only when by man's touch they are slightly differentiated, that they are separable, in evident function." When erected into place by the power of man's body and mind, in response to need, and "his desire, supported by the kindly earth [8]—a new, a primitive FORM appears without and within man." For this is the great capacity of man. He creates forms, even at the most primitive level of art. The most wonderful and moving quality about the pier and lintel is the power of the expressive mind which they exhibit. Architectures of great beauty, Assyrian, Egyptian, and Greek, are alike in basic form, yet greatly different in their rich and vivid display "of poetic expression, fertile fancy, and dramatic power." These prove that the powers that reside within man's structures reside within man himself.

And what is this power which lies within man, the architect? It is the power of creation itself. "It is related in Genesis that the Lord God formed man of the dust of the ground, and breathed into his nostrils the breath of life; and the man became a living soul. So did these peoples—the Assyrians, the Egyptians and the Greeks—and in the same allegorical sense—make their varied architecture of the dust of the earth, and breathe into the simple elements, lintel and pier, the breath of life, and they became living art, filled with the soul of the race, with the soul, the identity of those who made great architecture out of the dust, as the author of Genesis made man out of the dust." The pier and the lintel belong to architects everywhere. "Extrinsically and intrinsically they belong to no time, no people, no race." The architect must then realize the power of his forms. "Go, breathe into them the breath of your life, that, formed of the dust, under the urge of your need and your will, they become inspired of a living soul. You were born with spiritual power; for the Lord God, now as ever, breathes it into the dust from which man is continually making. You were at birth a living soul! See to it that the soul does not die within you." [9]

The three great civilizations of the past evolved their architecture from the primitive form of the pier and lintel. But there was another primitive form, the arch, which was of equal, perhaps of even greater importance than pier and lintel. "To the reflective mind the arch is a wonder, a marvel, a miracle." It is the third and last of our architectural elements. Pier, lintel, and arch are the three letters "which constitute the alphabet of our art—the briefest of them all. I wish deeply to impress upon you this simple fact; for it is of the utmost importance that you carry its significance ever in mind. It is a triune fact, the simple germinal phenomenon from which has arisen the vast, splendid, sumptuous Art of Architecture." [10] The arch is far more subtle, more intricate, and more subjective, and "has just so much more of man in it." We may view it "both as a triumph over an abyss and as the very crystallization of that abyss itself. It is a form so much against Fate, that Fate, as we say, ever most relentlessly seeks its destruction. Yet does it rise in power so graciously, floating through the air from abutment to abutment, that it seems ever, to me, a symbol and epitome of our ephemeral span. . . . The arch is, of all constructive forms, the most emotional. It is susceptible in possibility and promise to the uttermost degree of fulfillment that the creative imagination can forecast. Its plasticity is limitless. . . . It responds to every need. . . . In all its power it is a form so frail in essence, so gracious, so ethereal, that it must need ever touch the heart attuned to Nature's mysteries." There is much beauty in past use of the arch, but nowhere "do we see a full grasp and intensive comprehension of the arch as such." [11]

Sullivan then continues his discourse on the principles of architecture: "I am endeavoring, ever more fervently, to impress upon you the simple truth —immeasurable in power of expansion—of the subjective possibilities of objective things. In short to clarify for you the origin and power of *Beauty*: to let you see that it is resident in function and form." The pupil, far more apt than at the beginning of their walk, asks: "So is ugliness, isn't it?" The master admits that this is so, but only because the principle of "function and form," is so universal that it embraces all forms. The student then asks: "Why have you said nothing concerning the cantilever?" "Because," the master responds, "it is not primary. It belongs among those secondary structural forms which may be classed as expedients. It is neither one thing nor the other; neither pier, lintel nor arch, though it seems curiously to partake of their functions in a reverse or imitative way. It may assist pier, lintel and arch. Its essence is overhang. The pier, lintel and arch are in their simplest forms primary propositions. The cantilever belongs in the province of morphology." [12]

But what, asks the pupil, "would the modern bridge engineer do without the cantilever?" The master replies with some asperity: "That is his business. What he does with it does not change its nature, however wonderful the performance. The same may be said of his impressive development of lintel and arch. Because of his needs, and in response to his needs, he has raised the primitive cantilever to a position of high importance, but its nature remains unaltered. But I am not following the development of the science of engineering, however fascinating the topic may be. It is our immediate business to deal with the art of architecture." [13] The pupil, teasing his master for his verbosity and "philosophical, metaphysical and somewhat poetical way of talking," says: "If I get the drift, the abutments of the arch are essentially piers; and the two abutments, with the arch rising between them, form a triune-simple which does not differ in essence from the triune-simple you have visualized as a resultant type-form of the two piers and a lintel. . . . I infer [that you wish] me to conclude that these two triune-simples are so similar in their nature that they evidently derive from the single function SPAN." [14]

The development of the three great elements of architecture, namely pier, lintel, and arch, teach us that man's greatest power is his "plastic" power as a worker. As the pier gradually takes clearly defined form, it does so because "of its *own* plastic nature, for all materials, however refractory, yield to the will of the craftsman." Materials do not "yield" but "consent" to the hand and will of the master. Their nature and character must be understood. The craftsman and his material must then be thought of as a unison, not as separate and isolated. Even though the modern craftsman is no longer in immediate physical contact with materials, he must not lose actual, emotional, intellectual, and spiritual contact with them "any more than though seemingly isolated he shall lose contact with his people." [15] Architectural form must never be thought of as the "result" of forces or tradition. Art teaches us to think of man as a power, not the result of a force. What made man wish to make changes in the simplest form of the pier? "Was it not in response to some need—physical, intellectual, emotional?" But is it not true that the need at the bottom of all man's needs is the desire "to procreate his own personality, temperament; the need, the desire that the creation of his hands, of his brain should fit him—that he might feel at home with himself? That when he looked upon his creations they *satisfied* him: else why that singular allegory that the Lord God looked upon his works and declared them good? Are not all works to be judged by this basic standard, independent of a need, of a desire of the exercise of a power!" [16]

The great modern enigma in architecture is that in contrast to past civilization, we have "no present of our own except in a materialistic sense." The more we ransack the past for its historical styles, the more we understand that such styles are demonstrations of character, indexes of civilizations and the changes of mood within civilization. But we must recognize that these luminous symbols can only light up the past. The present is our concern. Our failure to rise above our techniques to create a form of architecture characteristic of our own time, the curious empty and amorphous quality of present time in American society, indicates to some that we are in a period of moral decay and spiritual degeneration. Others, however, think that our materialism signifies the beginning of a new epoch, "a gestation period of spirituality within the huge body of materialism." "How is one to decide?" the student asks. Does "this vast materialism signify and prophesy a terrific cataclysm of birth? . . . the coming release of the heart from its bondage to the intellect? Can it mean this or am I hoping against hope? . . . It seems as though I were living in a cocoon, a cocoon spun by the thought of the ages. I can dream of the past. I can, as it were, see the past and live in the past but I cannot see the world about me. I feel as though I were at the edge of an abyss—I totter." The master replies: "You are not at the edge of an abyss; you are climbing a summit. You are high enough now to see something of the past. Climb higher and you will see the present." [17]

Notes

[1] In a letter to Claude F. Bragdon he defines what he means by "objective." He is describing his purpose in writing *Kindergarten Chats*. "A young man who has 'finished his education' at the architectural schools comes to me for a post-graduate course— hence a free form of dialogue—I proceed with his education rather by indirection and suggestion than by direct precept. I subject him to certain experiences and allow the impressions they make on him to infiltrate, and, as I note the effect, I gradually use a guiding hand. I supply the yeast, so to speak, and allow the ferment to work in him. . . . This is the gist of the whole scheme. It remains then to determine carefully the kind of experiences to which I shall subject the lad, and in what order, or logical (and especially psychological) sequence. I begin, then, with aspects that are literal, objective, more or less cynical, and brutal, and philistine. A little at a time I introduce the sub- jective, the refined, the altruistic; and by a to-and-fro, increasingly intense rhythm of these two opposing themes, worked so to speak in counter-point, I reach a preliminary climax; of brutality tempered by a longing for nobler, purer things." This letter is found in the Introduction to the Scarab edition of *Kindergarten Chats,* and is reprinted in Appendix A of the Athey edition. See Louis H. Sullivan, *Kindergarten Chats and Other Writings,* ed. by Isabella Athey (New York: George Wittenborn, 1947).

[2] They are also considered, in architectural criticism proper, a sign of his "façade painting" or his penchant for the "picturesque."

[3] Frank Lloyd Wright, *Genius and the Mobocracy* (New York: Duell, Sloan and Pearce, 1949). Book Three, Chapter Three, "A Master Venerates Only Truth."

[4] This is reprinted in the Athey edition of *Kindergarten Chats*. It was read before the annual convention of the Architectural League of America, in Chicago, June 1900.

[5] He obviously disagreed with the concept of nature "red in tooth and claw" where the fittest survived through cunning, ferocity, based on "evolutionary theory, or luck" —a belief used in apologetics of the time for all kinds of authoritarian domination.

[6] These are the last words of "The Tall Office Building Artistically Considered."

[7] *Kindergarten Chats,* XXXVII, "The Elements of Architecture."

[8] As we shall see, Sullivan's "nature" is benign, kindly, spiritual, and beautiful. That is, he does not think of nature as an "environment" so much as a great stage which conditions human action. Nor does he think of nature as containing evil which must be guarded against and extirpated. Even in his moods of black despair, as in anguish over the "dark ages" of democratic society, "Democracy: A Man Search," it is mis- guided man, not nature, who is evil.

[9] Equating the architect with God as Superman is not, in Sullivan, a violation of a democratic ethic, for, as we shall see, the architect must communicate with people and educate them to the purposes and values of great architecture. He does not command, but persuades. He submits himself to them in open, free, and informed discussion of his purposes. Thus, while he is bound to his own standards of justice and honor, he is always responsible to the community in which these standards operate.

[10] Sullivan, *op. cit., Chat* XXXVIII, "The Elements of Architecture: Objective and Subjective: (2) The Arch."

[11] *Ibid.*

[12] *Ibid.*

[13] Sullivan's early infatuation with the engineer soon passed. His treatment of Jenney in *The Autobiography of an Idea* and perhaps even his break with Adler in 1895 in- dicate clearly that he no longer regarded the engineer as an ally of the architect seeking to make structure into art through giving it significant form. He respected engineers

for their capacity to face problems and to give their clients simple, honest buildings. But engineers were not architects. Architects could not be artists without being engineers, but neither could engineers become artists without deep and profound experience of art.

[14] Sullivan, *Kindergarten Chats.*

[15] *Ibid., Chat.* XXXIX, "Illumination."

[16] *Ibid.*

[17] *Ibid.* The master teaches that the architect must seek "illuminations" within himself. He guides his pupil into three such great moments of understanding in nature, among men, and in art—the sources, Sullivan taught, of all creative power. "Your illumination," the master tells his pupil, "will remain with you forever. You are born again. For illumination is but that cataclysm of birth of which you have heard me speak."

31

Sullivan's Principle of Plasticity:
Form Follows Function

SULLIVAN'S ESSAY, "The Tall Building Artistically Considered," which first appeared in 1896,[1] tells much of how, as well as what, he thinks about form. He begins by facing the new and unique problem of the tall office building. "The architects of this land and generation are now brought face to face with something new under the sun—namely, that evolution and integration of social conditions, the special grouping of them, that results in a demand for the erection of tall office buildings." To design such buildings we must begin by describing the social conditions which such buildings must meet.

Briefly, they are these: offices are necessary for the transaction of business; the invention and perfection of the high-speed elevators make vertical travel, that was once tedious and painful, now easy and comfortable; development of steel manufacture has shown the way to safe, rigid, economical constructions rising to a great height; continued growth of population in the great cities, consequent congestion of centers and rise in value of ground, stimulate an increase in number of stories; these successfully piled one upon another, react on ground values. . . . Up to the point all the evidence is materialistic, an exhibition of force, of resolution of brains in the keen sense of the word. It is the joint product of the speculator, the engineer, the builder.[2]

Every problem contains and suggests its own solution. We must seek the essence of the problem, and then proceed from general to specific considerations. The practical conditions of a tall office building are, first, a basement containing boilers, engines, and the power plant. Second, a ground floor devoted to stores, banks, etc., which require large areas and easy access. Third, a second story readily accessible by stairways and broken into large subdivisions, with liberal structural spacing, glass expanse, and broad openings. Fourth, above these an indefinite number of floors of offices, piled tier upon tier (similar to a cell in a honeycomb), all alike, nothing more, in short, than compartments. Fifth, and last, an attic which must house mechanical elements originating in the basement. Here the circulatory system of the building completes itself and makes its grand turn, ascending and descending. Finally, there must be on the ground floor an opening common to all who use the building.

This description of the content, or the functions, of the tall office building is a general description, common to every such building in America. Arrangements for light courts are not "germane to the problem," nor is the arrangement of the elevators. For these "have to do strictly with the economics of the building, and I assume them to have been fully considered and disposed of to the satisfaction of purely utilitarian and pecuniary demands." The architect soon discovers that the plan and floor arrangement of the tall office building are seldom determined by aesthetic values. "Aesthetic elements are considered only when the lighting court is external or an internal feature of great importance." The size of a standard office room of comfortable area and height "predetermines the standard structural unit and, approximately, the size of window openings." These arbitrary units of structure, in turn, form in "an equally natural way" the true basis of the artistic development of the exterior. The structural spacings and openings in the first or mercantile floor must be the largest of all; those in the second floor are somewhat the same. Attic openings are not necessary, since light may be brought in from the top of the building—hence no recognition of a cellular function is required in a structural spacing at the top of the building.

Now if we approach the problem of the tall building in terms of the elements already described and

follow our natural instincts without thought of books, rules, precedents, or any such educational impedimenta to a spontaneous and "sensible" result, we will in the following manner design the exterior of our tall building—to wit: Beginning with the first story, we give this a main entrance that attracts the eye to its location, and the remainder of the story we treat in a more or less liberal, expansive, sumptuous way—a way based exactly on the practical necessities, but expressed with a sentiment of largeness and freedom. The second story we treat in a similar way, but usually with milder pretention. Above this, throughout the indefinite number of typical office tiers, we take our cue from the individual cell, which requires a window with its separating pier, its sill and lintel, and we, without more ado, make them alike because they are all alike. This brings us to the attic, which, having no division into office-cells, and no special requirement for lighting, gives us the power to show by means of its broad expanse of wall, and its dominating weight and character, that which is the fact—namely, that the series of office tiers has come definitely to an end.

This bald statement is not yet an architectural statement, but it is at least a "thoroughly sound, logical, coherent expression of the conditions" of the building. An architect, if he will but make such a statement for himself, and take a direct and simple path from the problem to its solution, can produce a building far better than the "sinister" building "of the speculator-engineer-builder combination." For any architect, and not even a highly gifted and trained architect, can conceive of a building as a form, so long as the architect has a "strong, natural liking for buildings, and a disposition to shape them in what seems to his unaffected nature a direct and simple way. He will probably tread an innocent path from his problem to its solution, and therein he will show an enviable gift of logic." If he adds to this some gift for "form in detail, some feeling for form purely and simply as form, some love for that, his result in addition to its simple straightforward naturalness and completeness in general statement, will have something of the charm of sentiment."

Yet, with all this said, we have said little about the true meaning of architecture. We have passed through four stages in our thinking about the tall building. First, we described the social basis of the demand for such a building. Second, we itemized its literal material satisfaction. Third, we elevated the question of how to elevate design of the building above considerations of literal planning, construction, and equipment, to the plane of elementary architecture as a direct outgrowth of sound, sensible building. Fourth, we further elevated the question of design to the "beginnings of true architectural expression, through the addition of a certain quality and quantity of sentiment." But a building design may satisfy all of these needs and yet be far from "the adequate solution of the problem." To reach this we must take our final step in which we pay heed to the "imperative voice of emotion." To take the last, the final, the *architectural* step in our thought, we must ask:

What is the chief characteristic of the tall office building? And at once we answer, it is lofty. This loftiness is to the artist-nature its thrilling aspect. It is the very organ-tone of its appeal. It must be in turn the dominant chord in his expression of it, the true excitant of his imagination. It must be tall, every inch of it tall. The force and power of altitude must be in it, the glory and pride of exaltation must be in it. It must be every inch a proud and soaring thing, rising in sheer exultation that from bottom to top it is a unit without a single dissenting line—that it is the new, the unexpected, the eloquent peroration of most bald, most sinister, most forbidding conditions. The man who designs in this spirit and with a sense of responsibility to the generation he lives in . . . must realize at once and with the grasp of inspiration, that the problem of the tall building is one of the most stupendous, one of the most magnificent opportunities that the Lord of Nature in His beneficence has ever offered to the proud spirit of man.

Yet what have we done in our time with this opportunity to create not simply a new order of architecture? We do not even recognize that there is such an opportunity; indeed, we even deny that it exists. The reflective architect pauses before such "an exhibition of human perversity. . . ." In our search for a comprehensive solution to the problem of the tall building, we do not lack serious and thoughtful reflection on the nature of the tall building. Some hold that the true prototype of the tall building is the classical column with its base, shaft, and capital—"the moulded base of the column typical of the lower stories of our building, the plain or fluted shaft suggesting the monotonous, uninterrupted series of office-tiers, and the capital the completing power and luxuriance of the attic." Others, following mystical symbolism, "quote the many trinities in nature and in art, and the beauty and conclusiveness of such trinity in unity. . . . So they say, should the building be in three parts vertically, substantially as before, but for different motives." Another group of theorizers, of a more intellectual temperament, argue that a building design should be in the nature of a logical statement: "it should have a beginning, a middle, and an ending, each clearly defined—therefore again a building, as above, in three parts vertically." Yet others turn to the vegetable kingdom, to argue that a "design shall above all things be organic. They quote the suitable flower with its bunch of leaves at the earth, its long graceful stem, carrying the gorgeous single flower. . . . Thus, they say, should be the design of the tall office building: again in three parts vertically." Still another group, "more susceptible to the power of a unit than to the grace of a trinity, say that such a design should be struck out at a blow, as though by a blacksmith or by mighty Jove, or should be thought-born, as was Minerva, full grown. They accept the notion of a triple division as permissible and welcome, but nonessential. With them it is a subdivision of their unit."

Critics and theorists agree on one thing, however. This is that the tall office building must not be made a field for the

display of architectural knowledge in the encyclopaedic sense; . . . that miscellany is abhorrent to their sense; that the sixteen-story building must not consist of sixteen separate, distinct and unrelated buildings piled one upon the other until the top of the pile is reached. To this latter folly I would not refer were it not the fact that nine out of every ten tall office buildings are designed in precisely this way in effect, not by the ignorant, but by the educated. It would seem indeed, as though the "trained" architect, when facing this problem, were beset at every story, or at most, every third or fourth story, by the hysterical dread lest he be in "bad form": lest he be not bedecking his building with sufficiency of quotation from this, that, or the other "correct" building in some other land and some other time. . . .

But even the serious and thoughtful views of these various schools of tall building design, as much as they rightly censure the miscellaneous piles, still miss the mark. Such discussions "for the purpose of this demonstration . . . are . . . secondary only . . . and as touching not . . . upon the true, the immovable philosophy of the architectural art." Only when we take such a broad view can we bring to the solution of the problem a final comprehensive formula. This view is to be found in consideration of the relationship between form and function. All things in nature, as among men, have shape, that is to say, "a form, an outward semblance, that tells us what they are, that distinguishes them from ourselves and from each other."

The forms of nature "express the inner life, the native quality, of the animal, tree, bird, fish, that they are so characteristic, so recognizable, that we say, simply, it is 'natural' it should be so." Yet what an absorbing mystery is its simplicity and naturalness. "Unceasingly the essence of things is taking shape in the matter of things, and this unspeakable process we call birth and growth. Awhile the spirit and the matter fade away together, and it is this that we call decadence, death. . . . Yet to the steadfast eye of one standing upon the shore of things, looking chiefly and most lovingly upon that side on which the sun shines and that we feel joyously to be life, the heart is ever gladdened by the beauty, the exquisite spontaneity, with which life seeks and takes on its forms in an accord perfectly responsive to its needs. It seems ever as though the life and the form were absolutely one and inseparable, so adequate is the sense of fulfillment." "It is the pervading law of all things organic, and inorganic, of all things physical and metaphysical, of all things human and all things superhuman, of all true manifestations of the head, of the heart, of the soul, that the life is recognizable in its expression, that form ever follows function. This is the law." Why then is it so difficult for us to see that the shape, form, "outward expression, design or whatever we may choose [to call it], of the tall office building should in the very nature of things follow the functions of the building, and that where the function does not change, the form is not to change?" Does this not clearly show that the tall building will take on a special character suited to its special needs? In its very nature, its function shall equally be so in force, in significance, in continuity, in conclusiveness of outward expression?

And so "the design of the tall office building takes its place with all other architectural types made when architecture, as has happened once in many years, was a living art." And "when native instinct and sensibility shall govern the exercise of our beloved art; when the known law, the respected law, shall be that form ever follows function; . . . when it becomes evident that we are merely speaking a foreign language with a noticeable American accent, whereas every architect in the land might, under the benign influence of this law, express in the simplest, most modest, most natural way that which it is in him to say—then it may be proclaimed that we are on the high-road to a natural and satisfying art"—and an art for all the people, whose art is the only true fine art.

In his youth Wright rebelled against Sullivan's attempts to reduce the expression of function to plastic ornament. It was, Wright tells us, "my natural tendency to draw away from the mastery of his efflorescence toward the straight line and rectangular pattern, working my own rectilinear way with T-square and triangle toward the more severe rhythms of point, line, and plane. Never having been a painter I had never drawn more than a little 'freehand.' So at this time not only was it my instinct to go away from free-hand exercise, but my technique (such as it was) condemned me to T-square and triangle, which I came to love and prefer, but they compelled me to stay behind the sensuous expressions the master so much loved and mastered so surpassingly well." [3] In his final statement of his relationship to his master, *Genius and the Mobocracy*,[4] Frank Lloyd Wright characterizes his master as a lyric poet and a philosopher: "I . . . adored the lyric poet I had instinctively felt him to be and later actually came to know as the great philosopher he was."

Wright worked with T-square and triangle because he thought geometric forms more suited to the materials of building construction. "More and more . . . as the years went by I would instinctively draw toward expressions more appropriate to other building materials by way of T-square and triangle: just as purely instinctively rhythmic [as Sullivan's designs for ornament]—but more architectural ones." [5] He tells how Sullivan would sometimes reproach him. " 'Wright,' he would say [concerning details which the apprentice] was trying (as yet by instinct) to work with T-square and triangle more simply into the materials of building construction itself, 'bring it alive, man! Make it live!' He would sit down at my board for a moment, take the 'HB' pencil from my hand and, sure enough, there it would be. Alive!" [6] In his early years Wright continued to think of expression by T-square and triangle as "more architectural." But nearly a half century later, in 1949, he says:

I now know that "architectural" is not exactly the right word because the basis of architectural thought was there in what he did, but I know now that many a long lifetime must be spent to find the proper technique—each man for himself—to put into actual building practise the implications of the great philosophy to which the lyric poet dedicated himself in this sensuous efflorescence so peculiarly and so absolutely his own. But if a building was ever to be organic in the same sense that this deeply individual expression of himself was so and prophesied it, the lifetime, at least, is only a beginning. I felt this rather than knew it—then. Now I realize it and acknowledge it.[7]

Thus while paying full tribute to his master's statement of the principles of architectural form, and realizing in his later years that what had earlier seemed "baying at the moon" in Sullivan's talk and writing was part of a profound search for a democratic philosophy of architecture, Wright feels that Sullivan (like himself) made only a beginning. Actually, Wright tells us, the master's conceptions were sometimes greater than his performance. Given "a novel problem of that moment—like the troublesome skyscraper —his fine mind instantly saw its chief characteristic. *Aware of its nature* he got its real sense. It was Tall!" Yet Root's Monadnock, a "noble building [done] later [went] even further along. . . ." As the design of the tall building developed it was easy to look back and see that Sullivan really conceived of it as a column with base, shaft, and capital, with no direct or apparent relation to actual construction. It may also be said justly, Wright admits, that Sullivan's verticality is often picturesque, since he emphasizes height in terms of the façade, or what was then called the "countenance" of the building. But his revolt against the academic architecture went far beyond negation of current practice to a search for new principles of form. To appreciate this, Wright asks us to compare Sullivan's prophecy of the new order to come in architecture with the historic styles as practiced in his time. "I never heard the master once refer to Greek architecture,[8] but again see the Greeks, see Richardson, see the painter-architects of the Renaissance. See the stencilists' cliché of today. See them all for five centuries previous and past! Look back and see the interminable vistas of interior structure ignored or falsified in exteriors without any sense of the nature of the problem as you see a type in the Wainwright."

Wright tells us after nearly seventy years of practice as an architect, and at the end of a career of unsurpassed devotion to the art of architecture, "the task of making the countenance of building authentic of structure" will require the lifework of many architects yet unborn. As a young man in the master's office Wright sensed that what Sullivan called integrated or organic architecture would occur only when America became a culture as well as a civilization. "I 'felt' this then. I realize it now because he [Sullivan] was then what he was." Thus while it is impossible to say that any of Adler and Sullivan's buildings express an integration of form and function, we cannot be sure that we have yet achieved it in our time. Certainly simple functional expression of structure is (according to Wright) no more valid than the "façadism" of the Wainwright or the Auditorium. Structure is an expression, not simply of function, but of some idea of how the function should be formed.[9]

The excitement for Wright of Sullivan's structural work was its "prescience of a new world." It was a statement of principle, unfulfilled in execution, but illuminating, nonetheless, a path toward an architecture which would become a cultural order of expression and not merely another style. But in his ornament, Wright felt in his youth and even more deeply in his last years, Sullivan's execution matched his theory.

Yes, the significant implication of lieber-meister's gift to me was his practise *of—the—thing—not—on—it,* which I recognized and saw most clearly realized in his unique sense of ornament. Seeing this in his use of clay, when modeled under his supervision from the plastic mud itself, was always to me a prophecy and sheer joy. His sentient integral modulation by imaginative reason processing from generals to particulars always inspired me, as it must inspire anyone who can see into it as he drew it—or read the record when his designs were modeled as he wished them modeled. If he attended to the modeling himself (he usually did): perfection! His own soul's philosophy incarnate. Music its only paraphrase and peer. . . . Assertion of pure form as *integral* rhythmic movement was what made him a lyric poet. . . . It was that *quality* in him which fired my imagination.[10]

In his last attempts to help us understand the true significance of Sullivan's contributions to architectural form, Wright tells us: "I saw more clearly the spiritual implications of plasticity where space was a quality to be realized in building constructions. I learned the stimulating values of its implication wherever the life of the free individual might be served by the building." He learned this, as he tells us, mainly from Sullivan's ornament. But he learned something else, and in his later years he realized that it was the greatest lesson of all. He learned how to feel as well as think about architecture. He learned finally that art must develop "the capacity for love." Love, for Sullivan, was joy and gladness among men who found their individuality enhanced in community life, where they could share experience through forms created in art.

Notes

[1] First published in *Lippincott's* magazine for March, 1896, this is the only article Sullivan wrote for a popular audience.

[2] *Ibid.* This article is reprinted in "Additional Papers" in *Kindergarten Chats,* ed. by Isabella Athey (New York: George Wittenborn, 1947).

[3] Frank Lloyd Wright, *Genius and the Mobocracy* (New York: Duell, Sloan and Pearce, 1949), p. 55.

[4] Despite its title, and despite misleading reviews which treat this book as some kind of political preachment, it is really a confession. Wright's guilt over the fate of his master, their quarrel, and his too little acknowledged debt to his master shines through much of the discussion about democracy and art.

[5] Wright, *op. cit.,* p. 58.

[6] *Ibid.*

[7] *Ibid.,* pp. 58–59.

[8] In his writings Sullivan often refers to the Greeks as the masters of "static equilibrium." Wright did not like his master's writings and did not read many of them (he even made a point of *not* reading *The Autobiography of an Idea*). At times he says things about Sullivan which simply do not make sense. Thus to say that Sullivan was "untroubled by a social conscience" (see *Genius and the Mobocracy,* p. 40) and then

say later (see p. 80): "The capacity for love—ardent, true, poetic—was great in him as his system of ornament, alone—with no buildings—proves."—is contradicted by Wright's own words, as well as the writings of Sullivan's years of estrangement from Wright. Thus what Wright tells us of Sullivan must always be understood as a personal statement of what happened between himself and Sullivan. It tells us far more about Wright than Sullivan, and interpretations of Sullivan taken from Wright must be heavily discounted for this reason. This does not deny the greatness of Wright, nor his unique contributions to our understanding of Sullivan. The master and his apprentice were very different personalities. From the record left by both, they seemed to have had little in common as friends. Wright admits, in an extraordinarily frank passage in *Genius and the Mobocracy* that he hated his master's habits. "Although he did seem untroubled by a social conscience, he but seldom swore and in money matters was immaculate. Seeing only moral, no ethical, quality in either, I was heedless in both, believing punctilio with money tied up with meanness: Were they trying to make the damned thing sacred so they could keep on playing their game safely? Well . . . I've learned a lot about 'money' since. I regarded swearing as I was taught: as unbecoming —ugly, a bad noise, repulsive like a bad smell; ventilation really. I despised smoking, then, drinking, whoring, and do now. I despised *the habitual in any form*. And L.H.S. practised them in their many forms to a dreadful extreme. Poison himself to lose his real self for what? Why go around following a filthy incendiary sticking out of his face? Just to give an imitation of something on fire inside? I guess the cigarette is something of a relief to paws disengaged when the human animal rose upon its feet. But the animal in me wanted and expected more from him than just that!" But, as an old and mature artist looking back on his youth, Wright says: "Ah—arrogance! Of course, and—I see it now—I was a disagreeable character too." Sullivan's "habits" fitted much better into the young, masculine life of Chicago of the nineties than Wright's home, family, and woman-centered life in the suburb of Oak Park. Thus in the Chicago tradition, and in the memory of those who knew Sullivan, he is loved and cherished, with all his faults, or perhaps because of them, as a Chicagoan.

[9] Mies van der Rohe, who became Wright's opponent in the problem of how to make the "countenance of the building authentic of structure," is the first to admit this. In reply to why he repeated steel sections across the exterior walls of his apartment at 860 Lake Shore Drive in Chicago, so that the sections occur not only at window divisions, but also on the column of the building frame, he said (as reported in *Architectural Forum*, Vol. 97, No. 5 [November, 1952], pp. 93–111): "It was very important to preserve and extend the rhythm which the mullions set up on the rest of the building. We looked at it on the model with the steel section attached to the corner column and it did not look right. Now, the other reason is that this steel section was needed to stiffen the plate which covers the corner column so this plate would not ripple, and also we needed it for strength when the sections were hoisted into place. Now, of course, that's a very *good* reason," he laughs, "but the other reason is the real reason." Actually no one is more arbitrary about form than the so-called functionalists themselves. In the same article, Mies's work is characterized as follows: "He is an admirer of Louis Sullivan, his historical predecessor in straight steel building in Chicago, but he does not follow the ringing dictum of *Form Follows Function*." "We do the opposite" (Mies is quoted as saying). "We reverse this, and make a practical and satisfying shape, and then fit the functions into it."

[10] These quotations are taken from the chapter, "Of the Ground, Not on It," pp. 61–62 of *Genius and the Mobocracy*. Wright's italics.

PART FIVE

The Struggle to Create an American Architecture in Chicago

32

The Birth of a New World Architecture in Chicago from 1873–1891

FROM ITS REBUILDING after the disastrous fire of 1871 to the World's Fair of 1893 Chicago was the creative brain and heart of modern architecture. As Sullivan says in his autobiography, "the progress of the building art from 1880 onward was phenomenal." [1] Wright, too, tells us of the challenge of Chicago of these years to the young artist: "I wanted to work for [Sullivan] above all others because already the firm of Adler and Sullivan was known as revolutionary even in the architecture of that unconsciously —but naturally, thank God!—revolutionary time." As Sullivan's train rolled over the prairies of northern Indiana toward Chicago, his excitement mounted until he experienced an "illumination" as powerful and deep as those he experienced in nature and in the Paris rooms of Monsieur Clopet. He

was utterly amazed and bewildered at the sight of the prairies of northern Indiana. They were startling in novelty. How could such things be! Stretching like a floor to the far horizon,—not a tree except by a watercourse or on a solitary island. It was amazing. Here was power—power greater than the mountains. Soon Louis caught glimpses of a great lake, spreading also like a floor to the far horizon, superbly beautiful in color, under a lucent sky. Here again was power, naked power, naked as the prairies, greater than the mountains. And over all spanned the dome of the sky, resting on the rim of the horizon far away on all sides, eternally calm overhead, holding an atmosphere pellucid and serene. And here again was a power, a vast open power, a power greater than the tiny mountains. Here, in full view, was the light of the world, companion of the earth, a power greater than the lake and the prairie below, but not greater than man in his power. . . . The train neared the city; it broke into the city; it plowed its way through miles of shanties disheartening and dirty gray. It reached its terminal at an open shed. Louis tramped the platform, stopped, looked toward the city, ruins about him; looked at the sky; and as one alone, stamped his foot, raised his hand and cried in full voice: 'THIS IS THE PLACE FOR ME!' That was the day before Thanksgiving in Eighteen Hundred Seventy-three.

As he walked the streets of the city his wonder and excitement mounted. "Louis thought it all magnificent and wild: A crude extravaganza: An intoxicating rawness: A sense of big things to be done." [2]

Other engineers, architects, and builders shared in the excitement of Chicago's "sense of big things to be done." Civil War veterans such as Jenney,

Adler, Otto H. Matz, and Sooy Smith came to Chicago. In 1871, as the smoke cleared from the burning city and the extent of the damage became apparent, the task confronting builders was more than the erection of a few buildings according to established practices in design, construction, and financing. A city which had been all but destroyed had to be rebuilt. Architects were asked how many *hundred* feet, not how many feet, of street frontage they could build, and how soon they could build it. Thus, we read in the Chicago *Tribune* of October 9, 1872, that Burling & Adler had designed a hundred buildings aggregating 8,875 feet of street frontage, costing $4,022,000.[3] Swift and efficient construction—as well as destruction—was not new to Jenney and to Adler. After graduation from Harvard, Jenney had studied in Paris from 1857 to 1859. He had served with Grant's engineering staff until the battle of Corinth, and then, until the end of the war, was on Sherman's staff. Both Grant and Sherman fought "engineering wars." Campaigns like Vicksburg, with their emphasis on co-ordination between navy and army engineers, and the swift deployment of huge masses of men and materials, taught the armies of the West how to use their engineers. Sherman's argument that mobility in war must be the rule, not the exception, was so radical that its complete acceptance by Hitler's generals some seventy-five years later shocked France into defeat and nearly crushed England. "Getting there fustest with the mostest," as Forrest summed up the art of mobile warfare, was a principle which Sherman and his engineers extended far beyond the deployment of cavalry squads.

Grant's and Sherman's armies of Western troops reduced movement to a science. Sherman used his engineers (under Jenney) as others used their artillery. His planning began with carefully prepared topographical studies. One engineering officer in each division was appointed acting topographer. It was his duty to accompany his reconnoitering parties, to collect information as to distances of hamlets and houses, and to sketch roads, streams, and other features. This information was then co-ordinated at corps and army headquarters. Sherman's soldiers sometimes lost skirmishes, but not because they did not know the ground over which they fought. Sherman's army of sixty thousand men, forty thousand animals, and three thousand wagons and ambulances advanced by several parallel roads. The engineering exploits of his expert woodsmen from the Middle West, led by engineers trained in military and civilian engineering awed soldiers and civilians alike.

Dankmar Adler's school of draftsmanship was, not Paris, but the armies of the West under Grant and Sherman. He enlisted in July of 1862 in Company M of the First Regiment of Illinois Light Artillery, and served during 1862, 1863, and 1864, in Kentucky, Tennessee, and Georgia in some of the hardest fought battles of the war. In service with Sherman on his march to the sea he designed bridges, and, more important for the future of American architecture, he was able to pick up many books from the libraries of homes that were looted by the troops.[4] He secreted scientific and historical books in ammunition caissons and studied them whenever he could. During the last nine months of service, he was assigned as a draftsman in the Topographical Engineer's Office of the Military Division of Tennessee, where he gained engineering experience in projects of far greater scope than he could in field experience alone.

Victory road the rails in the Civil War, as our historians are beginning to stress. But she learned to ride it in the West, under Sherman and Grant in the Vicksburg and Chattanooga campaigns. The North, unlike the South, was not fighting on interior lines. Grant based his strategy on supply and he used his engineers to plan as well as fight battles. Turning toward Vicksburg from Grand Gulf and crossing the James River in June 1864 was the result of months and weeks of careful planning in which engineers played a leading role. The Middle West, the frontier of 1861, furnished very large quotas of men and supplied leaders who created a new art of war. It furnished more than one-third of the Union troops, and the new "commercial aristocracy" of Chicago supplied the troops with grain, hides, meat, cloth, and arms. During the long horrible years of war, few Union soldiers suffered from lack of food, ammunition, or clothes. At Lee's surrender at Appomattox, Grant fed Lee's starving troops out of northern stores, transported hundreds of miles through hostile territory, while Lee's army rations stood unused only twenty miles away.

The engineering skill of Sherman's army became legendary. In reminiscences of his service as a common soldier in Sherman's march to the sea, Upson tells us:

They [the Confederates] seem to think they have got us so far away from our base of supplies that they can hold us. . . . There is a story going around the camps that two Johnnys [rebels], one of whom was rather doubtful as to the result, were talking. One said, "Jo Johns[t]on has got old Sherman fixed now, and he will soon have to fall back for want of supplies as we have burnt all the bridges as we fall back."

"Gaunnou [go on now]," said the other, "Sherman had duplicates of all those bridges before he started [which was true] and he can soon replace them."

"Yes," said the first Johnny, "but we have blown up the tunnel."

"Oh you d—md fool, don't you know that he has a duplicate tunnel too?" [5]

General Haupt tells us in his *Reminiscences* that he kept interchangeable parts of bridge trusses, in spans of sixty feet. These were carried on flatcars, by ox teams, or otherwise to the place where they were needed. No trial fittings were required, and they were put together with such rapidity that one of his foremen claimed to be able to build a bridge "about as fast as a dog could trot." When the Massaponix bridge, six miles from Fredericksburg, was burned down one Monday morning, a new one was put in its place in half a day—a feat Haupt says which led some of the onlookers to say: "The Yankees can build bridges quicker than the Rebs can burn them down." The fears of Southern troops over the engineering skill of the North were fully justified. By 1862 Haupt and his men, using standing timber, replaced in a few days bridges which had taken months to build.

Thus at Potomac Creek, Haupt used three companies of Western troops (the Sixth and Seventh Wisconsin, and Nineteenth Indiana Regiments) to build a bridge over four hundred feet long and over eighty feet from the bed of the creek. None of these men was experienced in bridge building. Haupt spent three days in organizing and instructing them. While one crew hoisted and locked up the notched crib logs, others went into the rain-soaked woods to cut and trim selected saplings and fetch the long poles necessary to create trestleworks three stories high. At the second-story level tired and wet workers found it difficult to keep their footing. At the eighty-foot level only a small number of men could be relied on to work at all. Yet in twelve days, from timber growing at the site, and with no machinery more effective than simple hand tools, Potomac Creek bridge was built by untrained soldiers. After he traveled over this bridge, Lincoln told his War Committee in Washington: "I have seen the most remarkable structure human eyes ever rested upon. That man Haupt has built a bridge across Potomac Creek 400 feet long and nearly 100 feet high, over which loaded trains are running every hour and, upon my word, gentlemen, there is nothing in it but bean-poles and cornstalks."

Army engineering of 1862 was part of a well-established tradition. Until 1824 the U.S. Military Academy at West Point was the only engineering school in the United States. From 1824 to the Civil War, it was our leading technical school.[6] The Corps of Engineers had priority over the best graduates; the Corps of Topographical Engineers, the next best. Until 1838, army engineers made surveys for canals, roads, railroads, ports, and harbors. Almost all the great routes of internal communication were first explored, located, and projected by officers of the Corps of Engineers. From 1830 to 1840 several army engineers were loaned to railroads to superintend construction of their lines. Many graduates left the army to go to work for the railroads. In his history of the Illinois Central, Corliss states: No "railroad in the United States was the alma mater of more high-ranking army officers than the Illinois Central. Men who rose to places of great responsibility in the Union Army include Major Generals George B. McClellan, Grenville M. Dodge, Ambrose E. Burnside, Nathaniel P. Banks, John A. Logan, Thomas E. G. Ranson, Mason Brayman, and James C. Lane; and Brigadier Generals David Stuart, Henry L. Robinson, John B. Wyman, and John B. Turchin." [7]

We are told of Jenney that "he could scan a map or a landscape and tell precisely what materials the houses, shacks, mills, churches, etc., offered for bridges or other military works, for materials for the engineering department had mostly to be found on the ground as the army advanced." Sherman's "bummers," as his soldiers were called, not only lived off the land but carried improvised bridges and roads to replace those destroyed by the retreating enemy. Sixty thousand men cut off from their base marched three hundred miles in twenty-four days. These soldiers were trained to fight, to destroy, and to build, but they were also taught how to organize themselves to carry out such large and swift maneuvers.[8] To move 25,000 men, 10 batteries of artillery with their horses, and 100 cars of baggage, over 1,200 miles in eleven days—as was done during the Chattanooga campaign—required technical skill with material, but it also required ability to organize large bodies of men and supplies for swift and efficient movement.

Men such as Jenney and Sooy Smith, who contributed much to Chicago building, thus became far more than engineering technicians. They became organizers and administrators. The railroad, the army, and the building of a city destroyed by fire created a new school for the engineer—a school where practical and pressing problems had to be solved by whatever expedients were at hand. But this emphasis on practical expedients was not born of ignorance. Jenney, like Sooy Smith, Root, Sullivan, and Wright, was a well-educated man. Jenney studied at Harvard and in Paris. Sooy Smith was a graduate of West Point. Root was educated in England as a boy, where he passed the examinations for Oxford at the age of sixteen (in 1866), but he returned to America to enter the University of the City of New York, from which he graduated as an engineering major. Sullivan attended the Boston Latin School, M.I.T., and the Beaux-Arts in Paris. Wright attended the University of Wisconsin. Baumann and Edelmann were cultured men. There were no "detached" intellectuals or pure "artists" in Chicago in the last quarter of the century. Whether as professor, artist, aesthete, critic, or philosopher, a man was expected to be active in civic affairs and to get up before his fellow Chicagoans and speak out. As Sullivan kept repeating, a building was an *act*. Art, as Dewey taught in his Chicago years, was "experience," like business, politics, or religion. Professors at the new University of Chicago were asked what their learning had to do with life. President Harper made clear that "service to the city" was one of its best reasons for existence. Victor Lawson of the *Daily News* urged his reporters to write as they pleased—so long as they wrote about the city.

When the Fair opened in 1893 over one hundred buildings and structures of varying degrees of excellence, but all radical and new in design, stood ready for those Fair visitors willing to look beyond the official classical buildings on the Fair grounds. New forms of organization (as well as design) necessary to large-scale work in modern society had been created by Chicago architects and engineers. In 1890 Chicago offices were already training men who were to carry the Chicago tradition in building to the four corners of the world. Their ability to undertake building projects far greater in size and complexity than existed anywhere in America made Chicago a mecca (as it still is) for ambitious young architects, engineers, and builders. In 1873 Daniel Burnham and John Root, both from the employ of the Chicago architects Carter, Drake, and Wight, became partners. In the same year Sullivan went to work for William Jenney, whose Portland Block had attracted Sullivan to his firm. In 1880 Sullivan and Adler became partners; and in 1883, Holabird and Roche.

The size, complexity, and range of expression achieved in the work of these men made clear that Chicago of 1890 was the world capital of a new organization of master builders, architects, engineers, and bankers. These buildings ranged from straightforward engineering solutions, to problems of space, such as Jenney's Leiter II Building, to the sheer poetry of Sullivan's Getty Tomb. The soaring flanks of Root's Monadnock, a great unornamented block of sixteen stories, are a pure architectural statement of masonry composition. This, the last skyscraper to be built of solid masonry, and still this country's highest wall-bearing building, with ground-story walls some seven feet thick, moves into the sky with a grace and force which belies its massive construction. In sharp contrast to the great, flaring walls of the Monadnock stood Burnham's Reliance Building and Holabird and Roche's Tacoma Building, where for the first time structure becomes expression in itself. With walls practically of glass, divided by piers and mullions large enough only to provide fireproofing for the steel frame, these "beautiful glass towers of the nineteenth century" were prophetic of the great glass towers of our time. In these structures Sullivan's principle of "mobile equilibrium" found expression—the *vernacular* expression of the Chicago school, which was ready by 1890 to lead America and the world to a new order of architecture.

Even where there was precedent for the construction of buildings such as the Auditorium, as in the opera houses at Halle, Prague, and Budapest, continental and American mechanical practice differed so widely that plans copied from European models had to be redrawn, and alterations and improvements made by engineers who installed the hydraulic apparatus. As Sullivan said: "The problems that Mr. Adler had to meet in that building were simply heart-breaking. In those days there were few consulting engineers, and these few were employed mostly by the railroads, iron companies, and mines. There was one man who gave some attention to sanitary and heating matters, but that was almost all the professional advice Mr. Adler could call to his aid. He practically had to dig out his information for himself, and it was a tremendous proposition." [9] The most dramatic problem, and the one most talked about at the time, was the tower. Adler added to the height of the tower [10] to please Sullivan. Since all foundations had to be designed to settle uniformly in so spongy a soil, Adler decided that the heavy foundations of the tower would not settle fully until all the weight was applied to them, which would not happen until the tower was completed. But in the process of building, the office and hotel on either side of the tower, and of much less height, would settle much more rapidly. Unequal settlement would create cracks or ruptures along the lines where the buildings joined. Adler solved this by loading the tower floor artificially with lead and sand, as the building ascended, so that the load per square foot on the foundations of the tower was always the same as that on the foundations on either side. As the tower passed the tenth story, the height of the adjoining parts, he began to unload, so that at the time the capstones were being placed on the finished tower, workmen were wheeling the last load of sand and lead out the front door.

Even the best and most rigorously checked drawings and specifications were meaningless without the closest cooperation between designers and builders. Builders, too—such as young Ernest R. Graham, who was to become Burnham's superintendent of construction for the Fair, and Henry Ericsson, who worked with many of the great Chicago architects of his time —had to solve new problems in construction. "The builder's art," says Ericsson of his early days as builder of Van Osdel's Monon and Jenney's Manhattan Building, "was in a stage of transition, and one was left to meet new and trying problems of his wits and resources right on the job." "Our organization," Ericsson continues, "was simplicity in itself. I was contractor, superintendent, foreman, timekeeper and material clerk, running both the Monon and the Manhattan for a while at the same time." The "prize crew of laborers I had on the Monon were Swedish and Norwegian sailors, together with a Scotchman, Steve, who had sailed the seven seas." With Steve as boss, Ericsson began the construction of the first two buildings in

Sullivan in his early thirties, the years of the
Wainwright Building in St. Louis and the
Auditorium in Chicago. *From the files of
Richard Nickel*

Dankmar Adler in his great years as a leader
of the Chicago School. *From the files of
Richard Nickel*

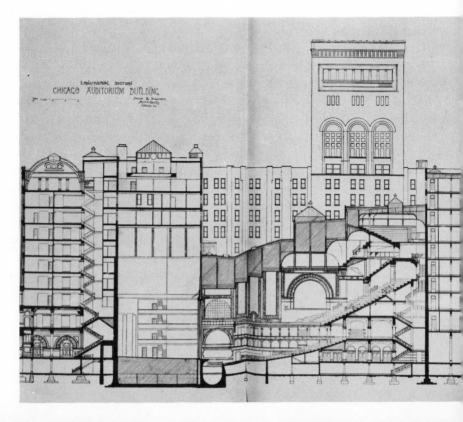

The tower of Adler and Sullivan's Auditorium Building. *Photo by Richard Nickel for the Sullivan Project of the Institute of Design, Illinois Institute of Technology*

(*Left*) A longitudinal section of the Auditorium showing the complexity of its structure and the many activities housed under one roof. *Courtesy Chicago Historical Society*

Chicago to reach thirteen and sixteen stories. "We had the biggest derrick that had so far appeared in the equipment of a Chicago builder." Available hoisting machines could not handle the ten-ton blocks of Bedford stone. A stout, heavy timber forty feet long had to be lashed to the derrick to raise the stone from the fourth floor. Here "even my hardy seamen failed me, and I had to do the job of lashing the great pole to the derrick myself, [for] workmen . . . had their fears and superstitions about attempting the new tasks and taking the risks that their construction at first entailed." The same Swedish and Norwegian sailors from Lake boats assembled and set the cast iron columns and wrought iron beams for the Monon Building. None of these men were workers in iron, nor had any of them ever worked in a blacksmith shop or a forge. "But they had the wits of men of the sea, took hold and did as good a job as willing hands always can do. Those great stones on the front of the Monon I set, every one with my own hands, but Steve managed the men in setting the interior columns and beams." It was not until the Ludington Building, which had an all-steel frame and the largest floating foundation ever to go under a Chicago building, that the structural iron worker came into being. "After the Monon I did not again have occasion to employ sailors to set iron work in a building." [11]

Notes

[1] Sullivan discusses Chicago's great period in the chapter "Retrospect" in *The Autobiography of an Idea*.

[2] This is the close of Chapter X, "Farewell to Boston," of Sullivan's *Autobiography of an Idea*, pp. 175–97.

[3] This is reported by Hugh Morrison in his biography of Dankmar Adler, which appears in his *Louis Sullivan: Prophet of Modern Architecture* (New York: Norton, 1935).

[4] Adler, the gentlest and most honorable of men, was always somewhat embarrassed at having come into possession of books in this way. His daughter was careful to explain to the author that her father always told his children that, since the books would be burned or destroyed in pursuance of Sherman's "scorched earth" policy, he did not commit such a crime after all.

[5] Theodore F. Upson, *With Sherman to the Sea*, ed. by O. O. Winther (Bloomington, Ind.: University of Indiana Press, 1958), p. 113.

[6] Liberal arts colleges then—as now—divorced engineering from art and the humanities. In his Chicago days, Dewey (like Veblen) taught that the common European distinction between "fine" and "applied" art, or between the machine and handicraft, did not fit American life. Even today in Chicago there is no resolution of the separation between engineering and art in the standard liberal arts curriculum of any university.

[7] Carlton J. Corliss, *Main Line of Mid-America: The Story of the Illinois Central* (New York: Creative Age Press, 1950), p. 129.

[8] J. F. C. Fuller, *The Generalship of Ulysses S. Grant* (Bloomington: University of Indiana Press, 1958) discusses Sherman's contributions to modern warfare.

[9] Louis H. Sullivan, "Development of Construction," *The Economist,* Vol. 56, No. 1 (July 1, 1916), p. 39.

[10] Wright tells us that Adler did this three separate times.

[11] Henry Ericsson, *Sixty Years a Builder: The Autobiography of Henry Ericsson,* written in collaboration with Lewis E. Myers (Chicago: A. Kroch, 1941) pp. 106–9.

33

The Flowering of the Chicago School: I. The Chicago Vernacular in Architecture: Adler and Edelmann

T HE REBUILDING of Chicago created a great stage for architectural and engineering talent. Yet it would be a great mistake to assume that the need for rebuilding "inspired" Baumann, Adler, Root, Burnham, Roche, or Sullivan. Boston and San Francisco were rebuilt after great fires, but they produced nothing comparable to even the minor work of the Chicago school. Nor does it make better sense to say, as even Wright does, that the men of the eighties were "unconscious" of what they were doing or, as others say, that they were "primitives" who were able to do good work because their clients were indifferent to style—good or bad.[1] Men such as Baumann, Edelmann, and Adler, of whom we hear very little in American cultural history,[2] were creative thinkers whose influence on American civilization continues to be more profound than many of the literary artists who figure so prominently in every conventional assessment of American culture.[3] Sullivan's architectural thought was created in discussion and talk with men like Baumann, Adler, Burnham, Root, Edelmann, and his apprentice, Frank Lloyd Wright. Discussion, debate, formal and informal oratory, and talk-for-talk's-sake were a great part of Chicago life.[4] Every gathering required a speech. Banquet oratory was a much-prized social art. Ability in humorous talk brought wide social acceptance. Sullivan describes his first months beside John Edelmann in Major Jenney's office as a kind of verbal euphoria. "In the Major's absences, which were frequent and long, bedlam reigned. John Edelmann would mount a drawing table and make a howling stump speech on greenback currency, or single tax, while at the same time Louis, at the top of his voice, sang selections from the oratories [of Handel]."[5]

Sullivan always paid high tribute to the wonderful talk of men like Baumann and Edelmann. Even Major Jenney, whom he did not think an architect "except by courtesy of terms" since his "true profession was that of engineer," wins his praise as a talker. "He was an excellent raconteur, with a lively sense of humor and a certain piquancy of fancy that seemed Gallic. In his stories or his monologues, his unique vocal mannerisms or gyrations or gymnastics were a rich asset, as he squeaked or blew, or lost his voice, or ran in arpeggio from deep bass to harmonics, or took octaves, or fifths, or sevenths, or ninths in spasmodic splendour. His audience roared, for his stories were choice, and his voice, as one caught bits of it, was plastic, rich and sweet, and these bits, in sequence and collectively had a warming effect. The Major was really and truly funny." [6] Frederick Baumann, another engineer, educated in Germany "to the point of cynicism," was a caustic joker but, unlike Jenney, "a man of brains." He was master of one idea, "A Theory of Isolated Pier Foundations." This essay, published in 1873, "was so coherent, its common sense so sound, that its simple idea has served as the basis of standard practise continuously since its day." [7] Baumann lived to be ninety-five. Sullivan met him frequently at the gymnasium, "and liked to talk to him to get his point of view." This he found not bitter but "Mephistophelian." He was "most illuminating, bare of delusion, and as time went on Louis came to regard him as a goat-laughing teller of truths out of school. . . . the world seemed to his sharp, mirthful eye, to grow more and more ridiculous."

But it was John Edelmann, Major Jenney's foreman, under whom Sullivan worked during his first months in Chicago,[8] who gave Sullivan his greatest help. "Louis instantly noted in John a new personality: brawny, twenty-four, bearded, his vocabulary an overflowing reservoir." He loved to talk, and even in a city of talkers,[9] it was great talk. Edelmann, like so many talkers of his time, was a "born orator—he must talk or perish." He was a profound egotist. "It speedily became evident that John was a hero-worshipper, as John blandly worshipped John in the presence of all; and Louis casually remarked that John's unconsciousness of his own personality was remarkable to the point of the fabulous and the legendary, whereupon they became fast friends." Edelmann's friendship meant much to Sullivan.[10] Few men received such high praise from Sullivan, and, so far as we know, their friendship continued without a break.[11] Sullivan was attracted mainly by Edelmann's mind. "It gradually dawned upon Louis that he had run across a THINKER, a profound thinker, a man of immense range of reading, a brain of extraordinary keenness, strong, vivid, that ranged in its operations from saturnine intelligence concerning men and their motives, to the highest transcendentalisms of German metaphysics. He was as familiar with the great philosophers as with the daily newspapers." As an "immediate psychologist, never before or since has Louis met his equal in vitality, in verity, and in perspicacity of thought. He, John, knew all that all the psychologists had written, and much, of his own discernment, that they but recently have begun to unveil. Louis found in John a highly gifted talker, and John found in Louis a practised listener, so their bond of union may be summed up in the token 'I myself.'" [12]

In their talks together John explained his theory of *"suppressed functions;"* and Louis, startled, saw in a flash that this meant the real clue to the mystery that lay behind the veil of appearances . . . a new, an immense idea came suddenly into being and lit up his inner and outer world as one." [13] Edelmann cautioned his eighteen-year-old friend to let the philosophers alone for a while. "He said that Schopenhauer showed some intelligence, because he was a man of the world, while the others were more like spiders, weaving, in the gloom of obscurantism, festoons of cobwebs in their dens, far from the light of the world of men and things." He advised Louis to keep his eyes on the world as it is. He would find plenty to interest him there, and if he had the vision, "he would find a great romance there, also a great tragedy." As John went on "preaching of the world of men and their significance, for worth or ill, in the social order," Louis again moved to new need for understanding what Edelmann meant by "social order." After a return from Iowa, where he had been playing "the game of farming" during a lull in work in Chicago, John entered the office of Burling and Adler. Here in the single, very square office room "he flooded with language; he literally 'ate up the work,' as he spouted." He "cut loose on his latest fad—single tax—and lauded Henry George in superlatives."

One day John asked Louis to come over to meet Adler. "He was a heavy-set short-nosed Jew, well bearded . . . a picture of sturdy strength, physical and mental. . . . It did not take many ticks of the clock to note that Adler's brain was intensely active and ambitious, his mind open, broad, receptive, and of an unusually high order. He was twelve years Louis's senior, and in the pink of condition." Months passed before they met again. John again brought them together. Adler had cut loose from Burling, set up independently, and, in collaboration with a resourceful promoter, was building the New Central Music Hall. John had discussed Louis with Adler. On this second call, there "ensued a mutual sizing up at close range, very friendly indeed." Louis was asked to take charge of Adler's office, and thus launched a partnership which was to revolutionize world architecture.

The vigor and profundity of Sullivan's architectural thought is obvious enough. But Adler's understanding of the art, as well as the science, of building was also profound. As Wright points out, Adler's article, "The Influence of Steel Construction and Plate Glass upon the Development of Modern Style," [14] remains one of our best statements of the "engineer's aesthetic." In his opening paragraphs he states that engineers or architects who think they can apply the new formula, "form follows function," without understanding that function in a building is a human problem, will do not better than those who think form must follow *traditional canons of beauty* in historic styles because their beauty alone is "eternal." "Every architectural work has a 'function,'" says Adler. This function is a "purpose which has called it into being, and its success is measured by the degree of approximation to fulfilment of 'functions' which characterizes its 'form.'" It is easy enough, Adler warns, for the architect "to divide into a few classes the functions to be served by architectural structures and to determine the form best adapted to each, and thus develop an infallibly correct system of architectural design from which none may deviate without incurring the reproach of ignorance and lack of culture." But such reduction of architecture and engineering to mechanical elements alone would be as "trite and as devoid of interest" as is the architecture "founded upon the principle, *Form follows historic precedent,* which stamps as barbaric every structure for which the architect has failed to provide an academically and historically correct mask and costume, and which treats as heresy an attempt to do, not as the Romans did in the year I, but to do as one thinks the Romans might have done in the year 1896." [15]

Adler stresses that "Mr. Sullivan's aphorism" is based "upon studies and observations of nature . . . [in which] an ever changing environment has produced an infinite number of species and innumerable differences in individuals of each species." Therefore, if form follows function, it does not do so "in a straight line, nor in accordance with a simple mathematical formula, but along the lines of curves whose elements are always changing and never alike." Further, the *human* environment cannot be thought of as we think of matter. For, "if the lines of development and growth of vegetable and animal organisms are infinitely differentiated, the processes of untrammeled human thought and human emotions are even more subtle in the differences and shadings of their manifestations, while the natural variations in conditions of human environment are as great as those which influence the developments of form in the lower organisms; and human work is further modified by necessary artificial conditions and circumstances." He then suggests that "before accepting Mr. Sullivan's statement of the underlying law upon which all good architectural design and all true architectural style is founded, it may be well to amend it, and say: 'function and environment determine form,' using the words environment and form in their broadest sense." If we take this view, Adler continues, we are ready to understand what is happening (in 1896) to "those conditions of the environment which comprise the structural and decorative materials at the disposal of the architect." We have inherited much from the past, but we are "still more blessed in being allowed the privilege of participating in the creation and in witnessing the birth of another epoch of architectural design." The form of modern architecture will be founded on "the discovering of the steel pillar, the steel beam, the clear sheet of plate glass, electric light and mechanical ventilation, all devoted to the service of functions or wants created by the greater intensity of modern life and by improved means of communication between places and men."

Every style of architecture "was called into being in obedience to new developments of function and environment, and each was in its own day an iconoclastic innovation upon well established and firmly founded practise." The proper study of the past, and a study which would be of great help to architects in the present, would be to "ascertain the creative principles and laws which underlie the architectural styles of bygone periods of greatest artistic achievement, and to apply these principles to the utilization of the means placed at the disposal of the architect of our day for satisfying the requirements of the day." This can be done if we study how the architects of the past strove "to utilize all the means at command, [so] that the form and expression of each structure might conform to its function, whether that were the worship of God, or the glorification of guild or municipality; whether intended to serve the lavish display of the wealth and dignity of the great noble, or to house the humble burgher." And finally, we must understand that each structure has its individuality, which "gives expression to the character and personality of its occupant." [16]

The architect "is of the world as well as in it." He is "not only an artist, but also an engineer, a man of science and a man of affairs." Were he simply an artist, the "giant strides which science and by its aid industry, communication and traffic have made in the past fifty years would leave him by the wayside, content as are his fellow artists of the brush and chisel to admire the onward rush." But this would mean that the architect would be "with [the modern world] but not of it, to be dazed by its splendor, and to thrive and wax fat under the patronage of those who imitate and control the movement of modern material progress." The architect must engage himself in the life of his times, for this is the only way to greatness in any art. Architecture differs from all other arts in modern times by its engagement in life. There is no "pure architecture," and aesthetic doctrines of art for art's sake cannot be applied to architecture. Architecture "is not permitted to remain placidly contemplative of the march of events. The architect is not allowed to wait until, seized by an irresistible impulse from within, he gives the world the fruit of his studies and musings. . . . The world of today has greater need of his aid than had any previous period, and he is pressed into its service and must work for it and with it, no matter whether or not urged by the spirit within him. The world must have buildings, it will have them adapted to its wants and functions; it will insist upon the utilization of the materials and processes which scientific and industrial progress place at its disposal."

The architect must then prepare himself carefully to meet the demands of his society. "The world calls upon him to do the work of today with the tools of today, not as a tyro, not as one who must first learn how, but as an architect, a master worker, as one of whom the world belies that familiarity which he has acquired with the processes by which the work of other periods has been accomplished makes him better fitted for the work of today, and that he will press into its service all the experience of many ages and epochs." In doing so we only emulate the great artists of the past.

Michelangelo was a painter, sculptor, architect, diplomat, but above all, and in all, an artist. An important factor in his greatness as an architect was his familiarity with the techniques of the auxiliary and subsidiary arts, sciences and crafts, the command of which devolves upon the architect. . . . Were he among us now, he would be in the front rank of the experts and specialists in all the modern arts and sciences which have arisen to perplex and worry the artist-architect wedded to the traditions, processes and materials of the past. And being Master of specialities and details, he would as General, muster them all into martial array for overcoming the difficulties incident to the expanded and diversified demands which our time makes upon the architect.

What distinguished Michelangelo (Adler continues), among other things, was his capacity for hard work. We may lack his genius but we can all emulate his zeal and capacity for hard work. He did not disdain to learn "the metal founder's, the quarry worker's, and other crafts. . . ." Modern architects, too, must become "impatient and contemptuous of the performance of auxiliaries and specialists, and dismissing them, can ourselves acquire a knowledge of the technique of their arts and sciences and crafts, and in the furnace heat of zeal and enthusiasm for the attainment of a great end, combine all that we honor in the lore and traditions of our profession with the discoveries and achievements of the science of today, pour all into the mold of contemporary requirements and bring forth our contribution to the architecture of the new world, the new age of steel, electricity, and scientific progress." The steel pillar, steel beam, and other contemporary contributions to the materials and processes of building construction in the modern business building, and many of the buildings called "monstrosities" by our "professors of art," are "legitimate contributions to architectural art, as were in their day, when first introduced, the stone pier and lintel, the brick wall or pier, the arch, the vault, the roofed temple, the vaulted basilica, the spired and buttressed cathedral. All that is wanting is the will and the ability to make proper use of these newly discovered agencies." Thus far the contribu-

The trestle bridge at Whiteside, Tennessee, taken by George N. Barnard in 1864. Barnard accompanied Sherman during the Atlanta Campaign and the march to the sea. *Courtesy Chicago Historical Society*

The Tacoma Building, designed by Holabird and Roche in 1889, was one of the early experiments of the Chicago School with what we now call the "curtain wall." *Courtesy Chicago Historical Society*

tions "which modern science has made to our power to command and utilize the materials and forces of nature, and the increased opportunities for the creation of useful and beautiful works which modern society has given us, have been looked upon askance."

But functionalists who argue that we should disregard art and follow utilitarian engineering approaches to form are equally wrong. New materials and processes, "the new requirements, should not, however, in their introduction into architecture and in their assimilation by our art, be treated as things apart and by themselves, but as related to and part of all that has gone before in the long history of human and artistic progress." Thus while we welcome "the prosaic output of furnace and mill" and "even the unpromising and garish sheet of plate glass," we must see to it that they are used "where they are wanted and as they are wanted and never where they are not wanted, nor as they are not wanted." The transmutation of "these utterances of scientific prose into the language of poetry and art" must be undertaken at once. "In the nature of things the block of rough stone, the lump of clay, the log of timber, all are apparently as uncompromisingly unpoetic and inartistic as these much dreaded and imprecated modern intruders into the programme of architectural composition. . . . What they have of poetic suggestion and significance they owe to the genius of man, and what man has done with them, man can do with other media." Let us not, then, stand back, "and admit that we are unable to learn from our predecessors how difficulties are overcome, how victory is wrested from apparent defeat."

When we add to the formula: "Form follows function," the modification that "function and environment determine form," we simply state what any builder knows. Our conditions determine our opportunities for form. Steel beams occupy so little space that "in order to enclose structures of which they are the essential supporting parts, they must be furnished with a filling if a space-enclosing structure is to be erected, and steel posts and beams, to be adequately protected against possible attacks of fire, must receive bulky fire protective coverings." Thus, even in the most functional building there are many opportunities for artistic treatment "which may be handled solely with reference to the desire to adapt 'form' to 'function.'" Adler thus sums up his position in the debate between the engineer and the architect by refusing to admit that either alone can create significant design. The "artist architect" must learn to think in terms of structure as determined by the use of the building, while the engineer must respect the transmutation "of scientific prose into the language of poetry and art." "If this is done the influence of the new materials and processes will tend to a more free and less tram-

melled treatment of architectural design, and . . . the striving for the creation of ideally perfect form will be less hampered by limitations incident to
the use of refractory materials of construction."

The leaders of the Chicago school hoped to convince their clients that
architecture had no hierarchy of content and that the distinction between
"useful" and "beautiful" buildings, or between "commercial" and "fine"
architecture, was false.[17] John H. Edelmann pointed out that even bridge
engineers attempt to make their works beautiful. Even the "most uncultivated persons speak of 'looks' as an important quality of a house," and
salesmen are the first to admit "architectural beauty has money value." Thus,
all agree that emotional expression "is the very essence of architecture." We
read past cultures, Edelmann continues, from their architecture, and we
must therefore be prepared to be read ourselves in turn. Our architecture
of the Civil War years and before the seventies—with its large, badly-
constructed, ill-arranged buildings, aping all manner of ancient styles,
covered all over with ill-assorted tawdry detail and badly rendered and
worse-designed ornament—are they "not eloquent of a people intoxicated
with material wealth finding their emotional expression in lavish vulgar
display? The buildings of that time, should they survive, would surely tell
their true story to a future investigator—the story of a people who believed
that money would buy everything, art included, and that a skilful buyer
could even cheat in the buying and get fine art at a bargain." [18]

Fortunately for America our architectural wares are improving, Edelmann continues. "Ever and again an architect escapes from the thralldom
of shop-keeping to become an artist, and finds clients instead of customers."
This advance is along two lines—scholarship and invention. All study more
carefully the great works of the past. The whole world is ransacked. "Even
the gentle Japanese are investigated by ardent enthusiasts who hope to transplant the only living national art to our own country." And these are good
traditional structures, as Stanford White's "Giralda Tower" indicates. This
is not a slavish copy but a reproduction "in form and spirit." But even a
piece of old Spain transplanted to America must remain an exotic, not rooted
in our soil. "At best it gives only negative expression to American ideas."
"Infinitely more crude" are the works of those who strive for originality
and dream of an "American style" to be "presently invented," or of those
who wholly ignore tradition and scholarship while they accept local conditions and requirements. The painful results we see in every American city,
especially in commercial buildings, where the supposed necessity for light
and the use of cast iron have resulted in a class of structures "without visible

means of support." Yet these buildings, crude as they are, are alive: "these childish, brutal, vulgar designs . . . spring from the soil." Foreigners recognize in them the "American architecture." And they are right, for out of these crude beginnings will come our great American architecture. "When all the elements have been distilled in the alembic of a great artist's soul we shall have a true national architecture."

"Richardson," Edelmann continues, "was undoubtedly the first great American architect. He alone has founded a school and has been recognized abroad as an artist distinctly American. It is true he used the Romanesque of the south of France, but he used it only as a point of departure; he was not a pedant and never permitted his scholarship to limit his freedom." The first quality of his art is simplicity. "His buildings are not 'cut up'; there are few parts, he delights in large masses, in huge forms, austere outlines; his walls are cyclopean. His rude simplicity is even ostentatious, so that one suspects him at times of playing a part and of laughing in his sleeve at the gravity of the audience. His detail is coarse and meager, but it is not essential to the effect. His early work was not in commercial building. Doubtless this was fortunate, for business is a hard and hostile master to the artist." His first business buildings were comparative failures, "both practically and in artistic tradition. But later, in the Marshall Field Warehouse done in Chicago, he created a new type." This "grim fortress of trade" disdained all petty subterfuges and make-believes of design. He gives us a square box with regular ranges for openings for light—"massive, simple, brutal, naive, the true expression of its inward character." But his insight has not been transferred to his followers. The work of his imitators creates amusement and disgust. His Romanesque becomes a fantasy of "crude eccentricities; brutal strength devolves into brutality, and so while the last of his work is barely completed his school is already in decadence."

Richardson's true heir, and indeed an architect of far "deeper insight than Richardson, and possessed of far greater power of expression, is Louis H. Sullivan," Edelmann tells us. Not because of "the first work that brought him into general notice, the Chicago Auditorium Building." This building is distinctly Richardsonian. "Although the detail is most individualistic, detail is lost in the huge mass. The tower which marks the passage that pierces the girdle of commercial structures encircling the half-commercial auditorium and which was designed doubtless to mark emotionally the entrance, is in itself very profitable to the very roof, and the emotional expression of the whole naturally rises no higher than the commercial ideal." Its "great size, simplicity, insufficient means, pride of attainment, unbounded ambition, are the qualities expressed, and the soot-laden atmosphere throws a grey shadow over all that well corresponds to the cynical pessimism of the society it serves and exemplifies." But the Auditorium, important as it is, must be taken as "the germ swiftly ripening to complete development."

Notes

1 This curious theory of culture—that the more ignorant the artist and his people the better are chances for good art—is often used to "explain" what happened in Chicago. Even thoughtful writers like Giedion invoke "anonymous history" as a kind of mystical historical force, as an explanation.

2 Dankmar Adler is not even included in *The Dictionary of American Biography*.

3 Cultural history is still mainly the history of literary culture, and furthermore, of written literary history. It is, in short, a history of what happened in books. Obviously, this limits our understanding of society. Until we have a theory of culture based on *all* the arts of expression, and theoretical models of human interaction based on the communication of significant symbols created in every art, our concept of culture will remain literary. How this limits our range of thought on culture, and how it has hindered the development of American criticism in architecture, will be obvious to anyone who compares our journals of architectural and literary criticism. The paradox of American humanism is that we live in a society where most characteristic expression depends on engineering and technological forms, but we are educated only in literary forms. Literary criticism is very superior to architectural criticism. We even read serious discussions of architecture where such phrases as "structure speaks for itself" occur.

4 Old Chicago saloons, George Ade tells us, were designed for talk over drink and food. There was no entertainment for the customers, rather, as in the English pub, they were given a place where they could entertain themselves.

5 Sullivan's love of Handel, shared in his generation by Samuel Butler, has been obscured by constant reference to his love of Wagner. In his autobiography he refers to Handel as well as to Wagner.

6 Sullivan then goes on: "Louis thought him funny all the time, and noted with glee how akin were the Major's thoughts to the vertiginous gyrations of his speech. Thus, we have a semblance of the Major's relations to the justly celebrated art of architecture." *The Autobiography of an Idea*, p. 204. Henry Ericsson, in his *Sixty Years a Builder* (Chicago: A. Kroch, 1942), saw Jenney from the practical view of a builder trying to get a building constructed, and was greatly impressed with Jenney's ability to supervise a job. In Chicago construction this was as prized a talent as accurate computation of costs, skill in labor relations, and all the other skills of the builder.

7 Its clarity of thought and expression is remarkable. The discipline of Chicago engineering thought as early as Van Osdel's time (he was Chicago's first architect and he trained Baumann) is obvious in Baumann's every line. "I advance [the Method of Isolated Piers] as a *scientific method* in opposition to the old *random method of continuous foundations*. I am aware that *isolated foundation-piers* are of old date. Such isolation of piers has been, however, the *exception*, not the *rule*. Its origin is from chance and circumstance, not from logic. I, on the other hand, advance a principle which *makes isolated piers* the *rule in all cases*, and *continuous foundations the exception*, where, for instance, piers of *uniform weights* are so close to each other that the bases

will interconnect." Quoted in Ericsson, *Sixty Years a Builder,* p. 211. Italics as given.

[8] Sullivan was seventeen when he first came to Chicago, and when he first met Edelmann he was not much older.

[9] As was discussed earlier, the spoken, not the written, idiom created the characteristic linguistic forms of the Middle West. In the oratory of Lincoln, the writings of Mark Twain, and the later Chicago school of writers a new language, the American language of our time, was created.

[10] Wright said in 1949: "Louis H. Sullivan venerated none except Adler, Herbert Spencer, Richard Wagner, Walt Whitman, John Edelmann, and himself." *Genius and the Mobocracy* (New York: Duell, Sloan and Pearce, 1949), p. 54. "Outside the initial impetus of John Edelmann in his early days, H. H. Richardson was the one whose influence the master most felt. And John Root, another fertile rival of that time who knew less than the master but felt almost as much. The master admitted that he sometimes shot very straight indeed. They were his only peers" (p. 79). In his *Autobiography,* Wright tells us: "Mr. Sullivan would still talk of John Edelmann who was his most respected critic, not to say teacher. I conceived a respect for John Edelmann, knowing no more than this about him."

[11] This was not the case with Adler, who left their partnership to sell elevators and thus in Sullivan's eyes deserted the cause of architecture.

[12] These are the considered opinions of Sullivan's last years, as given in *The Autobiography of an Idea,* pp. 206–7.

[13] This was the beginning of the search for a principle of architecture that was to end in Sullivan's famous formula: "Form follows function."

[14] From "The Proceedings of the Thirtieth Annual Convention of American Institute of Architects," 1896, pp. 58–64. In private conversations with the author Wright stressed that Adler ought to get much more credit for the accomplishments of Adler and Sullivan. Wright said: "Sullivan never could 'button up a building.'" Adler's articles indicate clearly the force and order of his thought. Hugh Morrison's *Louis Sullivan: Prophet of Modern Architecture* (New York: Norton, 1935) contains a biographical sketch and a list of Adler's writings.

[15] See "Influence of Steel Construction and Plate Glass upon the Development of Modern Style": a series of four papers read before the 30th Annual Convention of the A.I.A. at Nashville, Tenn., October 21, 1896, by J. W. Yost, Dankmar Adler, George F. Newton, and Robert D. Andrews. Adler's paper is a discussion of the doctrine "form follows function." It is printed in *Inland Architect and News Record,* Vol. 28, No. 4 (November, 1896), pp. 34–37.

[16] The sociology of architecture, if ever undertaken as a study in America, could scarcely find a better beginning than this article.

[17] Wright, often careless in giving others credit, always honored Adler, and in *Genius and the Mobocracy* is careful to mention this article of Adler's, as well as to assess the importance of Adler to his own development as an architect. The fame of Wright's Hull House lecture of 1901, "The Art and Craft of the Machine," has obscured this earlier but equally important lecture of Adler's. The small interest shown by American cultural historians in the art and architecture of the Middle West has obscured other important writings by Edelmann, Root, Jenney, Baumann, Bragdon, and Schuyler. Lewis Mumford, to whom we all owe so much for our understanding of modern architecture, gathered together some of these essays in his *Roots of Contemporary American Architecture: A Series of Thirty-Seven Essays Dating from the Mid-nineteenth Century to the Present* (New York: Reinhold, 1952).

[18] The "future investigator" appeared much sooner than Edelmann thought. Veblen's *Theory of the Leisure Class,* expounding his theory of "pecuniary canons of taste" as determinants of American spending, appeared in 1899. Veblen's ideas were current in

the Chicago school of architecture, as they were in the Chicago novels of Fuller and Ade's fables and stories. Chicagoans of the nineties, as well as the seventies and eighties, were experts at distinguishing the nuances of what Veblen called "conspicuous consumption." Veblen was really writing from a well-established point of view, as Edelmann's essay of 1892 shows.

34

The Flowering of the Chicago School:
II. The Organization of Building in Chicago

Eᴅᴇʟᴍᴀɴɴ's and Adler's writings show that the radicals gathering around Sullivan were highly self-conscious of their art. After the completion of the Wainwright Building in Saint Louis in 1890–91, architects of the Chicago school and their partisan critics, such as Schuyler and Bragdon, realized that in "commercial architecture" the synthesis between architecture and engineering had been achieved. The engineers of the seventies and eighties taught architects the science of constructing large and tall buildings, while the architects taught engineers the art of building. But the engineers came first and, in many ways, were far more responsible than the architects for "Chicago construction." Jenney and Loring published their *Principles and Practise of Architecture* in 1869. This was written from the engineer's point of view, although some sensitivity was shown to expression in structure. They admit the value of cast iron, but criticize its too frequent use "to counterfeit stone." Engineers initiated the manufacture of terra cotta in Chicago. Its fire-resisting qualities were highly prized by builders, who had seen their whole city burned out in 1871, and in 1874 again saw many new buildings destroyed by fire.[1] But even Jenney, who designed the first metal frame, had no idea (in 1869) of how to use terra cotta tile to protect iron beams, girders, and columns. The problem of fireproofing was finally solved in 1872, when city officials, architects, contractors, and Chicago dignitaries gathered at the Kendall Building of Van Osdel and Johnson to witness the laying of the first flat hollow tile arches, and the first hollow tile partition walls ever to go into a building in America.

Baumann, like George H. Johnson who solved the problem of fireproofing, worked with Van Osdel, Chicago's first architect. In his *Recollections,* Van Osdel tells us that up to 1856 there was no architect's code in Chicago. Indeed, there was no profession of architecture in the city at all. Builders of the city combined and asked Van Osdel to open an architect's office. The builders pledged that they would neither make plans of their own, nor construct any building of importance without architectural plans. Until this proposal was made "no one had ever used an architect, and it was difficult to convince proprietors of the necessity for such a branch of the builder's business." Thus, in 1844, with the opening of Van Osdel's office, Chicago obtained its first professional architect, and in 1856 twelve budding architects signed an "Architect's code" to regulate practice. In 1856 Chicago had four hundred lawyers as against twelve architects.[2] As we should expect in a business society, professions related to the market, such as lawyers and engineers, and those which priced services in conformity to market practice, such as doctors, soon rose to power. But they kept this power only so long as they controlled communication with their clients and were able to play a prominent public role. Architects had no clearly defined public role as guardians of justice, health, safety, wisdom, or morals, like the lawyer, doctor, engineer, teacher, or priest.

The function of architecture, as of art, was not clearly understood by the people, nor, for that matter, was it better understood among intellectual leaders of the time. The tension and contradiction between culture and democracy were resolved, when they were resolved, by flight to the past, as in Charles Eliot Norton's Harvard lectures on the "democratic art" of Greece, or by making art criticism subordinate to social criticism, as in the writings of Ruskin and Morris. "Aestheticism," which was dramatized by Oscar Wilde in his Chicago lectures in the eighties and upheld by the Chicago publishing house of Stone and Kimball, served only to complicate understanding of the artist's role among the general public. Art, aestheticians preached, existed only "for art's sake," but the slogans of the aesthete made little sense to engineers and architects who were trying to create forms suitable to life in a commercial society.

That Chicago architects were not working in a tradition of architecture was obvious enough. Attempts to overcome this lack of tradition by importing a tradition could succeed only if this could take roots in the new society. Sullivan, as well as Edelmann, Adler, and Root, argued that this was impossible because the life of Chicagoans was too far removed from that of Athens or Rome. Sullivan's jest about Chicago bankers wearing togas and greeting their customers in Latin made Chicagoans laugh, not because they did not like classical architecture but because the incongruity of a Chicagoan acting like a Roman senator was too great. Veblen's jokes over monastic real estate were well received because the young (and even some of the old) instructors at the University of Chicago knew that whatever they were they were not monks. And even Mrs. Potter Palmer and her imitators, who turned house design, like the design of their hats, into a majestic-plutocratic style, were somewhat ironic over playing their roles as Chicago hostesses on French, English, Spanish, and Italian stages. They were proud of being Chicagoans, even if they were not always sure of the basis of their pride, and of the role women were expected to play in creating the new city. Sometimes they wore their houses, like their hats, with an air of whimsy.[3]

But the failure to find a usable tradition was far less important than the failure of the artist to find a role comparable in power to that of the lawyer, doctor, priest, soldier, teacher, or engineer. Everyone knew why these professions were necessary to the community. The engineer knew how to build sound buildings and how to survey and build railroads, highways, and canals. Sanitary engineers were necessary to public health; civil engineers guaranteed public safety. Communities appointed engineers to their governing bodies as they did lawyers, doctors, and superintendents of education. At first this community acceptance of the engineer's role helped the architect. In the image of the engineer he was closer to public comprehension than the poet or the musician. An artist like Sullivan at least worked "with an engineer" to create great buildings whose importance was comprehensible enough, if for no other reasons than their costliness and their solution of problems in construction. But, as architects soon discovered to their own discomfort, it was the engineer, not the architect, who became the public hero. As Sullivan's practice decreased he realized (as Wright tells us) that clients had been coming to Adler the engineer, not Sullivan the architect. Chicagoans were, if anything, indifferent to what went "on" the building, and what went "on" the building was put on by the architect. They knew far more about construction than about design because they had been educated to think about structure and construction. The drama of Chicago, as reported in the local press, was an engineering as well as a political and economic drama. A man like Pullman was famous among Chicagoans for raising the city out of the mud, as well as for his skill in making money. Jenney was famous, not for creating a new form of art, but for "inventing" the steel cage.[4] As Giedion discovered years later in his Chicago research, even in 1940 Chicago manufacturers thought of form as an engineering, not an architectural, invention.

Sullivan watched Burnham change from an architect into an administrator and planner. Adler told young architects that to be a success in Chicago an architect had to be a "man of affairs." In his description of the architectural profession in Chicago Montgomery Schuyler singled out administrative skill as an important factor in the success of the architects. By 1885 Chicago architects were training themselves to do more than simply design forms. By 1892, as we see in Edelmann's essay, it was no longer a question of whether the architect should become a businessman, but of how to be a businessman and an architect at the same time. It was obvious that American art would be determined by money, and Chicago architects of the eighties saw nothing wrong in this. Indeed, as the custom developed in civic projects of awarding commissions on the basis of selection by a committee of "experts," and the classical mania took hold of civic officials, the businessman seemed a far better client than the politician.[5] At least in the business world men made their own decisions, unlike government, the church, or the school, whose committees of "experts" trained in architectural schools usually reached decisions by vote. This, as Frank Lloyd Wright pointed out in his refusal to submit plans to juries for prize awards of commissions, led to members of a committee selecting artists who would please a majority of the committee. An "expert" on a committee, after the classical World's Fair, was someone who had studied in the Beaux-Arts tradition.

What Chicagoans did not understand, Sullivan and his fellow architects soon discovered, was the *function* of architecture, or more broadly, of form itself. They understood that the structure of the Wainwright was determined by the offices within the building, but they did not seem to realize that office space was formed like any other space. They knew that the steel cages they saw standing against the sky were supports for the building, but they did not realize that even these "supports" were formed and designed like any other supporting element in classical and Gothic architecture. They knew that a building ought to "look good" and that some buildings were better-looking than others. The only people who seemed to know *why* buildings "looked good" were professors, who told them that a building ought to look like old buildings in Greece, Rome, and Paris. Chicago humorists were quick to point out that if we judged female beauty by the same canons, women's styles would be even more incredible. But, outside of a few radicals, no one seemed able to challenge the professors and the cosmopolites among the critics who found beauty everywhere but in their own country.

Worst of all, Sullivan decided, architects themselves did not understand the function of art in society. Even Edelmann argued that commercial architecture could never be great architecture because such buildings were being built for money. As Sullivan said, it was easy enough to argue that great architecture could not come out of patronage by the school, the church, or the government, but if business patronage was equally hopeless, where else in America could the architect turn? He could turn to the people—but who were the people, and how did one communicate with them? There was a general public, who read magazines and newspapers.[6] There were engineers and architects, who read their own journals and attended their professional and business meetings.[7] And finally, there were students, young architects in the schools, and apprentices in the offices of established architects. But the communication of architecture was, it turned out, far more than a matter of finding audiences for a message already formed. What was the message of the architect? The lawyer, doctor, priest, soldier, teacher, businessman, and engineer could state directly and forcibly why they were necessary to the community. Everyone knew that the engineer was the one who made the building safe. But what did the architect really do? What was any different about his design and the design of a woman's hat? And even if it was "beautiful," how important was beauty after all? And who was to say what was beautiful? How much should be spent on "beauty?" How much should an architect be paid, and how much attention should be paid to him when decisions on the efficiency of buildings and communities were being made?

Architects could not lead publics unless they could tell them why architecture was necessary to society. They must, Sullivan taught, be able to teach people how to discriminate among the effects of structure. They must be able to return the idea of environment to the idea of culture. The human environment was a symbolic as well as a physical experience. People must be taught how buildings are experienced. This meant eliciting the assumptions lurking in architectural forms, detecting the impulses they appeal to, and exposing the real purposes they serve. The result would be a heightened awareness of the language of architecture as an agency of civilization. This task, as Sullivan saw, could open a connection between sensibility and practical judgment which would deploy the resource of architecture in the service of the people. The engineers had already done this in their great bridges. In the rebuilding of Chicago after the fire of 1871, they taught Chicagoans that "invention was the mother of necessity," as Veblen said while he watched Chicago skyscrapers soar into the Loop sky.

The most baffling practical problem for Chicago's early builders and architects was how to build a foundation for a building of any size, even a brick building of two stories. As Ericsson, who came to Chicago in the seventies to begin a career which carried him from laying bricks to Building Commissioner of Chicago, says: "More buildings tumbled over in the early days than there is any record of, to say nothing of falling walls when building was under way. Even before [Chicago] was incorporated, the government engineers built a stone lighthouse fifty feet high, which promptly caved in." [8] The First Unitarian Church, whose cornerstone was laid in 1863, had to be abandoned within a few months because its tower sank twenty inches. Thus, long before the skyscraper era, the endless struggle to conquer foundation problems required a high degree of engineering skill. Until such problems were solved through the science of building there could be no art of building tall buildings. Until the work of Johnson and Baumann in fireproofing was developed, the great buildings of the eighties could not be created. Despite the loss of virtually half the city by fire in 1871 and 1874, fire protection was still more of a slogan than a reality. People assumed that such harsh lessons had taught builders to fireproof their buildings, but when the prize building of 1881, the Grannis Building (or Grannis Block, as the block-long six- and seven-storied buildings erected after the fire were called), went up in flames Chicagoans discovered that interiors were still constructed largely of wood. The bulk of the money in the "fireproof" Grannis (built by Burnham and Root) had been put in an imposing front. This rented the building and made its sale at a profit possible. Public indignation mounted as this use of stone and brick for sales, not safety, was exposed. The *Tribune* asked: "Why don't the men who build large and costly structures in the business center make them fireproof?" [9]

George H. Johnson's principles and materials of fireproof construction could not be applied, it turned out, by builders and architects who had been trained only as carpenters.[10] Working on steel, iron, terra cotta, cement, and glass demanded new skills and new types of building organization. The need for hoisting machinery to handle the cement and steel, as well as to erect the steel cage itself, required organization of work on the site which was entirely foreign to a wooden structure. As machinery became more expensive, the small carpenter-contractor could not afford to own more than a fraction of the equipment he needed to complete a building. The general contractor, who could organize the many crafts and skills necessary to a building and, above all, who could estimate costs of large and expensive structures, soon dominated the building industry. These contractors of the eighties soon developed into such firms as the George A. Fuller Company, whose 1904 list of buildings includes skyscrapers in New York, Philadelphia, Boston, Pittsburgh, Baltimore, Washington, and St. Louis—as well as Chicago, where this company built the Tacoma, Monadnock, Woman's Temple, Ashland Block, Venetian, Columbus Memorial, Reliance, Marquette, and other Chicago buildings. The Flatiron Building in New York was designed by D. H. Burnham and built by George A. Fuller, both Chicagoans.

Chicago architects and builders were such acknowledged masters of the tall steel building that they were called upon for construction throughout the country, particularly New York, whose vast construction in these years before World War I was done largely by Chicago builders. The shift to financing a building on paper, in contrast to the older method of financing it as a commodity, revolutionized the science and art of building. From the moment of its inception in the mind of the promoter, to the granting of a loan for construction, the building existed on paper. This required accurate drawings and specifications, good estimates of the market or rental value of the building, accurate ways of predicting upkeep costs, and some kind of presentation of the building to prospective investors and tenants, as well as to clients who commissioned the building. Since only a few clients paid cash for a building, architect, contractor, and client alike knew that final decision on their building would be made by those who supplied the money. The banker, in turn, based his risk on how quickly a building would sell if "thrown on the market," what kind of "yield" it would return in capital offered as an investment, or how it could be sold to investors.

Salesmen, in turn, based the vendibility of a building on what had already sold or rented well. What sold well was determined by how quickly and effectively it could be promoted and advertised. The influence of classical architecture was spread rapidly by the Fair, through the communication within a few months to millions who would never have known classical forms if they had not visited the World's Fair. Wright's prairie house was communicated to several hundred thousand readers through the *Ladies' Home Journal,* just as some fifty years later Wright's houses are again being communicated widely through the pages of *House Beautiful.* Business control of mass communication made possible the swift rise of the builder to power over engineering and architecture. The builder could advertise his services; but the architect who followed the ethics of his profession could not. Frank Lloyd Wright could lecture to a small audience at Hull House, but a builder could advertise whenever and wherever he liked.[11] As in every business two different types of builders emerged—those who wished to speculate and those who wanted a steady return on their money. The speculator wanted the building to sell as rapidly as possible. He wanted a "flashy" building which would be easy to publicize, and thus draw the maximum number of potential buyers in the shortest possible time. The determinant of risk in such buildings was not cost, but how quickly a sale would be made. The possibility of immediate and handsome profit, not income over a period of years, attracted speculative capital. And, since bankers, brokers, and salesmen profit each time a building is sold, not on how long it stays in the hands of one owner, the speculator always has many powerful—if unavowed—business allies. In "flush times," when there is great enthusiasm over future earnings, banks become highly speculative. Thus in 1892, we read, Chicago bankers became "riotously speculative" in their enthusiasm over the World's Fair. During 1892 the volume of building activity had been approximately 50 per cent greater than during the busy year of 1890, and much of the money necessary to finance this enterprise had come from Chicago banks. Even the older and larger banks were persuaded to advance money, while several of the newer institutions plunged recklessly into the wave of speculation with blithe enthusiasm.[12] Thus, the pressure of the market, for banker and speculator alike, soon made vendibility a prime determinant of value.

As he watched this change in Chicago building Sullivan, like Veblen, concluded that "The passion to *sell* is the impelling power in American life. Manufacturing is subsidiary and adventitious."[13] Estates, trusts, and individual owners, unlike the speculator, wanted security and calculable returns over long periods of time. The speculator thought in months, the investor of trust funds in years, sometimes even in generations. To the speculator a building was money; to the investor, and particularly local investors, a building was also a stage for gaining prestige and renown. The great Chicago real-estate trusts, such as the McCormacks, the Fields, and the Palmers, were controlled by families who wanted to be leaders of Chicago, not simply cosmopolites who used Chicago as a source of money to create stages for their plutocratic grandeur in New York, London, or Paris. These families had great pride in their city; they did not want to choose between pride and profit, but their attitude toward money was dynastic as well as speculative. The abstract, impersonal, and anonymous character of speculation became more subjective and personal when the building was named after a Chicago family.

In these great buildings space meant money. Rental and resale value determined financing. Search began for ways to maximize space at the lowest possible cost.[14] Thus, isolated pier foundations sustaining buildings of thick brick walls and brick partitions required so much basement space that sufficient room could no longer be found for the light and steam plants required for heat and power for elevators, or for the machinery of the new hydraulic elevators. To meet this problem, Burnham and Root developed the floating foundation, which they put first under the Montauk Building. Iron rails were crossed and crisscrossed and imbedded in Portland cement, so that the building load was distributed under the entire area of the building. As great piles of old steel rails mounted in Monroe Street in the autumn of 1881, and workers began to cross and crisscross them in piles over the blue clay, and then to pour Portland cement over them to make a smooth, shining floor that was to serve as the surface of the foundation, the building of the Montauk became a public event.

The month after the Grannis fire, the North Chicago Rolling Mills announced they would begin the manufacture of structural steel such as girders, beams, joists, and braces. The announcement read that manufacture of structural steel would be new not only to Chicago, but to the nation.

Jenney had invented a steel beam, which Andrew Carnegie agreed to fashion. It was in these Chicago mills that the first Bessemer steel rails in America were rolled. As the future of steel as a building commodity became apparent in Chicago, J. P. Morgan was persuaded that Carnegie Steel, with control of the Jenney invention, was the one indispensable unit to be considered for the economic and financial justification for the formation of the United States Steel Corporation. The drama of the first steel cage, Jenney's Home Insurance Building, Chicago's great gift to the art of building, took place on the northeast corner of LaSalle and Adams. Jenney designed the Home Insurance in 1883 and it was built the following year. The *Inland Architect* of September 1884 noted: "The Home Insurance Building is up to the third floor, and the massive granite walls are ready for the brickwork from this point." But what suddenly appeared to the startled eyes of Loop workers was something new, even in a city where experiments in building were common enough. A network of columns, piers, girders, and floor beams, "remarkable for [their] finished appearance," rose against the sky. This network rising above the massive granite walls was the first iron frame ever erected. "Chicago construction" had arrived, in the idiom of a new world architecture, at the steel age.

Fireproofing and hollow tile partitions greatly reduced weight relative to height, and the steel frame offered obvious possibilities of creating walls which did not bear the load of the building. Yet heavy brick walls, which in all cases except that of the Home Insurance Building carried the entire building load, continued to be used. Tallmadge even argues that Jenney himself did not visualize his skeleton as independently supporting the outside facing of the exterior piers.[15] Neither the floating foundation that Root had devised for the Montauk nor Baumann's isolated piers, where footings had to be kept within the lot which the building itself covered, was capable of any heavier loading. Jenney's cage frame indicated possibilities of pushing buildings higher than the ten or twelve stories already reached, but lack of adequate foundations prevented the inventors of the steel cage from using it to its full capacities, and traditional ways of thinking about walls as supports prevented the development of the modern wall.[16] Engineers solved the problems arising out of heavier loading by the adaptation of the cantilever, taken from the cantilever bridge, to the steel frame, and by using the pneumatic caisson which had been developed by Smith for a lighthouse at the Straits of Mackinac in 1867. When a foundation had to be kept within the building line to leave an adjoining wall undisturbed, the cantilever provided the best, and sometimes, indeed, the only means of distributing the load. In their design of the Rand-McNally Building at Adams and Quincy,

Burnham and Root in 1889 were among the first to provide such a solution for the difficult party wall problem.

Adler and Sullivan came to William Sooy Smith for help in solving the foundation problems of their proposed Odd Fellows Building. Like Frank Lloyd Wright's "Mile High" cantilever building of our day, this project for a thirty-six story building was greeted with suspicion and laughter.[17] The prospectus for the Odd Fellows Building said: "The concentration of immense loads incident to the construction of this building renders necessary unusual precautions in the construction of the foundations, and consultations had by our architects, Adler and Sullivan, with eminent engineers, among them General William Sooy Smith, have resulted in the design of a system of foundation construction which will, without excessive cost, carry the weight of the building down to the underlying bed rock, and, therefore, far below any disturbing influences that may occur in consequence of the construction of subways, etc. . . ." Although the Odd Fellows Building was never built ("an office tragedy," as Wright describes it), the circulation of this prospectus made clear that engineers were prepared to push buildings far higher than any thus far constructed.

Thus for many years the engineers were far ahead of the architects in their grasp of the principles of building and in adaptation of industrial processes to building construction. Architects even neglected construction devices common to their city. The engineering of the grain elevator was one of these. Elevators were built early along the river bank in Chicago. Frequent and sudden changes from light to heavy loads tested them severely, yet there were few failures in their foundations. Piling continued to be used in these structures. But pile driving, like isolated piers, was not practicable where party walls could not withstand the shock of vibrations from the pile driver.[18] So in the construction of their Chicago Stock Exchange, 30 N. LaSalle Street, Adler and Sullivan decided to try out Sooy Smith's caissons. Eight wells ranging in diameter from 5½ to 8 feet in diameter, and from 51 to 74 feet in depth, were sunk. At the bottom the wells were expanded into the shape of bells. These wells were filled with concrete tamped all the way to the top, making one solid pier of concrete. Now the steel cage had a foundation which would permit it to soar into the sky. The era of the skyscraper was at hand.

Notes

[1] The fire of 1874 swept sixty acres, roughly from Clark Street to Wabash and south of Van Buren to Twelfth Street. State Street was widened to Twelfth Street following the fire of 1874. It was discovered that buildings with brick walls built after the great fire of 1871 did more to stop the fire of 1874 than all the efforts of the fire department.

[2] This is Ericsson's figure. See Henry Ericsson, *Sixty Years a Builder* (Chicago: A. Kroch, 1941), Chapter III, "Struggles of the Early Builders."

[3] No one laughed harder than Chicagoans over the social activities of their "swells," as parodied and burlesqued by George Ade in his *Fables in Slang* and in the cartoons of McCutcheon and McMannus (*Maggie and Jiggs*). This robust laughter was very different from the "sophisticated" humor of William Dana Gibson in *Life*. In Chapter IV of Henry Blake Fuller's *With the Procession* (New York: Harper's, 1896), Susan Bates (who is heavily engaged in upholding plutocratic canons of taste) explains to Jane Marshall how the "social game" is played in Chicago: she suggests that many plutocrats' wives spend money with a sense of irony over keeping up their position in society. There was a good deal of playfulness in Chicago spending.

[4] The author was once asked by a Chicago landscape designer not to introduce him as a "landscape artist," but as a "landscape engineer." Edgar Lee Masters tells us how he had to write his verse under an assumed name so as not to arouse suspicions over his soundness as a lawyer. In the Chicago Loop there are firms that specialize in "human engineering," that is, testing clients for occupational capacities. "Engineer" is an honorific term in Chicago business and social life. Even students at such advanced schools as The Institute of Design become uneasy with lecturers who talk about the art of structure. "We," they say, "are solving problems, not creating art."

[5] Clergymen, if anything, were worse. The Unitarians in Chicago have commissioned some noteworthy churches, but even new sects like the Christian Science Church turned to traditional forms, in this case, classical. Wright always said that he preferred businessmen as clients. Certainly he did much of his best work for them. There is no public building designed by Wright or Sullivan in Chicago. The battles Chicago architects have waged against Federal Housing authorities—in such cases as the battle for inside bathrooms for apartment buildings—has done nothing to inspire any great faith in bureaucratic or socialistic patronage.

[6] Mrs. Trollope and, earlier, Tocqueville commented on how many American businessmen read newspapers and how avidly they discuss the news (although they read few books).

[7] Even at these meetings, business and professional motives were in open conflict. In our time, the American Institute of Architects is regarded as a trade, not an art, association by many architects. It is certainly true that the A.I.A. sponsors or sustains very little serious criticism of architecture.

[8] See Chapter V, "Building Comes of Age," of Ericsson, *op. cit.*

[9] Ericsson says that the *Tribune* only a year before in an article, "The Brick Era," had assured Chicagoans that "comparatively cheap and effective fireproofing methods . . . have been discovered during the last few years . . . and the result is that Chicago has many buildings the interiors of which, although almost wholly of wood, are as free of danger of fire as though they were constructed of brick, iron and cement."

[10] In his apprenticeship in Chicago during the seventies, Sullivan worked for architects trained in the generation of wood construction. Of them he says: "They were men of homely make-up, homely ways. Louis found them very human, and enjoyed their shop-talk, which was that of the graduate carpenter. He did not demur because

they were not [graduates] of the Beaux Arts. He preferred them as they were; much of their curious wisdom stuck to him. They were men of their lingering day." *The Autobiography of an Idea,* p. 245. It should be kept in mind, however, that these carpenters were responsible for the development of balloon construction, which made possible the cheap and easily built homes of the Middle West, and soon of all America. Frontier cities, such as Pittsburgh, Lexington, Louisville, and Cincinnati, had always been plagued by housing shortages. These were not the result of poverty, or lack of means, but of not knowing how to build houses quickly enough for people who wanted them and could afford them. Nor were these carpenter-built houses always crude and ugly. The Greek Revival plans, and the detailing of houses according to good Greek Revival and Colonial patterns, created a "Garden City" out of Chicago before the Fire of 1871. These simply built houses are still one of the most attractive architectural features of older Middle Western towns.

[11] The dependence of sales on communication has been given dramatic illustration in our times by the invasion of the American market by the "compact" foreign car. Americans bought what Detroit wanted them to buy—so long as Detroit controlled the communication of its images of the right car to buy.

[12] F. Cyril James, *The Growth of Chicago Banks,* 2 vols. (New York and London: Macmillan, 1938), Vol. I, p. 580.

[13] As his business declined after his break with Adler, Sullivan tried presenting his plans with a financial prospectus. Veblen's observations on salesmanship were developed in his Chicago years, where he saw the new art of American salesmanship develop. The Chicago "drummer" soon became a national legend. Dreiser describes him as a distinct social type in *Sister Carrie.* In his humorous tales of Chicago, George Ade depicts "drummers" taking small towns by storm.

[14] Design, too, affected rental, as we know from the premium rentals paid for office suites with many windows. The number of windows soon became a mark of prestige, as it still is, if we can believe current jokes about how to become a "four-window man." The "Chicago window" greatly affected the use of glass in office buildings.

[15] See Thomas E. Tallmadge, *Architecture in Old Chicago* (Chicago: University of Chicago Press, 1941), for a discussion of the Home Insurance Building (pages on the Home Insurance Building are listed in the index).

[16] The "skin-wall," that is, the non-load-bearing wall, is just coming into practice in the 1960–1970 decade—some 90 years after the steel cage made it entirely possible, and some 80 years after such buildings as the Tacoma and the Reliance of Chicago's Loop were built as "glass towers."

[17] Ericsson states that in 1885, at a banquet of the real-estate board at the Palmer House, the notion of a thirty-six story structure had been introduced "as mere jest in the raillery of the banquet." See *Sixty Years a Builder,* p. 230.

[18] "The use of piles," Randall tells us, "had not been attempted in the Loop [prior to 1890] for the simple reason that no satisfactory method of driving the piles had been discovered. The method then in use was to lift a four-or-five ton weight up to the head of the derrick, release it, letting it strike from a distance of twenty-five feet. The resulting vibration was so excessive that adjoining property owners objected and even enjoined the contractor from further driving. A little later a steam hammer for pile driving was devised. . . . This gave a light blow with great rapidity." Frank A. Randall, *History of the Development of Building Construction in Chicago* (Urbana: University of Illinois Press, 1949), p. 93.

35

The Flowering of the Chicago School:
III. The Development of Architectural Criticism
in Chicago

S ULLIVAN's Wainwright Building was to the art of architecture what Jenney's Home Insurance had been to the practice of steel construction. In 1892 Edelmann said: "I select the Wainwright [from all of Sullivan's work] . . . as the most complete expression of American commercial architecture." In 1896 Schuyler said: "I know of no steelframed building in which the metallic construction is more palpably felt through the envelope of baked clay. The designer has in this respect fully availed himself of the plasticity of his enclosing material." Wright, recalling his first view of the Wainwright drawing, says: ". . . when [Sullivan] brought the drawing board with the motive for the Wainwright outlined in profile and elevation upon it and threw the board down on my table I was perfectly aware of what had happened. . . . This was a great Louis H. Sullivan moment. The tall building was born tall. . . . here was the 'skyscraper': a new thing beneath the sun." The strength and vigor of Edelmann's analysis and the early articles of Adler, Root, and Sullivan indicate the depth and vigor of architectural criticism in Chicago during the nineties.

Engineers and architects trained themselves to write and speak, not only before colleagues in their professional societies, but before general publics at banquets, clubs, and civic affairs. Critics such as Schuyler and Bragdon, newspaper writers such as Julian Ralph,[1] and foreign travelers such as Paul Bourget—all of whom wrote in the nineties—did much to spread the fame of the Chicago school outside of professional circles. But Adler, Edelmann, Root, Schuyler—and, of course, Sullivan—went far beyond popularization in their writings. Their criticism is searching and serious, on both aesthetic and social planes. The stature of Chicago criticism, aside from the writings of Sullivan and Wright, is well illustrated by Edelmann's article, "Pessimism of Modern Architecture," which appeared in the April 1892 issue of *Engineering Magazine*.[2] This little-known essay makes clear that the architects of the Chicago school knew what they were doing and, as Edelmann's fear of the "money cult" indicates, were highly sophisticated in their concern over the social implications of their art. The problem of form, as Edelmann saw it in the eighties, was one of how to relate structure and expression, and on the social side, how to relate the profit motive to a democratic architecture. Edelmann's essay of the early eighties is a key to later debate in Chicago over the aesthetic and social implications of "commercial architecture," as the classicists called the work of the Chicago school.

The debate in Chicago on how to relate culture, democracy, and money took many forms. Among literary critics the argument shifted to discussion over standards in language, themes, and forms of expression. Garland argued for realism, Browne for the "beauty" of the classics.[3] This debate was not unique to Chicago, of course; Henry Adams's *Mont-Saint-Michel and Chartres* and *The Education of Henry Adams* described the spiritual struggle of America in the images of the virgin and the dynamo, with the dynamo as an impersonal "force" crushing beauty. Chicagoans such as Sullivan, Wright, and Veblen were on the side of the dynamo but for reasons opposite to those of Adams. They agreed with businessmen who argued that the machine would create a better standard of life, but they also argued that the machine could be related to art. Edelmann begins his essay by asking us to observe in the Wainwright "the complete absence of all conventional forms." He compares it with buildings in the East [of 1890] where "our most clever men are still building up their lofty structures, by super-imposing several old buildings one upon the other, and making serious sacrifices of structural convenience to vertical divisions into bays, pavilions, towers, etc. . . ." In the Wainwright "all this is brushed aside and the rectangular steel skeleton is expressed in rectangular outer forms." The building "is treated as one essential and integral growth. Instead of concealing the implicity of internal function it is emphasized by repetition of parts; instead of minimizing the height by horizontal divisions into three or more fields the height is made the artistic motive." Nothing could be more simple, Edelmann turns aside to say, "now that it has been done." As he reflects on the wonder of the Wainwright, he is struck, like Wright [then Sullivan's young apprentice], by Sullivan's mastery of problems which others had failed to solve in "years and lives [which] have been spent in vain attempts."

"The main piers," Edelmann continues, "are carried up through the first floor, the large openings covered with flat arches, the entrances marked by decorative carving, the story topped with a simple strong course which marks at once a change of internal function. Then the whole vast range of stories—having common uses—are treated alike, with only minor differences of detail; the vertical lines are clear and distinct and in themselves give a strongly emotional expression." The last story is "frankly sacrificed for a frieze of marvelous design pierced only by circular openings of small value

as windows . . . and all surmounted by a broad, straight cornice richly decorated in unconventional fashion." Commercial architecture is no longer "a
thing of shreds and patches and shams, but direct and complete in itself—an
embodiment of truth. . . ." Edelmann then comments on the proposed Fraternity Temple to be built by the Independent Order of Odd Fellows on a
site in the Chicago Loop. This project called for a skyscraper of tremendous
dimensions, taller and larger than any contemplated up to that time. The
building was announced to the public in September 1891, in a prospectus
describing in detail the building and how it was to be financed, its plan
accompanied by an exterior rendering by Adler and Sullivan. Schuyler and
Edelmann recognized that this projected building was a step beyond the
skyscraper. Edelmann said: "The recent climax of the spirit of commercial
architecture which aspires ever higher in the search for the 'Ultima Thule'
of profitable exploitation of the upper air, in a thirty-four story building,
fortunately has found artistic embodiment at the hands of Mr. Sullivan, for
he alone could do it artistic justice."

As Edelmann points out, Adler and Sullivan, in their "Fraternity Temple"
plan, anticipated the problem of light and air in the congested streets of
urban downtown areas. The "necessity for leaving air to breathe and some
light at least for the occupants of the lower stories, has led to new features in
the design. Even the broad Chicago streets will not suffice for thirty-four
structures built vertically on the street line." Sullivan recognized very early
that skyscrapers could easily become a threat to a humane development of
commercial centers. "The tall steel-frame structure may have its aspects of
beneficence; but so long as man may say: 'I shall do as I please with my own,'
it presents opposite aspects of social menace and danger. . . . the tall office
building loses its validity when the surroundings are uncongenial to its
nature; and when such buildings are crowded together upon narrow streets
or lanes they become mutually destructive. The social significance of the tall
building is in finality its most important phase." [4]

The "Fraternity Temple" is a complete anticipation of the modern set-back
style which the New York City Zoning Law of 1916 standardized for urban
building. But it was also, as Schuyler pointed out in 1896,[5] an extraordinary
projection of solutions to the humanization of the urban environment—solutions that are only now coming into general acceptance in the planning and
rebuilding of our cities. The projected "Fraternity Temple," Schuyler says,
"is worthy of preservation as an illustration of its architect's powers and
methods, but also and eminently of the *genius loci*." It is "immensely characteristic of Chicago that a building which bears the same relation to the
ordinary 'skyscraper' that this bears to the old-fashioned five-story building

of the pre-elevator period should have been projected by 'practical men' as a practical structure." "Given a detachment complete enough, indeed, and absolute protection against fire," Schuyler continues, "and there is no reason why a thirty-five-story building should be any more an example of 'incivism' than one of ten. One can even imagine a building of the dimensions of the Fraternity Temple at the center of each square mile, or even less, of a crowded city, so prepared for in its surroundings as well as so planned in itself as to involve no abatement of their utility, although in that case its owners ought perhaps to be the owners of all the land within its 'sphere of influence,' and the building of this to be planned with reference to the towering central structure."

The Chicago idea of a city of skyscrapers with parks between them reached full expression in the "City of Towers" of Le Corbusier. In *Vers une architecture,* originally published in 1923, Le Corbusier says:

Let us listen to the counsels of American engineers. . . . If we take as our basis the vital constructional event which the American sky-scraper has proved to be, it will be sufficient to bring together at certain points (relatively distant) the great density of our modern populations and to build at these points enormous constructions of 60 stories high. . . . In these towers which will shelter the worker, till now stifled in densely packed quarters and congested streets, all the necessary services, following the admirable practise in America, will be assembled, bringing efficiency and economy of time and effort, and as a natural result the peace of mind which is so necessary. These towers, rising up at great distances from one another, will give by reason of their height the same accommodation that has up till now been spread out over the superficial area; they will leave open enormous spaces in which would run, well away from them, the noisy arterial roads, full of a traffic which becomes increasingly rapid. At the foot of the towers would stretch the parks: trees covering the whole town. The setting out of the towers would form imposing avenues; there indeed is an architecture worthy of our time.[6]

The real task of Chicago architects, Schuyler explains, "is to produce sky-scrapers and homes—and factories, indeed, which architecturally are neither here nor there, but which occupy much of the attention and contribute much to the incomes of the busiest architects. Even before the introduction of the 'Chicago construction,' which first appeared in the Home Insurance building some six years ago, the sky-scrapers were noticeable for two Chicago characteristics, their extreme altitude and their strictly utilitarian treatment." In the evolution of Chicago architecture the share of the businessman has been no less "important than that of the architects," and no less "important for being in the main negative." Schuyler then quotes approvingly from "a very intelligent and a very candid foreigner, Paul Bourget, whose comments in *Outre-Mer* [7] are "so true and so well put."

Bourget entitles his remarks on Chicago as "Chicago in an autumn morning from the tower of the Auditorium." This tower, he explains, "is two hundred and seventy-five feet high, and it crowns and dominates a chaotic cyclopean structure which connects a colossal hotel with a colossal theatre. One's first visit on arriving should be here, in order to get the strongest impression of the enormous city, lying black on the shore of its blue lake." The

dark coloring of the city . . . is reflected back from the deeper azure of Lake Michigan, ploughed with steamboats like a sea. . . . you discern differences of heights among [the levels of the buildings]. Those of only six or seven stories seem to be the merest cottages, those of two stories are not to be distinguished from the pavement, while the "buildings" of fourteen, fifteen, twenty stories, uprise like the islands of the Cyclades as seen from the mountains of Negroponte. A mighty murmur uprises from below like that of no other city. . . . Yes, the scene is strange even to unreality, when one reminds oneself that this Babel of industry grew out of a tiny frontier post—Fort Dearborn. The irresistible devouring force of one of the most terrific conflagrations mentioned in history transformed this entire plain into a burning mass. . . . I leaned again over the balustrade of the tower, gazing down upon this prodigy, stunned with the thought of what men have done!

As Bourget reflects on the miracle of Chicago he feels (like Henry Adams) his inadequacy to analyze such new and terrible power. And, like so many observers of Chicago, he invokes the superhuman power of money as the new symbol of life in Chicago.

Men! The word is hardly correct applied to this perplexing city. When you study it more in detail, its aspect reveals so little of the personal will; so little caprice and individuality, in its streets and buildings, that it seems like the work of some impersonal power, irresistible, unconscious, like a force of nature, in whose service man was merely a passive instrument. This power is nothing else than that business fever which here throbs at will, with an unbridled violence like that of an uncontrollable element. It rushes along these streets, as one before the devouring flame of fire; it quivers; it makes itself visible with an intensity which lends something tragical to this city, and makes it seem like a poem to me.

As you descend from the Auditorium Tower, Bourget continues, to the

exuberant life, the exhaustless stream of activity. . . . You walk along the sidewalks of streets which bear marks of haste,—here flagstones, there asphalt, yonder a mere line of planks crossing a miry swamp. This want of continuity in road material is repeated in the buildings. At one moment you have nothing around you but "buildings." They scale the very heavens with their eighteen and twenty stories. The architect who built them, or, rather, made them by machinery, gave up all thought of colonnades, moundings, classical decorations. He ruthlessly accepted the speculator's inspired conditions,—to multiply as much as possible the value of the bit of earth at the base by multiplying the superimposed "offices."

These strange buildings, Bourget says, seem very remote from art. "One might think that [buildings "made by machinery" and made possible by speculators] would interest no one but an engineer. Nothing of the kind! The simple power of necessity is to a degree a principle of beauty; and these structures so plainly manifest this necessity that you feel a strange emotion in contemplating them. It is the first draught of a new sort of art—an art of democracy made by the masses and for the masses, an art of science, where the invariability of natural laws gives to the most unbridled daring the calmness of geometrical figures." The portals of the basements,

usually arched as if crushed beneath the weight of the mountain which they support, look like dens of a primitive race, continually receiving and pouring forth a stream of people. You lift your eyes, and you feel that up there behind the perpendicular walls, with its innumerable windows, is a multitude coming and going,—crowding the offices that perforate these cliffs of brick and iron, dizzied with the speed of the elevators. You divine, you feel the hot breath of speculation quivering behind these windows. This it is which has fecundated these thousands of square feet of earth, in order that from them may spring up this appalling growth of business palaces, that hide the sun from you and almost shut out the light of day.

Chicago, Bourget continues, cannot be comprehended by any known standard of urban civilization. Time as well as space has been broken into new forms.

Close beside the preposterous, Babel-like building extends a shapeless bit of ground, undefined, bristling, green with a scanty turf, on which a lean cow is feeding. Then follows a succession of little wooden houses, hardly large enough for a single family. Next comes a Gothic church, transformed into a shop with a sign in great metal characters. Then comes the red and pretentious ruin of some other building burned the other week. Vacant lots, shanties, churches, ruins,—speculation will sweep over it all tomorrow, this evening perhaps, and other "buildings" will spring up. But time is needed, and these people have none. These two years past, instead of completing their half-finished city, they have been amusing themselves in building another over yonder, under pretext of their exhibition. It is entirely white, a dream city, with domes like those of Ravenna, colonnades like those at Rome, lagoons like Venice, a fair of the world like Paris.

The people, like the buildings, are "the most cosmopolitan of human mixtures." These violent, turbulent people are never easy to control. The daily papers "continually tell of some 'hands up' performed in the taverns, the gambling-houses, or simply in a carriage, or on the tramway. . . . 'Hands up!' It is the classic command of the Western robber, as he enters, revolver in hand, his first business to make sure that you have not yours. How many times has it been uttered in the suburbs of this city, the meeting-place of the adventurers of the two worlds? How many times will it yet be uttered?" To hold such people in check strong measures are needed. "And as at Chicago, it seems that everything and everybody must be larger, more developed, stronger, so from block to block in the middle of these streets are posted, to maintain order, enormous mounted policemen, tall as Pomeranian grenadiers; gigantic human barriers against which break the seething eddies of this multitude." But the violence and the strangeness of Chicago should not blind us to the creativity of the city. The

spirit of adventure is also the spirit of enterprise, and if the size of the policeman of this surprising city attests the frequency of surprises attempted by [the criminals of the city] it completes its complex physiognomy; different, surely, from every other since the foundation of the world, a mosaic of extreme civilization and almost barbarism, a savage existence only partly discerned through the abruptness of this industrial creation. In short, it is Chicago, a miracle that would confound the dead of seventy years ago, if they were to return to earth and find themselves in this city, now the ninth in the world as to population, which when they were alive had not a single house.[8]

Edelmann does not share Bourget's enthusiasm over Chicago's linkage of business and architecture. Like Bourget, he thinks the new "engineering art" a great accomplishment, but he predicts that commercial art will never be great art. "Our craftsmen are politically free and highly-educated men, in theory at least. Economically—that is to say, actually—they are mere wares subject like other wares to the law of supply and demand; they are bought for the work they can do. Their interest is of course to give the least in exchange for the purchase price—i.e., the wages. And this view is enforced by the trades unions to which they must belong, for these unions know that increased efficiency of labor must, on the whole, lower wages, and hence do not encourage it." The architect, like the craftsman, is

almost always a ware bought and sold in competition with other wares, harassed by a thousand uncertainties and perplexities, [he] gives what energy he can spare to his life as an artist. He must pre-determine the exact form and shape of his buildings, specifying all material and labor, minutely describing all constructive forms, working out all decorative detail from the standpoint of money cost at least. For the building itself is a ware and its price settled by competition. The *lowest*, as a rule, is the *best*, bidder, and "if t'were done at all t'were well it were done quickly," for "time is money." If the architect is a man of extraordinary force and enthusiasm he will nevertheless work out his design with vast and loving care, securing the cooperation of young and ardent associates who work as much for love as money.

But even the greatest architect must place his design in the hands of contractors, to whom "profit is the first law." And whose workmen "cannot be expected to hold their work as higher than themselves," for they, too, are "wares." How then can we look for "art work from a commodity?" Under present conditions it is "wonderful how much we actually receive." Humanity is not to be "wholly expressed by the formula of trade, and people will after all give more than is paid for." The death of art at the hands of business is not peculiarly an American tragedy. "I have spoken here only of American art, but the world over the old joyous art is dead. Even in Japan it is dying and from modern commercialism no happy art can spring. If this phase of civilization is to prevail Pessimism must become its final expression and embodiment."

Notes

[1] The best early criticism of Chicago architecture, outside of the ranks of the architects themselves, came from newspaper critics.

[2] Vol. 3, No. 1, pp. 44–54.

[3] Eugene Field, George Ade, and other Chicago humorists soon popularized this debate into a struggle between "culture vultures" and "slobs." Newspaper writers were for realism—but urban realism, not the agrarian realism of Garland. The humorists were very suspicious of "horny-handed" Chicagoans who acted as guardians of the classical tradition. Any man who talked of beauty was like Veblen's man of fashion, a male "in the biological sense alone." Culture belonged to women in Chicago, as P. D. Armour made clear in his quip that in his family all culture was in his wife's name.

[4] Louis H. Sullivan, *The Autobiography of an Idea* (New York: Press of the Institute of Architects, 1926), p. 313. This was Wright's point. To show the true nature of the tall building as a tower, he later built the H. C. Price Company Tower at Bartlesville, Oklahoma, and designed the mile-high Illinois building for Chicago. Concern over the social significance of the skyscraper was shared by other Chicago artists, notably Henry Blake Fuller, whose novel, *The Cliff Dwellers* (New York: Harper's, 1893), uses a Loop skyscraper (supposedly the Tacoma Building) as a setting for the drama of life in Chicago. Norton of Harvard admired Fuller's Italian stories, but he objected to Fuller's Chicago stories such as *The Cliff Dwellers* (1893), and *With the Procession* (1895), because they went far beyond the accepted limits of literary propriety and failed to attain the high moral function of great literature. The "repulsiveness" of life in a Chicago skyscraper (as Norton found Fuller's description of it to be) is not a fit subject for art, any more than a tall office building.

[5] Montgomery Schuyler, "A Critique (with Illustrations) of the Works of Adler & Sullivan, D. H. Burnham & Co., Henry Ives Cobb," *The Architectural Record,* Great American Architects Series, No. 2, February, 1896.

[6] This is taken from the chapter, "Three Reminders to Architects," of Le Corbusier's *Towards a New Architecture,* trans. from the French by F. Etchells (London: The Architectural Press, 1952), p. 56.

[7] Published in 1895 by Scribner's of New York, based on observations made during his trip through America in the latter part of 1893. Chapter V, "Business Men and Business Scenes," is about Chicago and its architecture.

[8] Quotations from Bourget are taken from Chapter V, "Business Men and Business Scenes."

36

John Wellborn Root

Jₒₕₙ Rₒₒₜ had it in him to be great, as Burnham had it in him to be big." So spoke Sullivan of the only Chicago architect he recognized as his peer. As he looks back at his early years in Chicago he tells us that Root's death left "in Louis's heart and mind a deep sense of vacancy and loss." Root's death was also a great loss to the Chicago school of architecture. He was six years older than Sullivan, and his partnership with Burnham began in 1873, eight years before Sullivan began his career with Adler. Until the completion of the Auditorium in 1889, Adler and Sullivan did nothing comparable to the tall buildings in which Burnham and Root pioneered so many new principles of construction. The Montauk Block was completed in 1881, two years before the Revell Building, the first significant work of Adler and Sullivan. None of the buildings done by Adler and Sullivan from 1879 to 1887 exceeded six stories, and only one, the Ryerson Building, was strictly an office building, what architects of the time called elevator buildings.

The business buildings of Burnham and Root were the first tall buildings, as Schuyler says, "in which the conditions both of commercial architecture in general and of elevator architecture in particular were recognized and expressed." [1] Like Sullivan, Root owed much to Richardson. His early buildings are Romanesque, but just as Richardson's Romanesque underwent great change when applied to purely commercial purposes, as in the Marshall Field Warehouse, so did Root's Romanesque take on new functional elements, as we see in the entrance to the Phoenix Building. Schuyler characterizes this as "Richardson chastened and restrained . . . [and] one of the most noteworthy examples in this country of the art of architecture. . . ." [2] But the refinement of the Richardson tradition is only a small part of Root's contribution. The range in his expression, from the Montauk Block of 1882 to the Monadnock Building of 1891, is far greater than Adler and Sullivan's for the same years. Burnham and Root were the first to experiment with many of the new types of building arts which made the Chicago school possible. And even in style, Root's Montauk, Counselman, and Monadnock buildings were as functional as anything done by Adler and Sullivan in these years. Indeed, it is part of Chicago lore that a remark of Root's to the effect that "Louis couldn't build an honest wall without covering it with ornament," led to Sullivan's revision of his plans for the Auditorium.[3]

The Montauk Building of 1882 was an engineering landmark. As Tallmadge says, "The use of 'floating foundations,' a broad raft of concrete reinforced with iron rails, used here for the first time, revolutionized foundation construction and remained the accepted form until caissons were first used in 1892. It was the first thoroughly fireproof high building in Chicago because in it the columns were protected for the first time." New ways of organizing work on the site also were developed. It was the first building in Chicago in which work continued without pause through the winter months. The construction area was covered with a canvas tent and was heated.[4] A grillage of iron rails was used to reduce the volume of footings by eliminating the pyramids of dimension stone, as recommended by Baumann.[5] Cast-iron columns were used for the interior columns, with wrought-iron floor beams and heavy exterior bearing walls. As the building reached its tenth story it was called a "skyscraper." Until the twelve-story Mallers Building was built in 1884, the Montauk was the first skyscraper in Chicago and perhaps in the United States.

But the Montauk, like the Calumet Building of 1882–83 and the Counselman Building of 1884, were significant architectural as well as engineering achievements. As Tallmadge says: "We must not let the creative power of Louis Sullivan blind us to the equal originality of John Root. Sullivan was striving after light, but at the time he was experimenting with exuberant ornament applied often wherever he could find room for it. Root, with remarkable courage and taking great chances, put the ornamental side of his art behind him for the nonce and threw his soul into a functional expression of this new intensely Chicago problem, which meant solving problems of planning, foundations, fireproofing and utilities."[6] As a contemporary account noted, the Counselman Building, 145 feet high, has little exterior ornament, for the architects tried to achieve massive and durable effects. The Montauk was a clear expression of structure, with walls devoid of ornament and the floor levels marked by horizontal bands.[7]

Like Sullivan, Root probed deeply into the meaning of architecture. In his essays of the eighties[8] he argued that "utility" or "fitness" was the text of good architecture. For, of all the arts, architecture is dependent upon its public. That is why the architect must keep his mind open to "all those influences which lie most closely about him, with which he is most familiar because of daily association. Remote and unfamiliar aspects of nature or types of men or conditions of life cannot be felt with earnestness deep enough to fully permeate the work produced under their influence. In all the world's history it has been true and it must always remain true that art produced solely under foreign inspiration has been worthless." [9] Architecture in Chicago could become vital, Root argued, only if it accepted and expressed frankly the spirit of its environment.

There never was a picture that people loved, . . . nor a building that they went out of their way to see, which was not essentially local. Michelangelo did not paint Spanish beggars; nor did Jean François Millet paint Alpine mountains. So thoroughly have all great artists been permeated by the spirit of almost their very city that this spirit has often swept them away from a single art. Thus Leonardo, or Giotto, or Angelo, or a dozen others of the Renaissance were engineers, architects, men of science, men of letters, critics, all in one—compendia of all things about them. . . . For artists, thus surcharged by the spirit of the people and the aspect of things immediately about them, there has always been success and fame; and for artists here similarly imbued, await success and fame. What have we of inspiration to offer artists intent on thus bringing themselves into harmony with us? . . . Here we are content that artists should sit under a north sky-light and paint for us memories of Dutch peasants and Picardy apple blossoms, or even pictures of landscapes they have never seen. Can they do nothing better for us? Let them come down to us and try. Eternal thanks and deepest love to him who shall open our heavy eyes to the beauty about us! [10]

The Chicagoan is ready for good architecture, but as a client he

wants knowledge more than anything else, and what he needs when off the track is only information to put him right. To combat his whims with whims equally unreasoning, to fight his groundless notions of style with our groundless notions, to make him cease laying down absurd law by ourselves laying down law equally as questionable—all this is the height of folly. . . . Fashion becomes our only fortress. We fight our battle behind bulwarks made of stays and ruffs, laces and ribbons, baggy and tight trousers, snuff-boxes and smelling salts, 'Queen Anne' gables, and Neo-Jacobean bays and 'Romanesque' turrets. . . . For our own self-respect, for the dignity of our own position, for the sake of an architecture which shall have within it some vital germ, let us come out from our petticoat fortress and fight our battles in open field. In science and literature, in art, is heard, loudly calling, the voice of reason. For any branch of human knowledge or imagination or aspiration to shut itself from this cry is death.[11]

The architect must respect his client's needs and approach them as problems to be shared and solved in common. "In the present catholic condition of art there seems to be no reason for violent prepossessions or any shirking of persistent 'whys'; for any notions we may have of a possible solution for a problem as yet unstudied should have at least the merit of being suggested by the inherent elements of the problem; and this being true, a statement of the possible solution and its reasons will certainly carry weight. Much more will an equally frank statement carry weight when the problem has been in all its bearings carefully considered and the best solution arrived at." Reason, of course, has its limits in architecture, which, after all, is an art which reaches full attainment when the higher faculties of taste and imagination are brought into play. "Reason should lead the way, however, and imagination take wings from a height to which reason has already climbed." [12]

A good working relationship between the architect and his client demands a reasonable approach on both sides. This is as necessary for the architect as for the client, for the architect must remember that he is not a high priest of art. A "reasonable plane for the contact of architect and client removes from between them much of that false view which assumes that art is an arcanum too profound for uninitiated minds, a Court of the Priests upon which unwashed feet may not tread. There is no danger that great things or even good things in art will ever be born to the sterile mind, or that the creative gift of a true artist will be profaned by a perfect comprehension of the unwashed." [13]

Architecture is different from other arts in the extent of its "purely reasonable and (if the word be allowed) explainable side. Not to avail himself of this fact is for the architect a great mistake, for when the client has fully grasped the reasons for that part of a design which can be explained, he is inspired to completer trust for those parts which lie in the realm of the imagination and fancy." In any case it is not wise for the architect to think himself superior to his client. "It is not uncommon that an intelligent layman will have a breadth of view in architectural matters which will not be suspected if he is to hold rigidly to professional interviews. He lacks technical vocabulary; he fears perhaps to express an opinion which from a professional point of view will seem ridiculous; he hesitates to commit himself to what may be out of style." [14]

"All this is wrong and should be discouraged." For a client's opinions and tastes may be more than mere whims. "His opinions and tastes may be the result of careful study and close observation by a mind at once acute, discriminating and retentive." Often, indeed, a client's freedom from a professional approach is of the greatest value to the architect.

The technical and professional point of view in art is not always the truest. Artists are often victims to artificially acquired judgment, when unaided vision in daylight should be the only communication with the mind. How great would be the value to an architect of being able at will to free himself from all the prejudices and theories which in his practice have grown about him, and for an occasional hour see as an intelligent layman may see! . . . The temptation is almost irresistible often to take refuge in the books, among the Greeks, among the French; to seek cover in the darkness of the middle ages, or concealment in the glitter of the seventeenth century; to quote precedents, and turn to buildings erected by great men. All this is nonsense. [15]

The Chicago Woman's Temple, the national headquarters of the Women's Christian Temperance Union, designed by Root in 1891.
Courtesy Chicago Historical Society

No reason for a building is of any value that does not deal directly with the fitness of the building as a solution to problems in its intended use. Styles in architecture develop by "the careful study of all the conditions which lie about each architectural problem, and thus while each will have its distinct differentiation from all others, broad influences of climate, of national habits and institutions will in time create the type, and this is the only style worth considering." This can never lead to the "monstrous method . . . which would gather fragments from all the ages and build them into one hideous whole. . . . It means rather to . . . make sure that the particular thing chosen for the given purpose shall be the best fitted for that purpose—shall in short grow out of it. This is as obvious as to say that a man's exterior form shall be the result of his interior structure, that his skin and hair shall be colored by the climate where he lives; and being thus obvious it becomes the true position to assume in relation to the client." [16]

Thus far Root has said nothing (although he said it earlier) that was not also said by Sullivan, Adler, and Edelmann. But we must realize that Root is talking about homes as well as large office buildings. Root designed far more significant houses than any other Chicago architect of his time. Monroe lists 126 in her list of buildings designed and erected by Burnham and Root from 1882 until Root's death in 1891.[17] Morrison lists 38 for Adler and Sullivan, and until the Albert W. Sullivan and the Charnley residences of 1892, Root's domestic design is far superior to Sullivan's.[18] Earlier residences of Sullivan, such as the John Borden home, designed and built in 1880, are so undistinguished that it is difficult to believe [19] that Sullivan did much more than design some of the ornaments. This is all the more strange when we consider that Richardson, whose Marshall Field Wholesale Warehouse had such profound influence over Sullivan's designs for the Auditorium, also had designed and built in 1885–86 the Glessner house on Prairie Avenue. This is Richardson's greatest house, but it was used as a model by Root, not Sullivan.

The architect, Root continues, must begin thinking about his design for a house by asking: "What sort of a town is the house to be in? How wide are the streets it faces? Where do the prevalent winds blow from? How much hot and cold weather has the town? How much rain? Which way is south? How far from the street is the house to stand? Has the town smoky or clear air? What are the native building materials? What is the character of the workmen to be employed? Is the occupant of the house a student? a family man? a public man with many friends? one who has many guests? who gives many entertainments? Is he a man fond of display, or one who shirks it and rather prefers simplicity of 'solid comfort'?" The architect "will frankly accept the consequences involved in each answer, and will not be burdened by prepossession so strong as to prevent his acting dispassionately." [20] Architectural style cannot be reached through mere form, but through an understanding of the effect of form on those experiencing it. A building has a character, like a man. And just as we speak of the qualities of a gentleman in such terms as repose, refinement, self-containment, sympathy, discretion, knowledge, urbanity, and modesty, so may we apply them to a building.

Repose is the most essential of all qualities. "The instinct of the world has decreed that all large things should be quiet or slow-moving, and that only little things like bees and butterflies may flutter." Since buildings are the largest things made by man, a deviation in them from the quality of repose is the most elemental of mistakes. Many things may be pardoned to a little house, or one without public significance, which would be unpardonable in a larger or more important building. The great buildings of the world teach us that the inner principle of form is this: "What sentiment is the building designed to convey? Is it the restless aspiration of the soul after God, as embodied in the medieval cathedral? Is it the expression of the power and stability of a great corporation, as expressed in its office building? . . . The two are very different, but the design of each must be an expression of purpose." [21]

We can test the relation of design to expression by thinking about roof lines. "In large and important buildings, . . . and especially those built for commercial purposes, . . . experience will show simple sky-lines to be best, as best conducive to the quality of repose." The value of "plain surfaces in every building is not to be over-estimated." Strive for them, "and when the fates place at your disposal a good, generous sweep of masonry, accept it frankly and thank God." Color should always be kept "well subordinated to the general mass, whose largeness and dignity should be expressive of not only sober thought, but of the gravity becoming all great things." Refinement in architecture requires not only careful consideration of each detail but the relation of each to its neighbors and to the whole. For what may be good enough in itself "may be utterly vulgar in juxtaposition with other things." Refinement depends on taste. And despite all the difficulties in generalizing over taste there is doubt that it can be cultivated. The experience of great architectural works is, however, not enough. The architect must familiarize himself with all the arts.

The most significant form of architectural study is the human form. In the human body proportion and form reach their most refined and significant expression. The human body is the "perfect solution of the relation of exterior expression to interior arrangement." In the human body even herculean strength may be combined with the utmost refinement. When fully expressed in architectural design, such refinement means all that it suggests in the human form. "There is the same careful avoidance of useless features, the same perfect adjustment of each part to the function performed by it. Elephantine columns are not used to do the work of mice; necessary structural features are not emasculated by ornament too delicately wrought; purely decorative features are not so formed as to give a false suggestion of vital necessity." [22] The need to be original, to make every building "different," is one of the great difficulties facing the architect who seeks to develop a sound principle of design. Self-containment becomes almost impossible in times which force the architect to make buildings "fairly scream" to be seen among other "original" buildings. For now a building must advertise its owners. Hence, now, more than ever before in architecture, self-containment is a duty of the architect. Buildings last a long time; every "intemperate and hastily uttered thing about them remains to our discredit." [23]

Lack of sympathy for people's needs and desires is another great flaw among architects, Root told his audiences. "In each community there are certain tendencies of the people, certain peculiarities, full sympathy with which is essential to the successful designer." American architecture "has too much of the transplanted look which comes from the absence of this active sentiment." Where there is active sympathy for the people among architects, all styles "become quickly acclimatized and characteristic." We hold too tenaciously to the dry canons of mere architectural style. But a great building like the Parthenon, "becomes great not only because of its perfection as a solution of a given problem, but because in a hundred small respects it expresses the immediate influence of essentially local conditions." Variation in architectural forms which is the result of local conditions "always comes about of itself in time, and this may be in spite of architects." No importation of Greek architects could save Roman work from swift differentiation from Greek work. "Our attitude should therefore be one of readiness to accept and help forward the inevitable. By doing this we can insure that it will be the finer national characteristics, rather than the grosser, whose influence will be manifested." [24]

But sympathy with local needs and conditions must be matched with sympathy for the purpose of each building and the idiosyncrasies of each owner. If the building is "a warehouse, a dry-goods store, an office-building, or a hotel, the true points of view in designing them will be largely determined by these various commercial considerations." In this respect the architect differs from all other artists. He can never afford, "even when the artistic expression of his design alone is considered, to neglect a single condition not only in the larger matters of climate, national characteristics, general purpose, etc., but also in matters very trifling. I am confident that an architect designs a better grocery-store, if into his own professional view of the problem he will admit in all possible fullness the grocer's view. More than for all other artists does success for the architect depend on the activity and warmth of these sympathies." [25] Yet sympathy, unless tempered by discretion, is very dangerous. "Without discretion architecture is like a machine without a governor." Columns, roofs, gables, balconies are stuck on everywhere in Chicago homes. These effects are like "a drunken man swearing that he is what he pretends to be, while even a blind man could see there is not a word of truth in it." In their anxiety to induce belief by volubility of protest, many of them "look as if the source of their design had been a fireworks pin-wheel, while some assert by their combrous features, by their heavy brows and wrinkled skins that they are only wretched little pygmies. . . . What discretion have we, when we assume in the prevalent craze that because a type of design is good for a house 100 feet wide and high, it is equally good for a dwelling 25 feet wide and 30 feet high?" [26]

The same kind or the same scale of detail is not equally good for all buildings. "We don't sing Schubert's 'Lorelei' on the floor of the Board of Trade, nor shout the price of grain in our music-rooms." And yet we "spend a wealth of delicate ornament on our down-town edifices, and build our dwellings like Stonehenge." Ordinary discretion should teach us that the relation between dwellings and trade palaces is the relation between an orchestra and a brass band. "Whatever is to be spoken in a commercial building must be strongly and directly said. The very style of ornament should be simple enough, and the scale large enough, to be easily comprehended. . . . let us consider each quality our building will express, making sure that its expression be appropriate, and that it be well adjusted to the mood of the spectator; not lowered down to his plane, but, although above the sordidness of his daily thought, sufficiently in recognition of it to escape total neglect." [27] Genius in architecture is beyond the reach of most, but knowledge is accessible to all. Thus in our time ignorance must be regarded as a crime. The so-called "practical" architect who knows nothing of his art "beyond what has been grafted into him by the surgery of dry practise, is passing away." It is true there are large and acute minds whose ripe wisdom and nice taste have been acquired by long experience and observation. Yet these are not the men who deride learning. Often, indeed, they point out their early work "as monuments, not to their glory, but perhaps to their shame or misfortune, and warn us to push with all vehemence our acquisition of the knowledge thus early denied to them." The practice of the profession itself and the absorbing cares of an active life will give any architect enough practical knowledge. It is then a misfortune when he ceases to acquire "that form of professional knowledge which is entirely literary, and which may be related to his profession only by some side-light from another art, which architecture may borrow." [28]

Urbanity in architecture is the "expression of readiness to extend sympathy even before it is asked." In the past, "urbanity in a house was as unsuitable as a silk cap in a jousting tournament. The house was a castle, its owner its warrior defendant, and everybody outside it possible besiegers. But with the dawn of day after the long dark feudal night, the dwelling opened outward like a rose in the sun. Men like Jacques Coeur of Bruges built houses in which they delighted to express to all who passed the new-found peace and friendliness. In such houses was the frankest avowal of good fortune, the most charming confession of a desire to please." Nothing threatens our homes, yet we see a sudden growth of medieval castles "whose only lacking detail is a shriveled head thrust over the cornice on the end of a pike." We may be as aristocratic as we please, but if we are really gentlemen our houses will, like gentlemen, "doff their hats to their neighbors." In our business hours we may be brusque, and hence "my business house may follow . . . in the expression of this." But we should not be brusque with our neighbors. People who see our houses should be able to say: "Here lives a gentleman." This does not mean extravagant ornament nor lavish outlay of money, nor vulgar solicitation of notice. Urban architecture scorns these, for such architecture is "the natural grace of a graceful society, to which every man in it owes allegiance." [29] Architects should remember that their buildings will be subject to a criticism which has a long history. Self-assertive design has little chance to survive the scrutiny of such criticism. "All its cheapness and all its arrogance are revealed, and at last it stands forth a bragging humbug. Look at the splendid architecture of the second empire in France. Men of great talent created it. Millions were spent on it. Why did it fall short of enduring fame? It is not modest, it protests too much; it claims too much. It has the cheap bluster of a hired bravo, and the false beauty of the street cocotte. We must learn to suspect in our designs all that directly demands admiration as its right." [30]

Not until Wright's essays, and the erection of his prairie houses in the years from 1900 to 1910, de we find such critical understanding of the importance of architecture, and particularly of domestic architecture, to democratic society. Many of Wright's ideas are to be found in Root's essays of the eighties, and even the "open plan," which became so characteristic of Wright's work, is anticipated in Root's houses.[31] Root's homes are still within the tradition of

Richardson's Romanesque, but in the Goudy and Valentine homes, done in the eighties, we see walls treated as flat planes pierced by large windows. Even where Romanesque masonry effects are attempted, as in the Turner house, the wall is still treated as a plane and expresses the structure within. There was, then, a Chicago tradition in domestic as well as commercial architecture, upon which Wright and architects of his generation, the second generation of the Chicago school, could build.

Notes

[1] Montgomery Schuyler, "A Critique (with Illustrations) of the Works of Adler & Sullivan, D. H. Burnham & Co., Henry Ives Cobb," *The Architectural Record,* Great American Architects Series, No. 2 (February, 1896), "Part II—D. H. Burnham & Co." pp. 49–69.

[2] Schuyler also agrees with Sullivan that Root liked to experiment with new forms rather than develop principles of design. Of the Phoenix Building entrance he says: "Alas, it remains also, like so many other things, a monument to our inconstancy, and another proof that no sooner do we approach a common way of working and begin to attain some skill in it than the promise of a style is broken by the capricious introduction of a new fashion."

[3] Thomas E. Tallmadge tells this in his *Architecture in Old Chicago* (Chicago: University of Chicago Press, 1941), p. 160. He gives as his source Paul Mueller, who was Adler's assistant. Morrison published the preliminary and final designs in his *Louis Sullivan.* The progress toward simplicity is clearly indicated.

[4] As Schuyler (and others) tells us, Burnham's administrative and managerial skills matched Root's skill in design. The importance of this combination in an architectural practice is evident when we see the decline of Sullivan's work after he broke with Adler. After Root's death Charles B. Atwood became Burnham's designer, but was in no sense an equal who would stand up to Burnham and fight for principles of design he considered right. Atwood did as he was told, and Burnham considered himself as important to design as to administration of the office. Root had never tolerated much interference from Burnham on design.

[5] Burnham and Root had few followers in this radical departure until the building of the Rookery, where not only rails but combinations of rails and iron beams were used.

[6] Tallmadge, *Architecture in Old Chicago,* p. 147.

[7] This is illustrated in Frank A. Randall's *History of the Development of Building Construction in Chicago* (Urbana: University of Illinois Press, 1949), p. 69.

[8] In her study of Root's work, Harriet Monroe quotes at length from these essays. Root married Harriet Monroe's sister, Dora Louis Monroe, and thus Harriet Monroe writes from an intimate knowledge of Root's character, as well as from her own sensitivity as a poet. It is obvious she admired and loved Root. But her memoir is far more than a romantic tribute. It is one of our best sources for understanding the struggle of the Chicago architect of the eighties to resolve the tension between culture and democracy. See Harriet Monroe, *John Wellborn Root: A Study of His Life and Work,* with etchings and drawings by Charles F. W. Mielatz and facsimiles of designs by Mr. Root (Boston and New York: Houghton, Mifflin, 1896).

[9] Monroe, *op. cit.,* pp. 62–63.

[10] *Ibid.*, pp. 211–12. This same plea is made by Hamlin Garland in his *Crumbling Idols: Twelve Essays in Art Dealing Chiefly with Literature, Painting and the Drama* (Chicago and Cambridge: Stone and Kimball, 1894).

[11] Monroe, *op. cit.*, p. 65.

[12] *Ibid.*, p. 66.

[13] *Ibid.*

[14] *Ibid.*, pp. 66–67.

[15] *Ibid.*, p. 68.

[16] *Ibid.*, p. 69.

[17] Monroe tells us that records of earlier work were burned in the destruction of the firm's offices in the Grannis Block. See Appendix B of Monroe, *op. cit.*, for the list.

[18] We are told that Sullivan did not like to design houses, but did them only as a favor to his clients. This was, as Wright tells us, how Wright got his start (and the source of his quarrels with Sullivan). The Charnley house was turned over to him.

[19] The author was told by George Fred Keck, one of the few Chicago architects who kept the spirit of the Chicago school alive in the twenties and early thirties and who taught in the Institute of Design under Maholy-Nagy, that when Giedion was shown the Borden house he refused to believe that Sullivan had designed it.

[20] Monroe, *op. cit.*, p. 70.

[21] *Ibid.*, p. 81.

[22] *Ibid.*, p. 84. Sullivan and Wright use the tree, not the body, as their model.

[23] *Ibid.*, p. 85.

[24] *Ibid.*, p. 86.

[25] *Ibid.*, pp. 86–87.

[26] *Ibid.*, p. 88

[27] *Ibid.*, pp. 88–89. By this Root means that delicate ornament is wasted "if the unseeing eyes of busy men are daily saluted by delicate details" which they do not have the will or the leisure to contemplate. This, he argues, only vulgarizes ornament.

[28] *Ibid.*, p. 90.

[29] *Ibid.*, p. 92.

[30] *Ibid.*, p. 93.

[31] It was also anticipation in Richardson's Glessner house of 1886.

37

The Presentation of Chicago to the World:
Root's Plan for an American World's Fair

As the four hundredth anniversary of the landing of Columbus drew near, demands crystallized in America for an international exposition. The same generation of Chicagoans who rebuilt the city destroyed by fire decided that the Fair should be held in Chicago so that the culture as well as the money power of their wonder city could be told. From 1880 to 1891 Chicago's population increased from 503,298 to 1,099,850; her size from 35.79 square miles to 180.2 square miles; her wealth from $117,133,726 to $219,354,368; and her building from $8,207,000 to $47,400,000. The great Fire of 1871 made Chicago front-page news. Her growth, the drama of her politics, and the open and free discussion of her social problems served to keep Chicago on the front page. She became, in the eyes of Americans such as Henry Adams and European students of American life, typical of the new America of the West, and, indeed, of all America. Chicago was fast becoming "the American city."

Many American cities wanted the Columbian exposition. But none could show such a building as the Auditorium of Adler and Sullivan, the Rookery, Monadnock, or Reliance buildings of Burnham and Root, or boulevards and parks along the shore of a vast inland sea busy with ships. As William James, Henry Adams, and Charles Eliot Norton of New England and Harvard were soon to admit, Chicago could really "make culture hum." Some, such as Adams, said with an air of incredulous discovery what Chicagoans like Veblen, Sullivan, and Dewey had long accepted as fact—namely, that the center of creative force in America—for better or worse—was shifting from Boston to Chicago. With the completion of the Auditorium no city in America could boast of so beautiful and efficient a theater. Chicagoans were being called to every city in America to design and build after the forms developed in "Chicago Design" and "Chicago Construction." New Yorkers did not know how to design and build their own great buildings. Tuthill, who designed Carnegie Hall in 1889, called in Dankmar Adler as a consultant on acoustics.[1] The aesthetics of Chicago architecture could be questioned, but all admitted that no city in America, or for that matter the world, boasted of so many architects and engineers who could undertake vast buildings and whole areas of buildings, and do so in terms of fixed costs and time schedules.

In the contest between American cities for the international exposition, Chicagoans were distinguished by the faith in their capacity to raise money and do the job. In characteristic fashion, business leaders of the city organized promotional campaigns within and without the city. Businessmen pledged five million dollars even while other cities were still holding discussions on how to raise the money. In the winter of 1889–90 Chicago sent to Washington a committee of her foremost citizens,[2] fully empowered to make large promises and ready to assure Congress that if the exposition were granted to Chicago, it would not be used for political purposes. Chicago also had many choice sites available. New York did not convince Congress that she had such sites, or that she would keep the exposition out of the hands of politicians. On February 24, 1890, the House of Representatives passed the bill locating the Columbian Exposition at Chicago, fixing the four hundredth anniversary in October 1892 for the dedication of the buildings, and May to November, 1893, for the six months' festival. This bill soon passed the Senate and became a law in April by the signature of the President.

Both within and without Chicago questions were raised over the capacity or inclination of businessmen to produce anything more than "a cattle-show on the shore of Lake Michigan," as Eastern newspapers put it. But to the surprise of the East, if not to Chicagoans themselves, Chicago businessmen seemed very confident of the ability of their own architects and engineers. Their promise to "keep politics out of the Fair" was kept to the letter. The "feudal barons," as the radicals called them, were determined to get the best that money could buy. It was to be their show, and whatever failure or success it had was to be theirs. Like George H. Pullman, who created a model village, Jeffery, Gage, Ellsworth, and other Chicago businessmen knew how to plan and administer large-scale projects. The problem of how to landscape six hundred acres, erect a whole village with many large sumptuous buildings, and be ready to house, transport, and feed millions of visitors, all within a few months, did not seem insurmountable. To a generation of Chicago engineers and architects who had already lifted a city out of the mud and built the tallest buildings in the world on foundations sunk in mud and sand, the Fair was simply another challenge.

Financing the Fair was done by issuance on August 14, 1889, of 500,000 shares of stock selling for $10 per share. By April 9, 1890, the stock issue was fully subscribed. As Currey points out: "In making subscriptions to the stock of the World's Fair it was clearly understood that subscribers would not be likely to have a full return of the money thus invested, much less any profit therefrom. At the Centennial Exposition of 1876, the subscribers had one-third of their subscriptions returned to them afterwards, and it was thought as much might be expected from our own Fair. It is likely that a result as favorable as this might have been realized had it not been for the financial panic that broke upon the country during the progress of the Fair. As it turned out these subscribers eventually received fifteen per cent of their investment, which the final statements of the Fair will show in a later part of this history. It spoke well for the generosity and public spirit of the people that they subscribed as liberally as they did in the face of the dubious prospect of little or any returns from the investment in the stock of the World's Fair." [3] E. T. Jeffery, president of the Illinois Central Railroad, and O. Chanute, an engineer, were sent to Paris in 1889 to examine and report on the French Universal Exposition. Another committee was elected to report on sites. This committee asked Burnham to consult with them in regard to the site to be proposed in support of Chicago's claims before Congress. Congress created two commissions: one to take care and custody of the exhibits, including communications with exhibitors and all dealings with foreign officials, the other to be formed into a local corporation to build the exposition and conduct the Fair. Since each of these organizations had their own officers, discussions over possible sites soon became long and bitter. And since whatever site chosen would have to be accessible to rapid and cheap transportation, the site became a problem for railroad officials, as well as Chicago businessmen and their engineers and architects.

A few days before the Act of Congress was passed, a meeting of the Illinois corporation was held and forty-five directors were chosen. In selecting the board, "leading spirits in the movement aimed to choose from among the prominent citizens men whose business ability was recognized, and who would be counted on as possessing both time and the inclination to serve the interests of the proposed Exposition. The latter qualifications were considered most essential, and gentlemen of the greatest prominence and business ability withdrew in favor of younger men, who could be more easily drawn upon for hard service." [4] Lyman J. Gage, the banker, was chosen President of the Board of Directors. The official title, "World's Columbian Exposition," was soon changed by the people of Chicago to "The World's Fair." Chicagoans were determined to present their new city to America and to the world as a center of culture as well as commerce. But Chicagoans soon discovered that confidence in the power of the businessman as a standard bearer of culture was not shared so widely in the East. James William Ellsworth proposed that Frederick Olmstead, the leading American landscape architect, be consulted. Gage finally consented to this and agreed that Olmstead and his partner Codman be invited to visit Chicago to consult with Burnham, who had continued to act as informal adviser. But when Ellsworth visited Olmstead he found him "inclined not to have anything to do with a fair," as Moore tells us.[5] This attitude was shared by other Eastern artists. Ellsworth made clear that Chicago did not intend to do just another "fair." Six hundred acres were to be treated as Olmstead had treated Central Park and as Chicago was developing its world-famous park and boulevard system. There was, in the Fair project, every possibility of a great exposition area with waterways, canals, lagoons, and fine architecture—and fifteen million dollars was available. Olmstead accepted.

Seven sites were examined by Olmstead when he arrived in Chicago. Three of these were on Lake Michigan and four were inland. None of the sites possessed any natural scenery beyond marsh, sand, and water. The inland sites were eliminated quickly. Of the Lake sites, Olmstead preferred the north because the cost of preparing the ground would be comparatively small and a spectacular effect could be produced by the great marine commerce of Chicago passing in review before the grounds. But the railroads refused to spend the money required to provide transportation to the northern site.[6] As Olmstead tells us,[7] he turned with reluctance to Jackson Park. He knew the site well, for he and his partner, Calvert Vaux, had made a plan (in the eighties) for Jackson and Washington parks and the strip of land connecting them, which was known as the Midway, and is now the campus of the University of Chicago. Before making his formal report favoring Jackson Park, Olmstead discussed with Burnham and Root the distribution of buildings upon the sandy ridges of the shore of the Lake and the use of excavated material to back up retaining walls. It was a forbidding site at best, and engineers told Olmstead that by the time of the opening of the Fair the Lake would be four feet higher than it was at the time he was studying the plan.

Olmstead was retained as a consulting landscape architect on August 20, 1890. John Root was made consulting architect the next day. This appointment was amended on September 4, at Root's request, to include his partner, Burnham.[8] In October Root was made consulting architect, and Burnham chief of construction. They reported to E. T. Jeffery, chairman of the Grounds and Building Committee. Burnham was now forty-three years old. Burnham and Root had been in practice in Chicago since 1873; the firm had built nearly forty million dollars' worth of buildings. No other Chicago firm, and certainly few other firms in the country, had done as much. Besides their work in Chicago, Burnham and Root had built everywhere in America, with one exception—they had done no building in the chief cities of the East.

As matters stood in the fall of 1890, Olmstead's general scheme of land and water, which he and Root had worked out together for the Jackson Park site, was accepted. It was tentatively assumed that Burnham and Root could do the whole job. As Sullivan said, "The idea was sound in principle—one hand, one great work—a superb revelation of America's potency—an oration, a portrayal, to arouse that which was hidden, to call it forth into the light." But as Sullivan goes on to point out, "the work of ten years cannot be done in two. It would require two years to grasp and analyze the problem and effect a synthesis. Less than three years were available for the initiation and completion of the work entire, ready for the installation of exhibit." As a consequence, one firm, even Burnham and Root, the largest in Chicago and one of the largest in America, was not enough. What America and Chicago lacked, Sullivan tells us, was a "veteran mind seasoned to the strategy and tactics" of producing a Fair where the new American culture of Chicago could express itself.

"The White City by the Lake," as the Fair became in its final, classical form, was not Root's vision of the Fair. Though the Grounds and Buildings Committee intended to invite collaboration of other architects, it took no initiative in this, but allowed Root to form his own schemes. It was taken for granted by the majority of directors, the press, and the public that Root would be the designer of the principal buildings. Root's fellow architects also expected this. Eastern architects had no expectation of participating in the work, and Chicago architects suspected they might be excluded. Foot's conception of the Fair differed greatly from the classical White City. Monroe tells us that if Root had lived and if his ideas had prevailed, "the Columbian Exposition would have been a City of Color." The fundamental point, Monroe continues, in Root's creed and the creed of the Chicago school of the eighties, was that a building should frankly express its purpose and its material. "Thus it would have been impossible for him to design, as the chief buildings of the Fair, imitations in staff of marble palaces: these could not express their material; or to adopt a classic motive: this could not express the purpose of a modern American exposition."

Root wanted to express frankly in his design the temporary character of the Fair. It

would be a great, joyous, luxuriant midsummer efflorescence, born to bloom for an hour and perish—a splendid buoyant thing, flaunting its gay colors between the shifting blues of sky and lake exultantly, prodigally. Edifices built in pursuance of this idea should not be given the illusion of weight and permanence: they should be lighter, gayer, more decorative than the solid structures along our streets. To his mind the dominant note in our civilization was its youth, its newness, crudeness: manifestly things were beginning here,—beginning with a swift rush and turmoil of creative energies. He wanted to show its affluence, its sumptuous conquering enthusiasm. He wished to offer to the older nations a proof of new forces, new ideals, not yet developed and completed but full of power and prophetic of charm. He wished to express our militant democracy as he felt it, pausing after victory for a song of triumph before taking up its onward march.[9]

There is hardly a trace of a classic motif in all the sketches Root drew. Monroe, who watched these sketches grow into final forms, describes them as "unconventional or even bizarre, conceived in a lyric mood with delightful freshness and spontaneity." His idea of a "World's Fair would not have given the nations a Celestial City—it would not have been divine." Something perhaps, "more like the Kremlin or Nishni-Novgorod," which would "appeal to the popular imagination." This would have been done through color. This is why, Monroe thinks, Henry Ives Cobb's Fisheries Building and Sullivan's Transportation Building, "with its beautiful Golden Door, were the best example on the Fair grounds of Root's ideas of Fair architecture." Root's imagination was deeply affected by color. Even music translated itself into color to his imagination: "symphonies flashed themselves out to his eye as well as his ear." Monroe tells us that he "wrote somewhere of the 'reds and yellows of brasses, the greens of oboes and flageolets, the violets of cellos, and the blues of violins.'" He looked forward to the development of color as a great art of the future. In an essay on "The Art of Pure Color," he argues that in this art of the future "the arrangements of color will be written upon a score, like the notes of music, and we shall sit enchanted while the performer plays for us this symphony."[10] In a color symphony we shall see, as in Beethoven's *Eroica,* "the struggle of the human soul through mists of doubt, through darks of despair, into fullness of day, into the greenness of fields, and the bloom of flowers."

Root's vision of a great Fair filled with fire and color was approved by Burnham in the appointment of William Prettyman, a close friend of Root, as Director of Color for the Fair. He experimented in the tinting of staff with thin washes of pure transparent oil colors, believing that opaque paint of the ordinary kind would harden the delicate material, and that white especially would destroy its creamy translucency. Monroe and Tallmadge, who saw these experiments, tell us that beautiful results were obtained. "Any one who saw the Fisheries Building . . . when it was first completed in 1892, and noted the lovely amber tones of the staff melting graciously into the sunlight, could not fail to feel a painful shock when this seductive bloom was hidden forever under the heavier white. Somehow the poetry of the building seemed to have gone out of it."[11] As evidence of the great vitality

(*Top*) Sullivan's Transportation Building at the World's Fair. *Chicago Architectural Photographing Company*

(*Bottom*) Sullivan's Golden Door in his Transportation Building was a great dramatic splash of color and modernity in the white, classical Fair. *Courtesy Chicago Historical Society*

of Root's conception Monroe turns to Sullivan's Transportation Building. "I am convinced that the people would have responded with joy to an intelligent use of color in the treatment of buildings at the great festival, that it would have added a strong sense of beauty and gayety, and emphasized the grandeur of noble façades. The Transportation Building, with its beautiful Golden Door, was an interesting experiment in this direction, although Mr. Sullivan's sumptuous orientalism was scarcely given a fair setting as the only strong note of color among many classic façades of changeless white." [12]

Sullivan shared Root's vision of an American Fair, as we know from a passage in his autobiography and from his Transportation Building. We know, too, that the Transportation Building with its brilliant color and golden door, was as popular with the people as with foreign critics,[13] who thought it the only significant American building of the Fair. An American Fair, Sullivan says in recalling the hopes of the young radicals gathered under Root's leadership, would have arisen as "a gorgeous Garden City, reflex of one mind, truly interpreting the aspirations and the heart's desire of the many, every detail carefully considered, every function given its due form, with the sense of humanity at its best, a suffusing atmosphere; and within the Garden City might be built another city to remain and endure as a memorial, within the parkland by the blue waters, oriented toward the rising sun, a token of a covenant of things to be, a symbol of the city's basic significance as offspring of the prairie, the lake and the portage." [14]

Notes

[1] Carnegie Hall was recently saved from destruction by Governor Rockefeller because of its "wonderful acoustics" and the memory of great performances held there. Few press stories in April of 1960 even mentioned Dankmar Adler's name.

[2] Edward T. Jeffery presented to the Congressional Committee on the Location of the Columbian Exposition, a document certifying that five million dollars had been subscribed by Chicagoans. To this he added "some striking statistics" showing the construction activities of the city in the recent period, the receipts and shipments, the value of manufactured goods, the ability of Chicago to take care of a multitude of visitors, the railroad facilities, and the immense tonnage of its lake commerce. He also paid tribute to the energy and enterprise of the people of Chicago. J. Seymour Currey, *Chicago, Its History and Its Builders,* 3 vols. (Chicago: S. J. Clarke, 1919), Vol. III, p. 7.

[3] See Currey, *op. cit.,* Vol. III, Ch. XLI, "Formative Period of the World's Fair," for a discussion of the financial aspects of the Fair.

[4] *Ibid.* On p. 7 he lists the members of the Illinois corporation. This list bears out Lovett's contention that the World's Fair was the "swan song of the feudal barons of Chicago." On the policy level, where allocation of money was decided, there were few professional men, and engineers were selected because they knew how to make and spend money, not because of their skill as engineers. Chicago boards, such as that of the University of Chicago, are still heavily staffed by businessmen.

[5] Charles Moore, *Daniel Burnham, Architect, Planner of Cities,* 2 vols. (Boston and New York: Houghton, Mifflin, 1921), Vol. I, p. 32. This is the story of the Fair told from the classicist's point of view, just as Monroe's memoir on Root tells the story of the Fair through Root's eyes and Sullivan's autobiography describes it from the view of the Chicago school. Thomas E. Tallmadge, in his *Story of Architecture in America* (New York: Norton, 1936), tells it from the view of an architect who abandoned the principles of the Chicago school, and who thought the Chicago school had produced a style, but not an order, of architecture. There are many references to the Fair in the literature of the time. Norton's letters and Adams's chapter on Chicago in his *Education of Henry Adams* represent the views of the cultured New England and Boston elite. But there was also a popular literature on visits to the Fair, as indeed there was on the city itself.

[6] This was not the only time railroads forced Chicagoans to abandon civic projects. Today, in 1965, the redevelopment of Chicago's Loop waits on an agreement among the railroads.

[7] Frederick Law Olmstead, "The Landscape Architecture of the World's Columbian Exposition," a paper read before the convention of the American Institute of Architects, Chicago, 1893.

[8] Moore as champion of Burnham, and Monroe as champion of Root, do not agree on the role of Burnham. In the first months of planning, Burnham apparently had little to do with the architecture of the Fair. He was regarded as an organizer and administrator, not as a designer, by Chicago architects. Unfortunately for the future of American architecture, this was not Burnham's conception of his role. He thought of himself as a great architect. In her autobiography, *A Poet's Life: Seventy Years in a Changing World* (New York: Macmillan, 1938), Harriet Monroe tells us Burnham took Root's death as a personal affront by God. "Through the night watch [over Root's body] my Aunt Nettie . . . sat on the dark upper curve of the stairway which led directly from the living room of narrow Astor Street House. Afterwards she told a strange story of Dan Burnham's pacing out the hours and talking to himself at times under the room where his partner lay dead. He seemed to be rebuking supernal powers: 'I have worked, I have schemed and dreamed to make us the greatest architects of the world—I have made him see it and kept him at it—and now he dies—damn! damn! damn!' His snatches of soliloquy through that night of despair, before he emerged to new dreams, took the form of wrath, and he shook his fist and cursed the murderous fates as he paced back and forth between intervals of comfortless sleep on the living room couch" (p. 114). She then goes on to describe Burnham's megalomania (which increased with age, as Sullivan in agreement with Monroe, points out in his autobiography): "I mean no disparagement in telling this story. Burnham was a great man in the way of a powerful executive; he was one of those magnificent egoists who rule their world. It was instinctive with him to claim the credit for the firm's work. Root could and did call him down now and then [Sullivan also says this] as long as he lived; but the younger man [Root], humourous and amused, did not care much who got the credit while his solemn and impressive partner got the jobs for him to work at. But Burnham's belief in himself as the inspiration for the firm's buildings never wavered. About three years later, when I had one or two long talks with him while preparing my memoir of Root, I was amazed at his unconquerable egoism. It was not fraud or pose; he sincerely believed that he was the virtual designer of Burnham and Root's buildings, in spite of the complete change in his firm's whole system of design which occurred under Atwood, his new classical-minded partner, after the death of Root" (p. 114).

[9] Monroe, *op. cit.,* pp. 243-44. Monroe's description of Root's conception was based on many conversations with Root, as well as talks with others who worked with him.

Tallmadge, whose *Architecture in Old Chicago* (Chicago: University of Chicago Press, 1941) is one of our important source books, agrees with Monroe.

[10] Root was a musician, not merely an instrumentalist, possessed of (as Monroe says) "thorough musical scholarship and good training. He was proficient in harmony and counterpoint, and familiar with the development and history of music. He would sit in his easy-chair of an evening, and enjoy a musical score just as others enjoy a poem or a novel. Even among professionals one rarely encounters a musical memory so richly stored, so ready and available." Harriet Monroe, *John Wellborn Root: A Study of His Life and Work* (New York: Houghton, Mifflin, 1896), pp. 201–2. As he lay dying musical images thronged Root's mind. His last words were about music.

Like Sullivan, Adler, Edelmann, and Veblen, Root felt no antagonism between science and art. The two cultures, as we are hearing them called now, were, for the architects of the Chicago school, one culture. The lesson science taught art, they insisted, was how to deal with problems and to seek true solutions to them. Art must do the same. The "strange hostility" between science and art, says Root, is based on the wrong notion that science "deals with that which is, art with that which seems to be." But this is no longer true of science, "for the actual vision has been expanded a thousand fold, and is still expanding through the influences of greater knowledge. In nearly every art career in the world, on the other hand, has been seen the slow obscuration of pure vision, and the substitution of perverted judgement; and thus the artist finally fails to see truly what is. It is here, as elsewhere, that science may be helpful."

[11] *Ibid.,* p. 246.

[12] *Ibid.,* p. 245. Despite her sensitivity as a poet, Monroe was not a very perceptive critic of architecture. Her remarks on the Fair show that as she grew older her love of Root's architecture was rooted more deeply in her regard for him as a person than in her understanding of the principles of the Chicago school. She says in 1938, some forty-two years after her first appraisal of Root's work, "[The Fair] was exotic, anachronistic, no doubt—not Root's idea of a modern show pointing to the future; rather a dream of classic beauty, rising 'like an exhalation' out of the shining waters of Lake Michigan. . . . Even though the Renaissance palaces around its Court of Honor may have retarded that development of a modern style which we are following breathlessly today after two-score years, yet, like all great achievements of beauty, it became an incalculably inspiring force which lasted into the 'next age' " (Monroe, *A Poet's Life,* pp. 132–33). In 1915 she summed up the beauty of the Fair not so much in its classical architecture as in its landscape art. "Why was there a magic in the Columbian Fair which no other had possessed? . . . No other festal city has been so spacious by land and water, with buildings so nobly grouped beside larger lagoons. No other has achieved the Venetian magic of water life among palaces—little launches and gondolas moving from building to building between mirrored colonnades, or drifting around a wooded island as wild as a Sierran valley, and then passing out into the dark lake until the city was a string of jewels in the distance. And at night, when the palaces were hung with lights that trailed gold fringes in the water, when the boats drifted in and out of the shadows, and iridescent domes and towers faded off into darkness—then was a passion of great beauty evoked out of dust and fire; for a moment all unreal things were real, and dreams had the hardihood of marble. . . . No gala city was ever so beautiful as this Columbian city at night. We Americans are wasteful of our treasures, spendthrift even of memories" (*A Poet's Life,* p. 138).

[13] The *Union Centrale des Arts Décoratifs* awarded Sullivan a medal for this building. French observers, like Bourget, were far more impressed with the Transportation Building than with the classical Fair.

[14] Louis Sullivan, *The Autobiography of an Idea* (New York: Press of American Institute of Architects, 1926), p. 319.

38

The Defeat of the Chicago School at the World's Fair: Chicago Yields to the East

ALTHOUGH the general scheme of the Fair, as drawn by Root after consultation with Olmstead, Burnham, and A. Gottlieb, had been officially adopted by the National Commission on December 1, 1890, it was, as Moore says, "a crude outline without suggestion of architectural treatment or style." Up to this time, he continues, "nothing had been done or said as to the architecture proper, except idly and in a desultory way," although, as he admits, "Mr. Root was leaning to variety in style and color for the buildings." It was widely assumed that Root would be the designer of the principal buildings, and during the early stages of planning, as Monroe tells us, "Eastern architects had no hope of participating in the work." It was to be a Chicago Fair in architecture, planning, construction, and promotion.

But it soon became obvious that no single firm of architects, let alone any single architect, could take over nearly seven hundred acres of land, most of which was swamp, and plan, design, and build an Exposition within thirty-one months. And it soon became obvious, too, that if Root was to function as artistic director he must be responsible for the selection and direction of architects and artists who would regard themselves as his equal. Agreement could be reached only through persuasion; disagreement among equals could be resolved only through discussion and arbitration. This required a director who could function as an impartial judge. But to the degree that he was an artist he could not be impartial, and time and energy spent in judging impartially and holding meetings to persuade others to accept such judgment, was time lost from the creation of architecture. Chicago architects, Monroe tells us, "were bitterly suspicious of exclusion." [1] Root soon discovered that being responsible for direction as well as design was a heavy burden. "I remember how Root came home one evening, soon after his appointment, cut to the quick because one of these, always hitherto a friend, had apparently refused to recognize Mr. Burnham when they met at a club. 'I suppose he thinks we are going to hog it all!' he exclaimed, disheartened." Root decided not to design any of the chief buildings in Jackson Park. To be an impartial judge of the work of other architects, while accepting commissions for the same project, would be impossible, Root concluded. At the same time, both Burnham and Root wanted to give the Fair a "national character" by inviting the leading architects of the country to take part in it.

In December of 1890 Root presented a memorial to the Committee on Grounds and Buildings, describing impartially four possible ways of selecting architects. He began by stressing that Chicago must realize the importance of the kind of buildings to house the exhibits. These "buildings should, in their design, relationship, and arrangement, be of the highest possible architectural merit [for this is] of importance scarcely less than the variety, richness, and comprehensiveness of the various displays within them." The buildings, if not the exhibits, would be a cultural display. Money alone was not enough. There must be "thought, knowledge, and enthusiasm by men known to be in every way endowed with these qualities." And the "results achieved by them will be the measure by which America, and especially Chicago, must expect to be judged by the world." [2] The four methods of selection proposed in the memorial are described as first, the selection of one man to whom the designing of the entire work should be entrusted; second, competition made free to the whole architectural profession; third, competition among a selected few; and fourth, direct selection. The first would produce a coherent and logical result, but no single man could do good work in the short time allotted to him. Although successful in Europe, open competition would not work because too much time would be required to bring competitive designs into any kind of coherent plan, and many good architects in America would not enter such competitions because of the uncertain returns for the time and money spent in the preparation of plans. Limited and paid competition would be better, but again, far too much time would be required for the competitors to familiarize the purposes of the exhibits, etc. Direct selection of a number of eminent architects who would work together and agree on some general scheme of procedure would be best. Those selected would feel so deeply the honor of selection that they would place artistic excellence before money, and thus, "in a rivalry so dignified and friendly could not fail to produce a result which would stand before the world as the best fruit of American civilization."

After much discussion, the recommendations in the memorial were adopted. On request of the committee, Burnham and Root designated five architectural firms, and the committee promptly confirmed the selection. Richard M. Hunt, George B. Post and McKim, Mead, and White, of New York; Peabody and Stearns, of Boston; and Van Brunt and Howe, of Kansas City, were notified of their selection in a letter sent by Burnham. On receipt of Burnham's invitation, the Eastern architects met in the office of McKim,

Mead, and White. A common height of cornice was recommended, and, while there is no record of open discussion of style, Mead (who was present at this meeting) tells us that it "was the unanimous opinion of the Eastern architects that the classic motive should be used." [3] Burnham and Root's idea of a unified composition was acceptable to all. As Burnham's letter stated, these architects were to design the main group of buildings around the Court of Honor. Monroe tells us that Root intended that other buildings were to be designed by Chicago architects.[4] The appointment of the five firms, not one of which was a Chicago firm, shocked Chicago architects and business-men alike. As Monroe says: They "were no sooner appointed than strong opposition to the employment of outsiders began to impede the action of the committee. It was said that Chicago was paying for the Fair, and Chicago men should have the designing of it; and that, moreover, professional talent in this city, compared with that in the East, was fully as competent and more progressive. Under pressure from local architects and their friends in the directory, and from the spirit of local patriotism in general, there was danger . . . that the appointment of the five firms might be rescinded." But Burnham and Root argued, in and out of official meetings, that to appoint only Chicago architects would destroy the "national character" of the Fair.[5]

On December 27 Root proposed a compromise by asking that ten Chicago firms be designated to work with the Eastern firms. The committee cut the number of Chicago firms to five, and Burling and Whitehouse, Jenney and Mundie, Henry Ives Cobb, S. S. Beman, and Adler and Sullivan were noti-fied. All accepted and agreed to attend the first meeting of the architects on January 10, 1891. On January 1, 1891, Root went East to see the appointed architects and give them some idea of Chicago's hopes for their Fair. He explained what would be demanded of them and invited them to the confer-ence on January 10, in Chicago. It was a discouraging trip for Root. The strain of preparing for the Fair was beginning to tell, and, according to Monroe, "he was somewhat depressed by the attitude of the Eastern men, whom he found singularly apathetic, utterly incredulous that any association of Western business men would give art a free hand in the manner he set forth. . . . They shared at this time the general Eastern feeling that a Columbian Exposition in Chicago would be little more than a cattle-show."

The first Chicago meeting of the Easterners took place in the offices of Burnham and Root, with Hunt in the chair and Sullivan acting as secre-tary. After the meeting, Burnham drove the visitors to Jackson Park. It was a cold winter day with overcast sky. The surging lake was covered with foam. As they looked out over the sandy wastes of Jackson Park, Peabody of Boston broke the silence, "Do you mean to say that you really propose opening a Fair here by '93?" Burnham replied that such was their intention. Peabody replied flatly that this was impossible. Burnham answered that Chicagoans would see to it that the site would be ready, and that the Easterners could regard that point as settled. The Grounds and Buildings Committee acted as hosts for the city in the evening. Gage presided at the dinner. Jeffery spoke, and then Burnham took the floor. He said that in one sense the Columbian Exposition was to be the third great American event, comparable to 1776 and 1861. "In both these crises men came to the front and gave themselves up to the public. So the times now demand self-sacrifice. The success of this undertaking depends upon team work." [6]

Peabody's reaction to the sandy wastes of Jackson Park was shared by Hunt, Post, and Mead. Root complained to his wife and to Harriet Monroe that he could not get these Easterners interested in what he considered the greatest opportunity ever offered American architects. They were coming to the conference, but reluctantly; their hearts were not in it. The following evening the architects gathered at the Root home for tea. "In talking with them," Harriet Monroe tells us, "I was amazed at their listless and hopeless attitude toward the great undertaking which brought them to Chicago. Beautiful effects were scarcely to be expected in buildings so enormous and cheaply constructed; the level monotony of the ground surfaces in Chicago made effective grouping practically impossible; the time for preparation and construction was too short: these and other criticisms indicated a general feeling of disparagement." [7]

But underlying all talk about money, the shortage of time, and the inadequacy of the site was unstated but profound disagreement over style. The Easterners wanted classical buildings; the Westerners, led by Root, wanted an American style.[8] The January meeting of the architects did not settle problems of style. This was to be done at the next meeting in February. Burnham thought the best expression of American culture would follow from placing all important Fair designs in the hands of the Easterners. The culture of New England, and its expression in classical architecture, was far superior to that of the crude "commercial" architecture. Although in the December meeting Jeffery had forced Burnham to include Chicago architects, in the January meeting no allocations of buildings were made, for the problem of style and the degree to which either side would yield had not yet been faced.

But before the next meeting could take place, John Wellborn Root was stricken with pneumonia. On the evening following the first meeting on

January 10th he had invited the Eastern architects to his home. It was a cold raw night, yet he insisted on seeing each guest to his carriage. He caught a cold, which soon became pneumonia. As the pain in his chest deepened, he realized he was very ill, but he made no complaints and sent to the office for his drawing board. He was unable to work. As his strength ebbed, his mind filled with visions of color and music. The sounds of music grew louder as death approached. He turned to the women of the family gathered around the bed and said: "Do you hear that music?" And when they assured him that it was lovely, he put his hands on the counterpane and played, as if seated at a piano. His voice grew rich and deep once again for his last words. "That's what I call music—grand," and as he said this he lifted his hands from the imaginary keyboard, and died.[9]

Root's death shocked the city. Root was greatly loved for what he was—an artist and a Chicagoan who loved his city even as he realized its faults. Eugene Field, poet, humorist, and the first modern columnist, paid tribute to his intelligence, wit, and above all his great warmth and cordiality. "Successful to a remarkable degree and admired by all with whom he came in contact, his relations with all were tempered with singular modesty, thoughtfulness and benevolence; he was charitable, kindly, liberal; now that his strong brain and warm heart and willing hands are at rest, the stately edifices that bear witness to his genius, bespeak for him our reverential regard far less potently than does the memory of the brave, generous personality that shall gladden us no more on earth." As the preparations for the fateful February meeting went on, Sullivan, as well as other Chicago architects, realized the fearful blow their cause had suffered. "Louis missed him sadly. Who now would take up the foils he had dropped on his way, from hands that were once so strong? There was none!"[10]

Richard Hunt, acknowledged dean of American architects, was given the chair of the February meeting. Louis Sullivan acted as secretary. Burnham arose and began his speech of welcome. To the consternation of the Chicagoans and to the embarrassment of the Eastern architects, Burnham began by "progressively and grossly apologizing to the Eastern men for the presence of their benighted brethren of the West." This was more than Hunt could stand. He interrupted: "Hell, we haven't come out here on a missionary expedition. Let's get to work." Everyone agreed. Burnham accepted the correction of his bad taste and joined in discussion as a layout was submitted for approval. As the day progressed it soon became obvious that the Fair was to be a classical Fair. The East had won. Men trained in the schools of Europe, bound by precedents of a classical past, and led by a Chicagoan, Burnham, denied their city and watched Burnham destroy every ideal cherished by his dead partner. As the betrayal of the Chicago school went on, the enthusiasm of the classicists mounted. Burnham tells us:

The winter afternoon was drawing to an end. The room was as still as death, save for the low voice of the speaker commenting on his design. It seemed as if a great magnet held everyone in its grasp. Finally, when the last drawing had been shown, Mr. Gage drew a long breath. Standing against a window and shutting his eyes, he exclaimed, "Oh, gentlemen, this is a dream." Then, opening his eyes, he smilingly continued, "You have my good wishes, I hope the dream can be realized." . . . All day long Saint-Gaudens had been sitting in a corner, never opening his mouth and scarcely moving. He came over to me, and taking both my hands said, "Look here, old fellow, do you realize that this is the greatest meeting of artists since the fifteenth century!" [11]

Burnham's selection as Chief of Construction was amply justified. All were moved to admiration by his capacity for large-scale planning. Even Sullivan, who thought the Fair an "appalling calamity" and hated everything that Burnham stood for in architecture, admitted that Burnham performed in a masterful way, "displaying remarkable executive capacity." He was "open-minded, just, magnanimous. He did his great share." A few weeks before the Fair gates were opened to the public, Burnham's fellow architects and the citizens of New York honored him with a dinner. As James S. Norton of New York, who responded to the toast of Chicago, made clear, Chicago would now be known as a center of art as well as commerce. "This is, indeed, a new sensation for Chicago. Hitherto she has received from this quarter full recognition of her claims as a pork, beef, and grain market, and scant courtesy to her aspirations for art and culture. That now, in this city [New York] of accomplishments, her chosen representative should receive the plaudits of the very elect for his services to art, is at least a sweet surprise." [12]

J. S. Norton then went on to sum up the discovery of Chicago by the East. Visitors to the Fair would find Chicago

the most interesting city in the world to one who studies the evolution of cities. Elsewhere the phases of development have succeeded each other too slowly to be noted except in part through the imperfect medium of history. There the changes have come so rapidly within the field of view that the entire process may be seen. The whole marvelous transformation from the trading post to the chosen theatre of a world's pageant has come within the range of single lives far from spent. . . . We see her now, a field of prodigious activities, a marvel of brilliant achievement, a turbulent school of sociology. It has fallen to this generation to see the elements of society in violent agitation; and just now the storm-center seems to be over Chicago. . . . We know that in [Chicago] men are being moulded by the pressure of events; that the incessant urgency of life . . . is breeding a race of men fit for responsibilities; and that the same energy which has made her in half a century a great spectacular city, is now surely tending toward the better purpose of her life.[13]

Charles Eliot Norton, Professor of Fine Arts at Harvard and the most powerful architectural critic in America, acted as spokesman for architecture, sculpture, and painting. His talk created the surprise of the evening, and soon he became front-page news in the East. Norton had always disliked the West. In an essay published in 1888, "The Intellectual Life of America," he had said: "The prevailing spirit of the West . . . is not promising. It is not modest; it is not serious; it is not large-minded. In a word, it exaggerates the defects in the spirit and temper of the country at large." The only hope for the West was that its great energy might be turned to culture, as the businessmen of Florence and Venice had turned from making money to the cultivation of the arts. But such hope was at best a small hope. There was little in the West, or all America for that matter, to inspire belief in American culture. He taught his students at Harvard that the golden age of Athens, the flowering of the Gothic style in Venice and Florence, and the Renaissance in Italy were the great periods. The Renaissance was the terminal point in Norton's survey of art history. There was little significant art after 1600.[14]

To the amazement of his audience, and to the wonderment of Eastern intellectuals, Norton stated flatly that the Chicago Exposition was the highest art achievement in America's history.

The general design of the grounds and of the arrangement of the buildings was in every respect noble, original and satisfactory, a work of fine art not generally included in the list of poetic arts, but one of the most important of them all to America—that of the landscape architect. Of all American artists, Frederick Law Olmstead, who gave the design for the laying out of the grounds of the World's Fair, stands first in the production of great works which answer the needs and give expression to the life of our immense and miscellaneous democracy. The buildings which surround the Court of Honor, so-called, at Chicago, make a splendid display of monumental architecture. They show how well our ablest architects have studied the work of the past; and the arrangement of the buildings according to the general plan produces a superb effect in the successful grouping in harmonious relations of vast and magnificent structures.[15]

In closing he singled out Atwood's Palace of Fine Arts as a particularly noteworthy architectural design.

Norton's admiration of the Fair was such a change from his previously expressed opinions on the West that rumors began to circulate that he intended to forsake Cambridge and move to Chicago. When approached by the press Norton said that the rumor grew out of his saying to William James that if he were a younger man he should like to cast his lot in with a city like Chicago. A Cambridge newspaper, quoting from an interview with Norton, reported that Norton said with conviction: "I like Chicago. I like the spirit, the civic power of the place." After praising Atwood's art building and Olmstead's landscape work, the news story went on to say: "He [Norton] said more for Mr. Burnham's personal honor than the modest Director of Works [Burnham] would have believed he or any other Chicago man could win from the Harvard professor who is popularly reputed to admire nothing modern, not even the modern man. But to Mr. Norton the civic enthusiasm and success of Chicago seem to be embodied in Mr. Burnham." [16]

On May 1, 1893, the great Exposition opened its gates to the people. For most, it was a revelation of the art of architecture. Only a few among the millions of visitors had experienced great architecture. Even those who knew the glories of architecture were deeply moved.[17] In his *Story of Architecture in America,* Tallmadge says:

The Exposition as completed, with its banners fluttering in the breeze, its fountains splashing in the sunshine, its lagoons troubled by the course of the launches and gondolas which crashed into a million fragments a fairy vision reflected on their breasts, its emerald lawns jewelled with flowers and birds, and its tremendous and many palaces with their regal equipment of terraces, bridges and esplanades all bathed in sunshine against the azure setting of the lake, furnished a spectacle unequalled in the history of the world for the magnificence of its beauty. Imperial Rome in the third century might have approached but surely did not surpass it. Such was the conviction of my boyhood, and thirty-five years of increasing sophistication, which have included most of the architectural spectacles of the generation, have not dimmed the splendor of that picture nor changed in my mind the school-boy's verdict.[18]

Notes

[1] As events showed, their suspicions were justified. Monroe tells us that "Burnham and Root had determined weeks before in the December meeting when the first five firms were nominated upon their board of architects. . . ." Harriet Monroe, *John Wellborn Root: A Study of His Life and Work* [New York: Houghton, Mifflin, 1896] p. 238). But Root had no intention of doing a classical fair, as the appointment of Prettyman as Director of Color shows.

[2] There are two versions of this memorial: the earliest is given by Monroe (*op. cit.,* pp. 236–38) from the "original manuscript in his [Root's] handwriting. Another version is given by Moore in his life of Burnham (see Vol. I, pp. 37–41). Moore states the Burnham "drew up a memorial," while Monroe states that "Root [not Burnham] presented a memorial." Moore omits one very significant sentence in the original as given by Monroe: "The precise relationship between the directory and these architects might safely be left to the general conference, at which all questions of detail could be agreed upon" (Monroe, *op. cit.,* p. 238). As events proved, Burnham had every intention of turning the design of Fair buildings over to Eastern architects.

[3] Charles Moore, *Daniel Burnham, Architect, Planner of Cities,* 2 vols. (Boston and New York: Houghton, Mifflin, 1921), Vol. I, p. 42.

[4] There is no reference to this in Moore's life of Burnham, and, since Moore had access to the Monroe memoir, we must assume that this was never Burnham's intention. Moore treats Burnham as an Olympian figure who was above "petty bickering." He characterizes Monroe's life of Root as a "romantic memoir."

[5] Moore makes no mention of the struggle between Burnham and Chicago businessmen and architects over the selection of Eastern architects.

[6] Moore, *op. cit.,* I, 43. The implication here is that Burnham always intended using Chicago architects, but, as Burnham's letter of December 12 to the five selected firms shows, he was writing them "to secure the service of five architects to design the main group of buildings at Jackson Park."

[7] Monroe, *op. cit.,* p. 249. Again Moore and Monroe do not agree. Moore states that Burnham met "at dinner in New York [on December 22] Mr. Hunt, Mr. Post, Mr. Mead, and Mr. Peabody. . . . The Eastern architects were lukewarm. Chicago was a long way from home. They were skeptical as to funds. It took all of Mr. Burnham's power of persuasion to win them over; but once committed they became enthusiastic" (I, 42). Of the first Chicago meeting, which Monroe says did nothing to lift Root's distress over the attitude of the Easterners, Moore says: "There was fine response to Burnham's call for the spirit of 1776 and 1861. The Chicago men promptly responded to the old appeal of the Spirit of Chicago on which they had been brought up. From that night the spirit of cooperation never failed" (I, 43).

[8] Burnham admitted this. Moore quotes Burnham as saying: "I cannot, of course, believe that the architecture of the Exposition would have been better had he lived, but it certainly would have been modified and stamped with something of his great individuality" (Moore, *op. cit.,* I, 44–45).

[9] This is taken from Monroe's account, pp. 260–63.

[10] Louis H. Sullivan, *The Autobiography of an Idea* (New York: Press of American Institute of Architects, 1926), p. 320. Root typified the architect-artist as well as architect-engineer, to the city. Among architects he was always distinguished—as an *architect*—from Burnham, the promoter and organizer and administrator. After his death, Burnham took over the mantle of artist as well as administrator—to the people, if not to architects. Fuller and other Chicago novelists, such as Herrick, used Burnham as their model of the architect in Chicago.

[11] Moore, *op. cit.,* I, 47.

[12] This speech is quoted by Moore, *op. cit.,* I, 75–78.

[13] *Ibid.,* 78.

[14] See Kermit Vanderbilt, *Charles Eliot Norton: Apostle of Culture in a Democracy* (Cambridge: Harvard University Press, 1959), pp. 201–10, for a discussion of Norton's attitude toward the Fair. Norton's opinions on art had great weight. He was regarded as one of the most cultured figures in American life. He had been an intimate friend of Oliver Wendell Holmes and was considered the last of the Cambridge Immortals. John Ruskin, Matthew Arnold, and Thomas Carlyle considered him to be a leading American thinker and her greatest scholar. In 1895 he was drawing nearly five hundred students to his classes in fine arts at Harvard.

[15] Quoted from Moore, *op. cit.,* pp. 78–79.

[16] Quoted from Moore, *op. cit.,* p. 79.

[17] Henry Adams, Norton, William James, Harriet Monroe, and Tallmadge are but a few of the sophisticated observers who left testimonials of their admiration for the Fair.

[18] As a young architect in Chicago, Tallmadge was a follower of Sullivan and the radicals of the Chicago school. He worked for Burnham for about seven years, and,

like Burnham, turned away from the principles of the Chicago school. All his writings of Chicago architecture are born of long familiarity with the city and its architects. In *Architecture in Old Chicago* (Chicago: University of Chicago Press, 1941) he admits that his estimate of Sullivan and the Chicago school was wrong, as he also did in his revised edition of *The Story of Architecture in America* (New York: Norton), which appeared in 1936.

PART SIX

Sullivan's Creation of an American Philosophy of Architecture: A Resolution of Culture and Democracy

39

*The Lessons of the Fair: The Unresolved Tension
between Culture and Democracy*

To Sullivan the Fair was a catastrophe. From the morning of the
February meeting, when he realized that Burnham was turning over control
of design to the Easterners, to the last years of his life, when he was revising
Kindergarten Chats and finishing his *Autobiography of an Idea,* he searched
deeply for explanations for the defeat of the Chicago school. The real tragedy
in Sullivan's eyes was in the betrayal of the American people, who were
exposed to what he called "an imposition of the spurious, . . . a naked exhi-
bitionism of charlatanry in the higher feudal and domineering culture,
enjoined with expert salesmanship of the materials of decay." The American
people "had not had time nor occasion to become immune to forms of
sophistication not their own, [nor] to a higher and more dexterously insidious plausibility." These deluded people left the Fair joyously, "unaware that
what they had beheld and believed to be the truth was to prove, in historic
fact, an appalling calamity." [1]

The Fair, Sullivan insisted, honored neither Chicago, America, nor even
Columbus. The "structure representing the United States Government was
of an incredible vulgarity, while the building at the peak of the north Axis,
stationed there as a symbol of 'The Great State of Illinois' matched it as a
lewd exhibit of drooling imbecility and political debauchery. . . . South of
them, and placed on the border of a small lake, stood the Palace of the Arts,
the most vitriolic of them all—the most impudently thievish." [2] The landscape work alone was significant, for with its "genial distribution of lagoons,
wooded islands, lawns, shrubbery and plantings," it did much to "soften an
otherwise mechanical display." Aside from replicas of the three caravels of
Columbus and a representation of the monastery of La Rabida, there was no
homage paid to Columbus "and his daring deed, his sufferings, and his
melancholy end." There was no keynote, no "dramatic setting forth of that
deed which, recently, has aroused some discussion as to whether the discovery
of America had proven to be a blessing or a curse to the world of mankind."

But what disturbed Sullivan, and what Sullivan's young apprentice, Frank
Lloyd Wright, never forgot, was the architects' betrayal of themselves. It was

Burnham, not Jeffery, who handed the Fair over to the Classicists. Sullivan alone stood against Burnham. He insisted that his building be a statement of what it was—a great transportation display which would welcome people with a wonderful portal designed in the Chicago tradition. Cobb's Fisheries Building, "the swan song of the Romanesque," with its gay and charming ornament of sea horses, lobsters, and frogs, stood beside Sullivan's Transportation Building in revolt against Eastern classicism. But even this building, whose very essence was the play of color in light, was painted over with white to match the classical buildings.[3] As Sullivan looked back at Burnham's career, he concluded that Chicago architects had failed as artists because they did not understand the function of art in society or the specific relationship between art and democracy. "Daniel Burnham was obsessed by the feudal idea of power.[4] Louis Sullivan was equally obsessed by the beneficent idea of Democratic power. Daniel chose the easier way, Louis the harder. Both brooded incessantly." A democratic architecture demanded complete commitment to the struggle for form. The refusal of Chicago architects to take themselves seriously as artists left them powerless in a struggle against those, like Burnham, who knew what they wanted and believed deeply in their mission as American artists. To stand against men like Burnham, "a man with a fixed irrevocable purpose in life, for the sake of which he would bend or sacrifice all else," architects must believe deeply in the values of art in society.

Even Root failed to take his art seriously enough. In the midst of the great boom in Chicago architecture in 1890–92, when Root's buildings were soaring into the sky, Root said to Sullivan: "You take your art too seriously." Burnham had already warned Sullivan: "It is not good policy to go much above the general level of the intelligence." Yet it was Burnham with his mania for bigness, not Root, who possessed a fixed, irrevocable purpose in life. "John Root was so self-indulgent that there was risk he might never draw upon his underlying power." Adler, too, was not really a deeply committed artist but "was essentially a technician, an engineer, a conscientious administrator, a large progressive judicial and judicious mind securing alike the confidence of conservative and radical, plenty of courage but lacking the dream quality of Burnham; and such he must remain—the sturdy wheelhorse of a tandem-team of which Louis did the prancing. Unquestionably, Adler lacked sufficient imagination; so in a way did John Root—that is to say, the imagination of the dreamer. In the dream-imagination lay Burnham's strength and Louis's passion."[5]

Chicago businessmen, Sullivan warned his fellow architects, were not to blame for bad architecture. They believed in the power of money and possessed the will and imagination to impress this power on others. They were taking over American society because they realized the importance of communication. Money was nothing new in civilization; what was new was the development of a rhetoric of money. The businessman knew, if the architect often did not, that a building had a meaning, and whoever controlled the expression of such meanings would control society. More, the plutocracy knew what it wanted to communicate—the glory of money—and how to create such glory. "The populace looked on, with open-mouthed amazement and approval, at the mighty men who wrought these wonders; called them Captains of Industry, Kings of this, Barons of that, Merchant Princes, Railroad Magnates, Wizards of Finance, or, as Burnham said one day to Louis: 'Think of a man like Morgan, who can take a man like Cassatt in the palm of his hand and set him on the throne of the Pennsylvania!' And thus, in its way, the populace sang hymns to its heroes." [6]

The heart of business power was not in the "materialism" but the spiritualization of money, as exemplified by Burnham's visions of becoming the greatest architect in the world. Chicago businessmen dramatized money before audiences who were taught to identify with a new and exciting hero, the plutocratic hero expressing himself through money. In this new symbol there was promise of superiority as well as equality. Money, Sullivan's "feudal barons" knew, created a new kind of hierarchy in society. It destroyed the power of family lineage and aristocratic class, as it brought new freedom to the individual to rise in society. But in redress of traditional inequalities it created new kinds of inequalities which were considered just by businessmen because the "rules of the money game," not the will of individuals, "caused" them. And, since under these same rules status determined by money was open to all and there were few restrictions on how money could be spent, it was easy enough to equate money with freedom.

The people rejoiced, Sullivan said, because they could identify with the rich and powerful:

all rejoiced in the thought that these great men, these mighty men, had with few and negligible exceptions, risen from the ranks of the common people: That this one began as a telegraph operator at a lonely way-station, and this one was boss of a section gang on such and such a railroad; another started in life as a brakeman; that one was clerk in a country store; this one came to our hospitable shores as a penniless immigrant; that one was a farmer boy; and their hymn arose and rang shimmering as a paean to their mighty ones, and their cry went up to their God, even as a mighty anthem, lifting up its head to proclaim to all the world that this, their Country, was vastly more than the land of the free and the home of the brave; it was the noble land of equal opportunity for all; the true democracy for which mankind has been waiting through the centuries in blood and tears, in hope deferred. This, they cried, as one voice, is the

Hospitable Land that welcomes the stranger at its gates. This is the great Democracy where all men are equal and free. All this they sang gladly as they moved up and down the runways.[7]

Burnham's greatest power was his "dream-imagination." Like Pullman, he was able to conjure up whole communities and to plan the kind of organization necessary to make his visions real. He was the first architect in Chicago, and indeed in America, to see that architectural practice must shift from the studio to the office, where it must take on the corporate structure now necessary to large projects. When the young Sullivan first met Burnham (sometime in the late seventies), in the neighborhood of Prairie Avenue and Twenty-first Street, where several of Root's houses had been built, Burnham told Sullivan, "my idea is to work up a big business, to handle big things, deal with big business men, and to build up a big organization, for you can't handle big things unless you have an organization." In Burnham's eyes this was a democratic vision. There was never enough housing in the Middle West, and even when there was the varied and highly mobile life of the people created needs which made necessary building quickly and cheaply. Even in 1964, Chicago has few hallowed and cherished ruins.[8] Millions of Americans change residences every year, the young executive class lives in the same home for only three or four years. The Chicago (and American) environment has created a new psychology of time, a human time in which the future, not the past, determines the present. The American standard of living is an "ever-increasing" standard, not for a few but for all. We have a tradition in architecture. But it is a tradition of the new, not the old. We may live in a colonial house, but it must be a new imitation of traditional Colonial design.

Even the great office buildings of Chicago were not built to last, but to be amortized within twenty or thirty years. At the end of this time the building "paid for itself," and could be torn down or preserved, as income warranted. In a city which lived in the future, being "up-to-date" soon became a business tradition. A prestige location was a new and expensive location, a signification of the will and ability to spend money. The "vintage building" which evoked a hallowed past and the office where four or five generations had done business had no sacred traditional aura for Chicagoans—then or now. The money value of a building was a future value, and building design was thought of as a stage which evoked an orgiastic future where all would be shining, bold, and beautiful. In the first stages of the development of the Chicago school, business enterprise, as much as engineering and perhaps even more than architecture, was responsible for the development of the steel cage. As Sullivan says, "the Chicago activity in erecting high buildings finally attracted the attention of the local sales managers of Eastern rolling mills; and their engineers were set at work. The mills for some time past had been rolling those structural shapes that had long been in use in bridgework. Their own groundwork was thus prepared. It was a matter of vision in salesmanship based upon engineering imagination and technique. Thus the idea of the steel frame which would carry *all* the load was tentatively presented to Chicago architects." It needed the "flash of imagination" of the artist to create the steel frame. And to the honor of Chicago architects, they "welcomed the steel frame and did something with it . . . while the architects of the East" were appalled by it and could make no contribution to it.[9]

So long as the architect could master salesmen and engineers there was hope for the development of an indigenous American architecture. But the architect's task in mastering such conditions went far beyond design or thinking simply of a building as a façade. He could not accept the building as a given thing to which he applied design or ornament. The structure itself was a design in which the rhythm of space was determined by what Root, Sullivan, and Adler called "the conditions of the problem." That is, given a certain kind of act, such as selling groceries or worshiping God, how could the space in which this act is performed be so designed that the essential qualities of the act would be enhanced by the formed space in which the act took place? Sullivan tried to convince his fellow architects that this question of how to think of architectural space as a determinant of human relationships must be faced by architects if they were to control their own fate as artists in a democratic society.

Sullivan, like Dewey fifty years later in his reflections on art, wanted to bring architecture back to experience—but the experience of the urban democratic community. To do so he tried to appeal directly to those who were responsible for the new life of America. He taught that so long as the new men of the city (and their architects) were able to think about architecture as a spatial expression of the needs of acting human beings, the imagination of the architect and the power of the businessman could function creatively. For nothing betrays our misconception of the power of art, Sullivan argued, more than failure to understand that the businessman in Chicago needed the architect as much as the architect needed him. State Street merchants understood by 1900, as they had understood in 1875 and 1885, that the city must be designed as a stage for a new kind of life. A building was not a façade, but a structure related to many other structures, whose use was determined by movement *to, within,* and *from* it. And the movement to be studied was that of *customers,* not simply "people," "pedestrians," or "drivers" of cars. Burnham understood this. He did not think of architecture in

Sullivan tried to teach the architects of his time to accept the characteristic acts of the people of a free society and to stage them with all the beauty and power in their command. Carson Pirie Scott Store, looking south on State Street. *Photo by Len Gittleman, for the Sullivan Project of the Institute of Design, Illinois Institute of Technology*

Nowhere is Sullivan's principle of mobile equilibrium more clearly stated than in this façade of the Carson Pirie Scott Store. *Photo by Richard Nickel*

Chicago businessmen, not the exponents of "beautiful architecture," gave the architects of Chicago many opportunities to design freely, as we see in this view of the street level of the Carson Pirie Scott Store. *Photo by Richard Nickel*

terms of a building, but of a community, and above all of a community in motion.

The businessman wanted to bring people into the Loop, move them about in the Loop, and take them out of the Loop. He was interested in the human being as a customer, not a home dweller, a worshiper of God, a maker or enjoyer of art, a teacher or student, or voter. That is, he was not interested until he understood the relationship of these roles to making money. Burnham and the early planners taught businessmen that men could not live by trade alone. A community organized around commerce would end by having no commerce unless businessmen were willing to think of the urban world in terms of every human need. If they did not, they would lose control of the community to those who would. For money, like any other symbol of life, depended for its power on the kind of human experience it made possible. As we see in his autobiography and in the terrible rage and despair of *Democracy: A Man Search,* Sullivan realized that Burnham and his businessmen understood the function of the city as a great stage for spending, as well as earning, money. And to his horror, he discovered that Burnham, his evil genius of American architecture, understood the power of art. But the power he understood was, in Sullivan's words, the "feudal idea," which depends on mystification and fear. The tragedy of Burnham, as of Pullman, was that while both knew the power of architecture over the souls of men, they did not think as democrats but as autocrats. The tragedy of architecture was that architects themselves did not understand the importance of architecture to democracy. Their failure, as Sullivan realized, was a failure in social thought and, within the profession itself, a failure to develop significant and widely communicated criticism of the value of architecture to democracy.

Once the schools were committed to the classic style in their courses of architectural instruction, the classical architect could speak in the voice of tradition. The lack of tradition, the need for feeling that what one did was at least in some kind of cultural stream, haunted every Chicago artist. As Fuller said in his ironic stories in *Under the Skylights,* ignorance of art, or the confusion of art with craft, was all that kept many of the young painters and sculptors of Chicago at work in the nineties. The crisis in every career occurred when the artist had to define for himself the significance of art. The dilemma of the Chicago artist was not between honorable poverty in Bohemia, and art—but between loneliness, isolation, and sometimes even absurdity, and art. There was no Bohemia in Chicago, where poverty served as a badge of honor, as an identification with other artists, and at the same time a gesture of defiance toward the good burghers. There were studios, but even these were self-conscious imitations, and almost all of the artists gathered around the "Little Room" and other studios in the Fine Arts Building had some connection with wealthy Chicago women who used studio life for social ends.

Burnham, like so many Chicago artists, was a self-made artist. If the community could give these artists no tradition of art, neither could their families.[10] Burnham was nearly fifty years old before he took his first trip to Europe.[11] For Burnham, as for Fuller, the trip to Europe was a search for tradition, for something that would ease the anxiety of not really knowing what art was for, or what one stood for, in society. It was easy enough to laugh with Sullivan in *Kindergarten Chats* when he personified buildings and entered into dialogue with them as with a cast of disreputable and grotesque figures like the lecherous, thieving tramp in American burlesque. It was easy to laugh with Mark Twain over the art of Europe or the phony artists in *Huckleberry Finn,* but there was a difference between finding art—even traditional art—comic and finding it unreal. Until the Chicago artist was sure of his function in society, anxiety could not be overcome by laughter. For if comedy demanded anything it was an underlying seriousness which made the comic distinction between the ideal and the real resonant with meaning. But when the seriousness of art was not understood (or not properly valued when it was understood) laughter over traditional art could not be distinguished from laughter over all art. Sullivan discovered this in Baumann's ironic laughter. The engineers, it seemed, found all architects, not just traditionalists, ridiculous.

The search for tradition, then, was not simply a matter of making some kind of choice between one style and another, but of creating some kind of identity for the self of the artist. Thus Burnham records in his diary of his first trip to Greece: "I have the spirit of Greece once and forever stamped on my soul. It is the blue flower; the rest of life must be the dream and this land of Greece the reality." [12] Moore, Burnham's biographer, tells us that on a later trip to Europe as a member of the United States Senate Park Commission of 1901, Burnham was brought "face to face with things eternal" in Rome, where all "that man had done to express his nature in highest terms had been gathered . . . during the ages. The fleeting, the transitory, the ephemeral, the self-assertive, the struggle for originality, all seemed to drop out of mind, leaving a desire to discover and to use in the work of a new nation those forms which have satisfied age after age of men." [13] Even those who remained skeptical of the relevance of classical standards to Chicago found it difficult to challenge the linkage of classicism with the traditions not only of Europe, but of America itself. Burnham and his classicists taught that much of what seemed new and strange in classical form was really a return to early days, when the tradition of Wren had been followed in colonial architecture. For had not Washington and Jefferson insisted on classic precedents in planning America's earliest public buildings? Thus, in the last analysis, as Moore says, the adoption of classicism was "but a return to our better selves." Political leaders turned again to follow the steps of Washington and Jefferson, whose patronage of classical form stamped it with a sacred democratic aura. The linkage of political symbols with classical form soon became so deep that any civic building, to be really "civic," must be classical.[14]

But in Chicago itself, the heaviest blow to the Chicago school was its lack of acceptance for homes, clubs, or private buildings by leaders of Chicago society. It was not so much that the work of men like Root was considered a "commercial style" but that a house like the Charnley house of Wright (designed when he was still Sullivan's "pencil") evoked no social tradition. Even Root's houses, radical as they sometimes were in treatment of the wall as a plane and the grouping of windows, were still in the tradition of Richardson, whose prestige in high society was very great. Root's death was a severe enough blow to civic and commercial architecture, but to the future of significant design in domestic architecture it was even worse. Sullivan took houses only as a favor to Adler's clients, and even these he treated sometimes in a very perfunctory manner. When Root died, the link between high society and the domestic architecture of the Chicago school was shattered.

Chicago society leaders, like their artists, had no tradition of their own. Romanesque was at least a valid high society tradition. Its acceptance by such families as the Hay and Adams families in Washington and the Glessners in Chicago, placed its prestige beyond cavil. When there was any lingering doubt about style it was always possible to follow Mrs. Palmer and order a castle. If it could not be brought from Europe stone by stone, architects were available who made copies sufficiently grand to convey the majesty and power of money. For, whatever else the Potter Palmer mansion communicated, there was no doubt about its costliness. The dramatization of money was an easily understood function of architecture to Chicagoans of all classes. Only a few radicals, like Professor Veblen of the new University of Chicago, or John Root and Louis Sullivan, found a castle on Michigan Boulevard ridiculous. Readers of the society page did not know much about Veblen and Sullivan or, if they knew, were not much concerned with what they thought.

Even by 1908 Chicago society leaders were still fearful of playing their roles on stages created by Chicago architects. There was no question about the ability of men like Wright to design stages palatial enough for even the very rich, as Mrs. Harold McCormick discovered. But the question in 1908 was no longer one of how to let people know that one was rich, but of indicating to one's peers that one knew how to be rich "in style." The Palmers, like the barons of old, built their castle where it could be seen by all. But Mrs. McCormick was of a later generation. The glory of communicating with all Chicago was gone, and certainly there was no need to tell any Chicagoan that the McCormicks were rich. Now it was a matter of communicating with a new audience of peers who judged according to standards which plutocrats themselves upheld. McCormick turned to Charles Adams Platt, whose careful studies and measurements of Renaissance gardens in Italy had been published in 1894 in his *Italian Gardens*. A Platt "villa" was authentic, a clear indication to all that Mrs. McCormick, like a Henry James heroine, knew how to buy the "best" tradition.

Notes

[1] Louis Sullivan, *The Autobiography of an Idea* (New York: Press of American Institute of Architects, 1926), p. 321.

[2] This should be compared with the measured criticism of Tallmadge, who as late as 1938 still found these buildings a "façade of the greatest beauty and distinction." Moore thought Atwood's Palace of Fine Arts one of the great buildings of the world. "Mr. Burnham admired this design beyond even his power of expression; while he gave whole-hearted approval to Mr. Saint-Gaudens' opinion that Mr. Atwood's Art Building at the Fair had been unequalled since the Parthenon." Charles Moore, *Daniel H. Burnham, Architect, Planner of Cities*, 2 vols. (Boston and New York: Houghton, Mifflin, 1921), Vol. I, p. 85. Norton's enthusiasm about the West soon changed, as Vanderbilt points out: "The favorable impressions left by Chicagoans who, to Norton's astonishment, had shown a surprising degree of refinement and intelligence, began to disintegrate almost as rapidly as they had formed. After several months of settled reflection, Norton reconsidered his sanguine predictions about life in the West. These second thoughts centered primarily on the architectural expression of America embodied in the buildings at the Fair. Olmstead's landscape planning now became the only achievement Norton could wholeheartedly praise at Chicago. The other architects betrayed a defect both in education and imagination; because, Norton decided, there was little in the experience of the respective states that could inspire the highest poetic expression of the artist. The buildings mirrored in their confusing variety of forms and dazzling exteriors, in their decorativeness and "degrading accessories," both the ingenuity and the uncultivated tastes of a wealthy, immature people. The Columbian Exposition was "full of material promise. Was it full also of spiritual promise?" The best Norton could say was that the Fair offered promise of a better day. As he wrote to Henry Blake Fuller: "The Fair, in spite of its amazing incongruities, and its immense 'border' of vulgarities, was on the whole a great promise, even a great pledge. It, at least, forbids despair." (See Kermit Vanderbilt, *Charles Eliot Norton: Apostle of Cul-*

ture in a Democracy [Cambridge: Harvard University Press, 1959], pp. 203–4, where he analyzes Norton's attitude toward the Fair and Chicago).

3 Tallmadge does not mention this. Burnham ordered it done while Prettyman was in the East. Prettyman objected, and he was replaced by Francis Davis Millett, who supervised the application of white.

4 As we shall see in the discussion of Sullivan's *Democracy: A Man Search,* "feudal power" was the antithesis of democratic power.

5 Sullivan, *op. cit.,* pp. 288–89. Sullivan condemned Jenney for the same reason. His break with Adler, as with Wright, seems to have been rooted in the same idea, namely, that an architect must be completely devoted to the principles and practices of his profession.

6 Sullivan, *op. cit.,* p. 315. This was Veblen's point, too.

7 *Ibid.,* pp. 315–16.

8 Chicago has very few historical monuments of any kind. Even the Sauk Trail which Lincoln rode is poorly marked. The Douglass monument in Chicago, which contains the body of the "Little Giant," who so often forced Lincoln to greatness in speech, until the last few years was littered with filth. Sullivan's home is falling into decay in the midst of a slum. Only in 1960 was the restoration of the Auditorium Theatre announced by the trustees of Roosevelt University. Chicago has lost, and is losing now in 1965, many great buildings. But it is a great mistake to think that Chicagoans are without traditions simply because they have no past. They have a future, and thus "built-in obsolescence," so wasteful to Europeans and older Americans, is really honorific. As we waste in America we *hasten* the arrival, and encourage the use, of the new. Historical landmarks have until very recently been described as "places where something *happened.*" The fact that a building possessed a very beautiful window, like the original first story of the Gage Building, designed by Sullivan, was not considered a "historical event." The front was "modernized" so that the store would be "new" and thus rent more quickly and for more money. In Chicago there is no law to prevent such vandalism, nor is there even money available for adequate photographs or records of buildings slated for destruction. There is no belief in the past, so why preserve it? And further, how could a building done in 1890 be as good as one done in 1965 with "modern conveniences"?

9 Nor have they ever made any great contribution. Wright and Mies van der Rohe, both working in the Chicago tradition and living in the Middle West and Chicago, produced the next great forms of the tall building.

10 Dynasties of Chicago architects are now beginning to form in the Burnham, Root, Perkins, and other families. Wright, too, left sons and daughters who are active in architecture and the arts.

11 As Moore tells us: "The Fürst Bismarck, sailing from New York on January 28, 1896, carried Mr. and Mrs. Burnham for their first trip to Europe" (Moore, *op. cit.,* p. 117).

12 *Ibid.,* p. 127.

13 *Ibid.,* p. 157.

14 We have already mentioned the adoption of classic form by the Christian Science Church as a further element in the increasing use of classic form to create majesty and glory in many institutional forms of building.

40

Sullivan's Search for a Social Philosophy of Architecture

B y 1905 Sullivan's days of innocence, as he called his Chicago days of the eighties, were over. "Surely, he was an innocent with his heart wrapped up in the arts, in the philosophies, in the religions, in the beatitudes of nature's loveliness, in his search for the reality of man, in his profound faith in the beneficence of power." The individual, not society, interested him in these early years. "What delighted him was to observe the ins and outs of personality—wherein he was especially sensitive and keen to the slightest rhythm." [1] He had been singularly blessed, and cursed, in his relations with people. As he told Bragdon in 1903: "With me, architecture is not an art, but a religion, and that religion but a part of democracy." Whoever did not share such belief, or in any way threatened it, soon alienated him—as Wright, Adler, his brother's wife, and finally his own wife, Margaret,[2] discovered.

In 1895 Adler decided that he must make more money to support his wife and three children. Few blamed him. The panic of 1893 hit hard, and even at best dedicated architects such as Adler and Sullivan with their large office in the Auditorium Tower and a staff of over fifty draftsmen, engineers, and designers did not make great sums out of their professional fees. Adler accepted a ten-year contract as consulting architect and general sales manager of the Crane Elevator Company, at an annual salary greater than what he had made in any single year as an architect, and announced his acceptance by an open letter [3] in which he announced his retirement from architecture. To Sullivan, a serious architect could no more "retire" from his art than a devout believer could "retire" from religion. Such defections in his eyes were a denial of architecture, and thus of democracy. The architect was *creating* democracy. Architecture was as necessary to democracy as business, politics, education, or religion. Democracy was a system of relationships dependent on art, for only in art was there expression of joy, charity, and love based on natural powers which were subject to reason. The architect created the environment which made such relationships possible. This faith in art sustained Sullivan through his defeat at the Fair, his breakup with Adler, his separation from his wife and his dearly loved brother, Albert, and even the most terrible moments of all—the days, weeks, and finally years when he sat with nothing to do, in the bitter knowledge that other offices in the city were filled with work.[4]

In these terrible years Sullivan searched the foundations of his faith in democracy. Were the people of America really capable of sustaining good architecture? How was it that in the greatest democratic commonwealth in history there was so much bad architecture? Why had the great art of Greece, Rome, and Christianity failed to produce a just society? What was the relationship of money as a social symbol to other social symbols? Why was science failing to produce a good society? These questions mark Sullivan's departure from the easy faith of his youth in the beneficence of democratic art. "What my heart yearns for now," he wrote to Bragdon, "is justice, and a sympathetic interpretation of that which I have loved, and for which I have lived." The question must be faced: Were the people of a democratic society based on money capable of good art, and did good art, in turn, have much effect on the people of a free society?

After he finished the National Farmers' Bank at Owatonna, Minnesota, in 1908, Sullivan turned again to writing. In his talk of 1905, "Natural Thinking: A Study in Democracy,"[5] he compared the social context of "feudal" and "democratic" thinking. He argued that feudal limitation of thought to a leisure class of clerics and scholars grew out of a social system based on monarchy. Even the feudal God, Sullivan argues, was but a reflection of court life where a monarch upheld his mystery through keeping himself distant from his people. Such monarchs ruled through fear, as did their gods, who taught men to consider themselves sinful and unworthy. Democracy, Sullivan argues, is based not on mystification and fear but on reason and love, which are born and sustained in democratic fellowship. Democracy seems to lack the sublimity of feudal monarchy, but this is not because democracy is not sublime but because its sublimity has not yet been expressed. Such expression will be the task of a democratic art. In his next essay, "What is Architecture: A Study in the American People of Today," first published in the *American Contractor* in January of 1906, Sullivan turns again to analysis of social as well as individual problems. He argues that architecture is the best index to society since buildings stand "as social acts." The source of all social action, among aristocracies and democracies alike, is the people. All power, even the power of the feudal lord, rests upon the consent of the people. Consent is based in thought and reason. That is why it is wrong to study a society through its "styles" of architecture. Each "building of the past and present [is] a product and index of the civilization of the time, also, . . . a product and index of the thought of the people of the time and place." Now if we argue, as the classicists do, that architecture must not change, we are really saying that architecture was finished long before democratic society was born. Classical dogma admits no change in society or architecture. It tells the American people to give up democracy and return to feudal forms of life. It says, in a word: "The American people are not fit for democracy."

Perhaps, Sullivan continues, they are not. But if so we ought to ask how and why this has happened. We must ask: "[Is] this alleged unfitness . . . really normal and natural, or is it a feudal condition imposed upon the people by a traditional system of inverted thinking? We shall see if those whom we have entrusted with leadership in our matters educational have or have not misled us. We shall see, in a larger sense, if we, as a people, not only have betrayed each other, but have failed in that trust which the world-spirit of democracy placed in our hands, as we, a new people, emerged to fill a new and spacious land." But we must learn to read this in our current architecture and to check our reading by analysis of the thought and activity of the American people as they are expressed in other ways. "For, to be sure, what we shall find in our Architecture, we shall as surely find elsewhere and everywhere." The art of reading a culture must go far beyond words. Words have been the stock symbol of the scholastics, and through "scholastic fetishism" words have taken the place of reality, of the things and acts of life in society. If we would only turn from words to acts, and learn to understand men by how they act together, the power of scholastic verbal mystification would be broken. The scholastics and all those upholding feudal forms of education say that the common man cannot think and that there is something called "pure" thought which can be experienced by only a small minority. But the natural powers of thought "are vastly greater, [and] infinitely more susceptible to development than is generally assumed. Indeed, the contumacy in which we habitually underrate the latent powers of the average human mind is greatly to our discredit." This is sheer superstition, "traceable to the scholasticism of past centuries, and to the tenacious notion of social caste." Democratic education denies this to search out, liberate, and develop "the splendid but obscured powers of the average man, and particularly those of his children."

Our educated elites have exalted theory over practice until many of our university graduates lack ability to see clearly and to think concisely and constructively. Instead of having more faith in democracy, they have less. At the other pole, we have the "active-minded" but "uneducated" man who has so much to do with architecture. This man reads well whatever directly concerns him. His mind is active, practical, and superficial. In small and large enterprises he thinks the same way. He is concerned only with the immediate. His powers of reflection are undeveloped. This is not to say that such men, typical in so many ways of all America, are incapable of greatness. "The constructive thinking power of such men, the imaginative reach, the incisive intuition, the forceful will, sometimes amaze us." But when we look deeply we see that all this is a "brilliant superstructure." The hidden foundations are weak "because the foundation-thought was not sought to be placed broad, deep and secure in the humanities." This, then, is our dilemma: "we have at the poles of our thinking two classes of men, each of which believes it is dealing in realities." Yet both are dealing in phantoms, for between them they have studied everything but "the real thoughts and the real hearts of the people."

For, in society as in architecture, the thoughts and emotions of the people are the only source of social stability and social change. As architects we must return to a vital simplicity in our search for form. The source of this power is in the people. If "you would seek and express the best that is in yourself, you must search out the best that is in your people; for they are your problem, and you are indissolubly a part of them; it is for you to affirm that which they really wish to affirm, namely, the best that is in them, and they as truly wish you to express the best that is in yourself." For, "if the people seem to have but little faith it is because they have been tricked so long; they are weary of dishonesty, much more weary than you know, and in their hearts they seek honest and fearless men, men simple and clear of mind, loyal to their own manhood and to the people. The American people are now in a stupor; be on hand at the awakening. . . ."

Why, Sullivan asks, do we not have a vital architectural criticism? "Is it because our professional critics lack penetration? Because they lack courage? Is it because they, who should know, do not know? Do they not see, or will they not? Do they know such buildings to be lies, and refrain from saying so? Or are they, too, inert of mind? Are their minds, too, benumbed with culture, and their hearts, thus, made faint?" If this is so, how are people ever to learn about good architecture? "How is a people to know what, for them, a real and fitting Architecture may mean, if it is not first made clear to them that the current and accepted Architecture with which their minds are rapidly being distorted—is false to them! To whom are we to look if not to our trusted critics? And if these fail us, what then?"

Our architectural periodicals are not journals of criticism. "They float along, aimlessly enough, drifting in the tide of heedless commercialism— their pages filled with views of buildings, buildings, words, words, words. Buildings in this 'style,' that and the other; false always, except now and then and here and there in spots . . . where the architect, under 'compulsion,' has had to let the 'style' go—and do something sensible; or, rarely, where the architect, of his own free will, has chosen to be clean, and has expressed himself with feeling and simple, direct eloquence." The publishers of such periodicals tell us they are but mirrors of the times and publish what critics write and what their subscribers, who are mainly architects, want. Our more ambitious architectural criticism in books and monographs is weak, because it offers no way of testing conclusions by reference to contemporary work. Discussion is "left in the open air as a vapor; it is not condensed into terms of vital, present use." Thus those who are in search of architectural reality are being led "into a jungle within whose depths his guides are lost, and he is left without a star." He cannot judge the work of his own time because it has been tacitly assumed by our mentors that "Architectural Art is a closed book, that the word FINIS was written centuries ago, and that all, obviously, that is left for us moderns is the humble privilege to select, copy and adapt. Because it has not been assumed that ALL buildings have arisen, have stood, and stand as physical symbols of the psychic state of the people."

No distinction has been made between "WAS and IS" in architectural criticism. This false "historicism," which confuses historical with creative thinking, is even more absurd when we consider that modern science, "with devoted patience of research, has evolved, is perfecting and has placed freely at our service the most comprehensive, accurate and high-powered system of organic reasoning that the world has known." Yet such reasoning—the "breadth and fertility of this supreme search for the all-life-process, this most fruitful function of democracy"—is neglected by those who could use it most fruitfully, the architects of our time. The critic may reply in cynical despair: "What is the use of sincere thoughtful criticism for people who are neither sincere nor thoughtful? For in our time, "everybody else betrays everybody else." We are all false. Why then should a false people expect anything but a false architecture? "People get the architects they deserve. If people want real architecture let them become real themselves. If they do not want to be betrayed, let them quit betraying. If they want their architects to be loyal to them, let them be loyal to their architects. If they really want thinkers, let them do some thinking themselves. If they really do not want humbug architecture, let them cease being humbugs themselves." Serious students of American society would agree that such cynicism has much truth in it. If we believe in a democratic architecture, how are we to answer these questions?

There is no way, Sullivan admits, save through a testament of faith in democracy. Not, to be sure, the democracy we now have, but the democracy we could have if we had the courage, will, and understanding to achieve it. If we could but return thought to action, away from feudal dreaming, we could believe that "pure democracy is the deepest-down, the most persistent, while the most obscured desire within the consciousness of man." It is obscured by bad architecture. Our architecture is filled with hypocrisy and cant. It is ashamed to be honest, "but it is not ashamed to steal; so, then, by the unanswerable logic of life," people who live in such architecture are ashamed to be honest but not ashamed to steal. The architecture of our time "shows, ah, so plainly, the decline of Democracy, and a rank new growth of Feudalism—sure sign of a people in peril!" Such architecture has no serenity and is, therefore, a symbol of a people out of balance. It has no lucid guiding principle because the people have not yet evolved a lucid guiding principle. Our architecture shows no love of nature because our people despise nature. In it there is no joy of living because we do not know what the fullness of life signifies. In our buildings the dollar is vulgarly exalted because we place the dollar above man. We "adore it twenty-four hours each day: it is [our] God." Our buildings show no love of country, no affection for the people. So we have affection for each other, but secretly will ruin each other, even wantonly betray our neighbor and our own children, so great is our love for gold.

Complete despair is avoided only because we have here and there a building which does bespeak integrity. All is not false. "What leaven is found in your buildings—such leaven is found in you. Weight for weight, measure for measure, sign for sign—as your buildings, so are you!" Here and there stand buildings which are modest, truthful, and sincere. These prove the existence of a genuine democratic feeling. But these are intermingled with many more which bespeak a colossal energy which is not true power at all, but feudal arrogance. Feudal ways of thought have power over us because we have no philosophy, and, worse, we do not even think we need one. We exalt a cheap "philosophy" of common sense. What this really turns out to be is a philosophy of success, but of success in terms of money. Yet we pay a terrible price for such success. Drug merchants poison us, food merchants adulterate what we eat, industry fills our cities with smoke and filth. The price we pay for success is too great.

But what is a sound philosophy, and how do we achieve it in a democracy? It is essentially a social philosophy, "a balanced system of thinking, concerning the vital relations of a people." The dollar has betrayed us because it has destroyed the equilibrium of American life. We no longer think about the quality of our relationships, but the quantity of things and dollars. It is not skill we lack. No architecture in the world shows greater inventiveness;

few problems have not been met by the resourceful intelligence of our engineers and architects. And while this architecture is often barren of poetry, it contains a latent suggestion "which bespeaks dramatic, lyric, eloquent and appealing possibilities." It is not the fabled American inventiveness which is our real greatness. It is the unspoiled "American heart." This alone gives us hope, for "the heart is ever greater than the head." This is because the heart is "Desire; and, from it, comes forth Courage and Magnanimity." American men have been taught that listening to the heart is an unworthy weakness for men of brains and hard-headed business. But men must realize that to be a man we must cultivate sensibilities we ordinarily deride as feminine. The feminine principle of life is the hidden "well-spring of Intuition and Imagination." These are like our two eyes, without which the brain is powerless. Men are taught to deride poetry, but poetry is not only verse. There is a poetry of things, of thoughts, and above all, of action. So long as we persist in regarding print or language as the only readable or hearable things we will remain dull interpreters of "the voices of Nature, and of the acts and thoughts of the men of the present and the past, in their varied, but fundamentally alike activities." Poetry, properly understood, is the highest form of intellectual activity and the broadest in scope.

We are taught to believe that poetry deals only with metaphor and figures of speech, but what is daily talk but metaphor and figures of speech? "Every word, genuinely used, is a picture; whether used in conversation or in literary production." Poetry, like all art, stands for the quality of thoughts and acts in society. We have assumed that the art of expression is a fiction, something apart from life. We have said: "What do we want of an art of expression? We cannot sell it!" This may be true, "but if we have sold ourselves to our feudal masters, why then can't we sell art?" Look at business. "What is it become but a war of extermination among cannibals? Does it express democracy?" By what right can any man say: "I am! I own! I am therefore a law unto myself." How quickly among us has grown up: "I LEAD! BECAUSE I POSSESS! I BETRAY!" Did we fight a long and terrible war only to lose the right to the "fundamental art of expression whereby a people may, unhampered, give voice and form to the aspirations of their lives, their hopes, as they press onward toward the enjoyment of their birthright, the birthright of every man—the right to happiness!"

We are now, Sullivan concludes, in a time of crisis. Our time has come. We can still choose, but we must choose soon. We must make democracy a religion in which reverence for the integrity of individual man will determine our thoughts and our acts. Only as we learn to think in terms of democratic action will feudalism disappear. Feudalism is, after all, a frame of mind, a way of thinking. It is not force that keeps the feudal use of money in power, but thought and belief. All social power, for good or for ill, rests upon the thought of the people. This is the single lesson of history that is really worthwhile for us. Whatever has happened in the past, we must learn that our survival depends on the development of arts of expression characteristic of a democratic people.

Notes

[1] Sullivan discusses his days of innocence in *The Autobiography of an Idea* (New York: Press of American Institute of Architects, 1926), p. 291.

[2] We now have a biography of Sullivan in which some details of his personal life are given for the first time. See Willard Connely, *Louis Sullivan as He Lived: The Shaping of American Architecture* (New York: Horizon, 1960).

[3] Published on July 11, 1895, in the *Inland Architect*.

[4] The cruelest blow in Sullivan's career was in 1906, when the job of adding the south five bays at 21–29 South State Street (State side 285 feet, Madison side 140 feet) of his great Schlesinger and Mayer store was given to D. H. Burnham & Co. by the new owners, Carson, Pirie, and Scott. Burnham followed Sullivan's design, except in the attic story.

[5] This was given before the Chicago Architectural Club. The manuscript is in the Burnham Library in the Art Institute of Chicago.

41

Sullivan's Despair: Democracy: A Man Search, *I*

BEFORE 1906 and 1907, the years when Sullivan finished the first draft of *Democracy: A Man Search,* he argued as an artist who believed that democracy could exist only if adequate forms of architecture were created. People did not become democratic in their political, economic, or religious life, and then ask artists to express what they had become without the aid of art. People reached democracy in and through relationships made possible by the artist's creation of expressive forms. Every institution depended on such expressive forms because *how* it communicated determined *what* it communicated. Social integration did not involve a choice of art or no art, but of good or bad art.[1] The denial of the Chicago school of architecture by Burnham taught Sullivan that architects themselves did not understand the function of art in society. For if architecture was to express the needs of the people of Chicago, what did these needs have to do with those of Greece, Rome, or Paris of the Middle Ages? This question, so obvious to Sullivan, was not even understood by Burnham and his followers. For them the question was quite the opposite, namely: How can we create "beautiful" stages for the vulgar Chicagoan to act out his life upon—Greek, Roman, British, French, or Italian stages, as the case may be? For the classicists, as for Henry James and Henry Adams, the American businessman and his city, Chicago, could create power but not art. To Sullivan, as to Veblen, Dewey, and Mead, this was simply a denial of art. Art must express the needs of the people, of democracy itself, before the new American gentleman and lady who would create a poetry of action in society could emerge.[2]

Until the completion of the Schlesinger and Mayer department store, Sullivan was able to express himself fully as an architect. He wrote because he liked to write, not because he had to write. But after 1905 Sullivan discovered in bitterness and sorrow that an architect cannot create architecture unless his society asks him to do so. A writer may be persecuted or live in poverty—and still write, so long as he has pencil and paper. The reality of his form exists on paper. But the reality of architecture exists in the creation of structures whose completion requires the organization of men, money (or some kind of economic power), materials, sites, and skills of many kinds. The architect *must* be accepted by his people to exist as an architect.[3]

Chicago's traditional architects, led by Burnham, denied Sullivan and the Chicago school—but the people, too, denied him. Why had they done so? Was it because of ignorance, veniality, or bad leadership? And how could bad leadership of the kind supplied by Burnham so easily defeat good leaders in the struggle to dominate the expressive life of America? Sullivan decided that if the artist must be held responsible for bad art, so, too, must the people, who, when given choice, patronize bad art. To say that the American people possessed "latent" sensitivity to great architecture which society corrupted was close to saying that democracy corrupts a child who is born pure in heart. If the child is the father of the man, and the child was pure but is corrupted by "society," what grounds exist for faith in democratic society? Sullivan faced such questions as these in *Democracy: A Man Search*.[4] In this strange book Sullivan reaches the depths of his despair and anger. The distance between his own suffering and the form in which he expresses it often breaks down completely; it becomes a confessional, a prayer, and often a curse. Philosophy, invective, poetry, incantation, and prophecy follow in swift progression. Sheer horror, as in the forty pages of the "Dance of Death," haunts its pages. As we read on we realize that Sullivan is probing the anguish and sorrow he suffered to reach his deep and abiding love for democracy. In his earlier writings he faced the question: Why have architects betrayed the people? Now he faces the most agonizing question of all: Are the people of a democracy worthy, or even capable, of great art?

Sullivan's struggle to answer this question is highly dramatic. He divides the book into six "Groups." The first is called "Parting of the Ways." Man is at a crossroad. One path leads to feudalism and death; the other to democracy and life. The second group, "Face to Face," [5] depicts how we must face evils born of misuse of power in the feudalization of money and property. In the third group, "The Man of the Past," the tyrannies of feudal aristocracies, which denied the people, are exposed. In the fourth group, "Dreams," man's search for God and for the spirit of man is described. In Group Five, "The Man of Today," the struggle between the feudal power of money and the democratic power of the artist for the soul of modern man is drawn. In the concluding Group Six, "The New Way," the struggle between feudalism and democracy is resolved in the victory of democracy in alliance with art. It opens a way of life for man in nature and in society which does not depend on supernatural powers, but on the reasoned imagination of the artist as expressed in community life.

This drama of struggle between feudal and democratic powers has none of the genial comedy and soaring lyricism of *Kindergarten Chats*. The struggle now is tragic. Man stands at a point in the ways. He must choose between evil and good—and he must choose soon, so he can marshal his strength against the powerful and destructive forces of feudal leaders. The individual must move "either away from his people, or toward them." The ideological form of this struggle will be over ideas of property. New ideas of ownership and property must be created if democracy is to survive, for until we have new ideas of property, democratic consciousness cannot enlarge. So long as the feudal idea of property holds, men will be isolated from each other and no democratic community can develop. Property must no longer be thought of in terms of money or ownership of things, but "all that may be used and communicated in the community." The conscious, possessive, and isolative intellect must be subordinated to the creative power of the emotions as these are expressed in the forms of art.

The thoughts of a people are to be read in their acts, for acts are thoughts. We act in terms of specific problems in a present, and the "flow and pressure of tradition," but we are beginning to press forward to new goals. The awakening consciousness of the people is the new social fact of our time. Creative power in society lies in the imagination and will of the people. The American people (in 1908) suffer from spiritual, not material, famine. This hunger must be satisfied. Democracy will satisfy it, not only because it revolts against feudalism, but because it is a positive affirmation of the spirit of man, which can develop only in a free community which satisfies the emotions as well as the mind. Feudalism of money, like that of rank, denies this. Modern feudalism rests on control of money and has as its goal the enslavement of the people. It is the artist's task to make the nature of this struggle clear so that the people can choose wisely, but it is also his task to create great forms which will make possible the expression in democratic community life of spiritual and emotional needs.

Men must learn to face themselves and to look hard at the evils which beset them. In our time these evils originate and flourish in the deification of money. We have a god, but a "god of gold." No more cruel or vicious god ever existed. He lives off the blood of his victims. "The blood of little ones is so sweet that the god of gold must need drool and drowse with the glut of it. . . . The blood of women, too, is good and sweet, the women in his sweat shops and his stores." The "torn and maimed" we see in the human residue heaped beside the grade crossings of his railroads is further witness. The "god of gold" spells "the word dividends with the identical letters that others use to spell the word murder." This "god of gold" is made into a smiling "Sunday god" for the leaders of our universities and cultural institutions. Behind this Sunday god is the worshiper who murders, poisons, betrays, robs, and mangles in the sanctified name of the god of gold. While people worship their feudal god, Christ groans, the Sunday god looks foolish, and the golden god smiles and dozes. Before the veil these worshipers stand as brothers in Christ, but behind they stand ready to assassinate each other. For the ruling passion of man's mind is to destroy life, "because man's deepest fear, his ancient fear, is the fear of life." [6]

Two phantoms of the past still haunt the consciousness of modern man in his struggle toward democracy. These are the phantom of inflexible constant natural forces and the phantom of a capricious supernatural will. The idea of unchanging force has been fashioned into absolutes by philosophers, while the idea of a supernatural will has become the god of our priests. But any cosmic plan external to man is false; man's salvation lies within himself alone, for has it not been said even in religion that the "kingdom of God is within you." If this is so then man needs no priests or Gods, but an understanding of himself as an actor in society which would be reached through the forms created in art. Such forms depict our social roles in terms of the good and evil which arise in the enactment of human relationships. It is true enough that depiction in art is symbolic, but no social act can exist without the symbols of art, for they express in imagination what the goal, end, or future, of an act will be like, and thus help us to organize what we do in the real present as we act.

Man needs Christ because he symbolizes democratic teachings of brotherhood and love. These must be rescued from the established feudal churches which have imprisoned Christ in "an immense dungeon of forms and ceremonies." If we do not learn the lesson of Christ's love we will destroy ourselves, for what we call civilization is nothing but intricate cruelty and an elaborate denial of man. What we call reason is a blight, a disease. Western man is like a "huge giant with the beak of an eagle. He is predatory from tip to tip. He lives upon prey; and if there be not living prey—carrion will do." His madness is the madness of the conscious intellect which believes all things external to it and is itself external to all things and solitary. The tragedy of Western thought is that we believe that an idea can exist apart from man. Thus we still dwell in fear and trembling of supernatural sources of such ideas. We "whistle while we walk through the graveyard we call our philosophy." Our intellects "are slaughter houses, and our intellectual output is embalmed in hypocrisy and cant." [7]

Our whole civilization has become nothing but a "Dance of Death." [8] It is like a beautiful moor which changes from the beauty and joy of sunny mornings and cloud-swept blue skies into a charnel house at night, where skulls push through the earth and skeletons arise in ghastly light to honor death in their terrible *danse macabre*. The rising shrieks of the dancing skeletons become an exhortation to kill—as Christ was killed by the money changers. The skeletons, chanting of death and delighting in the memory of how Christ was nailed upon the cross, are the images of the feudal powers of our time who seek to enslave and destroy men through the power of money. Here in a noble land, so completely equipped with all the instrumentalities of advanced civilization, nothing but ugliness has arisen. Our cities are blemishes on the fair face of the land. They are inhabited by people with split souls. This is illustrated by the way city people talk. Every man has two systems of speech: the one "rather flat, formal and colorless, the other surprisingly forceful, compact, vivid and direct." The Chicagoan passes with a significant, almost unconscious freedom from one to the other. His formal speech repels "as much by its imitative sophistication and inadequacy, as [his natural] speech attract[s] by an ardent, almost youthful reach and force of its locutions." [9] He also thinks and acts in two very separate ways. These people declare they are free and democratic, yet they have failed to create in their lives in such a beautiful land a valid statement of Democracy. The people assert their freedom and democracy, but at the same time inoculate themselves "with a feudal taint which runs in their very blood and thought—and hence inevitably in its acts and their logical consequences." [10]

The "feudal taint" in America has existed alongside democratic ideals from the very beginning. American feudalism's first phase was slavery, "a terrible curse in the form of millions of black slaves, and ensuing gigantic internecine war, pathetic in its waste of lives, and its aftermath of progressive corruption." America has suffered, and still suffers, from feudalism. Never has the ancient doctrine of feudalism "wrought such unspeakable havoc among a people. No less than the people of Europe, Americans have felt the effects of a feudal philosophy, a feudal doctrine, and a feudal religion." But there is one difference. The feudal lords of our time, our money barons, do not act openly in their own right, but secretly through the church and the school, whose priests and teachers are used to poison the minds of men against democracy. The schools teach "a little of everything official and conventional, and nothing whatsoever concerning the realities of life." In our churches of 1908

what was preached carefully abstained from mention of the integrity of man, his normal and upright place in the integrity of Nature, his normal spiritual relation to his neighbor and to the vast, silent integrity of the Spirit of us all. The preachers were mere social parasites, kept by the well-to-do and the rich, like so many kept women. Now and then, if one of them by chance suffered an access of manhood and spoke aloud, he was ejected bodily, and branded as heretic to the church and to the feudal God of the church —because he had dared be loyal to man and the God of man. Hence, in that fair land man is honest at his peril—he speaks truth at his peril—and every man's hand is against every man. What wonder that a civilization whose basic motive is betrayal should now be swiftly moving toward the reckoning day which Nature had ever exacted from those who betray her? [11]

We are now at the maddest pitch of our Dance of Death, Sullivan goes on. The entire world stands at the hour of destruction—or birth of a new democratic culture. The hour has come—and it will pass. If we do not act for democracy, America will sink into the morass of the corruption caused by the unholy alliance between a feudal church, school, and business community. No people put action into thought so swiftly as Americans—when they see why they must act. But will they see? To do so they must take a great grip on the creative spirit, and thus, once and for all, "*create* their Destiny out of the heart, out of justice; and so hold it, safe and secure." Will they fail—or will they succeed? No one knows. The sadness and failure of our lives lie about us in the "Great City." Who can look at the filth in our streets, breathe the foul air, smell the stench of death which pours daily into the city from Chicago's mechanized slaughterhouses, and listen to the noise rising in our ever-deepening canyons of steel and brick, and not think he is in hell or a madhouse? Yet this hell is our own doing. We have succumbed to feudal thought because we have placed our trust in a feudal God, the Sunday School, rewards in an afterlife in heaven, and, worst of all, a belief in some kind of an elect who can do for us what we cannot, or will not, do for ourselves. We must realize that in a democracy we cannot escape personal responsibility and accountability. To realize this we must overcome the fatal split in our mind between the conscious and unconscious. Consciousness lives in reason, and discourse; the unconscious in feeling and a monstrous will in which the other is a slave, not a person. Consciousness enlarges in democratic relationships because these exist in discourse among equals. Feudal consciousness is subordinated to the unconscious because feudal relationships are based on fear.

We do not use our consciousness well because we confuse reason with intellect. Reason in man is dramatic and social, not analytic and solitary. We consider drama

as occasional, episodic; an artful presentation merely, as set forth on a stage within an isolated house called a theatre; and more or less well done, more or less inane, as the case might be. That is but a little truth. The broader, unescapable truth is that you are ever in the midst of the drama; a drama in the open. You are both spectator and actor therein. It is the drama of the Great City. This drama is unfolded within the action of the greater drama of Land and People. The drama of Land and People is in turn enfolded within the greater drama of the Nations and Peoples of the Earth. This latter drama is but the tidal continuation of the still greater drama of History; and the urge of it all sets forth the stupendous and pitiful drama of Man.

In the "drama of the Great City are enfolded lesser and lesser dramas—dramas growing ever acuter, more poignant, more intimate . . . dramas innumerable in the open, dramas of the day and night. The lesser drama keys to the greater drama, the greater a key to the lesser, and the least. Dramas, without end, within a roof and a wall. Terrible and subtle tragedies behind closed doors; behind the door the breath of life has blown to, to hold in tight the sordid and calloused soul." [12]

What is the Great City, Chicago, but a stupendous drama? "It is as a . . . monster . . . shuddering with the load of traffic in and the burden of traffic out. . . . And the monster groans and sighs. . . . the monster is without a definable brain—and without seeing eyes—bringing forth blindly, struggling turgidly, quivering and working without a clear thought—a Caliban in the Midsummernight dream of a new century, in a Land magnificently fair and filled with shimmering and hovering gaiety and beauty and wistfulness and delight—and a winging spirit of the Land, that laughs it to scorn, because the Monster does not yet know how to wish to be glad." Yet within the massive bulk of Chicago "a consciousness is struggling toward the slowly envoluming light of a dawning day. . . . And the seasons sweep over it in untiring succession. And the great shadow, night, sweeps over it silently. And the great orb of day moves over it, dazzling and silent—as the Monster broods in a fateful mood—dreaming by day and night, its inchoate and turgid dream —in the midst of the steadfast prairie—by the steadfast prairie—by the steadfast Lake. Unaware, unaware!—For the Great Feudal City, the man-created monster, has not yet dreamed of man." [13]

We have not dreamed of the greatness of man because we have not learned how to think of man as an actor in society. Thus we speak of the poor as the result of a red-clawed nature, in which the poor and weak must suffer and die for the rich because it is a law of nature that the unfit must not survive. Yet at the same time we affirm proudly that we are not subject to the laws of nature because we are endowed with reason. But the poor affect the drama of urban life. If they must live in suffering and death, so, too, must the actors who use the poor as audience to their majesty and power. For, in all their glory, the rich actors on the stage of life in the Great City know that they have won their eminence at the price of killing and destroying the very audience before whom they strut and play their parts. They know, too, that we are reaching a climax of human sacrifice in this ghastly drama. For what honor can there be for feudal plutocrats in playing parts before an audience they must destroy and kill? [14] The meaning of life is to be found among the poor. They have paid the cost of every civilization. Their sufferings arise from our failure to love and cherish each other. They are our masters, for until there are no poor there will be no culture. It is only the artist, the poet, and the so-called genius who can enter the life of the poor. For the poet and the poor are the primal stuff of society. "They alone, the great poet and the great poor, are elemental—hence creative." From the very beginning of time the poor have been the "pristine dreamers of dreams." They have lived close to earth, "they have exhaled the delicacy of the Earth-life; and have brought forth out of their earth-fertility, out of the mystic solidity and power of their teeming mass thought—the wonders of the past beheld, the wonders we behold!" [15]

Notes

[1] Failure to realize that what is communicated is determined by how we communicate it has been one cause of the woe and suffering Sullivan predicted would result from the victory of feudal power. Hitler, like Stalin, *staged* the drama of politics as a great, indeed the greatest, *community* drama. All communication by the government was considered as a *dramatic* communication. The German people were never given "facts," but acts. A speech was never a "report" but a community drama, as we see in the way Goebbels prepared, rehearsed, and staged his speeches. The "facts" of political life in Germany under Hitler were *dramatic,* as well as economic, facts.

[2] Some months after his final draft of *Democracy: A Man Search* (which was finished at 1:42 A.M., April 18, 1908, in the Chicago Club, where Sullivan was living at the time) Sullivan published in *The Craftsman* (Vol. 15, No. 4 [January, 1909], pp. 402–4), "Is Our Art a Betrayal Rather than an Expression of American Life?"

[3] The sociology of art, when properly developed, will therefore stress architecture as the social staging of community life. This is accepted in archaeology. But, if we know so much about the past through the study of architecture, why can't we learn as much about the present?

[4] Sullivan could find no publisher, and the Burnham Library of the Art Institute of Chicago, which owns the copyright, was not able to arrange publication until 1961 (aside from microcard publication in 1949 by the Louisville [Ky.] Public Library), when it was published by Wayne State University Press of Detroit. Nothing better illustrates the low state of architectural studies in America than the fact that this manuscript, the work of our greatest architect, was so long in being published. The contrast with the high development in America of literary studies is striking. The notebooks, letters, and other literary remains of our major, and in some cases of our minor (sometimes, indeed, very minor), authors are made available. Architecture is considered a technical, not a humanistic, study in America. Some, it should be noted, argue that this is the way it should be, for when the "literary" side of architecture is stressed, the architect is subordinated to the critic. This overlooks the fact that when the "practical" people dominate architecture, the architect is soon subordinated to the banker and the builder, or the politician—as he is now. The enemy of good architecture in 1964 is no longer the professor, but those who, without critical checks of any kind, use architecture

for profit alone, like the builder, or for popularization of their power, like the politician and the educator. They use architecture to communicate wealth and civic magnificence or as "learned tradition"—not art.

[5] Sullivan uses the same title for Chapter XIV of his *Autobiography*, in which he sums up for the last time the spirit of man in society. The two chapters that follow are about his life as an architect in Chicago.

[6] Louis H. Sullivan, *Democracy: A Man Search*, with an introduction by Claire Hedges (Detroit: Wayne State University Press, 1961). These quotations are taken from Group II, Chapter 2, "The Hermit," pp. 49–55. Many of Sullivan's images of money and the "feudal powers" of industry and finance are sheer grotesques. They are neither tragic nor comic, but expressions of horror, like the images of a nightmare. Such images originate not only in hate but in terror. It is this phase of Sullivan, as of Veblen, which belies the commonly accepted notion that Chicago thought from 1880 to 1910 was optimistic and failed to see into the dark recesses of man's hate. Both Sullivan and Veblen warned us before World War I that feudalism was far from dead. But their warnings were never communicated widely, because they argued that feudalism would dominate capitalism, despite what capitalists thought and hoped.

[7] *Ibid.,* pp. 61–62.

[8] This is the title of Chapter 5, of Group II. This is a poem, with interludes. It is one of the most violent attacks on Chicago's "feudal barons" ever written. Even the anarchists, who openly branded businessmen as thieves and murderers, did not create such horrible imagery of predatory monsters as does Sullivan. Veblen thought the businessman predatory and feudal, at his worst grotesque, but more often a clown or fool, gifted with a kind of low cunning. There is no such humor in Sullivan's writings of these years. The "god of gold," the "smiling Sunday god," now becomes the incarnation of evil and death.

[9] *Ibid.,* from "A Traveler's Tale," part of the interludes to the poem, "Dance of Death," p. 54. The two languages of Chicagoans were used by all Chicago humorists to produce some of their best effects. This thesis on American speech is the basis of Mencken's views on the American language. It was a truism in Chicago thought about American speech, and indeed all American expression, by 1885.

[10] *Ibid.,* p. 86.

[11] *Ibid.,* p. 88. Sullivan refers to the heresy trial of Dr. David Swing, pastor from 1871 to 1875 of the fashionable Fourth Presbyterian Church of Chicago (admired as "The Emerson of our American Pulpit"), for his denial of predestination, vicarious atonement, justification by faith alone, the Calvinistic doctrine of the elect, and his refusal to admit a hell of endless torment for sinners.

[12] *Ibid.,* pp. 101–2. "The Great City." This is Sullivan's final statement of what he means by the term "act." A building is an "act" because it is the stage of a drama—and all acts, and all phases of the act, must be thought of as dramas. "Function" thus becomes a dramatistic term, "form" becomes a term for dramatic, *not* mechanical, structure.

[13] *Ibid.,* Group II, Chapter 6, "The Great City," pp. 109–10.

[14] This horrible image is not the phantasm of a highly disturbed poet. German death camps, the Roman Circus, sexual sadists, public trials in the daily press—all teach that man needs an audience for his lusts, even if the audience must be beaten, tortured, ravaged, and killed as its heroes play before it. Sullivan's point, and one that Pascal, la Rochefoucauld, and Freud (among others) have well substantiated, is that we have unconscious—Sullivan called them "feudal"—lusts which do *not* remain secret or repressed, but demand expression. Man seeks to *enjoy* the dramatic enactment of his hate as well as his love. And whoever supplies the drama of hate dominates man. Until we believe this, Sullivan argued, we will continue to be ruled by more feudal monsters. This

bitter prophecy (shared by Veblen) of Chicago's greatest poet-architect has reached terrible truth in the anguished cries of Hitler and Stalin's victims. Before the real dramas of torture and death enacted in Germany and Russia the predatory businessman of Chicago, so feared and hated by Sullivan and Veblen, becomes almost benign.

[15] *Ibid.,* "The Luxury of the Poor," p. 116. Chicago artists from Sullivan to Algren have kept very close to the poor. Indeed, Chicago naturalism, or realism as it once was called, is almost wholly a depiction of middle- and lower-class characters and life. The source of creative resonance in Chicago art has been in the existence of poverty. This has been true, perhaps even more true, of Chicago's intellectual, moral, and political life. The poor are indeed the masters of the spirit of Chicagoans. Thus, while philosophical relations between culture and justice are not yet established, the conviction that eradication of suffering and want is the standard by which culture must be measured has been widely accepted. Perhaps this is why there is so little interest in the sufferings of the upper class or the tragedy of the gentleman and lady which is so characteristic of James and Wharton. Tragedy in Chicago art has never been over the death of great heroes of the past, but of the failure of democratic heroes to arise and take us into the promised land of democracy where all men will be brothers.

42

Sullivan's Search for Usable Traditions and Visions of the Future of Democracy:
Democracy: A Man Search, *II*

S ULLIVAN's dramatic view of society teaches that men turn to the past, as to the future, for help in acting in a present. We can act in a present only if there is a path to the future, for without goals we cannot organize action in a present—as Mead stressed. Even a return to the past is only a way of making the past a future, for how can we return to an irrevocable past? The new power in American life which increases opportunities for significant action is communication. Through communication we link man to the past and thus enlarge his consciousness of his role in society. But the seer and the prophet, the men of the future, the artists, storytellers, and wandering minstrels, have always formed the visions which direct community life to desired goals. Until dreams are given *form* by the artist, people could not know what their dreams or visions meant. The artist must turn his face to the people, as serenely as the philosophers and priests of the past turned their backs. Culture and democracy will be integrated when the artist gives people forms in which they can act out their social roles. Without the symbolic forms of expression there will be no democratic community life because human relationships can be enacted only through expressive forms created in art. And democratic art, unlike feudal art, expresses the life of man here and now in a human community of the earth, not of heaven or hell in a supernatural realm beyond the reasoned imagination of man.

Feudalism taught, Sullivan continues in *Democracy: A Man Search,* that servitude was necessary to self-preservation. The people of Europe worshiped a feudal God, and the "God-concept is ever in accord with the social conception." The heritage of feudalism makes it difficult for us to believe that man can be free and to identify power and wisdom with man himself, not some supernatural power or force. Evil in society—as in the individual —is the result of ignorance, not natural depravity. But this is the ignorance of the intellect, not of the imagination. Man's heart, his desire formed in imagination, has always been right. There is a fundamental urge in all men to work. When this urge can develop freely, as in a democracy, men desire deeply to work creatively in the service of their fellow men, as we see in the work of artists. This is not true of the man who is dominated by intellect, for intellect without the imagination of the artist is vain and absurd. Feudal thought ends in dualisms such as master and man, God and the Devil, or good and evil. Conflict in such dualisms is always resolved by the supernatural, who speaks through the superior, not the inferior. Supernatural authority cannot be disobeyed. The disobedient serf breaks not a rule, but a commandment. Like Adam, his disobedience is not simply a violation of a law, but a sin. Forgiveness for this sin can be obtained only through the master, as priest or lord, who intercedes with God. Since only superiors can protect inferiors, and since the power of feudal lords ends in the supernatural power of the greatest lord of all, the feudal God, free men acting together, following rules of their own making and subject to reason in society, cannot exist in feudal ways of life.

Man cannot exist without some kind of god. His gods are projections of his fear, hate, and love. The god of love—like the god of vengeance, and, indeed, all other types of gods, such as the gods of war, hunting, tillage, the family, or the state—has proved to be an illusion. For so long as men do not love and honor each other as men and cannot believe one another capable of reason, some kind of mystic symbol of the "man-idea" will always prevail. Man is the brain of passion, and hitherto his most daring and passionate outburst is the creation of the gods. It is characteristic of men to create gods. The god is really the human Ego. That is why gods will last as long as men, and will change as men change. But in the coming day of democracy, men will balance their historic power to create gods in the image of a master, against their "evident collateral power to create man in the image of man." [1] The development of the arts and sciences, and above all reason in the service of imagination in art, makes it possible to discover man for the first time. The average man is not weak, although he has been taught to think he is by those who seek dominion over him. He has always paid a heavy price to his warriors, politicians, and priests, because he is fearful of his own powers. But his leaders, like his gods, have all been created in his own image, and they have always been bound by his own power. Leaders cannot take men beyond their capacities and desires. Thus the leaders of the future who believe in freedom and democracy must help men to realize their full capacities. All of us, leader and follower alike, must dream and work for this new society. Our dreams and visions of a new day are great dreams, the greatest men have ever known. We can give these visions forms, and thus make them real, if we are willing to create a democratic culture in which men can express themselves freely. [2]

The greatest expression of the "man-search" in our civilization has been the image of Christ. Christianity, under the leadership of Christ, substituted love for hatred in the human mind. The new God proclaimed by Christ was to be a God of love. This was the "deepest, most gentle, most ecstatic of dreams . . . this dream of the myth-man of sorrows acquainted with grief." The dream soon began to pass away but there emerged "for a brief gleaming, the first glow of the brotherhood of man, the first ardent, flitting moment in the true man-search, the true God-Search, the first articulate cry of the free spirit of man." [3] There is a symbolism in the child's tale of the birth in the manger, and the man's tale of the last sigh upon the cross. This moment of death was also a moment of birth, the birth of democracy. But the tragedy of humanity is that this first aspiration toward democracy came to a speedy end. The loving God became a God of judgment, a feudal God. Men were not yet ready for democracy. It was a "local hour that was ripe, not a world hour." And democracy must have for "its field the whole broad world of man, and the consummation of his intellect in reason." But this must be social reason,[4] born of love in the imagination of the heart, such as we find in art. As art lightens the soul of men, the hour of redemption ripens once more. Men will cast off fear and live in brotherhood under the guidance of democratic artists, who will create forms in which free men can express their freedom in brotherhood and love.[5]

Why was Christianity taken over by feudal powers who denied the democratic teachings of Christ? The natural human teaching of the Christ seemed to suit "the common people, the lowly, the poor, the outcast." But it did not suit scholars, for they were obsessed by the pride of intellect. Christian teaching was too simple; the scholars had no use for the new theory of democracy. They did not know what democracy meant, or what to do with it, for these scholars were intellectual aristocrats. As they understood status in their world, it was necessary to make an aristocrat out of a humble and obscure man who died on the Cross. Thus, a feudal Christ replaced a democratic Christ. The church betrayed Christian teaching because it desired to enthrone feudal power and glory. It was able to do so because the people themselves, fearful and ignorant, wished to be enslaved. They thought this the only way to security. The leaders of the church knew this, and "responded more keenly to the overt evil in its world of men, than to the good which was hidden in them." [6]

We have not shaken off the power of this feudal church. Its power is not in its history and tradition, but in the feudal styles of thought and emotion it has created in the soul of man. We see this in our modern trusts, which have changed the Christ of compassion into the "Money-Christ." These trusts seek to acquire all that people have. "The modern trust, the Church, and the military empire of Rome are exactly alike in principles, differing only in the scenery." The spiritualization of money and the corporate principle are merely a variation of an old theme. The spiritualizing of things and men "had become a part of the business policy of the Church." Any lands or personal property it acquired, by any means, were immediately spiritualized. The church's dream of power advanced "to that phase of reckless arrogance, which we today can see forth in the tigerish hunger of our own magnates." The "modern combination of piety, cunning, brutality, insatiable greed, and a consuming, devastating, and suicidal dream of power" [7] is but a continuation of the feudal dream of power.

But even the powerful feudal church could not escape the "law of internal compensation; any more than can our modern sanctimonious pirates." Its reasons for "torture and repression were purely business reasons, as we today understand the term," and as we today say "business is business." The church was Roman in every sense. "Under new names, within new local colorings and conditions, it was the heir of that despotic and seemingly invincible empire. The methods of its predecessor in power, it revised, and reorganized, and [made] its special contribution to world-feudalism, that form of subtle betrayal behind the veil, to which we moderns give the name 'Business Enterprise?'" Thus in our search into its essentially feudal nature, "its hitherto tendencies, and its attitude toward the man of today and his inherent free creative spirit, do we find the story of origin, the growth, the hierarchy, and the working organization of the Church a clarifying agency. For it was the first, as well as the greatest of modern business corporations."

Our only hope for the victory of democracy over this powerful combination of businessmen and the church lies in their ignorance and stupidity. Our "modern trusts are made up of grossly ignorant men . . . imbeciles as to the fundamentals of human nature." This was not so with the church in its beginnings as a trust and a closed corporation. Back of it was the learning of the world: "its methods were always gentle and soothing where possible, always magnetic, seductive, aromatic and refined where possible, always was there the fragrance of sanctimony." But it had its savage side, which we see in our time as well as in the past. We also have an Inquisition and frequent assassination and ruin of men. If we understood the feudal roots of this our church and our business life, we might save democracy. "Such study may help us to discern in our midst a hierarchy of interests, whose siren song and whose ominous threats differ not a whit from the plaintive song and deep thunder of the Church." [8]

"Man is so much a dreamer that what he holds real and will wager his life upon, is naught else than the vivid working of his imagination." Man's greatest power is his ability to make "pictures of himself and within him-self." All that man does or can do is done by virtue of this picture-making power. "For man lives within a world of moving pictures; a picture-world within him and without." This capacity is shared by all, despite feudal teachings that imagination and will are possessed only by lords and masters. The common man does not understand that imagination awakens and stimulates the will and so "enables the will to hold the picture steady." The man who rises in a society is not the "fighter," as he superficially appears to be, but the man who "lets himself alone, lets his faculties work freely; who recognizes their inherent tendency and power to grow and unfold and thus beget an activity and strength," which finds expression in creative work. The average man does not let himself alone. He interferes constantly with the free working of his own natural powers by suppressing and repressing them. Hence he does not grow in imaginative strength and power of will. Nor does he hunger for mental activity, or the intense desire for achievement which constitutes virility.[9]

The average man has been taught that the artist possesses some kind of magical power which is beyond his native power. But if imaginative powers were not common to all, if we could not create images of our social roles, how could society exist at all? When the common man denies his own imagination, yet admires that of his leaders, he becomes the dupe of feudal masters who must convince people that they are inferior and thus incapable of the exalted achievements of their masters. The source of power for the artist is the people. The real drama of life begins for the artist (as for others) when he begins to think the thoughts of the people, to feel their feelings, to take on the life of their desires, to look through their eyes from within him, to feel the movement of their emotions, and thus become one of them. We must not regard man from the outside, remain indifferent to him, or manipulate him in masses. We "no longer regard him from the outside, stranger to stranger, this common man; we no longer take him for granted as he passes us in shoals; but we live the life within him, merge our person-ality with his and, thus, let our imagination work through his imagination that we may see as he sees, and dream as he dreams." As artists enter into the common man's heart and reach his spirit, they find their own creative strength.

For what, after all, do we mean by the *power* of man? We talk of man as a worker, a toiler, a fighter, a schemer, and a drone. But man's greatest power is his power to imagine, to create visions. He imagines what the results of work will be, and then works to achieve such visions. The "realism" of life is based on visions which give concrete form to our hopes.

Without such visions no one works, for how can we know the satisfaction of work unless its goals are made real to us? Yet this power of imagination, the greatest power of man, is the least known, and the least valued by the humble. But the common man must realize, for his own preservation, that his superiors, who tell him that their imaginings are a special gift of a divine providence, must be made to submit their imaginings to reason in society. It is not a matter of whether a revelation is divine, but of its use in society. For, if we do not submit the imagination to reason, it will breed monsters who will destroy us all.

There are three great dreams of power in men. These are the dream of work, the dream of might, and the dream of cunning. Only one of these is immortal—the dream of work, for this is the true dream of creative power. It is the one dream which includes "the normal ego of the other two." Work, the creative work of the kind we find in art, is the dream that means life. In his work to give form to the spirit, the artist upholds life against death. He struggles to give men control over spirit so that he may achieve a good life here and now. Man has been self-edified, and self-terrified through his belief in gods, angels, devils, fairies, goblins, elves, sprites, and ghosts. He must learn that he has created these out of the hunger of his heart and spirit, out of an inexhaustible fancy which must be satisfied. For man is a maker of symbols, a dreamer, a creator of visions, who does not yet understand his power as a maker of symbols. This is why we have been, and remain still, in the power of our feudal masters, who teach us that our visions of democracy are illusions. Yet they ask us to follow blindly visions which are real to us only because they express our fear, distrust, and hate of each other.

We say we do not know what life is, yet we talk endlessly about it, and often in feudal terms. We are taught to think of the world as composed of "I" and "not I." To what extent we are all conductors of the life flow of each other rarely troubles us. We do not understand that it is the quality of our desire to live which makes us a conductor or retarder of the flow of life in the community. Since we exist in terms of each other, whatever we do to weaken or block shared relationships with our neighbors harms not only the neighbor but ourselves. Morbid distrust of neighbors indicates clearly that our culture is founded on the constriction of fear, and not upon the openness of courage. Fear makes sharing impossible, while courage opens our hearts and minds to each other. Science once taught that man was apart from nature. Man found himself even more alone than he had with the feudal gods. Knowledge became an abstraction. Scientific knowledge was taught as "power," not love or understanding. Man would "conquer" nature. Thus was the old feudal idea of power, of the master and the slave reincarnated. Even in his personal life the scientist became monastic, a Brahman among men. He began to believe himself too profound for common men, and began to withdraw into an esoteric world of fictions—fictions which he took more seriously than he took man, his neighbor. These fictions seemed so real to him that he deified them. To his supreme fiction he gave the name Reason. This was his chief idol. He did not realize that the theologian he despised for worshiping idols had glimpses of truth far greater than his own, because he stayed much closer to the life of the people.

So, science came to a crisis. The search for truth was abandoned to dogmas and abstractions about matter, force, energy, and the atom. Man, it seemed, existed in a nature outside of him, and beyond his control. The old feudal dualism of the "I" and the "not I" appeared in a new guise. The "providence" of the priests, which was beyond the reasoning powers of man and could only be "revealed," was replaced by a nature whose "forces" functioned mechanically. They could be known but never created. But, unlike the Church, and to the good fortune of our democracy, "Science relaxed its Ego, grasped the golden moment and renewed its youth." It is beginning to "surmise that the notion of life within not-life, may perhaps be an illogical conception. . . . it is getting ready to part with the notion, I and not I." [10] In so doing, science will someday suddenly and dramatically discover man, and the human sciences will be born. Then we will all discover that we are our own providence, just as we are our own nature. We will begin to understand ourselves as creators, because we will understand that reason in society must be of the heart and the spirit, as well as the mind alone.

Notes

[1] Louis H. Sullivan, *Democracy: A Man Search,* with an introduction by Claire Hodges (Detroit: Wayne State University Press, 1961), Group IV, Chapter 1, "God-Search."

[2] *Ibid.,* Group IV, Chapter 2, "Man-Search."

[3] *Ibid.,* Group IV, Chapter 3, "The Nazarene."

[4] "Social reason" is distinguished as reason subject to discourse among men, not revelation from God, or commandments of masters.

[5] Sullivan, *op. cit.,* Group IV, Chapter 3, "The Nazarene."

[6] *Ibid.,* Group IV, Chapter 4, "Story of the Church."

[7] *Ibid.*

[8] *Ibid.*

[9] *Ibid.,* Group IV, Chapter 5, "The Dream of Power."

[10] *Ibid.*

43

The Man of Today and Tomorrow in American Democracy: Democracy: A Man Search, *III*

THE DRAMA of our time will be the awakening of the people to democracy. The evil of our time, the hideous drama of the rich and the poor, must be ended. The man of integrity, the creator who is the only efficient or sane man, must come to power. Laws must be established which will make men responsible not to some, but to all men. The first principle of the new day will be that all men are brothers. "The man hunt is over! Fear not! . . . a new conception of the thinker, the worker, the creator, the poet, the magician—Man!" The pith and substance of the new drama of man in our age is the "awakening of the Multitudes!" All of history has been but the prologue—the "real drama of man is about to begin:—the World Drama of Democracy!" Thus far in America, money has been used to brutalize us. We are taught that "money talks." It would be better to say that money calls to a ghostly savage which still dwells in each of us. Like a savage dwelling in the jungle, man replies to the call of money: "I kill . . . to gain the power of thy spirit . . . so that I may kill more, Lord! in thy name! . . . to have more." When asked, "Why have more?" the bloodthirsty savage replies, "to kill more—ever more—evermore. . . ." [1] It is the same with the expression "Business is business." What this really means is: "Business is Death." "The man-hunter is abroad in the land. He lurks like sunshine and shadows on the highways. . . . He glides through the green fields everywhere. . . . He melts into the secret places of the Great City." Unlike all other beasts, he preys upon his own kind. This hunt is called business.

Money has become a perverted symbol of life because we have learned to look upon it as a fetish of power and violence. We worship it because we have been taught by our feudal economists to fear it. In feudal teaching all powers are external to man, while in democratic teaching man himself is the source of the power of money, as of everything else. They created it all. It is what they are." Its power to buy and sell them will exist so long as they believe that life is a struggle in which we must kill or be killed. So long as we say the fittest shall survive, just so long will the fittest seek our lives to take them away." Man has chosen to make money and business symbols of death. He can also choose to make them symbols of life, for the power of choice is man's primal power, the power underlying all his other powers.[2] Our national drama unfolds like a play in three acts: "Money Talks," "Business is Business," and "Prosperity." We are in the third act now. The final intoxication, delirium, and madness of the white man terrifies us all. We hear "his raving incoherence, his horrible, ghostly cries: 'Buy! Sell!' " We listen as we "submerge and kill" our honest men while we cry, "Business is Business!" It is tragic "to behold a people killing its honest men, ridiculing them, while it laughs, mutters, sneers, whispers, 'Business is Business.' . . . it holds its own infants by the throat as it simpers 'Money talks.' . . . Would any but madmen kill their own young? . . . Is not our drama, Economy, a drama of murder? . . . Is not our 'Christianity' tragic and intolerable? Is not our third act the supreme crucifixion of mankind?"[3]

The horror of our economy is our complacency over killing. We hold it horrible to kill one, "but 'business' to kill many." It is a crime to kill at short range, but "an accomplishment" to kill at long range. Our lust for killing increases with advances in science and technology. But this is the thought and act of a madman, of white madmen going to pieces. "Is this, then, the real modern drama: That we kill at long range, poison at long range, steal at long range. Is not the suppression of the clean, clear, pleading warning cry of the true heart most tragic of all?" And how sickening it is to behold the "benevolence" of our murderers. "Are they not our chiefest in Charity? Is it not intolerable that [people], in their madness, accept Charity? Why then do men call such crimes economy? We are feudal; therefore it is normal for us to be ghosts, and measure our ponderous dance of death to the song of crucifixion."[4]

Americans are sound at heart. We are really a people of deep faith. We hunger for something of the spirit, of a life which we can share in brotherhood with our fellow men. We are generous to a fault. Our sympathies are quick, and we are certainly not a thoughtless people. We are ambitious and work hard. But for what? We think "indefatigably, intensely, constructively and passionately about Success." The successful man is "at once our mystery, our hero, our idol." But we recognize only the accumulation of money as success. For money has become our language, the "only language we know and use earnestly." In its terms: "we couch our hopes, fears, ambitions . . . our misery, our wretchedness, our despair."[5] But this worship of money is taking us too far away from the people. We need once more to honor plain, simple men of the people, not politicians, priests, warriors, financiers, captains of industry, merchant princes, and other "feudal ghosts" of the past. Our feudal heritage teaches us that, as individuals, we are greatly different from each other. We regard ourselves as separate, solitary, and distinct from other men. We feel this because we live within ourselves and for ourselves so much. Every American believes himself an isolated individual, separate from his fellows. But we also believe all things are external to us, and different from us. Nature, God, Society—these are forces which determine man but can never be determined by him. But so long as we believe this democracy is doomed. For the "heroic power of choice" is the mark of democratic man. Eliminate choice and man becomes meaningless. Choose boldly and man can reach the stars. In such choice feudalism will fade into nothingness.[6] This is the only way to be the "practical" men we pride ourselves on being.

We get the kind of eminent men we deserve. Eminent men, and the people alike believe in some kind of external, capricious will which creates one man thus, another man so.[7] If we make our gods authoritarian and capricious, why do we expect our heroes and demi-gods to be any different? A feudal people must have authoritarian demigods because they are such intense egoists. They believe that authority, not love, guarantees social order. From this follows their tenacious belief in castes, in slavery, and in all kinds of inequality. But it is monstrous to talk about these as grounded in human nature. They are grounded in society. No child enters the world corrupt. It is society, the kinds of relationships our feudal heritage has created, which corrupts us. None of us—eminent men and common people alike—really believes in himself. We say we are "self-made," but if we really believed this we would relate to each other in more benign ways. For why should people who really believe they can shape their own lives in community with their fellow men fear each other? [8]

Democracy, like consciousness and reason, flourishes in the light of open and free discourse. Too often in America politics is the "back door and the back stairs procedure." It is a strange paradox that a democracy founded on the belief that justice can be achieved through politics, uses "politics" as a word to describe bribery, corruption, and graft. When our political life is conducted openly it becomes subject to the authority of rules or procedures, and is judged by critical standards and not the authority of men. Rules, as invested in constitutions, are immortal because they can be changed by free will and free discussion to meet the problems of the day. But the authority of men, even at its greatest in feudal times, was limited by death and is thus subject to recurring crises.[9] That is, democracies can change, because they believe change is necessary to community life, while feudal powers regard all change as heresy and meet it with violence and death.

The vision of democracy is clear because it is a dramatic vision. It judges

The Chicago Maxwell Street neighborhood about 1906. Sullivan, like other members of the various Chicago Schools, saw, in such humble traders trying to make a living on their own, a promise and a hope for American democracy.
Courtesy Chicago Historical Society

men by their characters, not by supernatural powers, which, so feudal thinkers tell us, are beyond their control, or, as feudal scientists teach, by forces
which can be discovered but not created by man. But we must realize that
judging by character and thinking of man as an actor responsible for his
own choices place heavy burdens on democratic man. The haunting of poverty, death, and our feudal heritage of fear of life must be faced squarely.
The poor exist with the sanction of us all. When we regard every man as
our neighbor, in the best tradition of the Middle West, we will have no
poor. Before we busy ourselves with the reform of others, we must reform
ourselves. This will not be done after the fashion of the pious who say:
"Lord, we are miserable sinners all," for this is said confidentially to the
Lord. "It is not intended for worldly publication." It is far better to say
simply, honestly, and plainly: "I have injured my fellow-men because I have
thought evil and hence have chosen evil, and bred evil. I, even I, immaculate
though I appear, have actually done this thing." [10] This, and only this, will
make religion possible in democracy.

Truly, "no animal that roams the earth is so furtive, so timorous, so solitary and so unhappy as man." The struggle between democratic and feudal
values rages within our souls, as well as in the world around us. The agony
of our time will be resolved in one of three ways: in the victory of feudalism,
which means complete enslavement, in violent revolution, which will settle
nothing, or in enlightenment, which will come when we understand that
personal freedom depends on personal self-control. The powers of "might
and cunning are preparing for the final insane attempt . . . to enslave an
entire people." The hierarchy of today is monopoly. This hierarchy confronts the free spirit of today. "Its hand is poised—to kill." Monopoly
"relies on the multitudes to enslave themselves . . . in the belief that any
man, when put to the test, will betray and kill for money." Man has been
taught to be fearful of himself and mistrustful of the power of the human
community to regulate its own affairs through reason led by imagination.
He has been taught to say: "What is the use?" And when this pessimism
settles into conviction, he is ready to become "either a slave or slave-driver." [11]

The greatest victim of the feudal monopolist is the workingman. He thinks
himself shrewd and wise in the ways of economics and politics. But his trade
unions reveal that he, too, is nothing but a monopolist at heart. "His abiding
desire is to get something for nothing. His prime thought centers on wages,
that is, money; his second thought upon how little he can give in return,
that is, how much of that money he can steal." Like an operator on the
market, he dreams of cornering the labor market. He believes in might and
cunning. He denies the right of labor to other men when he can. He is an

aristocrat through and through, establishing ranks, grades, and distinctions among the working class.[12] Like the feudal monopolist, the feudal working-man has accepted money as a fetish of power. If his "working center of gravity—money around which his thought revolves in a small circle in common with all Americans, is suddenly and massively shifted at the right moment, he will be utterly and completely demoralized, and in his panic, will fly at the throat of his fellow working man." The stability of the workingman is not a matter of wages but of character, imagination and will power, and thought power. Like every democratic citizen, he must assume responsibility to, and accountability for, his fellow men. Class feeling is his deepest bond, but this bond will snap as soon as unemployment and hunger ravage the country. The monopolists know this, for they understand that the cry for bread will not be addressed to other workers. It will be addressed to the monopolists, who "now are arranging that it shall in due time be addressed to them." The cry "will be received gently, and benevolently." "Saviours of the people will appear," charity will be given—and that will be the end of labor leadership and labor solidarity against the bosses.[13]

When the feudal powers of modern society decide the time is ripe to take power, the vaunted labor unions will "be trodden into the mud." The worker will become a willing tool of tyranny, because he has already surrendered his conscience to his labor bosses. "Who has poisoned our foods? The working-man. And he knows it better and more intimately than anyone else. What good are his unions? Have they raised a voice in protest? Not a voice. Have they sought to protect you and me against poisoning. Not for a minute. On the contrary, they have worked hard to poison the people—for wages—that is blood money." Who makes the rot-gut whiskey which poisons workers? Who makes the vile nostrums and patent medicines? Who runs the freight cars into the yards of a favored shipper, and prevents their use to an unfavored shipper. Who really is helping the monopolist to enslave the worker? The worker himself. And what is his excuse for his denial of personal responsibility and accountability? His cry that he must earn an honest living, and that he must do what he is told or lose his job. The American people are beginning to see through the virtuous poses of the workingman and will soon hold him accountable for "doing the dirty work of the monopolist." [14]

Thus, if we analyze the feudal monopoly of our time we discover two feudal elements: "One, the cunning and malevolent mind hidden in the 'control,' and surrounded by its small group of 'big' men; the other, a great army of agents, clerks, etc., and workingmen, which makes an immense and powerful mass in unity of action." This whole system is essentially military. It is the "warrior-man in a new guise, in modern local color, with new names and labels." So it is not the cunning malevolence of a few minds we must fear, for were we to change our minds the power of feudal thought would vanish like a mist. What we have to fear is ourselves, as we realize the "appalling grip on us of that feudal thought we as a people hold in common." This feudal way of thinking and feeling is embodied in the idea that self-preservation must mean the "sacrifice of the neighbor, and if must be, the sacrifice of any and all." [15] Thus the day of the fanatic approaches. He is in the air of our times. So long as we base our social values on money as a force with power like the forces of nature, or the supernatural force of "God's law," we are doomed. Our only hope for salvation is in reverence for the nobility of man as man and the sacredness of man as neighbor. [16]

The divinity of man in democracy is in his work. But democratic work has nothing in common with feudal labor, which is the toil of slaves. The free worker in democratic society will not "labor," but he will work like the artist, who works in joy because he works in freedom and in conviction that what he creates will be of use to all men. The artist's belief in creative work is the kind of faith democratic workers need. The artist believes that man lives in his imagination, which he makes real for others, as for himself, by the forms he creates. It is then the worker-artist "whose name is life." The song of democracy is the song of work, the human song, "the inspiring song of Life, the worker—at Work!" In this song a new faith in man as free spirit is being born. For the deepest conviction of the democratic artist is that someday man "shall walk the earth as a free spirit," because, under the guidance of the artist, he will learn how to express himself freely.

Old gods are dying; new gods are struggling to birth. Will they be powerful enough to stand against the new devils, the feudal monsters, who are also coming to monstrous birth? "Man has but to open the door, and go through that portal of self OUT into the world." For the real imagination of man is of the spirit—the "white light of the liberated democratic ego, rather than the phosphorescent gleaming of the submerged and feudal ego." Modern man now has the power to interpret the past and forecast the future. He can be "seer of his own spirit" and its "incomparable power of choice." Through his magical imagination he can fashion his own future, and through reason in discourse and art he can face problems as they arise. But he must learn that reason must not be confused with the conscious intellect, for this is but a modern variant of the feudal ego, which can never give "utterance to a democratic social or racial truth." [17]

Reason without the heart and instinct will destroy democratic life. The conscious intellect is the weakest of man's powers. "Conscious intellect would have brought our forebearers to extinction long before recorded history began." Man, with his "I and not-I," has been only half conscious. What he has called dualism has really been nothing but a reflection of his own conflict between intellect and the heart—his age-long quarrel with himself. For man has but one nature—the spiritual. "There is but one fundamental human social instinct, and that is kindness. It seeks to flow from the heart of man as from a living wellspring. . . . It is the one broad impulse that can draw men together. When it flows into man's intellect that semi-conscious instrument will acquire full social consciousness and take on the beneficence of Reason." We will then cease to be madmen, because we will become like artists. "Conscious intellect smears its victims with its saliva of Kindness, preliminary to swallowing them. This is characteristic of the Politician, the priest, and the Plutocrat. . . . Conscious intellect is blind and deaf, in its arrogance and pride of isolation." [18]

Thus, while men betray, torture, and kill, they do so, not out of a depraved nature, but a vicious feudal heritage.[19] This heritage is a psychological as well as a historical fact. For some, this confrontation of our evil will lead to despair; for others, and for all those who would share in the democratic future, it will lead to hope. In such hope we discover art and the new sciences of man which make possible a new kind of culture, where, for the first time, the study of man as man becomes possible. Such study will be focused on how man acts in relation with other men, not how he thinks apart from other men and about subjects which are dissociated from human relationships. We cannot understand human relationships unless we understand art. "The significance of the word art has been so limited by us in its application to the social life, that the mere fact illuminates, as with a glare, the poverty of our present day thought concerning the social life itself, and the possibility of giving it sane organization and expression." When we limit our notion of art, we limit our notion of life, for the one determines the other. The social function of art is the expression of the "life of a people in the image of the true thought or integrity of that people." The fact that we think poorly about art shows plainly "that we have no valid social sense." For art and art alone teaches us how to think of life as interaction between actors on a stage of life. So when we assume that art is of no importance, as sensible practical men do, we assume at the same time that such men consider social health and strength to be negligible. When we hear a man say he "knows nothing about Art," we may assume "with certainty that he knows nothing valid about anything that concerns civilization; that he is . . . a vacuous morbid dreamer, living in a ghost-world of abstractions and destitute of the sense of plain and clamorous reality." [20]

We have been taught to think of art as "painting pictures, or something of the sort. Just so long as we assume this, we shall remain diseased. Painting pictures may be a special manifestation of Art; but the reality of Art consists simply and universally in this:—DOING THINGS RIGHT." And what is the test of right and wrong in art? "Clearly the things which make for social disease or health." And when we say that art creates human relationships, we must be prepared to define the kind of relationships art ought to produce. For how else can we be sure art is producing good relationships? The opposite is also true, of course. That is, we cannot have a good art unless we have a good society, for one cannot exist without the other. Artists and "practical men" alike must learn to think of the power and efficiency of art.[21] What are good relationships? Democratic relationships, in which man's "immortal dream of work awakens to a new dream of power—an Art of Civilization." [22] Art joins with science in its search for how to do things right. Democracy is the highest reach of science, as it is of art, because it puts man's finest powers of inquiry and research to wide social use. The scientist who withdraws from his community, or who deals in abstractions which cannot be related to people, is wrong. "Individualism without collectivism means sure destruction. Collectivism without individualism is an abstraction. Both are unscientific and inartistic." Just as art is "man the Worker," so is science "man the Inquirer." The "practical" mission of the scientist, as of the artist, is moral and social, as well as the development of his own craft. Science can never produce a sane social order so long as it ignores the heart and the basic "system of kindness" which alone upholds the moral order of community life.

When we reflect deeply on art and science we discover that both the artist and the scientist are transcended by the poet, who is the greatest of all men. The poet creates life. Poetry is the "soul of adventure—the going forth—the daring to do—the vision of doing and the how to do—the vision which creates a situation." "The poet is always a pioneer." He is always the master of men because his visions goad and drive us. He sees deeply into the meaning of society because he thinks of harmony—indeed, the form of poetry itself is a search for harmony. The poet is the man who sees things rhyme, and "rhyme is but the suggestion of harmony, and harmony is but the suggestion of rhythm, and rhythm is but the suggestion of the superb moving equilibrium of all things." [23]

> Come forth into my world, O, Man!
> This is what Art means.
> Art is a song of life.
> Utterance of man's free spirit—at work.
> Hence man's immortal dream of work awakens to a

> new dream of power—
> an Art of Civilization.
> This is what Democracy means.
> It is its very soul—its spirit—its ego.
> It is its answer to the wish and will of
> the All-Spirit—in the image of its
> integrity: The Spirit that inspires in Life
> an utterance of the Song of Songs.[24]

The poet teaches us to think "in situations" not "in tasks." To think in situations is to think in terms of dramatic action; it requires using thought to plan. "We have not been taught to plan, because we have not been taught to think scientifically and artistically." The final value of thinking "consists in its use in planning—that is, in the creation of new situations." All efficient action depends on theory, and only through the power of thought to create situations in advance can we act at all. We cannot separate thought and action any more than we can separate mind and body, or the spiritual and the physical. Mind and body, spirit and matter, all meet in consciousness, and the experience of consciousness is all we really know. We speak bravely of matter, as if it alone were real, but its reality exists in consciousness.[25]

The song of life is the song of Ego. Men sing of death—the song of fear, the song of distrust. But this is because we do not yet understand the Ego. We exist in terms of each other, and therefore the greater the other, the greater the Ego. Integrity is, then, the highest form of self-preservation, just as democracy is the highest expression of socialization. If we deny democracy, and the art which makes democracy possible, we deny life. Then all that remains is the feudal "Dance of Death" and the terrible feudal "Song of Death." Mankind is now at the parting of the ways. Our time has come. "The cock is crowing the shrillest dawn that the world has known. You must declare for an art and science of civilization or against it. . . . To create, to construct, to build, to put forth out of himself is man's natural work. It is the free and full expression of Ego." If men discover the new power of art, then will awaken a "dream of power." Poetry, "long sleeping," will awaken, and men "will vision forth." The dawn is breaking. "NOW BEGIN." [26]

Notes

[1] Louis H. Sullivan, *Democracy: A Man Search,* with an introduction by Claire Hodges (Detroit: Wayne State University Press, 1961), Group V, Chapter 3, "Business is Business."

[2] *Ibid.,* Group V, Chapter 4, "Economy."

[3] *Ibid.*

[4] *Ibid.*

[5] *Ibid.,* Group V, Chapter 6, "The Practical Man."

[6] The Calvinistic doctrine of the elect and the evolutionary idea of the survival of the fittest were closely related in Sullivan's thinking. The fusion of these two powerful ideas, as taken over (with whatever validity) by Protestant industrialists, was very powerful by 1890. We have already commented on the attempts of liberal churchmen in Chicago, such as Graham Taylor, to break away from what they considered a perverse linkage of Christianity and "rugged individualism" in business.

[7] Sullivan, *op. cit.,* see Group V, "The Eminent Man," and "The Self-Made Man," for these discussions.

[8] *Ibid.,* Group V, Chapter 9, "The Politician."

[9] *Ibid.,* Group V, Chapter 11, "The Monopolist."

[10] *Ibid.*

[11] *Ibid.*

[12] *Ibid.*

[13] *Ibid.*

[14] *Ibid.*

[15] The Middle Western ideal was not taken from the patriarchal family, but from the democratic community. Man was not a brother but, for Whitman, a comrade; for Jane Addams and Sullivan, a neighbor.

[16] Sullivan, *op. cit.,* Group V, Chapter 12, "Dusk of Gods, Dawn of Ego."

[17] *Ibid.,* "Instinct" was used by Sullivan and Veblen in a very different way from the usual biological use of the term. Thus Veblen entitles a book, *The Instinct of Workmanship* and talks of the *creative* instinct. In Sullivan the term is linked with emotion, heart, art, love, and imagination, as opposed to intellect, calculation, aristocratic disdain, isolation, and feudal science. As we shall see in the discussion of Sullivan's *Autobiography of an Idea,* instinct as imagination and the "heart" is the wellspring of art in the individual, as, for Veblen, the instinct of workmanship in the technological worker is the source of democratic solidarity in the democratic community. In short, "instinct," as used here, *creates* goals in action through imagination; it is not a drive which "impels" man to act in certain ways.

[18] For our generation, which lived through the worst evil thus far recorded in human history, namely, the German death camps, Sullivan's belief (shared by Mead and Dewey) that kindness will be enough to draw men together seems incredible. To our sorrow and despair we have been made to realize that hate is as firm a social bond as love. But it would be doing Sullivan great injustice to assume that he was not aware of hate as a social bond. For did he not say that man is the only social animal who preys on his own kind? And did he not forecast, in poetic imagery of a dance of death, the horrors of our time? He was not alone in this, of course. In America we have not yet learned to take our artists seriously. Instead we follow politicians, economists, educators, business leaders, and a "social gospel" that taught us that "sharing" would naturally lead to sharing good—not evil. We have paid a heavy price for our neglect of art and science as human studies.

[19] Sullivan, *op. cit.,* Group IV, "The New Way," Chapter 2, "Art." As if to dispel any doubt about this grounding of art in society, Sullivan says in these concluding chapters: "To trace all these diverse thoughts [of the people] to their common birth in the view of Life [as art], and to show clearly that, in all their variations of aspect, they are true images of the view a people holds concerning life, is the purpose of this book. . . ."

[20] Veblen, it will be recalled, exhorted his "practical" Chicagoans, to believe that in-

vention, or art, is the mother of necessity, which was a reversal of the proverb, quoted so often by engineers and practical men, that necessity was the mother of invention. State Street merchants understood well the power of art—in so far as it was related to their own profit, as did those who staged the community drama of American politics. Veblen also pointed out that educators such as Harper—"Captains of Erudition," as he called them—well understood the power of art in their use of monastic stages to mystify the unlearned and to lull the pious by linking learning with piety through the use of Gothic architecture.

[21] Sullivan, *op. cit.,* Group VI, Chapter 2, "Art."

[22] *Ibid.,* Group VI, Chapter 3, "Science."

[23] In his peroration on the poet in Chapter 4, "The Poet," Sullivan ends with the same image: that of moving equilibrium, which he uses to characterize good form in architecture in *Kindergarten Chats.* This is his basic aesthetic image of beauty in art.

[24] Sullivan, *op. cit.,* Group VI, Chapter 2, "Art."

[25] *Ibid.,* Group VI, Chapter 6, "Ego."

[26] *Ibid.*

PART SEVEN

Sullivan's Description of the Development within the Individual of the Idea of Architecture

44

Sullivan's Theory of Plastic Form:
A System of Architectural Ornament According with a Philosophy of Man's Powers

F R O M   T H E completion of *Democracy: A Man Search* in 1908 to the first weeks of the New Year in 1922, Sullivan wrote only a few scattered essays and designed only eleven buildings. By 1920 the greatest architect of his time was reduced to penury. His last two small rooms in the Auditorium were closed to him. His cottage at Ocean Springs, where he had experienced one of his greatest illuminations and where he existed most purely in spirit, was given up in 1908.[1] At about the same time he separated from his wife. In 1909 he auctioned off his library and art collection. In the autumn of the same year George Elmslie, who had replaced Wright as Sullivan's chief designer, left his master. Sullivan moved his office to cheap quarters at 1808 Prairie Avenue and took up lodgings nearby at the Warner Hotel, where he paid nine dollars a week for two small rooms. Friends supported him with loans and fellowship when they could. But fellow architects, such as Max Dunning, and critics, such as Bragdon, who loved and supported him, could not get him what he needed most—work as an architect or orders for writing.

Years of enforced inactivity, loneliness, and poverty weakened his body. The despair over architecture and democracy, which he voiced for the first time in *Democracy: A Man Search,* almost destroyed him. At such times he shut himself off from people, and drank.[2] His faithful companion of these years, a "loyal little henna-haired milliner," as Wright recalls her,[3] was not considered fit for "good society." By 1917 it seemed as if Sullivan was finished. At sixty-one his powerful body was still sustaining him, but it was obvious to his friends that he was aging rapidly. He had been deserted by the people whom he loved so deeply, and for whom he had designed some of the greatest buildings of our time. He now carried himself like an old man. As Wright says of these years, "[His] body was disintegrating; his heart irretrievably damaged."[4]

But Sullivan's spirit did not die. He lived in hope that he would get work to do. Friends, such as Bragdon; Chicago architects such as Wright, Rebori, Dunning, and Nimmons; and executives of several terra cotta companies, such as Gates, Lucas, and Hottinger, tried to do what they could. But it was very difficult to get work for a writer whose major writings could find no publisher, and whose architectural designs were considered "commercial" and "vulgar." But in June of 1918 Bragdon urged Sullivan to rewrite "Kindergarten Chats" in book form. Sullivan agreed, and returned to the manuscript he had begun seventeen years before, in 1901. He worked through the summer and autumn. On fine days he worked at his favorite bench in Washington Park; in the evenings, at a table in the Cliff Dwellers Club. But Bragdon's enthusiasm proved to be ill-founded. No publisher would accept the revised edition of "Kindergarten Chats." This manuscript joined "Natural Thinking: A Study in Democracy" of 1905, and "Democracy: A Man Search" of 1908, in his file of unpublished work—nearly a thousand pages of typescript.

But if Chicagoans did not honor and support Sullivan, neither did they let him die in neglect. George Elmslie and Frank Lloyd Wright visited him, as did Dunning and Rebori. Young architects from abroad asked to see him when they visited the city. Bruce Goff wrote a eulogy of Sullivan for the *Western Architect* (August 3, 1920). The Cliff Dwellers honored Sullivan and helped him greatly by giving him a Loop home where he could sit by the fire, or write at a secluded desk, into the morning hours. The American Institute of Architects—and particularly its *Journal,* under the editorship of C. A. Whitaker, who had been responsible for the serialization of "Kindergarten Chats"—kept in touch with Sullivan. The spectacle of their master— the once imperious leader of their profession, who had created for the first time a concept of American architecture as a new order of design—slowly making his way along Michigan Boulevard struck deep. Elmslie, Wright, Dunning, Andrew Rebori, and Nimmons, like Bragdon and Schuyler, knew that the glory of American architecture now flamed fitfully in the dying body of their master.

Max Dunning and George Nimmons searched for ways to make the last years of their master productive. Dunning had served on both state and national boards of housing and was a director of the American Institute of Architects. Nimmons had studied at the Art Institute of Chicago, served his apprenticeship as an architect in the office of Daniel Burnham (died in 1912), and in 1920 won the gold medal award for industrial buildings given by the American Institute of Architects. They decided that they could support Sullivan as a writer and artist, if not as an architect. They asked him if he would design a set of twenty plates in folio to illustrate his philosophy of ornament, and accompany this with a narrative of his life—the narrative to be serialized in the *Journal of the American Institute of Architects.* He was to be paid for both, and Dunning and Nimmons assumed responsibility for raising funds and for ensuring publication. The Burnham Library of the Art Institute advanced five hundred dollars toward designing the plates. Members of the Cliff Dwellers subscribed another five hundred dollars, assigned Sullivan a table to serve as a writing desk, and paid for his meals and incidental expenses at the club. C. D. Gates, president of the American Terra Cotta Company, whose modeler, Christian Schneider, had always been loaned to the Sullivan office, offered Sullivan free office space for his drawing equipment and remaining furniture at the company headquarters at 1701 Prairie Avenue.

For two years, the last two years of his life, Sullivan drew and wrote, hoping that he would be spared to finish what he knew was his last, yet he hoped his greatest, statement of the power of art in democratic life. On January 27, 1924, he wrote the "Prelude" to his drawings of ornament in four folio pages entitled "The Inorganic and the Organic." The task was now done, and Sullivan put aside pencil and pen. He was never to take them up again. During March he could no longer make the journey to the Cliff Dwellers Club. His companion of many years, the "little milliner," worn with anxiety and sorrow, fell ill and was hospitalized. Her departure crushed Sullivan. He phoned Max Dunning and took to his bed. Dunning saw that the last hours of the master had come. Sullivan's only concern now was to see copies of the *Autobiography* and his *System of Architectural Ornament*. Dunning telegraphed the American Institute of Architects Press. A finished copy of each was rushed to Chicago.

Wright tells us of his master's reception of his first published manuscript.

I continued to see him oftener than every week if I could. . . . Some weeks passed. A telephone call to Taliesen from the Hotel Warner. . . . He had now fallen worse than sick. Spells of violence came over him more and more often. . . . The manager was really devoted to Sullivan as he said he was, but he was now at his wit's end. . . . "Don't leave me, Frank," he begged. "Stay." I stayed and he seemed to be himself again toward evening. We talked about his forthcoming book, "The Autobiography of an Idea." He hoped there might be some income in it—for him. Hope—always hope. . . . In town a few days later, I went to see him again. He seemed better. There—at last—the first bound copy of the "Autobiography"! The book had just come in and was lying on the table by his bed. He wanted to get up. I helped him, put my overcoat round his shoulders as he sat on the bed with his feet covered upon the floor. He looked over at the book. . . . "There it is, Frank." . . . I was sitting by him, my arm around him to keep him warm and steady him. I could feel every vertebra in his backbone as I rubbed my hand up and down his spine to comfort him; and I could feel his enlarged heart pounding.

The master spoke eagerly to his great pupil:

"Give me the book! The first copy to you, Frank! . . . A pencil?" He couldn't lift his arm. Gave it up with an attempt to smile. . . . Was he cursing a little? Gently enough. His eyes were still deeper in their wan sockets, but still burning bright. He joked about the end he saw, and—under his breath—said something. For the first time he would admit to himself that the end was near. But to me he looked as though he were better notwithstanding that helpless arm. But the man in him seemed indifferent. He didn't want to talk about it any more, either way. Life had been pretty hard on him. Such friends as he had could do but little to make up for the deep tragedy of his frustration as the greatest architect of his time.

And even though Wright thought little of his master's writings, the plates for the *System* and the sheaf of drawings the master had given him a few days before moved him deeply. "But his ornament was his inextinguishable gift to the last. . . ." [5]

In the "Prelude" to his *System of Architectural Ornament According with a Philosophy of Man's Powers,* Sullivan makes his final statement about the meaning of art in life. Man's spiritual power "masters the inorganic and causes it to live in forms which his imagination brings forth from the lifeless, the amorphous. He thus transmutes into the image of his passion that which of itself has no such power. Thus man in his power brings forth that which hitherto was non-existent." Man's powers are natural, or congenital; they are not gifts received from any outer source, but are phases of that "integral solitary *ego.* . . . this *ego,* precisely in essence of principle, [is] what the seat of power in the germ is to the future plant form. . . . the *ego* is not merely the seat of intellectual consciousness, but, what is of vastly greater importance, it is primordially the seat of *instinct:* it *is* instinct—the intellect is but one of its powers." Knowledge is not understanding until it is inspired by sympathy, which is the "power to enter into communion with living and with lifeless things." To repeat, all these powers are natural. Even "when dormant, suppressed, or inarticulate they are potential." Genius "is potentially universal," and thus "natural man" is the seat of genius.

Man's powers are physical, intellectual, emotional, moral, and spiritual. Through his physical powers man can effect changes in his environment. He creates his situation. His intellectual powers begin in curiosity but end in "highly sophisticated manipulation." When we say that man reasons we mean "the construction of a diagram or model purporting to show how curiosity works to satisfy its craving for orderly form." The emotional powers embrace "every impulse, every power of feeling; an enormous volcanic complex—the basis of action. . . ." Such action is "of *instinct.*" This is the great power that really moves the world—even though people are busy denying it—"even as they exalt Intellect to the rank of fetich." Moral powers are the great stabilizing powers. The central moral power of man is "*free-will* choice," and the struggle to recognize this and face it will be the great struggle of our time. To be free, man's spirit "must liberate and organize his instinctive powers. His intellect has held them too long in bondage. Spiritual power is the power of vision. . . . It seems as in a dream; it feels as in the depths of instinct." It concentrates its vision on man himself, to awaken man to consciousness of himself, "to a realization of his own nature and his own powers; to evoke his kindness, his faith and his courage—to dispel his fear."

In the practical affairs of life, man's powers are concentrated in certain roles. The physical man becomes the worker, the artificer. The inquirer becomes a scientist. The emotional man "dramatizes the activities. He colors life." The contemplative, speculative man becomes the philosopher. "The moral power of man urges on toward democracy (the great dream)." The dreamer-man becomes "the seer, the mystic, the poet, the prophet, the pioneer, the affirmer, the proud adventurer. He dreams his dream with open eyes, with clear vision of realities, . . . with intense persistent concentration upon an idea, a purpose. His power utilizes and manipulates all powers—focusing their aim upon a program of genuine achievement." Thus the physical man, the worker or artificer, becomes stronger through inquiry and science; stronger still through emotion, which finds its expression in dramatization; stronger still through philosophy; stronger still through moral poise, as expressed in human responsibility and accountability; and strongest of all in his visions and dreams. For here he reaches the summit of his powers, because all his other powers are "enfolded in his fear of creative power, and he rises to the heights of that utterly simple artificer . . . who materializes his dreams in the every-day world—for the good of mankind!"

"To seek and find man is the modern adventure." The path to an understanding of man is blocked by many preconceptions. Most of these come from confusing the man of the past with the natural man. But when the veil is lifted we will see that man is not what we believe him to be. The real man, "the dreamer of dreams, the creator of realities, the greatest of artificers [is] the *master craftsman*." All men "in their native powers are craftsmen whose destiny it will be to create, courageously, wisely and worthily, a fit abiding place; a sane and beautiful world. . . . And thus does the nature of universal art begin to emerge within the glow of this modern light." Following this final statement of the function of the artist in society, which must "constantly be borne in mind by the student" as he draws, "we shall now begin to set forth a specific aspect, in the technical form, of the application of such powers to material things." For, as the master made clear in a letter to Charles H. Whitaker: "The graphic work, to have the greater value, must be founded securely on philosophical prelude outlining man and his powers, and the idea of the prelude carried out in the series of plates." The master then begins to illustrate these principles.[6] Each plate contains notes on this theory of ornamentation.

Plate 1 begins with a "blank block" which is developed "through a series of mechanical manipulations." This type of manipulation is continued through ten stages, until the eleventh drawing, which is "developed with increased freedom, but still largely in the mechanical mode [with the] beginning appearance of the imaginative element." Plate 2 is entitled "Manipulation of the Organic." It contains seven drawings of "simple leaf-forms," seven of "compound leaf-forms," and fourteen showing "technical morphology of No. 7 into No. 12: plastic changes, following nature's method of liberating energy" while thirteen and fourteen, are enriched expression of the "same method." He then takes the motif of the thirteenth and the twelfth and develops them into larger and more complex drawings. He states in his subheading to the seven drawings of simple leaf-forms that "by manipulation any of these forms may be changed into any of the others through a series of systematic organic changes known technically as "morphology." Compound leaf-forms, as illustrated in the seven drawings, are derivatives of the simple leaf-forms, "but, organically, expressions of different identities of the seed-germ."

The image of the seed-germ dominates both the drawings and the text. The legend of the book begins with a "diagram of a typical seed with two cotyledons." These are "specialized rudimentary leaves containing a supply of nourishment sufficient for the initial stage of the development of the germ." The idea of the germ is basic to all art. "The Germ is the real thing; the seat of identity. Within its delicate mechanism lies the will to power: the function which is to seek and eventually to find its full expression in form. . . . The seat of power and the will to live constitute the simple working upon which all that follows is based—as to efflorescence." Plate 2 contains another drawing of the seed with its two cotyledons, bearing the legend: "Remember the Seed Germ," and on Plate 5 this drawing is repeated again to illustrate the theory of the axis in drawing as "a container of energy." In the "Prelude," which is entitled, "The Inorganic and the Organic," we are told:

. . . for the germ of the typical plant-seed with its resident powers, [man] may substitute, in thought, his own will as the seat of vital power in a figurative or imagined seed-germ which shall be the utterly simple energy-basis of a theory of efflorescence involving concordantly a theory of plastic control of the inorganic. These two elements of our premise are not to be considered separate conceptions to be harmonized, but as two phases of a single impulse of man's creative imagination and will—the will to create in the likeness of his emotions and his intellect; the passion to create in the image of his own power; the urge to create companions of his inmost thought.

But there is another kind of manipulation. This Plate (No. 3) is entitled: "THE INORGANIC . . . Manipulation of Forms in Plane-Geometry . . . MOBILE GEOMETRY." This mobile geometry is illustrated in drawings of basic forms: the circle; circles containing a triangle, a square, a pentagon, a hexagon, a septilateral polygon, an octagon; and finally a circle containing all these. The notes on these drawings describe the difference between supernatural, magical, and natural uses of art as an expression of man in democratic society. "These simple forms, of ancient discovery and use, were given esoteric meaning and occult powers by the men of that day in an effort to control, by means of formulas and secret ritual, the destiny of man amidst the powers of nature. With mystic numbers and other phenomena they formed part of an elaborate system of magic to which the world pinned its faith."

But in this new "mobile geometry" a "new faith is advanced." This is a faith that "man, with his natural powers, developed and free, may and shall control his destiny through the finer magic of his enlarged vision, and of his will to attain. Master of the inorganic and the organic, he will, when he has found himself, become master of himself." Inorganic forms, "rigid in their quality," are to be considered, in this new philosophy of form, as "containers of radical energy, extensive and intensive." In the "progress of his demonstration," Sullivan illustrates the principle of "extensive" form by showing how lines or axes radiate from the center of the basic forms. The principle of intensive form is illustrated, in turn, by showing how lines or axes radiate from the periphery toward the center. We can assume, too, he continues, that energy is resident in the periphery of the basic forms, and that all lines can be treated as "energy lines." Such development of the inorganic may be called "plastic geometry." The fusion of the inorganic and the organic "into a single impulse and expression" becomes possible, then, when we consider rigid geometric forms as "containers of energy" upon which a "germinal, liberating will is imposed by man's free choice, intelligence and skill." We see this all about us in plants. The plant derives its impulse from the seed-germ, and its growth develops subcenters of further growth. This can be illustrated through a series of drawings (in Plate 4) showing the "awakening of the pentagon." In six steps the form of the pentagon may be developed by geometric development, until in a seventh step we can draw a "pentagon in action." Here our geometric axes are respected, but now, as we elaborate freely along these axes, a new element is created. This is mobility. The rigid pentagon has vanished. It has now become "mobile."

Any line, straight or curved, may be thought of as an axis because an axis is always a container of energy and thus "a directrix of power." This is illustrated in Plate 5 by a line which bisects vertically the seed-germ with its two rudimentary leaves. There is no limit to possible variations or combinations, or to the morphology of such an axis. Axes may be expanded, restrained, combined, subdivided, made rigid or plastic, or mobile, or fluent. They may be developed inorganically or organically. There is always supposed to be a main axis, however, and even though it is overgrown or overwhelmed by the vitality of its subaxes, we can discover it through the use of imagination. Axes, with or without subaxes, selected at random, illustrate this (as in the drawings of Plate 5). Plate 6 illustrates how three elements, "A," "B," "C," of a single form may be drawn. Each may be selected as a dominant motif, but it is only (as in the final drawing on Plate 6) when "A," "B," and "C" are combined in one drawing, where we seek an equilibrium of these three axes, that a truly mobile equilibrium appears.

The next theme in the drawings is that of parallelisms. In brief review (Sullivan states) of what has gone before, we find that the "Prelude" to the series of plates sets forth in literary form Man's Natural Powers as the foundation of his deeds. Then begins, as illustrated in the plates, the development of a technical thesis, with the objective in view of exposing these powers in action, as applied to a specific form of activity called Architectural Ornament. The "out-working of the thesis as a science and an art is of necessity technical, inasmuch as it involves a new conception of energy—and new philosophic and practical deductions therefrom."

For the main task of the new democratic art is to break down the barriers between science and art and, specifically, to integrate engineering and architecture. We must humanize science so that it energizes art, and so exhibit the masterful fluency of art that it in turn can illuminate science. Between science and art there appear at first view separate parallel activities. That is, science and art, the bases of all culture, never seem to meet, although the scientist and the artist work side by side in the pursuit of wisdom in democratic society. So, too, with the parallelism between man and nature, and between man and his works. "These are self-contained within the all-embracing domain of life, the universal power, or energy which flows everywhere at all times, in all places, seeking expression in form, and thus parallel to all things." Man stands as a solitary ego, within himself both witness and participant. By virtue of his powers he is a "co-creator" for his creations are but "parallels of himself."

A scientifico-poetic theory, or at least conviction, of the doctrine of parallelism must be done by graphic illustration, so as to unfold gradually to the physical eye what the "Interlude" makes clear to the inner eye. Science and poetry, as well as other parallelisms, are integrated by the powers of man's imaginative will. For imagination is the greatest of "man's single working powers." The natural tendency of axes is toward fluency when they are liberated from rigid geometry, as illustrated in Plate 7. The drawings on this plate show the values of parallel axes. They teach us that distinctions between the organic and the inorganic cease in the struggle of the artist to create form. The "creative reality of form lies within a continuous series emanating from a single primal life-impulse seeking and finding manifold expression in form. Life itself is thus manifested as a constant flow into countless multitudes of specific forms." Thus, through words and drawings, we learn that there cannot be life without form and that the study of form is the study of life itself.[7]

Notes

[1] "After eighteen years of tender care, the paradise, the poem of spring, Louis's other self, was wrecked by a wayward West Indian hurricane. . . . 'Twas here Louis did his finest, purest thinking. 'Twas here he saw the flow of life, that all life became a flowing for him, and so the thoughts the works of man. . . . 'Twas here Louis underwent that . . . spiritual illumination . . . which is life's sublimation, timeless, and spaceless." Louis H. Sullivan, *The Autobiography of an Idea* (New York: Press of the American Institute of Architects, 1926), pp. 297–98. "The West Indian hurricane" was a figurative way of describing his loss of the cottage to the Hottinger tile factory in Chicago. Connely tells us that the house, furniture, and the wonderful rose gardens, were left intact. "Sullivan had neither the heart nor the purse to go down and remove even a few of his things." Willard Connely, *Louis Sullivan as He Lived: The Shaping of American Architecture* (New York: Horizon, 1960), p. 249.

[2] Sullivan's drinking seldom interfered with his work. Wright's attitude toward Sullivan's social life is always colored by Wright's dislike of "urban vices" such as drinking, smoking, gambling, and whoring. But, as Wright was the first to admit, Sullivan was very meticulous about debts. He kept a diary and entered every loan, however trivial and casual. He paid his debts when he could. As he aged, his temper and his youthful arrogance mellowed greatly, although he suffered occasional outbursts of rage and violence. Sullivan lives in the memory of Chicagoans who knew him best as a man of nobility as well as genius.

[3] We know very little about this woman who did so much to ease Sullivan's last years. Her name is not given by Morrison, Wright, or Connely.

[4] See Frank Lloyd Wright, *Genius and the Mobocracy* (New York: Duell, Sloan and Pearce, 1949), Chapter Five, for Wright's description of Sullivan's last years.

[5] *Ibid.,* Chapter Five.

[6] These drawings were finished on June 11, 1923, when they were sent off to the engraver. The original drawings are in the Burnham Library of the Art Institute. They were published in 1924 as *A System of Architectural Ornament According with a Philosophy of Man's Powers,* by Louis H. Sullivan, Architect (New York: Press of

the American Institute of Architects, Inc., 1924). The drawings, in pencil, are about twelve by twenty inches.

[7] On Plate 2 and again on Plate 5, the student is referred to *Gray's School and Field Book of Botany* for "a simple exposition of plant function and structure," while the advanced student "who wishes to investigate the power that antedates the seed-germ (which in reality is a sort of embryo) is referred to that remarkable work by Professor Wilson, *The Cell in Development and Heredity.*"

45

The Imagination of the Architect

The Autobiography of an Idea, written to accompany his plates on ornament, is the story of Sullivan's quest for a philosophy of democratic architecture.[1] The anger and bitterness of *Democracy: A Man Search,* over the betrayal of America by its feudal powers, had passed. As he lay dying Sullivan searched deeply in his own life for foundations of belief in the capacity of men to live in beauty and brotherhood. He did not believe one was possible without the other. If men were to be saved from feudalism and if the terrible prophecies of coming tyranny were to be forestalled, men must turn to art as they were turning to science and the intellect. But they must turn to art as an idea, a philosophy, as well as a craft or a tradition. How was this done? The *Autobiography* is the record of Sullivan's search for an answer.

This discovery of art as the great human power of his own time, the twentieth century, and in his own place, Chicago, is told in the form of a voyage. Thus Sullivan's *Autobiography* joins Whitman's poems and Mark Twain's song of the river, *Huckleberry Finn,* as one of the most characteristic forms of American art and life—the voyage of exploration in search of a great transcendent moment of democratic communion. Like *Walden,* the *Autobiography* is a great affirmation of the American spirit. Sullivan reached the end of his voyage at the end of his life. His chronicle is not a hope or a dream, but a record of the hard-won spiritual triumph of an American artist. In his last days, as he corrected proofs of the *Autobiography,* there was little in the life about Sullivan to sustain his faith. In one terrible cry of despondency he turned to Wright and said: "Frank, our people have stopped thinking! It would be harder now to do radical work and more difficult to get radical work accepted than it ever was." Yet out of such despair and anguish Sullivan created one of our greatest testaments of faith in democratic culture. The time in which he wrote was no easy time of faith but a time of blood and terror.

The world is in travail, smeared with blood, amid the glint of bayonets; the feudal idea has reached the pitch of its insanity. . . . It requires courage to remain steadfast in faith in the presence of such pollution. Yet it is precisely such courage that marks man in his power as free spirit. . . . one gives out words of . . . prophecy . . . announcing the new man and the culture of faith. . . . It seems fitting, therefore, that this work should close with the same child-dream in which it began. The dream of a beauteous, beneficent power, which came when, winter past, the orchards burst into bloom, and the song of spring was heard in the land. . . . That dream has never ceased. . . . It was this unseen nearby presence, messenger of Life in its flowing, that sang its song of spring to the child, and the child heard what no one heard; the child saw what no one saw.[2]

Sullivan believed that the artist was born in moments of illumination. He describes many such moments in his *Autobiography*. He also grades them on an ascending scale toward the greatest moment of all—the moment when the "Creative Dreamer"[3] envisions the forms which he must forge into reality. "In childhood his idols had been the big strong men who *did* things. Later he had begun to feel the power of men who could *think* things; later the expansion power of men who could *imagine* things; and at last he began to recognize as dominant, the will of the Creative Dreamer: he who possessed the power of vision needed to harness Imagination, to harness the intellect, to make science do his will, to make the emotions serve him—for without emotion nothing." What was the source of this belief? This steadfast belief in the power of man (as artist) was "an unalloyed childhood instinct, an intuition and a childhood faith which never for a day forsook him, but grew stronger, like an indwelling daemon."[4]

The poet is born in childhood. No one, not even Wordsworth or Whitman, believed more profoundly in the intimations of immortality of the child. The mystical trances of childhood which Wordsworth describes so poignantly and so beautifully in his great Ode[5] were also a part of Sullivan's childhood, as of his youth and manhood. At the end, as at the beginning, of his *Autobiography* Sullivan invokes the pure intuitions of childhood as the wellspring of all art. Democratic education must "recognize that every child is the seat of genius; for genius is the highest form of play with Life's forces . . . [and] that the child, undisturbed, feels in its own way the sense of power within it, and about it. . . . [for] by intuition the child is mystic—close to nature's heart, close to the strength of Earth." A democratic art was possible then, because *every* child, not just the gifted, was capable of art. The dreams of the child, "its wondrous imagination, its deep creative instinct, its romance," are a sacred trust.

Whence came this capacity in the child, and how are we to explain its perversion in the bad art of our times? And if the child is capable of pure intuitions of beauty, and the child is father to the man, what is the source of corruption in the child? This, like the ancient problem of evil, which required the devout to explain why a good God had created an evil world, had to be solved, in reason if possible, in faith if not. Sullivan held to both reason and faith. The child was born with capacities for art, but he was also born with "feudal fear," which, if not eradicated, will lead to destruction. The feudal fears of the child are survivals of a dark past which can be dissolved "with gentle ridicule." The child must be taught prudence and the obvious consequences of acts. "No child that can toddle bravely is too young to know what choice means, when presented objectively and humanly." We must therefore teach the nature of choice at the very beginning of life.

Nearly half of Sullivan's *Autobiography,* his account of the development of the *idea* of architecture, is about his childhood. The first four chapters are about his early childhood. In them he describes the birth of the artist, for in his eyes the experience of art begins early. The images experienced in early childhood became the basis of his work as an artist. His parents gave him many of these experiences. His father was a dancing teacher who had learned his art from the leading masters of Paris. "In those days dancing was a social art of grace, of deportment, and of personal carriage. . . . It was an art of elegance. Artificial it largely was, yet humanizing, and beneficent." His father was deeply moved by nature's beauty, particularly "its more grandiose moods," which "inspired an ecstasy, a sort of waking trance, a glorious mystic worship." His mother was a skilled piano player. "Her sense of rhythm, of sweep, of accent, of the dance-cadence with its reinforcements and languishments, the *tempo rubato*—was genius itself." [6] At the age of two he was deeply moved at the sight of street cleaners at work. In this experience there "upsprung a life-fascination,—the sight, the drama of things being done." As the first rank of four men armed with huge red watering cans swung into the rhythm of their sprinkling the thrill began. The child breathed hard. "Then followed the second rank—four men with huge brooms made of switches; they also, two-fisted, swung one-two, one-two, shaping a windrow in the gutter. Then came the glory of it all, the romantic, the utterly thrilling and befitting climax—an enormous, a wonderful speckled gray Normandy horse, drawing a heavy tip cart, and followed as a retinue by two men, one sweeping the windrows into hillocks, the other with shovel and with mighty faith, moving these mountains into the great chariot." The sight of this "Pageant of Labor" left the child thrilled "with a sort of alarm of discovery, held by an utter infatuation." Such early experiences, Sullivan decided in the last months of his life, were "a budding sense of orderly power. Indeed, the rhythm of it all!" [7] All through his childhood he was moved by this "song of work, the song of action."

At about the same time (his third year) another of Sullivan's "illuminations" occurred. This became a family legend and was often told by his mother. One afternoon, as his mother was playing a nocturne "with the fervor and melancholy sweetness that were her sometime mood," she became lost in the dreamland of her music. Suddenly she heard a "voice, low-pitched like a sigh, a moan." As she paused, her son pressed himself tight to her bosom—"tears, tears, an ecstasy of tears, a turmoil of embraces, the flood gates open wide, a wonder, a joy, a happiness, an exaltation, an exultation supreme over the world. The child did not understand. . . . Had a new world begun to rise, this time a wonder-world within himself? Had there been awakened a new power within the child of three,—a power arising from the fountainhead of all tears?" [8]

The next illumination was the beginning of a series of mystical moments in nature. He spent most of his time with his father on their vacation in Folly Cove on Cape Ann. "He would sit beside his father on a great boulder watching him fish with pole and line. He would remain patiently there, inspirited by the salt breeze, listening to the joyous song of the sea as the ground swells reared and dashed upon the rocks with a mighty shouting, and a roaring recall, to form and break and form again. It seemed to lull him. It was mighty. It belonged to him. It was *his* sea. It was *his* father fishing." One day his father rowed far out to sea and dropped below the horizon. The child shrieked in alarm. His father reappeared. The child, "dumbfounded, ran to meet his father, in wild excitement." His father explained as best he could how it was possible to drop beyond the horizon. But the child "knew, all of himself, and beyond the knowledge of others . . . that the sea was a monster, a huge monster that would have swallowed up his father, like one of the giants he had told his grandma about, if his father had not been such a big strong man. He felt this with terror and pride. Thus arose in prophecy the rim of another world, a world of strife and power, on the horizon verge of a greater sea."

This magical summer of his third year was followed by his first experience with the prison house of the world. The family returned to Boston, where he was sent to the public school. His recollection of his stay there is but "a gray blank. Not one bright spot to recall, not one stimulus to his imagination, not one happiness. These he found only at home. He learned his letters, he followed the routine. That is all. . . . The primary school had, for the moment, dulled his faculties, slackened his frank eagerness, ignored his abundant imagination, his native sympathy. Even the family influence could not wholly antidote this. The neighborhood was growing disreputable." [9]
The family decided to send Louis to his grandfather's farm at South Reading. Free from the prison house of the school and the city, the poet was born

again. Again, as he had thirty-two years earlier in 1899, he describes the awakening of the poet's imagination in nature. In his 1899 talk [10] on the artistic use of the imagination he described the link between the sensual and the emotional, the direct experience of things and feelings, and the emotion in imagination. Emotion

is simply the attention that the heart gives, and is as natural and easy as the attention that the sense of sight or hearing gives; when we think at a glance of the infinite variety of objects and actions that may be seized on by the eyes, the ears or the hands, separately or collectively, it becomes easy to see how immense may be the corresponding variety of emotions, reaching from the simple, the calm, the sedate, the joyous, through the serious and melancholy, to the complex, the turbulent, the sublime.

For the artist is gifted with "a capacity to receive impressions, and to transmit them in a more or less permanent form." What distinguishes him from his fellows is not the impressions he receives, but his ability to create forms which express a quality of spirit characteristic of himself. This individual quality is as "natural to him as is his walk, or his gestures, or the inflexions of his voice: and [as] the work of his hands first begins to assume that definiteness of form announcing growth, he for the first time, and with a certain joyful surprise notes those peculiarities . . . which mark his work as a something existing more or less independently of the work of his fellows." The peculiarities are like a man's first sight of his own visage, in a mirror, which "unmistakably exists, and which, though he did not and could not create it, he nevertheless feels to be his own." [11] The artist must be quick to perceive the beginnings of his difference and uniqueness. He must be careful

to mark their tendency, and to foster their growth; for he instinctively knows them [the forms he creates] for true children of his emotions, and he is pleased with the likeness. He knows that he has had within him certain thoughts, certain feelings, certain longings; that the people and the objects daily surrounding him produce on him certain attractions and repulsions from which his aptitudes and the drift of his ambition take their rise and shape their course. He knows that many sights and sounds are food for him, that some make a stifling, others a wholesome air to breathe.

The artist, it is true, seldom reasons much about these things, "for the true artist is, as he should be, rather a creature of instinct than of reason." Reflection in the artist cannot be confused with the operation of the intellect, as the work of the craftsman or the scientific technician. "It is only when, to the qualities of artist are added those of the poet, that reflection takes a powerful hand in shaping the results."

This does not mean that the artist abandons reason to seek some kind of orgiastic revelation in feeling and emotion. The artist "will naturally seek in thought to project the line of his tendencies toward its goal." He is like "the mariner outward bound, after many days [who] looks anxiously for the land." The voice of the topman shouting "Land ho!" does not bring the land any nearer, "for the wind must blow, the sails be trimmed, the helm shifted, soundings made, the pilot Prudence taken aboard and time elapse before a safe haven can be made and the cargo called secure." The artist "is much such a ship,—a creature of wind and current, rising and falling on an unstable and capricious sea. Yet he has a compass and determined rudder, and if storms be not too fierce he will arrive." Perhaps it would be better to say that the artist is like "a rounded year, ushering in with a clamorous and nimble springtime, bearing charming flowers in his heyday, sobering and quieting with the heavy growths of summer, bearing rich fruitage in the mellow autumn." Like the seasons, the development of the artist cannot be forced. The lapse of time works these varied changes, "and the lapse of time alone can cause the artist flower to ripen into fruit." This flower "is his own sensitive nature." Perhaps the artist, like the flower which reaches fertility in bloom, needs the "presence of the busy bee of self-deception and complacence." Before long

one by one the pretty petals fall and the serious business of growth and ripening proceeds. For a long time the fruit is green and unsavory, but it promises much and in the end fulfills when maturity with color and sweetness come to it. . . . Some natures indeed are like the persimmon and need a sharp frost to bring out their flavor. . . . Or is it more apt to say that the artist is like an orange tree,—bearing, continually, flowers, and ripeness in every stage,—pendant golden thoughts in the last,—fruits of all that sap we call imagination.

But whatever our analogy for the development of the artist, his growth will be slow. Its normal course cannot be hastened. "To produce vigorous results in art the emotions must follow close upon the mind and give it sure support. Sometimes the mind, in its own perversity, travels on ahead and alone; there then comes about that disjointed condition which Solomon characterized as the 'Pride which goeth before destruction,' and which, in more homely parlance we call the 'big-head.'" But the imagination must also be fed and nourished on homely experience of nature and man. For it is our daily experience of people and things that supplies the foundations upon which the imagination, like a great tower, rests. These small, homely, daily experiences must be of two distinct kinds to produce a real result. First, there must be the "prosaic and sometimes tiresome happenings and learnings of every day, the patient coming into touch with many things through the senses and the observation." We must be willing to "do one thing at a time and give [our] whole attention to it." For it is axiomatic that "to know one must touch; from every touch there comes a sensation, and it is this sensation that we call experience."

Such experiences are preserved intact for us in our memory. The longer we live "the greater does the accumulation become, and the more elastic our feeling of strength, the more secure our equipoise in difficulty, because the more precise and ready our sense of reality." What is really striking about a masterpiece is the "vast wealth of small experience that is to be seen stored up in it. They do not give it its quality of mastership, that were indeed a puny view to take of a large thing, but just as surely it would not be a profound work without them." For the imagination "is impotent without this basis of common and matter of fact experience and can no more make its spring than can the line without a firm footing." But we should not confuse the practical with the real in art. An "exact sense of reality" in art requires a second and distinct set of experiences "which amplify the practical and give to it the keen intuitive incisiveness of life, namely, the emotional."

The sensations of the true artist are very complex, for, "to susceptibility of the senses he adds susceptibility of the heart." Every object and every experience with people give him a double sensation, "specifically the sensual and the emotional." As the artist matures, the sensual and the emotional come to be so "interblended that they will appear to be one impression." But for all, artist and spectator alike, the fusion of sensation, or feeling, and emotion in the experience of form "can be nothing less than an artistic experience." This does not mean that the artist is some kind of god whose emotions are supernatural, beyond common experience. Emotion "is simply the attention that the heart gives, and is as natural and easy as the attention that the sense of sight or hearing gives. . . ." Emotions, unlike feeling or the sensual, are born in society. The "more important of one's experiences are those derived from contact with his fellows, with the works and thoughts and experiences and qualities of those who have gone before."

We see, then, that if the artist possesses a simple and wholesome nature, his surroundings will appeal to him, and we see the ways in which he will answer such appeals. "Into all that he sees he enters with sympathy; and in return all that he sees enters into his being and becomes and remains a part of him. For, in the words of Walt Whitman:

There was a child went forth every day,
And the first object he looked upon and received with wonder, pity, love, or dread, that object he became,
And that object became part of him for the day, or a certain part of the day, or for many years, or stretching cycles of years.

The early lilacs became part of this child,
And the grass, and white and red morning-glories, white and red clover, and the song of the phoebe-bird,
And the Third month lambs, and the sow's pink-faint litter, and the mare's foal, and the cow's calf,
And the noisy brood of the barnyard, or by the mire of the pond-side,
And the fish suspending themselves so curiously below there—and the beautiful curious liquid,
And the water-plants with their graceful flat heads—all became part of him.

The field-sprouts of Fourth month and Fifth month became part of him,
Winter-grain sprouts, and those of the light yellow corn, and the esculent roots of the garden,
And the apple-trees covered with blossoms, and the fruit afterward, and woodberries, and the commonest weeds by the road,
And the drunkard staggering home from the outhouse of the tavern, whence he had lately risen,
And the school-mistress that passed on her way to the school,
And the friendly boys that passed—and the quarrelsome boys,
And the tidy and fresh-cheeked girls—and the barefoot negro boy and girl.

His own parents,
He that had fathered him, and she that conceived him in her womb, and birthed him,
They gave this child more of themselves than that,
They gave him afterward every day—they and of them became part of him.

The mother at home, quietly placing the dishes on the supper table,
The mother with mild words—clean her cap and gown, a wholesome odor falling off her person and clothes as she walks by;
The father, strong, self-sufficient, manly, mean, angered, unjust,
The blow, the quick loud word, the tight bargain, the crafty lure,
The family usages, the language, the company, the furniture—the yearning and swelling heart,
Affection that will not be gainsaid—the sense of what is real—the thought if, after all, it should prove unreal,
The doubts of day-time and the doubts of night-time—the curious whether and how,
Whether that which appears so is so, or is it all flashes and specks?
Men and women crowding fast in the streets—if they are not flashes and specks, what are they?
The streets themselves, and the façades of houses, and goods in the windows,
Vehicles, teams, the heavy-planked wharves—the huge crossing at the ferries,
The village on the highland, seen from afar at sunset—the river between,
Shadows, aureola and mist, light falling on roofs and gables of white or brown, three miles off.
The schooner near by, sleepily dropping down the tide—the little boat slack-towed astern,
The hurrying tumbling waves, quick-broken crests, slapping,
The strata of colored clouds, the long bar of maroon-tint, away solitary by itself—the spread of purity it lies motionless in,
The horizon's edge, the flying sea-crow, the fragrance of salt-marsh and shore-mud;
These became part of that child who went forth every day, and who now goes, and will always go forth every day,
And these become part of him or her that pursues them here.[12]

Notes

[1] As a chronicle of his life, it ends in his thirty-eighth year, and it tells us little about his family life and private life after his sixteenth year.

[2] These quotations are taken from the last paragraphs of Louis H. Sullivan's *The Autobiography of an Idea* (New York: Press of the American Institute of Architects, 1926).

[3] Sullivan's use of the word "dream" is closer to our use of the word "vision." That is, for him "dream" means a conscious imaginative construction, not a fantasy of the unconscious.

[4] Sullivan, *op. cit.*, pp. 247–48.

[5] In his introduction to his *Ode on Intimations of Immortality from Recollections of Early Childhood*, Wordsworth says: "Nothing was more difficult for me in childhood than to admit the notion of death as a state applicable to my own being. . . . it was not so much from feelings of animal vivacity that *my* difficulty came as from a sense of indomitableness of the Spirit within me. . . . I was often unable to think of external things as having external existence, and I communed with all that I saw as something not apart from, but inherent in, my own immaterial nature. Many times while going to school have I grasped at a wall or tree to recall myself from this abyss of idealism to the reality. At that time I was afraid of such processes. In later periods of life I have deplored, as we have all reason to do, a subjugation of an opposite character. . . . To that dream-like vividness and splendour which invests objects in child-hood, every one, I believe, if he would look back, could bear testimony, and I need not dwell upon it here: but having in the poem regarded it as presumptive evidence of a prior state of existence, I think it right to protest against a conclusion, which has given pain to some good and pious persons, that I meant to inculcate such a belief. It is far too shadowy a notion to be recommended to faith, as more than an element in our instincts of immortality. But let us bear in mind, that though the idea is not advanced in revelation, there is nothing there to contradict it, and the fall of Man presents an analogy in its favor. Accordingly, a pre-existent state has entered into the popular creeds of many nations; and, among all persons acquainted with classic literature, is known as an ingredient in Platonic philosophy. Archimedes said that he could move the world if he had a point whereon to rest his machine. Who has not felt the same aspirations as regards the world of his own mind? Having to wield some of its elements when I was impelled to write this poem on the 'Immortality of the Soul,' I took hold of the notion of pre-existence as having sufficient foundation in humanity for authorizing me to make for my purpose the best use of it I could as a poet." Wordsworth then quotes in conclusion and as epigraph to the Ode the last three lines of his "My Heart Leaps Up When I Behold."

> My heart leaps up when I behold
> A rainbow in the sky:
> So was it when my life began;
> So is it now I am a man:
> So be it when I shall grow old,
> Or let me die!
> The Child is father of the Man;
> And I could wish my days to be
> Bound each to each by natural piety.

[6] Sullivan, *op. cit.*, pp. 15–16.

[7] *Ibid.*, pp. 17–18.

[8] *Ibid.*, p. 20.

[9] *Ibid.*, p. 24.

[10] In his paper, "The Artistic Use of the Imagination," which he read before the Chicago Architectural Sketch Club, on October 7, 1889 (at about the time the Auditorium Building was completed), Sullivan ends by quoting in full Whitman's "There Was a Child Went Forth." This paper was published in the *Inland Architect and News Record*, Vol. 14, No. 4 (October, 1889), pp. 38–39.

[11] Sullivan, "The Artistic Use of the Imagination." The following quotations in this chapter are from this paper.

[12] This version of "There Was a Child Went Forth," from Whitman's *Autumn Rivulets*, is that of the 1860–61 edition.

46

The Individual Development of the Architect

DURING THE WRITING of his *Autobiography* Sullivan was careful
to compare the illuminations of his own childhood with those necessary
to the artistic use of the imagination, as he had described them in his early
essay of 1889. *The Autobiography of an Idea,* written some thirty years
later, is a personal record of his search for an understanding of art and the
role architecture must play in society. It is personal only in so far as it is a
record of his birth and development as an artist. He reached maturity as an
artist, he tells us, at the time of the Fair. From his arrival in Chicago on
the day before Thanksgiving, 1873, at the age of seventeen, to the closing of
the Fair in 1893, he is concerned with his struggles to achieve a philosophy
of architecture. On the remaining thirty years of his life, he is silent.[1]

As we see in the 1889 essay on the imagination, Sullivan was always concerned about the artist's development as an individual. But he believed that
the artist's individuality developed only through active participation in the
practical daily life of his time. For, if experience in nature supplied inspiration for form, the experience of the artist in society supplied the meaning
of form.[2] Sullivan's principle of form is always a social, as well as an aesthetic,
principle. His thoughts as he entered his fateful partnership with Adler in
1891 clearly indicate this.

After long years of ambitious dreaming and unremitting work, . . . at the age of 25,
Louis H. Sullivan became a full-fledged architect before the world, with a reputation
starting on its way. . . . Now Louis felt he had arrived at a point where he had a foot-
hold, where he could make a *beginning* in the open world. . . . He could now, undisturbed, start on the course of practical experimentation he long had in mind, which
was to make an architecture that fitted its functions—a realistic architecture based on
well-defined utilitarian needs—that all practical demands of utility should be paramount
as a basis of planning and design; that no architectural dictum, or tradition, or superstition, or habit should stand in the way.[3]

For his view, his conviction, was this:

That the architectural art to be of contemporary immediate value must be *plastic;*
all senseless conventional rigidity must be taken out of it; it must intelligently serve—

it must not suppress. In this wise the forms under his hand would grow naturally out of the needs and express them frankly, and freshly. This meant in his courageous mind that he would put to the test a formula he had evolved, through long contemplation of living things, namely that *form follows function,* which would mean, in practice, that architecture might again become a living art, if this formula were but adhered to.[4]

Ten out of sixteen chapters of the *Autobiography* deal with childhood, boyhood, and youth. In these the life of the artist is personal and subjective. But the content of this subjectivity, the search within, is a search in the experience of art. Sullivan is concerned with himself, his family, his friends, and his environment in terms of his development as an artist. And since, in the last months of his life, as in his early essays of the eighties, he believed that the supreme faculty of the artist is his imagination, the life of an artist, on whatever level, is always a record of his struggle to develop this supreme faculty. Sullivan does not try to describe himself as a man, but as an artist. Thus, even in his most intimate moments of revelation, it is his early intimations, his struggle to discover a universal principle of art and finally to create form in architecture, that engross him. His "life story" is what the title states—the autobiography of an idea, and above all, the *idea* of art. He writes in the third person, as if desiring to keep distant from himself so that he can be objective about his search. He asks us to share a journey in understanding of the development of the artist in American society and particularly in Chicago, where, in terrible pain and suffering, he fought and won some of the most decisive battles of the spirit in our time. But, he insists, this journey of understanding must be subject to reason as reason arises in discourse between equals. The romantic hortatory tone of the architect-poet and priest, and the rage and hate of the dishonored prophet, have gone. Passion still lives in the pages of Sullivan's autobiography, but it is the passion of reasoned imagination—the imagination of the form-giver in art.

In Sullivan, passion lived with irony, for as he grew older his passion became more and more a passion of the mind and spirit. The bitterness and cursing of *Democracy: A Man Search* changes into genial but profound irony. The comic spirit replaces the tragic. In the *Autobiography* smiles and laughter banish tears. The pain and suffering of life are transcended by a stoical comic spirit which will not close the mind to reason, even though reason opens sudden and terrible visions of man's corruption and savagery. As Mark Twain looked back on the boy, Huck, to tell us of the birth of his imagination, so does Sullivan recall his own childhood as a similar time of delight and wonder.[5] There is deep sadness in Sullivan's joy over his childhood—the sadness of all falls from grace. For the grace of chidlhood—*every* childhood, if we but knew it, Sullivan argues—is art. Men live in misery and gloom because they no longer hear the voice of art within them. Sullivan's irony over adult rejection of art arises in questioning why men disregard the golden moments of joy in art which they knew in childhood. Why, given choice, the basis of all moral and aesthetic experience, do men choose art that brings them misery, to art that could give them joy? Why, when beauty is so natural to man, is there yet so much ugliness? But the haunting question of whether men, all men, are really capable of creating and living with art is now settled. Sullivan *hoped* and *believed* they were, but he wanted to ground his faith in reason.

Sullivan refused to abandon reason in his last months of pain and despair. As he lay dying in poverty and neglect, he was not even sure that his principles would survive among the people he so deeply loved. Yet he decided once again to probe deeply into the foundations of his belief in art and to open these beliefs to reason. He does this through irony, for he believed always that reason lived in irony and comedy as much as tragedy. In *Kindergarten Chats* he turned to irony and comedy as the form proper to instruction of the young. The irony of the *Autobiography* is far more gentle than that of *Kindergarten Chats,* in which we saw master and pupil through each other's eyes and each exposed to the other and to the reader incongruities between ideals and life.[6] But in the *Autobiography* the master chooses the role of an ironic friend who asks us, as another old and wise artist, to view with him the journey of "Louis, the child, into the kingdom of art."

The use of the child to symbolize the awakening of the artist to beauty and his calling in life creates a compassion and tenderness between the reader and the artist. The student in *Kindergarten Chats* arouses our sympathy, but he always remains to us what he was for his master, an audience who is at his best when he stimulates the master to great talk. But "Louis" is the artist growing up in society. In smiles, sometimes in laughter, we witness the childish eagerness, boyish bravado, and youthful arrogance of the artist making his way into a world at once strange, alien, hostile—as well as friendly, warm, and loving. We witness, too, wonderful moments of possession when the mystic power of art sweeps over the soul of the child and youth. Our smiles hide tears over the innocence of the "little hero" who dares to affront the world of practical men by becoming an artist. But the ironic sadness of the *Autobiography* is the sadness of love for those who must live in fear and misery because they do not know how to enter the kingdom of beauty. Art, the great guardian of the human spirit, exists as surely as the kingdom of God exists in the compassion of Christ. And in democratic art, just as in early Christianity, we are equal because we are

Ornament, Sullivan taught, should be "of," not "on," a building. Farmers and Merchants Union Bank (1919), Columbus, Wisconsin. *Photo by Len Gittleman for the Sullivan Project of the Institute of Design, Illinois Institute of Technology.*

brothers. Our passion and love are for men as comrades and brothers, as well as lords and slaves. Sullivan's irony is not based on doubt of art, but on the spectacle of man suffering in self-inflicted gloom and misery, while the golden joyous kingdom of art lies so close at hand.

The child-artist in Sullivan has not fallen from a paradise of beauty, as he has in Wordsworth. There is no state of pre-existent artistic grace, or Platonic essence buried in some mythological past, to which man turns his eyes in sadness and remorse as he stumbles through life in pain and anguish. Man is not attended by the brilliant but melancholy light of life's star which

> Hath had elsewhere its setting,
> And cometh from afar: [7]

but the great radiance of a democratic commonwealth, which men can reach once they banish ignorance and fear through art. Like an ironic god, Sullivan smiles, as we smile, over the spectacle of men living in the dark because they dare not lift up their eyes to light and beauty. But Sullivan asks us to smile at men, and thus at ourselves, in hope that someday men will find the courage and wisdom to take themselves to the golden kingdom of democratic art whose dawn will light a new day of freedom and dignity among men.

One of the earliest illuminations of the child was the sight of a tree, whose image became the image of all structure for Sullivan (as a tree also did for Wright). On his way to his first day in school in South Reading, accompanied by his beloved Grandma, they

leisurely mounted a gentle grade until the crest was reached. At this exact point, just behind the stone wall to the right of the road—marvel of marvels—stood a gigantic, solitary ash tree. . . . of a sudden there it stood, grand, overwhelming, with its immense trunk, its broad branches nearly sweeping the grass, its towering dome of dense dark green; . . . The child stood transfixed, appalled. A strange far-away storm, as of distant thundering, was arising within his wonderself. He had seen many trees, yes; but this tree—this *tree!* He trembled strangely, he wished to cry; with gentle scolding he was dragged away.

The next morning he began school. "All details settled, he was to come the next morning, which he did, after successfully passing the magnet tree, while saluting it affectionately in a calmer mood. Day after day he passed the tree. It became *his* tree—his Great Friend." [8]

The school he entered at South Reading was Sullivan's first profound experience with his peers and with a social group outside of his family. The response of the child-artist was characteristic of his later dramatic view of society.

The school-room was large and bare with two wooden posts supporting the roof. The teacher sat at her desk on a raised platform. . . . The children sat at rows of desks (a row per grade). . . . There were five grades in the single room. Teacher sat at her desk, ruler in hand to rap with or admonish. All the children studied their lessons aloud, or mumbled them. . . . Everything was free and easy; discipline rare. There was however a certain order of procedure. Came time for a class to recite. They flocked to the wall and stood in a row; neither foot nor head at first. Questions and answers concerning the lesson of the day. Teacher's questions specific: pupils' answers must be definite, categorical. Teacher was mild, patient; the answers were sometimes intelligent, more often hesitant, bashful, dull, or hopelessly stupid. Each answer was followed by a monotonous "go to the foot," "go to the head"; and all the time the hum went on. . . . This label merged or deliquesced into a monotone; there seemed to be a diapason, resonant, thick, the conjoined utterance of many souls trying to learn, entering the path of knowledge that would prove short for most of them. The children were all barefoot and rather carelessly clad; notably so in the matter of omissions. One thing is certain and the rest is lies: This school was of, for, and by the people. . . .[9]

The child was given his proper place in the lowest grade, or class, or whatever it was called. . . . He seemed to feel the importance of his entry into this new world, so different from home. . . . Somehow he did not fit into the curriculum or the procedure. . . . He seemed to be nothing but a pair of eyes and ears not intended for books, but for the world little and big about him. In this immediate sense he was almost devoid of self-consciousness. His normal place was at the foot of the class. But one day he awakened to the fact that unawares he had become interested, not in books, but in procedure; said procedure consisting in the oral examinations and recitations of the grades above his own, as they, in accordance with the arrangement of the school-room, stood directly in front of him, drawn up in line, undergoing the routine torture.[10]

He began to notice their

irregular mass-effect and their separate persons. He followed their fortunes in going to the head. He transferred himself to them. He noticed, too, which girls were the prettiest and which boys were the gawkiest. He learned the names of all. He became solicitous of their personal fortunes, in their struggle for knowledge or their attempts to escape it. For him, it became a sort of drama, a sort of stage performance, and he began to note with growing interest what they said and what teacher said, which answers were correct, which were failures. Over and over he saw and heard this until he came to know the groundwork of what all grades above him were struggling with.[11]

Even the arithmetic problems were recast in the child's mind as a drama.

. . . he followed the upper grades so intently that he became critical: What was this about four men who built so many perches of stone wall in three days, and two other men who were to build some wall in six days. What did it amount to anyway? The real question was *where* was the wall to be built? For *whom* was it to be built? What was his name? What were the names of the men who were building the wall, (for it was becoming a real wall)? Were they Irish or Scotch? Where did they get the stone to build the wall? Did they get it from the rough quarry across the road from the schoolhouse? Did they gather up boulders from the field? Was not this matter of four men and two men irrelevant? The information was too sparse, too unconvincing. He could not *place* the wall, and what good was any wall he could not see? And thus he went on, unaffected by the abstract, concerned only with the concrete, the actual, the human.[12]

But the child-architect's intense interest in the drama of the classroom and his dramatic interpretation of elementary problems in arithmetic—an interest that was to ripen many years later in his treatment of buildings as stages for the enactment of human relationships—was not appreciated by the teacher. She wrote to his grandparents, the Lists. "One evening when all were at home, a letter arrived addressed to Grandpa. He opened the envelope and read the letter aloud. . . . his grandson was a dull boy . . . inattentive, would not study his lessons, was always at the foot of his class, but he was a nice boy. Could not Mr. List bring influence to bear to induce Louis to reform his ways?" [13] At this point, conflict between society and his individuality entered the critical time of his childhood—the years, so he believed, when the artist is born. What part would his parents and grandparents take in this conflict between child and society? In his outline of his "mongrel origin," as Sullivan described his ancestry, Henri List is the intellectual force of the Sullivan family. Henri List

was straight German of the Hanoverian type—6 feet tall, well proportioned, erect carriage, and topped by a head, full, clean-shaven face, thick lips, small gray eyes, beetling brows and bottle nose. He was of intellectual mold, and cynically amused at men, women, children and all else. . . . Henri List was reticent as to his past, but the family gossip had it that as a young man he was educated for the Catholic priesthood, rebelled at the job and ran away from home. . . . The intervening years between this hegira and his arrival in Geneva, Switzerland, are a blank. . . . was he a Professor of Greek in the University, or did he coach rich young English gentlemen through their university course? In any event he was highly educated, and he prospered.[14]

Anna Mattheus, Henri List's wife and Louis Sullivan's beloved grandma, was "a miniature woman of great sweetness and gentle poise. . . . Like a true *mère de famille,* she ruled the roost, as was the custom in French society of the Middle Class. Her mind was methodic, her affection all-embracing." Her daughter, Adrienne, "seemed French, but was not wholly so. She had typical eyelids, expressive hazel eyes, an oval face, features mobile. She was a medium stature, trimly built, highly emotional, and given to ecstasies of speech." Patrick Sullivan, Louis's father, said that his father was a landscape painter, a widower, and he an only child. Together they used to visit the county fairs in Ireland. At one of these fairs he lost his father in the crowd and never saw him again. "Thus at the age of twelve he was thrown upon the world to make his way. With a curious little fiddle, he wandered barefoot about the country-side, to fiddle here and there for those who wished to dance; and of dancing there was plenty." [15]

No one knows how Patrick Sullivan became interested in dancing as an art. "As to the grim determination of his character, his pride and his ambition, there can be no doubt." In London he placed himself under the "tutelage of the best—most fashionable—masters, and in due time set up an academy of his own." Not content with this, he journeyed to Paris, where he took instruction under the leading masters. To him "the art of dancing was a fine art of symmetry, of grace, of rhythm." But Patrick also possessed a hunger for beauty. In him "Nature's beauty, particularly in its more grandiose moods, inspired an ecstasy, a sort of waking trance, a glorious mystic worship." [16]

Patrick was a strange paradox. His highly "virile and sensitive powers" were embodied in an unlovely person.

His medium size, his too-sloping shoulders, his excessive Irish face, his small repulsive eyes—the eyes of a pig—of nondescript color and no flash, sunk into his head under rough brows, all seemed unpromising enough in themselves until it is remembered that behind the same mask resided the grim will, the instinctive ambition that had brought him, alone and unaided, out of a childhood of poverty. . . . he had not found time to acquire an "education," as it was then called and is still called. He, however, wrote and spoke English in a polite way, and had acquired an excruciating French. Hence by the standards of his time in England he was no gentleman as that technical term went, but essentially a lackey, a flunkey or social parasite. Perhaps it was for this reason he revered book-learning and the learned. He knew no better.

Patrick reached Boston in 1847, "set up an academy and was successful. He was always successful. His probity was such that he could always command respect." [17]

Each grandparent reacted to this crisis in the child's life in characteristic ways. When Grandpa read the teacher's letter, he

dropped the letter on the floor, burst into volcanic laughter, roaring until the lid of the heater rattled, rocking forward and backward on his chair, clapping himself on the knee, in a series of subsiding outbursts, ending in a long-drawn spasmodic chuckle, expressive of his cynical sense of humor, his infinite contempt for those who had eyes and yet saw not. To call his sharp-eyed grandson a dullard! Why, he said, one might as well call Sirius a flap-jack, and other joking words to that effect, for he was fond of teasing his grandson, whom he had so long watched out of the corner of his eye.

Grandma took the side of society. "With her grandson at her knees, a bit abashed, a bit afraid, after giving her six propitiatory kisses, his arms about her neck and cheek to cheek, she found it, oh, so hard to scold him. Instead she told him gently how necessary it was to acquire an education; how necessary to that end little boys, particularly her own grandson, for the family's pride, should attend industriously to his lessons. Could he not do better, would he not do better? He said he could and would; and all was peace." [18]

With the capacity for single-minded devotion to a task interesting to him, which was to characterize Sullivan all his days, the six-year-old boy, "shutting out all else," pitched in to his studies. He was soon head of the class. But he could not remain engrossed in being at the "head of a row of dull-wits." His downfall was lapses of attention caused by "a twitching squirrel in a tree nearby the window, or a beautiful white cloud curiously changing shape as it slowly drifted through a beautiful blue sky. . . ." And then came winter with the drama of sports, and work, especially the work of men cutting ice. "How exciting it was to watch men at work. They used large hand saws to cut ice into square blocks and there was one strange saw drawn by a horse. Then men with poles shoved and dragged the ice-blocks through the clear water to the bottom of the runway, and then it was hauled up the runway by a horse that walked away with a rope that ran through a pulley and then back to the ice cake. The ice seemed very thick and clear." [19]

And then there came his first experience of nature in winter,

splendid snow-storms, decorating the trees, forming great drifts through which he struggled in exultation, every now and then stumbling and falling with his face in the snow. How he rolled over and over in glee in the snow of a white world, a beautiful world even when the gray skies lowered. . . . And the sleigh rides. Oh, the sleigh rides in the cutter with the horse looming so high, and the row of bells around the horse's collar, jangling and tinkling in jerky time. . . . It was his first experience within the pulchritude of a winter in the open. His mother came frequently to see him and caress him. He could hardly understand why she loved him so; he had so many other personal interests and distractions. But he hailed her comings and deplored her departures.[20]

Soon after his sixth birthday another social crisis faced the family. "While his name was Louis, he had other names—interesting ones, too." It seemed difficult for a family of such diverse temperaments and backgrounds to settle on a single name for their child. He had not been christened or baptized. A family council was called. "The father, a nominal Free-mason, not sure whether he was a Catholic or an Orangeman or anything in particular, expressed no serious interest; he would leave it to the rest. Grandpa, as usual, vented his view in scornful laughter. Grandma, a Mennonite, was opposed to baptism. But mother in her excited way was rampant. What! Would she permit any man to say aloud over the body of her pure and precious infant that he was born in sin and ask for sponsors? Never! That settled it and they named him Louis Henri Sullivan." [21] The Sullivans had difficulties with their Irish heritage.

It has been declared and denied that the name was given in order to heap honors upon Napoleon III. Be that as it may. The name Henri, obviously, was to deify Grandpa. The Sullivan could not be helped. It was scorned by all but its owner. They detested the Irish, whose peaceful penetration of Boston had made certain sections thereof turn green. Even his wife could not stand for it, much less for Patrick. So sometimes she gallicized the name; which wasn't so bad, when she used it in the third person, nominative, singular. Then she had an inspiration, an illumination one might say, and invented the word Tulive, whatever that may have meant, as a general cover name, and thus secured a happy, life-long escape.[22]

Later on, at about the age of twelve,

the scion asked his father about this name Sullivan, which seemed to coincide with shanty-Irish. So his father told him this tale: Long ago in Ireland, in the good fighting days, there were four tribes or clans of the O'Sullivans: The O'Sullivan-Moors, the O'Sullivan Macs, and two others. That *We* were descended from the O'Sullivan-Moors, and that all four tribes were descended from a Spanish marauder, who ravished the west Irish coast and settled there. His name it appears was O'Soulyevoyne or something like that; which, translated, meant the Prince with One Eye. Now, however great was the glory of this pirate chief, his descendant, Louis Henri Sullivan O'Sullivan-Moor–O'Soulyevoyne, had this specific advantage over him of the high seas. The prince had but one eye that must have seen much; the youngster of six had two eyes that saw everything, without desire to plunder.

Such then, was the family and the world of Louis Henri Sullivan until the age of six. And, as Sullivan quotes Whitman,

These became part of that child who went forth every day, and who now goes, and
    will always go forth every day.
And these become part of him or her that peruses them here.

Notes

[1] We know far less about the personal life of Sullivan, who died in 1924, than we do about many artists who died before 1800.

[2] Sullivan was always wary of "arty" talk. "To discuss architecture as an art is interesting enough in a way. It is amusing, after a fashion, and hurts nobody. But to discuss architecture as the projected and written life of a people is another story."

[3] Louis H. Sullivan, *The Autobiography of an Idea* (New York: Press of the American Institute of Architects, 1926), p. 257. Sullivan's italics.

[4] *Ibid.*, pp. 257–58. Sullivan's italics.

[5] In *Kindergarten Chats,* the "young architect" has lost the intuitions of his childhood in school. The master seeks to rediscover them by returning his pupil to the imagination and the heart. But this is done through the mind, as well as through highly emotional moments in nature.

[6] That is, the young graduate student trained in the best schools turns out to be very ignorant; the master, who is supposed to be teaching the young architect how to think about buildings, soars off into clouds of poetic rhetoric about the seasons of the year, etc.

[7] See stanza V of Wordsworth's ode, *Intimations of Immortality from Recollections of Early Childhood,* and the ode's introduction as given in Ch. 45, note 5. Although Wordsworth, Whitman, and Sullivan write about the pure artistic intuitions of the child, the source of these intuitions is very different. Whitman and Sullivan find it in the future. The past is not the "home" ("but trailing clouds of glory do we come/From

God, who is our home") nor the time of God's creation, but a time of wandering and darkness. The future is the glory in Whitman and Sullivan, where "These became part of that child who went forth every day, and who now goes, and will always go forth every day." Here, the child as artist *progresses* to his kingdom.

8 Sullivan, *op. cit.,* pp. 28–29. Sullivan's italics and capitalization.

9 *Ibid.,* p. 30.

10 *Ibid.,* pp. 30–31.

11 *Ibid.,* p. 31.

12 *Ibid.,* p. 32.

13 *Ibid.*

14 *Ibid.,* pp. 11–12. Baumann, the Chicago engineer who befriended Sullivan in his first years in Chicago, was another German of intellectual mold, cynically amused at men. But these German liberals were not cynical about democracy, so long as democracy was based on free, open, and informed discussion.

15 *Ibid.,* pp. 12–13.

16 *Ibid.,* p. 14.

17 *Ibid.,* pp. 14–15.

18 *Ibid.,* pp. 32–33.

19 *Ibid.,* pp. 34–35.

20 *Ibid.,* p. 35.

21 *Ibid.,* p. 36.

22 *Ibid.*

47

The Illumination of Nature in the Life of the Architect

Lᴏᴜɪs, the child, did not know, because of the city life he had led in Boston, that the bare fields left by the rains would soon give rise to a spectacle of entrancing beauty—his first spring.

The grass appeared as a delicate deepening influence of green. Did not the child soon find the earliest pussy-willows, the first crocuses in the garden? Did he not note the delicate filigree appearing as a mist on tree and shrub, and the tiny wild plants peeping through the damp leaves of autumn in his favorite woods? Did he not really see things moving? . . . The outburst of bloom upon peach tree, cherry and plum, evoked an equal outburst of ecstasy and acclaim, an equal joy of living. Was not something moving, were not all things moving as in a parade, a pageant? . . . Was not something moving with great power? Was there to be no end to the swet, clamorous joy of all living things, himself the center of all? Could he stand it any longer? [1]

Suddenly the apple orchards "sang aloud!" What was this marvelous power in nature? "Was it something serene, sweet, loving, caressing, that seemed to awaken, to persuade, to urge; yea, to lure on to frenzy, to utmost exaltation, himself and the world about him, the new, the marvelous world of springtime in the open—a world that became part of this child that went forth every day, a world befitting him and destined to abide with him through all his days? Oh, how glorious were the orchards in full bloom! What mountains of blossoms! What wide-flung spread of enravishing splendour!" The child was overwhelmed. He "became unstrung! His heart found relief from suffocation in his running about, his loud shouts of glorification and of awe, his innumerable running-returns to the house to say breathlessly, 'Come, Grandmama! Come see! Come see!' He wished to share his joy with all. These wonder-orchards were *his,* the fields, the woods, the birds were his; the sky, the sun, the clouds were his; they were his friends, and to this beauteous world he gave himself." [2]

He soon became a "son of the soil. Hatless, barefooted, his short pants rolled above his knees, and unkempt with activity," to the passer-by "he was a stout, stocky, miniature ruffian, let loose upon a helpless world." Only "two fine eyes, clear and bright," which "saw all things as they were" betrayed the fire within the child. "Exceedingly emotional—though unaware of it—the responses of his heart, the momentary fleeting trances, the sudden dreaming within a dream, perturbed him. He wished to know about these, he wished to know what it was that enthralled him time after time." He did not find out, for "that which perturbed him lay far deeper than his thoughts —a living mystic presence within the self-same open that was his." [3] But what was the nature of this mystic presence? Was it to be found in religion? "[His] father had some nondescript notions, without form and void. He was attracted by the artistic. . . . He had tried church after church seeking what he wanted. What he wanted was not priest or preacher, but a thinker and orator. At last he found, in Theodore Parker, the satisfaction of his quest. Going alone, he attended regularly. From this it may be inferred that he leaned toward Unitarianism. Nothing of the sort—he leaned toward oratory. If Unitarianism went with it, well and good. It was of no moment. He praised Parker highly." Mother had a fixed idea that "existence was continuous in a series of expanding becomings, life after life, in a spiral ascending until perfection should be reached in a bodiless state of bliss. This ethereal belief opened to view the beauty and purity of her heart. Moreover, she read with avidity Renan's *Vie de Jesus*." [4]

"Grandpa looked upon religion as a curious and amusing human weakness—as conclusive evidence of universal stupidity." Grandma alone was devout. She believed in her God; but she did not seek to proselyte. She was satisfied to abide in her faith, undisturbed and undisturbing. Perhaps this is why her grandson loved her so. Innocent of creed, of doctrine and dogma, he loved her because she was good, he loved her because she was true, he loved her because to his adoring eyes she was beautiful. Such was Grandma." [5]

Grandpa, who ridiculed so many things and scoffed at religion, worshiped the stars. He retired to his room early in the evening, and as the boy passed the open door of Grandpa's room, he "always looked in, and always saw Grandpa stretched full length in bed, reading by the light of a student lamp some book on astronomy." The child did not intrude, for he knew these moments were sacred to Grandpa. "He knew full well that however much Grandpa ridiculed so many things, he never poked fun at the solar system. In this domain, and the star-laden firmament, he lived his real life. This was his grand passion. All else was trivial. The vastness awed him; the brilliance inspired him; he kept close track of the movements of the planets. He read endlessly about the moon and the vast, fiery sun, and the earth's spiral path." [6]

Grandpa "went forth in the early hours of night to make vigils with the stars, to venerate, to adore this panoply of constellations, to be wholly lost within the splendour of the sky." Here Grandpa found his mystic presence, and he tried to open a way to it for the child. For Grandpa recognized very early in the child's life that he had one supreme gift—imagination. The child in turn felt, if he did not understand, the depth and wonder of his Grandpa's veneration of the starry skies. "What communion he held within the stillness of night, within his own stillest hour, no man shall know. Now and then he would, bit by bit, endeavor to impart a little of his knowledge. But he knew well enough that his grandson was not of age." [7] But his grandson was able to imagine what the keen and erudite mind of Grandpa could not conceive.

One evening they were walking together along the garden path. The crescent moon was smiling just above the tree-tops to the westward. They had been silent, thus far, when Grandpa of a sudden asked, "Louis, have you ever seen the penumbra of the moon?" When the meaning of penumbra had been asked and answered, when the child had grasped the idea that it was the rest of the moon next to the crescent, he said, "Yes, Grandpa, I see it." Grandpa asked: "What is it like?" The child replied: "It is curved at the edge and flat the rest of the way. It is pale blue, like a fog. It is beautiful." Grandpa was moved deeply. He recognized the power of the artist in the child. "Ah! . . . how I envy your young eyes! I have never seen it. I have tried with opera glasses, but still could not see it. It must be wonderful—and I shall never see it." And then Grandpa made his prophecy. "You see things that I cannot see and shall never see. When you are older you shall know what I mean." [8]

Grandmama's gift of a loving nature was not matched by the gift of imagination. "In place of this divine power she had well-defined, solidly settled ideas concerning decorum, breeding, formal and informal social intercourse, and a certain consciousness that Mrs. Grundy resided as definitely in South Reading as elsewhere." She was oblivious to hypocrisy and cant. "In this instance, she differed diametrically with her daughter Adrienne, who railed bitterly at that cloak of respectability which to her view camouflaged the sins of the world. . . . Candor and sincerity were her ideals of conduct." Grandmama soon settled on the Baptist Church, "attendance upon which would at one and the same time insure to her unquestioned respectability, and nearly as possible, coincide with her individual views of doctrine." She began regular attendance, and soon decided Louis was of age to attend divine service. "Thus another world was to arise above the limited horizon of his experience." [9]

On a Sunday morning, "fair to look upon, in early summer, . . . the family set forth, following the dusty road to the village. . . . Upon arrival at the church, a white-painted wooden structure in imitation of stone, pretentious, and ugly,—as if indoctrinated with sin,—so much talked about within—the family entered." They entered a large, dim, barren room, and reached the family pew. "Louis immediately felt a pang of disappointment. There was nothing here to recall an echo of the spring song he had shared in the open.

He thought there should be. Looking about at the congregation, he was astonished at the array of solemn faces; Why solemn? And the whispering silence: Why whispering? What was to follow? What was to happen? He inquired, and was hushed. He awaited. The service began; he followed it eagerly to the end, noting every detail." [10]

The details the child noticed, like those in the schoolroom, were dramatic details. It was the expression in pantomime, not the content of the sermon, which fascinated him. "He greatly admired the way the minister shouted, waved his arms terrifically, pounded the big Bible magnificently, and then, with voice scarcely exceeding a whisper, pointed at the congregation in dire warning of what would surely befall them if they did not do so and so or believe such and such. He roared of Hell so horribly that the boy shivered and quaked. Of heaven he spoke with hysterical sweetness—a much of syrupy words." His vigorous sermon, in which he "painted the same word-pictures year after year; [and] worked himself to the same high pitches and depth," moved his congregation. "His listeners, now thrilled, relaxed, expanded, held these sermons, these prayers, these hymns as precious; for the man looming in the pulpit was of their world. He gave pith, point and skilled direction to those collective aspirations and fears, which otherwise would have lacked symmetry and power." [11]

The child's first experience with religion was a violent one. The "total effect was one of confusion, perturbation, and perplexity." For the child-artist it was a spectacle of fear and hate, acted out on an ugly stage.

One particular point puzzled him most: Why did the minister, when he prayed, clasp his hands closely together and so continue to hold them? Why did he close his eyes? Why did he bow his head and at times turn sightless face upward toward the ceiling? Why did he speak in whining tones? Why was he now so familiar with God, and then so groveling? Why did he not shout his prayers as he had shouted and roared through his sermon? Why did he not stand erect with flashing eyes, wave his arms, clench his fists and pound the big Bible, and walk first this way and then that way, and otherwise conduct himself like a man? He seemed afraid of something. What could it be? What was there to be afraid of? [12]

And what was the reason for attacking the Papists?

Why so bitter, why so violent, why so cruel as to wish these people, whoever they were, to be burned throughout all eternity in the flames of awful hell? . . . The boy asked at home what Papists were. Grandma said they were Catholics, Grandpa said they were imbeciles. Then he asked what were Catholics, and Grandma said, simply, they were not Protestants. And what were Protestants? And Grandma said, as simply, but with a touch of detail, that they were not Catholics, to which Grandpa added that they, also, were imbeciles. But at the end of the next sermon the minister explained it all. He declared in his wrath that they, the Papists, were pagans, heathen, infidels, idolaters, worshippers of saints, low beasts, vile savages, ignorant, depraved, the very scum and slime of earth whom God in his mercy had segregated from the elect, in this world, in order that he might damn them totally to Hell in the next.[13]

The minister acknowledged himself a sinner, "and frequently proclaimed, as with a sort of pride, that his entire congregation, individually and collectively, were miserable sinners; and they agreed. He told them, moreover, the wages of sin was death. He told them also, with unction, of the bloody source whence came the wages of purity in redemption." The child suffered in the midst of all this fear, violence, cursing, threatened torture, and blood. He appealed to Grandpa. Grandpa said the minister "was an idiot full of wind and nonsense." The child continued to suffer. Nothing in this new world of religion agreed with the world of the child-artist. "It was all upside down, all distorted, cruel and sugary. It was not like his beautiful springtime, it was not even like his beautiful winter. There was no laughter, no joy as he knew these things." Perhaps Grandpa was right. "After more sermons, and prayers, and denunciations, he began to feel distinctly that his world, his life, which he had frankly felt to be one, was being torn in two. Instinctively he revolted." [14]

As he looked back from his last months of life at his revolt against the church, Sullivan realized that the child, Louis, had already reached the deepest source of his being in beauty. "He would *not* have the beauty of life torn from him and destroyed. These things he did not say; he felt them powerfully. A tragedy was approaching. He was about to lose what he loved, what he held precious in life; he was about to lose his own life as he knew or felt life." The services irritated him more and more. He asked to be transferred to the Sunday School. "The Old Testament amused him and pleased him with its interesting stories. He could almost live them over." But "when it came to the crucifixion he rebelled again in spirit, this time so ardently that it was thought prudent at home to release him from Sunday School and church alike."

The child had other battles to wage in his struggle to find himself. The hillside school irked him ruthlessly. He could not understand why he must be punished at school when he was never whipped or punished at home. He struggled to keep his eyes from the sky and the trees, as he sat in the schoolroom. But he could not, for the call of "a wooded ravine through which wandered a noisy rivulet" called to him. One morning the call overwhelmed him. After stuffing his blouse with rolls, doughnuts, and cookies, he hurried to his ravine, whose tall arching oaks sheltered the gurgling stream which passed hurriedly over a bed of fieldstones. Here was erected the first Louis

H. Sullivan structure. It was an ideal site for a dam. "He got immediately to work. He gathered the largest field stones he could handle, and small ones too. He had seen Scotchmen and Irishmen build frame walls and knew what to do. . . . He found a rusty remnant of a hoe, without the handle; with this he dug up some stiff earth. So with field stones, mud, twigs, and grass he built his dam. It was a mighty work." And, as it turned out, it was another powerful illumination, the discovery in a mystic moment of creative work of a new joy in the life of the child, and indeed, of a joy in creative work that marked all the remaining years of his life.

The child was lost to everything about him save his dam.

The impounded waters were rising fast behind the wall, and leaking through here and there. He must work faster. Besides, the wall must lengthen as it grew higher, and it leaked more at the bottom. He had to plug up holes. At last child power and water power became unequal. Now was at hand the grand climax—the meaning of all this toil. A miniature lake had formed, the moment had arrived. With all his strength he tore out the upper center of the wall, stepped back quickly and screamed with delight, as the torrent started, and with one great roar, tore through in huge flood, leaving his dam a wreck. What joy! He laughed and screamed. Was he proud! Had he not built the dam? Was he in high spirits? Had he not built this dam *all by himself*? Had he not planned in advance just what happened? Had he not worked as hard as he had seen big men work? Wasn't he a strong boy for his age? Could anything at home compare with this? Exhausted with work and delight he lay stretched on his back, in the short grass, looking far up at the spreading branches, glimpsing bits of blue between the leaves, noting how these self-same leaves rustled softly, and twinkled in the sunshine.[15]

After going afield to hunt up a cow ("All cows were his friends") to milk, he settled to his meal near the site of his triumph.

Then he loafed and invited his soul as was written about a big man about the time this proud hydraulic engineer was born. But he did not observe "a spear of summer grass"; he dreamed. Vague day dreams they were,—an arising sense, an emotion, a conviction; that united him in spirit with his idols,—with his big strong men who did wonderful things such as digging ditches, building walls, cutting down great trees, cutting with axes, and splitting with maul and wedge for cord wood, driving a span of great work-horses. He adored these men. He felt deeply drawn to them, and close to them. He had seen all these things done. When would he be big and strong too? Could he wait? Must he wait? And thus he dreamed for hours.

The next great moment in nature for the child was his experience of the setting sun. As Louis waded into Tyler's Pond, to immerse himself in the "evening chant to the invisible King of all frogs," he noticed that the surface of the pond was crimson. As he waded ahead the ripples of the pond turned silver and crimson as they moved away from him. He looked straight ahead from where he stood in the water, and in the woods beyond he saw the setting sun, the trees silhouetting against it, and the lower sky aglow. The sun sank from sight, "the western sky softened into gray, twilight deepened into gloaming as the child stood knee deep in the warm shallow water, lost in reverie so faint, so far, so near, so absorbing, so vibrant that the once noisy chorus seemed a tranquil accompaniment to a melody that was of earth and sun in duo with his dream." [16]

As he wakened from the dream the child decided he must speak to Grandpa about the sun. Grandpa was willing, but careful. "He knew a child's mind was a tender thing. He was keenly observing, but said little. He quietly, even eagerly observed his grandson, as one might watch a precious plant growing of its own volition in a sheltered garden, but far was it from him to let the child suspect such a thing. . . . But this time, when his grandson in eager child-words dramatized the sunset and climaxed all by a sudden antithesis, saying he had never seen the sunrise. How did it rise? Would Grandpa tell him? Would Grandpa please tell him? Then Grandpa wide-eyed knew a mystic golden bell had struck the hour." [17] It was difficult for Grandpa to explain the rising and the setting of the sun over the horizon in a hilly country, and to a child who had never viewed the open sea. But with a "strategy of simple words, and easy similes he produced a sort of image for the child." He explained that the sunset could be viewed from the land westward of the house. The child asked: "But Grandpa, is the sunrise as beautiful as the sunset?" His Grandpa assured him it was. "Far more so, my child; it is an epic grandeur; sunset is lyric, it is an elegy." Thus the old German cynic opened his heart to the child. The child felt, but did not understand, the mystic presence of the sun and the stars for Grandpa. Grandpa, in turn, was embarrassed at slipping into a lyric outburst which the child did not understand. He returned to his gentle teasing of the child. "But you must know that in summer the sun rises very early, earlier than I; and I scarcely believe my young astronomer will get out of his comfortable bed long before daylight, just to see the sun rise out of *his* bed." [18]

But Grandpa was wrong. The child could scarcely sleep in anticipation of the dawn. He arose at twilight, made ready quickly, and passed up the road leading to the great ash tree, whose companionship he ever sought on high occasions.

Here, under the wondrous tree . . . here in stillness of oncoming dawn punctured here and there by a bird's early chirp, and chanticleer's high herald call heard near and far, raucous, faint, and even fainter far away; the few remaining stars serene within the dome of pale passing night, he stood gazing wistfully over the valley toward a far away range of dark blue drowsy hills, as the pallid eastern sky, soon tremulous with a pink suffusion, gave way before a glow deepening into radiant crimson, like a vanguard of fire—as the top of the sun emerging from behind the hills, its slow-revealing disc reaching full form, ascended, fiery, imperious and passionate, to confront him.[19]

The child now experienced one of his great mystic moments in nature.

Chilled and spellbound, he . . . became impassioned with splendour and awe, with wonder and he knew not what, as the great orb, floating clear of the hilltops overwhelmed him, flooded the land; and in white dazzling splendour awakened the world to its work, to its hopes, to its sorrows, and to its dreams. Surely the child, sole witness beneath his great ash tree, his wonder-guardian and firm friends sharing with him in its stately way as indeed did all the land and sky and living things in the open—the militant splendour of sunrise—the breaking of night's dam—the torrent and foaming of far-spreading day—surely this child that went forth every day became part of the sunrise even as this sunrise became forevermore part of him.[20]

Notes

[1] Louis H. Sullivan, *The Autobiography of an Idea* (New York: Press of the American Institute of Architects, 1926), pp. 39–40.

[2] He remembers, too, his first experience of war: "For how could he know, that far, far from this scene of love, of pride and joy, men were slaughtering each other. . . . True, at the appointed hour, he had run about the house shouting 'Fort Donelson's taken! Fort Donelson's taken!' and equally true he had made *Monitor*s out of a bit of lath and the bung of a flour barrel, and with greater difficulties a *Merrimac*."

[3] *Ibid.,* pp. 41–42.

[4] *Ibid.,* p. 42.

[5] Sullivan's attacks on the church in *Democracy: A Man Search* are based on the conviction that the established church had betrayed Christ. His reverence for the Passion of Christ was deep and abiding. For Sullivan religion meant love. As he tells us, he learned this from Grandmama, who possessed the gift of love. *Ibid.,* p. 43.

[6] Sullivan, *Autobiography,* p. 44.

[7] *Ibid.,* pp. 44–45.

[8] *Ibid.,* p. 45.

[9] *Ibid.,* p. 46.

[10] *Ibid.,* p. 49. Huck Finn, like Louis, objected to the dreariness of religious practice. "The widow rung a bell for supper, and you had to come to time. When you got to the table you couldn't go right to eating, but you had to wait for the widow to tuck down her head and grumble a little over the victuals, though there warn't really anything the matter with them."

[11] *Ibid.,* p. 49. Sullivan completes his dramatic sketch: "The sermons invariably ended with a tirade against the Papists. This epilogue appealed to all as a most satisfying finale. After the closing words of benediction the congregation remained for a while outside the church, gathered in groups, the men swapping lies and horses, the womenfolk exchanging idiosyncrasies. This was routine. Then they went home."

[12] *Ibid.,* p. 50.

[13] *Ibid.,* p. 51.

[14] *Ibid.,* pp. 51–52.

[15] *Ibid.*, p. 56.

[16] *Ibid.*, pp. 58–59.

[17] *Ibid.*, p. 59.

[18] *Ibid.*, pp. 59–60.

[19] *Ibid.*, pp. 60–61.

[20] *Ibid.*, p. 61. As he grew older, Sullivan was to experience many such moments, and, as we have seen, he always returned to nature (as he carried his young architect to nature in *Kindergarten Chats*) to revive his spirit.

48

The Illumination of Man and His Works in the Life of the Architect

THESE MYSTIC MOMENTS in nature refreshed the child's keen interest in the world and its work. His elders were not disturbed by his strange trances, because "between spells" he was "ridiculously practical."

As a matter of fact Louis was living almost wholly in the world of instinct. Whatever there was of intellect consisted in keen accuracy of observation, and lively interest in all constructive affairs. Without reflection he admired men at work. To see men at work, and himself to work, especially if he could participate, was his childish joy. . . . Though he was his grandparents' pet, disparity in age, occupation and thought left him much to himself and he did mostly as he pleased. What marked him apart and comforted his elders was an entire absence in him of destructive tendency.[1]

His first morning task was his garden. Here was born the wonder of seed, of the seed with its two cotyledons, whose image was to infuse the drawings of his last work, *A System of Architectural Ornament According with a Philosophy of Man's Powers*. When the young gardener discovered a nasturtium cut down by a cutworm, he asked:

How could a cut-worm do such a shocking thing? Had he not reared all these beauties from the very seed? Had he not watched them growing, day by day, from infancy to blossom time—putting forth tender leaf after leaf, and unfolding their tiny buds into lovely flowers? Had he not watered them and weeded? How often had he wondered at what made them grow. How often, on hands and knees—close up—had he peered and gazed long, hungrily, minutely at them one by one, absorbed in their translucent intimacy; indeed worshipped them in friendship until he seemed to *feel* them grow; that they were of his world and yet not of his world; that they seemed to live their own lives apart from his life.[2]

He soon returned to his ravine, where he had first experienced the joy and excitement of engineering. The song of nature and of work filled his spirit. He wandered eastward out of the heavily wooded ravine, into a broad field of meadow grass, where the busy stream flowed quietly and tranquilly. As the child lifted his eyes to the meadow,

there, solitary in the meadow, stood the most beautiful tree of all. He knew it at once for an elm; but such tall slender grace he had never seen. Its broad slim fronds spreading so high and descending in lovely curves entranced him. He compared it with the two . . . elms [on the Thompson place next door]. They were tall and spreading but stiff and—they were *pruned* from the ground way up to the big strong branches, while this lovely sister of the meadow, beneath her branching plume, put forth from her slender delicate frothy branchlets reaching almost to the meadow grass. Her beauty was incomparable.[3]

As he stood entranced before the great elm he thought of his other tree, his great ash tree. "How different it was—so grand, so brooding, so watchful on the crest of the hill; and at times, he firmly believed, so paternal—so big-brotherly." But this elm was far different.

. . . the lovely elm was his infatuation—he adopted her at first sight, and still gazed at her with a sweetness of soul he had never known. He became infiltrated, suffused, inspired with the fateful sense of beauty. He melted for an instant into a nameless dream, wherein he saw [s]he was sufficient unto herself, that like his garden plants she lived a life of her own, apart from his life. Yet they both lived in the same big world—they both, for the moment, stood in the same green field. Was there nothing in common? Did she not know he was there?[4]

His trance passed, leaving the child's senses keen and open to the song of nature. As he continued his first exploration of the stream, following its windings, wading as he went, he came upon the deep, clear wellspring from which the rivulet flowed. As he continued his journey, the "little stream began to ripple and sing sweetly to the child all alone in the meadow in the full sunshine—all alone; with plenty of company. Then the rivulet began to hurry and gurgle. Louis scaled the fence quickly to see the water descend all at once in a beautiful cascade of about his own height. After this, noisily foaming, it poured among the boulders to the lower level where he had built the dam."

And then the child knew joy, the deep joy of nature that lasted throughout his life and was one of the great illuminations that lighted his struggle to create art for the people of a democratic community.

He had reached his sanctuary in the shady grove, and sat a while on the lower or northern bank, to watch the squirrels. It seemed so funny to see a gray squirrel run head first down a tall tree, sit up straight in the grass, frisk his tail, wag his head, scamper to the next tree, run up and out to the end of a branch and jump from that to a branch of the next tree. He laughed gleefully at these antics. Meanwhile came from the undergrowth the note of the brown thrush, and from above various twitterings, chirpings, and distant floating meadow songs. . . . [And there was the marsh beyond] —how beautiful—covered with water half-knee deep, filled with groups of tall bulrushes, of reeds of blue flag, and slender grasses; and bright flowers here and there along the wavering edge. What joy to wade and wade, lengthwise and crosswise . . . following the margin to seek out hidden flowers. It was too much; too much at one time for one small boy. . . . Now the . . . boundaries of his domain [were] established.

The domain was his very own . . . no other boys should enter these lovely precincts. No other boys could understand. Besides, he loved solitude as he loved activity, and the open.[5]

For a whole month the truant boy played alone in his kingdom in the woods. "Not a soul came to disturb him." Like Thoreau at Walden he had much company in his solitude. "Rabbits, squirrels, birds and snakes were company enough." But while his heart was fixed in the woods, he made journeys into the other world he loved; the world of work. He called on many farmers and shoemakers. "He even went so far one day as to enter the stove foundry beside the tracks, near the depot. He went frankly to a work-man, watched him a while and told the man he liked to see him work." The moulder, much amused at the eagerness and curious innocence of the child, set about to show him how his work was done. The child spent the whole afternoon with his moulder, who "carefully explained to him every large and minute procedure." The child Louis was amazed. A "new world had opened to him—the world of handicraft, the vestibule of the great world of art that he one day was to enter and explore." [6] He also visited another craftsman, Boardman, the shoemaker. He was a swarthy little man, with black beard, black beady eyes, who worked and chewed tobacco—both furi-ously. From him he learned every detail of making pegged and sewed shoes: "He saw them built from beginning to end." The shoemaker and the boy soon became fast friends. Sometimes he would stop work, and "to amuse the child, would extinguish the life of a fly on the opposite wall with an unerring squirt of tobacco juice. Louis danced with joy. What a wonderful man to spit like that. . . . Then the Boardman man would catch flies with his hand and eat them, or pretend to eat them. Then the shoemaker would return to his furious work, and Louis in admiration would wander on." [7]

Neighbors said that Boardman was a "lowdown sport who stayed sober and worked hard only to get money to bet on the races—whatever that meant." But the child knew no social distinctions. People existed for the child in dramatic terms, and the most interesting drama of all was that of work. Often he visited Farmer Hopkins to watch him break a field with his "monstrous team of oxen, swaying and heaving heavily against the yoke, with low-bending heads and foaming mouths, as the man, with one booted foot in the furrow, guided the ploughshare as it turned up the beautiful black soil of the bottom land, while the man said, 'gee-haw'; 'haw'; 'haw-gee.'" The child made many such trips to his heroes in the drama of work. But he always visited his secret domain in the woods before each trip. At home in the evenings he teased Julia, the Irish servant, to tell him Irish fairy tales.

How lovely, how beautiful they were, with fairies, elves, gnomes and a great company, weaving spells of enchantment in the moonlight. He lived them all. Julia was a robust Irish peasant who remained with the family for nine long years. . . . She had a temper that came and went like a storm. She was not long since come to America. Many evenings her Irish women friends called and they talked Irish together. He had never heard anything so sweet, so fluid, except the rivulet. He could listen by the hour; and Julia taught him a few words.[8]

Thus for a whole month the child wandered freely, passing from one mystic moment to another in nature, in work, and in the beauty of words. He lived in a house of love and learned to love men. No hand was ever raised against him, and whatever moved the child to wonder also moved Grandmama and Grandpa. They loved him, and they talked with him. The child knew no fear at home, and thus when he ventured away from home he took no fear with him. He was taught that curiosity was natural and good, and that beauty was the heritage of all men. But this great month in which Louis H. Sullivan, the architect, was born, came to a sudden end. Teachers wrote to the Lists about their truant grandson. No one had said anything during this month of exaltation. No questions were asked, nor were any asked when the letter arrived. He was simply sent back to school, where "he languished in misery." But help soon came. Patrick, his father, had opened a summer school in Newburyport. "Father decided that the grandparents were too soft; they had let his child grow up like a weed; they had pampered him outrageously; it was high time his son was brought to him that he might establish in him a sense of respect, order, discipline, obedience." The child's mother came by train to South Reading. "She looked at her son with a sadness he could not understand, but she found it not in her heart to chide. The day of their departure arrived. With many a sob he said good-bye to all."

The train journey to Newburyport continued the song of work in the child's life. Work brought him into the world; our "poet, he of the dream life, crawled forth from his cave of gloom and began to take notice. Soon he was all notice and no gloom." The awakening of the child to the world about him on the train soon matched in intensity his illuminations in nature. His questions soon wore out his mother. But in another workman, Luke, the brakeman, he found a friendly mentor for the voyage. He soon exhausted the brakeman's store of knowledge of links, pins, couplings, engines, telegraphs, as well as his opinions on how to run a railroad. The brakeman showed the boy through the train, and watched in horror as a strange man yanked the child from underneath the train, where he had gone to examine the tracks.

At Newburyport the child was introduced to another art—the art of the

Ornament on the Getty Tomb of 1890. Sullivan's geometric forms, like his organic forms taken from nature, are plastic and rythmic expressions of structure. *Photo by Richard Nickel*

Frank Lloyd Wright called Sullivan's Getty Tomb in Graceland Cemetery, Chicago, a "requiem in architecture" comparable to the great requiems in music. *Photo by Richard Nickel*

human body. His father, the dancing master, was determined that his son should learn the grace and power of the body. "This program he set in motion by pulling his son out of bed at five in the morning, standing him upright, hurrying him into his clothes and leading him by the hand straight to the town pump." Here the day began with a full cup of cold water, a sharp quarter-mile run, followed by a two-mile brisk walk. At the end of the walk they came to a beautiful sequestered pool with deep, clear green water.

"Strip!" was the order. Strip it was. No sooner done than the high priest dexterously seized the neophyte, and, bracing himself, with a back-forward swing cast the youngster far out, saw him splash and disappear; then he dived, came up beside a wildly splashing sputtering unit, trod water, put the child in order, and with hand spread under his son's breast began to teach him the simple beginnings of scientific swimming. "Must not stay too long in the water," he said. "Would Sonny like a ride astride Papa's shoulders to a landing?" Sonny would and did. He gloried as he felt beneath him the powerful heave and sink and heave of a fine swimmer, as he grasped his father's hair, and saw the bank approach.[9]

In his father's body he discovered another nature, a companion to his beloved nature of earth, sky, water, flowers, and animals. "On land he took notice of his father's hairy chest, his satiny white skin and quick flexible muscles over which the sunshine danced with each movement. He had never seen a man completely stripped, and was pleased and vastly proud to have such a father, especially when the father, an object lesson in view, made exhibition dives and swam this way and that in lithe mastery." And thus a new ideal was born—"he had a new ideal now, an ideal upsprung in a morning's hour —a vision of a company of naked men, with power to do splendid things with their bodies."

But he found new visions in the real world—a world, it turned out for the child, much vaster than the small pond or the busy brook at Grandpa and Grandmama's farm in South Reading. On picnics with his parents, which always ended in sketching, he discovered a great river, the Merrimac, and a wonderful bridge which seemed to float in the air. Here, too, he had his first view of the concerted action of a group of craftsmen in a shipyard. "The child had never seen a river. Was it not wonderful, this river so wide, so dark, so silent, so swift in its flow? How could such things be? Why had he not known?" As the child watched, fish jumped, leaving a pretty circle of ripples, and then

arose into the air an enormous sturgeon, to fall heavily back, making a great hole whence came a rush of circles expanding magically to the shores, causing sky and trees to totter and twist; then all would be calm again and silent, as the great stream flowed on and on careless of trifles; on and on, so Papa said, until its waters should mingle with the sea's; on and on, day and night, winter and summer, year after year, before we were born, when we are gone, so Papa said, its waters had flowed and would flow and would evermore flow to the sea.[10]

Here on this river everything was large, and strange, and wonderful.

As he trudged up a hill into a heavy grove of woods, musing on the great river Merrimac, so different from his rivulet, his dam, and his marsh at South Reading, he felt lost in this new world. It was growing "so large that it seemed out of proportion to him—too great for his little size, too bewildering for his untutored mind." As he peered through the trees awe and foreboding seized him. Something "large, something dark, was approaching unperceived; something ominous, something sinister that silently aroused him to a sense of its presence." As he peered through the foliage he saw a huge, long, dark shape. What was it? "He thought of turning back, for he was but a little boy, alone in the woods bordering a dark-running river whose power had stilled him, and the lonely grove that stilled him. . . ." The dark thing came nearer and nearer, seeming to draw the child against his will. In the stillness of the wood, the dark thing became broader, looming, and then, as the child stepped out of the wood, changed itself into "an enormous terrifying mass that overhung the broad river from bank to bank."

He saw great iron chains hanging in the air. "How could iron chains hang in the air?" His fancy wandered to the magic of Julia's fairy tales with their giants. Perhaps he had invaded the home of these great creatures? Might there be fairies in the woods? And then, "He saw a long flat thing under the chains; and this thing too seemed to float in the air; and then he saw two great stone towers taller than trees. Could these be giants? And then of a sudden, mystery of mysteries, he saw a troll, not much bigger than a man, come out of the fairy forest, driving a fairy team. The troll went right across on the flat thing that floated in air, and vanished." Only a wicked wizard could do this, the child decided. Surely a giant who could do these things would soon come to eat up the little boy, as the giants in Julia's tales of enchantment often did. The trees echoed the child's thoughts.

And the tree murmured: "Yes; a wicked wizard has done this thing—a giant will come to eat up the little boy—good-bye, little boy"—and the river said: "Good-bye, little boy." The child screamed for Papa. Papa, searching for his lost child, and determined to punish him for wandering off, halted in alarm at the glazed and terrified eyes of his child, "Oh, Papa," said the child, "see the big iron chains hanging in the air, see the two giants turned to stone, see the flat thing floating in the air. A troll just came over it with horses and wagon. I am to be eaten by a giant. The troll with the magic wagon is coming to get me now. I am to be eaten by a giant, Papa; the trees have just said good-bye, little boy; the river has said good-bye, little boy; Oh, Papa, did the good fairy send you to save me?" [11]

After warning his son that fairies lived in their enchanted land only in people's fancy long ago when Ireland was young, and that Irish heads were often filled with queer notions, he told the boy that they would exorcise the spell by visiting the bridge. But the child was still fearful. "What is a bridge, Papa?" His father assured him that the bridge would not harm him. Then the dancing master explained to his son, as he had to many little tots, how a form or figure was made. His skill and patience in explaining the bridge were fine art. Gradually he brought his son out of the land of dark enchantment to the light of reality. "For shameful fear, he substituted in his son's heart confidence and courage." And thus was the child's mind "freed again to wonder what men could do; to adjust itself to the greater world into which it had been suddenly catapulted from South Reading's tiny world. Within that little spot of earth he had never seen a river, never seen a bridge." The child looked back in awe and love upon the great suspension bridge. "There, again, it hung in air—beautiful in power. The sweep of the chains so lovely, the roadway barely touching the banks." And most wonderful of all, it was made by men, not supernatural creatures from enchanted lands. How "great must men be, how wonderful; how powerful, that they could make such a bridge. . . ." And again the child "worshiped the worker."

The song of work rose to greater harmonies in the fancy of the child. Father and son visited the shipyards, where ships were being built on the ways while others were being rigged in the slips. One was but a skeleton, another was ready to launch.

The strident song of the caulking iron saws the air; odors of tar everywhere. . . . Here in the shipyard were crowds of men working, doing many things, all moving at the same time—all urging toward a great end. The child was in seventh heaven; here were his beloved strong men, the workers—his idols. What a great world it was into which he had been thrust—the great river, the wonderful bridge, the harbor, the full rigged ships so gallantly moving. And what new words too—circulation, calisthenics, catenary, dietary, suspension, bridge, and others, that seemed very long, very strange indeed. Was he also entering a world of words? Were there many more such words? [12]

The child found such a rush and crowd of things that were new to him that he was "joyfully dazed—very happy, very serious. It was his first view of the power of concerted action. But the child still thought of it as the work of individual men, a great crowd of men each doing his own work in his own way. But he sensed keenly the greatness of the work. What could men not do if they could make a great bridge—suspended in the air over the Merrimac?" At the launching of the ships the child had another "spasm of wonder." As the ship went down the ways his father recited: "She seems to feel the thrill of life along her keel." This was poetry, his father said, because it all rhymed. So the child "learned at once what poetry was—it was a new *world*." He learned also from his father's explanations that there was another new and utterly unsuspected world—"the world of pure knowledge—vaster than the sea, vaster than the sky."

This new world, the world of words, took its place in wonder and beauty beside nature, men, and work. When he saw his first ship disappear beneath the horizon he ran to his father, crying, "Papa, some of those ships are sinking! One is all gone but the top of the masts; one is just beginning to sink!" His father, who taught children to dance, now wished to teach his son something of the earth. But how was one to explain to a seven-year-old boy the curvature of the sea, the horizon, and thus prove to the child that the ships were not sinking. "Little by little the child grasped the idea; he brightened with intelligence. His father had opened for him then and there a new, an utterly unsuspected world—the world of pure knowledge—vaster than the sea, vaster than the sky. And for the child, the portal to that limitless world was an illusion—a sinking ship."

Thus ended the childhood of Louis H. Sullivan. For within a few days the seven-year-old boy was to leave Newburyport and plunge into a new life in the city of Boston, where the fields and ponds of South Reading soon became a memory of things far off and long ago. His childhood was over, the prison house of the city was soon to close over him. But in this child the illuminations of his childhood would never die. They remained for him the most important moments of his life. For in these great moments, in the deep visions and trances of childhood, Sullivan found himself. The child became indeed the father of the man whose spirited voyage stands beside those of other heroic American voyagers—Hawthorne, Melville, Whitman, and Mark Twain—into the kingdom of Art.

Notes

[1] Louis H. Sullivan, *The Autobiography of an Idea* (New York: Press of the American Institute of Architects, 1926), pp. 62–63.

[2] *Ibid.,* p. 63.

[3] *Ibid.,* pp. 63–64.

[4] *Ibid.,* p. 64.

[5] *Ibid.,* pp. 67–68.

[6] *Ibid.*, p. 68.
[7] *Ibid.*, pp. 68–69.
[8] *Ibid.*, p. 70.
[9] *Ibid.*, pp. 78–79.
[10] *Ibid.*, p. 81.
[11] *Ibid.*, p. 84.
[12] *Ibid.*, p. 90.

PART EIGHT

The Idea of an American Architecture in the Life of Louis Henri Sullivan

49

The Childhood of the Architect as a Parable of the Birth of Imagination in the American Artist

SULLIVAN'S PAGES on his childhood in *The Autobiography of an Idea* are the greatest pages he ever wrote. They were written at the end of a life whose last years were lighted by the brilliant memory of early success —a brilliance which only increased the poignancy of years when he sat with idle hands. Not, as in Frank Lloyd Wright's years of idleness, because of economic depression, but by something far more difficult to endure—conscious neglect by his countrymen and by his fellow architects, such as Burnham, who could have brought work to him if they had wanted to do so. Yet there is little bitterness in the *Autobiography*—even in the last chapters, where he deals directly with other architects. The pages on his childhood are written in tenderness, passion, and love, and they are written to be far more than a memoir of the childhood of one man.[1]

Sullivan himself makes this clear. Before he turns to his boyhood in Boston, he tells us very explicitly that the thoughts, feelings, emotions, and waking dreams of the child govern and determine us through the course of our lives "with compelling power." What the "child accepts we accept, what the child rejects we reject." It is because of his deep conviction in the importance of the child to the artist, and indeed to every man,[2] that he places great stress upon an authentic study of child life. As if to underscore this, he turns aside both at the beginning and the end of his *Autobiography* to discuss his theory of childhood separately from the chapters on his boyhood years in Boston.

In one of his most obscure passages, Sullivan argues that when one is intent "not upon recalling but upon re-entering"[3] the past, two movements of imagery occur. There emerges a broad vision which assumes the color and movement of a life once lived, but the soul also moves eagerly forward, "descending through intervening atmospheric depths toward this oncoming solid reality of time and place. . . . So moving, the two great illusions, the two dreams of the single dreamer, accelerating, rush onward, and vanish both into a single life which is but a dream; the dream of a past enfolding and possessing the dreamer of today; the dreamer of today enveloping, entering and possessing the dream-reality of the past; all within the inscrutable stillness of a power unknown, within which we float, with our all, and believe ourselves real."

We are taught to believe too much in reality as determined in our strenuous hours, our practical doings, and in our "exclamatory moments." We also are taught to believe in the importance of dreams in sleep. We even extend the importance of dreams to men's ambitions, as when we say a conqueror had dreams of empire. But only occasionally do we acknowledge that "such dream had taken full possession not of a man we read about, or see in the plenitude of his power, but that the dream arose within the child, in broad daylight—as night-dreams do in their way—and aroused in him a passionate desire." This is because we are not taught to associate the "idea of dream" with our strenuous hours of thought and deed in broad daylight. But neither "do we see the stars at noon—but they are there. So is the dream there, within every human, ever—day and night unceasingly." [4]

We "impeach" the dream idea, but when we do so we forget that "we could not put one foot forth before the other were we not dreaming; so artificial and sophisticated are we in our practical moments." And even as we banish the thought "from the abysm of Memory's stillness" that out of the child we have grown inevitably to be what we are, the child comes into being "within Life's dream, within the dream of eternal time and space"; and in the child we behold what we were and still are. Environment may influence the child but it cannot alter him. Childhood preserves, in mystical continuity, the spirit of man. It is the child that creates "the flowing environment of thought and deed that shall continuously mature in its due time." In memory mirror of childhood we rediscover ourselves. As we search memory to find a true reflection of ourselves as we believe we are, the image dissolves as the features of a long-forgotten child confront us. In this memory of the forgotten child we discover our true, that is, our artistic, self.

As we turn from ourselves and look about in society, we discover that children are the true radicals. We see children moving on and on through time. Their life is the new life, ours the old; and, "as ancients, we move on, unchanged from the children that we were—leaving our thoughts and deeds as a beaten trail behind us." That is why it is necessary to place great stress upon an "authentic study" of child life. In their fatuity men believe they cause "replicas of themselves" to be born of woman and that they create children "like themselves for themselves." They are unaware that they are but instrumental in bringing forth grown men and women whom they may never see, but who are in essence of being with them at birth yet specifically different from them. The "unceasing flood of child personalities" accepts or rejects influences in an environment they had no share in making. Historically, and in the mass, children are victims of Fate rather than Masters of Destiny. But Destiny and Fate are born in the acceptance or rejection of the child.

The dreams of childhood are forms of "mystical illumination." These illuminations of the child become art through the imagination which "passes beyond reason and is a consummated act of Instinct—the primal power of Life at work." [5] The task of democratic art and education is to liberate instincts which are akin to the dreams of childhood, and which, continuing on through children, shall be a "guide evermore." Thus the child is our "unsullied well-spring of power." The chief business of all education must be to pave the way for children who may grow wholesome, proud and stalwart in their expression of native powers. In doing this we shall uncover the "amazing world of instinct" in the child, the world in which genius arises with its "swift grasp of the real." [6] At the very end of Sullivan's summary chapter on his search for the idea of architecture, the child-artist emerges as the hope of democracy. Democracy will stand or fall by the education of its children. Such education must allow the child to dream, to express his wondrous imagination, his deep creative instinct, his romance. Every child, not simply a chosen few,[7] "is the seat of genius; for genius is the highest form of play with Life's forces." The child must be educated in a wholesome atmosphere of "activities." He must be regarded as a garden awaiting careful cultivation. We must accept as "fact the capacity of the child mind to understand things and ideas, which we now suppose in our pride of feudal thought" to be far beyond his reach. The child "is mystic—close to nature's heart, close to the strength of Earth."

The apparent contradiction between the idea of a child who cannot be altered by environment, and yet whose natural powers come to nothing unless they find suitable nurture, is resolved through art. For in art we bring the reveries of the child and the artist to form, and thus to consciousness in experience. The mystic powers of the child, his purity of response and vision, weaken and die because they are not expressed, as they are by the artist. The natural love of the child for all men is born of free expression, for we live in fear and misery only because "feudal doctrines" and conventional religions teach us that we must fear free expression among men. The child regards men as individuals, not as members of a class, religion, or race. The same view of men is held by the artist. He regards each man as unique, unlike the scientist (of the intellect) who abstracts certain qualities from all men, and then describes each individual in terms of these abstract qualities.

Sullivan is not alone in the Middle West in his haunting memories of childhood and boyhood. William Dean Howells, Mark Twain, Hamlin Garland, and many other writers of this generation recall a golden day of childhood. *Huckleberry Finn* is the story of a boy and his friends who seek to find in nature what they cannot find in the town life of their elders. But we soon discover that Huck is seeking more than nature; he also wants to live in brotherhood and joy. Joy comes from art, brotherhood from democracy. For all, childhood alone is a hallowed time of art and brotherhood. By 1900 artists of the Middle Border who had spent their childhood, boyhood, and early youth on farms and in towns, were faced with ugly cities filled with strange and alien people who knew nothing of the democratic town and farm life of agrarian America. Beside the ugliness, and the terrible extremes of poverty and wealth in the city, the town and farm life of the child in nature, in fellowship with animals and with men who created with their own hands, became a poignant memory. For many, the poignant memories of this lost paradise deepened into tragedy. Others stood perplexed and bewildered before the city. Older American artists turned away from the present to a romanticized rural past of youth, adventure, romance, and nature. For them democracy was of the town and the farm. Democracy existed in such art, but not in the forms comprehensible to city people. Only in Chicago, where the shock of immigrants and the city was far greater and far more swift than in any American city from 1880 to 1910, did the artist stand firm in his belief in democracy as a way of art as well as a way of life. No city in the world laid itself so bare and was so open about its problems. There were no hiding places, no genteel refuges where the artist could retreat.[8] In Chicago, the artist, like everyone else, stood in the middle of the battle. He survived, if he did survive, only through his toughness and skill in confronting the new urban life of his time.

The blackest hours of Sullivan's boyhood and youth were spent in his first experience of city life in Boston. As he says, "Boston City swallowed him up." He likens the effect of city life on his boyhood to a flourishing plant which has been removed from the open to a dark cellar where it is imprisoned. The miasma of the city "poisoned a small boy acutely sensitive to his surroundings." In the people about him "already city-poisoned" (even his own kin) he found no solace. "Against the big city his heart swelled in impatient, impotent rebellion. Its many streets, its crooked streets, its filthy streets, lined with stupid houses crowded together shoulder to shoulder like selfish hogs upon these trough-like lanes, irritated him, suffocated him; the crowds of people, and wagons, hurrying here and there so aimlessly—as it appeared to him—confused and overwhelmed him, arousing amazement, nausea, and dismay."[9] The ugliness of Boston seemed senseless to the boy. He was greatly shocked and bewildered by his first experience of urban squalor and ugliness. His bitter disappointment could find no adequate utterance or relief. He kept his suffering to himself and "became drugged" to the point of lassitude and despair. The thought of a whole winter to be spent in the ugliness of the city, shut out from the open world that had been growing so large and splendid for him, filled him "with a sudden frantic desire to escape." [10]

He was just beginning to recover from the first shock of the city when his "ruthless father" placed him in the Brimmer School on Common Street. Louis found it "vile; unspeakably gloomy; a filthy prison for children." Here he learned nothing, as there was no one to teach him. The winter passed with Louis looking, "ever aimlessly, yearning, for *a teacher*." This yearning became a fervent hunger, a yearning within for a kindred spirit who might illumine him, and in whom he might rejoice as a spirit utterly human that would break down "the dam made within him by sanctioned suppressions and routine." He longed to break the "gathered cesspool" so that the waters of his life might again flow on.[11] During this time he slowly came to grips with the city. This began with long and searching walks up and down the streets of Boston. He searched out every street, alley and blind court, and dock and wharf from "end to end and crosswise within the limits of Boston" [12] and made partial explorations of Charlestown, Chelsea, and South Boston. He began to understand the city as a great stage of life where men and women were relating in new ways. Gradually there arose within him a consciousness of what a city means objectively as a solid conglomerate of diverse and intricate activities. He began to sense the city as a power, "a power that extended the range and amplified the content of his own child-dream of power as he had seen it manifested in the open within the splendid rhythm of the march of seasons." [13]

Even as a boy he knew that, for better or worse, the city was the great cultural reality of his time. This did not lessen his dislike of the city, but it made him determined to understand it. He saw in his "boy-way" and felt strongly the great mysterious contrast between the city and the country. In the open all was "free, expansive and luminous." In the city all was "contraction, density, limitation, and a cruel concentration." He felt that between himself and the city lay a "harsh antagonism" that seemed insoluble. The city seemed to have been made by men "when they were mad," and as it grew it "mastered and confined them." Yet there seemed to be some moments of openness and freedom: "men, women and children seemed to move about freely enough at certain hours." Waves of doubt and apprehension over city life came and passed, but each wave left "its precipitate" in the boy's quizzical mind. It was difficult at best to understand the city. The school was of little help, but what little there was had to suffice.

But in these unhappy city years, another great vision, the vision of form, and the beginning of wonder over the mystery of form, was born. On one of their walks his "ruthless" father took him to South Boston and made him run up a hill, on the top of which was a reservoir. A great view spread before him. The boy at once became "exalted with awe at the living presence and expanding power of Mother Earth." As the boy gazed in wonder his father called attention to points of beauty in the land and waterscape, finally coming around to the Blue Hills which stood in blue enchantment in the haze of the far horizon. The father asked his son which of the two hills was the larger. "He replied that the larger one was the larger—and why did Papa ask? Then the trap fell—knocking Louis senseless—for Papa said (beyond a doubt maliciously he said it) that *the smaller was the larger.*" Louis protested vehemently that such things could not be, but "Papa said he had been there and knew." Then, "relenting, believing he had carried his practical joke far enough, he told his son, seriously, that the effect, the appearance, the illusion was, in fact, due to what he called PERSPEC-TIVE." His father then went on to explain the nature of this particular perspective, and perspective in general. He explained, as he always did explain factual things, with skill, simplicity, and many illustrations. But the boy, instead of receiving this information with acclaim and joy as a new world opening before him, was deeply "saddened and perturbed."

The boy's inner world was crumbling under the challenge of knowledge, and the reality of external things which had laws of their own. His father, sincerely believing he was educating his son, "came near to destroying him." He had built up his own cherished world of dreams, of practicalities, of deep faith, of unalloyed acceptance of externals. Now this world was trembling and tottering on its foundations, threatening to collapse, or to vanish "before this new and awful revelation from the unseen." This "ghostly apparition" which his father called "perspective" terrorized him. His father's explanations did not help, for behind the perspective the father saw "was a perspective that, although plain enough to the child, was invisible to the father." [14] Behind his father's explanation Louis, the child, sensed the "mystery that lay behind appearances, and within appearances, and in front of appearances. . . ." But this mystery, the boy sensed, might hide a great kind of knowledge, for if it was penetrated he might explain and clarify all, "as his father had explained and clarified a little." But what was the nature of this mystery which moved him so deeply? "Did this mystery reside also in his lovely slender elm tree? Was his great friend the ash tree involved in mystery? Was the surprise that had glorified him and the earth around him part of this mysterious perspective that lay behind appearances, that lay behind even the clear apparition his father called perspective? Must he lose faith in what seemed real?" [15]

In the groping, excited imagination of the boy was born the beginning of Sullivan's life-long quest for a law of form. As he tells us, he sensed, dimly yet deeply, that ideas and forms must be as real and as necessary to man as the nature he knew on the farm at South Reading. Was it possible that the ugliness of Boston, and everything within it, was but "a mask and a lie?" Could there be within it and behind it a perspective, a mystery which if understood might make it intelligible to him? The boy resolved then, as later in his studies in Paris, that this mystery would be solved. "He was determined it should be, soon or late—and that he would do it." This high-pitched emotion of a child could not last. Such visions were bound to fade as in a day-dream. But within the dream "there awakened a deeper dream that has not passed." [16]

But the deeper dream, the dream which was the first stirring of Sullivan's struggle toward life as an artist, was shattered by the brutality of the school and the streets. He returned to school, where each boy was ranked according to the size of those whom he could lick and of those who could lick him. Here, in addition to some geography and arithmetic, Louis picked up every form of profanity, every bit of slang, and "every particle of verbal garbage he could assimilate." He was one of the gang, and a tough. For the first time in his life he began to take pleasure in destruction. Only his sense of honor compelled him to refrain from "licking the good boys just because they were good." And this, he tells us, could not be said of some of the boys in his gang.[17] The artist within the boy, so deeply stirred by his first glimpse of the mystery of form, seemed about to die in the streets and public schools of Boston. Although he liked music,[18] his mother's attempts to teach him piano failed. The same five-fingered exercises, "arranged as stately composition," which he was always teasing his mother to play, bored him when he tried to play them for himself. Listening to Handel oratorios in the Boston Music Hall had opened up to him a new and revealing world of choral harmony. But making music was never to be a part of the boy's life.[19] It was the same with the drawing lessons of his father. "His son detested drawing. The prospect of copying a lithographic plate setting forth a mangle, a step-ladder, a table, a mop and a pail, was not alluring. . . ."

But if the streets of Boston were a stage of ugliness and violence for the boy, they were also a stage for tragedy. His sense of the mystery of human suffering, and the terrible capacity of men to wound and kill each other, developed in the ugly streets of the city. One day the boy of nine heard the sound of drums as crowds gathered on the sidewalks. The sadness of the drums "pulsing to a labored measure of weariness and finality, as a faint bluish mass appeared. The sidewalk crowds thickened; men, women and children stood very still as the mass of faded blue undulating to the pathos of the drums approached." [20] The drummers passed by, and in the growing silence, came on and passed "ranks of wearied men in faded blue, arms at right shoulders, faces weather-beaten, a tired slow tread, measured as a time-beat on the pavement, the one-two of many souls. And to these men, as they marched, clung women shabbily clothed, with shawls drawn over their heads, moving on in a way tragically sad and glad, while to the skirts of many of these women clung dirty children." Thus passed by in order and in silence a regiment of veterans with their women and their children. As they passed onward between two tense rows of onlooking men, women and children, triple deep, many of them burst into tears. This heartrending drama of return from the wars stirred the boy deeply until he overflowed with compassion. "When he had ceased weeping upon his coat sleeve, Harrison Avenue was vacant; but not so the boy—he in fullness of sympathy was ill with the thought of what all this might mean. What was the mystery that lay behind these men in faded blue? He found no sufficing answer. The men had been mustered out, he had been told; that was all." [21] Thus the streets of the city, with all their ugliness and violence, were, the boy realized, the stage of a new mystery, the tragic mystery of man's guilt and suffering.

Notes

[1] In this they are like Mark Twain's chapters on his childhood and boyhood in his *Autobiography*. These contain some of Mark Twain's warmest writing, and since much of *Huckleberry Finn* was taken from his own boyhood, Mark Twain's use of his childhood was of profound importance to the artist, as well as to the man.

[2] As we have seen in the discussion of Dewey and Mead, Chicago educators were deeply interested in the child. Dewey talked about educating the emotions as well as the intellect. This was to be done through educating the child in terms of a theory of action, not of knowledge or intellect alone. And since Dewey and Mead both considered the experience of art to be the "characteristic" experience upon which knowledge of action in society should be based, we see that in his concern with the childhood of the architect, Sullivan was sharing in Chicago's concern with education for democracy. Despite Dewey's far greater reputation as a child educator, there is nothing in his pages to match those of Sullivan on *how* the child experiences his world. Frank Lloyd Wright,

too, placed much emphasis on his childhood, because it was then, he believed, that his mother determined his life as an architect.

[3] We now say, "re-enacting the past."

[4] For the interlude on the meaning of childhood, see the first four pages of Chapter VI, "Boston," in Louis H. Sullivan, *The Autobiography of an Idea* (New York: Press of the American Institute of Architects, 1926).

[5] These phrases occur in Sullivan's description of his visit to Rome. See Chapter XII, "Paris," of the *Autobiography*.

[6] See Chapter XIV, "Face to Face." In this chapter of the *Autobiography*, Sullivan finishes his search for the idea of architecture. The remaining two chapters, primarily on Chicago, are a historical statement of the great days of the Chicago school.

[7] Sullivan hated all doctrines of the elect—whether in religion, art or society—which presupposed that elites differed in kind, and not in degree, from the people.

[8] And there are none now. The artist in Chicago must *convince* people that art is a social good. There is no leisure class whose status depends on taste in art. Whatever is done in Chicago is judged in terms of how it benefits the largest number of people. Thus, even the Art Institute justifies its existence by the number of people who use its facilities, not simply by the excellence of its collections. The Chicago artist of today still finds deepest meanings among the life of the people. The hero in Chicago writing of our time is the "little man" betrayed by leaders who hate and fear democracy.

[9] Imagery of sheer physical reaction to buildings abounds in Sullivan's work. A building affected him as a person did. His criticism of architecture is singularly free from discussion of form, but very rich in discussion of the meaning to the individual and to society of architectural form. He tells us that even in childhood he possessed a high degree of "sensitiveness to externals which, always with him, took on character, definition and, as it were, a personality" (*Autobiography*, p. 103).

[10] Sullivan, *op. cit.*, p. 99.

[11] In his theory of function determining form in nature, as in art, Sullivan included "suppressed functions." Functions could be expressed only through form, but there is also a "need" to function in the organism, as there is a need to express himself in man. This need may or may not be expressed, and it may or may not be expressed well. But it must be satisfied in some way, and if it is not, man sickens and dies in spirit until he lives in fear and hate—of himself as well as others. Thus to Sullivan guilt is "aesthetic" as well as religious. We suffer because we cannot express ourselves freely, or because we must suppress what we yearn to express. In Sullivan "freedom" means freedom of expression.

[12] Sullivan explored thoroughly the streets of Philadelphia and Chicago. Chicago writers of Sullivan's time, such as Dreiser, George Ade, and Henry Blake Fuller, and the journalists (literary and otherwise) also knew their city intimately.

[13] Sullivan, *op. cit.*, p. 102.

[14] *Ibid.*, p. 104.

[15] *Ibid.*, pp. 104–5.

[16] *Ibid.*, p. 105.

[17] James T. Farrell, the Chicago novelist, describes the ugliness and violence of growing up in such a world in his *Studs Lonigan* trilogy and in its continuation, the *Danny O'Neill* tetralogy. Depictions of the ugliness, injustices, and sheer terror of growing up in Chicago still mark the vision of the Chicago writer, as in the work of Willard Motley and Nelson Algren.

[18] Sullivan's first great love in music was Handel; it continued through his life. His love of Wagner began during his Chicago years.

[19] Sullivan finally concludes that his hands were at fault. "Louis' hands were not made for the piano. Louis did not know it; yet there lay all the trouble."

[20] Sullivan, *op. cit.,* p. 10.

[21] Boys of this generation who later became artists have left us accounts of the deep sense of tragedy in the return of the veteran. The Civil War brought a sense of personal tragedy, probably the deepest America has ever known, into the lives of more Americans than any experience in our history.

50

Sullivan's Early Awareness of Architectural Form

B UT LOUIS was saved from the streets of Boston. His mother was stricken with diphtheria (for the fifth time) and her life endangered. In the summer of 1869, Louis' thirteenth year, Patrick Sullivan moved his family to Chicago. Louis was left behind to live with his grandparents and continue his education. He was much relieved to say good-bye to his father, for now he was free once again to roam the fields around the farm at South Reading, where he could hold close the enchantment of nature in his beloved ravine.

A new interest entered the boy's life. He became interested in buildings. Boston had depressed Louis ever since he became engulfed in it. "These structures uttered to him as in chorus a stifling negation, a vast No!—to his yea-cry for the light-hearted." In their varied utterance these buildings "denied the flowers of the field." Some "were austere, some gave forth an offensive effluvium of respectability, some fronted the crowded street as though they had been there and that the streets had come later; some seemed to thank God that they were not as other buildings, while others sighed: I am aweary, aweary." [1]

To the boy of twelve, buildings were "personalities." He felt them to be "physiognomies, . . . presences, sometimes even as personalities. . . ." Thus the State House with its golden dome seemed to him "a thin, mean, stingy old woman; while Park Street Church seemed to tower as a loyal guardian above its ancient graveyard, and as friendly monitor of the crowds below." On their walks together Grandpa and the boy shared common responses to buildings. As they looked at Faneuil Hall, Grandpa said of it: "The Wild Ass of the City stamps above its head but cannot break its sleep." This sounded "thrilling and imaginary to Louis, like a wild thing out of Julia's land of enchantment; but Grandpa said he got it out of a book and that its meaning was too deep for the boy—that he was talking to himself." [2]

Thus, early in his life, buildings spoke to Louis Sullivan, "in their many jargons." Some said "vile things, some said prudent things, some said pompous things, but none said noble things. His history book told him that certain buildings were to be revered, but the buildings themselves did not tell him so, for he saw them with a fresh eye, an ignorant eye, an eye unprepared for sophistries." He soon began to think of buildings as forms in themselves, as well as "personalities," and to respond to them as architecture. A "vague sense of doleful community among buildings slowly suffused him. They began to appear within his consciousness as a separate world in their way." This world of separated things, of architectural forms could not be understood by the mind alone, for it was a "message from an unseen power." [3]

This message reached him through one building in particular. This was a Masonic Temple which stood at the northwest corner of Tremont and Boylston streets. "It was . . . built of hewn granite, light gray in tone and joyous of aspect." He returned again and again to this building, for it was "the single one that welcomed him, the solitary one that gave out a perfume of romance, that radiated joy, that seemed fresh and full of laughter. How it gleamed and glistened in the afternoon sunlight. How beautiful were its arches, how dainty its pinnacles; how graceful the tourelle on the corner, rising as if by itself, higher and higher, like a lily stem, to burst at last into a wondrous cluster of flowering pinnacles and a lovely, pointed finial." Thus the boy raved about his new discovery of form in art, as he had earlier of form in nature. As the old artist looked back at the boy's first love in architecture, he smiled in gentle irony. "It has often been said that love is blind! If Louis chose to liken this new idol of his heart unto a certain graceful elm tree, the pulchritudinous virgin of an earlier day, surely that was his affair, not ours; for he who says that love is blind may be himself the blind—and love clairvoyant." [4]

And then the boy who loved and hated buildings saw an architect, the man who made these buildings which gave him a new kind of joy and sorrow. One day, as he was strolling down Commonwealth Avenue, he saw a large man of dignified bearing. The dignity was unmistakable—"all men of station in Boston were dignified; sometimes insistently so, but Louis wished to know who and what was behind the dignity." He was told by one of the workmen that the dignified man who had just departed was the "archeetec of this building." What was an "archeetec?" The "archeetec," the boy learned, was the "man who drawed the plans for this building." The boy was amazed: "What! What's that you say: Drawed the plans for this building?" "Sure," the workman went on: "He lays out the rooms on paper, then makes a picture of the front, and we do the work under our own boss, but the archeetec's the boss of everybody." [5]

He asked the man if there had been an "archeetec" for his beloved Masonic

Temple. He was assured that there was an architect for every building. "Louis was incredulous, but if it were true it was glorious news. How great, how wonderful a man must have been the 'archeetec' of his beloved temple! So he asked the man how the architect made the outside of the temple and the man said: 'Why, he made it out of his head; and he had books besides.' " The "books besides" repelled Louis: anybody could do that; but the "Made it out of his head" fascinated him. How could a man make "so beautiful a building out of his head? What a great man he must be; what a wonderful man." And then and there, in conversation with a simple workman in Boston, Louis made up his mind to become an architect and "make beautiful buildings out of his head." He confided his ambition to his informant. He was warned: "You got to know a lot first. You got to have an education. Of course us mechanics has our books too. That's the way we lay out stairs, rails and things like that. But you got to have more brains, more experience, more education and more books, especially books, to be an archeetec." [6]

Just before his father left Boston for Chicago, Louis told him of his resolve. Patrick seemed relieved to discover that his son, the dreamer given to illuminations, had settled on something definite. Architecture was a great art, his father declared, but if Louis was so fond of the farm and life in the open, why not think of becoming a scientific farmer? Patrick had agreed that his son was to be educated until he was twenty-one. After proper preparation, Louis would be sent to an agricultural college. Louis was dazzled by his vision of a "scientific farmer." Before him arose the woods, the fields, the cattle, the crops, the great grand open world as a "narcotic phantom of delight." His father grew eloquent on the joys of scientific farming. "The boy wavered for a moment. He sat in long silence, on his father's knee, lost to the world. Then he said: 'NO: I have made up my mind.' " Father and son agreed then that Louis was to remain in Boston to complete his general education. This completed, he was to go on to technical school, and someday he could finish his education abroad.

The boy soon discovered that the world of art and men could be entered only through knowledge. But how did one get knowledge? And especially how did one get the ordered kind of knowledge that came from books? For the secret of architecture seemed to be order, an order which did not exist in nature, but in man's head before it became a building. In looking back at these years when the disciplined mind of the artist was born, Sullivan tells us of the struggle of the boy to find order in his mind. During the years preceding his decision, "Louis, in practise, was essentially scatter-brained." His varied activities and preoccupations,

The façade of the Wainwright Building is an early example of Sullivan's attempt to subordinate ornament to structure and yet to give "warmth" and "emotion" to a building. *Photo by Richard Nickel*

The Wainwright Building in St. Louis, which, as Wright tells us, was the birth of a great new principle in architectural form. *Photo by Richard Nickel*

his keen power of observation, his insatiable hunger for knowledge at first hand, his temperamental responses to externals, his fleeting mystic trances, his utterly childlike flashes of intuition, his welcoming of new worlds, opening upon him one after another, his perception that they must grow larger and larger, his imagination, unknown to him as such; all these things, impenetrable to him in their vast significance within the gigantic and diverse world of men and things and thoughts and acts, a world as yet sealed tight to him; all these things seemed to exist within him formless, aimless, a disconnected miscellany rich in impulse but devoid of order, of form, of intention.[7]

Yet some kind of "presiding order, a primal impulse, was governing and shaping him." His experience of the art of men, their manifestations of power, "his constant wonder at what men could do; at men's power to do what they willed to do; deepened." And deeper even than his wonder at the power of men, was the call of a power he had heard in "the Song of Spring, and which awakened within the glory of the sunrise." This new power, surging within him, could not be satisfied in introspection. Nor could it be guided by teachers, for until his fourteenth year there were no good teachers available to him. He must learn how to get at books and the ordered ideas they contained, in spite of his teachers. Fortunately the gloom and ugliness of the old school no longer existed; he had been transferred to the new Rice Grammar School building. Its lightness and brightness and cleanliness raised his spirits. In the light and joy of the new building, he decided to immerse himself in the world of books as he had once entered into the magic realms of nature and fancy as a child at South Reading.

For it had become clear to him that in books might be found an increase in power; "that books might be—and he later said they were—storehouses of what men had done, an explanation of their powers to do, and that the specific knowledge stored within them might be used as tools of the mind, as men used tools of the hand." His first deep experience in this new world of books and study was in grammar. Here, for the first time in all his schooling, "a light began to shine within a book and illumine his brain. Here opened, ever enlarging, a world of things said, and to be said. The rigid rules became plastic as he progressed." As the end approached "there came forth from the book as a living presence, as a giant from the world of enchantment, with shining visage, man's power of speech." [8]

As he grasped the idea of grammar, words suddenly became plastic expressions of a principle of form which his imagination, if not his powers of analysis, made clear to him. And, "as usual," his imagination far outsped any possibility of reasonable accomplishment. Louis, "as usual, saw too much at one time. He saw, at a glance, ends that would require a lifetime of disciplined endeavor to reach." He had grasped the idea of grammar at one stroke of the imagination; his other studies appealed to him in the same way, but without the enthusiasm of his enchantment with words. There was little romance in arithmetic. He saw its practical use, and accepted it as a daily task to be learned. It was not his fault but his misfortune that "it was handed to him dry." He liked geography. He could visualize it, but topographically and racially he could not see into it. In history he "was lied to shamefully, but he did not know it." History did not interest him greatly because the people described did not seem "human like the people he knew, and the story was mostly about wars. He got the idea that patriotism always meant fighting, and that the other side was always in the wrong." [9]

Immersing himself in his books brought problems in the classroom. He learned too much, too soon, about the magic of words. The topics assigned in composition seldom fired his imagination; "as a rule they were academic, arid, artificial, having no relation to life experience, concerning which he might have said something worth while had he been given a chance." Declamation, or "speaking pieces," was another difficulty. He simply could not orate nonsense, for even at twelve his sense of irony was well developed. He was bashful enough before the class, and when he could not speak with conviction he could not speak at all without tortures of self-consciousness which made him angry and rebellious.[10] He took his revenge in cutting criticism of the speaking pieces, and finally one day launched a full-voiced parody of the "spread-eagle" style of oratory which "Old Ironsides" usually invoked.

This affront to the majesty of tradition and class decorum brought on a visit to the headmaster. As he entered the office of Mr. Wheelock, who "wore a blond beard, had rather high color, merry blue eyes . . . and was judicial, considerate and human in his dealings," he found an angry man, "gray of face, sinister of eye, holding in his left hand a long rattan." Louis, "fearless and aggressive by nature," apologized for insulting his teacher. But he made clear that he regarded the poem as bunkum. "Mr. Wheelock sneered. [Louis] then went on to take the poem to pieces, line by line, stanza by stanza. Mr. Wheelock looked puzzled; he eyed Louis quizzically . . . he dropped the rod." Louis let go, "he waxed eloquent, he spread out his views—so long suppressed; he pleaded for the open, for honesty of thought, for the lifting of a veil that hid things, for freedom of utterance. He passionately unbosomed his longings." Louis discovered that he had found a man, if not a teacher. The headmaster sat, chin in hand, looking steadily at the boy. His face was grave and sad. As Louis ceased, the headmaster remained silent. He then said, "That was a pretty fine stump-speech, young man. When you got through with Holmes, you left his poem as tattered as his ensign. As for the rest: Irish accounts for that. I'm glad we had it out though. I might have thrashed you in anger. Go back to your class now, and hereafter be considerate of a woman's feelings." [11]

Louis returned to his room and plunged into his grammar. Louis worked on and on, alone, "digging into the solid vein of knowledge as a solitary miner digs; washing the alluvial sands of knowledge as a miner sifts—a young prospector grub-staked by an absentee provider now settled on the shores of a vast lake far in the West." He was living with his grandparents and thus "felt at home once more." The farm at South Reading (now called Wakefield) offered refuge from the "bareness and baldness" of the city. He studied hard in the evenings. He lost interest in playmates; waved aside all girls as nuisances and inferior creatures until they became nonexistent. He rose very early, "at all seasons and all weathers." Before the family awakened he walked a mile to the depot, took the train to Boston, walked a mile to breakfast, and then another mile to school. Thus Louis studied, "in gluttonous introspection," with a fixed idea, "an unalterable purpose, whose goal lay beyond the rim of his horizon, and beyond the narrow confines of the casual and sterile thought of the day." Louis was graduated with honors in June of 1870, when he received proudly his first and last diploma as a scholar. Never again did he regard life "with the gravity, the seriousness and the futility of a cloistered monk."

The world of men, and the expression of man's power in engineering, called again. Grandpa List decided to visit his second daughter, who lived on a three-hundred-acre farm at Lyon Falls in New York. Louis begged to go. His geography told him that there were big things in the West, where the outdoors got bigger and bigger. The boyish cry was a cry for expansion, a defining hunger for larger vision; perhaps the boy was "outgrowing his cocoon." Grandpa and Louis departed in the evening. Louis waited, restless and sleepless, for his first view of mountains and the spacious scale of life in the "west."

The hour came near dawn. The thrill of action began with the "uprearing of imposing masses as Louis clung to the solid train now purring in the solitudes in ever-lengthening swings—deep valleys below—until, amid mists and pale moon gleaming, arose the mighty Berkshires, their summits faint and far, their immensities solemn, calm, seeming eternal in the ghostly fog in the mild shimmer, clad in forests, uttering great words, runic words revealing and withholding their secret to a young soul moving as a solitary visitant. . . ." It was indeed another mystic moment for the boy who heard the engines crying: "We will!" the mountains replying: "We will!" To an expanding soul listening within its own shimmering dream, "to the power without and within, amid the same echoes within and without," a stillness being, as though through "mists of mind and shimmer of hope, SUBLIMITY, in revelation, had come to *one* wholly unprepared, had come to *one* who had known mountains only in books." [12]

But it was not the sublimity of nature alone which held the boy in trance. It was the power of man, which the child had known in the village workers and craftsmen, but which the boy now saw expressed on a far greater stage. The thought struck deep "that what was bearing him along was solely the power of man; the living power to wish, to will, to do." Man had entered the sanctity of these towering hills and "like a giant of Elfinland had held them in the hollow of his hand." Many saw engines and rails, but "*one* saw what lay behind them. In the murky mist and shimmer of moon and dawn, a veil was lifted in the solitude of the Berkshires." [13]

But the power of man, his power as engineer, was not matched by power in architecture. As the train approached the bridge across the Hudson at Albany, he was struck by its lack of "bigness, beauty, and romance. . . . It appeared to creep, cringing and apologetic, across the wide waters which felt the humiliation of its presence." How different from this appearance was the shock of elation as the train moved slowly along the bridge. As "he gazed downward upon the flowing waters, again he marvelled at what men could do; at the power of men to build; to build a bridge so strong it would carry the weight of a great train, even with his own precious and conscious weight added thereto. And Louis mused about the bridge; why was it so mean, so ugly, so servile, so low-lived? Why could not a bridge perform its task with pride? Why was not a proud bridge built there?" [14]

How strange was the meanness of spirit in great cities compared with what he now saw. "Was not [New York] called in his geography 'The Empire State'? . . . Then why so shabby an approach?" He envisioned a noble proud bridge which would be a great salute between the sovereign states of Massachusetts and New York—"even as Almighty God proclaimed unto Noah of old and his sons: 'I do set my bow in the clouds, and it shall be for a token of a covenant between me and the earth.'" Louis felt keenly that "this venomous bridge was a betrayal of all that was best in mankind." [15]

The Mohawk Valley soon made him forget the power and ugliness of man's work. Here in the valley were freedom and expanse; he followed its wondrous immensity as mile after mile of the valley passed by. His mind now at peace, Louis "passed into wonder that such open world could be, and now he marvelled not at man's power and his works, but at the earth itself." A mood of reverence swept over him as he began to see what "Mother Earth, in her power, had done in her varied moods, and to surmise as best he could what more she had done that he knew not of." As the Mohawk wound its limpid way, Louis, "softening into an exquisite sympathy, cast his burden upon the valley, and there he found rest; rest from overintrospection, rest from overconcentration; freed from suppression and taboo." [16]

The mystic moment returned in nature, as it was to do so often in later years at Ocean Springs. As the train passed through the valley, Louis became freshened with new growth "as a tree in spring." He felt a new power rising within him. He was cleansed "as by a storm, and purified as by fire." There arose from the valley a still, small voice, "and Louis heard the voice and recognized it as his own returning to him, and he was overjoyed and strengthened in his faith and became as one translated into the fresh, free joy of living; for in this valley, this wilderness of light and earth he had found surcease." [17]

Louis turned at once to Grandpa, as he had so often in the past, to share his mystic moment. Grandpa sensed the boy's excitement. He asked with a lazy smile if he had found the "big things," and how the "shut-in life was faring." Louis overflowed. Words tumbled out about the Berkshires, the Hudson, and the Bridge. But he was silent about the valley—"*that* was sacred." As he finished, Grandpa began teasing the boy. "As to your bridge, young man, I know nothing; as to the Hudson, you know nothing; as to your Berkshires, they are an impertinence." As he watched the boy's crestfallen face he relented (as always) and entered the heart and mind of the boy, and began a monologue which stirred Louis, and which he carried with him all the days of his life. "Louis," he began, "what good does the study of geography do you? . . . Have your teachers ever told you anything of value about a river? Any river? . . . Have they ever given you a word-picture of a river, so that you might at least summon up an image of it, however short of reality?" And then he warned him, your teachers "are not inspired. They are victims of routine, wearied on the daily treadmill until they can no longer see into the heart of a child." [18]

Grandpa looked searchingly at the boy and, from the depths of his love and understanding, said:

Now, I have watched you since you were a babe in arms, and I have mostly let you alone for fear of meddling with nature's work; for you were started right by my daughter, the mother who carried you and yearned for you. She is sound to the core. She alone of my children might fittingly wear the red cap of liberty. Yet you do not know your own mother. *I* know *you*. I know your abominable selfishness—come from your father; and your generosity and courage—come from my proud daughter. You have a God-given eye and a dull heart. You are at one and the same time incredibly industrious and practical, and a dreamer of morbid dreams, of mystic dreams, sometimes clean, brilliant dreams, but these are too rare.

What you have said, from time to time, concerning man's power to do, has astounded and frightened me, coming from you. *That idea* you never got from any of us. *There* shines the light of the seer, of the prophet, leading where?—to salvation or destruction? I dare not think how that flame may grow into conflagration, or mellow into a world-glow of wisdom. But I know, worst of all, that adolescence is at hand; that you are in grave danger of a shake-up. Hard work and clear thinking may pull you through: that is my sincere hope.[19]

And then Grandpa, aroused to eloquence, created a flowing word-picture of the Hudson, from Albany to the sea, that brought out all the rare qualities of his fine mind and so aroused Louis "that he made the journey with him —lost to all else." At this moment the train pulled to a full stop. They were in a ravine with high walls of rock, jagged and wild, and through this gorge came "dashing, plunging, swirling, sparkling, roaring over the ledges in cascade after cascade, laughing and shouting in joy, the same Mohawk River that had flowed as gently as the footsteps of a veiled nun, through the long, quiet valley that it had traversed." Louis was in ecstasy. Exultantly he leaped from the train, "waved his hat, and in spirit sang with the waters the song of joy."

Notes

[1] Louis H. Sullivan, *The Autobiography of an Idea* (New York: Press of the American Institute of Architects, 1926), p. 117.

[2] *Ibid.*, p. 117.

[3] *Ibid.*, pp. 117–18.

[4] *Ibid.*, p. 118.

[5] *Ibid.*, pp. 118–19.

[6] *Ibid.*, p. 119.

[7] *Ibid.*, p. 121.

[8] *Ibid.*, pp. 122–23.

[9] *Ibid.*, pp. 123–24.

[10] Sullivan is careful to point out that the bashfulness he suffered in the classroom did not extend to the streets, where he fought boldly and with confidence, even though he was sometimes beaten.

[11] Sullivan, *op. cit.*, pp. 126–27.

[12] *Ibid.*, p. 131. (Sullivan's italics and capitalization)

[13] *Ibid.*, p. 131.

[14] *Ibid.*, p. 132.

[15] *Ibid.*, pp. 132–33.

[16] *Ibid.*, p. 134.

[17] *Ibid.*

[18] *Ibid.*, p. 135.

[19] *Ibid.*, pp. 135–36.

51

Teachers of the Heart and Mind

At fourteen Louis fell in love. This was his first deep relationship with anyone near his own age, although even here Minnie was four years older than Louis. It was not his first profound relationship with women. His first lessons in compassion and love came from Grandmama. Julia, the Irish maid of the Lists, who loved Louis—even when he teased her unmercifully —took him into the enchanted land of fairy tales. She, too, tried to give Louis the gift of love and compassion by making her brilliant, but self-centered, boy understand something of the life of the poor and the humble. Louis's mother, too, with her deep hatred of social injustice and all the snobbery and affectation of class, taught Louis to cherish people as individuals. Thus, the boy knew the power of women as well as men. This was the power of the heart, the capacity for love, which Louis finally came to believe was the greatest power of all, in art, as in life.

Louis knew very little of the world and of people. His memories of early years are filled with older people, and until he lived in Boston he knew nothing of the life lived by the poor and the helpless. His first great moment of compassion for the poor and humble was the sight of returning Civil War veterans. Their sad, worn faces, and the shabbily clad women with children clinging to their skirts as they marched beside their men, moved him to tears. As the "aching drama of return" from battle unfolded on the streets, the boy was overwhelmed by the mystery of human suffering. He sought out Julia, "to whom alone he could bare his heart." To her he opened his heart about the weary soldiers in faded blue with their wives and children hanging on them. Why was it so sad? Why did people cry? Why did he have to cry? What did it all mean?

Julia tried to explain to the boy sitting beside her.

Well, Louis dear, ye know war's a sad business; those men ye saw had just been mustered out of the army; they were good fighting men, but all tired out. From the shawls the women wore and the dirty childer, I know the whole crowd was Irish and poor; and as everyone knows, the Irish won the war. . . . It's a tender heart indade, ye had likewise to be lookin' at thim dirty childer hangin' to the mithers' skirts! It's a big heart ye had and a fine education ye have that ye didn't think at wanst whin ye saw thim that ye haven't a care in the world, that ye've niver known rale hunger, niver a rale sorrow, niver a heart-break, niver despair; niver heard the wolf bark at the door as yer blood went cold! And yerself, Louis, wid yere big, big heart and small head couldn't see with yer own eyes and without any books at all, that thim very childer was part of what as ye say lies behind it all? God! me heart aches in the tellin'; for the min ye saw come back wuz not all the min that wint out; but I'm through. I'll tell ye no more. . . . I want to knock a bit of sinse into yure empty skull. Yere all sintiment, Louis, and no mercy.[1]

Julia always mocked Louis's good fortune, but like Grandpa she did it out of love for the boy. For those who knew him best and loved him most were afraid of his egocentricity. All recognized his gifts. Even Grandpa, whose cynicism over human folly ran deep, was stirred by the boy's depth of feeling and imagination. But the boy's heart, his growth into love and compassion through understanding people, was undeveloped. Louis was loved and cherished by his elders, but he took their love for granted. He knew what being loved was, but he knew little of loving in return. His grandparents, his parents, and Julia realized Louis was very innocent of the world. Louis in turn found it difficult to talk about people and his feelings for them. Only with Julia could he express openly what he felt, as well as what he thought or imagined. He was too young to understand Julia's sorrows, but when she talked of the sufferings of her countrymen, she set him "vibrating at the suggestion of an unseen power." This new power was society, the world and its people. Louis resolved to penetrate the mystery that seemed to lie back of this new world.

Louis met Minnie at the farm home of Mrs. Jenny List Whittlesey, Grandpa's other daughter. Minnie told Louis at once that she had been longing for his arrival. She also told him that she was eighteen, and now a young lady in Utica society, of whose mysteries she promised to enlighten him. She had been reading French books for a month and speaking French with Aunt Jenny. Louis was taken unawares by Minnie. He hardly knew what to say when she told him that they were now chums and then asked Louis if he would like her. When he dared at last to look into Minnie's gray Scotch eyes, she seemed "endowed with an endless fund of merriment, of badinage, of joy, of appeal, of kindness, and saturated with an inscrutable depth beyond all these." She was not beautiful, but of an irresistible and pervasive charm.

Minnie took charge of Louis. She drew him out of himself and taught him the joy and delight of love and companionship with a girl. Her dreams were not of great dark powers, but of light and joy among people. She, too, had her enchanted ravine. This was filled with rock ledges, tall trees, and a rivulet with green along its banks. It was, she said, a solitary oasis in a desert of hay-land. Here she took Louis and here they read and talked. She read Tennyson, "making her selections carefully varied, feeling her way through Louis's responses to see where she could reach his heart, how she could bare it, and then keep her secret." She read from Byron and recited many other poems "with a skill unknown to elocutionists." Louis, in turn, told her about his reading of Captain Mayne Reid's books, of Cooper and Maryatt, stories he had read from the Bible. He recited for her, verbatim, the story of Elijah, the whirlwind, and the still small voice.

Minnie and Louis went often to her oasis. As they sat together on one of the great stones, Minnie put Louis at ease and asked him about his home and life at school. She wanted to know every detail. Soon the boy was telling her not only the story of his life, but the story of everyone and everything there-with connected: Minnie saying: "Fine, fine, how well you tell it," in running comment. "He even told her one of Julia's fairy tales. Minnie in turn talked about herself and her home. She told him in great detail about finishing school, and mimicked its follies. She shared her enthusiasms about her adored brother, Ed, fresh from Yale. She told him of her debut in Utica society, and about her set, the landed aristocracy, the old families, the exclusive, the best people." [2]

Louis learned from her talk that people were graded. He had never been taught this at home. Only Grandma placed much store in the conventional world's judgment, but this seldom weighed heavily on Louis. Now class divisions suddenly became real. Louis was pained at many of the things Minnie described so casually. She revealed too much. As she came to a full realization of Louis's profound ignorance of the world, "of social organiza-tion both in its ephemeral and its momentous inert and stratified aspects," and realized that he was "provincial, . . . honest, frank, and unsuspecting, she became alarmed. . . . and determined to prepare him and in so doing, she lifted at least a corner of a sinister and heavy veil that lay behind appear-ances." She did so with great skill, a little at a time, making her case in every instance by direct illustration and none too complimentary observations on people. But she refused to be serious for too long a time. She preferred laugh-ter, nonsense, and high spirits, and thus kept Louis dazed in her land of enchantment.

Minnie became Louis's "precious teacher." She made him feel that he was not being taught, but "entertained with gossip." Minnie was "both worldly and unworldly. With nature she was dreamy; but when it came to people, she became a living microscope, her sharp brain void of all illusion, for her true world was of the world of people—there she lived—as Louis's world had been a world of the wide open—of romance." Louis idolized Minnie: "An aching in her guarded heart was soothed by him; and he became for her a luxury." She was determined not to let her feelings go too far. Louis was to be enjoyed fully in the present, and to become a precious memory in the future. She filled the air with laughter and delight—"meanwhile feeding honey drop by drop—just to see upon a human face the rare, the precious witching aspect of idolatry."

They loved each other in the wonderful purity of adolescent friendship. They spoke out of their hearts, for they both knew they soon must part. As the time drew near, Louis had another of the mystic moments which illuminated his life's path. He learned what it meant to be a friend and a companion. To the boy who had been long adapted to elderly people, "she was held . . . as in a shrine, to be the only truly human he had ever known." Her kindness in "adopting him, and making him her own, not for a day, but for all the glad summer long, made him feel as though his life, before her floating into it had been a blank." She had come, it seemed, out of the "invisible that lies behind all things, all dreams, to be his faerie queen." At the end of his life, Sullivan still possessed the vision of Minnie and their days in the woods. As he closes his reminiscences of Minnie, he pauses for a moment to say: "And now it seems as though half a century had stood still." [3]

As Grandpa and Louis journeyed back together, Grandpa began to tell the boy something of his life. Louis was busy with his own thoughts. Grandpa was hurt by this indifference. The boy, whose fourteen years "had been filled to overflow with vivid episodes, with active thoughts, with dreams, mysteries, prophetic intuitions and rude industrious practicalities," was innocent of the world—ignorant, "grossly innocent and careless of the vicissitudes and follies of a seething human world." Grandpa "shuddered momentarily at the chasm that lay between them." He knew that Louis "was now paying in ignorance the penalty of a sheltered life." [4]

Upon their return, Louis decided against the Latin High, and chose the English High. It was one of the most important decisions of his life, for he met his greatest teacher, Moses Woolson. His first visit to the school was not reassuring. "It was a barn-like, repellent structure fronting on a lane as narrow as the prevailing New England mind of its day." The classroom was "dingy rather than gloomy." Louis glanced at the teacher. He was above medium height, his movements pantherlike. He did not even bother to welcome his class but began at once to harangue them with an air of "authority and pugnacity, like . . . a first mate taking on a fresh crew." He was tense and determined, but he did not swagger. He was a man of passion,[5] and determined, as his words made clear, that his students would know the passion of learning. "I will give to you all that I have; you shall give to me all that you have." For, he told them, "you are here under my care, . . . as wards in my charge; I accept that charge as sacred." He made clear that he would keep pace with any boy who wanted to extend himself.

He laid down five rules. The class was to be silent, strict attention must be given, and each pupil must be alert. The fourth rule: "You shall learn to LISTEN; to *listen* in *silence* with the *whole* mind, not part of it," for, explained Master Woolson, sound listening is a basis for sound thinking. Finally, he went on, students must learn to observe, to reflect, and to discriminate. This, he made clear, would be difficult and could not be done without due preparation. He promised that he would not start the class "with a jerk, but tighten the lines bit by bit until I have you firmly in hand at the most spirited pace you can go." As he finished, "a dangerous smile went back and forth over his grim set face." [6]

Louis was "amazed, thunder-struck, dumb-founded, over-joyed." At last a teacher—a man who could help him give form to the chaotic thoughts, feelings, emotions, and dreams of his childhood and boyhood. In this man's utterances his yearnings for some kind of order and the discipline of learning found voice. In "a flash they became defined, living, real. A pathway had been shown him, a wholly novel plan." Louis saw that true freedom could come only through "discipline of power," and he interpreted the master's words to mean that discipline of the self was the way to power. His days of lonely study, "of longing for a teacher who would train his mind, had ended." He knew little about teaching, but when he heard Moses Woolson promise himself to the class, Louis was deeply moved by his first experience of a new creative force in life, the teacher. "You are here as wards in my charge; I accept that charge as sacred; I accept the responsibility involved as a high exacting duty I owe to myself and equally to you. I will give you all that I have; you shall give to me all that you have." In these words, "there stood forth not alone a man but a TEACHER of the young." [7]

On the journey back to Wakefield Louis felt like a wanderer who had come into home port at last. His recent journey by rail, river, and sea, with its inspiring thoughts and emotions and reveries, had now been drawn into himself and shaped into a single imposing drama which was to serve as a prelude to a new and greater life. But this prelude was really a return, a return to his childhood. His childhood domain, holding, "within the encircling woods, . . . his great green field, his tall, beauteous, slender elm; land of his delight, paradise of his earth-love, . . . sanctuary of his visions and his dreams, had seemed at first, and hopefully, to extend itself progressively into a larger world as far as Newburyport and Boston." But there it had stopped, remaining "fixed and bound up for seven long years." [8]

During these seven years from his eighth to his fifteenth year in Boston, Louis had been held back "as by a sinister dam," which contained a "larger, urgently growing Louis, held also back within it, impatient, repressed, dreaming of power, storing up ambition, searching for what lies behind the face of things, agitated and at times morose, malignant." When the dam breaks, as it did in Moses Woolson's class, "the child-domain . . . rushes forth, spreading over the earth, . . . pouring its power of giving and receiving far and wide over land and sea, encompassing mountains and broad valleys, great rivers, turbulent waterfalls, a solemn boundless forest enfolding a lustrous lake, and again a noble river mountain-banked, an amazing harbor, and the great salt waves of the sea itself." This provided deep and sound foundations for the "masterful free spirit, striding in power, in the open, as the genius of the race of purblind, groping, striving, ever hoping, ever dreaming, illusioned mankind." [9]

Louis was becoming stronger and surer of his own powers. His trip with Grandpa had opened his mind and spirit. He now awaited confidently the beginning of what he foresaw "was to be a long and arduous disciplinary training, which he knew he needed, and now welcomed." He was anxious now to learn how to give form to his feelings and his dreams, to express in some way the surging power he felt within him. He came to feel that this power within him was "a ward in his charge; that he must accept the responsibility involved as a high exacting duty he owed to himself and equally to it; that he must give to it his all, to insure that it might give to him its all."

Louis placed high value on Algebra, Geometry, English Literature, Botany, Mineralogy, and French language. Algebra startled him. He entered a new, and unsuspected, world of symbols. The symbol x "flashed at once as a key to the unknown but ascertainable." He viewed this x in surprise "as a mystic spirit in a land of enchantment, opening vistas so deep he could not see the end, and his vivid imagination saw at once that this x, expanded in its latent power, might prove the key to turn a lock in a door within a wall which shut out the truth he was seeking—the truth which might dissolve for him the mystery that lay behind appearances." For him this x was manipulated by means of "things unknown." [10] He looked far ahead toward the time when he would be mature and understand "what lay behind appearances."

Geometry delighted him because of "its nicety, its exactitude of relationships, its weird surprises—all like fairy tales, fairy tales which could be proved, and then you said: Q.E.D." He did not perceive, as he did later, the rigidity of Euclidian geometry compared with the fluency of Algebra. He was at home in Botany, for he had always been a keen observer of trees, shrubs, vines, flowers, of the field, the orchard, and the garden. His love for them only increased as he learned their secrets of structure and form, and the organization of the plant world. In Mineralogy the common stones began to "talk to him in their own words." He studied French assiduously, for he meant to visit France when he could.

But his greatest experience in these years was in English literature. This opened to him the "great world of words, or ordered speech, the marvelous vehicle whereby were conveyed every human thought and feeling from mind to mind, from heart to heart, from soul to soul, from imagination to imagination, from thought to thought." Literature rose before him "as a vast treasure house wherein was stored, in huge accumulation, a record of the thoughts, the deeds, the hopes, the joys, the sorrows, and the triumphs of mankind." Master Woolson taught Louis how to experience the form as well as the content of literature. "He delighted in taking apart passages and lines, to show the value of each word in respect to action, rhythm, color, quality, texture, fitness." He then put these together again in a renewed recital of the passage which now became "a living moving utterance . . . a new world, a new land of enchantment." [11]

The function of literature, its social purpose, Master Woolson explained, was to give form to the innate qualities of the heart and mind of a people. For the culture of a people existed in expression. This meaning of culture, taken, Master Woolson explained, from Taine's *History of English Literature,* was new to Louis. He was bewildered and excited by it. Here perhaps was the key to unlock the mystery of the relation of art to society. "Culture" thus became for him a living word, "a sheer veil through which, at first, he could but dimly see; but living word and sheer living veil had come from without to abide with him. It seemed indeed as though Moses Woolson had passed on to him a wand of enchantment which he must learn to use to unveil the face of things." Master Woolson also loved nature. After recess there was a period of nature study with open book, chiefly Gray's *School and Field Book of Botany.* Professor Asa Gray of Harvard, out of regard for Master Woolson's devotion to botany, came occasionally to talk to the boys about botany.

Under Moses Woolson's tutelage, Louis changed from a "crudely promising boy" into a mental athlete. "He had brought order out of disorder, definition out of what was vague, superb alertness out of mere boyish ardor." He nurtured all that was best in the boy. He made him "consciously courageous and independent; had focused his powers of thought, feeling and action; had confirmed Louis's love of the great out-of-doors, as a source of inspiration; and had climaxed all by parting a great veil which opened to the view of this same boy, the wonderland of Poetry." Louis was not a brilliant or flashy scholar, but he was adept at the art of listening. He wanted to get every ounce of treasure out of Moses Woolson. He felt neither love nor affection for Moses Woolson, and there was no reason to think Woolson felt any different about him. What Louis did feel was "a vast admiration . . . [for] the power and the vigor of his intense and prodigal personality."

Louis doubted whether Moses Woolson ever knew what he had done for the boy. But Louis knew it, and "there came gradually over him a cumulative reciprocity which, at the end, when he had fully realized the nature of the gift, burst forth into a sense of obligation and of gratitude so heartfelt, so profound, that it has remained with him in constancy throughout the years. There may have been teachers and teachers, but for Louis Sullivan there was and could be only one." All he could do in his last tribute to Woolson was but small payment for his debt to him. "And now, in all too feeble utterance he pleads this token, remembrance, to the memory of that ONE long since passed on." [12]

As Louis learned of love and wisdom in his fourteenth and fifteenth years, so did he also learn of death. Early in 1871, Anna List, Grandmama, was taken sick. Louis was forbidden her room. After days of quiet, furtive comings and goings, and whisperings, Louis was told he might see Grandmama. He went directly into her room. "The white shades were down and all was light within. On the bed he saw extended an object fully covered by a sheet. He advanced, drew aside the sheet, rashly pressed his lips upon the cold forehead, drew back as though stung. . . . Standing erect he gazed steadfastly down upon rigid features that seemed of unearthly ivory. . . . Grandmama had vanished!" She could no longer see, hear, feel, move, speak, and she could no longer give the love her boundless heart had bestowed so often on the boy. Now she was gone, and all that remained was "an ivory mask which repelled, which instantly he rejected, as a ghastly intrusion." His true Grandmama was in his heart "and would remain there until his own end should come. He replaced the shroud. Dry-eyed, and as one filled with a cold light, he left the room." [13]

The funeral service in the "spare room" reduced Grandpa to a flood of hysteria and tears. Louis gazed at him "in wonder that a strong man could be so weak." He cursed the Baptist minister's sermon "of sensuous words in praise of human bloodshed." The "whining quartet" drove him to desperation. He ran from the house to sit under a tree and "damn them all to perdition." Why had he been dragged into this "gross orgy of grief? Could he not be left alone and in peace, to revere in memory that Grandmama who still lived on within his heart? The others with their noisy and their mercenary grief would soon forget. He, never." And as he raged in his grief, he looked about and saw a peach tree in full bloom. "He hastened to it as to a friend, in dire need."

The joyous presence of the tree in the garden gave him courage, "for spring again was singing her great song." A choir of resurrection filled the air. Here, in the beauty of the blossoms of springtime, "was resurrection and the life. It seemed to him not in the least incongruous that his beloved had vanished into that great life whence she came—whence he had come; and that as Life was within him, so was his beloved within him as life within a life to be treasured evermore." Death, Louis felt, as he stood near the full blooming peach tree, must be accepted as "an envanishment." Life was the power of all powers, for Life, through the song of Spring, seemed like a great rainbow glowing through the dark clouds of death. The cloud with the glowing rainbow in its heart "might well stand forever as a symbol of a token of a covenant between Life, and Man's proud spirit, and the Earth. Thus Louis dreamed." And in his dream a small voice, the voice of Minnie coming from afar, seemed to say: "If one must dream let the dream be one of happiness." [14]

The home of Henri List vanished, and with it the childhood and boyhood refuge of Louis Henri Sullivan. Louis was offered a home by the John A. Thompsons, the next-door neighbors, so that he could finish school. John A. Thompson was "gifted with extraordinary deftness of hand and a high spirited intelligence." He became a "wonder and an inspiration to Louis, who spent the following two years in this charming household where epicureanism prevailed." Louis spent the spring and summer of 1871 in the fields around Wakefield where he "botanized and mineralized with incessant ardour." He learned why things must be named, and what order and classification "meant in the way of organized intelligence, and increased power of manipulation of things and thoughts." His insight into the "relationship of function and structure" deepened rapidly. Many things began to cohere and arrange into groups. Logical connections began to form in his thinking.

He began to seek order in his daily life. Here he was helped by Thompson, who possessed a highly developed sense of order. In the fall Louis returned to school, but not to Moses Woolson. He entered the Second Class under a submaster named Hale. This "respectable and approved lay figure" could do little for a boy trained intensively for a year by Moses Woolson. At the end of his second year, George Thompson, Louis's friend, asked him why he did not try out for "Tech" (Massachusetts Institute of Technology).

Thus encouraged, Louis took the entrance exams, passed easily, and entered in the fall of 1871, the time of the great Chicago fire. As the news of Chicago's destruction swept the nation and the world, Louis received word that the family was safe and sound "beyond its fearsome ravages." With this assurance Louis now felt "safe and strong to face in 'Tech' his first adventure, as prelude to an architectural career."

Notes

[1] Louis H. Sullivan, *The Autobiography of an Idea* (New York: Press of the American Institute of Architects, 1926), pp. 113–14.

[2] *Ibid.*, p. 147.

[3] *Ibid.*, p. 150.

[4] *Ibid.*, pp. 156–57.

[5] "Moses Woolson was not a deep thinker, nor was Moses Woolson erudite or scholarly, or polished in manners, or sedate. Rather he was a blend of wild man and of poet. . . . His one weakness was a temper he all too often let escape him, but his high strung, nervous make-up may be averred in part extenuation, for this very make-up was the source of his accomplishment and power. He surely gave in abundance, with overflowing hands, all that he had of the best to give." (*Ibid.*, pp. 164–65).

[6] *Ibid.*, pp. 158–59.

[7] *Ibid.*, p. 160.

[8] *Ibid.*, p. 161. Sullivan believed in what he called "suppressed functions."

[9] *Ibid.*, pp. 161–62.

[10] *Ibid.*, p. 163.

[11] *Ibid.*, p. 166.

[12] *Ibid.*, p. 169.

[13] *Ibid.*, pp. 169–70.

[14] *Ibid.*, pp. 171–72.

52

Sullivan's Years of Apprenticeship:
Student and Draftsman

Louis's two years' residence with the Thompsons in Wakefield and his work at M.I.T. introduced him to the world of culture, "as culture then existed in Boston." It was highly intellectual, and in Louis's mind, at least, materialistic. "A certain materialistic clarification of intellect was proceeding within a new light which enabled him to see things superficially and to share in that state of illusion concerning realities which was the common property of the educated and refined." For the first time—and the last—Louis even turned his back momentarily on the mystical illuminations of his own childhood. The dreams of childhood, the "form of mystical illumination which enables the little one to see that upon which the eyes of its elders seldom focus," were eclipsed for the moment. "In one less romantic and willful by nature, [they] would have vanished permanently from active consciousness in the usual and customary way." [1]

The conflict between intellect, or adulthood when we put away childish things, and the deep intuitions of childhood had been resolved in Boston on the side of learning and intellect. The birth of the imagination of childhood was relegated to obscurity, and when referred to at all, dismissed as inconsequential and "childish." Yet Sullivan felt such banishment of childhood did not destroy it, for it lived "sequestered within us unchanged." We may obscure it by an overlay of sophistication, and deny it in our pride and disdain, but if we do, we really deny our maturity. "For where lives the man who does not firmly believe in magic and in fairy tales; who does not worship something with a childlike faith, who does not dream his dreams, however sordid or destructive, however high, however nobly altruistic?"

The purpose of architectural education at M.I.T., Louis soon decided, was not to create, but to study and classify architecture. Professor Ware, of the Boston architectural firm of Ware and Van Brunt, lectured on the theory and history of architecture. There were, it seemed, "Five Orders of Architecture." In Boston these had reached their final transcendence as eternal verities. Students traced the five orders and learned about "diameters, modules, minutes, entablatures, columns, pediments and so forth and so forth, with the associated minute measurements and copious vocabulary, all of which items [Louis] supposed at the time were intended to be received in unquestioning faith, as eternal verities. And he was told that these 'Orders' were 'Classic,' which implied an arrival at the goal of Platonic perfection of idea."

The meaning of these orders was fixed for all time, so Louis was taught. But something in him rebelled against this. "These rigid 'Orders' seemed to say, 'The book is closed; Art shall die.' Then it occurred to him: Why five orders? Why not one? Each of the five plainly tells a different story. Which one of them shall be sacrosanct? Now it would appear by the testimony of the world of scholarship and learning that Greek is sacrosanct; and of all the Greek, the Parthenon is super-sacrosanct." The Parthenon was unique and perfect, other structures could, at best, only be measured against it. After "centuries of ruin the Parthenon is dead; therefore all is invalid, Art is dead." As he studied the books on architecture Louis discovered that there were many buildings of the past which did not have pediments and columns. But these were considered "styles," and styles, it seemed, were not sacred, but merely human. Thus, there was a difference in kind between a style and an order. There was a difference, too, in the intellectual, and therefore the social scale, between a style and an order. "Thus passed the days, the weeks, the months in a sort of mish-mash of architectural theology." [2]

But Louis's faith lay in the "oft-seen creative power and glory of man. His faith lay indeed in freedom." The belief that art was dead seemed to him romantic; much like a fairy tale. "And this is all that he gathered from the 'Orders'—that they really were fairy tales of the long ago, now by the learned made rigid, mechanical and inane in books . . . wherein they were stultified, for lack of common sense and human feeling." The worldly pose and the poise of the cultural Boston of the time, as exemplified by Professor Ware, who created and maintained an air of legitimation and approval, derived from Boston and Cambridge crusades to "save" and "refine" American taste.

But his year at "Tech" and his two years in the Thompson home were not wasted. Louis turned to the study of music under John A. Thompson's tutelage. He also learned to draw, and, as he tells us, "to draw very well," by tracing the five orders "in a manner quite resembling copper plate." His first hearing of the great oratorios of Handel revived "his childhood's sensibilities and faith." But he acquired some knowledge of their structure, "some definition and labeling of the wondrous chords and modulations that had exalted him to an agony, and had borne him along in a great resplendent stream of song." As he studied the oratorios (particularly those of Handel) his sense of wonder increased over the capacity of men to create forms "out of their own heads." He dreamed again, as he had in childhood, "of that power within man of which no one had told him; for he had heard only of the power of God."[3] In this special vision he had always seen man "as a magician bringing forth from nothingness, from depths of silence of a huge world of sleep, as though, by waving of some unknown unseen wand, he had evoked this sublime, this amazing fabric; which equally would pass away and vanish with the sound of the last note, even as the bare thought of such passing left a haunt within."[4]

Thompson, "he of the precise, the articulate, the exact, the meticulous, the hard intelligence," brought Louis from the clouds of enchantment over music to a study of musical form. Thompson brought him, bit by bit and with great subtlety, into the "world of fact and technique." The first effect of this teaching was to arouse in Louis a "new interest—an interest in technique—in the how." He realized that these great oratorios brought profound moments of order into Thompson's life. "He clung to them indeed as though imagining he was a shipwrecked mariner and they a saving raft." Yet while Thompson lived in "Puritan New England where large utterances of joy and faith in the Earth, of faith in Life, of faith in Man, were few and far between,"[5] he was in heart and mind an epicurean, "quiet and gleeful amid the dangers in the open sea of sound." Louis's "utter innocence of music's artful structure, form and content was John A.'s joy, his secret delight."

Louis became deeply curious of musical form. He amassed technicalities and names "as one might collect precious curios." It seemed to him that "in giving names to all these sounds and movements he had heard and felt, it was much like giving names to the flowers and shrubs and trees he had loved so well." But one difference haunted him. The name of a plant form did not affect the reality of the plant, while naming musical expression did. "Thus while his plants and trees in spite of their names lived on in mystery, and slept their winter sleep, to be again awakened by the call of Spring, giving names to music had dispelled the mystery, and had caused its sweet enchantments one by one to pass in defile into a group of words, which might mean much or nothing according to as one first had felt the living power without their aid." There was danger that music might become "enslaved to the intellect and might nevermore be free. For as he began to see the full bulk of the mechanics, the mechanisms, and the tyranny of rules he became alarmed that music might die." Louis did not yet grasp the intellectual reality of form, even though he was highly sensitive to its emotional effects. "For he could not yet see that here also, in spite of names, the mystery, the enchantment would live on even though it be in winter sleep, and, at imagination's rousing call, again and again would renew its onward flow of rejuvenescence, and thus retain its magic power to stir the heart." [6]

Boston's cultural world, "within which were the blest, without which were the damned," was an intellectual world of theory, "of conjecture, of analysis and synthesis; the world of idea of Abstraction, of tenuity, of minute distinctions and nuances, filled with its specific belief in magic, its own superstitions, its aberrations, its taboos, denials and negations." Yet at the same time "it was a world of vast horizons . . . of immense powers of ethereal flight . . . accumulating a vast fund of how and why, wherewith to record, to construct, to upbuild." The intellect, powerful as it was, could not stir without the "willful power of Imagination." Boston overlooked the "living relationship" between intellect and instinct. Intellect "is recent, and neuter, and unstable in itself, while instinct is primordial and procreant." Instinct is that power of all time "that sleeps and dreams; it is that power within whose dream we dream,—even as in our practical aspect, our hard headed, cold-blooded, shrewd, calculating suspicious caution we are most obviously dreamers of turbid dreams, for we have pinned our faith to Intellect; we gaze in lethal adoration upon a reed shaken by the wind." [7]

He felt this more keenly as he listened to music other than oratorios. The music of Patrick Gilmore's "World Jubilee," in Boston in 1872, made him feel that music, and particularly the single voice, was the perfect instrument to "interpret and convey every state of feeling and of thought." The secular music of the Jubilee contrasted sharply with the somber, tragic note of the oratorios. "This blossoming of music exotic to all he had known hitherto, made him glad, made him gay, relaxed his sobriety, refreshed his outlook on life." Music was a new kind of beauty, "a beauty that seemed free and debonair, like a swan in the pool, like rain on the roof, like roses on a garden wall, with groves, and a turquoise sky; like bold and joyous horses, . . . and like unto furtive gentle creatures of wood and stream, and like curling breakers when close by, or the tossing of trees in a hearty gale." [8]

But society as well as art engrossed Louis. He began to enjoy companionship with those of his own age. This was a marked change. "Hitherto he had been entirely neglectful of his school comrades, caring neither who nor what they were as persons." At M.I.T. there was "space, freedom of movement and continued personal informal intercourse." In his portraits of student days at M.I.T. we see Louis beginning to put on "a bit of swagger, to wear smart clothes, to shave away the down and to agitate a propaganda for inch-long side whiskers." A photograph of that date, Sullivan tells us, shows him "a clean cut young man, with a rather intelligent expression, a heavy mop of black hair neatly parted for the occasion, a pearl stud set in immaculate white, and a suit up to the minute in material and cut." Yet as he looked back on the college "swell" of these years, Sullivan decided that while "Louis posed a bit, sensing the reflected prestige and social value of a student at 'Tech,' . . . he did not altogether make a nuisance of himself, nor a complete nuisance, for he was toppy [9] rather than vain."

The great drama of Boston in 1872 was the great conflagration in November. Louis was one of a dozen who saw the holocaust begin with a small flame curling from the wooden cornice of a building on the north side of Summer Street. As the flame spread, the city seemed doomed. "It was a magnificent but terrible pageant of wrathful fire before whose onslaught row after row of regimented buildings melted away." As far as the eye could reach "all was consuming fire, and dire devastation; an inferno, terrible and wonderful to look upon." When the ruins cooled, the streets were unrecognizable. At night he stood guard as a member of the M.I.T. battalion. "Clad in full uniform with a Springfield rifle and fixed bayonet at right shoulder," he walked his post for two nights. Order was restored and the rebuilding of the city began. For Louis "it was a terrifying experience; so sudden, so overwhelming, so fatalistic, so cruel."

His two days of military service, and the spectacle of a city in flames, turned Louis's thoughts to war, destruction, and social injustice. He liked military drill as "discipline in play." But he hated and loathed war, "as the wild dream of madmen who stood safely behind the evil." Louis was beginning to sense and understand what lay behind social façades. "Social strata had become visible and clear, as also that hypocrisy of caste and cant and 'eminence' against which his mother, time and time again, had spoken so clearly, so vehemently in anger and contempt." Among the thirty students registered in the architectural course at M.I.T. a few were rich men's sons, "to whom the architectural profession seemed to have advantages of tone." A few were poor men's sons who worked hard to become breadwinners. "What certain others were there for, including Louis, is a somewhat dubious surmise." The relationship between social hierarchy and the forms of life, thought, and art, were not difficult to grasp in Boston or M.I.T. in 1872. Bostonians scarcely bothered to hide them, and the students at M.I.T., like college students everywhere in 1872, were sure that, whatever else they were, they were members of the American elite.

Louis did not question the kindness and fundamental decency of his teachers at M.I.T., or the Bostonians he met in the Thompson home. Nor was there any question that Boston honored intellect. But it was not the creative intellect, but that of the cognoscenti and the intelligentsia. These men and women were interested far more in judging and classifying than in creating art. Historians, scholars, critics, theologians, and professors of "fine" art were the cultural heroes of Boston. The proper Bostonian respected culture, but he seldom loved it enough to commit himself to its creation. Creation demanded passion, the passion of the artist who seeks to create forms which, he believes, create community among men, because it is in and through the forms of art that men communicate and have their being.

Louis did not yet know what he needed to educate himself for architecture. But as the year began to close at M.I.T. he felt an emptiness in himself and his work became like the "play of marionettes." "He felt the need and the lack of a red-blooded explanation, of a valiant idea that should bring life to arouse his cemetery of orders and of styles, or at least to bring about a *danse macabre* to explain why the occupants had lived and died." He also discovered that the School of Architecture was but "a pale reflection" of the École des Beaux-Arts. Why not then go to the source? Perhaps there he would find a teacher like Moses Woolson. He reflected in despair that "neither immaculate Professor Ware nor sweaty, sallow, earnest Eugene Letang [10] was a Moses Woolson. Ah, if but Moses Woolson had been versed in the story of architecture as he was in that of English Literature, and had held the professorship; ah, what glowing flame would have come forth to cast its radiance like a rising sun and illuminate the past." [11]

He was not even sure he knew what it meant to be an architect. All he was getting at "Tech" was a "polite introduction to the architectural art." He wanted something more, something that would move him as the tower of the Brattle Street Church moved him. This was "conceived and brought to light by the mighty Richardson, undoubtedly for Louis's special delight; for was not here a fairy tale indeed!" The only way to learn how to keep alive such architecture was to live in the stream of life, to be impelled by the power of living. Perhaps it would be best, before going to the Beaux-Arts, to see what it was like to practice architecture. It would be advisable, he decided, to spend a year in a good architect's office, so that "he might see concrete preparations and results; how, in effect, an actual building was brought about."

His mind made up, Louis decided to go to Philadelphia, where his uncle and Grandpa lived. He stopped over for a few days in New York, where he talked with Richard M. Hunt, "the architectural lion there, and the dean of the profession." He was told to look up the firm of Furness and Hewitt in Philadelphia. But Louis wanted to see for himself what Philadelphia had to offer. As he had done in Boston, and was to do in Chicago, Louis began a systematic walking survey of Philadelphia, "looking quizzically at buildings as he wandered." On South Broad Street a residence, almost completed,

Sullivan's Meyer Building, designed in 1893, is an early example of his search for an architecture that would express function in structure, and thus integrate form and function. *Photo by Richard Nickel*

"caught his eye like a flower by the roadside. He approached, examined it with curious care, without and within." Here was something "fresh and fair to him, a human note, as though someone were talking. He inquired as to the architect, and was told: Furness and Hewitt. Now, he saw plainly enough that this was not the work of two men but of one, for he had an instinctive sense of physiognomy, and all buildings thus made their direct appeal to him, pleasant or unpleasant." [12]

Louis decided that he would work for Furness and Hewitt. They were "to have no voice in the matter, for his mind was made up." He presented himself to Frank Furness and informed him he had come to work for him. "Furness looked at him half blankly, half enraged, as at another kind of dog that had slipped in through the door." Louis was fascinated by Furness. "He affected the English fashion," and let out "a string of oaths a yard long." When he found that Louis had no experience, and had just come from M.I.T., he exploded. "This answer was the detonation that set off the mine which blew up in fragments all the schools in the land and scattered the professors headless and limbless to the four quarters of earth and hell!" Louis was a fool and an idiot to have wasted his time in a place "where one was filled with sawdust, like a doll, and becomes a prig, a snob, and an ass. As the smoke blew away he said: 'Of course you don't know anything and are full of damnable conceit.' " [13]

After more oaths, and humble admissions from Louis that he had much to learn, Louis told Furness about his unaided discovery of the house on Broad Street. He must work under the master who had produced this house. He looked Furness steadfastly in the eye and told him that "here he was and here he would remain." Then he sang a song of praise "like a youthful bard of old to his liege lord, . . . placing all on a high plane of accomplishment." Here in this office, Louis went on, one could really learn something. Furness agreed there was some truth in what Louis said, but turned aside further compliments by saying: "Only the Greeks knew how to build." He then turned to Louis and told him to come in the morning for a trial, and predicted darkly that Louis would not last out the week. At the end of two weeks Furness told Louis that he could stay as long as he liked. And thus began the career of Louis H. Sullivan as an architect.

It was a fortunate beginning. George Hewitt was a clean draftsman. Louis admired him as a draftsman, if he did not admire his "Victorian Gothic in its pantalettes [which he did] when a church building or something of that sort was on the boards." Frank Furness, unlike George Hewitt, who found his inspiration in books, made buildings "out of his head." His freehand drawing was extraordinary. He hypnotized Louis, especially when he drew and swore at the same time. John, George's younger brother, ran the shop. He took a fancy to Louis. He was the "practical man" and Louis ran to him for advice whenever he found himself in a tight place. "John was patience itself and made everything clear with dainty sketches and explanatory notes. These drawings were beautiful and Louis frankly told him so. He begged John to teach him 'touch' and especially how to 'indicate' so crisply. This John did. In fact it was not long before he had made Louis a draftsman of the upper Crust . . . , and Louis's heart went out to lovable John in sheer gratitude." [14]

Sullivan always paid high tribute to the training he was given in the Furness and Hewitt office. "In looking back upon that time," he tells us, "Louis Sullivan gives thanks that it was his good fortune to have made his entry into the practical world in an office where standards were so high —where talent was so manifestly taken for granted, and the atmosphere the free and easy one of a true workshop savoring of the guild where craftsmanship was paramount and personal." Yet he could not have taken advantage of such training without Moses Woolson's teaching. "We may say in truth that Moses Woolson put him there. For without that elastic alertness and courage, that grimness Moses Woolson imparted, it is sure that Louis would not have broken through the barrier of contempt in that first interview." Louis worked hard "day and night." [15] As always, he turned to nature, here Fairmount Park and Wissahickon Valley, for comfort and surcease.

One warm day in September, the sounds of shouts from the street reached the office. As Louis looked out he saw a swarming mass of frantic men jammed from wall to wall. Jay Cooke and Co. had just closed its doors. The panic of 1873, one of the worst in our history, was on. Louis was shocked and appalled. "He was too young, too inexperienced, to understand what it really meant, even when told it was a panic in finance, that credit had crumbled to dust, that men were ruined, and insane with despair: that this panic would spread like wildfire over the land leaving ruin in its wake everywhere. And still he could not understand what had brought it all about." One day in November Frank Furness came to Sullivan's desk and told him that he must go. But not without telling him: "You've done well, mighty well. I like you. I wish you might stay. But as you were the last to come it is only just that you should be first to go." With that, "he slipped a bill into Louis's hand and wished him farewell and better times." [16] Within a week, Louis was on his way to Chicago.

Notes

[1] Louis H. Sullivan, *The Autobiography of an Idea* (New York: Press of the American Institute of Architects, 1926), p. 175.

[2] *Autobiography,* pp. 187–88.

[3] Much has been made of the conflict between science and religion in our cultural history. But there was also a deep-seated conflict between art and religion, as Sullivan so often stressed in his writings. The conflict between science and art, which was raging in Chicago when Sullivan arrived in 1873, still continues. The University of Chicago, which pioneered in so many branches of the social studies, has never been able to resolve the tension between art and science in its cultural studies. History, for example, is taught in the social sciences. The humanities have produced nothing to compare with the brilliance and boldness of the work done in the physical and social sciences.

[4] Sullivan, *op. cit.,* pp. 176–77.

[5] Three cities, Boston, Paris, and Chicago, inspired Sullivan. The tension between intellect and faith in Boston culture was resolved by Moses Woolson, whose passion for learning was creative, not antiquarian, and certainly not religious. This was the New England of Sullivan's time at its best. Class, race, religious bigotry, and cultural snobbery were, for Sullivan, its worst vices. Paris, unlike Boston and Chicago, honored the artist as a social type and gave him a definite place in its social life, as well as honoring the intellectual, as Boston did. Chicago, as we have seen, honored art so long as it was related to democracy. The Chicago vice was indifference to art. Sullivan thought this could be overcome by education. Chicagoans were ignorant, not corrupt, like New Yorkers, and they trusted the heart, unlike Bostonians.

[6] Sullivan, *op. cit.,* p. 178.

[7] *Ibid.,* pp. 179–80.

[8] *Ibid.,* pp. 180–81.

[9] *Ibid.,* p. 186. "Toppy" is an American slang term meaning: preeminent, ambitious to excel, a member of an elite, etc.

[10] Professor Ware's assistant in charge of student projects.

[11] *Ibid.,* p. 189.

[12] *Ibid.,* pp. 190–91.

[13] *Ibid.,* pp. 191–92.

[14] *Ibid.,* pp. 193–94.

[15] *Ibid.,* p. 194.

[16] *Ibid.,* p. 196.

53

The Search for an Idea of Architecture in Practice: Chicago

L o u i s 's first impression of the West and Chicago was one of overwhelming power. As his train crossed the Alleghenies into the long descending Horse-Shoe Curve, Louis was aroused by a new sense of space. The prairies of northern Indiana left him "utterly amazed and bewildered." They were entirely new to him.[1] "How could such things be! Stretching like a floor to the far horizon,—not a tree except by a watercourse on a solitary 'island.' It was amazing. Here was power—power greater than the mountains." Then came Lake Michigan, the great inland sea. "Soon Louis caught glimpses of a great lake, spreading also like a floor to the far horizon, superbly beautiful in color, under a lucent sky. Here again was power, naked power, naked as the prairies, greater than the mountains. And over all spanned the dome of the sky, resting on the rim of the horizon far away on all sides, eternally calm overhead, holding an atmosphere pellucid and serene."[2]

The horizon of prairie, water, and sky, which stretched into eternity, moved Sullivan deeply. But this new power of nature was dominated by a still greater power in Chicago, the power of men. "And here again was a power, a vast open power, a power greater than the tiny mountains. Here, in full view, was the light of the world, companion of the earth, a power greater than the lake and the prairie below, but not greater than man in his power: So Louis thought." As the train broke into the city, Louis's excitement mounted into ecstasy. "The train . . . plowed its way through miles of shanties disheartening and dirty gray. It reached its terminal at an open shed. Louis tramped the platform, stopped, looked toward the city, ruins around him; looked at the sky; and as one alone, stamped his foot, raised his hand, and cried in full voice: THIS IS THE PLACE FOR ME!"[3] Louis had reached his magic city, the city of Chicago.

In his first exploration of Chicago, Louis met people whose energy and power matched the prairie, the lake, and the horizon. Chicagoans were telling the world that Chicago had risen phoenixlike from its ashes, although in 1873 many ashes remained. Ruins and new buildings stood side by side in newly laid and repaired streets. It was, Louis thought, "magnificent and wild." The ruins could be endured because time in Chicago was of the future; in the eyes of Chicagoans the ruins were but cryptic symbols of a glory yet to come. There was a "sense of big things to be done." Chicago was to rebuild, not the simple "Garden City" of the past, but the greatest modern city in the world. Louis had heard something about Chicago braggarts. The genius of the West for seeing in the future things which older eyes could not, or would not, see, was a constant wonder and amusement to Easterners. Louis agreed that these Chicago "boomers" were the "crudest, rawest, most savagely ambitious dreamers and would-be doers in the world."

But these savage dreamers, so different from the intellectual, bookish Bostonians, were not mad dreamers, but prophets. Louis soon learned that their dreams, even the wildest, often became true. "All this frothing at the mouth amused him at first," but he soon realized that Chicago had a way of making dreams come true. "He saw the primal power assuming self-expression amid nature's impelling urge. These men had vision. What they saw was real, they saw it as destiny." Certainly, unless one shared their visions, Chicagoans seemed vulgar braggarts, and the city itself nothing but a vast mudhole over which hung the stench of death as the daily kill at the stockyards mounted higher and higher. For those of aesthetic sensibilities who could not see the visions of Chicagoans, the city and its people were grotesque. The pavements were foul and dirty; mud and slime erupted everywhere. The Chicago River was one vast, open sewer. The elevated wooden sidewalks, with steps at each corner, seemed "shabby and grotesque" to Louis. But when he learned that the city was determined to lift itself another three feet out of the mud, he began to see the present in terms of a golden future. Chicagoans were not fools or madmen, but heroic. There were "big men" here, men of destiny to play their parts on the heroic stage set for them in the boundless prairie and beside the mighty lake.

Even in the midst of the great depression of 1873, Chicagoans were not fearful. The panic, which brought business to a standstill in Boston and Philadelphia, was considered a "set-back," a temporary halt to progress. Chicagoans were determined to make their city what they already saw it to be in their visions, and what they were beginning to call it—namely, a "wonder-city." The terrible destruction of the fire forced rapid and cheap construction. "When Louis came to understand the vast area of disaster, he saw clearly and with applause that this new half-built city was a hasty improvisation made in dire need by men who did not falter." Yet even in the midst of such rapid building, a few showed talent. One of these was the Portland Block, a four-story structure of pressed brick and sandstone at Washington and Dearborn streets. He learned that Major William Le Baron Jenney had designed it.[4]

Major Jenney was a new kind of architect for Louis, as indeed he was for America and, as it turned out, for the world. He was an engineer, more than an architect, but this does not mean that he was uncultured.[5] Born in 1832, he was educated at Phillips Academy, the Lawrence Scientific School, and the École Centrale des Arts et Manufactures in Paris, where he studied art and architecture and graduated with high honors in 1856. He returned to the United States, where he became an engineer for the Tehuantepec Railroad Company of New Orleans on the Isthmus of Tehuantepec. After a year in this position he returned to France and spent another eighteen months in the study of architecture. Shortly after the outbreak of the Civil War he enlisted in the Federal army. He was assigned, as a captain, to Grant's staff as engineering officer. He served with Grant from Cairo to Corinth and then, at Sherman's request, was put in charge of the engineering work at Memphis, Tennessee. He became chief engineer of the XV Army Corps. He came to Chicago in 1868 to begin his practice as an engineer and architect. In 1860 he published *Principles and Practice of Architecture*.

Even Jenney, Adler, Sooy Smith, and Maatz, who came to Chicago from war service to practice as engineers and architects, did not "bring" engineering and architecture to the city. As early as 1856 Van Osdel's account books contain the signatures of Chicago architects: G. P. Randall, P. A. Nicholson, Robert Schmid, A. Bauer, Edward Burling, John M. Van Osdel, O. S. Kinney, O. L. Wheelock, W. W. Boyington, T. V. Wadshier, and A. Carter. Van Osdel became in 1841 the first architect to practice in Chicago or in the West.

In 1837 there were not more than twenty brick buildings in Chicago, out of a total of nearly a thousand. The hundreds of frame buildings, and the many thousands to follow, were made possible by George W. Snow's invention of the balloon frame method of construction. This one invention practically changed building in wood from a complicated craft, practiced only by skilled labor, to an industry.[6]

Edward Burling, like so many of the early Chicago architects, started his career as a carpenter. He came to Chicago in 1843, worked with several builders, and then began his own practice in the early 1850s. His office and wholesale building at 200 West Adams, which he and Whitehouse did in 1888, is remarkable for its adaptation of the masonry wall to the architecture of interior framing.[7] But even as early as 1865, Burling, with Baumann's help as draftsman, built a Chamber of Commerce which soon became famous for its lack of architectural bombast and fussy ornament. A. T. Andreas, whose three-volume history of Chicago appeared in 1884–86, indicates the ambivalent attitudes of the time toward the relative simplicity of the building. "The design was not strictly in accordance with any known style of architecture, the aesthetic element in art being kept in subservience to the practical uses for which the building was planned and restricted by the economical limitations to the cost of the proposed structure. It was, however, when finished, with one exception the most pretentious and substantial edifice in the city, and, although severely plain in its outward adornments, was symmetric in its proportions, massive in style and an ornament to the growing city." [8]

Burling also trained John J. Flanders, whose Mallers Warehouse at 225 South Market Street, which was completed in 1893, stood beside the Tacoma and Reliance buildings as first examples of what we now call the glass tower.[9] Indeed, Condit says that "this warehouse represents the most nearly complete dematerialization of the wall that one can find before the work of Le Corbusier in the early 1930's." It is a glittering prism of glass, "all the more brilliant because of its setting among the begrimed buildings of the Market Street wholesale area." The absence of any ornament (except at the entrance) makes the Mallers Warehouse "the purest revelation of steel framing until one comes to the work of the so-called International School in Europe—the bauhaus, the Van Nelle Tobacco Factory, the Swiss Dormitory, the Maison Clarte." As Condit goes on to point out, it is but a short step from this functional and unpretentious warehouse to Mies's glass towers of the 1950s in Chicago. "In fifty-five years the new architecture has come full circle, from Chicago through France and Germany and back to its native home."

Edward Baumann, who befriended Sullivan in his early years in Chicago and whose monograph, *A Theory of Isolated Pier Foundations,* published in 1873, did much to create the engineering practice necessary to skyscraper construction, was consulted by Jenney for his Home Insurance Building, the first building using a steel cage for framing. When Sullivan arrived in Chicago, Baumann was thirty-five years old. He came to Chicago in 1857, and within a few years was used by Van Osdel, Burling, and Maatz as a consultant. In 1862, after a few years as a contractor, he returned (with a cousin as partner) to architecture, and lived to attend meetings of the Illinois Chapter of the American Institute of Architects up to the 1920s. W. W. Boyington, Augustus Bauer, Otto Maatz, and others practicing in Chicago before and after the Fire created structures which added to the importance of Chicago as an engineering and architectural center. The brilliant improvisations of Van Osdel, Snow and Burling and the important engineering contributions of Baumann did not stand alone.

It is true enough that Snow, Van Osdel, Baumann, Burling, and Flanders did not follow accepted traditions of building. But this was not because they were ignorant or untrained, but because they were trying to solve new problems. As we have already pointed out in our discussion of Van Osdel's Monon Building, Chicago architects had to create not only building designs, but a whole new organization of the building art. Ericsson, one of the great Chicago contractors who worked on buildings designed by Van Osdel and Jenney, tells us that to build the Monon and the Manhattan he had to create a new organization, invent machines and equipment, and train workers in new skills, before he could follow Van Osdel's and Jenney's plans. The plans themselves were radical enough, so radical indeed that no existing engineering tables could be used to estimate stress. Men like Jenney, Burling, Adler, Johnson and Edelmann thought it only natural to design and supervise the construction of their own buildings.

In one sense these men were highly traditional. They returned architecture to building and construction. Chicago architects of this generation thought of themselves as builders, not "artists." Indeed, they were almost cynical about the "art" of architecture. They despised bookish architects. As Sullivan said, a man should get a building "out of his own head." He should also be able to boss the construction of his building, not just visit the site to "consult" with the builder. And it was not uncommon for the architects of this generation to help promote and finance their buildings. For engineers, the "art" of architecture was necessary to make the building "appealing." Pretty façades "dressed up" the building and thus attracted tenants and customers. But the real job of building was not the façade but the structure, and respect and honor was given to the man who could "button up the building in the back," [10] as well as decorate its front.

Another distinction between the early Chicago engineers and traditional architects was the interest of the engineers in planning. Jenney was engineer and architect for the West Park Commission from 1859 to 1875. By 1885, Humbolt, Garfield, and Douglas parks, with their boulevards, and the boulevards designed as "elongated parks" to connect with parks on the north and south side, comprised 353 acres of improved land with 50 acres of lakes, 119,564 planted trees, 68,736 lineal feet of drives, 45,916 lineal feet of walks, and many buildings of various kinds.[11] Few architects in the country, or for that matter in the world, were given opportunities for such large-scale works in urban environments. Jenney's park work in the 1870s was to be continued by Jens Jensen in his school of "naturalization" in landscape design, and by Burnham in his great Chicago Plan of 1906–09.

In his first months in Chicago, Louis found himself in conflict over men like Jenney who were highly "practical," or, as we now say, "functional," in their approach to building. What disturbed Louis, who was seeking to discover universal principles of architecture which could be applied to new world architecture, was the lack of self-consciousness in such men as Jenney, and lack of belief in art as a constituent part of reality in such men as Baumann. "The Major was a free-and-easy cultured gentleman. . . . he disposed of matters easily in the manner of a war veteran who believed he knew what was what. . . . All in all the Major was effusive; a hale fellow well met, an officer of the Loyal Legion, a welcome guest anywhere, but by preference a host. . . . Louis thought him funny all the time, and noted with glee how akin were the Major's thoughts to the vertiginous gyrations of his speech." His absences from the office were "frequent and prolonged." Was Jenney an architect? By "courtesy of terms" only; his "true profession was that of engineer." But a few lines later Sullivan denies even this. "Louis soon found out that the Major was not, really, in his heart, an engineer at all, but by nature, and in toto, a *bon vivant,* a gourmet." [12]

But Jenney's foreman, John Edelmann, was not like Jenney. He was incredibly vain, a hero-worshiper. "John blandly worshipped John in the presence of all." Yet when Louis remarked casually to John that "John's unconsciousness of his own personality was remarkable to the point of the fabulous and the legendary . . . they became fast friends." John was a new kind of personality to the young Bostonian, whose idea of architects had been formed on Professor Ware, the Hewitts, and Frank Furness. He was "brawny, twenty-four, bearded, unkempt, careless, his voice rich, sonorous, modulant, his vocabulary an overflowing reservoir." He was a born orator and loved all kinds of talk. His vitality and humor were overpowering. In the Major's absences, "John Edelmann would mount a drawing table and make a howling stump speech on green back currency, or single tax." [13] Like John Root, Edelmann talked and drew at the same time.

But the curious difference between John Edelmann and the men Louis knew in the East was the extraordinary range of Edelmann's interests, and his ability to move quickly from abstruse speculation to practical application. His ability to relate thought to action, indeed his insistence that thought, to be thought at all, must be related to action, was new to Louis. "It gradually dawned on Louis that he had run across a THINKER, a profound thinker, a man of immense range of reading, a brain of extraordinary keenness, strong, vivid, that ranged in its operations from saturnine intelligence concerning men and their motives, to the highest transcendentalisms of German metaphysics." John Edelmann was as familiar with the "great philosophers as with the daily newspapers. As an immediate psychologist, never before or since, has Louis met his equal in vitality, in verity, and in perspicacity of thought." [14]

Edelmann, like the Chicagoans Dewey, Mead, and Veblen, searched for values and meaning in the life of his own time, and in his own city, Chicago. It was not a matter of knowing German philosophers or reading Schopenhauer, but of knowing their relevance to the new life of Chicago. Moses Woolson taught Louis principles of knowledge and art, but John Edelmann taught him to think about the value of principles in action. Edelmann was concerned with architectural principles, and was always willing to discuss them with Louis. Despite his vanity and loquacity, and even though he was accepted as a master by Louis, who was seven years his junior, their relationship was not that of teacher and pupil, so much as fellow craftsmen. What Louis learned from John—and he learned a great deal—he learned in companionship, through the give and take of open and friendly talk.

Edelmann was interested in the idea of architecture in general, and of the specific application of general principles to American architecture. For him, American architecture was not a matter of themes (Indian, etc.) or of newness as such. He argued that thought in art, the reason of art, had little to do with utility or mechanical function. As we have seen in his essay, "Pessimism of Modern Architecture," he believed that emotional expression was the very essence of architecture. Such expression alone "distinguished it from mere engineering, where material expedience and convenience are the standards. . . . The attempt to meet the emotional want has in all times and places produced architecture in our country, as in all others." But if the functionalism of the engineers could easily degenerate into a sterile functionalism, there was danger, too, that effective theories of architecture could lead to sentimental and picturesque art. The only escape from either of these pitfalls was to search for an idea of architecture which would include *both* form and content. That is, what kind of experience was architectural experience? How did the form of architecture create experience? And above all, how did one create an architecture that would not only "relate to," but enhance, democratic life?

Even a genius of seventeen, or the brilliant, far-ranging mind of a twenty-four-year-old designer, living in a city where bold and original thought was common enough, could not be expected to answer these questions. The wisdom of these young architects and engineers lay in the questions they asked, not in their answers. John taught Louis that while functions of forms become real only when expressed, functions can also be suppressed. "Thus with John's aid, Louis saw the outer and the inner world more clearly, and the world of men began to assume a semblance of form, and of function." He warned Louis, too, that many thinkers were like spiders, "weaving, in the gloom of obscurantism, festoons of cobwebs in their dens, far from the light of the world of men and things." Louis, John said, should keep his eye on Chicago. He would find plenty to interest him there, and if he had the vision "he would find a great romance there, also a great tragedy."

John was right. Louis found romance of the spirit and the mind. Chicago of 1875 loved its visionaries, as it loved its young. But above all it cherished men as free individuals. A man was expected to "make it on his own." Being "self-made," as an artist as well as a businessman, was highly honored. In the morning of life in the new city, the city of youth and dreams, all things seemed possible. Among his friends at the Lotus Club, whose members had boathouses on the bank of the Calumet, William B. Curtis, one of the great amateur athletes of his time, offered Louis another example of power. A consumptive in his youth, Curtis had disciplined his mind and body through study and rigorous exercise. When he walked in sunlight to the end of the pier for a plunge, "he was a sight for the Greeks, and Louis was enraptured at the play of light and shade." He was the exact opposite of John. He detested display, talked little, and was "too cynical to brag." But, like John, he loved Louis and was his friend. As they wrestled, raced, swam, and read together in joy and laughter like young Greeks, the world seemed not a sad pilgrimage, but a mountain shielding a paradise which could be won by those daring enough to try.

Notes

[1] As they were to many travelers. There are many moving accounts in travelers' reports of the great "sea of grass," the prairie. Jens Jensen created a philosophy of landscape art based on the "Prairie Line." His moment of mystery in his art was in long horizontal lines representing the line of the horizon, where sky, or water and sky, met the land. Wright's early houses were called "Prairie Houses," and in them he created a mystique of the "Prairie Line."

[2] Louis H. Sullivan, *The Autobiography of an Idea* (New York: Press of the American Institute of Architects, 1926), pp. 196–97.

[3] *Ibid.*, p. 197. Sullivan's capitalization. This was on the day before Thanksgiving, 1873.

[4] Louis learned also that the Portland Block had really been designed by a clever draftsman named Cudell. "This gave him a shock. For he had supposed that all architects made buildings out of their own heads, not out of the heads of others." His experience in the office of Furness and Hewitt had given him this erroneous idea. But this knowledge cheered him, too. Perhaps someday he might "make buildings out of his head for architects who did not have any heads of their own for such purpose." (*Autobiography*, p. 202)

[5] It is necessary to stress the education and culture of early Chicago architects, if for no other reason than to correct the impression fostered by such critics and historians as Henry-Russell Hitchcock, who tells us on pages 240–41 of his *Architecture: Nineteenth and Twentieth Centuries* (Baltimore; Penguin Books, 1958), that "If the Chicago architectural scene had any virtues around 1880 they were largely negative ones: no established traditions, no professional leaders, and ignorance of all architectural styles past or present. Among the architects who had settled in Chicago in the seventies was a Dane, Dankmar Adler (1844–1900)." More mistakes could scarcely be made in two consecutive sentences. Major Jenney worked in a great Chicago tradition, the tradition of American engineering. The architectural profession in Chicago, even in the eighties, had highly self-conscious leaders in Burnham, Root, Adler, Sullivan, and Jenney. They founded Western societies of architecture, wrote codes for practice, created journals of criticism and professional news, wrote dozens of articles, and gave many talks on architecture. Dankmar Adler was not a Dane, but a German Jew, and he did not settle in Chicago in the seventies. He was the son of Liebman Adler, rabbi and cantor of the Jewish Congregation Bethel. In July, 1862, he enlisted in Company M of the First Brigade of Illinois Light Artillery. He saw service in the campaigns of 1862, 1863, and 1864 in Kentucky, Tennessee and Georgia, and fought in some of the greatest battles of the war. He was wounded, but managed to escape serious injury. After the war, Adler came to Chicago and went to work for Augustus Bauer. He then entered the office of O. S. Kinney. In 1871 he went into partnership with Edward Burling. In 1872 he married Dila Kohn, daughter of Abraham Kohn, head of one of the first Jewish families of Chicago, and the founder of Anshe Ma'arive Congregation, for which Adler and Sullivan designed a temple. (See the biographical sketch of Dankmar Adler which Hugh Morrison included in his book, *Louis Sullivan: Prophet of Modern Architecture* [New York: Norton, 1935].) Neglect, as well as shoddy scholarship, haunts the student of Chicago architecture.

[6] For a good discussion of Snow's invention, see Sigfried Giedion, *Space, Time and Architecture,* 3d ed. (Cambridge: Harvard University Press, 1954), pp. 344–52. Without balloon framing, the settlement of the Middle West and the plains in such a short time would have been impossible. There was no timber in many areas of the West. Prefabricated units, designed and built by balloon frame methods, were shipped to the West from Chicago in the 1890s.

[7] Carl W. Condit discusses Burling's work in *The Rise of The Skyscraper* (Chicago: University of Chicago Press, 1951). See also Thomas E. Tallmadge, *Architecture in Old Chicago* (Chicago: University of Chicago Press, 1941).

[8] A. T. Andreas, *History of Chicago from the Earliest Period to the Present Time,* 3 vols. (Chicago: A. T. Andreas, 1884–86), II, 358.

[9] Condit illustrates this building (still standing in 1964) and describes it in his discussion of Flanders (see p. 207, Condit, *op. cit.*). Flanders was born in Chicago and trained in the offices of Bauer, Wadskier, and Burling. He remained two years with Burling and opened his own office in 1874. The first Mallers Building, an office building built in 1884 on Quincy and LaSalle streets, was the first twelve-story office building in Chicago. Andreas tells us that in 1885 "it was admired as a monument of architectural skill." Tallmadge, who denied the greatness of the Chicago school (but recanted in his later years), thought this early building was superior to the one Condit admires so greatly, the Mallers Warehouse.

[10] This is a phrase used by Frank Lloyd Wright in conversation with the author. Wright was careful to explain the importance of Adler, the "Big Chief," as he was called by Wright, to the creation of Adler and Sullivan's buildings: he knew how to "button up" a building.

[11] Andreas, *op. cit.,* describes the early stages of city planning in Chicago.

[12] Sullivan, *op. cit.,* p. 203.

[13] "While at the same time Louis, at the top of his voice, sang selections from the oratorios, beginning with his favorite, 'Why Do the Nations So Furiously Rage Together'; until all the forces furiously raged together in joyous deviltry and bang-bang-bang." *Ibid.,* p. 205.

[14] *Ibid.,* p. 206. Examples of Edelmann's critical acumen have been given in Chapter 33. Sullivan's capitalization.

54

The Search for an Idea of Architecture in Theory: Paris

CHICAGO, Louis soon learned, was a world of work and action. A city had to be rebuilt, and it had to be rebuilt quickly. The immediate problems to be solved were engineering problems, and the first questions asked of the architect were practical questions. Van Osdel, Burling, Adler, and Jenney had little time for discussion of design. But for Louis design was important, for if the architect did not have a theory of art, how could he justify himself? Chicago engineers knew how to make a building work. They also knew how to think about structure, and, when left alone, knew enough not to corrupt a building with ornament that betrayed the structure of the building. The fact that walls were still too heavy and that the spirit of the tall building had not yet been invoked was not the fault of engineers. If there was any failure, it was in the art, not the science, of building. Louis knew, or thought he knew, what architects ought to be doing. How to do it, how even to think well about architecture, was another matter. He decided to go to "the fountain head of theory," the École des Beaux-Arts. Eight months of practice in Chicago was enough for the time being.

But Louis was not going to Paris to be taught "about" theory in architecture. He made the long journey from Chicago to find answers to questions which had been haunting him since his childhood. The questions began in wonder over the mystery of the forms he saw in nature. Why were they so beautiful? What, in the form of a tree, moved him so deeply? As he discovered bridges, buildings, and finally Richardson's Brattle Square Church in Boston, the mystery of form in art also engrossed him. He decided long before he came to Paris that the creation of form was a natural power in men, as in nature, but nature did not create buildings. These were created by men. It was simple enough to discover the relationship of form to function in a leaf, just as it was easy enough to describe the mechanical functions of a building, but this was not the *human* function. What, for example, did we mean by work? What kind of satisfactions were proper to the act of work? How did the architect create the stages which made possible these satisfactions?

Of one thing Louis was very clear. He wanted to create, not to judge, promote, or write about, architecture. He knew that despite all that had been said about architecture, nothing had really been said in America about its social function. In architecture, as in nature, delight and joy characterized his experience of form. He believed that the desire for beauty was an instinct, common to all men. For if this were not so, how could we talk of a democratic art? And if there were no instinct of beauty, how could Louis explain the raptures and trances (his illuminations) of his childhood and youth? Historical criticism and depiction of architecture, evolutionary theories of the development of forms, and logical theories of architecture derived from the formal analysis of great buildings—these said nothing about the simple but overwhelming fact that some buildings aroused joy and delight, and others did not. The secret, the reality behind the veil of appearances, as Louis had talked about it since his childhood, must lie in form. For this was what the artist struggled to create. But what was the secret of *good* form? And how could form be related to democracy? That is, what was the content of form proper to democratic life?

Paris, the home of art and, above all, the great center of art criticism, must have the answer, just as Chicago, the great vital center of architectural engineering, had the answer to construction. No one in Chicago, certainly not Jenney, was concerned about theories of art. Chicago architects such as Burling, Baumann, Adler, and Jenney did not talk about art at all. They were engineers and inventors, not artists. Inspiration came from solving problems, not from philosophizing about art. Jenney's creation of the steel frame was born in the search for a practical solution to the problem of supporting weights great enough to make taller buildings possible. During the bricklayers' strike of 1883—so the Chicago legend runs—Jenney went home early one afternoon. When he arrived home Mrs. Jenney thought he was ill. As she rose hurriedly to greet him, she placed the heavy book she was reading on top of a bird cage which stood on a table. At the sight of this, Jenney asked himself: "If the frail frame of the bird cage could hold such a heavy book, why couldn't a similar frame of cast iron or steel hold the weight of a building?" [1]

In Paris, Louis found another great teacher. This was Monsieur Clopet, the tutor in mathematics recommended by the American Legation. Like John Edelmann, Clopet was interested in first principles. But where Edelmann searched for them in society, Clopet sought them in the mind. In his gentle, polished, yet forceful mind, Clopet was the antithesis of Edelmann. Clopet relied on logic and demonstrations. "As a drill master he was a potent driver, as an expounder he made good his word to Louis in a method and a manner, revealing, inspiring, as he calmly unfolded, step by step, a well reasoned process in his demonstrations. . . . so there was not a book in sight; but ever in sight was Monsieur Clopet, making something teachable out of what at first seemed an abstraction in three dimensions." [2]

Louis found that he had little use for what was then called "proof." "In his secret heart he did not believe that anything could be *proved,* but believed as firmly that many things might be *shown*." He became convinced that all abstractions were assumptions—"that abstract truth was a mirage." Searching for abstract truth made Louis feel imprisoned within his inner consciousness, instead of the "free open" of outward consciousness. Abstract reasoning was a working of the intellect "detached from reality," and therefore detached from life. And while it was necessary (to pass his entrance exams) to learn the kind of abstract reasoning used in the science of arithmetic— which demanded that one could prove by "rigorous logic" that two and two make four—he rebelled against the "impertinence" of such logic. And, he decided, "once we assume an abstraction to be real, we lose our anchorage which is in the real." Thus, despite the clarity, elegance, and power of French thought, the lessons he had learned in his first months in Chicago from the highly practical engineers were not forgotten.

But if the search for abstract truth seemed fruitless to Louis, the constant attempt to clarify thought through logic and reason did not. And, even though he was not in sympathy with the science of arithmetic, he was deeply moved by Clopet's insistence that any logical demonstration must be judged by its universality. As Clopet examined the books Louis had been told to obtain by the American Legation, Clopet pointed out that a demonstration with five exceptions, a theorem with three special cases, another with nine, and yet others with exceptions and special cases, should be disregarded. He told Louis quietly: "I suggest you place the book in the waste basket; we shall not need of it here; *for here our demonstrations shall be so broad as to admit of* NO EXCEPTION!" At these words Louis stood "as one whose body had been turned to hot stone, while his brain was raging." If this could be done in mathematics, why not in architecture?

For all their differences, Paris and Chicago had much in common for Louis. England seemed alien and old. He recognized the strength of English tradition, but he did not understand it. The poverty and squalor of London dismayed him. He was at home in Paris as he had been in Chicago. He realized now that he was no longer a proper Bostonian, but a proper Chicagoan. Parisians seemed "rather like his own people of the Middle West." They were more cultured, more polite, and more refined, but between "raw Chicago" and "finished Paris" there was a temperamental likeness, just as there was between Boston and London. Parisians and Chicagoans possessed the "same lighthearted spirit of adventure." Paris, though filled with historic monuments, did not seem old; it gave rather an impress of ever-renewing youth and its people seemed lighthearted. The children were "like flowers" and the nurses in the Luxembourg Gardens were like stately flowers. "Never had he seen such child-happiness, such utter joy in living; and he felt convinced this must be the child-key to France. . . . Yes, there was an atmosphere; this atmosphere was Paris; Paris was to be his home; its air of hospitality, of world-welcomer and host, found in him a ready and a heartfelt response." [3]

And Paris, like Chicago, gave Louis confidence in his own power of constructive imagination. He knew he could draw, and his months in Philadelphia and Chicago gave him enough practical experience as a draftsman to assure him that he could be an architect, as architecture was then practiced. But what he did not know when he came to Paris was whether or not he really possessed the kind of imagination necessary to great achievement in architecture. The day of his great trial, the examinations for admission to the school, soon approached. The real test would be in the oral exams. These were conducted in little amphitheaters, with a professor presiding and each aspirant free to come and go during the others' exams. Louis waited his turn with other students. The professors of the École, waiting to judge them, were guardians of the greatest architectural school in the world—the École des Beaux-Arts of Paris. But what kind of spirit these professors guarded, Louis did not know.

As Louis stepped forward for his exam in mathematics, the examining professor made clear that he wanted to test his understanding, not his memory. "For over an hour—Lord knows how long it was—he put Louis through a steady gruelling—always kindly however—such as Louis had never known, never dreamed of, never believed could be so." After a heartbreaking crisis when he almost lost hold, he suddenly found himself "*thinking* in terms of mathematics." He relaxed and let his mind go free. "The professor's interest quickened. He increased the difficulties of his questions. Louis was stimulated by the challenge. From beginning to end he did not make a fluke." At the end the professor reached over and pressed Louis's hand and said: "I felicitate you, Monsieur Sullivan: you have the mathematical imagination which is rather rare. I wish you well." Louis was astounded at his success. Of all things Louis felt he did *not* possess, mathematical imagination was among the first. He had learned mathematics from books, where drill, and not imagination, was required. But here in Paris he suddenly discovered that mathematics was an act of the imagination, and an act he could perform well. [4]

Louis was equally startled by the method of questioning in history. Only three questions were asked. "Monsieur, will you be kind enough to tell me the story of the Hebrew people?" "I would like an account of the ten emperors of Rome." Give me "an intimate account of the times of Francis First." The charm of answering these strange questions lay in the fact that Louis was encouraged by the examining professor "to give a pictorial and rather dramatic recital, and the professor's frequent questioning concerning what Louis had said and as to why he thought thus or so." At the end of the hour and a half the professor informed Louis that he possessed to a high degree the faculty of constructive imagination. "In you," he told Louis, "it is vivid, amazing, and rash." Louis respected the judgment of these men. Paris had opened his mind to a new kind of thought, French thought—rich, firm, solid, and severe, disciplined beneath a smooth surface.

Louis's search for some way to resolve the problems of democratic art, by relating architectural form to a democratic content of experience as community experience, was aided by another aspect of French thought. This was Hippolyte Taine's social philosophy of art. From Taine's works he derived "three strong impressions, so strong indeed that they came as a shock." First, that there existed such a thing as a Philosophy of Art; second, that according to Taine's philosophy, the art of a people is a reflex or direct expression of the life of that people; third, that one must become well acquainted with that life in order to see into the art. All this was new and exciting. He knew it was true of Boston and Chicago. But Taine did even more than open a path for Louis's journey into an understanding of the social function of art; he also introduced him to Michelangelo.

Louis spent three days in Rome. Two of these were spent almost alone in the Sistine Chapel. Here ended his quest for the man of superpower, the great and glorified man of whom he had dreamed in childhood, as he watched his big strong men "build stone walls, hew down trees, drive huge horses." He discovered his culture-hero in the artist. "Here he communed in the silence with a superman. Here he felt and saw a great Free Spirit. Here he was filled with the awe that stills. Here he came face to face with the first great Adventurer. The first mighty man of Courage. The first man with a Great Voice. . . . The first mighty Craftsman." The "powerful presentiment which he had seen and felt in the glory of the sunrise; which he had heard in the voice of spring; and which, personified through the haze of most mystical romantic trances, he believed in, he had faith in—that faith which is far removed from fancy, that faith which is near its source and secure. . . . Now was he in that veritable dreamed-of Presence." [5]

As he kept vigil in the Chapel, pondering over the miracle of art, his

Sullivan's design was created out of a deep commitment to life as lived in Chicago and the Middle West. But, he taught, the architect must enhance, not follow, function, as in this graceful and elegant entrance to the Carson Pirie Scott store.
Photo by Richard Nickel

mystic moment of communion with art deepened. "Here was power as he had seen it in the mountains, here was power as he had seen it in the prairies, in the open sky, in the great lake stretching like a floor toward the horizon, here was the power of the forest primeval. Here was the power of the open —of the free spirit of man striding abroad in the open." But it was more than the power of nature, great as this was. It was the power of man, the creator. "There seemed to come forth from this great work a mystery. . . . From beneath the surface significance there emerged that which is timeless, that which is deathless, that which in its immensity of duration, its fecundity, its everpresent urge, we call LIFE."

And if life depended on the creation of the artist to come into being, then surely the great power of the artist was imagination. "For no hand, unaided, could do this; no intellect unaided could do this; Imagination alone could do this; and Imagination, *looked into,* revealed itself as uncompromising faith in Life, as faith in man, and especial faith in his wondrous powers." And thus imagination and all art pass beyond reason. For imagination is a "consummated act of Instinct—the primal power of Life at work." The artist must sink his roots deep in life. "It was his purpose to *live,* . . . to absorb, to contemplate." Not so that he could witness, but create, life.

His hunger to create drove him to new exertions. "Nightly he sat at his desk, a candle at each side, and, pondering his books of history," created a living drama out of the past. The processional of races and nations seemed to coalesce into a "mass movement of mankind, carrying the burden of a *single* thought." What was this thought? "He did not know. He could not see. But he knew it was there. . . . Thus became vaguely outlined an image of Man as a vast personality, within which were gathered all the powers, all the thoughts of the races, all vicissitudes of the civilizations. . . . He would someday locate this phantasm. . . ." It was in this sense of history as a great moving drama that he studied the history of architecture. These silent hours of the night were the hours of deepest contemplation, and in them was begun his real education, the self-education of the architect.

The Atelier Vaudremer, where Louis finished his training in Paris, accommodated about twenty "young ruffians." Vaudremer, remembering his own youth, criticized firmly, but with a regard for the individuality of the student. "Louis thought the exigent condition that one hold to the original sketch in its essentials, to be discipline, of an inspired sort, in that it held one firmly to a thesis." As time passed, and he was accepted as a comrade by his European classmates, he felt more deeply the differences between Europe and America. "He began to realize that Paris was not of a day, but of busy and sad centuries." As time went on, it became clearer and clearer to him what the power of culture really meant. He studied the theory of the École des Beaux-Arts. He decided that its brilliant results originated in its "theory of plan."

Yet with all its brilliance, the greatest architectural school in the world was not enough. Something was lacking. A theory of plan was, after all, a highly abstract, and as it turned out, a highly local theory. It was "an abstraction, a method, a state of mind, that was local and specific; not universal." Worse, "there was for him a fatal residuum of artificiality, which gave him a secret sense of misery where he wished but too tenderly to be happy." Beneath the law of the school there was a great law—the law "he had seen set forth in the stillness of the Sistine, which he saw everywhere in the open of life." This was that architecture was not a method, but a primal inspiration whose forms created life within space, because it made possible the life which formed space contained and expressed. As Louis struggled to express these thoughts, he knew that his life in Paris was over. He was "becoming solitary in his thoughts and heart-hungry." Now he must go his way alone, and now he must return to Chicago, where architecture could be more than a method of plan: the stage for a great new democratic civilization.

Notes

[1] This is Ericsson's account, and one that he stuck to through all the argument about who had created the steel frame. "As a bricklayer and a budding mason contractor at the time, I feel that I understand the temper of the men and the situation of the other interests involved, and, as I later came to know Jenney so well, the incident has remained unshaken in my mind through all the dispute and controversy, now settled, over the origin of the steel frame." Ericsson was on the side of the builders and engineers. His faith in Jenney's excellence was not based wholly on the man's Chicago work. As a military engineer, Jenney had been credited with a share in Grant's "engineering campaign" at Vicksburg. "In a few hours of the night after the battle of Champion Hills at Vicksburg, he had bridged the Black River, and by dawn a division of Grant's army, with artillery and baggage wagons, had crossed in safety. . . . So proficient was Jenney that, in connection with Sherman's March to the Sea, a Southern newspaper stated that it was useless for the retreating armies to burn the railroad bridges because Sherman carried a full line of ready-built bridges with him!" *Sixty Years a Builder: The Autobiography of Henry Ericsson,* written in collaboration with Lewis E. Myers [Chicago: A. Kroch, 1942], p. 217. Ericsson's irony is somewhat naïve. Sherman's army did carry ready-built trusses, if not whole bridges, with them. They also carried something of vastly greater importance: the idea of cage construction— light, open frames, made from timber, to support great weights. The principle Jenney saw in his wife's bird cage supporting a heavy book had been used many times in his military engineering, and indeed, in all bridgework. But Jenney, like Burling, Van Osdel, Sooy Smith, Johnson, Baumann, and Adler—and unlike the architects—adapted military and civil engineering techniques to building. They were not haunted by aca-

demic preconceptions of beauty or style. Ericsson's account is another illustration of how those who know how to ask questions, and persist in their questions, often find solutions in "accidents which mean nothing to those who are not searching for solutions."

[2] Sullivan, *The Autobiography of an Idea* (New York: Press of the American Institute of Architects, 1926), p. 224.

[3] *Ibid.*, p. 227. Sullivan became a Chicagoan very quickly. He decided the Middle West was "his own" after only a few months in Chicago.

[4] Sullivan ends the paragraph with a cryptic remark: "And now from the secret places of this new world there came a Siren call which perturbed Louis sadly for many years. Toward this new world Louis turned many a wistful thought thereafter: It was a land of Romance" (*Autobiography*, p. 230).

[5] Sullivan, *op. cit.*, p. 235.

55

Chicago Regained: The Birth of Modern Architecture

THE PHYSICAL BEAUTY of Chicago's setting always moved Sullivan to delight and wonder. His descriptions of the natural beauty of the city often became rhapsodies. He kept his offices in the Auditorium Tower as long as he could, and indeed long after he was able to afford them, because from the windows of his tower he could see the city, the lake, and the prairies. "There was a time a city stood beside the shore of a great and wonderful lake with a wonderful horizon and wonderful daily moods. Above the rim of its horizon rose sun and moon in their times, the one spreading o'er its surface a glory of rubies; its companion, at the full, an entrancing sheen of mottled silver. At other times far to the west in the after-glow of sunset the delicate bright crescent poised in farewell slowly dimmed and passed from sight." [1]

The Garden City of 1870, with its charming Greek Revival cottages, survived only in the suburbs by 1875. "Around this city, in ever-extending areas, in fancied semi-circles, lay a beauteous prairie, born companion of the lake; while within this prairie, at distances of some seven to twelve miles from the center of the Garden City, were dotted villages, forming also an open-spaced semi-circle, for each village nestled in the spacious prairie, and within its own companionable tree growth." [2] To the north and west of the city there grew in abundance "lofty elms and oaks; to the south the section-line dirt roads were double rowed with huge willows all swayed toward the north as the summer winds year by year had set them when sap was flowing strong; while scattered through this tract were ancient cottonwoods rising singly or in groups, in their immense and venerable strength." Further to the south "there appeared fantastic dwarf pines and scrub oaks, while at the Lake Shore, neighboring them, stretched a mile or more of heavy oak groves that might be called a forest. Within it were winding trails; within it one seemed lost to the world." [3]

In 1875, Sullivan continues, Chicago was more than a large village, as were so many American towns of a quarter million population. It was a village "grown robust with an impelling purpose." The drama of the city was central to the lives of its inhabitants. Families lived near, and indeed within, the central business district. Residences and near-by churches on Court House Square, still resisted commerce. There were few streetcars. "Horse-and-buggy was the unit; and on the Grand Boulevard fine victories, blooded-high-steppers noisily caparisoned in shining brass, liveried driver and footman, were daily on view to the populace—wealth was growing breathlessly." But the city still possessed an organic quality. The business section passed insensibly into the residential, "where trees and gardens began." The city "bloomed in its season."

Chicago had only three seasons, winter, summer and autumn.[4] "In winter was the old time animation which came with heavy, lasting snows, with cutters, jangling bells, and horses of all shades and grades, and the added confusion of racing; for everybody who was anybody owned at least one horse." And then came "equinoctial spring; crocuses appeared; trees, each after its own kind, put forth furtive leaves; for 'April Showers' all too often were but chilling northeast rains." But in June "the Garden City had come again into its own. From a distance one saw many a steeple, rising from the green, as landmarks, and in the distances the gray bulk of grain elevators." The river, with its two branches, divided the Garden City into three commercial sections, where no gardens grew and where shanty towns were waiting to become the slums of our time.

But Chicago was more than a Garden City bustling with commerce. It was also a great inland port. On occasion, when a spell of hard weather had held the lumber fleet in port, one "might see the schooners pour in a stream from the river mouth, spread their wings, and in a great and beautiful flock, gleam in the sunlight as they moved with favoring wind, fan-like towards Muskegon and the northern ports." The memory of these ships and the sight of Lake Michigan in her many moods moved Chicagoans—as it did Sullivan. One, Montgomery Ward, who started an immense mail-order house in a loft and became very rich, loved the lake front almost to madness—or so sane Chicagoans thought. He said the lake front belonged to the people, and that buildings should be kept off the shore, at least for a mile or two bordering the downtown district, so that the lake could always be seen from the streets along its shore.

Through many years, this pioneer businessman spied out and crushed every effort to erect by the lake a permanent structure tall enough to count as a building. He refused to listen to schemes for "attracting conventions" to Chicago. Even a project to put up an armory did not meet with his approval. He kept a corps of lawyers busy drawing injunctions and forti-

fying his resolve. Four times, at least, he fought contests to the last ditch
—that is, to the State Supreme Court—and he always won. Even the Art
Institute nearly lost its site in Grant Park. Other Chicago businessmen, led
by Burnham, followed Ward. By 1909 the Chicago Plan made the improvement of the lake front the first step in the creation of a new Garden City.
Within a few years the Forest Preserves, the ring of woods and meadow
around Chicago, was created. The setting for Sullivan's visions of a new kind
of city, a city where men could live in harmony with each other and with
nature, was now created.

When Louis returned from Paris, he found the Chicago dream of commercial empire slightly clouded. The Fire of 1871, followed by the devastating panic of 1873, had benumbed the city. There were no jobs for architects,
certainly not for one with a "new-fangled imported education." As he had
done in Boston, Philadelphia, London, and Paris, Louis took to the streets.
"Daily he made his twenty miles or more in the course of a systematic recon-
naissance on foot. When his adventure had come to its end, he knew every
nook and corner of the city and its environs, and had discovered undisturbed
all that had formed the prairie setting of the living Garden City, and all that
had remained undestroyed." The city, gutted by fire and stunned by financial
panic, was far from commonplace; it was a symbol of the struggle of
America to create a civilization.

For Louis, the drama of Chicago began with the Chicago River. "He had
followed the branches of the Chicago River, had located the lovely forest-
bordered River Des Plaines, and the old-time historic portage." This carried
him to "Parkman's vivid narrative of LaSalle and the great Northwest, and
his wonder stories of Marquette and Joliet, and he shared in mind the hardships of these great pioneers. Thus he came to know the why and wherefore
of the City." As Chicago began to stir from its ashes and the worst effects
of the Panic of 1873 were dispelled, the imagination and will of the city
reasserted itself. The Garden City, Louis saw, "had vanished with its living
story. That tale could not be twice told; that presence could not be recalled.
It had gone forever with the flames." A new urban drama must be created.
It was this new drama that excited Louis. After exploring the spirit as well as
the terrain of the city, he returned to work. "He worked briefly now, at
intervals, in the office of this or that architect, until he had nearly covered
the field." The men he worked for in these years were men of "homely
make-up, homely ways. Louis found them very human, and enjoyed their
shop talk, which was that of the graduate carpenter. He did not demur
because they were not *diplômés* of the Beaux-Arts. He preferred them as they

were; much of their curious wisdom stuck to him. They were men of their lingering day. To them Louis was a marvel of speed."[5] They could build, Louis could draw.

There was a toughness and a will to build in these men. And, whatever they called themselves and however the world regarded them, they respected first of all the man who could build.[6] To them, distinctions between fine and applied art were meaningless. This was not because of their ignorance of art, but because of their conviction that art was the solution to problems in moving through, and living within, space. Form to them was structure, a solution to the containment of space, not a decoration of surface. Among these men a young architect soon became familiar with engineering—for if he did not, he was soon relegated to decorating. No one had any doubts about Louis's ability to draw. In 1875, when Louis was working for Johnson & Edelmann, he designed frescoes for Sinai Temple. This was followed by designs for the frescoes of the Moody Tabernacle. These received, as the Chicago *Times* of May 21, 1876, reported, the highest praise from leading architects of the city, who declared the "invention of power" of Mr. Louis H. Sullivan to be "wonderful."[7]

But to become a builder in the Chicago tradition, an architect, no matter how highly trained in art, had to become an engineer. Architectural engineering was learned in practice through apprenticeship in the offices of men like Jenney, Edelmann and Johnson, Baumann, Burling and Adler. There were few textbooks. Because of this, Louis made Trautwine's *Engineer's Pocket Book* "his Bible." Jenney and Loring published their *Principles and Practise of Architecture* in 1869. Baumann published his monograph on foundations in 1873. Engineering journals followed closely current structures such as bridges and railway construction. But Chicago architectural engineers solved their own problems. Their daring and determination soon attracted new audiences to the drama of building. As reported in the press, and as seen by the people who watched the new buildings go up, construction was an engineering drama.[8]

The spirit of Chicago was that of the engineer, not the "artist." The city owed its existence to her engineers, and much of the daily drama of life in the city was engineering drama. The construction of buildings was reported in the press. The engineer was a public figure, a hero on his own stage, the building site, where people could see him directing the construction of his building. As Louis worked his way up in the ranks of local draftsmen, the power and fame of engineers were so great that he dreamed briefly of becoming a great bridge engineer. But, he decided, if the "artistic" approach alone was weak, the engineering view was equally limited. The architect "could not or would not understand the real working of the engineering mind because it was hidden in deadly literal attitude and results, because of the horrors it had brought forth as misbegotten stigmata; while the engineer regarded the architect as a frivolous person of small rule-of-thumb consequence." The problem for Sullivan, Root, and later Wright, was not how to become either engineers or architects, but how to create design which would somehow capture the significance of both.

The resolution of the tension between architecture and engineering produced the best work of Adler and Sullivan, and created the basis for the architecture of our time. Unlike Root, and later Atwood, Sullivan believed that the dialectic of architecture must be between the engineer, with his science, and the architect, with his art. Neither the engineer nor the architect could work alone. To do good work the young architect must find an engineer sensitive to design as an organic part of structure, just as the architect, in turn, must sensitize himself to the relationship between structure and ornament. Adler and Sullivan found in each other the kind of sensitivity which inspired each to his greatest heights of expression. When he entered into partnership with Adler, Sullivan decided that he could "start on the course of practical experimentation he long had in mind, which was to make an architecture that fitted its functions—a realistic architecture based on well defined utilitarian needs—that all demands of utility should be paramount as a basis for planning and design; that no architectural dictum, or tradition, or superstition, or habit, should stand in the way." [9]

The idea of architecture, the principle Louis had been seeking all his life, was plasticity, a new kind of moulded space. His conviction was that "the architectural art to be of contemporary immediate value must be *plastic;* all senseless conventional rigidity must be taken out of it; it must intelligently serve—it must not suppress. In this wise, the forms under his hand would grow naturally out of the needs and express them frankly, and freshly." He would put to the test "a formula he had evolved, through long contemplation of living things, namely that *form follows function,* which would mean in practice, that architecture might again become a living art, if this formula were but adhered to." [10]

As important commissions for mercantile structures came into the Adler and Sullivan office, Sullivan treated each one "experimentally, feeling his way toward a basic process, a grammar of his own." The immediate problem in these buildings was how to bring in more light. He met this by using slender piers, tending toward a "masonry and iron combination." Such was the beginning of the "vertical system," which changed so radically building science and art. As different buildings came to his hand, he struggled to develop a "system of artistic expression." This was a "system of form and function" created in the conviction that "architectural manipulation, as a homely art or a fine art, must be rendered completely plastic to the mind and hand of the designer, that materials must yield to the mastery of his imagination and will; through this alone could modern conditions be met and faithfully expressed." For if the idea of architecture, that form follows function through expression in plastic space, was to become a principle and not simply another style, it must become a system of technique.

But technique, even a system of technique, would not be enough. The architect must be deeply committed to the democratic life of his own time. For if he lacked deep conviction over what kind of society he wanted his forms to create and sustain, his forms would soon be taken over by those who had other convictions. This is why Louis feared Daniel Burnham and felt that, despite all of John Root's brilliance, Burnham's ideas might win out in the end. It was the same with John Edelmann. Louis loved and admired both Root and Edelmann, but he recognized their lack of conviction, a failure to achieve a fixed purpose in life. Even as a youth of seventeen he sensed that talk for John Edelmann, was "merely luxurious self-indulgence and a luscious hour with parade of vanity." John Root was "vain to the limit of the limit of the skies." Yet beneath his "immediate ambition to shine" there was a man of power, who might yet free himself to become a friendly rival to Louis in the common cause of architecture.[11]

Daniel H. Burnham, Louis realized, was the man of power in Chicago architecture. Whichever way Burnham went was the way architecture in Chicago, and America, would go. Until Root's death in 1891, Burnham's talents as a promoter, organizer, and administrator were subordinated to the indigenous Chicago ideals of design which his partner did so much to develop. Burnham thought little about architectural form as such, but he thought a great deal about the organization and promotion of architecture as a professional and a business. If Sullivan wanted architects to be prepared in spirit, Burnham wanted them prepared in organization to undertake what he regarded as the future of American architecture. This was nothing less than the development of whole communities, or what we now call "planning." He foresaw, and indeed did much to change, the practice of architecture from a profession of art to the big business corporation of today, where the architect is but one voice, and sometimes a very weak voice, in the corporate "we" who "design" a building.

Sullivan watched Burnham's rise in sadness and despair.[12] He realized that the roof of their difference was not in devotion to architecture or a lack of conviction over what architecture should be used for in community life. No one could accuse Burnham of not being serious about whatever he undertook. The difference, as Louis saw it and as the Classical Fair proved, was that Burnham was obsessed by a feudal idea of power, while Louis was equally obsessed by a democratic idea of power. And, unfortunately for the future of American architecture, Adler lacked Burnham's vision and his will to become a great architect. "Adler was essentially a technician, an engineer, a conscientious administrator, a large progressive judicial and judicious mind securing alike the confidence of conservative and radical." Adler lacked the "dream-quality of Burnham; and such he must remain—he lacked the sturdy wheel-horse of a tandem team of which Louis did the prancing. Unquestionably, Adler lacked sufficient imagination; so in a way did John Root— that is to say, the imagination of the dreamer. In the dream-imagination lay Burnham's strength and Louis's passion." [13]

As he looked back over his life in Chicago, Sullivan realized that the imagination of the dreamer had been the source of Chicago's greatness, and the secret of his own development as an artist. For the businessmen of his youth, the McCormicks, Potter Palmer, Pullman, Armour, and Field, and the greatest business architect, Burnham, were men of great visions—feudal visions in Sullivan's eyes, but great visions none the less. To stand against the power and will of these men, Sullivan realized that architects must equal and surpass them in vision and power. He believed this could be done because the great artist was the new type of man democracy needed, the only man who could bring a democratic society into being because he alone could give it form. In his childhood, his leaders were the big, strong men who did things; later, in his student days, he turned to the great power of men who could think things. In early manhood he was moved by the power of men who could imagine things. But after he began to practice in Chicago, he "began to recognize as dominant, the will of the Creative Dreamer: he who possessed the power of vision needed to harness Imagination, to harness the intellect, to make science do his will, to make the emotions serve him —for without emotion nothing." [14]

This idea of the power of art was, Louis realized, a complete reversal and inversion of the commonly accepted intellectual and theological concept of the nature of man and the understanding of power in society. But, as he asked in the last months of his life in the summation of his search for a democratic idea of architecture, who had created the gods? Man himself, he answered, in all his weakness, terror, and depravity. Why does man bring so much woe upon himself and others? Because he does not yet understand his imagination, the least studied and poorest understood of all the human faculties. The "tricks of imagination are universal and beyond numbering in variety, permeating all phases of the social fabric. Hence man's vagaries and follies and cruelties are beyond computation." But all these spring from the same source, "namely the [ignorant] individual, unconscious that his imagination is incessantly at work. Because he is not acquainted with its nature, and unaware that he is its puppet, his waking hours are a continuing dream of inverted self." [15]

Until men learn to train and control imagination, they will live in fear, hatred, ugliness, and destruction. Until we "come as pioneers, to seek out and know imagination as such, to view it clearly defined as an erratic and dangerous power, to be controlled; until we have observed with realistic clarity its multifarious doings from black magic upward to mighty deeds of hand and head and heart, we shall remain remote from man's reality, and from the splendor of his native power." How de we know that imagination is really a great native power, common to all men? From our own youth, the golden memories of a time when the self was free and yearned for frank utterance and brotherhood. For the natural man, the man who alone can make a rendezvous with Life, is "sound to the core and kindly, yet innocent of himself as the seat of genius, as container of limitless creative powers of beneficence." [16]

What are these powers, and what is this new democratic man who will find freedom because he will learn how to express himself freely? And if we affirm that man is sound and kindly, and that there is nothing in any man which was not there in latency at birth, how must we think about man? He is, first of all, a worker and a wanderer. He can make new situations. He manipulates. He creates an environment of his own because he creates the forms of his environment. When, to the power to do, we add the power to inquire, man, the worker, gains new power to change situations and to make new situations for himself. When man throws a bridge across a chasm in one great leap, it is man himself who leaps the chasm. Through the coordination of his power to inquire and his power to do, the natural man enlarges his range of beneficence. "He reverses the dictum 'I think: Therefore I am.' It becomes in him, *'I am: Therefore I inquire and do!'* It is this affirmative 'I AM' that is man's reality." [17]

Other human types, the warrior, philosopher, and priest, have failed because they have turned their backs on man. For them it was settled long ago that man is corrupt and depraved. But now for the first time we are beginning to see that man in his power is "Free spirit—Creator, Man is stirring from the long night of 'mystical unconsciousness.' His deeds are about to become conscious deeds in the open. The beauty, the passion, the glory of the past shall merge into a new beauty, a new passion, a new glory as man approaches man, and recognizing him, rejoices in him and with him, as born in power." As man learns to bring the dark fears of his unconscious into consciousness through art, he will discover that "feudal thought simplifies into a basic concept of self-delusion and self-fear." For man can choose, and in such choice lies his whole moral being. The will to choose aright "lifts him to the peak of social vision whence he may forecast new and true situations." [18]

The creative spirit, the free spirit, is the spirit of joy. This spirit "delights to create in beauty. It is unafraid, it knows not fear. It declares the Earth to be its home, and the fragrance of Earth to be its inspiration. It is strong, it is mighty in beneficence. It views its powers with emotions of adventure. Humility it knows not. It dreams a civilization like unto itself." Such dreams become real through imagination in which we "picture forth . . . the power to act in advance of action; the power that knows no limitations, no boundaries, that renders vivid both giving and receiving; the inscrutable dynamic power that energizes all other powers." This spirit, as embodied in the new American architect, will go forth as a seer, a prophet, and as an evangelist proclaiming his faith, "in certitude as worker, to build a new home . . ." for the American people.

To say that all men are alike in native possession of creative power does not mean that there is little difference among men. No two human beings are alike. Each is unique, although each shares in the immense fecundity and industry of Life. "The individual and the mass become *one,* in a new phase of power whose stupendous potency of creative art in civilization stuns the sense of possibility." But this is possible only in democracy, and this is why we must open our spirit to the Democratic Vista. For then we unfold the power of the "*only one* in multiple, and the *One* become a vast complex of unique powers inspired of its free spirit founded on the full emergence of courage—the envanishment of fear!"

The idea of self-preservation has become a feudal idea, poisoned at the core by the virulent assumption of "Master and man, of potentate and slave, of external and internal suppression of the life urge of the only one—of its faith in human sacrifice as a means of salvation." Feudal thought denies the ego, but if we are to recognize our uniqueness as individuals, "we must recognize that the Ego is the most precious of man's powers," the source of all the marvelous diversity among men. Without Ego man becomes nothing. "Ego signifies Identity. It is the free spirit." It is not a tenant, "it is the all in all." It is what we call "the spiritual, a term now becoming interchangeable with the physical. It is the sign and symbol of man's immense Integrity—the 'I am that am.' To it the Earth, the world of humanity, the multitudes, the universe—become an Egocosm." In this view of man, the "ghostly feudal scapegoat with its burden of sin . . ." vanishes.

Thus, in the center of the drama of our time stands man as a moving center of radiant energy, awaiting his time to create a new world in his proper image. Out of this dream of man's abounding power to create in beauty and joy a dwelling place devoid of fear, a new man, a master builder, possessing a mighty spirit of adventure, and of masterful craftsmanship, will arise to the challenge of the "new art of all arts,—the art of upbuilding for the race a new, a stable home." The power of this new democratic man will not arise from a welter of pallid abstractions, nor from any cut and dried system of economics or politics. It must and will "arise out of the heart, to be nurtured in common honesty by the intelligence, and by that sense of artistry which does not interfere with the growth of a living thing, but encourages it to seek and find in its own befitting form." Thus the living idea of man, "the free spirit, master of his powers, shall set forth the highest craftsmanship, the artistry of living joyously in stable equilibrium." [19]

At his death Sullivan believed that feudal thought and feudal styles of life still dominated our civilization. People were still being taught "to deny themselves" and to huddle together in mutual fear of life and of themselves. Tyrants were born of such fear. Men submitted to the force of these tyrants because they were guilty over their own corruption and hate, and believed that their dark powers could be held in check only by fear and punishment. To keep men in fear, and to assuage guilt caused by the idea of sin, the idea of force was decked out in splendor and glory as an outward show of domination. American artists, like artists everywhere, have been suppressed, and their expression subordinated to powers who seek to enslave the spirit of the people. In their terror of the unknown, and in fear of supernatural powers, the people surrendered their immense unconscious power to those they raised above them. In fear and trembling they asked those they had raised to treat them as slaves and to punish them for their disobedience.

Those raised to power by the multitudes who accepted their own servility, soon became the great feudal parasites who denied man their rights and used them as beasts to toil the fields beside animals and to hunt each other down like wolves. But force and tyranny breed their own destruction. The feudal use of power ends in violent crises, recurring cycles of collapse and renewal. Times, places, names, local colors, mechanisms, and countenances change. The feudal idea persists through the ages, and will persist, so long as men live in fear. Yet what are men really afraid of but themselves? All sanctioning power, whether of gods or kings, comes from the people themselves. The majesty and pomp of the greatest monarch is nothing but the people's dreams of glory taking shape vicariously in their times and places. The "spectacular and imposing groups and summits of the feudal super-structure have no other base, no other sanction. Like towering cumulus clouds they float upon thin air."

But within the feudal dream there is another dream. This dream of the reality of man is the modern ideal. "The great drama we herein have called the Modern, unique in the story of mankind, beginning with a small tele-scope, advancing to the radio, to the measurement of the stars, to the search-ing out of the utterly minute in Life's infinitude of variety . . . constitute[s] the first act in the drama of the universal education of mankind through a series of imposing object lessons, changing situations, shifting scenes." The image of man as Moral Power—power based on choice, and determined by bringing into consciousness the many suppressed powers of men, will create a world of beauty and joy, and thus cause to dissolve into thin air, as though it had never existed, the "baleful feudal superstition of dominion and blood-sacrifice. . . . This moral power residing in the multitudes and awakening to voice, is what Democracy means." [20]

But democracy is not merely a mechanical, political, or economic system. The democratic idea must branch endlessly into science, art, all industrial and social activities of human well-being. It must be fed by human kindness and intelligence. For, when all is said and done, kindness is the sanest of powers, and the final test of democracy. "Kindness, seemingly so weak, is in fact the name of a great adventure which mankind thus far has lacked the courage, the intelligence, the grit to undertake." Democracy flourishes only in clarity born of the reasoned imagination of the artist. All "sound thinking and clean action, all sciences, all arts, all activities, become sentimentally, emotionally, dramatically and constructively imbued with the stirring, the self-propelling impulse of the democratic idea."

Democracy can be achieved only if we recognize that the race between democracy and catastrophe in another feudal night of the soul can be won only by education based on art. This education will begin with the child, for every child contains natural powers of understanding and love. The purpose of education must be to give vent to the child's wondrous imagination, its deep creative instinct, its romance and understanding. For these powers, natu-ral to all men because natural to all children, will lead if properly formed to a wholesome social order based on joy and delight in fellowship. To train the highest faculty of all, the imagination, we must turn to art. For only art is the imagination given "constructive foresight, in the feeling for real things, in the uses of sentiment, of emotion, in the physical and the spiritual joy of living; to stabilize the gregarious into a social sense; to set forth the dignity of the ego and all egos." As men are taught to recognize themselves, the cruel feudal chaos born of fear and hate will vanish. Democracy, born of free expression in art, will create a new world, where men walk the earth in dignity and freedom because they walk in beauty.

Notes

[1] Louis H. Sullivan, *The Autobiography of an Idea* (New York: Press of the American Institute of Architects, 1926), p. 241. From a practical view, the site of Chicago could scarcely have been worse. It required engineering genius to create, as well as sustain, a city on such soil and in such a location.

[2] Chicagoans have been "fleeing" to near-by villages, and making suburbs out of them, since 1875. The highly compressed downtown Loop, with its adjacent slums, and the outlying suburbs are closely related. The lack of urban tone in Chicago life has been marked for many years. Chicago is not "citified" in the same way as New York, or the cities of Europe. Indeed, for some, notably New Yorkers, Chicago is still a "hick town" in the "sticks."

[3] Sullivan, *op. cit.*, p. 241. The parks, boulevards, forest preserves, and the lake front parks of Chicago were designed mainly as natural parks. Jens Jensen fought at every attempt at formalization and the use of non-indigenous plants, trees, and shrubs. Jensen owed much to Sullivan's teachings on nature.

[4] The extremes of climate in Chicago, with temperatures ranging from twenty degrees below to one hundred degrees above zero, along with the sudden shifts in wind and treacherous soil conditions, have made Chicago a severe testing ground for architects and builders. Wright once pointed out that a Chicago structure had to withstand a hundred degree range of temperature. Meeting this challenge produced good builders, for if you could build well in Chicago, you could build well anywhere.

[5] Sullivan, *op. cit.*, p. 245.

[6] Condit quotes a letter from Elmer C. Jensen, who worked for Jenney from 1885 to 1907, the year of Jenney's death. "While [Jenney] felt [that] he was contributing to the making of new architectural forms, that was not his notice. His main purpose was the development of more efficient structural features. My personal opinion is that while he was fully conscious that his ideas and buildings were developing new forms, his main purpose was to create structural features which increased the effective floor areas and made it possible to secure more daylight within the buildings. . . . I do not recollect that he made any remarks about creating new forms although he did remark that skeleton construction would bring about a revolution in the design of office buildings." (Carl W. Condit, *The Rise of the Skyscraper* [Chicago: University of Chicago Press, 1951], pp. 132–33.)

[7] Willard Connely discusses this in Chapter Six of his biography of Sullivan. See *Louis Sullivan as He Lived* (New York: Horizon Press, 1960).

[8] In his *Genius and the Mobocracy*, Wright stresses, even more than he does in his *Autobiography*, that Adler was far more important than Sullivan to the clients of the firm. He makes clear, too, that Sullivan owed much to Adler. "Adler never lost faith in that growing phase of Sullivan's genius [as a designer]. . . . the grand chief knew enough about building construction for two or more. And the Sullivan schooling in practical planning of building actually began then and there under ideal auspices: ideal because the chief was not only an experienced engineer but was also a splendid planner

himself; a good critic, as his choice of a 'designer' was to prove" (p. 44). Wright also tells us that "I, with no graduation or architectural engineering degrees to speak of as such, was not only directly under Louis H. Sullivan but more and more, because of Mr. Sullivan's absences, I was under Dankmar Adler" (p. 47).

[9] Sullivan, *op. cit.,* p. 257.

[10] *Ibid.,* p. 258.

[11] Sullivan had great hopes for Root, despite his recognition of Root's lack of seriousness. "Louis, true to his form of appropriating to himself and considering as a part of himself the things and personalities he valued—as he had done with Moses Woolson, Michael Angelo, Richard Wagner, *et al.*—immediately annexed John Root to his collection of assets; or, if one so wills to put it—to his menagerie of personalities great and small."

[12] He often watched in rage, as well—especially in the years after his breakup with Adler when he sat idle in the midst of an architectural boom led by Burnham.

[13] Sullivan, *op. cit.,* pp. 288–89. Whatever credit we give Adler, and he deserves far more than he has received, he did resign formally from the architectural profession.

[14] *Ibid.,* pp. 257–58.

[15] *Ibid.,* pp. 261–62.

[16] *Ibid.,* p. 263.

[17] *Ibid.,* p. 265.

[18] *Ibid.,* p. 269.

[19] *Ibid.,* p. 275.

[20] *Ibid.,* p. 279.

PART NINE

Conclusion

56

The Legacy of Louis Henri Sullivan and the Chicago School

SULLIVAN BELIEVED that art must become a value in democratic society that could stand beside business, politics, science, and religion in shaping the mind and heart of America. The study of architecture was the study of society because what happened in architecture determined what happened in society. "Therefore, by this light, the critical study of architecture becomes not merely the direct study of an art—for that is but a minor phase of a great phenomenon—but, *in extenso,* a study of the social conditions producing it; the study of a newly shaping type of civilization." In this view, the study of architecture "becomes naturally and logically a branch of social science; and we must bend our facilities to this bow if we would reach the mark." [1] In a democratic society, form must follow function; functions, in turn, must be given proper form to *become social functions,* otherwise, as John Edelmann taught Sullivan, they remain "suppressed." Thus, while form "followed" function, it did so by evoking and expressing the function it "followed." A building was, then, an "act," and what we did with our buildings, the kind of stages we created for action, determined how we related as citizens of a democratic community.

In saying a building was an "act," Sullivan brought architecture back to life, as Dewey was to bring art back to experience some thirty years later. Art became the complete and pure expression of "doing," because it was in and through the forms of art that men communicated. And since the ways in which men communicated determined how they related, the study of these forms was the study of the "social" in human relatedness. Something like this had been suggested by Charles Sanders Peirce and by James, and the elaboration of this "functional" view of art in Dewey's philosophy was to become a cornerstone of American pragmatic theory on the function of symbols in society. As James discovered when he reviewed Dewey's *Studies in Logical Theory* (edited by Dewey and published by the University of Chicago in 1903), the "Chicago school of philosophy" (as James called it) was seeking to place mind and the self *in* society as well as in nature, or the structure of the "mind itself."

How to place the mind in society was, of course, the problem. If thought was related to science, then pragmatism must show how the relation between science and thought could be validated. But, as Cassirer pointed out in his discussion of Einstein's theory of relativity (published in 1921), in which Cassirer, too, refers to *Studies in Logical Theory,* if thought is an expression of "doing," then each hypothesis of knowledge can be justified only to the degree that it succeeds in intellectually organizing and harmoniously shaping the originally isolated sense data of action. To shift meaning in social action from being to doing, without defining doing, did not clarify the nature of social action. But neither did the substitution of scientific thought for all thought, unless it was made clear just how science was related to action in society.

On the one hand, Sullivan taught, the social meanings of architectural forms are their "function," or *use* as social stages; on the other, they are "functions" of architectural thought, which is both artistic and scientific. Architectural forms have *both* existential *and* ideational meaning. These two meanings represent the difference between the *use* and the creation of a form. It is important to keep clear the distinction between creation and use, but it is equally important not to subordinate the one to the other. The use of a building determines its form, but architecture gives spatial and temporal form to our environment, and in doing this it orders social experience. Through architecture we create the social stages upon which we mount the social dramas necessary to community life in a free society.

Form and function are interdependent. They exist as both signs and symbols of relationship in society, and both symbol and sign are existential events. Architectural form is drawn, seen, discussed, criticized, and judged purely as form; that is, *as* a form it functions as a universal in architectural discourse. These architectural universals are called "orders," and it is in and through the use of these orders that we think, write, and talk about architecture as art. They supply, so to speak, the *language* of architecture. The advantage of this language (like any language) is that it provides tools of architectural thought that can be manipulated quite independently of external events. It removes architecture from use to thought, but this capacity for abstract manipulation as a language of form is at once a blessing and a curse. What begins as a solution to a social need often ends in a form whose "purity," "beauty," or "holiness" removes it from any test of relevance to social action. The more successful the form, the more it determines the content of social experience; the more proper, right, and sacred the form becomes, the more it fails to satisfy our need for change and flexibility.

But while the language of architectural form takes us away from the actu-

The proscenium in the Schiller Building, 1891–92, later the Garrick Theatre (which, to the eternal disgrace of Chicago, was destroyed to make way for a parking lot), was one of Sullivan's most moving examples of clarity, power, and richness in design. *Photo by Richard Nickel*

alities of social relationships to the symbolic realm of architectural forms (the "orders"), it can be used to bring us back to life in the community with a better means for identifying, recognizing, understanding, and ordering our social needs. Social relationships are no longer just "had," or "endured," as habits, but are meaningful acts. In such meaning, reason (the reason of art as well as science) transcends habit; we know a new depth in our relatedness because now we have forms which make such relatedness a shared *conscious* experience in thought, discussion, inquiry, and consummation. We no longer live in a world of signals, or of functions suppressed in the unconscious, but in a world of meanings. The ways in which architectural forms can be used are vastly multiplied. Inference about architectural form need no longer be a matter of luck or intuition; it can be grounded, indeed, *must* be grounded, in science as well as art, and it can become subject to fresh inquiry. Thus architectural form is a *way* to create and control social relationships, in so far as such relationships are determined by the stages within which we enact our social roles. Architecture must become a "grammar of form," but its form is the form of a stage within which as members of a community we play our social roles.

As James pointed out in his famous essay of 1907, "What Pragmatism Means," he was only saying what Peirce had said in 1878 in his article, "How To Make Our Ideas Clear," which appeared in *The Popular Science Monthly* for that year. As he says, Peirce, "after pointing out that our beliefs are really rules for action, said that to develop a thought's meaning, we need only determine what conduct it is fitted to produce: that conduct is for us its sole significance." As the concept of "conduct" became central to pragmatism, it became obvious that what James, Dewey, Mead, Cooley, or Park meant by "conduct" would be what they meant by "thought." It turned out that for James thought was the kind of thinking that went on in science, not as knowledge of man in society, but in nature. In his review of the development of pragmatism, he links the development of pragmatism with the development of natural science.

Everywhere, these teachers [scientists such as Poincaré] say "truth" in our ideas and beliefs means the same thing that it means in science. It means, they say, nothing but this, *that ideas (which themselves are but parts of our experience) become true just in so far as they help us to get into satisfactory relation with other parts of our experience,* to summarize them and get about among them by conceptual short cuts instead of following the interminable succession of particular phenomena. Any idea upon which we can ride, so to speak; any idea that will carry us prosperously from any one part of our experience to any other part, linking things satisfactorily, working securely, simplifying, saving labor; is true for just so much, true in so far forth, true *instrumentally*. This is the "instrumental" view of truth taught so successfully at Chicago, the view that truth in our ideas means their power to "work". . . . Messrs. Dewey, Schiller, and their allies, in reaching this general conception of all truth, have only followed the example of geologists, biologists and philologists.[2]

But, as Sullivan, Veblen, Mead, Cooley, and later Dewey himself were careful to stress, the pragmatism of the Chicago school was based not only in science but also in art. Sullivan's "functionalism," Veblen's "instinct of workmanship," Dewey's "instrumentalism," like Mead's "consummatory phase of the act," Cooley's "sympathetic understanding," and finally, the "social process" as a "communicative interaction" of Park and Burgess,[3] had little to do with science as the study of nature (as science was really defined by James). For the Chicago school, conduct was not only a way of *thinking* about the physical world, as in science, but of *acting* in it, as in art. Veblen drew his analogies of "workmanship" from the arts, as the full title of his book, *The Instinct of Workmanship and the State of the Industrial Arts,* indicates. In his favorite essay, "The Place of Science in Modern Civilization," which appeared in *The American Journal of Sociology* in 1906, Veblen says: "The ideal man, and the ideal of human life, even in the apprehension of those who most rejoice in the advances of modern science, is neither the finikin skeptic in the laboratory nor the animated slide-rule."

Veblen distinguished sharply between what he called "pragmatic expediency" and art and science. Folklore, mythology, and what we call the dramatic arts, are at best, "an amiable inefficient formulation of experiences and observations in terms of something like a life-history of the phenomena observed." Art of this kind is neither expedient nor "systematic knowledge, of matter-of-fact." But it is "quest of knowledge, perhaps of systematic knowledge, and is carried on under the incentive of idle curiosity." In this respect "it falls in the same class with the civilized man's science; but it seeks knowledge not in terms of opaque matter-of-fact, but in terms of some sort of spiritual life imputed to the facts." Art is thus "romantic and Hegelian rather than realistic and Darwinian." The logical necessities of its scheme of thought are necessities of spiritual consistency rather than of quantitative equivalence." That is, in so far as we need to live by "spiritual consistency," we turn to art. And, although Veblen had little to say about *how* art produces this "spiritual consistency," he was adamant in his belief that the proper study of an art such as literature was not philology or history, but the discipline of taste and the development of a cultivated sense of literary form and literary feeling.

In Paul Arthur Schilpp's collection of essays on Dewey, and in Dewey's own reply to his critics, *Art as Experience* (which appeared in 1934) is regarded as Dewey's best general statement of how to think about conduct in society. Joseph Ratner, who edited so much of Dewey's work and who contributes the essay "Dewey's Conception of Philosophy" to the Schilpp collection, says: "'Intelligence' for Dewey is a quality of human behavior which is completely actualized when the experience of living has become an intelligently cultivated art. It is not unnatural therefore that one finds Dewey's best and profoundest exposition of his integral conception of philosophy, or the nature of intelligence, in his *Art as Experience*." In his essay, "The Significance of Dewey's Philosophy," William Savery says: "The crown of Dewey's philosophy is in his esthetic theory. *Art as Experience* is perhaps his most profound book. It is a consummatory theory of art, and it forms the natural complement to the instrumental theories of truth and goodness." Professor Stephen C. Pepper says: "I am personally convinced that *Art as Experience* is one of the four or five great books on esthetics." Dewey himself, in his reply to Pepper, says: "There are situations in which self-enclosed, discrete, individualized characters dominate. They constitute the subject-matter of esthetic experience; and every experience is esthetic in so far as it is final, or rouses no search for some other experience. When this complete quality is conspicuous the experience is denominated esthetic."

It was easy enough to say that art determined society. But if art determined society, as society determined art, *how* did this occur? To say simply that art was "social" was not enough, for if it was not social, what was it? On the other hand, to say that art was some kind of perfect form which in and of itself determined the structure of the world (of men as well as art) made even less sense. Those of Sullivan's generation who reduced art to the social, as Tolstoy had done, made art nothing but a "message," while those who abstracted art into some kind of pure form, as did the upholders of the architectural "orders," destroyed all hopes for a democratic art. The bitter lessons of the classical "White City" of the Columbian Exposition made this clear. To say that art must be "American" sounded good enough, but when the "American" turned out to be some kind of romanticized American rural past, how could this be tested for relevance to problems in a modern city? To say that art in Chicago must be disciplined by international standards of taste or that local artists must learn by copying masterpieces made little sense to artists.

To say, as did the "cosmopolites" of Chicago who brought back from European trips some sense of responsibility for the cultivation of art, that the upper classes must guide the taste of their inferiors and (as Ruskin taught) "raise them always to the nearest level with themselves of which those inferiors are capable," certainly had the weight of tradition and history behind it. For when, really, had the people supported good art? Art, so every professor of art history taught, had always been supported by an elite. Popular art, at best, was a kind of folk art which belonged to the "childhood of man" in primitive society, or to the "unformed tastes of the masses" in civilized urban life. And certainly, as Chicagoans were told, art accepted by the people was hopelessly vulgar. In the eyes of the cosmopolites, busy stuffing the public libraries, museums, and schools with "classics" and keeping the classical spirit of the Columbian Exposition alive by helping to found the American Academy in Rome, the art of Sullivan was "commercial art." So, too, was the newspaper art of Ade, Field, Dunne, and Ring Lardner, and novelists like Dreiser who wrote "without any style."

If a building was an "act" whose form was not to be determined by the classical architectural orders, what kind of an act was it, and how should it be analyzed? The image of the act was used in different ways by Sullivan, Veblen, Dewey, Mead, and Cooley. For Sullivan a building was a stage whose form evoked or expressed the action which took place on it. For Veblen, the act was "workmanship." For Dewey, the act was communication. For Mead, the act was taking the role of the other (as "the other" in turn took our role) so that we could respond to our internalization of his role. For Cooley, the act was a dramatic rehearsal in the imagination. But however various these stresses, they were a common attempt to place the act within the psyche of individuals whose relationships with other individuals was determined by communication. For, as Dewey said in *Democracy and Education* (published in 1916): "Society not only continues to exist *by* transmission, *by* communication, but it may fairly be said to exist *in* transmission, *in* communication. There is more than a verbal tie between the words, common, community, and communication."

As we see, then, the action frame of reference of the Chicago school was grounded in a theory of communication as participation in community activity. The symbols created and used in such acts could best be analyzed in terms of models of action taken from the arts. Shared activity in communication was symbolic activity which existed in its most characteristic forms in the moments when common action, not simply thought about action, was required. And since problems were solved in a present, the solution to a problem must be found within the problem itself (As Sullivan said, "Every problem contains its own solution."). This could be done only through the use of imagination, as the artist used imagination, to create ideal forms of acts which could serve as guides to action in a present. These forms could be taken from the past, or the future, but they must be tested by their relevance to the present. As Sullivan taught, we must ask: What kind of action is supposed to take place in a building, and how do we solve the problem of staging such action?

Action meant social action and this, in turn, meant relatedness. The forms of the architect *created* relatedness. That is, we do have relationships and then turn to the architect to "draw" the forms which will make possible the relatedness we have in mind. If we knew how to do this we would not need architects, but draftsmen who could "carry out" our intentions. The architect is important to democracy because we cannot have democratic relationships unless the architect gives us spaces in which such relationships can occur. If our buildings are arrogant, pretentious, domineering, pompous, sentimental, or archaic, so, too, will be our social relationships. For a building, like a name, forms a relationship. If banks were designed as warm, intimate, neighborly places, where people could meet in face-to-face relationships and where the banker and his customers could meet and talk, money could become a democratic force in the community.

Sullivan returned architecture to society long before Dewey returned art to experience. When Dewey arrived at the University of Chicago in 1894, he entered a city of vigorous and searching debate over the function of architecture (and all art) in society. Preparations for the Columbian Exposition, the problem of how to plan a new university, and finally the bold decision to plan a whole city in the Chicago Plan of Burnham—these brought discussion of the function of art in society to a central place in the intellectual life of Chicago. From 1885 to 1909, the date of publication of the *Plan of Chicago,* Chicagoans began to realize that the kind of lives they would lead in their new city would be determined by the kinds of stages of life created for them by their architects. The University of Chicago, like the Fair, was discussed as a planned community, and it was planned by an architect, Henry Ives Cobb, just as the University of Virginia had been planned by another architect, Thomas Jefferson. Clearly there was no separation of architecture from life in Chicago. In one very profound sense, architecture *was* its life.

As Dewey, Veblen, and Mead struggled to save the University of Chicago, the gray Gothic center of learning, from its restoration of a feudal past, they soon found themselves involved in the great Chicago debate. This debate, which was to set the terms for all future discussion on the function of art in democracy, was a search to determine how art could be a form of knowledge like science and, at the same time, a form of action like religion. We know the world because we act in it as men, not because we contemplate it like remote gods. We act in terms of belief, but belief is not grounded in supernatural laws or the commandments of gods, but in rules which men themselves make in their struggle to achieve order in their relationships. We act in relationships whose forms arise, and continue to exist, in communication. And these forms must be studied after models of action founded in art, and a new science of man, sociology, must be created out of the study of communication. Such were the themes of the great debate in Chicago.

To undertake to make art a form of truth, to offer it as a source for the creation of a model of socialization, and to insist that the ideal form of socialization was democracy and that the proper study of democracy was sociology—these were great undertakings. Success in grounding art in democracy and, at the same time, democracy in art would revolutionize America and the world. Sullivan knew this. He knew that in what he called his "illuminations" an idea of a new world was being born. His architecture, and all art, was a form of life, just as the democracy brought to life by architecture was a new form of community. In his later years, as he pondered the lessons of the betrayal of American art at the Fair, he realized that a radical reconstruction of social philosophy and of the idea of the function of art in society was necessary.

The revolt Sullivan led flamed into greatness in the spirit of his pupil, Frank Lloyd Wright, and in the work of Mies van der Rohe of the Bauhaus, who found a home for his spirit in Chicago. In him today, in his seventy-eighth year, the spirit of Sullivan still lives in Chicago. In the younger men trained by him in the great days of architecture at the Illinois Institute of Technology, who are now putting up some of the most beautiful buildings in the world, the spirit of the master endures. Chicago is still the spiritual home of modern architecture, the "great city" for young architects the world over. But the spirit of Sullivan soon passed beyond architecture, to find a new home in the spirit of Veblen, Dewey, Mead, Cooley, and Park. Dewey said in his own *Reconstruction of Philosophy,* in the passage checked by Sullivan in his copy of Dewey's work:

When the liberation of capacity no longer seems a menace to organization and established institutions, . . . When the liberating of human capacity operates as a socially creative force, art will not be a luxury, a stranger to the daily occupations of making a living. Making a living economically speaking, will be at one with making a life that is worth living. And when the emotional force, the mystic force one might say, of communication, of the miracle of shared life and shared experience is spontaneously felt, the hardness and crudeness of contemporary life will be bathed in the light that never was on land and sea.[4]

Notes

[1] Louis H. Sullivan, *Kindergarten Chats,* ed. by Isabella Athey (New York: George Wittenborn, 1947), p. 24.

[2] William James, *Pragmatism* (New York: Meridian Books, 1955), p. 24.

[3] Robert E. Park and Ernest W. Burgess, *Introduction to the Science of Sociology* (Chicago: University of Chicago Press, 1921). This influential work, done by members of the department which founded American sociology, advocated the study of communication as necessary to the study of society.

[4] W. G. Purcell, a surviving member of the Chicago school, has Sullivan's copy of Dewey's *Reconstruction in Philosophy.* For this quotation see John Dewey, *Reconstruction in Philosophy* (Boston: The Beacon Press, 1948) p. 211.

Index